Between Borders

Essays on Mexicana/Chicana History

Between Borders

Essays on Mexicana/Chicana History

Edited by
Adelaida R. Del Castillo

Giselle K. Cabello, Series Editor

La Mujer Latina Series

Floricanto Press

La Mujer Latina Series

ISBN 0-915745-14-3

Order from:

Floricanto Press
16161 Ventura Blvd., Suite 830
Encino, CA 91436
(818) 990-1885

TABLE OF CONTENTS

PART IV   Gender, Patriarchy and Feminism

In Memory

This book is dedicated to the memory of Magdalena Mora, activist, author, once student who worked with, researched and wrote about Mexican women and the Mexican working class. She wrote of the interrelation of national and international factors in the formation of the Mexican working class and the importance of these factors in the historical development of the southwestern United States.

Magdalena Mora was born in 1952 and raised in Tlalpujahua, Michoacan, a small mining town with a long history of labor activism. Her father had been a miner and leader in the area's labor movement during the 30s and 40s. Later, he came to the United States as a *bracero* and farmworker. At the age of thirteen, Magdalena came to California where she continued her schooling and worked in the fields and the canneries of San Jose. She completed her undergraduate studies at Berkeley and attended graduate school at UCLA where she majored in history.

Her collaboration, at the age of 23 (while a member of CASA-Hermandad General de Trabajadores) in the Toltec Foods strike in Richmond, California contributed to the successful planning of the strike and victory in 1975. The Toltec strike represented one of the few triumphs in the U.S. history of rank-and-file unionism by a predominantly undocumented, female labor force. Magdalena was a leader of sound politcal judgement, a kind and compassionate human being who had taken to heart the plight of the undocumented worker.

Her untimely death in 1981 was a loss to the organizational efforts of the undocumented in this country.

i

In Memory

Preface

In the last two decades conferences, publications and the inauguration of courses have influenced the formation of and contributed material to Mexicana/Chicana history. Among these is the "Mexicana/Chicana Women's History International Symposium" held in Santa Monica, California in March of 1982. The symposium, funded by the Fund for the Improvement of Postsecondary Education (FIPSE) and headed by Professor Juan Gómez-Quiñones, involved the participation of scholars and activists from Mexico and the United States who share research interests and teaching expertise on the history of Mexican women and organizational experiences. This collaboration underscores the benefits of international exchanges in Chicano Studies and in the history of Mexican women on both sides of the border.

The essays published here reflect the maturation of the field in the 80s. Some were presented in preliminary form at the symposium, others were written later. In keeping with the bilingual/bicultural tenor of Chicano Studies, contributions written in Spanish are presented in their original form, prefaced by abstracts in English.

Preparing a volume of this size is a collaborative effort. So it is with heartfelt graditude that I thank the contributors for their patience, ready collaboration and loyality to the publication's integrity: their commitment made this book possible. The late Ralph Segura gave expert advice on publication rights. Thanks also to Arturo Madrid, Manuel Gomez and others at FIPSE for having made the symposium possible.

The book could not have been completed without the help and moral support of colleagues and friends Juan Gómez-Quiñones, Oscar R. Martí, Devra A. Weber, Teresa McKenna, Yvaniza Abaunza, Kate Vozoff and Lourdes Arguelles. Special thanks to my publisher, Roberto Cabello-Argandoña, who took an aggressive interest in the completion of the book.

Introduction

by

Adelaida R. Del Castillo

The need to know and understand the past and its meaning for the present has made the study of history basic to ethnic and women's studies. This is certainly true of Chicana Studies. Since the inception of Chicana Studies courses in 1968 the historical significance of gender, class and ethnicity have been the foci of curricula in Chicana Studies programs.

Direction and growth in this area occured despite serious obstacles. First, there existed a stark division between Chicana activists who felt feminist concerns were irrelevant and distracted attention from the immediate goals of the Chicano Movement and Chicanas who felt sexism undermined the principles of a liberation movement. Chicana feminists, however, could not reconcile their needs as feminists and ethnic women to the goals of the broader women's movement because of the latter's insensitivity to and ignorance of the importance of race, class and ethinicity. Ostracized from the Chicano Movement and alienated by the women's movement, Chicanas found alternatives for exploring the dynamic of gender, class and ethnicity. These interests led to the formation of Chicana Studies courses and in turn encouraged curriculum development, scholarly interest, and research useful to traditional disciplines.[1]

In the last two decades Chicana history has been much enriched by a growing number of theses, doctoral dissertations and research on Mexicans on both sides of the U.S.-Mexico border. Most importantly, Chicana history, as evidenced by recent research and the contributions herein, is developing a more systematic approach to theoretical and methodological issues not likely in the past for want of interdisciplinary research but presently more accessible through recent scholarship. To date, the general lack of informed, unbiased work on Mexican women in the United States and inattention to theoretical concerns has been the Achilles' heel of Chicana history.

The Mexicana/Chicana

The historical, cultural and demographic basis of the composite term 'Mexicana/Chicana' derives from a community's common prehispanic and colonial origins and a contiguous international border which facilitates the revitalization of common cultural roots. Chicana history negotiates between national, political and cultural borders of a once common geography, the United States, and Mexico and, being essentially linked with Mexican women's history conceptually may be described as the history of Mexican women in the United States. Conventionally, the term 'Chicano' is used to refer to persons of Mexican descent born or residing in the United States. Hence, the history of early Mexican settlements in the Southwest is subsumed under Chicano history[2] even though this region did not become part of the United States until 1848, a benchmark date for the periodization of Chicano history which may be in need of reconsideration.[3] Be that as it may, the relation between the history of women in Mexico to that of Mexican women in the United States is one between a people who share a similar historical, cultural, linguistic, demographic and, at one time, a similar geographic experience. Historically, commerce between Mexicans has been commonplace despite the imposition of political borders on once Mexican territory or despite recent immigration laws which selectively discriminate against Mexican immigrants to the United States This community's *transnational dimension* has infused both Chicano and Anglo communities with the language and culture of more recent Mexican immigrants. This phenomenon is sharpest in border communities where a distinct border culture exists. Not surprisingly, Mexican cultural symbols also transcend borders, temporal and spacial, as do *La Virgen de Guadalupe, La Malinche* and *La Llorona*. Limon's treatment of the latter examines, for example, how South Texans recount and relate to the crime and pain of this weeping woman, disclosing in turn a people's social consciousness and class concerns.

Paradoxically, the regional integrity of Mexicano/Chicano communities remains strong as evidenced by the unique historical presence of *hispano, tejano* and *californiano* communities in the southwestern United States. More recently, this presence has extended to the Midwest. Año Nuevo Kerr's study of three Chicago neighborhoods during this country's Great Depression contributes to a growing literature on the diversity of Mexican women's social roles and the distinctive character of midwestern Mexican communities. Theoretically, notes Sánchez, these and other distinctions account for variation between groups of Mexican women and the dominant population that help to define the parameters of Chicana historiography. Hence, greater consideration must be given to the *complexity* and *diversity* of Mexican women's experiences as surveyed by an interdisciplinary approach to Mexicana/Chicana historiography. *Between Borders: Essays on Mexicana/Chicana History* represents such an approach.

Theoretical Issues and Conceptual Frameworks

With these considerations in mind *Between Borders* begins with a discussion on theoretical positions and conceptual frameworks important to the history of Mexican women. Aspects of these debates are familiar and not limited to history inasmuch as it is argued women have been uniquely affected by patriarchal, socio-political and economic structures which have confined females to the role of mother and nurturer. Clear in the discussion is the polarization between those who argue women's history (ethnic or otherwise) is best conceptualized from a historical materialist perspective and those who answer Marxism has little or nothing to contribute to a critique of racism, sexism or patriarchy.

The arguments presented in Part I represent variations of this polemic with specific reference to Mexican women. Dixon et al. argue that Chicana history is the history of Chicano and Mexicano people representative of a transnational labor force in the context of global capital accumulation. Sexism and racism, according to them, are the outcome of this capitalist world economy and serve to rationalize the oppression of working-class women and people of color and their use as a cheap labor force.

Sánchez prefers to stress the importance of treating this population as heterogeneous and subject to a multiplicity of social, sexual and cultural variables which also have had an impact on the class formation of Mexicans in the United States. Klor de Alva, on a different note, sees the concerns of Chicana history as being similar to those of women's history in general because Chicana history is for him subsumed under women's history. He argues that the theoretical tenets of women's history are equally germane to the history of Mexican women, save for considerations of class and ethnicity which remain subordinate to gender-specific issues.

Gómez-Quiñones, however, points out that an emphasis on gender raises an important theoretical consideration: "What must be considered ... is the possibility of a gendered differentiated epistomology for if demonstrated it would be a paradigmatic revolution of unprecedented proportions," which, of course, he thinks unlikely. Rather he sees free will and the material conditions which incite and inspire human behavior as the stuff of history for men and women alike. Gómez-Quiñones argues that scholarship in women's studies (be it English, French or American) has made its contribution not at a conceptual or methodological level but in the empirical treatment of social and cultural issues.

Method and Sources

The historiography of Mexican women presented in Part II applies and examines several methodological alternatives employing oral history, demographic history and the content analysis of written sources. First, Chicana history lends itself to oral history methods due to strong oral traditions among rural-origin and older generation Mexicans. Rubio-Goldsmith examines the usefulness of the oral history approach vis-a-vis Mexican women and Weber makes use of oral sources in her examination of the participation of Mexican women in the 1933 California cottonstrike. Oral histories present the historian with methodological dilemmas long confronted by anthropologists in their interviews of cultural informants. Rubio-Goldsmith considers the 'insider/outsider' dilemma in which the dynamics between the interviewer and interviewee influence what the latter will share with the former depending on the linguistic, cultural, class or gender distance between the two which may or may not work to the advantage of the interviewer. Weber's concerns are of a different kind. She makes use of oral histories to examine questions of *consciousness* and *purpose* among actors in history. Second, census data found in the parish, baptismal and marriage records of the colonial period comprise a basic source of demographic information indispensable to Chicana historiography. Utilizing computer analysis Lara-Cea examines records and census reports and develops a composite of the diversity of women's roles in California's first Mexican settlement. The Mexican historian, Elsa Malvido, uses similar data to examine gender-specific issues critical to the control of women's bodies in colonial society in New Spain. Third, though literature alone will not suffice as a primary historical document, it can be suggestive, argues Ramos Escandon, of period lifestyles, cultural norms and belief systems. Literary sources also may be supplemented with historical records as Castañeda has done in her treatment of nineteenth century stereotypes of Early California *mexicanas*. González also analyzes the content of literature, in this case the verse and prose of Sor Juana Inés de la Cruz, in exploring vestiges of incipient nationalism by *criollos* (Spaniards born in Mexico) during Mexico's colonial period. Finally, research on the colonial period of Mexico's far northern frontier is facilitated by Castañeda García's guide to the use and availability of nineteenth and twentieth century sources on women housed in Guadalajara's historical archives. These archives are an important repository of material on California's colonial period and contain historical documents relevant to the geographical expanse extending from San Diego to Monterey once governed by the Audiencia of Guadalajara.

Together, these articles provide the reader with, for example, a well-rounded purview into particular historical periods. The articles by Antonia Castañeda, Ramón A. Gutiérrez, Helen Lara-Cea, and Douglas Monroy all speak to the colonial period of Mexico's far northern frontier. Mexican *mestizo* women in California, for example, played an important role in the evolution of a regional culture mistakenly referred to as "Spanish." In her study of this period Antonia Castañeda examines North American literature written during U.S. expansion into Mexican territory prior to the Mexican American War of 1848. Her work documents how racism, sexism and classism served to discredit and undermine early Californian society. The manipulation of prejudices contributed to the generation of stereotypes and negative moral judgements against Mexican women and, by extension, Mexican society which justified the Anglo takeover of more than half of Mexico's territory.

Mexican colonial society was itself stratified with its own rules of social status based on class, race and gender. Whereas Monroy believes California's colonial period shows greater tension over matters concerning relations between the sexes than of class, Gutiérrez examines the interplay of gender and social status through a dramatic case of seduction in colonial New Mexico disclosing a markedly different relationship to patriarchy for different groups of women within the same society. Gutiérrez combines historical methodology with anthropological approaches to the study of normative behavior and symbolic systems in his study of the belief and value systems of colonial society.

Lastly, Lara Cea's work finds colonial women were not confined to traditional societal roles, but actually exercised a considerable degree of responsibility and leadership roles in their communities. Her examination of the parish records of California's first *pueblo* settlement of San Jose which today roughly represents Santa Clara County reveals a surprising diversity of public responsibilities assumed by women in the late eighteenth century. The author considers these roles important to the functioning of colonial society and believes they are illustrative of the level of integration and worth attributed women's public participation in colonial society.

Work Experience and Labor Activism

The record of contemporary labor history of Chicana women is presently unfolding and speaks to the potential of research material available. Among these, studies on the work experiences and labor organizing activities of women have been most auspicious.[4] Part III of *Between Borders* examines this history.

Important to these efforts is the study and analyses of the labor experiences of a superexploited sector of our economy, the undocumented Mexican worker. The labor of undocumented Mexican women is an integral and indispensable contribution to our economy acknowleged by scholars and community activists and attested to in the work of the late activist historian, Magdalena Mora, to whom *Between Borders* is dedicated. Only recently have their work conditions and labor struggles been described in detail.[5]

Women who are part of the transnational, low paid female labor force which migrates seasonally from Mexico to the United States are in a uniquely vulnerable position. Arguelles examines the anxiety ridden existence of undocumented Mexican women who are subject to arrest, deportation and separation from their families. Her work gives voice to the psychological stress, cultural shock and social isolation suffered by immigrant Mexican women, many of them from rural peasant societies. The response by these women to conditions encountered to what may immediately seem an egocentric, consumer-oriented, media-conscious society is among other things, a change of consciousness, both psychological and political.

This concern for providing a more holistic approach to the community profile and lifestyles of particular groups of working class Mexicana/Chicana women is evident in the work of Año Nuevo Kerr. The intra- and interlocal community characterisitics of areas in Chicago where Mexicano/Chicanos have long migrated to illustrate how the formation and patterns of behavior of Midwest Chicano communities differ from those of the Southwest. According to Año Nuevo Kerr, Mexicana/Chicana women in these communities do not necessarily conform to general conceptions we may have about Chicanas because their cultural, working-class, and immigrant experiences have been influenced by the inter-ethnic plurality and dynamics of Chicago communities.

On the other side of the border, beneath the debris and ruins of the 1985 Mexico City earthquake begins to emerge a tragic chapter in the contemporary labor history of the Mexicana/Chicana. This earthquake precipitated the exposure of an unseen infrastructure servicing Mexico City's clandestine garment industry. Clandestine, Arbeláez tells us, because the low wages, long hours, poor working conditions, and lack of worker benefits are prohibited by Mexican law. The industry depends on the labor of hundreds of unskilled, lower-income women with families to support but with little chance of employment in the city's formal job sector. Arbeláez came to know and interview these women whose vigil amid the rubble outside places of employment began calling public attention to them. Who were they and what did they wait for? Arbeláez answers these questions by placing Mexico City's garment industry in historical context, profiling the needs and priorities of workers and management and, finally, by chronicling unionization efforts.

These and additional studies on Mexican women as a transnational labor force (Dixon et al.), Mexican women's participation in California's cotton strike of the 30s (Weber), the labor organizing leadership of Manuela Solis Sanger and Emma B. Tenayuca in Texas during the 30s (Calderón and Zamora), Chicana cannery workers in California before and during World War II (Ruiz), and women's involvement in labor issues for twentieth century Mexico (Ruiz Funes) convey a comprehensive picture of the working class experiences of the Mexicana/Chicana.

Gender, Patriarchy and Feminism

Many of us became involved in Chicana Studies and women's issues as a result of participation in the political activism of the late 60s. A coming to terms between ourselves, Chicano men and the country's feminist movement over gender-specific issues played a pivotal role in the articulation of Chicana feminism and the rationalization of Chicana Studies itself. The varied manifestations and roots of woman's oppression as well as her response to these remain central to Chicana Studies and comprise Part IV of *Between Borders*.

The proximity of the border and the adeptness with which a transborder traffic negotiates movement between the United States and Mexico has historically made possible a cross fertilization of political ideas and organizational activism. The persecution of Mexican revolutionaries during the Portiriato drove groups into exile in the United States from which they continued to agitate for social and political change.

One such group was the Partido Liberal Mexicano (PLM), an anarcho-socialist organization which helped precipitate the Mexican revolution and whose ideology called for an end to the oppression of women as essential to the liberation of the working class. In her study of the PLM's gender ideology Pérez notes the often lopsided analyses of women's oppression by class conscious researchers who see her condition as primarily the outcome of class oppression. Pérez corrects this oversight by taking into account the manipulation of gender ideology and finds that although the PLM theoretically advocated the equality of women it left much to be desired in practice. She argues, however, that women of the PLM through their active participation in the revolution defied the confines of woman's traditional sphere and, subsequently, modified the PLM's ideology on women.

The documentation of women's nonconformity to prescribed gender roles has helped undermine belief in the omnipotence of patriarchal socio-political structures even if this behavior is often linked to extraordinary periods of social change whereby women will assume roles otherwise denied them. The trouble with this perspective is that it tends to accept the notion that gender roles are clearly defined and that normally individuals live according to

xii

a set of social roles and rules which allow for little doubt, ambiguity, confusion, manipulation or contradiction between rules or social roles. Perhaps women's nonconformity to prescribed gender roles is actually more prevalent than we are led to believe and may not always involve premeditation (of socio-political goals or their elaboration in cohesive ideological statements). At times, nonconformity may express very specific dimensions of personal choice. Blanco informs us that women in Mexican society were capable of defying prescribed gender roles despite a proper upbringing, superior social rank or advanced age when these interfered with personal drives of sexual expression. Vasquez reminds us, nonetheless, that Mexican women's roles from prehispanic times to the present have been shaped by cultural, religious, socio-political and, more recently, economic considerations which have contributed uneven change in the status of women despite a history of feminist activism aided by sectors of the power elite sympathetic to their cause.

During the early 1900s Mexico's feminists found support and collaboration in progressive sectors of the state apparatus and, as Soto argues in her paper, this support was critical to the women's movement in Mexico. Ruiz-Funes describes how the government gave unprecedented support to the Mexican women's movement during the liberal administration of President Lázaro Cárdenas (1934-1940). She is cautious, however, of its long term benefits. Dependency on government support, argues Ruiz Funes, has placed the Mexican women's movement in a precarious situation due to the idiosyncratic nature of social reforms resulting from the political propensities of each administration. In her own assessment of Mexico's feminist issues, Ruiz Funes pays particular attention to the specific needs of women in Mexico, 45 percent of whom are still peasants. Their demands as women encompass political and social dimensions which speak to their actual political oppression in the countryside.

Conclusion

The themes presented in this collection of essays are basic to feminist studies: the relationship between female prescriptive norms and actual behavior; the influence of tradition and innovation in women's lives; the disjuncture between the theory and practice of the left as concerns the liberation of women; urbanization and labor force participation as a catalyst for cultural change; the patriarchal oppression of women; women's choices and sources of strength; and women as agents of social change. These topics take on a new significance when placed within the context of the historical past of Mexican women.

It is the intention of *Between Borders: Essays on Mexicana/Chicana History* to offer a reader of broad topical diversity, scope and consciousness on Mexican women's history comprised of an unprecedented collection of interpretive essays and original research on the theory, method and content of Chicana history. Together, the works presented here attest to the potential of growth in the field and interdisciplinary contributions to Mexicana/Chicana women's history.

Notes

1.   In southern California, college level Chicana Studies curricula were inspired by the feminist activism and leadership of Anna Nieto Gomez who while a student at then California State Long Beach helped organize and teach courses on La Chicana in the late sixties. While at Long Beach, she and a group of student women founded the newspaper *Hijas de Cuauhtemoc* in which women discussed sexism and condemned its practice in the Chicano student movement. Nieto Gomez was also the catalyst behind the publication of the first Chicana feminist journal, *Encuentro Femenil*, which provided a forum for the discussion and debate of Chicano movement issues by feminists and community leaders. Later in 1974 under the auspices of the University of California, Nieto Gomez developed and published a curriculum guide on Chicana Studies. That same year she published "La Feminista" in *Encuentro Femenil* which along with the work of Marta Cotera of Texas represents one of the most important statements of Chicana feminism of the period.

2.   Nonetheless, it must be emphasized that any reference to Mexican patriots of the colonial period as 'Chicanos' is inaccurate although some scholars suggest the term has prehispanic origins and argue it is a corruption of the word 'Mexica.' In the past, the term has been used by Mexicans in the Southwest to refer to commmon folk, often in a derogatory sense. More recently, the widespread use of the term 'Chicano' is the result of the political renaissance of the 60s which led the Mexican American community to define itself as 'Chicano' and identify those endeavors resulting from their efforts as 'Chicano' (thus, Chicano

history, Chicano Studies, Chicano Research Centers, etc.). Also, Chicanos (unlike colonial settlers of Mexico's far nothern frontier) have since the annexation of Mexican territories encountered distinct processes of acculturation vis-a-vis North American dominance most evident in changes in language use.

3. Some historians have suggested 1600 to be a more appropriate date from which to chronicle the origins of Chicano history since it documents the first Mexican settlement of Mexico's far northern frontier by Mexicans in El Paso. This date is also preferred for its emphasis on socio-economic factors more appropriate to women's history than traditional periodization based on events related to internecine conflict.

4. Paul Taylor's seminal work (see Bibliography) on Mexican women workers of the late 20s and 30s and, more recently, studies by Mario T. Garcia, Laurie Coyle et al., Devon Peña, Patricia Fernández-Kelly, Magdalena Mora, Vicki L. Ruiz, and Patricia Zavella (see Bibliography for their work) on El Paso women, the Farah strike, *maquila* women workers, undocumented women workers, and cannery workers provide a diverse body of work on which to build.

5. See Margarita B. Melville, "Selective Acculturation of Female Mexican Migrants," in *Twice a Minority: Mexican American Women*, ed. Margarita B. Melville (St. Louis: The C.V. Mosby Co., 1980), pp. 155-163; Idem, "Mexican Women Adapt to Migration," in *Mexican Immigrant Workers in the U.S.*, ed. Antonio Ríos Bustamante (Los Angeles: Chicano Studies Research Center Publications, University of California, 1981), pp. 119-124; Magdalena Mora, "The Tolteca Strike: Mexican Women and the Struggle for Union Representation," in *Mexican Immigrant Workers in the U.S.*, pp. 111-117; and Lourdes Arguelles in this volume.

Theoretical Issues and Conceptual Frameworks

Part I

Theoretical Issues
and
Conceptual Frameworks

THE HISTORY OF CHICANAS: A PROPOSAL FOR A MATERIALIST PERSPECTIVE

by

Rosaura Sánchez

Historical discourse, although constantly being rewritten, has in the past not addressed women as historical subjects and for that reason women have been largely neglected in historiography. Since the Civil Rights and the anti-Vietnam War Movements, new discourses which interpellate women and ethnic minorities as discursive subjects have emerged to challenge the dominant discursive practices in history and in academia. These counter-discourses have not only empowered new discursive subjectivities but led as well to a resistance against the subjugation to which non-Anglo, non-male and non-dominant individuals have been subjected for centuries in the United States.

This challenge of dominant discourses has led feminist historians to call for a new conceptual framework that is woman-oriented and that rejects masculine categories in determining what is of social significance:

> Historians' neglect of women has been a function of their ideas about historical significance. Their categories and periodization have been masculine by definition, for they have defined significance primarily by power, influence, and visible activity in the world of political and economic affairs.[1]

1

Since women have rarely been in positions of power, their experience has been largely overlooked. The little available on women is limited to four general categories, according to feminist historians:

> Women who look to the current body of historiography in order to gain a better understanding of the social forces which have shaped their lives will find that writing on women falls into four categories: 1) institutional histories of women in organization, 2) biographies of important women, 3) histories of ideas about women and their roles, and 4) social histories of women in particular times and places.[2]

The first type of history is said to be generally concerned with feminist and suffragist movements.[3] The second is largely devoted to the lives of exceptional women.[4] The third deals with child-rearing practices, marriage, divorce customs and sexual mores of particular periods.[5] The last category, which feminists find the most promising, includes studies which relate women's movements as well as women's roles and functions to major social changes.[6]

Beyond thematic differences, these feminist historical studies can be distinguished in terms of methodology. Some follow a methodological position which focuses on micro-level explanations involving only individuals and their properties.[7] This methodological individualism is in sharp contrast with macro-level studies focusing on aggregate social entities which exist in a variety of relations to each other. A macro-level approach thus takes into consideration that all social phenomena are explicable not simply in terms of the properties of particular entities but rather, given the relational character of properties, in terms of the macro-level phenomena to which they are linked. Only an anti-reductionist position takes into consideration both micro and macro-level phenomena. Thus an analysis of the situation of women in society and in historiography cannot proceed simply from an explanation of the activities, properties and relations of the particular individuals to be studied but must consider social structural conditions and different kinds of class formations.

Feminist attempts to explain the historical neglect of women simply as the result of historians' sexist biases overlook social structural conditions which have encouraged historians to concentrate on dominant white male figures within the superstructure (government, military, political, religious and educational institutions) ignoring the vast majority of both men and women. The absence of women within historiography cannot then be seen strictly in terms of gender but must consider related social aggregates like class, national origin, and race. Let us not forget that Chicano as well as Black men have also not been considered worthy of historical research. The lack of subject status does not then respond solely to gender differences but is explainable as well by social and material processes which determine particular positions and discourses. Changes in historiography and the inclusion of minority and female historical subjects correspond then to changes in discursive and nondiscursive practices, of which recent ethnic and feminist scholarship forms a part.

Historical Discursive Process

The word *history* has two principle references: a) objective (non-discursive) reality (i.e., everything that exists (or has existed) and that is constantly in the process of becoming, of developing, is history), and b) the discursive process of describing and interpreting this reality. We are concerned then with a dual process that considers both the objective world and the discursive analysis of that material reality. Since historical conditions are marked as much by ruptures and discontinuities as by continuities, a historian's textualization of the world is also constantly in flux, as is the network of discourses which are always ideological and implicated with structures of power.

Recognition of the ideological and, therefore, contradictory nature of signifying practices does not necessarily lead to relativism (that is to the proposal that "history" is purely subjective) if we are ever conscious of the fact that objective reality exists beyond and outside of any mind and independent of it.[8] Although relativists recognize variable social conditioning, they erroneously reduce historical discursive practices to a subjective process where history is no more than thought about history.[9] Post-structuralists similarly reduce history to textualization. History, however, cannot be reduced to a discursive process, for material reality cannot be reduced to concept and form, although it is also the case that material conditions assume social meaning through discourse.[10] In the process of textualizing social differences--be they of class, gender or race--one initiates struggle which can lead to changes in the nondiscursive sphere.

Both the discursive and non-discursive then are part of social being, but the non-discursive is not reducible to the discursive for the non-discursive is vaster than any conceptualization of it. History is thus both a non-discursive and a discursive process, but even the discursive is objectively determined and it exists only in historically-determined forms which are part of reality.

The historian, in selecting historical material, is objectively conditioned by social factors and discursive practices which are always multiple. One is always before a social network of interacting, signifying or discursive practices which conceptualize and reconceptualize social differences according to changes in society. The historical text is thus always intertextual, bearing traces of a multiplicity of discourses. By the same token, it is contradictory, like society itself. As transformations take place in non-discursive practices, the historical cognitive-discursive process is also transformed; this does not deny that transformations can be initiated at the discursive level.

The discourses of resistance can be said to counter or dis-identify with dominant discourses, projecting in the process new subject positions and identities. In the process these counter discourses compete with the dominant ideological hegemony, a complex of dominant class discourses which affirm particular practices, sanction others,[11] and in the process serve to mask and displace the class nature of society.[12] Although contradictory in nature, as are all ideologies, these dominant ideologies create a framework, a set of ideological strategies of containment by which everything is explained and organized, ensuring thereby the consensus of the dominated and their consent to their domination. There are various mechanisms of subjection, as Therborn has explained, but the principal ones involve accommodation, resignation and identification.[13] Counter-ideologies arise then from a context of subjection; the primary strategies here are dis-identification, resistance and organized counter-ideologies.

In some cases, counter discourses may merely question certain aspects of the dominant framework rather than dis-identifying with the entire structure. Mainstream feminist discourses, for example, generally question the patriarchal organization of society but more often than not leave unquestioned the class structure of society. In fact, following Pecheux, one could say that counter discourses by definition operate within existing frameworks.[14] Thus to project a feminist counter-discourse is to postulate gender difference as primary, affirming thereby what it negates: domination on the basis of gender.[15] This is not to deny that within a patriarchal society which oppresses the female sex one must resist the subordination of the feminine gender, but one also has to recognize that the problem of exploitation and oppression goes beyond the boundaries of gender for working class and ethnic minority women. We need to remember that class exploitation is gender blind, that women are equally adept at exploiting other women as well as men. The real working of power goes beyond gender.

Chicano women then are interpellated by a series of different, competing and overlapping ideologies, including class and non-class ideologies. For this reason Chicano female historical discourses cannot be primarily feminist in nature for the subject positions and identities which they articulate emerge from a complex material reality which includes class, ethnicity, national origin, religion, gender, age, family, locality and education. Interpellated by a series of ideological discourses, the Chicana historian responds by affirming or rejecting particular subjectivities and particular non-discursive practices in society. The historical representation is thus mediated by discourses which constitute the theoretical framework; it in turn determines the questions to be posed, the observations to be made, and the ideological interpretation of history.

Issues in Feminist History

Any work attempting to situate Chicana historiography must consider the abundance of feminist studies which have appeared in the last two decades. Four principal theoretical frameworks based on biological, cultural, materialist or linguistic perspectives are typical of most feminist studies today, be they in sociology, history or literature. In many cases, feminist scholars adopt a combination of these theoretical constructs. All, however, presuppose that sex or gender constitutes the essential difference to be analyzed or historicized.

If one were to assume that gender is the difference which subjects women to a particular position in the world, then one could perhaps question the need for studying Chicanas separately rather than as part of women's history. Perhaps Chicano women should not be studied as a separate component with its specific historical particularities but merely as a subcomponent within feminist studies. The latter would, of course, be ludicrous for many Chicano women. Yet, despite our proposal for historicizing

Chicano women within the context of class and national origin, one must be aware of the latest issues in feminist studies, for other women form part of this context.

Feminists today distinguish between gender, which is culturally defined, and sex, which is biologically defined. In *The Second Sex* Simone de Beauvoir argues against biological reductionism by declaring that women were not born but made. For culturalist feminists, the important factor in the creation of a sex-gender system is assumed to be culture rather than nature. Culture here does not refer to a specific culture within a particular historical context but rather to civilization in general. The notion is thus pan-cultural and universal. Jean Bethke Elshtain best summarizes this culturalist description of a sex-gender system:

"This system dictates social roles, purposes, and norms. It inhibits, punishes, and devalues women, while enabling, rewarding and valorizing men. Generic human, the 'biological raw material,' goes in and gendered 'social products' come out. This system is operative in all societies, for 'all sex-gender systems have been male dominated,' hence driven to assign social gender at birth 'on the basis of genitalia.' Women are consigned to the sphere of reproduction or unfree nature; men are assigned to the world of production or are free to seize their freedom. The dominant male is constituted variously as a true agent, a layer down of Law (of the Father), and a transcendent being-for-himself who occupies the productive sphere of history-making, the superordinate arena of social existence."[16]

It is the process of socialization then that leads to the assignment of different roles and hence the devaluation of women in society. Juliet Mithcell in *Psychoanalysis and Feminism* declared partriarchy to be "culture itself."

In some cases gender difference is seen to emerge as a stage in psychological development which determines the subjection of women to the Law of the Father, to the universal patriarchal culture or discourse, at the level of the unconscious. This psychological gender identity is said to be further reinforced through socialization. Chodorow, for example, believes women's mothering is crucial in the learning of gender role behavior for both boys and girls.[17]

6

Materialist feminists do not focus on gender as either a psychologically or linguistically determined difference but rather as a social difference. Women's subordination and oppression is explained in terms of a social hierarchy dominated by men. Many feminists, among them Eisenstein, distinguish between oppression and exploitation. Exploitation is understood as economic exploitation of the labor force by the owners of the means of production. The sexual oppression of women, on the other hand, is seen to be determined by the patriarchal sexual hierarchy wherein women function as mothers, domestic laborers and consumers. For Eisenstein, "oppression is inclusive of exploitation but reflects a more complex reality." She sees oppression as deriving from sex, race and class. Thus, although patriarchy and capitalism are seen to complement each other and together form the political economy of society, Eisenstein views patriarchy as preceding capitalism "through the existence of the sexual ordering of society which derives from ideological and political interpretations of biological difference."[18]

Other socialist feminists, however, propose that women's oppression has a material base. Thus, materialist studies generally link women's subordination to exploitative class relations and marginalization from social production as well as to patriarchal family structures. Some feminists like Christine Delphy, however, see an oppression specific to women even while rejecting all biological and psychological explanations of gender difference. The difference she notes between the two sexes are those of power. For Delphy, materialist studies must account for the oppression of women as a result of social relationships of domination.

All of these issues and theoretical discourses are central to a study of Chicano women for it is undeniable that Chicano women are part of the biological group of women. But the real underlying question is whether women form a separate sociological group characterized by subjection and oppression based fundamentally on gender. Feminists have often answered this question affirmatively. Kuhn and Wolpe best summarize this position as follows:

Women, irrespective of nationality and class positions, were seen to comprise a homogenous group bound together by one characteristic held in common--their 'oppression' in all walks of life.[19]

While no one would question that all women form part of a sex group, it is incorrect to state that women form one sociological group, for history has shown that material conditions surrounding different groups of women distinguished by race, nationality, ethnicity, class, caste or tribe are significantly distinct and consequently determine different experiences and ways of life. But the same could be said of studies basing difference on ethnicity, as if all Chicanos constituted one sociological group when in actuality Chicano men and women can be distinguished not only by gender but by class, origin and power. The problem of incorporation into historiography has been not one of sex primarily, but of political and economic power. For this reason Black, Chicano, Asian and Native American men have rarely been the subjects of dominant history.

Any study of Chicanas then must recognize that women form one biological but various sociological groups. Those feminists advocating that sex is a significant factor in determining self-identity, like class, race, religion and national origin, cannot, however, ignore the fact that all women do not share the same positions in the world. One simply cannot generalize and speak of some universal "oppression" as if a middle-class woman in the U.S. were as oppressed and exploited as an Indian woman in Ecuador who attends not only to domestic chores in her mud hut but also bundles her baby and carries it on her back while she picks potatoes barefooted on the *hacienda* with nothing but a sack of toasted barley to eat day long. Statements like the following are thus facile generalizations:

> I would like, therefore, to define feminism as a view of women as a distinct sociological group for which there are established patterns of behavior, special legal and legislative restrictions, and customarily defined roles.[20]

That women form different sociological groups has not, however, impeded their organizing politically *as women* at particular junctures, although even feminist movements have for the most part organized along class lines and not simply in terms of gender. Class differences between women have led to diverse and contradictory experiences, as indicated by Lerner, and thus to diverse political and ideological positions as well. In her analysis, Lerner points to women deprived of power yet closer to power than most men; exploited yet often among the exploiters; dissatisfied with their conditions, yet reluctant to change society;

8

conservative, interested in maintaining the status quo while often joining forces as organized feminist groups with more progressive elements in society.[21] Thus, as feminists, women may take liberal positions while also taking reactionary or conservative positions in regards to issues affecting others. Even when issues relating to sexuality have arisen as in the case of abortion, pregnancy leave, sexual discrimination in employment and women's suffrage, women have been divided. In the particular case of suffrage, history has shown that middle class women in the United States united along class and racial lines with the support of white middle class males interested in suppressing the rights of Black and immigrant voters.[22] Thus even when sexual oppression and subordination at particular levels have necessitated the political organization of women as a sexual group, the feminist movement has been fragmented by significant class and ethnic differences; in cases where unity has prevailed and legal rights have been achieved, once the particular struggle was over, class and racial distinctions have continued to operate and the semblance of unity has disappeared.

Women in the feminist movement today continue to reflect different positions and political strategies. Schulman divides them as follows: bourgeois feminists--"embodied in the organization NOW and the publication *Ms*"; socialist feminists--represented in journals like *Feminist Studies*; conservative feminists--"surfacing most strongly in the recent anti-pornography movement"; radical feminists--evident in the "consciousness-raising" groups of the late sixties and early seventies; lesbian-separatists; cultural feminists and various other groups organized to protest against or advocate for particular issues.[23] As Schulman explains, these various groups "unite and split in many different ways over particular issues like ERA, abortion, pornography, protective labor legislation, divorce reforms, child custody" and so on.[24] These divergent strands of feminist tendencies, which emerge from different class interests and ideological perspectives are also evident within the Chicana population, as are anti-feminist and non-feminist positions.

In addition to these feminist discourses, Chicana history must consider a vast array of other cultural practices which affect both men and women for Chicanas reside not only within the Chicano community but within the larger society as well. The point that needs to be borne in mind is that they are constantly receiving the impact of dominant ideologies and changing trends in society since these ideas, values, myths of mobility, and notions of everything from what constitutes beauty, popularity, and success to what

9

constitutes "the good life" are constantly disseminated through schools, churches, media (radio, T.V., newspapers, journals, magazines, comic strips, films, etc.), the workplace and the home. Chicanas are thus acculturated to society's dominant values and norms even while standing outside the dominant sphere. Within the Chicana sphere, however, there is also diversity. Were we to assume Chicanas form one homogenous group, that all are members of one class, have the same norms, the same psychological makeup or suffer the same degree of oppression, are of the same status within their families and communities, or have the same sexual roles in relation to men we would be making a grave mistake.

That there are significant differences within this one group forces us to contemplate an integrative approach wherein the cultural, the economic, the social and the psychological interact to produce changing patterns of Chicana experience. As has been pointed out previously, given the dominant ideologies at work, various "lived experiences" or interpretations of that reality are produced as well. Thus although Chicana history cannot be studied as a mere extension of feminist historiography, in studying Chicanas, historians must be fully aware of current trends (occupational, legal, educational and health), affecting all women in society, in greater or lesser degrees, as well as of the theoretical premises underlying feminist studies. Scholars of Chicana history can profit from the methodology being developed and the discourses emerging from the analyses of women in various disciplines even though they are ethnocentric and to a large extent address primarily white middle class women.

These feminist studies, however, also offer criteria and conclusions which we are forced to reject. A good number of studies published on women, for example, are reductionist and focus strictly on the oppression, subjugation and general subordination of women at all levels to the point where, as indicated by Lerner, the victimization of women is the only aspect considered.[25] These studies fail to consider that not all women are "equally unequal" and that women have been more than passive entities upon whom history has forced its changes. Women have been active agents of change, have supported changes, have impeded change and have contributed to both progressive and reactionary movements throughout history as we have discussed. Thus women cannot be explained as mere objects in history for they have been participants in social change alongside men. Recognizing the importance of studying women's subordination as

10

feminists have advocated does not then imply accepting that women are passive objects, totally and mechanistically determined by their social and sexual conditions. Women are subjects, capable of effecting change, as indicated by Emma Goldman:

> True emancipation begins neither at the polls nor in courts. It begins in woman's soul. History tells us that every oppressed class gained true liberation from its masters through its own efforts. It is necessary that woman learn from that lesson, that she realize that her freedom will reach as far as her power to achieve her freedom reaches.[26]

Thus change will only come with women's analysis of their material conditions--social and sexual--that is, through consciousness of both economic and sexual contradictions followed by active efforts to change these conditions, not only at the discursive level but through continued struggle for transformation at a non-discursive material level as well.

Chicana Historiography

The history of Chicanas has been only partially written, and this not only in the sense that history always offers partial and tendentious truth about society, an event or a period, but in the sense that the history of Chicanas and Mexicanas has been of relatively little importance to Chicano and Mexican historians. Yet, the history of Chicanos, limited though it is to a handful of studies and monographs, has undoubtedly laid the groundwork for studies on Chicano women, especially that dedicated to labor history.

Feminist historians have also offered numerous thematic schemes for the study of women's history that are useful for a study of Chicanas: sexist attitudes toward women, women and sexuality, women's organizations, reproduction, social roles and classes, socialization, social and economic roles and life styles of women.[27] Mitchell suggests the study of four key structures: production, reproduction, sexuality and the socialization of children.[28] In England socialist feminists associated with the *History Workshop* journal have focused on working class women and the working class family.[29] There, British feminist historians have especially sought to investigate themes on women as workers, as members of the working class, as militants and participants in

11

struggle, and as members of a capitalist society.[30] Other feminists, among them Rowbotham, are critically examining analytical postulates like that of "patriarchy" which are being reconsidered for failing to account for its different formations in different societies.[31]

A materialist perspective in Chicana historiography, far from ignoring the importance of any of these themes, would propose that they all be studied as processes that are socially and historically conditioned, that is, determined by conditions of material existence. Only a historical approach to sex-gender relations can allow us to see how changes within capitalism, which have led to changes in technologies, mass communication and production, have also led to changes in political control and to more subtle ways of controlling women, workers and dissent.

When one considers the oppression of women in the Third World, be it in Brazil, India, the Middle East or Africa, women who are brutalized psychologically as well as physically, mutilated and killed outright by husbands or male kinsmen, and compares their subjugation to the abuse suffered by women and children in an advanced capitalist society, then one has to acknowledge that the oppression of women in the Third World calls for much more than just a liberal feminist framework; the degree of abuse and political impotence of these women calls for radical revolutionary measures, as do other forms of oppression and exploitation in the Third World. We do, however, have to recognize that women in modern capitalist societies, despite efforts to resist subordination and oppression, also continue to be subjected to male violence and control, even if not always to the same extent.

Chicana historians must thus consider a network of relations, power relations which emerge as a product of numerous factors. For this reason only a macro-level analysis which considers a number of inter-related practices, discourses and subject positions can begin to explain the particular situation of Chicano women in the United States. The trend, however, in the first few studies on Chicano women was to concentrate on exceptional women--"women worthies," as Lerner calls them--while ignoring the experiences and history of the mass of women.[32] This tendency was true of all early compilers, who, Lerner indicates, sought "to praise anything women had done as a 'contribution' and to include any women who gained the slightest public attention in their numerous lists."[33]

The desire to focus on individuals can be found in the work of Martha P. Cotera, who offers a compilation of "worthies."

Although perhaps a necessary first step, micro-level analyses cannot account for social phenomena nor should these compilations be seen as justifying our historical discourses on women. Other such sketches of "exceptional" women appear in the work of Mirandé and Enríquez, who provide brief mentions of different women in the history of the Southwest, whether these be wives or lovers of important colonial leaders or soldiers or Chicana labor leaders. These and other compilations run the risk of reducing history to anecdotes or brief sketches about the ruling class or to vignettes of famous women, like Lucy Parsons, Sara Estella Ramírez or Emma Tenayuca. Since these types of studies are fairly popular, we also need to begin questioning our criteria for selection of particular women for these compilations. School readers, for example, often reflect the selection criteria of the dominant society and provide sketches of movie stars, singers, politicians or politicians' wives, and women in federal government posts, this to the exclusion of an in-depth analysis of the conditions of the vast majority of Chicana workers and housewives.

The experiences and struggles of Chicanas since 1848 offer ample opportunities for research without the need to resort to the idealization of ancestors or a glorious past. Thus works tracing Chicana roots in Mexican history need not postulate direct links between us and La Malinche or Sor Juana Inés de la Cruz. References to Aztec goddesses similarly prove absolutely nothing and in fact have been used to idealize the status of Aztec women in pre-hispanic society, both in creative and historical projects, despite documentation which points to the subordinate status of women in pre-Columbian society.[34] In short, Chicana historians need fewer myths and more historical analysis. In all cases, whatever the focus, references to women included in these histories should be accompanied by information on the class status of the historicized figures, for we are often provided information which pertains only to the ruling classes in Mexico.

An important work tracing the roots of feminism in Mexico from 1890 to 1940 is that of Anna Macías, *Against All Odds*, which documents the participation of working class, middle class and upper class women in the feminist, revolutionary, labor and even conservative movements of Mexico.[35] It is interesting to see that many of the cases documented by Macías involve public school teachers, typographers, journalists, typists and office workers. History is after all not the product of exceptional men and women but the history of class struggle and of its impact on the mass of men and women who participate in these struggles. The history of Chicanas must thus necessarily acknowledge that Chicanas are a varied group of socio-political beings who have struggled within specific materials conditions. In order to study the "ensemble of social relations" which distinguishes Chicano women, we need to look at various periods of Chicano history within which women's roles, functions, and status can be assessed and which have led to the development of class and gender consciousness.

Chicano Historical Context

Chicano history *per se* begins in 1848 when the Mexican origin population residing in the Southwest became a national minority in the United States. The history of Chicanos is a history of immigration, social and political subordination, and geographical and occupational mobility. This population which is currently over 80 percent urban was once primarily rural, although characterized by seasonal changes in residence, from farms to small towns in the Southwest. Despite its urbanity today, its roots are still rural, for older generations as well as incoming immigrants, whether documented or undocumented, are often rural in origin, although not necessarily, given the increasing number of urban immigrants from Mexico. Urbanization and migration have played a significant role in social changes affecting the family, reproduction and women's roles and status within the family and community. This urbanization is likewise tied to occupational mobility, the result of industrialization of the Southwest which brought the mechanization of agriculture and the development of capital intensive industries. The development of a dual labor market which separated workers employed in large industries from those employed in secondary industries further subordinated Chicano workers who have been primarily restricted to the secondary sector. While labor stratification has meant better wages and greater benefits and privileges as well as job stability for those hired in primary industries, the opposite has been true for those employed in secondary spheres where minorities and women are concentrated.

These changes which took Chicanos from agricultural work into blue-collar occupations and the service industries have also meant the incorporation of Chicano women into the secondary labor market and their increased participation in the service sector which includes paid domestic work, often on a part-time basis. Improvements in wages and the contribution of the wife's salary to the family budget have allowed some Chicanos to leave the barrio for integrated residential areas. But whether in or outside the barrio the Chicano family has been significantly affected by changes in the labor process, particularly wives, mothers and daughters who, though still within an economically low income group, have gained greater personal liberties, through employment, education, contact with other women, access to media, recreation, mechanization of domestic work, and the consumption of various goods and services as the family's income has increased. Acculturation to the dominant ideologies is a constant to be considered. Thus we find that as material conditions for this population have changed, so have expectations for women and views on what is appropriate for women to do, say, and think.

Although we can speak of different periods in Chicano history, with World War II as the key transitional point after which Chicanos were increasingly incorporated into urban areas and blue collar and sevice work, it is important that we be conscious of the heterogeneous conditions prevalent within Chicano communities in terms of generation, immigrant status, rural/urban origin, language dominance, literacy, employment status, age, occupation, civil status (single, divorced, separated, widowed, married, cohabitating), number of children in the family, income, place of residence (barrio/integrated community) and church affiliation. All may be of Mexican origin but this population is as diverse as any other living group of people. There can be no simple labeling which can encompass the diversity represented by this population, despite the fact that there are certain general social changes which have affected the entire population, changes which need to be described and explained so that we understand not only what happened but also why it happened and what impact it has had on the entire Chicano population and, in particular, on Chicanas.

Marx once said, as a metaphor, that the human anatomy provides us with the key to understanding earlier forms of the species. In other words, as Schaff explains, a higher stage of historical development provides us with the effects and results produced by events of the past and allows us to understand the underlying "tendencies and driving forces" of that past.[36] Thus a study of the Chicana today, within the varied social conditions described above, provides us with an entire spectrum of what

Chicanas are, have been, and are becoming. History is a recount of this process of becoming, which is evident in changes affecting the labor process and ideology, changes which in turn affect our entire being. What Chicanas are today is thus evidence of their labor, sexual, reproductive, family and other social experiences which necessarily need to be studied in relation to what has changed, that is, in relation to what Chicanas were before 1940 and even before 1900.

Current Issues in Chicana History

The best work providing a history of Chicanas presently includes work done by sociologists, anthropologists, newspaper reporters, labor leaders and others. Their works furnish us with short but illuminating studies dealing with a range of issues including sterilization,[37] the garment industry,[38] women in the Chicano Movement,[39] domestic workers,[40] acculturation of female Mexican migrants,[41] pink-collar workers,[42] women as innovators[43] and abortion[44]. Theses and dissertations, like that of Shirlene Soto on the participation of women in the Mexican revolution, are an important source of historical material. In the area of psychology and education several theses have examined factors influencing Chicano women's enrollment in institutions of higher learning.[45] Through interviews, case studies, statistical surveys and personal observations, these writers are providing basic information, indicating the heterogeneity of the Chicano community and the importance of incorporating an economic analysis into these studies. Historians dealing with la Chicana now consider many different sources for information, especially oral interviews and even products of popular culture like songs and ballads which reflect popular attitudes and problems. Chicano literature, whether written by men or women, has also become a valuable source of information on prevalent male attitudes towards women and a resource for examining how a complex reality is translated into "lived experience." All of these studies provide indispensible data, and a wealth of resource material but the selection and interpretation for historical analysis remain to be done. One group currently and actively contributing to the interpretation of Chicana historiography is MALCS (Mujeres Activas en Letras y Cambio Social). Its efforts have been spearheaded by Ada Sosa Riddell, a leading Chicana feminist.

We then see that the history of Chicanas is being recorded in various types of texts. In any discussion of these texts, however, one has to distinguish between "feminist" works and those that simply focus on women. Despite differences in feminist theories, feminist works not only originate from a feminist framework, but in their analysis of the condition and experience of women provide a critical feminist account of gender inequality. An empirical, quantitative study of female industrial or domestic workers is thus not necessarily a feminist study. Similar studies on women workers are now available by Chicano males. Mario T. García, for example, has written on women workers and on the Chicano family and though he provides a materialist analysis, his work is not feminist (and this is not simply because he is male) because the overriding factor in his work is not gender, sexism or patriarchy.[46] This points to the fact that, in many studies on Chicano women, positing "gender" as the essential difference explaining the oppression of Chicanas is out of the question since Chicana scholars must consider class as well as ethnicity in their analyses.

Feminists who see an oppression which is specific to women cannot understand why Black and Chicano women use race/ethnicity and class concepts to explore the oppression of minority women nor why this oppression is always linked to that of minority men. If, as Delphy indicates, men are the agents and beneficiaries of the subordination of women, then men are the main enemy. This radical perspective appears in the work of some Chicana writers, especially in the work of some Chicana poets concerned with sexual oppression, but for the most part Chicana scholars, like their Black counterparts, have found it is not possible to understand the oppression of Chicano women without also taking that of Chicano men into consideration.

Most work on Chicanas has not dealt with theoretical formulations, although there are exceptions like that of Maria Linda Apodaca,[47] but rather has consisted of empirical studies on particular groups of women, grouped according to participation in a particular category of employment or labor organization or according to a type of oppression, as in the case of sterilization. Presently, with the growing (although at a snail's pace) representation of Chicanas in institutions of higher learning, research on Chicanas by sociologists, anthropologists, psychologists, historians and literary critics is increasing.

Generally speaking, material on Chicanas has been most accessible through anthologized texts. Three social science anthologies on Chicanas (two of them published by the UCLA Chicano Studies Research Center) have long been available: *Essays on La Mujer, Mexican Women in the United States,* and *Twice a Minority* (published by Mosby Press). There are also articles on Chicanas scattered throughout in journals and books. Anthologies on feminist studies however are more likely to include articles on Latin American women than on Chicanas but there are exceptions, as in the case of *Sisterhood is Powerful,* edited by Robin Morgan. From Arizona comes the Renato Rosaldo Lecture Series Monograph on *La Mexican/Chicana,* published in 1985, which contains three articles on labor activism, political organization and oral history. The volume entitled *Women in the U.S.-Mexico Border,* edited by Vicky L. Ruiz and Susan Tiano and published in 1987, offers studies on both Mexican and Chicano women workers, with a strong emphasis on *maquila* workers along the border. Oral history and testimonies ("testimonios") are one type of text now gaining acceptance. *Las mujeres,* published by the Feminist Press and McGraw-Hill Book Co., is a collection of autobiographical testimonies by Chicanas from New Mexico [1980].

A number of journals like *La Palabra,* [Vol. 2, no. 2, Fall 1980], *El Fuego de Aztlán* [Vol. 1, no. 4, Summer 1977], *Revista Chicano-riqueña* [Vol. XI, nos. 3-4, 1983] and *Imagine* [Vol. II, no. 1, Summer 1982] have dedicated issues to the literature of Chicano women. Bilingual Press recently published a series of essays on Chicana literature, *Beyond Stereotypes,* edited by María Herrera-Sobek, 1985, and various other journals have included articles on Chicana authors. A number of Chicana poets among them Ana Castillo, Angela de Hoyos, Sandra Cisneros, Yolanda Luera, Lorna Dee Cervantes, Bernice Zamora, Gina Valdés, Evangelina Vigil, Margarita Cota-Cardenas, Alma Villanueva, Lucha Corpi, and Xelina have published books of poetry. Marta Sánchez has published through the University of California Press, 1985, the first book-length study of four Chicana poets titled *Contemporary Chicana Poetry.* Short stories by Chicanas have also appeared in various journals and magazines. Gina Valdés has published her first novel *There Are No Madmen Here,* and in 1987 added a collection of poetry. Literature is possibly the discipline in which more work by Chicanas and on Chicanas has appeared. Yet even here the number of creative writers and critical studies of this literature is not large.

The following discussion will briefly review four research articles and is intended to provide a sense of the focus and direction of recent studies on Chicanas. The work by Vicki L. Ruiz, "Obreras y Madres: Labor Activism among Mexican Women and Its Impact on the Family"[48] is based on field research and statistical evidence, and looks at Chicana workers' participation in the labor force and in labor unions from a culturalist perspective (as previously described). Ruiz accepts the assumption that socialization produces "warm, nurturing" women whose main goal in life is to minister to the needs of husband and children, especially the latter. She states: "Mexican women, much as other women in other cultures, have been socialized to devote their entire lives to satisfying the physical and emotional needs of their children." Ruiz finds that this image of the nurturing woman can be reconciled with that of labor activist since devotion to family and especially to children often becomes the motivation for joining a labor union and going on strike for higher wages and benefits. The traditional family structure generally condemned for its patriarchal structure is here seen to be conducive to labor struggle. Ruiz does, however, recognize that in some cases this labor activity can lead to family stress, strife and divorce, problems attributed to "the values and attitudes of the husband and wife toward the role and function of women in society." Ruiz' argument accepts the assigned nurturing role of women and uses it to explain labor activism and indirectly family strife. The question here would be whether it is in fact family roles that lead to labor activism or whether it is a particular type of production which leads both to particular family roles and to a particular type of exploitation which calls for resistance. Although the article does not critically analyze the family structure in the Chicano community or take issue with basic assumptions on female roles, except to reinforce them, it does, however, by synopses of interviews, provide a forum for Chicano women workers to voice their opinions, an important task in itself.

In the area of cinema, the article by the Chicana filmmaker Sylvia Morales, "Chicano-Produced Celluloid Mujeres," looks at the image of Chicano women in films made or directed by Chicano men.[49] Morales acknowledges that the intent of these filmmakers has been to counter the image of Mexicans as violent, dirty, thieving and stupid, but she questions whether the traditional image of women has changed at all in these Chicano films. In the case of *Raíces de Sangre* she notes that the roles of both men and women are traditional ones, with the woman seen as dependent on men. In Luis Valdez' *Zoot Suit* Morales rejects the "worn out portraits of Mexican women" and their exclusion from political organizing and activism. The film *Seguín* is said to provide an idealized vision of Mexican women, ever nurturing, ever sweet and unthreatening. The only image that Morales finds to be positive is that of the female translator in *The Ballad of Gregorio Cortez*. This woman is a middle-class, self-supporting woman who toward the end of the movie becomes politically active in raising funds for Cortez' defense.

The article itself is a dialogue with Chicano male filmmakers. The rejection of the various film images points to a rejection of particular roles and functions and to a rejection of patriarchy, but there is no specific discussion of the relation between these culturally determined roles and society at large. The relation between these images and the other ideological discourses of the films themselves is also not explored. The film critic simply assumes that within existing society it is possible to make another type of film which will not malign women. The question then would be: is it possible? Since films are commodities as well as artistic and ideological products, they are produced for profit, that is, for massive consumption. This necessarily establishes financial constraints and guarantees that only those films offering a "preferred reading" of Chicanos and Chicanas will be funded. Actually, the image of Chicano males in these films is just as distorted and accommodating as is that of Chicanas.

In the article "A Double Edge Sword: Hispanas and Liberal Feminism," María Linda Apodaca offers a materialist analysis of liberal feminism from its origins in the nineteenth century to contemporary American feminism and then compares this movement to Chicana feminism.[50] In exploring the positive and negative aspects of liberal feminism, Apodaca finds that contemporary Chicana feminism has also been a middle-class movement despite the large percentage of working-class Chicano women in our communities and despite their participation in labor struggles. Her own theoretical approach, especially in the latter half of the article, resembles that of socialist feminism as she begins to question whether any meaningful change is possible without a change in the capitalist mode of production. This is one of the few Chicana papers concerned not only with providing data but with discussing the theoretical framework with which such data is to be analyzed. It is to be hoped that it will be the first of many more to come.

The Mexican feminist journal, *Fem.*, has now published two thematic issues on la Chicana. The October/November 1986 issue contained a translated article by Adelaida R. Del Castillo on the education of Chicanas, "Sobre la experiencia educativa chicana."[51] Here Del Castillo reviews various sociological, anthropological, psychological and educational approaches which have been used to account for both the low and high educational attainment of Chicanas and their high drop-out rates. For each study the determining variable is different: the family, parental attitudes, teacher attitudes, socio-economic status, lack of counseling, language, the influence of a strong mother, early marriage, the work ethic and an individual desire to excel. What is important in this article is that the writer proposes that the problem needs to be explored in terms of a number of factors. It does not propose one particular framework but does reject the fragmentary and atomistic way in which various studies seek to explain the problem of low educational attainment. The implication is that all of these issues are highly complex and must be seen as part of the larger historical context. Although not specifically feminist in its orientation, the article comes near to an integrated interdisciplinary approach.

Chicana history must thus consider all those social elements which interact and affect Chicano women. It must necessarily deal with labor struggle, labor stratification, immigration, deportations, racism, low wages, occupational and residential segregation, low educational attainment, lack of political power, as well as urbanization, industrialization, occupational mobility, social mobility, consumerism and ideological assimilation. Within this broad material context, historians must also examine patterns of socialization, sexual freedom and restriction, reproduction, female roles and functions, and the extent of personal liberties for women in the Chicano community, for all of these social, economic, political and sexual factors interconnect and affect Chicanas in diverse and contradictory ways. The victimization and oppression of Chicanas which result from these conditions is undeniable, but so is social change, however minor, which is constantly affecting Chicano women and changing their social relations and social life.

Socialization of Women

As indicated before, the family is the primary institution for socialization, for acquiring not only language but the various ideological codes of society. Primary indoctrination of children in the home is practiced, for the most part, by the mother whose primary function has been that of nurturing and socializing the

21

young. It is at home, then, within the sphere of the Chicano family that Chicanas learn particular sex roles and modes of behavior. Although socially conditioned, at home women act as subjects in charge of the socialization process. Thus, if women come to accept their subordination, it is a lesson well taught by their own mothers. Women have been willing accomplices serving as ideological apparatuses of the culture transmitting from one generation to the next the same wornout expectations of female behavior, the same discourses, whether this ideological function has been conscious or unconscious. Chicano mothers have taught their daughters that men come first, that their brothers are more important, and that women's education is less important. Thus Chicano women have been brainwashed into accepting their subordinate roles by other women. It is from other women that women learn that life without a man is not worth living. Women are at times their own worst enemies.

Even though men and women are socially conditioned by the interacting and competing practices and discourses in their environment, they are also capable of transforming social order and ideology, once they become conscious of their conflicts and contradictions and counter the existing practices. Women, and here specifically, Chicano women, will have to stop the proliferation of these discourses which disseminate forms of social constraint and produce discourses which resist domination. The discourse of struggle and resistance must become a greater part of the community network of discourses, if we are to effect change at the level of nondiscursive practices as well.

Unfortunately, the discourses of submission are often masked and misrepresented as legitimate and necessary, but they merely allow for the continuation of domination. There are, however, women who enjoy playing the defenseless role, who enjoy a patriarchal system which allows them to live as children protected by a male. That they then feel betrayed once this protection is withdrawn or once it turns into abuse indicates that they do not enter this contract on equal footing. Although all social practices involve constraints of some type, those that reduce a woman to the role of servant, sexual object, lap dog and punching bag must be resisted both by the victim and observers of victimization. We need then a study of all the cultural constraints imposed on women in the community, the types and degree of control exercised, the degree of consent and consensus to this domination and the degree of resistance evident in the lives of all Chicano women, whether single, married, or divorced.

Socio-Sexual Factors

If women are socialized into accepting their subordination, they are also taught to accept their sexual roles within the patriarchal family. The two major issues to consider here are reproduction and sexuality. Again both of these must necessarily be studied within concrete historical conditions which have facilitated technological strides, especially in medicine and in communication.

Television especially has revolutionized the home since families once isolated to a certain extent within the confines of privacy now spend hours "glued to the tube," sharing their time with countless strangers and their problems. Television has made us all aware of endless commodities and services as well as placed us in contact with the rest of the world. Minority families are thus not only provided with information that in the past was accessible to only a few but are indoctrinated with the dominant values of society; in the process they are exposed to changing trends and styles of life. The impact of television on the Chicano family, beyond the consumption of particular commodities, has still to be studied.

Technological changes have undoubtedly affected the population at large in all aspects of life, providing time-saving household appliances, faster means of transportation and improved medical services and prescriptions, easily packaged and made available to the general public. One of the most important products which has revolutionized sexual practices is the use and availability of contraceptives. Minority women also have taken advantage of the pill, reducing fertility rates in the community, although not to the extent of the majority community. The Census Bureau estimates the future fertility rate for Hispanics, the Spanish-origin population, will increase substantially in the near future. A low fertility rate (1.6) would mean a population of 43,948,000 and a high fertility rate (2.3) one of 85,478,000 persons by the year 2080.[52] Low estimates would assume some type of birth control among the population born after 1982. In order to project what will occur in the future, it would be important to study what percentage of Chicano women today are on the pill, where they obtained their information on birth control, whether

23

the pill was the woman's decision, a joint man-woman decision or whether it was imposed by a third party. It would also be important to research the length of time that it takes first-generation immigrant women to make use of the product, especially when Mexican radio stations also promote birth control through their "smaller families live better" promotions.

Technology has thus made it possible for women to have greater control over their reproductive lives. But birth control has its grim side. Third World and minority women have been exploited and used as guinea pigs to test contraceptives. In some cases, birth control has been forcibly imposed on minority women through the intervention of welfare and medical agencies which have been known to illegitimately impose tubal ligations and involuntary sterilizations upon often unsuspecting minority women. Within a capitalist society, one has to remember, technological advances are generally industrial schemes for greater profit making. The sole interest in profit leads to the marketing of defective and cancer-causing substances that a gullible public consumes, as was evident in the sale of the Dalkon Shield. Often these marketing objectives have resulted in the widespread use of experimental products by minority women in the U.S. and women in the Third World. Technological progress, like everything else within the capitalist system, is full of contradictions and has had a definite impact, both constructive and destructive, within the Chicano community.

Birth control practices, however, do not represent the end of sexual repression, an important feminist issue. Contraceptives may on the one hand lead to greater sexual expression, but on the other may facilitate the sexual exploitation of women as commodities without the fear of added economic burdens on the family. That for heterosexual men gaining or retaining sexual freedoms has never been an issue but a personal choice indicates that sexual freedom is a power issue, the private choice of those whose personal freedoms are not determined by others. Women, on the other hand, especially Chicano women, always have been subjected to this type of control. True, urbanization and economic independence have allowed for a greater degree of sexual freedom. This is true even for Chicano women, especially for women who live alone, but within traditional families, sexual freedom for women, even working women continues to be taboo in the Chicano community. The problem is greater and goes far beyond the community when we consider that abortion clinics may soon be available only to middle-class women, since a total of 35 states as of 1984 forbade the use of public funding for abortions.[53] The discourse of sexual freedom is in this way accessible only to those who can afford to pay for it.

Despite the double standard in the Chicano community which permits males sexual freedom but restricts women's sexual activity, changes in patterns of social contact between men and women have facilitated sexual encounters for many young women living at home, as is evident in the number of unwed mothers in Chicano households and in the number of teenage weddings and divorces. Yet even here there are differences which need concrete research, for today unwanted pregnancies among today's teenage girls are no longer the great family tragedies of the past. Sexual restrictions have of course always co-existed with deviations from the imposed norms as is evident in popular expressions and jokes about cuckolds. Yet these very expressions confirm that sexual norms were meant not only to restrict and protect women as private property but also to present them as "defenseless" creatures. Paternalism can be a most subtle form of male domination.

There are other types of female repression which need to be studied in the community. Among these are the numerous cases of child abuse and rape, often by male family members. The battering of women is also gaining more attention, thanks to community efforts, the media and to the availability of a handful of abuse centers throughout the country. Media coverage has also allowed us to see the number of Latina women living out in the street, often with children in tow. As families have fragmented and single or divorced women with children have established residence apart, the sense of obligation, of having to "take in" less fortunate family members has also been lost. Thus, even though industrialization and urban residence have brought greater information, education opportunities, and employment, as well as greater access to the welfare system, battered-women shelters, day-care centers, counseling centers and abortion clinics, all of these social changes which have altered the community's views of what is acceptable sexual behavior, yet changes in production and consumption have also brought about unemployment, double exploitation at home and at work, social fragmentation, and the further impoverishment of minority women and children.

Conclusion

Given the material conditions--economic, political, social-- which form the historical context of minority women in the United States, it is not surprising that Chicano women scholars have focused on the larger issues affecting the entire Chicano community rather than simply on the oppression of Chicano women. It is in analyzing at a macro-level the material conditions present within this country, that their relation to patriarchal ideology, sexism and the subordination and oppression of all women becomes clearer. Within this broader context we can then begin to explore the many issues that affect Chicano women: exploitation, poverty, wife and child abuse, sexuality and violence, unemployment, ideological conditioning, fears and phobias, domestic life and housework, the function of the family in late capitalism, the impact of divorce, the plight of single mothers, Chicanas' participation in different types of production, work hazards faced by Chicana workers, and the racism and discrimination faced by Chicano women workers and students.

But we also need to go beyond descriptive or empirical studies that provide information and statistical data. It is important to develop our own counter-discourses, however much they overlap with other competing or complementary discourses, to analyze the situation of a growing population in this country. We must formulate our own critique of existing frameworks adopting what is useful and rejecting those constructs which do not take into account the specific historical context of Chicano women. The history of Chicano women must deal with the combination of differences which constitute us: gender, class and national origin. Our multiple subjectivities must be addressed.

Notes

1. Ann D. Gordon, Mari Jo Buhle, and Nancy Schrom Dye, "The Problem of Women's History," in *Liberating Women's History: Theoretical and Critical Essays*, ed. Berenice A. Carroll (Urbana: University of Illinois Press, 1976), p. 75.
2. Ibid., p. 76.
3. Ibid., p. 78.
4. Ibid., p. 79.
5. Ibid., p. 81.
6. Ibid., p. 82.

7. Andrew Levine, Elliot Sober, and Erik Olin Wright, "Marxism and Methodological Individualism," *New Left Review* 162 (March/April 1987): 69.

8. Adam Schaff, *History and Truth* (New York: Pergamon Press, 1976), p. 157.

9. Ibid., p. 103.

10. Ernesto Laclau and Chantal Mouffe, "Post-Marxism Without Apologies," *New Left Review* no. 166 (November/December 1987): 79-106.

11. Goran Therborn, *The Ideology of Power and the Power of Ideology* (London: Verso Editions and NLB, 1980).

12. Stuart Hall, "Culture, the Media and Ideological Effect," in *Mass Communication and Society*, ed. J. Curran et al. (London: Arnold, 1977).

13. Therborn, *The Ideology of Power*, pp. 96-99.

14. Michel Pecheux, *Language, Semantics and Ideology* (New York: St. Martin's Press, 1982).

15. Michel Foucault, *The History of Sexuality* (New York: Random House, 1980).

16. Jean Betke Elshtain, "The New Feminist Scholarship," *Salmagundi* 70 and 71 (Spring/Summer 1986): 11.

17. Nancy Chodorow, "Mothering, Male Dominance and Capitalism," in *Capitalist Patriarchy and the Case for Socialist Feminism*, ed. Zillah R. Eisenstein (New York: Monthly Review Press, 1979), pp. 83-106.

18. Zillah R. Eisenstein, "Developing a Theory of Capitalist Patriarchy and Socialist Feminism," in *Capitalist Patriarchy*, p. 25.

19. Annette Kuhn and Ann Marie Wolpe, "Feminism and Materialism," in *Feminism and Materialism: Women and Modes of Production*, ed. Annette Kuhn and Ann Marie Wolpe (London: Routledge and Kegan Paul, 1978), p. 1.

20. Hilda Smith, "Feminism and the Methodology of Women's History," in *Liberating Women's History*, p. 370.

21. Gerda Lerner, "New Approaches to the Study of Women in American History," in *Liberating Women's History*, p. 351.

22. Alix Kates Schulman, "Dancing in the Revolution: Emma Goldman's Feminism," *Socialist Revolution* 61.

23. Ibid., p. 33.

24. Ibid.

25. Gerda Lerner, "Placing Women in History: A 1975 Perspective," in *Liberating Women's History*, p. 358.

26. Quoted in Schulman, "Dancing in the Revolution," p. 43.

27

27. Sheila Ryan Johansson, "'Herstory' as History: A New Field or Another Fad?," in *Liberating Women's History*, pp. 400-430.

28. Juliet Mitchell, "Four Structures in a Complex Unity," in *Liberating Women's History*, p. 385.

29. Samuel Raphael, ed., *People's History and Socialist Theory* (London: Routledge and Kegan Paul, 1981).

30. Anna Davin, "Feminism and Labour History," in *Peoples History and Socialist Theory*, p. 176.

31. Sheila Rowbotham, "The Trouble with 'Patriarchy'," in *People's History and Socialist Theory*, p. 364.

32. Lerner, "Placing Women in History," p. 357.

33. Lerner, "New Approaches," p. 349.

34. Iris Blanco, "Participación de las mujeres en la sociedad prehispánica," in *Essays on La Mujer*, ed. Rosaura Sánchez and Rosa Martinez Cruz (Los Angeles: Chicano Studies Center Publications, University of California, 1977), p. 48-81.

35. Anna Macias, *Against All Odds: The Feminist Movement in Mexico to 1940* (Westport, Conn.: Greenwood Press, 1982).

36. Schaff, *History and Truth*, p. 95.

37. See Adelaida R. Del Castillo, "Sterilization: An Overview," in *Mexican Women in the United States: Struggles Past and Present*, ed. Magdalena Mora and Adelaida R. Del Castillo (Los Angeles: Chicano Studies Research Center Publications, University of California, 1980), p. 65-70; and Carlos G. Velez-I., "Se Me Acabó La Conción: An Ethnography of Non-Consenting Sterilization Among Mexican Women in Los Angeles," in *Mexican Women in the United States*, pp. 71-91.

38. See Lisa Schlein, "Los Angeles Garment District Sews a Cloak of Shame," in *Mexican Women in the United States*, pp. 113-116; Laurie Coyle, Gail Hershatter, and Emily Honig, "Women at Farah: An Unfinished Story," in *Mexican Women in the United States*, pp. 117-143; and Mario Vasquez, "The Election Day Immigration Raid at Lilli Diamond Originals and the Response of the ILGWU," in *Mexican Women in the United States*, pp. 145-148.

39. Adelaida R. Del Castillo, "Mexican Women in Organization," in *Mexican Women in the United States*, pp. 7-16.

40. Vicki L. Ruiz, "Obreras y Madres: Labor Activism Among Mexican Women and Its Impact on the Family," in *La Mexicana/Chicana*, Renato Rosaldo Lecture Series, Vol. 1, Series 1983-84, Summer 1985 (Tucson: Mexican American Studies and Research Center, University of Arizona), pp. 19-38.

41. Margarita B. Melville, "Selective Acculturation of Female Mexican Migrants," in *Twice a Minority*, ed. Margarita B. Melville (St. Louis: The C.V. Mosby Company, 1980), pp. 155-163.

42. Denise Segura, "Labor Market Stratification: The California Experience," *Berkeley Journal of Sociology* 29 (1984).

43. Linda Whiteford, "Mexican American Women as Innovators," in *Twice a Minority*, pp. 109-126.

44. Maria Luisa Urdaneta, "Chicana Use of Abortion: The Case of Alcala," in *Twice of Minority*, pp. 33-51.

45. Frances Nelda Sanchez, "Motivational and Demographic Factors Which Influence Mexican American Women to Enroll in Higher Education," (Master's thesis, Texas Woman's University, 1983).

46. Mario T. Garcia, "La Familia: The Mexican Immigrant Family, 1900-1930," in *Work, Family, Sex Roles and Language*, National Association for Chicano Studies (Berkeley: Tonatiuh-Quinto Sol, 1979), pp. 117-139.

47. See Maria Linda Apodaca, "The Chicana Woman: An Historical Materialist Perspective,' in *Women in Latin America: An Anthology from Latin American Perspectives*, ed. William Bolinger et al. (Riverside, Calif.: Latin American Perspectives, 1979), pp. 81-100; and Idem, "A Double Edge Sword: Hispanas and Liberal Feminism," *Crítica: A Journal of Critical Essays* 1 (Fall 1986): 96-114.

48. Ruiz, "Obreras y Madres," pp. 19-38.

49. Sylvia Morales, "Chicano-Produced Celluloid Mujeres," in *Chicano Cinema*, ed. Gary Keller (Binghamton, New York: Bilingual Review, 1983).

50. See Apodaca, "A Double Edge Sword," pp. 96-114.

51. Adelaida R. Del Castillo, "Sobre la experiencia educativa chicana," *Fem.: Publicación Feminista Bimestral* 48 (octubre-noviembre 1986): 7-10.

52. Gregory Spencer, "Projections of the Hispanic Population: 1983-2080," in *Current Population Reports*, Series P-25, no. 995 (Washington, D.C.: Census Bureau, 1986), p. 9.

53. See "North America: United States. Developments in the States in 1984," in *Britannica Book of the Year, 1985*, (Chicago: Encyclopaedia Britannica, 1985), pp. 570-572.

CHICANAS AND MEXICANAS WITHIN A TRANSNATIONAL WORKING CLASS

by

Elizabeth Martínez and Ed McCaughan

> *The following is a revised version of a paper originally written for the Chicana History Project and Symposium in 1982. The data have not been updated, but the analysis has been amended to reflect the authors' more recent thinking. We wish to acknowledge Susanne Jonas' contribution to this article.*

Introduction

The experience of Chicana and Mexicana women in the United States is a story of workers and also the story of half a people. To understand it, we have to trace several simultaneous processes of colonialism. Before we begin to do that, let us lay out some theoretical premises and concepts.

A. The Capitalist World System. Beginning with the Spanish conquest, the Mexicano and Chicano peoples have developed as super-exploited populations within the framework of a capitalist world-economy. A capitalist world-economy is not defined per se by the existence (or exclusive existence) of wage-labor, but rather by the relationship of that population to the evolving capitalist world-economy. More generally: We take as the defining characteristic of capitalism neither the exploitation of free waged labor by capital (though such exploitation is the highest form of capitalist relations of production) nor the predominance of exchange on a market. Rather, we understand capitalism as production solely for capital accumulation, based on the appropriation of surplus value from the direct producers, where the greater part of the surplus value is reinvested; the market *under capitalism* is organized so as to maximize capital accumulation. Capitalism is the only mode of production in which

31

capital accumulation is maximized for its own sake (irrespective of human use value), which creates a pressure for constant expansion. Capitalism is a world-system whose dynamic is: expand or die.[1]

B. *Proletarianization.* Using a model of capital accumulation means that we do not restrict ourselves to the existence of wage-labor as the defining characteristic of a capitalist world-economy. Rather, the capitalist world-economy is characterized by a *process of proletarianization*: the increasing degree to which wage-labor is the predominant labor relation as a result of the incorporation of populations into the capitalist world-economy. This process proceeds along a continuum of types of household incomes. Wallerstein and Hopkins, in "Patterns of Development of the Modern World-System,"[2] discuss three varieties of workers' households in terms of how subsistence or income is obtained:

1. Subsistence-redoubt households: "... households truly external economically to the development of the (capitalist) system, albeit located geographically within, whose subsistence (however mean or luxurious) results from production unrelated to the capitalist world-economy's division of labor."[3] An example within the history of the Chicano/Mexicano people would be the pre-Colombian native households.

2. Lifetime proletarian households: "... households whose subsistence or maintenance, throughout the whole of their lives, results from production within the world-economy, the products they consume to live consisting of payments in kind from those they work for, provisions from public authorities, or commodities purchased 'in the market' with the payments in money (wages) they receive from those they work for. Production within the world-economy thus provides for their material wants and so 'reproduces' them, as labor, not only weekly or annually but generationally as well."[4] Examples would be the coerced labor system of the California missions under Spanish colonial rule, or the modern day urban proletariat.

3. Part-lifetime proletarian households: "... households who receive part of their life income from 'employers' or market-purchasers and part from direct production either by themselves or others (who may be kin). As a result, the full cost of reproduction is not borne by 'employers.' A good example would be the migrant laborer. A key question, however, is the degree to which they receive from their 'employers' a 'proportionate' share of the costs of reproduction."[5] An example from

Chicano/Mexicano history would be workers in the Bracero Program.

According to this paradigm, it is clear that the proportion of lifetime proletarian households has been growing (proletarianization) as a result of the expansion of the capitalist world-economy; yet the most costly form of labor to capital is lifetime proletarian households, since part of the cost of the production and reporduction of labor power must be reflected in wage levels. This is why, in moments of expansion of the capitalist world-economy (or one of its nation-state units), the number of lifetime proletarian households, increases. However, in moments of contraction, we find the re-emergence of the cheapest form of lifetime-proletarian household, employment by means of "putting-out" (contracting piecework to be done in the home) or in various forms of unregulated sweatshops. If the period of economic contraction is very severe, there is the likelihood of reversion to part-lifetime proletarian households, resulting in the cheapest labor costs.

Under capitalism, there is a transition from forms of non-wage-labor to predominantly wage-labor. This transition has occurred as part of the development of capitalism and the extension of the law of value into all aspects of life, including the family. In Wallerstein's terms, we are looking at an historical process by which, over time, the proportion of lifetime proletarian households has come to replace the subsistence/redoubt households and part-lifetime proletarian households which predominated in previous eras.

C. Chicanos and Mexicanos as a transnational labor force. To understand the social position and economic role of Chicanas and Mexicanas today, we must understand the total social milieu of the Chicano/Mexicano population of the United States and the continuous interrelationship between Mexico and the southwestern United States. The essential relationship between Mexico and the United States, in turn, defines the interrelationship between Mexicans and U.S. populations of Mexican origin.

The United States is a major core state within the capitalist world-economy. Mexico stands as a semiperipheral country in a neo-colonialist relationship to the United States. As a consequence of the historically unequal exchange relationship between the United States and Mexico, deliberate North American policy, and the more recent transnationalization of capital, a *transnational*

33

labor force has been created. It serves primarily as a reserve army of labor for U.S. agricultural and manufacturing enterprises.

The transnational labor force is distinct from the historical groups of European immigrants who settled in the United States. In our conception, it is a population increasingly not limited by national boundaries, but is defined by the division of labor between two neighboring but unequal areas within the capitalist world-system--in this case, the United States and Mexico. The transnational working class is in itself stateless: the state of origin promotes emigration as a "solution" to these impoverished masses, the state which receives them is willing to exploit, but not adopt them. They are the world's "industrial reserve army of labor," the world's underclass, living on the fringes in the core states.

Today, with the increasingly transnational operation of capital, and a corresponding subservience of U.S. immigration policy to that capital, the transnational labor force is a growing and ever more significant sector of this country's labor force. In addition, as a result both of the world capitalist crisis, and of capital's increasing ability to operate independently of nation-states, we are seeing the creation of transnational zones of labor in many parts of the United States--the generalization of what at one time existed primarily in the U.S.-Mexico border region.

The ebb and flow of labor power across the U.S.-Mexican border is older than the European guest worker program. Yet, with the possible exception of the Bracero Program, it is rarely perceived as an earlier and more pernicious species of the modern European guest worker system; nonetheless, both the European and North American situations are analogous. In Europe the guest worker program was initiated by the need for cheap labor on the part of European capital as the world crisis of capital accumulation created a demand for reductions in the cost of production among the European Common Market countries. Similarly, cyclical market fluctuations in this country have traditionally demanded an ebb and flow of cheap labor from the vast surplus labor reserves of Mexico. Given the contemporary world crisis of capital accumulation present within this country's national economy, the same demand for reductions in the costs of production has intensified the demand for acutely undervalued labor to replace capital-intensive production with cheaper labor-intensive forms of production.

The existence of a long-term Mexicano transnational labor force means that we cannot view the U.S.-Mexican border as if it represented discrete national boundaries, with Chicanos (Mexican

Americans) on one side and Mexicanos (Mexican citizens) on the other. There is, of course, a substantial Chicano population in the United States today with stable residency and employment and relatively little direct, personal contact with Mexico or Mexicans. However, historically speaking, even this sector is a creation of the transnational labor force that has been a constant and ever growing feature of the vast U.S.-Mexico border region and beyond. Even after two or three generations within the United States, the entire social milieu of the Chicano community is still very much shaped by the transnational migration of Mexican workers and various concomitant realities ranging from depressed wages and indiscriminate deportations to the constant rejuvenation of Mexican cultural expressions. Thus, when we speak of the transnational labor force, we are dealing with both Chicanos and Mexicanos. Whether or not Chicanos actually cross and recross the so-called border (and in fact they have been forced to do so in times of indiscriminate deportation), they must be considered part of the transnational labor force in the United States, with the understanding that they form the most stable component of that labor force.

None of this is to deny the differences that do exist within the Mexican immigrant community in the United States. The most obvious are the class differences, as some sectors of the Chicano community have escaped from the transnational working class into the petty bourgeoisie, which was consciously fostered by state policies in the 1960s. There are also the critical juridical differences of immigration status imposed by the state, which has left some sectors of the community more vulnerable and defenseless than others; yet even these differences wear thin during times of indiscriminate raids by federal immigration authorities. Immigration status creates the conditions for the existence and perpetuation of a transnational labor force (and a transnational reserve army of labor).

D. Reserve army of labor. The term *reserve army of labor* refers to a variable proportion of the labor force which may be employed when capital has a need for labor, and unemployed when the need declines. That is, surplus labor over and above the numbers *who* can be employed at any given time. Thus, the reserve army of labor shrinks in times of prosperity and grows in times of crisis. Furthermore, a reserve army of labor is essential to keep wages at a level acceptable to capital, for troublesome workers may be laid off and compliant workers hired--that is,

35

competition among workers for jobs (which depresses wages) is guaranteed by having a constant supply of unemployed, able-bodied workers.

In the core countries, there has tended to be a constant supply of workers held in reserve, this constant supply guaranteed by both racism and sexism. We see the reserve used, for example, in times of war when women and national and racial minorities are hired to replace a male labor force conscripted into armies. However, periods of unparalleled economic growth in the core countries, including the United States, lead to protracted periods of relatively full employment. At such times, the reserve army is limited and new reserves need to be obtained; needless to say, if the new reserves are made up of cheap labor, so much the better. At the same time, in the semiperipheral countries, unequal exchange operates against their full economic development, producing a large surplus of labor with little or no hope of employment. In the case of Mexico, this presents a major problem to the Mexican government that is partially alleviated by the "safety valve" of emigration to the United States.

E. Colonization. We would also like to clarify our use of the term *colonization.* We see colonization as the initial mechanism for incorporation of the Southwest into the capitalist world-economy and the creation of a transnational labor force. We do not perceive a colony in the sense of a population having a national/territorial base or constituting a nation within the United States. We do use the terminology of colonization to mean that the particular forms of exploitation of the Chicano and Mexicano population within the United States are very similar to those which have been used in colonial or neo-colonial situations in other parts of the world.

F. Superexploitation. A final word about terminology: we use the term superexploitation to mean a reduction of wages below the level necessary for the production and reproduction of labor power. To be more precise: "The concept of superexploitation ... does not mean higher rates of exploitation, in the sense of beginning to talk about superexploitation after exploitation reaches a certain level. Rather, superexploitation involves exploitation when the latter violates the value of labor power ... The forms of superexploitation that capitalist exploitation can assume are fundamentally three: increase in the intensity of work, extension of the working day, payment of labor power below its value."[6] Workers in the Third World, as well as racial and national

36

minorities and women in the core countries, have traditionally formed the superexploited sectors of the world's proletariat. In this current crisis, however, even broader sectors of the working class within the core face the potential of superexploitation as various forms of degrading and cheapening labor power are imposed.

* * *

The first section of our paper presents an historical and theoretical framework of colonization and the creation of a transnational labor force. In that context, we then analyze the role of the Chicano/Mexicano family, and the women of those families. This analysis addresses two simultaneous processes. One is the historical process by which the labor of Chicanas and Mexicanas became commodified, and the intensification of that process in the last quarter-century. We refer here not only to the undervaluation of Chicana and Mexicana labor in the workplace, but also to the devaluation of Chicana labor in the home where women's work in the production and reproduction of the labor force is unwaged. On both levels, we are dealing with the world-historical process of capital accumulation. The second process occurs superstructurally, and is the process by which bourgeois morality masks the domestic labor of Chicanas and Mexicanas (as of women generally, under capitalism) and the ways in which bourgeois morality is compounded in a colonized population to produce what is commonly known as *machismo*. These ideological aspects of the oppression of Chicanas and Mexicanas are reinforced by the institutions of capitalism (e.g., the church under capitalism), but at the same time are undermined by the intensified proletarianization of Chicanas and Mexicanas today.

I. Chicanos and Mexicans as a Transnational Working Class

Colonization and the Historical Process of Proletarianization

Viewing the history of what is now the Southwest within the framework provided by Wallerstein and Hopkins, we see that Spanish colonization incorporated this region--as a peripheral area--into the evolving capitalist world-economy. Whenever a western capitalist economy has impinged upon an indigenous economy, certain consequences followed for that society. In the case of what is now Mexico and the southwestern United States, the consequences were particularly brutal.

The process began with the violent expropiration of land and resources. The indigenous peoples living on those lands were transformed from societies of subsistence/redoubt households, whose maintenance resulted from production unrelated to the capitalist world-economy's division of labor, into societies where part-lifetime and lifetime proletarian households predominated. Those Native Americans who escaped genocide came to subsist-- over a lifetime--on the basis of labor performed for the production of commodities and, thus, surplus value. This labor was, at first, almost totally coerced.

We would agree with Wallerstein and Hopkins in rejecting the developmentalist view of coerced labor as feudal or precapitalist. In the examples of forced labor on colonial institutions such as the missions and *presidios*, surplus value was being extracted as a result of labor's participation in production for the capitalist world-system. As we shall see, coerced labor rapidly gave way to its successor, wage-labor, when North American colonization further integrated the region into the capitalist world-economy.

The U.S. imperialist war against Mexico in 1846-48, and the ongoing repression and extermination of Native Americans, brought vast acres of land and resources under the domain of the United States. The courts of the new state apparatus quickly secured the new lands--already concentrated into huge holdings under Spanish and Mexican rule--for North American capitalists. In California, where capitalist development was most rapid, the Gold Rush created capital and vastly strengthened markets; the stage was nearly set for the rapid capitalist development that was eventually to take place all over the Southwest. Only one crucial factor was missing--a sufficient supply of cheap, exploitable labor.

The labor scarcity in California, which if unresolved would mean higher labor costs for the new capitalists, resulted in part from the genocide of the Native Americans who succumbed to starvation, disease, and exhaustion under the conditions of coerced labor imposed by Spanish, Mexican, and North American colonization. The *mestizos* who already resided in California in 1848 (those who immigrated from central Mexico during the colonization and those created through intermarriage with the indigenous population) did not meet the need for cheap unskilled labor, in part because they were not yet willing to take on such employment.[7]

38

At California's Constitutional Convention in 1849, delegates were well aware of the labor scarcity, but sharply divided over the relative advantages of slave versus free labor. Ultimately, California did not enter the Union as a slave state, but it did opt for the organized importation of thousands of foreign workers-- the seeds of today's transnational reserve army of labor. California capitalists first attempted to meet their labor needs with the importation of Chinese workers, who were later excluded from immigration. Following the Chinese, there were experiments with Japanese, East Indian, Armenian, other nationalities, and finally Mexicans--all of whom were actively recruited to work for California agribusiness.[8]

Meanwhile, the Mexicanos already in California were thrown out of work by the destruction of the pastoral economy and the shift to capitalist agriculture. Many returned to Mexico. Those who remained were proletarianized and deskilled, plunged from the level of artisans and skilled workers to laborers in the lowest stratum of the proletariat. By 1880 seventy-nine percent of the Mexicano workers in California were unskilled laborers.[9]

The institutions of North American colonialism in California and elsewhere in the Southwest were directed at establishing control over the existing *mestizo* population as well as over the new non-Anglo immigrant workers. Methods of control ranged from the use of terror, violent repression (and, after 1920, the threat of deportation), to ideological manipulation. Racism served as the justification for this process and a powerful tool in combating the widespread resistance of Native Americans, Mexicans, and others who did not willingly submit.

While the Southwest was being rapidly and forcibly incorporated in the capitalist world-system between 1850 and 1900, Mexico, too, was being integrated as a peripheral area of the world-economy. As in all times of expansion, capital was moving from the core into the periphery. Mexico received significant investment by United States, British, and other European capitalists in the late 1800s. At the same time, the liberal bourgeois reforms of Juarez and Porfirio Diaz helped to transfer vast acres of land into the hands of a newly emerging capitalist class in Mexico while violently dispossessing thousands upon thousands of peasants and traditional Indian communities. By 1900, ninety-six percent of all heads of rural families in Mexico were landless,[10] a clear indication of the destruction of the subsistence household and the creation of a mobile, surplus proletariat in excess of the labor needs of the peripheral Mexican economy.

As a result of the situation in Mexico, combined with the ongoing need for cheap labor in the United States, Mexican immigration grew rapidly in the late 1800s. Thousands of workers were imported or came to find work on the railroads, in the mines, industry, and agriculture. The expansion of international capital in Mexico from 1900-1920 and the social upheaval of the 1910-1920 Mexican revolution, sent new waves of Mexicans into the U.S. at precisely the moment when World War I and the post-war economic expansion created new demands for labor in the United States. More than a half-million Mexicanos came during the twenties alone, not only to the Southwest but all across the country from Los Angeles and San Antonio to Chicago and Pittsburgh.

The decades around the turn of the century were also a time of increasing class conflict in the U.S., and Mexicanos, like other workers, engaged in wave after wave of labor protests. One of the real advantages to capital of a reserve army of immigrant labor originating in a neighboring country became clear by the 1920s. The state began to repress Mexican workers through the use of immigration laws and deportations--both the selective repatriation of labor leaders and massive deportations which took place during the depression of the 1930s. As a result, the Mexican population in the United States was reduced to nearly half its size.[11]

As a consequence of the peripheralization of the Mexican economy and the labor needs created by the expansion of the North American economy, the existence of a transnational working class--neither precisely Mexican or North American, but a mobile, *transnational labor force* pushed and pulled by the dictates of capital--was by the first decades of the 1900s a permanent feature not only of the permeable U.S.-Mexico border area but the Southwest in general.

This labor force has been sustained by racism, both ideologically and institutionally. Racism developed as the ideology of an expansionist, originally European, capitalism which incorporated non-European regions of the world as peripheral areas of an emergent capitalist world-economy. In the case of Mexicanos and Chicanos, North American capitalism incorporated non-Anglo areas--the Southwest and Mexico--as peripheral areas. Wallerstein has described racism as the ideological legitimation of global unequal exchange, the structural antinomy of core and periphery. Thus racism is not simply a product of capitalism but, rather, integral to the functioning of capitalism as a world-system. Without presenting a full analysis of racism and the transnational labor force, we must be very clear about the integral role played by racism in the development of that labor force as well as in the superexploitation of Chicanos as a sector of the U.S. working class.[12] Racism was enforced by every political, economic, and social institution which confronted Mexicanos and Chicanos in the United States.

Proletarianization and the Expansion of the Transnational Working Class Since World War II

Since World War II there has been an increasing integration of the world-economy. Particularly, until the late 1960s, and despite periodic recessions, that world-economy was expanding. On a world scale, expansion meant increasing shifts of capital from the core to the periphery, increased migration of labor from the periphery to the core, and the nearly constant shift of households toward the lifetime proletarian household.

Within the United States, World War II produced a domestic labor shortage which created new demands for Chicano and Mexicano labor--new demands to increase the transnational pool of labor central to capital accumulation in the region. The armed forces and defense-related work drew thousands of Chicanos from the rural villages of areas like New Mexico, where part-lifetime households were still common, into the cities as much more fully proletarianized households. By the 1940s, the majority of Chicanos and Mexicanos were living in urban areas.[13] At the same time, the war years also saw renewed growth of agribusiness, providing new jobs both in the fields--particularly for family labor which was necessitated by the extremely low wages--and in the packing sheds and canneries where Chicanas and Mexicanas were employed in significant numbers.

A combination of factors worked to push labor costs up and force capital to seek new sources of cheaper labor. On the one hand, the expansion of the Chicano/Mexicano population was dramatically curtailed in the Southwest by the deportations of the thirties. Those who remained in the U.S. were rapidly moving toward full-lifetime households, which always results in higher labor costs to capital since the cost of production and reproduction of labor power is increased by the household's increasing dependency on the purchase of commodities. On the other hand, in Mexico, the gains of the revolution and the liberal bourgeois agrarian reforms of the Cárdenas period temporarily expanded the possibilities for rural households in Mexico to subsist on the collectively worked *ejido*; this, among other factors helped to slow the natural process of proletarianization and thus the pressure to emigrate northward.

In this context, the U.S. government actively intervened to guarantee a cheap supply of labor for agribusiness by creating the Bracero Program under which contracted Mexican labor would be seasonally and temporarily imported. As Ernesto Galarza has written, "In 1942 the spontaneous and irregular migration that had prevailed gave way abruptly to one that was supervised and regulated by government .... The agricultural industry made its choice in favor of governmentally administered migration of Mexicans."[14]

The braceros, all men, could be paid at a much lower wage because the cost of the production and reproduction of labor power within the man's family was much lower. The family was usually a part-lifetime proletarian household in rural, peripheral Mexico, where living costs were far less than in the United States. (This process has its parallels in Africa, where contracted labor for the mines is brought from villages in which the existence of part-lifetime proletarian households and lower costs of production of labor power persist.) The impact of the Bracero Program was to make farm labor organizing much more difficult, to dramatically depress agricultural wages, and to increase the gap between agricultural and industrial wages in the United States.

In the prolonged period of general expansion and further integration of the world-economy that followed the war years, the transnational reserve army of Mexicano and Chicano labor began to grow anew--but on a vastly enlarged scale. Mexico's continuing integration into the world-system has been characterized by the expansion of capitalist agribusiness, which constantly forces workers off the land, and by the monopolization and concentration of Mexican industry in the hands of transnational corporations, a development which creates inflation and structural unemployment. This process produces an enormous surplus of proletarians who move northward by the millions. The Mexican phenomenon is not dissimilar to the peripheralization of the Puerto Rican economy and the consequent emigration of Puerto Ricans to the U.S. East Coast. However, in the case of Mexico, undocumented immigration quickly surpassed legal immigration and overshadowed the Bracero Program.

In this way, the transnational working class of the U.S.-Mexico border area is constantly enlarged and depressed by the influx of unemployed proletarians. Within this transnational work force, Chicanos have differentiated themselves to varying degrees from the newly-arriving immigrants, through acculturation and the incorporation of some into the petty bourgeoisie, as well as by the very concrete difference of possessing certain rights of citizenship or legal residency. However, in general, Chicanos have remained part of the transnational reserve army of labor. Both Chicanos and Mexicanos came to be concentrated in the lowest-paid blue collar jobs (mostly as operatives and laborers) and service work. Those in white collar occupations were mainly low-paid saleswomen and office clerks.[15]

In the late 1960s, the world-economy entered a new and much more prolonged period of crisis. Subsequently, the importance of the transnational working class of Chicanos and Mexicanos to capital's resolution of the crisis has become critical. Increased competition from Europe and Japan, along with a declining rate of production and profits in the United States, contributed to a restructuring of the international division of labor and new investment strategies. In brief, to solve its own accumulation crisis, capital has chosen to boost profits by increasing *absolute* exploitation--that is, by absolutely reducing labor costs through employment of the very lowest-paid, least organized sectors of the workforce. During a crisis, capitalists do not want to invest in capital, but they do want cheap labor. This is the reason that, for example, along with massive layoffs in steel, auto, and construction, some twenty-five percent of the new jobs created in the United States from 1976 to 1978 were in the service sector, and labor-intensive and/or high-technology industries (as opposed to capital-intensive industries) received substantial investment.[16]

In its drive to reduce labor costs, capital has depended heavily on the transnational labor force of Chicanos and Mexicanos, particularly women--as we will discuss in the next section of this paper. It is the perpetuation and further pauperization of the transnational labor force that explains U.S. immigration policy. Key to the issue of cheap labor is workers' rights--the right to organize, to protective legislation, to legal recourse, to protest, to strike. The federal immigration policy specifically aimed at maintaining a reserve army of labor that has no rights is at the heart of the issue of documented versus undocumented immigration. North American corporate interests have no intention of closing the border (not that they could if they wanted to) or stopping the flow of undocumented immigration. The policy is one of repression, terror, and selective deportation, all designed to assure capital a supply of unorganized, submissive labor stripped of any and all civil and political rights.

For capital, the transnational labor force of Mexicans (and, in fact, of Central Americans and Caribbean workers) represents more than additional workers; these workers represent a labor force that: (1) is stateless and, stripped of most legal and political rights, is therefore defenseless; (2) is largely isolated from the rest of the working class and, even within itself, is atomized among various national groupings; (3) is composed of individual workers who can be deported with relative ease when they cause trouble or are temporarily expendable, deportation meaning, in the case of Central Americans, possibly a return to political persecution; (4) can be submitted to levels of degradation which are socially unacceptable for other sectors of society because of the historical workings of colonialism and racism; and (5) produces and reproduces its labor power at a much lower cost to capital (and to the North American state) both because undocumented immigrants are denied many of the social services available to the rest of the working class, and because the immigrant's family often remains in the peripheral home country where subsistence levels are lower and where the home state absorbs much of the costs of education, health care, and so forth.

At a time when the United States ruling class is attempting to weather the crisis by reproducing within the United States the conditions of capital accumulation which have existed in the periphery, such a labor force is critical.[17]

II. The Commodification of Chicana/Mexicana Labor

We now turn to a specific examination of the role of women and the family within the transnational labor force. We will, in broad strokes, trace the transformation of the family, the commodification of women's labor, and the proletarianization of women beginning from the period of Spanish colonization. First, however, we would like to present our theoretical understanding of how this process has proceeded historically for all women.

As argued in *Women in Class Struggle*,[18] capitalism brought about the transformation of the family from an extended kin grouping that formed a basic production unit, which was central to the economy and produced many of the family's necessities, to

44

a largely consumption unit, dependent upon the sale of labor power for the purchase of commodities to sustain the family. Labor within the family was simultaneously transformed into the commodity labor power, whose price is wages. Accompanying this process was the breakdown of the extended family into a nuclear family defined by contractual marriages.

Thus the family came to be viewed as outside society--the capitalist society based on commodity production--and as a private institution. This apparent marginalization of the family resulted in the apparent marginalization of women's domestic labor. We stress apparent because the real function of the family under capitalism, as described by Engels, is the production and reproduction of the commodity labor power. Clearly capitalist society is totally dependent on the production of that commodity, and the entire family produces it; moreover, the wages paid to workers are in reality paid to the entire family as the unit which produces labor power. But capitalism has mystified and concealed the family's true function; and above all made it appear that a woman's domestic labor is not the socially necessary production of a commodity (labor power) but a private service to the husband-- thus devaluing her labor. By separating the *market price* of labor power--the husband's wage--from the *real value* of labor power (which is the collective product of the family), capitalism increases its profits greatly. Male supremacist definitions of women and their labor are a handy method for keeping down all labor costs under capitalism.

At the same time, capital benefits from the exploitation of women's underpaid labor on the job. Thus we speak of the superexploitation of working women: first, through the direct appropriation of surplus value in commodity production, and then a second time through the indirect appropriation of value from domestic labor.

Colonization and Proletarianization of Women

For the vast majority of the indigenous Mexican population, but particularly for women, imperialism's integration of Mexico and what is now the Southwest into the capitalist world-system was a brutal, degrading process. Indigenous women were not only raped, they were also branded as slaves and forced to work in mining communities, missions and *presidios*, and as domestic servants.

45

Over the centuries which followed the conquest, the family was now truly marginalized, no longer either the prevailing economic unit, nor primarily a production unit (except for its function as producer and reproducer of labor power). Women's work in the home was devalued as it became less obviously central to the economy. At the same time, since indigenous women now produced and reproduced labor power at home while also producing surplus value outside the home, they began to experience women's "double day" of superexploitation.

With North American colonization, the Native American family's existence as a production unit outside the world-system would be brought to a final end. For the Mexicana, this meant a devaluation of her labor in the home; massive proletarianization; wage competition with men; and, as we shall see later in this paper, a vicious form of sexism.

The new capitalists faced a serious labor shortage. It is not surprising, then, that we find the Mexicana rapidly moving out of the home and into the work force, particularly in California. Camarillo provides an example of the proletarianization of Mexicanas in the 1880s which, although it refers to Santa Barbara in particular, probably applied anywhere that the capitalist economy was expanding: "The most dramatic change was the entrance of the Chicana and her children as important wage earners .... As male heads of household faced persistent unemployment, their migrations to secure seasonal work in other areas of the county or region became more frequent. In these instances the Chicana assumed the triple responsibilities of head of household, mother, and wage earner. No longer able to subsist solely on the income of the husband, the Chicana and her children were forced to enter the unskilled labor market of Anglo Santa Barbara. The work they performed involved domestic services and agriculture-related employment."[19]

While the Mexicano family as a whole was being transformed into part-lifetime and lifetime proletarian households, the superexploitation of the women also became established. Those who did household labor and also sold their labor power outside the home experienced this superexploitation at an astounding rate. For example, many Mexicanas and their children (as well as the men) worked in the walnut harvest near Santa Barbara in the 1890s; the Walnut Growers Association boasted a huge profit based on labor costing only one percent of sales. This superexploitation was extended in southern California in the 1890s, with Mexicanas working as domestics, fruit cannery and packing shed workers, laundresses and seasonal farm laborers who migrated with their children and husbands. This work was almost never permanent, usually part-time or seasonal. The percentage of Mexicanas who were heads of households increased dramatically during this time, more than tripling in Los Angeles.[20]

The Mexicano family work-unit became a preferred form of exploitable labor among capitalists--mainly agribusiness--in the Southwest during certain periods. The 1919 Child Labor Laws excluded agricultural workers, and child labor was widespread, from the Imperial Valley to the beet sugar fields of Colorado and the Winter Garden of Texas. The use of child labor in agriculture has continued to this day.

As proletarianization, urbanization, and the ongoing destruction of the extended family proceeded, the burden of maintaining the family fell increasingly upon the Mexicana woman alone. In Los Angeles, in 1850-80, for example, twenty-one percent of the Mexican families were headed by a woman.[21] Thus, from the early days of North American colonization, Mexicana women have been superexploited, performing the unrecognized and unwaged labor of producing and reproducing labor power in the home while filling the lowest-paid, most exploitative jobs outside the home. This superexploitation was vividly described by a female agricultural worker of the 1930s--and her example still rings all too true today: "I am an agricultural working woman. I came to this camp with my husband and baby. I have to get up before the men get up. I feed my baby and then I am supposed to help in the kitchen. If I don't help in the kitchen, people will say, 'What kind of woman is she?' Although there is a paid cook, I am supposed to help. I have to go out to work with the men at the same time, taking my baby with me. When we finish work at suppertime, I have to do the cooking and wash the dishes. At night when the baby cries, I have to be extremely careful because we live in a rooming house and the partition has thin walls. Sometimes I have to take the baby outside in order to quiet the baby. Really I am suffering doubly. There must be several thousand women like me in the fields."[22]

Proletarianization Accelerates

World War II created labor shortages in the Southwest that forced capital to seek new sources of cheap labor. Consequently, the data for this period clearly indicate an accelerated incorporation (likely re-incorporation) of Chicanas and Mexicanas into the workforce and their increasing employment in nonagricultural jobs. The war industries employed thousands of Chicanas and Mexicanas who acquired new occupation and communication skills. For example, they made up eighty percent of the work force employed by the Eastern-based garment firms which doubled their number of plant locations in the Texas-Mexican border area during these years.[23] Chicanas and Mexicanas also moved into domestic work as Anglo women were integrated into the war economy.

Proletarianization of Chicanas and Mexicanas accelerated throughout the 1960s and 1970s. On the one hand, the absolute reduction of real wages in the U.S., imposed by state austerity policies since the Nixon era, forced ever greater numbers of all working-class women into the work force. On the other hand, capital actively sought to boost profits by investing in labor-intensive operations (including runaway shops/*maquiladoras*, such as the garment and electronics industries), many of them located in this country's Southwest, especially in the border region. These industries employ low-skilled, low-waged labor, particularly women and immigrants and, therefore, Chicanas/Mexicanas.

The drive to reduce labor costs within the core to the level of cost within the periphery has also brought about a return to some of the earliest, most exploitative systems of extracting surplus value--such as the putting-out system. It has been estimated, for example, that as much as fifty to sixty percent of all garments produced in California are sewn illegally in the home. Not only in small, fly-by-night garment sweatshops, but increasingly in the main-line, brand-name apparel firms, work is being contracted out for women to do in the home. In particular, the simplest and most tedious operations--like making button-holes--are being contracted out to thousands of deskilled Chicanas and Mexicanas, who are forced by the lowest piece-rate wages to work long hours and to rely on the additional labor of children for survival. Capital supplies nothing but the raw materials; all other costs, including simple machinery, electricity, and rent, are now borne by the family. These workers are isolated, dispersed throughout the city in their individual homes, making it nearly impossible to enforce protective labor legislation or organize them into unions.

Beginning in the 1960s, women began to form an increasing portion of Mexican immigration to the United States--a reflection of the crisis and ongoing proletarianization in Mexico. The study done by Gil Cárdenas of Mexican immigrant women in Houston,

Texas indicates that over ninety-five percent of the respondents in a survey of undocumented Mexican women came to the United States after 1960, and over half of them came since 1975. Half of the women gave economic reasons for immigration, in particular, the desire to get a job or lack of money (as opposed to reunification with the family, which has often been considered to be the primary motivation of immigrant women). Over eighty-three percent reported being unemployed in Mexico before leaving.[24]

The immigration of women and entire families in contrast to the migration of male braceros reflects: (1) the further shift towards lifetime proletarian households within the transnational labor force; and (2) the transformation of women from a latent component of the transnational reserve army of labor to employed workers, as it becomes more impossible for the family to survive in Mexico or the United States on the wages paid to the husband alone.

As a result of all the above factors, half of the Chicanas/Mexicanas residing in the United States were part of the workforce by 1980, the great majority in low-paid jobs as clerks, employees in the service sector, and operatives.[25] The same economic pressures that have brought Chicanas/Mexicanas into the work force have also steadily increased the number of other family members who must work in order to sustain the family. By the end of the 1970s, approximately fifty-six percent of the Chicano/Mexicano families--clearly fully proletarianized households--have two or more family members in the work force (but not always employed by any means).[26]

But the real meaning of these statistics becomes clear only when we recall that although many were in the work force, only eleven percent of Spanish-surname women worked fulltime, year-round in 1970[27] and that their unemployment rate in 1979 was far above the national average.[28] Chicanas and Mexicanas in almost all occupations earn less than Anglo men, less than Chicano/Mexicano men, less than Anglo women, for the same work.[29] That fact, combined with their concentration in the lowest-paid jobs, meant that median yearly earnings for Chicanas/Mexicanas in 1978 were barely a third of earnings by men in general and half of what Chicano/Mexicano men earned.[30] Over forty-seven percent of Chicano/Mexicano families headed by women had incomes below the poverty level in 1978.[31] Thus, Chicanas and Mexicanas stand at the bottom rung of the ladder within the work force, and their superexploitation serves to undermine the wages of the working class in general.

To summarize then, the historical development of capitalism has brought about for Chicanas: (1) the transformation of the household from a basic production unit that was largely self-sufficient and central to the economy, toward lifetime proletarian households that rely on the sale of labor power for the purchase of commodities to sustain the family; (2) the breakdown of the extended family into a nuclear family in which the domestic labor of the woman and the family--socially necessary for the production and reproduction of labor power--is made to appear as a private service to the husband; and consequently (3) the devaluation of women's labor and thus the superexploitation of her unpaid labor in the home and her underpaid labor as a member of the transnational reserve army of labor.

III. Devaluation of the Chicana/Mexicana as a Woman

We have seen how imperialism transformed women's role by destroying the family as a production unit and commodifying the labor of the native/*mestizo* family. Her status, or social definition, was also transformed. Capitalism made it appear that women were dependent upon their husband's wages; this apparent dependency was used--as it is today--to justify the perpetuation of male supremacy. Under capital's mystification of wages, the husband appears as the source of all value, hence, the autocrat. Along with the material bases for the transformation of woman's status, we need to recognize the role of superstructural forces. Among these, the Catholic Church stands out. We agree with Adaljiza Sosa Riddell when she states, "The Catholic Church is as responsible for the conquest of Mexico as the Spanish soldiers,"[32] and we could add only that the same can be said for the colonization of California and the Southwest. The church literally came with the conquest; cross and gun went hand in hand. Historically, it has been the function of the church as an institution to support the ruling class, and by its ideology, to facilitate the imposition and maintenance of wage-labor under capitalism. Its counsel of patience and acceptance of exploitation on earth, in hopes of a better after-life, is but one example.

A key component of the church's ideology always has been patriarchism, which it imposed on this continent--along with racism--to a degree of oppressiveness never known before. As

50

Sosa Riddell commented, the church "stands as a guardian and perpetrator of an ancient tradition whereby women were unequal to, and in need of the constant surveillance of men, preferably white Catholic men."[33] The church made the indigenous woman of Mexico a subject of both the subjected and the subjugators, justified by its ideal of the female as submissive, chaste, and unworldly. The downward transformation of woman's status was integral to the entire colonization process; the church's patriarchism, along with racism, served as a major tool of domination. Together they justified the economic rape of entire peoples and the sexual rape of women.

The same might be said of religious institutions in other colonial situations--Protestant missionaries in Africa, for example. But the Catholic Church was unique in its emphasis on women as breeders of children, a role from which escape has been stifled by the ban on birth control. Thus, today, the church is an absolute bastion of bourgeois morality with its insistence on monogamy for women, negation of women's right to control their own bodies, the definition of women as primarily sexual objects, promotion in women of a self-identification primarily as wives and mothers (or wives and mothers-to-be), repression of women's own sexuality, and control of sexual style, including the doctrine of homosexuality as unnatural.

Studies have called into question the church's influence on Chicano and Mexicano people. Survey data on their religious practice and attitudes in Los Angeles and San Antonio in the 1950s and 1960s showed much less frequent attendance at Mass than among Catholics nationwide. Only thirty-three percent agreed with church teachings on birth control, compared to much higher percentages among Catholics nationwide.[34] But this does not negate the church's role in the historical process of colonization, nor can we conclude that all male supremacist norms of the church have been rejected.

The Church's emphasis on women as breeders of children has a corollary: masculinity defined as sexual virility. This brings us to the question of *machismo*, a concept which must be addressed because it is so relevant to the liberation of Chicano and Mexicano people from exploitation as a transnational working class.

It has been said that *machismo* is a myth and a stereotype; Chicano and Mexican people have never been able to afford the woman who remains primarily at home, chaste, untouched by the world, nor have the men had the time or energy to make assertions of masculinity a matter of grave concern when the mere struggle to survive is clearly the priority. Other authors have deduced that the patriarchal family has never been the behavioral norm among Chicanos, only an ideal, and that patriarchal values and belief in the stable family became cultural ideals "at least in part *because* of the weakness of both the family structure and the male role."[35] We would strongly agree with the idealist aspect emphasized by such writers but cannot dismiss *machismo* as a myth. Again and again, *machismo* has been a concrete impediment to the incorporation of women in community organizing, labor organizing, the Chicano movement of the 1960s,[36] and today's struggles.

What makes *machismo* seem part of a stereotype is viewing it as strictly a cultural phenomenon, some kind of "weird" Latin characteristic, rather than as a form of male supremacist ideology serving capital accumulation. We would begin, then, by seeing *machismo* as a concept of masculinity in terms of domination, a masculinity which is linked to and ultimately dependent upon the negation of woman's full humanity. Under capitalism, we see *machismo* as based on three factors: the disguised value of Chicana/Mexicana domestic labor, workplace competition between men and women, and displaced agreession.

First, *machismo* is based on the disguised value of women's domestic labor in that it is a form of male supremacist ideology, which serves to mystify the family's real function under capitalism, by creating the appearance of a woman's domestic labor as a private service to the husband. Within this framework, Chicanas and Mexicanas are seen as dependent on men for subsistence, while the man responsible for the wife's support also possesses a lifetime slave by contractual marriage. Thus, despite their massive proletarianization from the 1880s onward, Chicanas and Mexicanas are still portrayed by bourgeois ideology primarily as homemakers, mothers, wives, and not workers.[37] Taylor's interviews with immigrant Mexican women and workers in Los Angeles in 1928, and their statements as to why they left the home to find waged labor, show how they internalized this definition.[38] The usefulness to capital of such definition and self-definition is enormous; in essence, *machismo* permits the capitalist to undervalue all labor power by its devaluation of women's domestic labor.

A second basis of *machismo* is the competition between men and women in the work place. The woman's wages serve to depress those paid to the man, thus encouraging the view among Chicanos and Mexicanos that women belong in the home and not

52

the labor force. Sosa Riddell comments, with reference to the immigration of Mexican farmworkers, that females were dealt with by employers "only through the males until they attempted to compete for jobs. It was when Chicanas began to seek work outside of the family groups that sexism became a key factor of oppression along with racism."[39] We see parallels in the black community, where women have been able to find gainful employment when men cannot. (We can also recall Camarillo's study of Santa Barbara and southern California, where, within the Chicano/Mexicano labor force, women found jobs before men in the 1880s; women sales and clerical workers were the only sector of that labor force with any upward mobility in 1910-20.)[40]

These first two bases of *machismo*, which are material, are found throughout the general society, although competition on the job is greatly aggravated when the factor of racism is added. One might then ask, why speak of *machismo* rather than sexism in general? But there is a third basis of *machismo*, which is subjective, and rises from the particular experience of colonization. We would call it *displaced aggression*, a term that incorporates a whole complex of subjective factors.

Displaced aggression is caused by anger and frustration with social and economic conditions which cannot with impunity be taken out against those who perpetrate such conditions and are therefore transferred to another target--women. The opening for displacement is created by Catholic mores. In its most extreme form, a man who cannot strike his boss instead strikes his wife. He can do this with impunity because it is implicitly acceptable in a religious world view that sees women as chattel, to be kept barefoot and pregnant, lifetime slaves bound by contractual marriage in homes where the husband is autocrat.

Again, we find displaced aggression throughout the working class of this country, as the mystification of women's labor in the home displaces the husband's hostility and frustration away from capital and onto the wife. He then becomes an unwitting accomplice of capital in subjugating and exploiting women. Again we may ask: what happened to the Chicano/Mexicano family that made it different from Anglo families with respect to displaced aggression?

We have already indicated the influence of the Catholic Church in generating machismo. In addition, we think that displaced aggression is greatly intensified as a result of negative self-images imposed by imperialism and its racist exploitation: self-images of impotence and worthlessness that are concretized in

53

stereotypes whose purpose is to justify that exploitation. Thus, virility is an expression of power which assumes special importance to individuals who find themselves in an objectively powerless, exploited position. In short, under some conditions machismo can take extreme forms--for which cultural, including psychological, reasons exist--that are founded in the historical experience of colonization and creation of a transnational working class.

Like other forms of male supremacist ideology, machismo has by no means remained static and unchanging. Studies made in Mexican and Chicano communities in the 1960s reveal a decline in sexist attitudes, particularly in the equation of masculinity with domination and within the family. We see these changes resulting from development of the same force--capital--that perpetuated sexism in the first place. The key to this change lies in the proletarianization of Chicanas.

Men (and women) may retain sexist images, but the realities of industrial and monopoly capitalism impinge on them. Taylor's interviews with the Mexican women workers in Los Angeles suggest this as early as 1928. He comments "... their labor was looked on as temporary, merely a help during hard times. The men folks did not like to have them work regularly. It appeared generally, only after many long and repeated periods during which it was necessary for them to work, that the old idea was relinquished."[41] The point is: the old idea *was* relinquished.

We see this change reflected in the history of Chicana and Mexicana militancy on the labor front. Beginning in about 1900, the list grows of women who participated in and sometimes led massive strikes and other forms of worker protest. In that same period, we find numerous all-women's organizations being formed, some of which explicitly denied men a vote.[42] In the era of the Mexican revolution, we find Mexico's Liberal Party (the *Partido Liberal Mexicano*), a revolutionary organization influential in California and the Southwest, taking a progressive stand on equal rights of women. In the fields and packing sheds and canneries of the late 1930s and 1940s, Chicanas and Mexicanas played a leading role in labor organizing as they did in the Farah strike of the 1970s. In the current crisis of capitalism, and the past twenty years of accelerated integration into the work force, changes in the family and the image of the Chicana/Mexicana woman have intensified along with reactionary pressures to put her back in the home.

IV. Nationalism and Racism

The current economic crisis has brought a renewal of racist attacks and a variety of responses. Within these responses, the social definition of women may have a progressive or reactionary character. Like other racial and national minority people in the United States, Chicanos/Mexicanos have historically responded to racism with what is commonly called nationalism. As members of a transnational working class, Chicanos and Mexicans find themselves in a lower position within the United States working class. There is a significant correspondence between people deemed "inferior" by racism and the lower sector of the working class. It is not surprising, then, that the class consciousness of the "inferior" people will be expressed in the form of "nationalist" consciousness.

In the 1960s, this expression came to be called *Chicanismo*, in some ways a more satisfactory term than nationalism. With certain exceptions, Chicanos and Mexicanos have not literally meant to affirm nationhood but rather a sense of peoplehood, of uniting for the sake of survival in the face of racist oppression, a refusal to accept negative stereotypes, a rejection of cultural assimilation, a taking pride in one's culture, language, and history--in short, an affirmation of nothing less than one's humanity. Such affirmation has been a common phenomenon historically among racial and national minority people.

We see the *Chicanismo* of working-class people as a movement against exploitation and oppression, a reflection of the reality of living in a racist society where the working class is segmented along racial lines. Rod Bush's comments, addressed to the black community, apply equally here: "It is a tactical nationalism ... It is not opposed to class unity in principle, but has real questions about the reliability of white workers in the struggle. The point here is that members of this section of the working class, even when they express their class interests in nationalist clothing, are not an 'ally' to the working class, as some assert, but constitute a central and decisive part of our movement."[43]

Conclusion

We have presented an analysis of Chicanos and Mexicanos as a transnational working class and, within that, the role and status of women. This analysis has addressed the past, as a means of understanding the present and with a view to changing the future. It is an analysis that calls for more research; many questions are raised by this paper for which even minimal data often do not exist.

When we look at the present, we find today one fact of all-encompassing import; there is a worldwide capitalist crisis which has profound implications for the future of Chicanos and Mexicanos, and for women in particular. Without analyzing the crisis in detail in this paper, let us review certain points of particular relevance:

1. The dynamic of the economic substructure of the whole system of western capitalist core countries has changed. Therefore, we see capital reorganizing the economy in various ways. One of these is relocating industry from high-wage to low-wage areas, so that there is an increase in plant closures and runaway shops to Mexico and other foreign countries--at least until the labor force in those areas ceases to be controllable. Another form of that reorganization is the increase of "putting-out" and other types of labor in the home, a method of exploitation that produces profit rates at minimal cost to capital and maximum cost to humanity-- above all, women.

2. The non-white working class and the "under-class" (the permanently unemployed) are being massively immiserated. In particular, the welfare state is under severe attack and threatened with extinction. Although its programs did not end the exploitation and oppression of racial and national minority people and all women, welfare programs meant the difference between life and death for the aged, people on Social Security and welfare, women who head households and others (particularly women) who find themselves at rock-bottom in the Chicano/Mexicano community.

3. The gains won by racial and national minorities from the struggles of the 1960s are being eliminated; no pretense of concern for minority people or women is maintained.

4. The ruling class is aggressively using racism and sexism as weapons to divide the working class, prevent it from developing unified opposition to capitalist policies, and legitimate the superexploitation of minority workers and women.

This situation contains innumerable political implications. The right-wing forces, which gained great strength under Reagan, seek to place women in a total stranglehold of the bourgeois morality with its view that women belong in the home, submissive and subservient as mother and homemaker; women should have no control over their own bodies which are seen as the property of men. While this ideological assault does not in itself remove women from the labor force, it does justify their being paid lower wages and their lack of job security. In the face of this assault, the rejection by both men and women in the Chicano/Mexicano community of any male supremacist ideology becomes more important than ever. *Machismo* is objectively the ally of these right-wing, reactionary forces, an alliance that is illogical and intolerable for an oppressed, exploited population.

As noted above, one of the hallmarks of the 1980s has been a form of "reindustrialization" designed to use the cheapest possible labor and to minimize the social costs to the employer. Alongside the growth of labor-saving high-technology, this has meant the revival of sweatshop operations, for example, in the garment industry, which reproduce conditions reminiscent of the nineteenth century, and putting-out systems, piecework production in the home. Given the drastic cutbacks in social programs, Chicanas and Mexicanas and other minority women are increasingly forced to work under conditions previously defined as intolerable within the United States. Capital's attempt to send minority women back into the home as a workplace is not only a way of cutting costs, but also has profound social implications in de-socializing women's work, thus undermining the possibility of union organizing.

This examination of a transnational labor force sets in sharp relief the glaring reality of transnational exploitation and thus the need to organize across the border. Against transnational capital, we need transnational labor organizations. To say this is nothing new; many committed activists have pursued the vision of borderless organizing for years. Today, both the need and the hope can be seen more clearly than ever. The more that capital gears its recovery to exploitation of such labor markets as the Chicana-Mexicana, the more crucial resistance becomes. But hope also exists.

Political challenge from the Mexican left in 1988 broke a 60-year old tradition of one-party rule in Mexico, affecting the consciousness of many Mexicans coming to this country or already here. The passage of new immigration legislation in the U.S. heightened the potential for organizing. The influx of Central American political refugees must have an internationalist influence, even while also generating competitive tendencies. Chicanas and Mexicanas coming together across the border on such issues as toxic wastes are setting new examples of women's activism. It is much too soon to say where these and other recent developments will lead, but it does seem that the transnational working class has new possibilities for building a long-needed transnational political strength.

Notes

1. Susanne Jonas and Marlene Dixon, "Proletarianization and Class Alliances in the Americas," in *Contradictions of Socialist Construction* (San Francisco, Calif.: Synthesis Publications, 1979, p. 2.

2. Immanuel Wallerstein and Terence Hopkins, "Patterns of Development of the Modern World System," *Review* 2 (Fall 1977): 134-35.

3. Ibid.

4. Ibid.

5. Ibid.

6. Jaime Osorio Urbina, "Superexplotación y clase obrera: el caso mexicano," *Cuadernos Políticos* Núm. 6 (octubre 1975): 6-7. Cited in Andre Gunder Frank, *Crisis: In the Third World* (New York, Holmes and Meier, 1981), p. 161.

7. Albert Camarillo, *Chicanos in a Changing Society: From Mexican Pueblos to American Barrios in Santa Barbara and Southern California, 1848-1930* (Cambridge, Mass.: Harvard University Press, 1979), pp. 51, 87-88.

8. Peter Baird and Ed McCaughan, *Beyond the Border: Mexico and the U.S. Today* (New York: NACLA, 1979), pp. 123-125. For other sources on this period, see the references given in this book.

9. Camarillo, *Chicanos in a Changing Society*, p. 88.

10. Lawrence D. Weiss, "Industrial Reserve Army of the Southwest: Navajo and Mexican," *Southwest Economy and Society* 3 (Fall 1977): 20.

11. Rosalinda Méndez González, "A Review of the Literature on Mexican and Mexican-American Women Workers in the United States Southwest 1970-75," unpublished manuscript, University of California, Irvine, 1976, p. 36.

12. For a fuller analysis, see Rod Bush's article "Racism and the Rise of the Right," *Contemporary Marxism* 4 (1982).

13. González, "A Review," pp. 35-36.

14. Ernesto Galarza, *Merchants of Labor, The Mexican Bracero Story* (Santa Barbara, Calif.: McNally & Lofton, 1964), pp. 14-15.

15. Laura E. Arroyo, "Industrial and Occupational Distribution of Chicana Workers," *Aztlan: Chicano Journal of the Social Sciences and the Arts* 4 (Fall 1973): 349-50.

16. Baird and McCaughan, *Beyond the Border*, p. 155.

17. For a further elaboration of this analysis see Marlene Dixon, Susanne Jonas and Ed McCaughan, "Reindustrialization and the Development of a Transnational Labor Force," *Contemporary Marxism* 5 (Summer 1982).

18. Marlene Dixon, "On the Super-Exploitation of Women," in *Women in Class Struggle* (San Francisco, Calif.: Synthesis Publications, 1978).

19. Camarillo, *Chicanos in a Changing Society*, p. 91.

20. Ibid. See chapters 4, 6 and 7 for general reference, specifically pp. 93, 137.

21. Richard Griswold del Castillo, "A Preliminary Comparison of Chicano, Immigrant and Native-Born Family Structures 1850-80," *Aztlán: International Journal of Chicano Studies Research* 5 (Spring 1975): 91.

22. Margo McBane, "History of Women Farm Workers in California," unpublished senior thesis, 1974, p. 1.

23. Marta Cotera, *Profile on the Mexican-American Woman* (Austin, Texas: National Educational Laboratory Publishers Inc., 1976), p. 91.

24. Gilbert Cárdenas, "Immigrant Women in the Labor Force," unpublished manuscript, University of Texas, Austin, 1981, pp. 78, 85.

25. Fred E. Romero, *Chicano Workers: Their Utilization and Development* (Los Angeles: Chicano Studies Center Publications, University of California, 1979), pp. 82-85 and Bureau of the Census, *Current Population Reports. Population Characteristics: Persons of Spanish Origin in the United States: March 1979*, Series P-20, No. 354, October 1980, p. 29.

26. Bureau of the Census, *Current Population Reports*, p. 13.

27. Romero, *Chicano Workers*, p. 88.

28. "Spanish surnamed" is the category used by the Census Bureau. Bureau of the Census, *Current Population Reports*, p. 29.

29. Ibid., Table 11.

30. Ibid., p. 30.

31. Ibid., p. 16.

32. Adaljiza Sosa Riddell, "Chicanas and El Movimiento," *Aztlan: Chicano Journal of the Social Sciences and the Arts*, 5 (Spring & Fall 1974): 158.

33. Ibid.
34. Leo Grebler, Joan W. Moore, and Ralph C. Guzmán, *The Mexican-American People: The Nation's Second Largest Minority* (New York: The Free Press, 1970), pp. 473-4.
35. Ibid., p. 360.
36. Adelaida R. Del Castillo, "Mexican Women in Organization," in *Mexican Women in the United States: Struggles Past and Present,* ed. Magdalena Mora and Adelaida R. Del Castillo (Los Angeles: Chicano Studies Research Center Publications, University of California, 1980), pp. 7-16.
37. Grebler et al., *The Mexican-American People*, p. 361.
38. Paul S. Taylor, "Mexican Women in Los Angeles Industry in 1928," *Aztlán: International Journal of Chicano Studies Research* 11 (Spring 1980): 106.
39. Sosa Riddell, "Chicanas and El Movimiento," p. 159.
40. Camarillo, *Chicanos in a Changing Society,* p. 179.
41. Taylor, "Mexican Women," p. 106.
42. Camarillo, *Chicanos in a Changing Society*, p. 151.
43. Rod Bush, "Racism."

CHICANA HISTORY AND HISTORICAL SIGNIFICANCE: SOME THEORETICAL CONSIDERATIONS*

by

J. Jorge Klor de Alva

> *"Historians' neglect of women has been a function of their ideas about historical significance."*
>
> Gordon, Buhle, and Schrom Dye
> "The Problem of Women's History"

Given the limited amount of work completed to date on the history of Mexican women in the United States, any attempt to elucidate the theoretical issues underlying Chicana history should be considered a necessary but tentative exercise. This paper is no exception. Though it is critical that we begin a serious dialogue on the subject, it is equally crucial that any conclusions should be tempered with reserve and accepted with skepticism. The points I make in this essay are not meant to imply closure, they are aimed at suggesting points of departure and paths for future exploration. These cautions are in order because of the current state of the study of the Chicana past; they do not imply that Chicana or women's history is not a proper object for significant generalizations. Gerda Lerner has concluded, and I agree with her, that "women's history is the history of the *majority* of humankind" and, therefore, "only a history based on the recognition that women have always been essential to the making of history and that *men and women* are the measure of significance, will be truly a universal history"; short of that, "all history as we know it is, for women, merely prehistory."[1] Chicano history can hardly claim to be the history of Mexicans in the United States if the role of females who make up half or more of the group is neglected. In this sense, Chicano history to date is, for the most part, prehistory.

---

* This work is dedicated to my mother, Maria de los Angeles de Alva, and Cathy Romero.

61

Women's history in general, and Chicana history in particular, have challenged the dominant-culture, male-oriented criteria for selecting what is historically significant. History cannot be written without criteria for distinguishing the historically meaningful from what seem like limitless possibilities. However, the miniscule number of Chicana historians (or of Chicano scholars interested in the area) and the compelling need to focus on content and method in outlining the Chicana past have meant that little attention has been paid to either articulating the theoretical bases of the challenge or to making explicit the proposed revised criteria. Because of the obvious advantages of numbers, research, and educational opportunities, women's history in the United States has developed significantly more theory than Chicana history.[2] While women's history has yet to fully encompass the study of the Chicana past, much of its theory is applicable to Chicana history. As a consequence, this paper will frequently draw form the former to elucidate the latter.

Criteria to determine historical significance must be systematically integrated into the historiographical process at three distinct points: in the selection of data, in the determination of the explanatory theory that will be applied to the data, and in the choosing of the narrative style that will attempt to reflect in prose the events said to have occurred in the past. These three elements are dialectically related. A change in the critieria utilized at any one point is sure to affect the other two. That is, in general, the choices made concerning one element will modify the decisions made regarding what will "count" as appropriate for the other two. Futhermore, there is a "precritically accepted paradigm," that informs the historical consciousness at a deep structural level. This metahistorical mode represents "a deep level of consciousness on which a historical thinker chooses conceptual strategies by which to explain or represent his data."[3] Without wishing to engage in a discussion of the role of gender in psychology, I would argue on the basis of the nature of traditional historiography to date that this metahistorical paradigm is deeply rooted in the basic psychological and epistemological structures of the historian and as a result is not very susceptible to fluctuations arising from changed material conditions. The paradigm is generally determined by the gender of the historian and since most known historians have been males, they have shared a somewhat similar metahistorical paradigm. Though male historians have frequently had neither a data base, a theory, nor a similar narrative style in common their psychological concerns generated by their gender and phenomenally shaped by their epistemologies have determined some conventions with regard to what is considered historically relevant. Had things been otherwise, women's history would be neither new nor polemical today.

The data base, theory, and mode of historical discourse that combine to make up a history have varied dramatically over the course of traditional historiography, unlike the gender of historians. Male-oriented topics have dominated what is today called history and have been limited, for the most part, to "those aspects of human experience in which men are active: wars, diplomacy, statecraft, and business."[4] With minor exceptions, what historians traditionally looked for in the documentation of history were materials concerning the acquisition, transmission, exercise, and maintenance of power in its myriad guises; only these topics were worthy of historical attention.[5] Since women had long been "excluded from the seats of power," they were necessarily ignored by historians. All but the few women who did exercise power were invisible in historians' chronicles.[6] Of course, Chicanas have suffered the same fate. Until very recently, they have been invisible in history on three counts: as women, as members of an oppressed racial/ethnic minority, and as working-class people who have enjoyed very little socio-economic or political power.[7]

The nature and content of women's history has changed over time and continues to do so. Females in the United States who in the nineteenth and early twentieth centuries wrote about women focused primarily on "compilations of woman's 'contributions,'" including their efforts on behalf of abolition, the woman's rights movement, and the struggle against male oppression.[8] In the period following the adoption of the Nineteenth Amendment, Mary Beard's work turned to recounting "the positive achievements of women, their social role, and their contributions to community life."[9] These studies were complemented and followed by others which analyzed the economic behavior of women, their activities in the various reform movements, and their role in the family.[10] However, the focus of women on women's issues during the new feminist era of the 1960s and 1970s included a fundamental challenge to male-oriented history. "Compensatory history" and revisionist works aimed at recording and reinterpreting the role of women in the past by using social history techniques and, quite frequently, Marxist and neo-Marxist theories.[11] In the process of these revisionist endeavors women interested in history slowly began to appreciate that something more was needed than merely new interpretations of old topics or the incorporation of "'missing facts and views'...into the empty spaces of traditional history."[12]

With the emergence of female historians interested in women's history, the resources needed to create a new metahistorical paradigm were at last present. Perhaps the single most important "discovery" needed to initiate the shift from male-centered decisions concerning historical significance to female-centered ones was the realization that history did not always affect men and women in the same way. In 1969 Gerda Lerner argued that "the economic role of men predominates in their lives, but women shift readily from one role to another at different periods in their lives. It is in this that their function is different from men and it is this which must form the basis for any conceptual framework."[13] Hilda Smith raises a number of critical distinctions in the differential effects of history on men and women when she notes that women had been frequently excluded form "the general 'progress of mankind'" which had often "worked to her detriment." In effect: "Women have fared better in nonstructural, nonintellectual, localized institutions and have been excluded from institutions which set rigid standards and operate on the basis of an established hierarchy. Women gain most from periods of social dysfunction such as war or rebellion in which the normal connections of power are severed." As a consequence, "two major developments of modern society have harmed women-- professionalization and industrialization."[14] In summarizing the thrust of various essays in their *Becoming Visible: Women in European History*, Renate Bridenthal and Claudia Koonz conclude "that the major political upheavals that fill so many pages in standard historical surveys have had only a temporary impact on the lives of women. Far more important have been transformations in social structure.... [And] the greatest of these changes has been the Industrial Revolution." In agreement with Hilda Smith, they add that the effect on women of this historical process was overwhelmingly detrimental.[15] These and similar conclusions derived from empirical studies clearly point to the importance of gender as a valid historical variable. But what does this variable consist of that makes its effects different from those of class, race, or ethnicity?

In *Is There a History of Women?*, Carl Degler underlines two important factors that distinguish gender from class, race, or ethnicity: women "are half of the population, or perhaps more than half" and they "are a sex." Because of the former, "it is hardly accurate to write about the consequences that affect men only as if they were the effects on society as a whole"; that is, "very little that we may find out about other minorities [males and females] can alter our generalizations so drastically, for no minority bulks so large in numbers as women." Because women are a sex, "women are evenly distributed from the top to the bottom of the social structure [thus] they are divided by class, while every other minority is usually united by class."[16] Degler adds that, "because women are a sex they are divided by more than class; they are divided too by the fact that they have an interest in the other sex and in the product of that interest, namely their joint offspring."[17] And, therefore, women are "both oppressed and intimately related to [their] oppressor at the same time." The fact that "the husband is *always* a member of the oppressor class" means that "the wife's identification with women of other classes or with women in general" is necessarily diverted or obscured; politically speaking, this means that more than any other minority, women have a "record of organized, internal division over causes for [their] own advancement."[18] Lastly, because they are a sex, rather than merely a social group, many of their health problems are unique as are the effects of being the bearers of children, the problems surrounding the practice and nature of birth control, and abortion. Nor can one disregard the nature of their sexuality, which has been manipulated by males who have denied it or feared it at different moments in history.[19] Given the physiological differences, the patterns of women's socialization as a sex and the psychological effects of that indoctrination have been different from those experienced by men. Thus, their respective interests and roles have often been divergent if not opposed so that, as has been noted, history has often affected and been affected by the sexes differently.[20]

For Lerner, women's "culturally determined and psychologically internalized marginality seems to be what makes their historical experiences different from that of men."[21] But the internalization of a marginal or subordinate condition is a psychological phenomenon shared by many male members of oppressed minority groups. And women, after all, belong to many more social groups beyond those determined by their sex. Gender, therefore, is not the only factor that has determined the past of women. Women's roles have been limited by family needs throughout history, however much they have undergone transformations; they have had more limits on their opportunities than males of their own class, particularly because sexuality and reproduction were inevitably linked for women. Still one must be careful not to oversimplify the complex historical situation of women by a too broad and reductionist distinction between the experiences of the two sexes.[22] Linda Gordon wisely asserts that a model that "finds female/male the most fundamental and constant dichotomy and contradiction in society" denies or minimizes "the importance of class and race divisions" and leads one to suspect that for one holding such a view, "class and race exploitation and oppression are not dominant problems."[23]

Having briefly delimited the importance of gender as a valid historical variable and pointed to the nature of women's history in general, I will now focus on Chicana history. The obvious point of departure is the following question. Why and how should the theory (and methodology?) of Chicana history differ from women's history in general?

The most compelling initial response is that Chicana history, like that of Black or Native American women, must take into consideration not only gender and class but also the cultural differences engendered by ethnicity and the socio-economic restraints imposed by a race-conscious dominant society. This is not the place to argue that race and ethnicity are key variables affecting a people's historical condition; Mario Barrera, among others, has done a superb job of outlining the reasons.[24] Here we merely underline that a theory of women's history that does not incorporate the historical effects of ethnicity and race in determining the socio-economic and political circumstances of women necessarily fails to present a coherent and credible picture. A women's history confined within the borders of the United States will also be unsuccessful in its attempts to outline the reality of Chicanas, whose social, economic, and cultural networks extend across political boundaries into Mexico. Therefore, beyond gender, class, race, and ethnicity, the international context of Chicanas must be fitted into any conceptual scheme that pretends to elucidate the full complexity of the Chicana past. While "standard" or white women's history has been primarily content to study gender and, at times, class, Chicana history is necessarily another genus in the family of women's history because it must integrate these five variables in complicated and as yet unanalyzed ways.

It is difficult to speculate on how the theory or methodology of Chicana history should differ from that used in the history of women. First, little has been published that can be reasonably categorized as Chicana history. Second, for the most part, what has been written that could genuinely be labeled historical continues to apply male-centered criteria to determine historical significance. Broadly speaking, Chicanas and Chicanos have initiated investigations into (1) the past of Mexican females who have individually or collectively pursued self-affirmation, status, or power and (2) the institutions, ideologies, and conflicts by which they sought to acquire or maintain power, status, or economic security. A history of Chicanas that concerns itself solely or primarily with the activities of women seeking power or heroically resisting it does not need a revised criteria of historical significance beyond that found in either traditional history, that focuses on female exemplars, or the new social history, that emphasizes the plight of the working class and their struggles against oppression. Thus, too frequently the study of the Chicana past has assumed the male-oriented paradigm and sought only to fill in the gaps left in the historical record by searching for information about women and female activities considered significant when judged by male standards. Martha Cotera's work is in this tradition.[25] She has concentrated on women worthies, the lives and deeds of exceptional or deviant women; compensatory history "which tries to redeem the anonymity of the many through the brillance of the few"; and contribution history, "describing women's contributions to, their status in, and their oppression by male-defined society."[26] Furthermore, the theoretical tools that have been used to outline the history of the Chicana have been limited to those used in standard male-oriented history, though the content and meaning of history as defined by the historians of the dominant class is clearly defied by the focus on women and the powerless. Alfredo Mirandé and Evangelina Enríquez's *La Chicana* is similar to Cotera's *Diosa y Hembra*, except that it attempts to introduce an internal colony model of historical explanation.[27] These types of histories of the Chicana differ from women's histories in general, and traditional histories in particular, only in their content which concentrates on Chicanas and their significant deeds (using a male-centered criteria of significance); or differs in their theoretical base (Marxist, neo-Marxist, or social history perspectives) which highlights the lives and circumstances of "ordinary" and working-class people. While these studies are extremely useful and necessary endeavors, they do not represent a theoretical challenge to the male-oriented criteria and, therefore, advance our understanding of Chicanas, *as women*, very little.

Ultimately, Chicana history must differ from white women's history because the two groups of women do not share many critical socio-economic and cultural factors. Their histories are not only dissimilar in content (which would hardly call for a separate theoretical perspective or methodological approach), but they have antithetical structures. White women are distributed among all social classes, with the middle and upper sectors dictating the cultural standards. Chicanas participate in infinitesimal numbers in the upper class and only marginally in the upper-middle sectors. Most Chicanas function in the lower-middle and lower socio-economic sectors and their culture, as Chicanas, is determined primarily by the women in these working-class sectors. Therefore, the traditions, needs, and past experiences of most Chicanas are not only greatly different from those of white women but, quite frequently, diametrically opposed.[28] For example, in order to write a history of Chicana domestic workers, one would need to revise the criteria used to elucidate the history of their female employers, some of whom, freed from the drudgery of routine household chores, found time to devote themselves to the advancement of women in white society.[29] Given the international and ethnic context of Mexican women in the United States, even a history of white or Black domestics would have to be structurally distinct from that of their Chicana counterparts. The fear produced by the immigration authorities, the threat of deportation by dissatisfied employers, the linguistic and cultural obstacles, and the differences in social networks and survival strategies all combine to make unique not only the story of Chicanas in the domestic labor force, but also the theory by which one can explain and determine the relevancy of the data.[30] Lastly, though the program of empirical research still requires the creation of a new conceptual framework for the history of women, we know that women of different classes have divergent (if not always opposed) historical experiences. Furthermore, when they are distinguished by culture, race, and ethnicity we can also be sure that they "experience their historical subordination differently." In addition, women have differential access to education and information in the United States and different patterns of sex roles predominate in diverse households. Therefore, the history of the consciousness of themselves as women is bound to be dissimilar for the various groups of females who differ by class, race, or ethnicity.[31]

The preceeding remarks make evident, once again, that women cannot be studied as though they were a minority. Not even Mexican women can be wholly analyzed via the male-centered conceptual framework that presently dominates the histories of oppressed minorities. The reason is ovious: Chicanas as women are a sex before they are anything else. No other category fixes their historical reality more firmly than their gender. However, this must be tempered by the knowledge that Chicanas are also clustered in the lower socio-economic sectors and that they share a culture and ethnicity distinct from that of other women. The synthesis of these disparate variables is the task of Chicana history. But the difficulties involved in this endeavor are truly great. Unlike ethnic/racial minorities that are not very integrated into white culture, Chicanas are very integrated into Chicano male culture.[32] Though they are members of a sex, Chicanas are more closely allied to Chicanos than they are to women of other classes and races. Chicanas are also primarily responsible for indoctrinating their children, males and females, "in the very values by which they themselves have been indoctrinated to subordination"; as Lerner states, the subordination of women "must therefore be essentially different in nature from other forms of human subordination."[33] Yet, because of their more extensive integration into Chicano culture than into white female life, "whatever subordination [Chicanas] experienced must be described and analyzed within the context of the oppression of the males of their group."[34]

We now come to two related questions. How are the various forms of oppression, by which Chicanas have been subjected, to be historically assessed? And, is Chicana history limited to that of an oppressed group and its struggles against oppression? The vacuum that exists due to the dearth of empirical research on Chicanas has been partly filled by impressionistic or sketchy studies. Unfortunately, these studies do not yield a clear outline of the relations between the various mechanisms by which Chicanas are kept in a subordinate state. Feminist scholarship has come a long way since Robin Morgan declared in *Sisterhood Is Powerful* "that capitalism, imperialism, and racism are *symptoms* of male supremacy-sexism."[35] In the same volume Elizabeth Sutherland, writing about Chicanas, noted that "for the woman of a colonized group, even the most political, her oppression as a woman is usually overshadowed by the common oppression of both male and female."[36] Her words were seconded by Enriqueta Longauex y Vasquez who stated "when a family is involved in a human rights movement, as is the Mexican-American family, there is little room for a woman's liberation movement alone. There is little room for having a definition of a woman's role as such.... The family must come up together."[37]

This "political familism" was perceptively studied by Maxine Baca Zinn and her conclusions were guarded but hopeful: "Political familism itself does not transcend sex role subordination.

But within the varied expressions and manifestations of El Movimiento are changes in sex role relationships and family structure, as well as the seeds of new roles for the women and men of La Raza."[38] The need for a dual or triple liberation of the male and female from socio-economic, racial, and sexual subordination has also been commented on by others. Mirandé and Enríquez speak for many when they conclude that Chicanas, "aware of colonial oppression, ...reject Anglo feminism for the very reason that Anglos neglect the issue of racism. The Chicana feminist seeks to eradicate poverty and racism as well as sexism."[39] While Margarita Melville speaks of Mexican American women as being "twice a minority" most scholars write about a triple oppression, variously described as based on nationality, working-class status, and sex;[40] or due to their colonial status, the effects of sexism, and internal oppression within the culture.[41] Some authors even assert a quadruple oppression based on race, sex, socio-economic status, and lack of language skills;[42] or heterosexism, racism, sexism, and "being just plain poor."[43] Martha Cotera claims that "as pressing as [the Chicana's] socioeconomic problems are, the real barriers to development are matters of 'image' and 'self-concept.'"[44] Beyond a lack of concensus concerning the elements of oppression, the historical relations between these forms of subordination are not known with any specificity.[45] Therefore, the question posed about how the historical oppression of Chicanas should be assessed does not yet have a historically valid answer, and for the present, must serve only as a suggestion for future research in Chicana history.

Of course, speculative assessments concerning the relative significance of the modes of subjection have been discussed. Some Mexicanas have claimed either that a ranking of oppressions is not useful[46] or that the oppressions (male chauvinism and class oppression) are too closely linked to be ordered in a hierarchy.[47] Other writers have pointed to the possibility that one factor has been more critical than another. However, there is little agreement as to which elements have been the most determinative. For Márquez and Ramírez the "essence of women's oppression" is primarily the product of "her relations to the means of social production in society, not...her relations to men at home."[48] Mirandé and Enríquez argue that the effects of oppression on Chicanas "are not additive. Their socioeconomic oppression ... is greater than would be predicted from the cumulative effects of race and gender."[49] And, at least with regard to what determines unemployment, they conclude the "ethnic background is more significant than gender."[50] Though she plays down a class analysis, Margarita Melville ranks socio-economic factors as "more clearly the determinants of people's options than are tradition, ...ethnicity per se," or gender.[51] The primacy of class interests has been emphasized by Del Castillo and others who adhere to a Marxist or neo-Marxist analytical framework.[52] Whether systematically linked or easily ranked, the forces oppressing Chicanas are varied and pervasive. But should they exhaust the subject of Chicana history?

The weight of scholarship in women's history is firmly on the side affirming that the history of women cannot be profitably compared to that of an oppressed minority, if for no other reason than because women are a sex and make up at least half of the population.[53] While the oppression of Chicanas, in all its forms and combinations, should make up a critical part of the content of their history, to limit the analysis of their past to the same framework that has dominated the interpretation of oppressed minorities "would not only be unimaginative," but "could lead to an intellectual *cul-de-sac* once all the forms of oppression are exposed."[54] The problem has been summarized as follows: "analyses of women based on static concepts such as caste or oppressed group render history an external process, a force which presses against women's lives without a reciprocal interaction. Women become in the truest sense the *objects of history*, bound by their peculiar situation as victims of oppression."[55] However much the limiting "compensatory history" and "great women syndrome" approaches have governed the study of the Chicana past to date, the fact remains that Chicanas have been much more than the objects of history or its passive victims. They have preserved and defended many of the values, traditions, and institutions necessary to the survival of Mexicans in the United States. They have also contributed immensely, albeit often through their exploitation or resistance to exploitation, to the formation and development of working-class urban and rural societies where they have predominated.[56] But, most important of all, Chicanas have a history intrinsically important for its own sake in which they have functioned as subjects, dynamically creating their own history.

Chicanas' status and role, both within and without the family, have been changing over time.[57] They have been a critical segment of the working force; they have been active in reform movements seeking to ameliorate the plight of Mexicans, male and female; and they have participated in community and institution building both within and outside of religious, social, educational, labor, and civic organizations.[58] Moreover, Mexican women in the United States have their own sexual history, which needs to be researched and recorded. We still know very little about the transformations they have undergone and caused as reproduction patterns have varied over time. The traditional link between sex and child-bearing has been displaced due to economic reasons, diseases, contraception, sterilization, and abortion; child-rearing practices have been altered as a consequence of immigration, socio-economic, demographic, and geographical factors. Transformations in Chicana sexuality may have an effect in other areas of the community: they may be behind the drives for sex education in local schools serving Chicano neighborhoods; they may be serving to lessen the sexual harassment to which Chicanas have been subjected; and they may have resulted in the sexual politics that impinge upon the lives of Chicanos and Chicanas. The new possibility of Chicanas talking frankly about sex may also be reflected in positive changes in the sexual behavior of the two sexes. Similarly, sex-role patterns determining the relation between child-bearing and child-rearing have been affected by modifications in employment, cultural and marital patterns, and innovations in sexual attitudes, belief systems, and female consciousness. Access to and quality of education and mass media have undoubtedly transformed aspects of sex-role indoctrination.[59]

Chicana female consciousness, even independent of acculturation, has also evolved through time.[60] In the light of this, we need to know what the culture of Mexican women has been and what phases it has gone through. This includes a stage by stage assessment of their separate occupations, within and beyond the house and place of employment; their experiences as women; their rituals, entertainment, and folklore; the status patterns within their separate culture and how these have been determined; their communication, survival, and supportive networks; how they have internalized partriarchal assumptions; how they have fought, consciously and unconsciously, to assert their autonomy and maintain their integrity as women; and how they have mediated the conflicts between male and female cultures.[61]

To progress beyond Chicanas as victims to Chicanas as agents of social change and historical transformation requires that we study not only Chicana culture but also how changes in this culture have affected male culture and history in general. First, variations in Chicana sexuality have had an impact on changes in the relationships between males and females. These, in turn, have caused changes in the divorce rate, age of marriage of both partners, and have led to sexual anxieties among Chicanos. Some have even attributed the rise of Chicana feminism to Chicano resistance to changes in Chicana consciousness. Indeed, in the late 1960s and early 1970s, efforts by women of all colors to make themselves heard and to have their needs recognized within the various social movements met with such adamant opposition on the part of males that many women opted to focus on their concerns in exclusively female groups.[62] Conceivably, Chicano resistance to Chicana demands promoted in no small part the rise of feminist consciousness among these women, whose reaction to this subordination helped, eventually, to further radicalize and raise the consciousness of males themselves.[63] Consequently raising consciousness between women of different ethnic and class backgrounds was also important but problematic. Too often Chicanas had little impact on white feminists who found working-class and ethnic demands irrevelant to their needs if not outright antithetical.[64]

The effects of Chicanas on males and the society at large go far beyond what I have described above. For instance, we need to explore to what extent Mexican women in the United States have had an impact, through their variable reproduction patterns, "on both the existence and welfare of local" and regional populations.[65] We need to know how Chicanas' have responded to traditional norms favoring large families and how their having children has affected present Chicano fertility patterns and the status of legitimate, illegitimate, single-parent children. How Chicanas "cooperate with or initiate new ways of raising children" also needs to be assessed, since different socialization styles produce different types of family units and individuals who can promote or destabilize ongoing social patterns.[66] As was made evident by the symbolic power of the zoot suit during southern California's riots of the 1940s, changes in dress, hair sytles, or use of cosmetics by Chicanas are "often the most visible part of widespread role discontent or the collective desire for role redefinition."[67] Women can profoundly influence their social and economic milieu by accepting or rebelling against predominant social roles. Yet females have "often been involved in spectacular role revolts, which tend to get overlooked by historians" because they are sometimes "diffuse [sic] and disorganized changes of mind and behavior that are similar in form to changing fashions."[68] Though Chicanas do participate singly and collectively in role revolts, these have yet to be identified and their causes and effects recorded.

Similarly, more needs to be known about the role of Mexican women in determining the quality and type of popular culture, life-style, and moral values prevalent among Mexican Americans. As consumers and food processors, they veto or promote trends in everything that touches barrio life from foods to clothes, from swearing to music. They are critical to the family's attempts at "keeping up appearances," retaining Spanish as a viable language or Catholicism as a belief system in the home and community. As mothers, wives, sisters, and sweethearts, Chicanas have had a profound influence on the attitudes, values, morals, and beliefs of males. Despite obvious socio-economic forces limiting their options, they ultimately decide who is or is not an attractive male type; who is or is not a desirable mate; and what it takes to be an acceptable breadwinner, a praiseworthy protector, or a respectable leader. Chicanas can support or stymie social movements, often they can make or break the local religious institutions, and they are pivotal to electing new leaders or maintaining the status quo. How this has taken place is still mostly unknown. Already research has been initiated into how the slow and painful work of Mexicanas in professional, civic, charitable, and socio-political organizations has led to changes in the form and content of welfare legislation, education, health delivery services, and labor relations. Progressive advances often have been the product of sustained strikes and organized protests mobilized and led by Chicanas. Though research continues to grow, the economic and social roles of Chicanas as industrial operatives, agricultural workers, domestic employees, small merchants, artisans, service workers, managers, professionals, midwives, folk healers, informal counselors and therapists has yet to be fully investigated.

Lastly, we need to know how Chicanas have affected patterns of migration, rural flight, and the geographical distribution of Mexicans. Their contribution to sex ratio imbalances in certain communities requires the need to explore age-specific patterns of dying, overall life expectancies, and the role of Chicanas as domestic distributors of scarce foodstuffs and critical resources during times of extreme shortages.[69] We must also come to understand how Chicanas have shaped Chicano history in general through the complex process of community-building, the transmission of culture to their children, and the creation of "social networks and infra-structure that provide continuity in the community."[70]

In conclusion, Chicanas have wielded considerable influence in their homes and communities and have functioned as dynamic agents of history. Of course, Chicanas have been oppressed in myriad ways. Nonetheless, it is important for historians to keep in mind that though, "women accept and sometimes even defend some of the conditions of their oppression, usually in order to protect themselves from worse penalities, [at] the same time they not only resist but usually succeed in fundamentally altering, in having some constant effect on, the terms of their subjugation. Sex relations, like class relations, can only be understood dialectically. The ultimate domination of male power and sexist ideas is only a net domination, not an absolute one; every aspect of male supremacy is affected by women's accommodation and resistance to it.[71] Or, as Lerner argues: "Women often participated in their own subordination by internalizing the ideology and values which oppressed them and by passing those on to their children. Yet they were not passive victims, but always involved themselves actively in the world in their own way. The history of women is the history of their on-going functioning *on their own terms* in a male defined world. It is also the history of their finding their own consciousness."[72] In other words, Chicana history is neither an endless list of examples of oppression nor a paean announcing the heretofore unknown power of Mexican women. What is historically significant about Chicanas is the processes by which they have mediated their subjection with continual affirmations of autonomy and integrity. Chicanas are both subjects and objects. While Chicana history can serve to refute the stereotypes produced by a focus on the latter, it should not lead to the creation of new stereotypes by a myopic fixation on the former.

The preceding discussion on the role of oppression has necessarily led me to argue for what the content of Chicana history should be. But further clarification on this last point is in order. I would like to begin by introducing an important distinction to Chicana history if we are to elucidate the theoretical bases of its challenge to traditional history and the proposed revised criteria of historical significance it represents. Though I do not wish to multiply categories unnecessarily, I propose that we distinguish "the history of Chicanas" from "Chicana history." I suggest that the former be reserved for those aspects of Chicana life that, because they are interchangeable with those of males, can be adequately studied through the male-centered criteria of the historical significance of data, theory, or narrative style. This includes much of what concerns Chicanas as they pursue socio-economic power or as they resist those who exercise it whether at home, school, field, factory, marketplace, in the streets and on the picket lines. Beyond current Marxist, neo-Marxist, and social history techniques equally applicable to males and females little else is necessary, theoretically speaking, to understand the relation of Chicanas to the mode of production or their roles as wage earners, labor organizers, revolutionaries, or corporate lawyers. As it is, Chicano labor, urban, social, political, and immigration histories have progressed well in their task of recording and explaining the Chicano historical experience.[73] Admittedly, few works by professional historians have focused on Chicanas. In one of the best of these, Mario T. Garcia has wisely observed that "the history of Chicanos, especially Chicano workers, is only half-complete without an appreciation of the contributions Mexican women have made."[74] This suggests that most Chicano historians to date, male or female, are concerned with the lack of attention to Chicanas, rather than with a revised critieria of historical significance.

It has been primarily Chicanas, and not necessarily historians (since there are extremely few of them), who have advocated the exploration of female-centered questions concerning sociocultural issues and female reality.[75] What they have pointed to goes beyond the standard fare served up by neo-Marxist theories or social history approaches. Their interest in the "female experience" requires a woman-conscious paradigm and a female-centered criteria of historical significance. I propose that the term "Chicana history" be limited to the elucidation of the status and transformations of those aspects of Chicana life that are uniquely female. Many of these aspects already have been outlined above; many more are still in need of articulation. The proposed revised criteria for Chicana history call for new data, new interpretive frameworks, new theoretical approaches, and, perhaps, new styles of historical narrative. Not only must a search continue for as yet undiscovered sources, but novel questions must be asked of known sources to elicit relevant information about Chicanas. To evaluate properly the activities and achievements of Chicanas, new analytical categories must be developed that reflect female rather than solely male actions and triumphs. Women's roles are frequently different from those of males: "obviously their achievements must...be measured on a different scale."[76] Relevant women-centered historical categories will make possible the realistic assessment of female activities (such as reproduction, household maintenance, and informal communication networks) previously devalued when analyzed through male-centered conceptual schemes. Chicanas will then figure prominently in their own right in areas other than entertainment, sports, politics, religion, or the military, where outstanding individuals are highlighted. That history often affects women different from how it affects men means that the periodization of traditional Chicano history will have to be modified. The paucity of information on the Chicana past makes it impossible to tell what this periodization will be. The chronological framework for Chicanos can continue to serve the history of Chicanas, but Chicana history will call for radical departures as new historical categories are introduced which redefine the significant periods of change.[77] In the future, we might focus on such watersheds as, for instance, the socio-cultural transformation of Mexican women resulting from changes in the link between sexuality and reproduction due to the widespread use of efficient contraceptives.

I would like to close this brief theoretical discussion by posing a final question. Is Chicana history a methodology in and of itself? The answer should be obvious by now. Theory delimits the type of data that will be assessed as adequate. The data available may well determine the theory that will be applied. The form of historical discourse employed is influenced by both the theory and the data base used and, in turn, the data base and the theory will be modified if the narrative style favored is such as to make one or the other unacceptable. Thus, both the data and theory of Chicana history emphasize the role and status of Mexican women as women. In turn, data and theory must be combined in some sort of narrative; these three factors joined compose history. A woman-oriented paradigm is not a method; it is a conceptual, epistemological framework that permits one to discriminate between data, methods, theories, and modes of discourse so that those that yield female-centered interpretations and information can be adopted when desired.[78] In short, Chicana history (and women's history in general) combines methodology, theory, and content.

Finally, given that Marxist and neo-Marxist scholarship has dominated a substantial part of the discourse on the Chicana past, I will briefly address this topic. Marxian-inspired methods of analysis have contributed immensely to our understanding of the role in the history of Chicanas of class conflict, the relation between modes of production and ideology, and the significance of economic subordination as a key historical determinant.[79] However, some caution should be exercised in the application of these conceptual schemes. First, women are a sex and sexual struggle cannot be theoretically equated with class struggle.[80] Nonetheless, "the history of production under capitalism, from a feminist perspective, is not simply the class struggle between the producer and the owner of the means of production. It is also the development of a particular form of the sexual division of labour in relation to that struggle."[81] That is, gender is often critical to class relations; witness, for instance, the role of women as a reserve pool of labor and their function as depressors of male wages through their unpaid (and, therefore, undervalued) housework.[82] Whether there is or is not an "unhappy marriage of Marxism and feminism,"[83] gender, like race and ethnicity, is not a secondary category which can be dismissed as an idealistic addition to material reality.[84] An over reliance on male-centered theories that focus primarily or solely on class and economic issues can lead to overlooking the sexual, ideological, and psychological elements critical to an elucidation of the female experience.[85] One example will suffice. Hilda Smith argues that: "as a possible alternative to viewing women's class outside of the context of their husbands' occupations, I would contend that number of children is as determining a factor in a woman's class as her husband's income...a woman whose husband's income qualifies her for middle-class status, but who has seven children, may lead a more encumbered existence than one whose husband is poorer, but who has only one or two children."[86] I believe the essence of this observation is correct even if class is determined by the relation to the mode of production rather than solely by income. Thus, however persuasive, if the theory does not raise and explore female-centered questions, it will not adequately explain the daily life and psychological reality of women. With regard to Mexican women in the United States, not only must they be studied with class and gender categories in mind, but with attention to critical historical variables of ethnicity, race, and international context. Therefore, no single conceptual framework will be able to fully capture the complexity and nuances of the Chicana past. Chicana history calls for the recognition of the historical significance of all these factors and their integration through a women-oriented perspective. Without that, the history of Chicanas cannot be Chicana history.[87]

Notes

1. Gerda Lerner, *The Majority Finds Its Past: Placing Women in History* (New York and Oxford: Oxford University Press, 1979), pp. 159, 167, 180.

2. Bell Hooks, *Ain't I a Woman?: Black Women and Feminism* (Boston: South End Press, 1981), p. 10; and Asuncion Lavrin, ed., *Latin American Women: Historial Perspectives* (Westport, Conn.: Greenwood Press, 1978), p. 5.

3. Though my analysis is not a tropological one, this paragraph draws from the work of Hayden White, *Metahistory: The Historical Imagination in Nineteenth-Century Europe* (Baltimore and London: John Hopkins University, 1973), pp. ix-xii.

4. Carl N. Degler, *Is There a History of Women?* (London: Oxford University Press, 1975), p. 5.

5. Gerda Lerner, "New Approaches to the Study of Women in American History," *Journal of Social History* 3 (Fall 1969): 53.

6. Gerda Lerner, *The Woman in American History* (Menlo Park, Calif.: Addison Wesley, 1971), p. 5.

7. "Letter to Our Readers," *Frontiers* 5 (Summer 1980): iv; Margarita B. Melville, ed., *Twice a Minority: Mexican American Women* (St. Louis: C.V. Mosby, 1980), p. 1.

8. Lerner, "New Approaches," pp. 53-54.

9. Ibid., p. 55.

10. Ibid., p. 55-56.

11. Roxanne Dunbar Ortiz, "Female Liberation as the Basis for Social Revolution," in *Sisterhood Is Powerful*, ed. Robin Morgan (New York: Random House, 1979), pp. 477-492; Mary S. Hartman and Lois Banner, eds., *Clio's Consciousness Raised: New Perspectives on the History of Women* (New York: Harper Colophon Books, 1974), p. vii.

12. Lerner, "New Approaches," p. 59; cf. *The Majority Finds Its Past*, pp. 177-180.

13. Lerner, "New Approches," p. 60.

14. Hilda Smith, "Feminism and the Methodology of Women's History," in *Liberating Women's History: Theoretical and Critical Essays*, ed. Berenice A. Carroll (Urbana: University of Illinois Press, 1976), p. 382; see also Degler, *Is There a History of Women?* pp. 9-14.

15. Renate Bridenthal and Claudia Koonz, eds. *Becoming Visible: Women in European History* (Boston: Houghton Mifflin, 1977), p. 255, cf. 280; see also Gerda Lerner, ed. *The Female*

Experience: An American Documentary (Indianapolis: Bobbs-Merrill, 1977), p. xxxii.
16. Degler, *Is There a History of Women?* p. 21.
17. Ibid., p. 23.
18. Ibid., p. 24.
19. Ibid., pp. 25-30; see also Degler, *At Odds: Women and the Family in America from the Revolution to the Present* (New York and Oxford: Oxford University Press, 1980) p. 18.
20. Degler, *Is There a History of Women?* p. 20; Lerner, *The Female Experience*, p. xxvi.
21. Gerda Lerner, "Placing Women in History: A 1975 Perspective," in *Liberating Women's History*, p. 365; and *The Majority Finds Its Past*, p. xxxi.
22. Bridenthal and Koonz, *Becoming Visible*, p. 474; Lerner, *The Majority Finds Its Past*, p. 155; Linda Gordon, "A Socialist View of Women's Studies: A Reply to Editorial," *Signs: Journal of Women in Culture and Society* 1 (Winter 1975): 562.
23. Gordon, "Socialist View of Women's Studies," p. 562.
24. Mario Barrera, *Race and Class in the Southwest: A Theory of Racial Inequality* (Notre Dame and London: University of Notre Dame, 1979).
25. Martha Cotera, *Profile on the Mexican American Woman* (Austin: National Educational Laboratory Publishers, Inc., 1976a); *Diosa y Hembra: The History and Heritage of Chicanas in the U.S.* (Austin: Information Systems Development, 1976b); and "Feminism: The Chicana and the Anglo Versions, A Historical Analysis," in Melville, *Twice a Minority*.
26. Lerner, *The Majority Finds Its Past*, pp. 145-146; Lavrin, *Latin American Women*, p. 4.
27. Alfredo Mirandé and Evangelina Enríquez, *La Chicana: The Mexican-American Woman* (Chicago and London: University of Chicago Press, 1979), pp. 9-10.
28. Rosaura Sánchez, "The Chicana Labor Force," in *Essays on La Mujer*, ed. Rosaura Sánchez and Rosa Martinez Cruz (Los Angeles: Chicano Studies Center Publications, University of California, 1977), p. 3-15; Elizabeth Waldman, "Profile of the Chicana: A Statistical Fact Sheet," in *Mexican Women in the United States: Struggles Past and Present*, ed. Magdalena Mora and Adelaida R. Del Castillo (Los Angeles: Chicano Studies Research Center, University of California, 1980), pp. 195-204.
29. For Latin America see Margo L. Smith, "Domestic Service as a Channel of Upward Mobility for the Lower Class Woman: The Lima Case," in *Female and Male in Latin America*, ed. Ann

Pescatello (Pittsburgh: University of Pittsburgh Press, 1973), pp. 191-207; Shoshana B. Tancer, "La Quisqueyana: The Dominican Woman, 1940-1970," in *Female and Male in Latin America*, pp. 209-229; for Blacks in the United States see Gerda Lerner, ed., *Black Women in White America: A Documentary History* (New York: Pantheon Books, 1972); for a preliminary look at Chicanas see Melville, *Twice a Minority*, pp. 155-163; and "Mexican Women Adapt to Migration," in *Mexican Immigrant Workers in the U.S.*, ed. Antonio Ríos-Bustamante (Los Angeles: Chicano Studies Research Center Publications, University of California, 1981), pp. 119-124.

30. Melville, *Twice a Minority*, pp. 155-163, and "Mexican Women Adapt to Migration," pp. 119-124; Roland M. Wagner and Diane M. Schaffer, "Social Networks and Survival Strategies: An Exploratory Study of Mexican American, Black, and Anglo Female Family Heads in San Jose, California," in *Twice a Minority*, pp. 173-190.

31. Lerner, *The Majority Finds Its Past*, pp. xxviii-xxxii, 146, 160.

32. See Gordon, "Socialist View of Women's Studies," p. 561.

33. Lerner, *The Majority Finds Its Past*, p. 170.

34. Ibid., p. 171.

35. Robin Morgan, ed., *Sisterhood Is Powerful* (New York: Random House, 1970), p. xxxiv.

36. Elizabeth Sutherland, "Colonialized Women: The Chicana - An Introduction," in *Sisterhood Is Powerful*, p. 376.

37. Enriqueta Longauex y Vasquez, "The Mexican-American Woman," in *Sisterhood Is Powerful*, p. 384.

38. Maxine Baca Zinn, "Political Familism: Toward Sex Role Equality in Chicano Families," *Aztlan: International Journal of Chicano Studies Research* 6 (Spring 1975): 24.

39. Mirandé and Enríquez, *La Chicana*, p. 243; see also Adelaida R. Del Castillo and Magdalena Mora, "Sex, Nationality, and Class: La Obrera Mexicana," in *Mexican Women in the United States*, p. 2; Lerner, *Black Women in White America*, p. xxv; Hooks, *Ain't I a Woman?*, p. 13.

40. Mirta Vidal, *Chicanas Speak Out: Women, New Voice of La Raza* (New York: Pathfinder Press, 1971), p. 6; Evelina Márquez and Margarita Ramírez, "Women's Task is to Gain Liberation," in *Essays on La Mujer*, p. 192; Del Castillo and Mora, "Sex, Nationality, and Class," pp. 1-4; Carlos Vasquez, "Women in the Chicano Movement," in *Mexican Women in the United States*, p. 28.

41. Mirandé and Enríquez, *La Chicana*, pp. 12, 130, 241.

42. Theresa Aragon de Valdez, "Organizing as a Political Tool for the Chicana," *Frontiers* 5 (Summer 1980): 7.

43. Cherríe Moraga, "La Güera," in *This Bridge Called My Back: Writings by Radical Women of Color*, ed. Cherríe Moraga and Gloria Anzaldúa (Watertown, Mass.: Persephone Press, 1981), p. 29.

44. Martha Cotera, *Profile on the Mexican American Woman*, p. 197.

45. Maxine Baca Zinn, "Gender and Ethnic Identity Among Chicanos," *Frontiers* 5 (Summer 1980): 18-24.

46. Anna Nieto-Gomez, "La Feminista," *Encuentro Femenil* 1 (1974): 37; Moraga, "La Güera," pp. 29, 33.

47. Maria Linda Apodaca, "The Chicana Woman: An Historical Materialist Perspective," in *Women in Latin America: An Anthology from Latin American Perspectives*, ed. William Bolinger et al. (Riverside, Calif.: Latin America Perspectives, 1979), pp. 83, 96.

48. Márquez and Ramírez, "Women's Task," p. 192.

49. Mirandé and Enríquez, *La Chicana*, p. 13.

50. Ibid., p. 121; Baca Zinn, "Gender and Ethnic Identity," p. 23; cf. Tacho Mindiola, "The Cost of Being a Mexican Female Worker in the 1970 Houston Labor Market," *Aztlan: International Journal of Chicano Studies Research* 11 (Fall 1980): 231-247; Beatriz Pesquera, "A Border Society in Transition: The Maquiladoras of Tijuana" (Paper presented at the Conference on the Cultural Roots of Chicana Literature: 1780-1980, Oakland, California, October 16, 1981).

51. Margarita B. Melville, "Introduction," pp. 8-16, and "Selective Acculturation of Female Mexican Migrants," pp. 155-163 in *Twice a Minority*.

52. Adelaida R. Del Castillo, "Mexican Women in Organization," in *Mexican Women in the United States*, p. 16; Marlene Dixon, "The Rise and Demise of Women's Liberation: A Class Analysis," in *Mexican Women in the United States*, p. 40; Gordon, "Socialist View of Women's Studies," p. 562; Juliet Mitchell, *Woman's Estate* (New York: Pantheon Books, 1971); cf. Sheila Rowbotham, *Women, Resistance and Revolution* (New York: Pantheon Books, 1972); and Lydia Sargent, ed., *Women and Revolution: A Discussion of the Unhappy Marriage of Marxism and Feminism* (Boston: South End Press, 1981).

53. Lerner, "New Approaches," pp. 54, 57-58, 60; Gordon, "Socialist View of Women's Studies," p. 561; Degler, *Is There a*

History of Women? p. 8, 20-25; June E. Hahner, ed. *Women in Latin American History: Their Lives and Views* (Los Angeles: Latin American Center, University of California, 1976), p. 1; Lerner, *The Female Experience*, pp. xxi-xxii; Lavrin, *Latin American Women*, p. 5; Lerner, *The Majority Finds Its Past*, pp. 150, 170; Degler, *At Odds*, p. 18; Hooks, *Ain't I a Woman?*, p. 8.

54. Lavrin, *Latin American Women*, p. 5; see also Lerner, "New Approaches," p. 54.

55. Ann D. Gordon, Mari Jo Buhle and Nancy Schrom Dye, "The Problem of Women's History," in *Liberating Women's History*, p. 88.

56. Sutherland, "Colonized Women," p. 377; Baca Zinn "Political Familism," pp. 15-19; Cotera, *Diosa y Hembra*; Mirandé and Enríquez, *La Chicana*, pp. 115-117; Mario T. Garcia, "The Chicana in American History: The Mexican Women of El Paso, 1880-1920-A Case Study," *Pacific Historical Review* 49 (May 1980): 322-323.

57. Leo Grebler, Joan W. Moore, and Ralph Guzman, *The Mexican-American People: The Nation's Second Largest Minority* (New York: The Free Press, 1970), pp. 350-377; Robert Staples, "The Mexican-American Family: Its Modification Over Time and Space," *Phylon* 37 (1971): 179-192; Peter Uhlenberg, "Marital Instability Among Mexican Americans: Following the Patterns of Blacks?" *Social Problems* 20 (Summer 1972): 49-56; Richard Griswold del Castillo, "La Familia Chicana: Social Change in the Chicano Family of Los Angeles, 1850-1890," *Journal of Ethnic Studies* 3 (Spring 1975): 41-58; Maxine Baca Zinn, "Chicanas: Power and Control in the Domestic Sphere," *De Colores* 2 (1975): 19-31, and "Political Familism," pp. 13-26; Cotera, *Diosa y Hembra*; Nathan Murillo, "The Mexican American Family," in *Chicanos: Social and Psychological Perspectives*, ed. Carrol A. Hernandez, Nathaniel N. Wagner, and Marsha J. Haug (St. Louis: C.V. Mosby, 1976), pp. 15-25; Betty Garcia-Bahne, "La Chicana and the Chicano Family" in *Essays on La Mujer*, pp. 30-47; Alfredo Mirandé, "The Chicano Family: A Reanalysis of Conflicting Views," *Journal of Marriage and the Family* 39 (November 1977): 747-758; Lea Ybarra, "Conjugal Role Relationships in the Chicano Family" (Ph.D. diss., University of California, Berkeley, 1977); Michael Miller, "Variations in Mexican American Family Life: A Review Synthesis of Empirical Research," *Aztlan: International Journal of Chicano Studies Research* 9 (1978): 209-231; Mirandé and Enríquez, *La Chicana*.

58. Cotera, *Diosa y Hembra*; Sánchez, "The Chicana Labor Force," pp. 3-15; Laura E. Arroyo, "Industrial and Occupational Distribution of Chicana Workers," in *Essays on La Mujer*, pp. 150-187; Mirandé and Enríquez, *La Chicana*; Garcia, "The Chicana in American History," pp. 315-337; Magdalena Mora and Adelaida R. Del Castillo, eds., *Mexican Women in the United States*; Magdalena Mora, "The Tolteca Strike: Mexican Women and the Struggle for Union Representation," in *Mexican Immigrant Workers in the U.S.*, pp. 111-117.

59. Ibid.; Baca Zinn, "Gender and Ethnic Identity," pp. 18-24; Melville, *Twice a Minority*.

60. Baca Zinn, "Political Familism," p. 13.

61. Lerner, *The Majority Finds Its Past*, pp. 158-159.

62. Rowbotham, *Women, Resistance and Revolution*; Sargent, *Women and Revolution*, pp. xii-xxii; Hooks, *Ain't I a Woman?*, p. 5.

63. Vidal, *Chicanas Speak Out*, pp. 5-6; Mirandé and Enríquez, *La Chicana*, pp. 2, 235-238; Del Castillo "Mexican Women in Organization," pp. 7-16; Roxanne Dunbar Ortiz, "Toward a Democratic Women's Movement in the United States," pp. 29-30.

64. Sylvia Lizárraga, "From a Woman to a Woman," in *Essays on La Mujer*, p. 91; Mirandé and Enríquez, *La Chicana*, pp. 1, 139-239; Marta Cotera, "Feminism: The Chicana and Anglo Versions, A Historical Analysis," in *Twice a Minority*, pp. 226-228, 233; Aragon de Valdez, "Political Tool for the Chicana," p. 10.

65. Sheila Ryan Johansson, "'Herstory' as History: A New Field or Another Fad?" in *Liberating Women's History*, p. 418.

66. Ibid., pp. 418-419.

67. Ibid., p. 419.

68. Ibid., p. 419-421.

69. Ibid., pp. 421-426.

70. Lerner, *The Majority Finds Its Past*, p. 179.

71. Gordon, "Socialist View of Women's Studies," p. 565.

72. Lerner, *The Female Experience*, pp. xxvii, xxxv.

73. Juan Gómez-Quiñones and Luis Leobardo Arroyo, "On the State of Chicano History: Observations on Its Development, Interpretations, and Theory, 1970-1974," *Western Historical Quarterly* (April 1976): 155-185.

74. Garcia, "The Chicana in American History," p. 337.

75. Baca Zinn, "Gender and Ethnic Identity," pp. 18-20; Cordelia Candelaria, "Six Reference Works on Mexican-American

Women: A Review Essay," *Frontiers* 5 (Summer 1980): 75; Lea Ybarra, "The Status of Research on Chicanas," unpublished manuscript, 1981, pp. 9-12.

76. Lerner, "New Approaches," p. 62.

77. Lerner, *The Majority Finds Its Past*, pp. 154-155, 169, 175; Judith Sweeney, "Chicana History: A Review of the Literature," in *Essays on La Mujer*, p. 100.

78. Cf. Lerner, *The Majority Finds Its Past*, pp. xiv, 168; see also Lavrin, *Latin American Women*, p. 6.

79. See, for instance, Rosaura Sánchez and Rosa Martinez Cruz, eds., *Essays on La Mujer* (Los Angeles: Chicano Studies Center Publications, University of California, 1977); Apodaca, "The Chicana Woman," and Mora and Del Castillo, *Mexican Women in the United States*.

80. Juliet Mitchell, *Psychoanalysis and Feminism* (New York: Pantheon Books, 1974), p. xxiii.

81. Sally Alexander, "Women's Work in Nineteenth-Century London: A Study of the Years 1820-50," in *The Rights and Wrongs of Women*, ed. Juliet Mitchell and Ann Oakley (New York: Penguin Books, 1976), pp. 59-60.

82. Sheila Rowbotham, *Woman's Consciousness, Man's World* (Baltimore: Penguin, 1973); idem, *Hidden from History: Rediscovering Women in History from the 17th Century to the Present* (New York: Pantheon Books, 1976); Wally Secombe, "The Housewife and Her Labour Under Capitalism," *New Left Review* 82 (January-February 1974): 3-24; Gordon, "Socialist View of Women's Studies," p. 563; Ann Oakley, *Women's Work: The Housewife, Past and Present* (New York: Vintage Books, 1976), pp. 3-78.

83. Sargent, *Women and Revolution*; and Rowbotham, *Woman's Consciousness, Man's World*.

84. See for instance Barrera, *Race and Class in the Southwest*; Sargent, *Women and Revolution*; Hooks, *Ain't I a Woman?*; Cherríe Moraga and Gloria Anzaldúa, eds., *This Bridge Called My Back*; Gloria I. Joseph and Jill Lewis, *Common Differences: Conflicts in Black and White Feminist Perspectives* (Garden City, New York: Anchor Books, 1981).

85. Lerner, *The Majority Finds Its Past*, pp. 155-157.

86. Smith, "Methodology of Women's History," p. 383.

87. This essay was written in the Spring of 1982. Since then much that is relevant has been published, but nothing that changes the thesis I present here. For a comparative overview of issues relevant to questions of historical significance among Latinas, see

Cary Davis, Carl Haub, and JoAnne L. Willette, "U.S. Hispanics: Changing the Face of America" and J. Jorge Klor de Alva, "Telling Hispanics Apart: Latino Sociocultural Diversity," both in Edna Acosta-Belén and Barbara R. Sjostrom, eds., *The Hispanic Experience in the United States: Contemporary Issues and Perspectives* (New York: Praeger Publishers, 1988). See also Edna Acosta-Belén, ed., *The Puerto Rican Woman: Perspectives on Culture, History, and Society* (New York: Praeger Publishers, 1986).

Questions Within Women's Historiography*

by

Juan Gómez-Quiñones

Introduction

Among the most consequential social charge in contemporary times is the alteration of gender relations and the empowerment of women, incremental to be sure, but irreversible. Thus, the evolution of empowerment is a central concern in the historical study of woman including Mexican women. Efforts to elucidate facts about women from the historical record are commendable for equilateral and psychological reasons and certainly these facts add to the historical record of human society. This granted, it is equally certain women's political role in history, though under-reported, is undeniable. Woman's history, like the history of workers, peasants and minorities, is one to be reclaimed, with many questions to be posed and answered. As in the case of laborers, the observation could also be applied to the 'silent presence' of women in history, they too have endured but too often been ignored. Such is the case for the history of Mexican women.

Inequitable recognition of women in the forming of history is certainly not a unique feature of the Mexican social record. In Mexico as elsewhere, male chauvinism and sexism have existed in correspondence to the level of social, economic and political development. What is historically specific is the particular evolution of the status and role of women from ancient societies

---

* This paper is based on lecture notes on the political economy of Mexican women in the far north, 1500-1900.

87

to the present in Mexican society, which is to say the analysis of women's position is related to the analysis of social change in Mexico.

In most Mexican historiographical literature an awareness of women's lives and struggles surfaces only occasionally.[1] Usually, when women are mentioned, it is in the context of the family, everyday life in the home or in connection with social activities. Some attention is assigned to patterns of marriage and inheritance, less to non-conformity. Relatively few documents on individual women's lives exist, especially in the pre-twentieth centuries. Research has been done on political activism among Mexican women, books and articles written, but often this material is incomplete in its data and perforce in analysis, on occasion it is counterproductive to initial analysis. Whenever individual activist women are mentioned, they are likely to be presented only as exceptions in the predominantly male realm of public and political life. Often, these outstanding women become representative figures for issues that may have been only partially women's. Rather than cause for historiographical pessimism, these deficiencies should be an incentive for further investigation because they raise questions about women's specific experiences.

Woman's Changing Status

There are several reasons for the little known participation of Mexican women in formal empowerment: Hypothetically, in the pre-hispanic period there was loss of leadership roles in the shift from matriarchal societal patterns to patriarchy in ancient indigenous societies. Among these societies there is some evidence to suggest high ranking Indian women with resources and political access to maintain their positions as such, the power of these matriarchs did not continue through the colonial period beyond the first and second generations after the conquest. At the time of the conquest the Western European tendency to further limit women to the domestic sphere was ascendant. The exclusion of women in war and male supremacy ultimately results in the Spanish conquest being an entirely male-dominated venture (this is not to deny the involvement of Spanish women). Moreover, the outcome of the conquest saw the rise of all male rulers who subjugated both Indian women and men, and defined European woman as adornments and assets. In this crisis women made no gains as was to occur in other periods of political and social upheaval. During and after the conquest the propagation of Catholicism as primarily an ideology for domination eliminated a formal space of potential nonconformism among women, religion. European women offered no immediate precedent for emancipatory opportunities because of the restricted role of the Spanish woman in Spain. Ideologically, moral codici and notions of 'propriety' and honor invalidated women's personal freedoms. Without access to the priesthood in the Catholic Church, the major institution outside of the state, nuns fell under the leadership of a bishop; this limited institutional paths of empowerment for women. In the colonial situation for both Indian and European women, exaggerated cultural stress on childbearing, family duties and early marriages confined woman to the home. Woman's general work responsibilities in the field and domestic service in and outside the home inhibited the building of female resources independent of inheritance. Acute deprivation of the vast majority of women generation to generation lessened the incremental momentum of what little progress occurred during one generation. The relative lack of education for women was crucial in impeding the questioning of the status quo even among elite women. Obviously, intentional exclusiveness from political activities eliminated female participation. From the time of Mesoamerican civilization to the settlements in the Southwest, Mexican women constituted an essential part of society, yet they remained unrecognized and were discriminated against because of their gender, their class if laborers, and ethnicity if Indian, mestiza or mulatta.

In contrast to the above were the antecedents and precipitates for progressive change. Women enjoyed some status and control over their pertinent activities in the Mexica days of the early sixteenth century, this tradition persisted albeit weakly. Undoubtedly, during the initial social stages of the conquest women were important to the Spaniards; women shared and shaped the formation of the colonial society, their equities and claims could not be completely denied. The seventeenth century witnessed for women increasing dispensations in Mexican society though convents, and through a more varied formal culture and increased wealth. However, most women were producers and laborers rather than the administrators or owners of sales or production units, or major intellectuals, social leaders and political brokers. But there were exceptions. At the end of the seventeenth and the beginning of the eighteenth century women became more prominent economically and politically, with respect to the latter, at still on informal level. They became actors as well as consumers and producers. The dynamics of their informal power was based on the family unit, material wealth and ideological force. Their social affairs, ownership of lands, and their ability to deal in trade increased. The Church could not force complete ideological submission, nor could women be kept ignorant of worldly occurrences, nor could they be kept as only supplemental partners by the head of the household. Independence, republican statutes, increases in production in the nineteenth century allowed inroads for women. They courageously participated in their country's nineteenth century struggles for independence, and Mexico's defense against the United States and France. In effect, they were actors in the survival of their country as well as on behalf of the enhanced future of consequent political persons. The late nineteenth and early twentieth century increased women's independence from the Church, and the family, and enhanced opportunities for women beyond the female elite population. Employment and educational needs and participation led to female labor and civic activism. The years between 1600-1900 brought some objective changes to a gender-discriminant society and also some awareness that society was indeed gender-divided politically, economically, and socially. Although male authority remained, the empowerment of female capability advanced incrementally. For many, it was unfeasible to subjugate women completely and some women were sufficiently wealthy and educated to resist or escape subjugation. In summary, the politically progressive and economically significant social change impacting Mexican society was reflected in the transition of woman's roles from 1600 to 1900. Confronting one disadvantage after another, Mexican women succeeding in maintaining and advancing an identity for themselves as political actors.

Historically, continuity and change for women are part of major developmental processes. Rudimentary comparisons of components in the advance and impediment of women's political progress raise larger questions pertinent to major formative transitions.

Historiographical Questions

Examination of the historical evolution of Mexican women beyond the discovery and construction if a specific history presents comparative dimensions to date not addressed. The pre-

Western, pre-feudal and early capitalist phases in Mexico's development are chronologically closer and informationally more accessible than those preceding Periclean Athens which inspired the "Golden Age" matriarchal hypothesis of nineteenth century European writers. Mesoamerica, a historical and coherent identifiable civilization situated in a geographical homeland, offers a range of patrilineal and matrilineal practices and a setting where examples of both were apparently the more efficient, aggressive, and influential. How does the history of ancient Mexico compare with other prefeudal or precapitalist societies in regards to women? If it is true Mexica society offered more latitude for women than did the Castillian state, what exactly are the specifics of the gender regression which occurred? And if both Mexican and Iberian societies offered women greater latitude, comparatively speaking, than did most European societies (and, undisputably, more so than did Asian and Muslim societies) what is the significance of this for women's threshold of equity in the modern period? As understood by research scholars there was no feudal mode of production in Mexico but whatever limitation or vitality is identified in its mercantile or emergent capitalism phrases, in Mexico there was a range of forms of property and labor practices. Are there identifiable contrasts in the role and status of women according to these particular formations? Mexican culture and society similarly offered a range in family and child rearing practices with formal bourgeois marriage exclusivity and seclusion for women, a decided minority practice. How did this diversity impact in the content of patriarchy? To date, feminist writers for the most part look at women in their own societies from the perspective of upper and middle class sectors and generalize ideologically from this bias. Ideologically, Mexican society offers in sharp relief the co-existence of pre-European female archetypical lores and figures, as well as their continuing tradition. These are concurrent with the historical and cultural introduction of anti-woman Judaic biases and the Western Middle class cults of domesticity and maternity. What is the interface of these? Lastly, in Mexico there has existed the salient presence of one institution in relation to women in particular, the Mexican Catholic Church. This institution has been both protector and oppressor; the midwife to legal protection for women and a rationale for the disenfranchisement of women. Because women are closely associated with the Church, their progress has been denied by otherwise progressive elements for alleged fear of this association or so it is rationalized. What is the substance of this paradox? Not least in Mexico, there is the overlay of conquests, setbacks and advancements, the confrontation between Spaniards and Indians, the formation of the republic, the tortured progress of Mexican Liberal-Conservation disputation, and the United States aggression on the Mexicans. How have women fared though these political changes?

At present, no one denies the participation and significance of women in history nor their exploitation. A brief analysis of Mexican women's history leads to a number of basic verities. More is known about the propertied wealthy and urban sectors than the impoverished and rural sectors who were the majority. Women were an important part of the population and were distributed among all class and status groups. This diversity must be taken into account, and a sophisticated chronology of women's diverse participation established. But it will not do to posit rudimentary chronological or exclusively economic frameworks of analysis which trace the evolution of a primitive golden age, early kingdoms and confederations, feudalism, emergent capitalism, monopoly capitalism, and finally emancipation. These approaches are not serviceable in Mexican women's historiography nor are those perspectives which are idealistically premised on a human nature which is divisible into a depraved male and virtuous female exponents where misogynist patriarchy rules and is eventually undermined and overthrown by heightened female consciousness. Woman's history is not wholly accessible by looking only at property and profit; nor by looking only at the consciousness of the few. Available material suggests that there has been both dissent and conformity by women within Mexican and, subsequently, Mexican-American society and culture. The measurement for this may be explored in the relatively acknowledged role Mexican women have held in the economic and domestic spheres in comparison to European or North American societies. Thus, it may be asked if in a culture which explicitly recognizes a sphere of their own may not integration and separation be more delineable? Of course Mexican culture is predominantly patriarchal but it also clearly has matriarchal elements. The history of the Mexicana seems to support the notion that family, class and ethnic allegiance have commonalities and a unique significance for them which is why 'Anglo' women's concerns and theories can only be partially relevant.

Male domination has meant unequal distribution and exploitation along gender lines and the propagation of values and interpretations which sustain this disadvantage among Mexicans.

To understand the course of women in history and their situation at any given time requires understanding particular production priorities and organization of society in relation to how production is organized and how the young are cared for and trained. This means understanding how the society survives, seeks individual and collective gain and profit and how it is educated and governed. Since substantive transition occurs in the areas of work, education and governance, these must be examined in both their material and ideological sense in order to begin to approach women historically.

Theoretical Concerns

Undeniably obvious to sensitive observers including Rouseau, Marx and Engels, from the nineteenth century to the present woman's oppressed and exploited state has called for two contrasting explanations. The more patent of the two is characterized by economistic reductionism. This upholds the division of labor, private property, and the family (with some attention to psychological characteristics) as basic premises for explaining the evolution of women's status. One extreme mode of this argument emphasizes profit, inheritance, and chauvinism. A contrasting explanation lends itself to psychological reductionism. It emphasizes male dominance, maternity as mystique, and the objectification of women and female character. At its extreme it argues female superiority and male conspiracy.

A current psychological linguistic variant of this idealist position is both troubled and tantalizing.[2] Making an ideological distinction between women's history which is a record and feminist history which is a unique voice, feminist history is argued to be grounded in a distinct theory and epistemology. Available theories, categories of knowledge and methods, be they materialist or idealist, are seen as intrinsically male-oriented which means, to be sure, that there is male and female knowledge and both of these are to be addressed. Though the starting point was the absence of the acknowledgement of women, the gist is gender difference or identity and male domination as ideological, explainable as due to values stemming from gender identity. History is to document the difference and indite patriarchy. Ironically, these psychologically linguistic views make positive the traditional dual spheres notion and the discredited beliefs of gender, physiological and intellectual inequality. It also makes men the subject of history through its focus on patriarchy. Since this approach is biased in the direction of its subject, i.e., the individual experience, although what is sought is group understanding, psychology and language are the conceptual and hence mythological foci. Human social evolution is not a journey from nature or barbarism to culture and an ever freer society but rather a regressive state resulting from nature to oppression. This is understood through language since it assertedly codifies power relations and preserves their record. Thus, male voice and female voice are to be studied. In effect, this approach is a feminist version of Levi Strausian post-structuralism, no more or less male than other conceptualizations with an emphasis on physiology, maternity, and motherhood, i.e., mothers train children. If patriarchy is ideology propagated by both men and women, where is women's history in this conceptual conundrum?

What must be considered in any case is the possibility of a gendered differentiated epistemology for if demonstrated it would be a paradigmatic revolution of unprecedented proportions. But whether this is true or not there is indeed abundant scientific evidence showing a wide and rich diversity of male and female behavior as well as paternal and maternal nurturing in animal life as Bettyann Kevles has encyclopedically documented.[3] Animals, however diverse, are encoded to follow species biological and ecological mandates; humans are free to choose from the spectrum of behaviors, and freedom and its material conditions are the subject of history, including that of women. The material is basic but interactive with the subjective.

Writers from Husserl to Kuhn have advanced the proposition that all theory is ideological including that which revises previous models. The anti-woman content in the sciences, social sciences and humanities as well as that of culture itself was summarized in the major and as yet unsurpassed synthesis of Simone de Beauvoir's, *The Second Sex*. Feminist writing is either an elaboration or correction of this magnificent critique which is the fulcrum of women studies discourse and at its base is undeniably Marxist and Western. Recently, feminists in the sciences and philosophy rather than in the social sciences have made the most significant statements to date among there are Evelyn Fox Keller's *Reflections on Gender and Science* and the collection of essays by Sandra Harding and Merrill Hintikhan in *The Crisis of the European Sciences*.[4] Whether writings on woman have focused on class relations as among the English, sexuality as among the French, or the sociology of roles and gender as in the United

States the most innovative insights are social and cultural rather than conceptual or methodological, i.e., how we know and are taught as opposed to how we organize and gather what we know. Reality and rationalization are equal foci of historical attention but facts are indispensable.

Unfortunately, the work of Mexican women on women is not yet extensive empirically or conceptually. Though the number of researchers on women in the social sciences is increasing, the number who do history is small. In Mexico and in the United States the most competent work has been empirical and descriptive, work as apart as that of Asuncion Larvin or Marta Tienda.[5] Among the contributions studies on the colonial period and nineteenth century have been the most informative and social history favored over political history. While white women's history has large numbers of practitioners and an extensive academic infrastructure, Mexican women's history is markedly limited in regard to professionals and resources.

Setting aside that as yet a historical matrilineal age is not demonstrable nor is it known what the pristine state of female or male psychology may be, there are a number of observations which a reasonable Mexican women's history framework must consider: Adequate explanation must account for the material and subjective factors of status diversity, changes in family structure and sexual practices, the uneven development of gender egalitarianism (which regresses and progresses), and for the similarity in skills, intelligence and endurance across gender lines. Further, the account must explain how the state of women has come to be despite numerical equality and the obvious significance of their social participation within the context of changes in modes of production.

Undoubtedly, ideology, sexuality, the family, and child bearing together have contributed disadvantages for Mexican women resulting in changes not entirely accounted for by economics or psychology. Nonetheless, the alleged physical disparity between men and women did not prevent women's work and their participation in war and construction. True, maternity does affect women exclusively, but not all the time and not all women. Certainly, the trend toward emancipation is evident though not linear nor universal and increasingly women's liberation is a normative ideal. Clearly, these conclusionary observations call for an approach which examines production, reproduction, socialization, and politicalization in a specific society because the social coercion of women is not only economic, it is, in fact, political.

Conclusion

Ultimately, Mexican women's history requires like other fields delineation of scope, conceptualization, literature, sources and narrative. To date, apart form some solid initial published research by a handful, the discourse has been limited to recriminations on the absence of women in the historiography, and calls for new conceptualization, periodization, or methods which are simplistic or redundant. Paradigms, sources, periodizations are available as is a base historiography but a new field requires critical discourse, narratives and interpretations, it should not be limited to the singling out of lacunae and errors. History as an unfolding process is objective, interpretations of its knowledge are subjective; the latter in the part has been exclusionarily partisan, but presently reality and its cognition involve women, women's history is inclusive. Distinctions between the exceptional, the sub-groups and the group are useful reminders, however, pejorative distinction between autobiographical, institutional, intellectual, and social foci is sophomoric in historiographical evaluation. Surely, this invidiousness is not the new dispensation. Each of these alternatives suggests the study of political struggle is the study of mass impact.

Women are part of history in interaction with others; they are part of a community with numerous subdistinctions such as class and ethnicity and are impacted by major developmental or formative processes among them community formation, survival strategies, urbanization, proletarianization, and ideologicalization. Women can only be visualized as a separate society or community in the abstract. In real life they are intermeshed in all aspects of life and share in all attributes of a community. Common sense or observation of reality reveals women are not passive nor are they mere victims; progress occurs as women are participants in this. The issue of women's history is not its validity but its standards and comprehensiveness. Some topics and fields will lend themselves more easily than others to women's history. Progress for women when visible is related to emancipatory surges for both men and women. Men and women make history together and together will make a future.

Notes

1. For the Mexican literature see Eli Bartra et al. *Mujer: Una Bibliografía* (Mexico D.F.: Universidad Autónoma Metropolitana-Xochimilco, 1983); for literature on Latin American women see Meri Knaster, *Women in Spanish America: An Annotated Bibliography from Pre-Conquest to Contemporary Times.* (Boston: G.K. Wall, 1977); for Mexican American women see Roberto Cabello, Juan Gómez-Quiñones and Patricia Herrera Duran, comps. and eds., *The Chicana, A Comprehensive Bibliographic Study* (Los Angeles: Chicano Studies Center, University of California, 1976).

2. See Liz Stanley "Whales and Minnows: Some Sexual Theorists and Their Followers, and How They Contribute to Making Feminism Invisible," *Women's Studies International Forum* 7 (1984): 53-67; and Barrie Thorne and Nancy Henley, *Language and Sex, Difference and Dominance* (Massachusetts: Newbury House Publishers, 1975); and Dale Spender, *Man Made Language* (London: Routledge and Kegan, 1980).

3. For a commendable, exhaustive and suggestive recording and interpretation of animal behavior see Bettyann Kevles, *Female of the Species* (Cambridge: Howard, 1986).

4. Evelyn Fox Keller, *Reflections on Gender and Science* (Hartford: Yale University Press, 1985) and Sandra Harding and Merrill B. Hintikhan, eds. *Discovering Reality, Feminist Perspectives on Epistemology* (Hingham: Reidel, 1983).

5. For works by Asuncion Lavrin and Marta Tienda see note 1.

Method and Sources

Part II

Method and Sources

FUENTES PARA LA HISTORIA DE LA MUJER EN LOS ARCHIVOS DE GUADALAJARA

Abstract

Dr. Carmen Castañeda García, former director of the Archivo Histórico de Jalisco, Guadalajara, offers a guide on the primary sources of the Archives of Guadalajara useful to research on women. Archival sources are divided into six categories spanning three centuries of collected letters, notarial records, and government documents. The six categories address the social and economic conditions of women during the 18th century; women and religion in the 19th century; the education of women in the 19th century; women's wage labor in the 20th century; women and unionism in the 20th century; and women and prostitution in the 20th century. The location of items is given and bibliographic sources which have made use of these materials are included. Examples chosen to illustrate topics focus on sectors of society from other than the affluent, educated or propertied classes which tend to be over represented in written records.

FUENTES PARA LA HISTORIA DE LA MUJER EN LOS ARCHIVOS DE GUADALAJARA

by

Carmen Castañeda García

Es muy difícil para un historiador empezar una investigación histórica si el problema no se ha planteado. Generalmente las investigaciones se inician si se tiene material sobre algún tema y no a partir de un problema dado. Lucien Febre dijo que "plantear un problema es, precisamente, el comienzo y el final de toda historia. Sin problemas no hay historia."[1] Si no planteamos problemas o si planteándolos no formulamos hipótesis para resolverlos, no llegaremos más allá de una mera transcripción de documentos. El historiador, sin embargo, no puede plantear problemas de investigación, y ni podrá resolverlos sin consultar antes bibliografías y relaciones de documentos.

En este sentido se presentan aquí algunas fuentes que se localizan en los archivos de Guadalajara y que permiten hacer investigaciones relacionadas con la historia de la mujer en México. Estas fuentes se clasifican en seis temas generales:

1. La situación social y económica de la mujer en la época colonial (siglo XVIII)
2. La mujer y la religión (siglo XIX)
3. La educación de la mujer (siglo XIX)
4. El trabajo femenino en la industria (siglo XX)
5. El sindicalismo femenino (siglo XX)
6. La mujer y la prostitución (siglo XX)

Para comprender mejor el contenido de estas fuentes se presentará una descripción de cada tema general, dando ejemplos e indicando el archivo donde se localiza ese tipo de material. Se dará también la información que ofrece la fuente presentada, datos bibliográficos de algunos trabajos sobre historia de la mujer que han utilizado documentos de los archivos de Guadalajara.

1. *La situación social y económica de la mujer en la época colonial (siglo XVIII)*

Trabajos recientes que examinan las actividades de la mujer en la época colonial han utilizado fuentes más inovadoras como son los archivos notariales. En estas fuentes se encuentran más datos sobre las mujeres ricas o educadas o propietarias que sobre las trabajadoras. Por esta razón se presenta un documento procedente del Archivo Histórico Municipal de Guadalajara[2] que es una comunicación dirigida al Ayuntamiento de Guadalajara para plantear la utilidad de la fábrica de cigarros como fuente de trabajo para las mujeres (en esta y en las demás citas se sigue la ortografía original).

N.Y.C. y R.

Jamás se ha pensado un projecto tan interestante al Rey, Público y Particulares, como la establecida Fábrica de Cigarros, en esta ciudad, que destituida de arbitrios, para la honesta ocupación y útil destino del sobresaliente número de mujeres que la pueblan, vemos felizmente empleadas las vergonzantes doncellas: socorridas las viudas: auxiliadas las solteras y sin distinción sobreadamente abastecidas, las que de todas clases y edades han ocurrido.

De tan constante verdad son fieles testigos los confesores: los padres de familia: los comercios, la misma plebe. Pues no puede ocultarse que este deboto sexo abastecido como lo esta frecuenta como vemos las Iglesias, socorre en lo posible a sus padres y bien emplean el jornal que debengan con la obra de sus manos. Por eso acuden diariamente de esta y otras poblaciones mujeres que instruidas a fondo de tan proficuo establecimiento decean ser admitidas a la maniobra, y participar de la válida que las otras, y más a vista del arreglado método afable trato y prudentes máximas con que se ha manejado el visitador desde la creación de esta oficina.

Más sin embargo de tan serias consideraciones como el tanteo de la fábrica no pueda extenderse a más de quatro oficinas o piezas, y estas por su corta capacidad, se surtan completamente con poco más de quinientas mujeres será preciso aunque doloroso al precitado visitador, y jefes que se encarguen de ellas despedir las que sólo citen su acomodo y cerrar la puerta a tantas infelices, que se presenten en lo sucesivo hasta el considerable número de dos o tres mil según lo basto de esta ciudad y sus immediaciones.

Desde que comenzó la fábrica con poco más de docientas han acudido tantas que hacienden hoy a más de quinientas mujeres con que se han ocupado las oficinas todas aun estrechadas por benebolencia y caritativa piedad del Director, sin arbitrio para las otras que se presenten y por lo mismo en obsequio de Dios y de el Rey a vista de los lamentos y aun lágrimas de tantas que ven imposible su admisión, juzga ... el procurador mayor acercar a V.S. esta representación para que parándola a la Real Audiencia superior Govierno, e Illmo. Prelado, le suplique ... para con el Exmo. a fin de que tenga a bien, mandar la extención de oficinas que basten al general consuelo de todas las que bien instruidas en el exercicio se califiquen proporcionadas al cumplimiento de su obligación ... Guadalajara nobiembre 4 de 1778.

Con documentos como éste llegaremos a una mejor comprensión de la situatión social y económica de la mujer en la época colonial y conoceremos más de las mujeres olvidadas por la historiografía como son las doncellas, las viudas y las solteras.

Otros trabajos que han utilizado fuentes de los archivos de Guadalajara, son: Carmen Castañeda, "La Casa de Recogidas de la ciudad de Guadalajara," *Boletín del Archivo Histórico de Jalisco* 2 (1978): 3-8, y su "La educación en Guadalajara durante la época colonial, 1552-1821," (tesis, El Colegio de México, 1974); y Asunción Lavrin y Edith Courturier, "Dowries and Wills: A View of Women's Socioeconomic Role in Colonial Guadalajara and Puebla, 1640-1790," *Hispanic American Historical Review* 59 (1979): 280-305.

2. La mujer y la religión (siglo XIX)

La relación entre la mujer y la religión se ha estudiado principalmente desde el ángulo de la participación de la mujer en la vida religiosa o conventual. Es más raro encontrar estudios que se refieran a las actitudes de las mujeres comunes y corrientes frente a problemas religiosos.

Un ejemplo que ilustra esto último es la "Representación que las Señoras de Guadalajara dirigen al Soberano Congreso

Constituyente, sobre que en la Carta Fundamental que se discute, no quede consignada la Tolerancia de Cultos en la República."[3]
Sobre este documento Alma Dorantes en su libro *Intolerancia religiosa en Jalisco* comenta que las señoras de Guadalajara:

> [A]ún cuando no gozaban del derecho de ciudadanía, y a sabiendas del asumbro que causaría a todos el que unas mujeres 'cuyo destino se cree en la sociedad estar reducido al cuidado y desvelos del hogar doméstico,' suscribieran una Representación al ... Congreso ... para destruir la 'fascinación irreligiosa' que con gran tristeza veían desde hacía tiempo, se apoderaba de algunos de sus conciudadanos. Quisieron interponer entre aquel 'hechizo' y éstos, los consejos que les dictaba su condición de esposas, de madres y de hermanas.[4]

Estas mujeres en 1856 creían que la gente ignorante en México se dejaría llevar por otros cultos "que no respetaban principios morales." También afirmaron que no estaban de acuerdo con el protestantismo pues "ultrajaba y despreciaba a la Santísima Virgen y sostenía la disolución del matrimonio."[5] En resumen, se declaraban partidarias de la intolerancia de cultos.

3. *La educación de la mujer (siglo XIX)*

Este es uno de los temas que cuenta con mayor número de estudios, aunque muchos no han utilizado la diversidad de fuentes que ofrecen los archivos. Por ejemplo, en el Archivo Histórico de Jalisco, en el ramo *Instrucción Pública* se encuentra información de la situación educativa en Jalisco desde la mitad del siglo diecinueve hasta fechas recientes.

Para ilustrar el tema se ha seleccionado un expediente relativo a las escuelas para niñas que había en el Departamento de Jalisco en 1866. Este expediente se formó cuando la emperatriz Carlota pidió informes sobre el estado de "los colegios de niñas primarios y secundarios" a las señoras de los comisarios imperiales.[6]

Los informes del Departamento de Jalisco ofrecen información sobre 43 escuelas para niñas, número de alumnas que tenían, sus maestras, los programas de estudio que seguían y su financiamiento. De acuerdo a este expediente la característica más sobresaliente de la educación fue la preponderancia de escuelas particulares frente a las municipales, es decir el predominio de la enseñanza privada sobre la pública.

4. *El trabajo femenino de la industria (siglo XX)*

Para este apartado tenemos numerosas fuentes de información en el Archivo Histórico de Jalisco, clasificados en el ramo *Trabajo*. Un ejemplo lo constituye este documento:[7]

Lista de operarios, con especificación de sexo y edad, que trabajan en la Fábrica de Cartón y Cajas de cartón 'El Aguila' ubicada en la calle de Manzano No. 414, de esta ciudad, propiedad de los señores Francés Hermanos.

Trabajo	Nombres	Sabe leer y escribir	S	Edad
Maestro	J. Jesús Vargas	sí	M	24
Cobrador	Ramón Díaz	sí	M	48
Chofer	Rómulo Rodríguez	sí	M	26
Carpintero	J. Jesús Rosales	sí	M	45
Conductor	Pedro Rodríguez	no	M	25
Aprendiz	J. Jesús Rubio	sí	M	15
Pila	Hilario Tapia	sí	M	31
Ayudante	Roberto Rosales	sí	M	19
Portero	José Godínez	no	M	33
Satinador	Ramón Torres	sí	M	38
Ayudante	Salvador Sánchez	sí	M	20
Patio	David García	sí	M	38
Cortador	Juan García	no	M	45
Ayudante	Juan Flores	sí	M	20
Ayudante	J. Jesús Guerrero	sí	M	22
Forradora	María González	no	F	29
Forradora	Victoria Padilla	no	F	18
Forradroa	Ma. Refugio Vargas	sí	F	21
Forradora	María López	sí	F	18
Forradora	Ma. Guadalupe Flores	sí	F	18
Forradora	María Puga	no	F	50
Forradora	Luisa Sánchez	sí	F	25
Forradora	Ma. Guadalupe Ponce	sí	F	18
Forradora	María Valenzuela	sí	F	18
Forradora	Sabina Delgadillo	sí	F	38
Forradora	Margarita Ibarra	sí	F	16
Forradora	Ma. Jesús Flores	sí	F	15
Forradora	Ma. Guadalupe Ramírez	no	F	16
Forradora	Martina Contreras	sí	F	16
Forradora	Ma. Jesús Villarruel	sí	F	15
Forradora	María Bernabé	sí	F	23
Forradora	María Dolores Cervantes	no	F	20
Forradora	Ma. Trinidad Pérez	sí	F	18
Forradora	Zenaida Copado	no	F	31
Forradora	Inés González	no	F	14

Guadalajara, 18 de febrero de 1928
Francés Hermanos.

Con este tipo de documento se puede saber qué porcentaje de mujeres trabajaban en esa fábrica, qué clase de trabajo desarrollaban, cuál era su edad y quiénes sabían leer y escribir. En esta forma se encuentra que en esa fábrica trabajaban veinte mujeres y quince hombres, lo que da un porcentaje de trabajo femenino de un 57 porciento. Todas estas mujeres desempeñaban el mismo tipo de trabajo y eran muy jóvenes pues tenían una edad promedio de veintiún años, mientras que las edades de los quince hombres alcanzaban un promedio de treinta años y todos realizaban diversos oficios. En cuanto al analfabetismo el índice era más alto entre las mujeres con un 35 porciento mientras que entre los hombres era de un 20 porciento.

El trabajo que desempeñaban estas mujeres no requería ninguna especialización y era muy mecánico. Esto, el índice mayor de analfabetismo y la edad, influyeron con toda seguridad en el horario, condición de trabajo y salario. Las declaraciones de los mismos trabajadores lo comprueban: "Ramón Torres de 30 años de edad, manifestó que trabaja 60 horas a la semana a razón de 14 centavos la hora ... María Guadalupe Ramírez, de 16 años de edad, dijo que entraba a trabajar a las 8 horas saliendo a tomar sus alimentos a las 13, regresando nuevamente a las 15 y volviendo a salir a las 18 horas, trabajanado a destajo ganando como máximo $2.50 y como mínimo $2.00 semanales." Un trabajo sobre el tema es el de Dawn Keremitsis, "Working the Double Day in Guadalajara, 1910-1940" en *Primer Encuentro de Investigación Jalisciense: Economía y Sociedad* (Guadalajara, 1981).

5. El sindicalismo femenino (siglo XX)

Sobre este tema también existen documentos en el Archivo Histórico de Jalisco clasificados en el ramo *Trabajo*:[8]

Al Ciudadano Jefe del Departamento del Trabajo

C. Ignacio Campos
Salud:

Nos es grato hacer del conocimiento por el precente oficio a ese Honorable Departamento del Trabajo que nos hemos constituido en organizadas, unicamente, para la prosperidad de nuestra sagrada doctrina social; que, por el centimiento de lo oprimido de nuestros compañeros, nos hemos constituido en organización para alludar a defender su causa de justicia; que esta unión feminista esperamos llebar a cabo, para que se sienta la preción y el peso de la proletaria organizada que, hará valer los derechos y la ley constitucional y la ley del trabajo vigente en el Estado, a lo que cueste del sacrificio del proletariado y proletariada.

Lo que ponemos en el conocimiento de ese honorable Dept. para los fines a que halla lugar.

Manifestamos nuestras por la dictadura proletaria.

Reitegramos su respeto.

Unidas por la Justicia.

Piedra Bola/Ahualulco, Jalisco/6 de febrero de 1927.

Secretaria general Secretaria del interior
Lucila E. Quiriarte Micaela Becerra

Esta "unión feminista" fundada en 1927 por cíncuenta y cuatro mujeres en un pequeño pueblo minero del municipio de Ahualulco, Jalisco, muestra la conciencia que tenían estas mujeres de las condiciones de trabajo de los hombres, sus "compañeros," esposos o hermanos. Conocían la lucha que estaban llevando a cabo los mineros y sabían de la existencia de leyes que reglamentaban el trabajo. Pero sobre todo entendían la importancia del sindicalismo y de la unión para luchar por los intereses de los trabajadores.

6. *La mujer y la protitución (siglo XX)*

En el Archivo Histórico de Jalisco se encuentran en el ramo *Gobernación* varios documentos que se refieren al estado de la prostitución en Jalisco. Se cita aquí el oficio que dos mujeres dirigieron al governador del Estado suplicando la apertura de sus casas de asignación en la ciudad de la Barca, Jalisco, en 1929:[9]

Al C. Gobernador Interior del Estado de Jalisco.
Guadalajara.- Jalisco

MARIA MARTINEZ y MARIA DE JESUS GONZALEZ, mayores de edad, libres de matrimonio y con domicilio en la calle de Torres número 9 de esta ciudad, y declarando previamente estar al corriente en el pago de impuesto sobre la renta, ante Ud. respetuosamente exponemos:

Somos dueñas de dos casas de asignación que tenemos establecidas, por la calle de Torres, al sur y en los suburbios de esta ciudad, no encontrándose al frente de ellas otras casas ni habitantes, si no solamente un terreno de sembradio.

Con fecha 26 de noviembre próximo pasado fueron clausuradas estas casas, por orden del Presidente del Consejo Municipal de esta ciudad, obedciendo según nos manifestó el encargado de la clausura, ordenes de esa Superioridad.

Nuestras casas tienen ya más de cinco años de establecidas en el punto indicado y jamás hemos dado motivo de queja, porque siempre nos hemos sujetado a las órdenes que se nos dan para su explotación y en atensión a esto se ha considerado necesario su establecimiento por las siguientes razones: 1ª Estando las casas establecidas, toda mujer pública tiene que recojerse a ellas, si no por su voluntad si obligada por la Autoridad, de no ser así dichas mujeres vivirían con toda libertad en cualquier punto de la ciudad, causando con esto un grave inconveniente para la sociedad en general y más aún para el servicio de policía que no cuenta con los suficientes elementos para vigilar a cada mujer en el lugar donde vive. 2ª Por ordenes extrictas y terminantes de la Autoridad, tenemos en nuestras casas servicios de sanidad en el cual se internan las mujeres que por alguna circunstancia se enferman y no se les da de alta, hasta que completamente no se alivian, con este servicio garantizamos a nuestra costa la salud pública en general, de no ser así y viviendo las mujeres libremente en sus domicilios, cada una de ellas se convertiría en un foco de infección, mas si se toma en cuenta que el municipio de esta ciudad, no cuenta con los elementos necesarios para la curación de las enfermedades, estos elementos a pesar de ser gravosos para nosotros, siempre se nos han exigido, y con gusto los tenemos tanto para garantía de nuestras casas, como para evitar que los males se generalicen.

Sabemos perfectamente bien que algunos elementos femeninos de poca significación y que sólo por alardear de moralidad, han pedido a Ud. la clausura de nuestras casas, sin tomar en cuenta lo antes expuesto y consideran la casa de asignación como un mal, pero un mal que es necesario, por que biene a salvar a la sociedad de otros peores, tanto en el orden material, como el higiénico y moral.

En consideración a lo expuesto, atentamente suplicamos con todo respeto, a Ud. C. Gobernador Interior del Estado, se sirva reconsiderar el acuerdo en que se ordenó la clausura de nuestras casas de asignación ordenando el Presidente del Consejo Municipal de esta ciudad, cancele la orden de clausura y ordene su reapertura ... La Barca, Jal. diciembre 9 de 1929.

Esta petición que no fue aprobada por el gobernador muestra la situación denigrante de "las mujeres públicas" en una ciudad del Estado de Jalisco, sujetas a vigilancia policiaca, obligadas a vivir en casas de asignación y expuestas a enfermedades.

Para concluir, las fuentes citadas muestran varios ángulos desde los cuales se pueden examinar las diferentes situaciones en que las mujeres han vivido. Aquí sólo se aspira a despertar el interés en los historiadores por la localización y utilización de fuentes de primera mano en los archivos, para que así más tarde puedan ofrecer una imagen más cierta de la historia de la mujer.

Notas

1. Lucien Febre, *Combates por la historia* (Barcelona: Editorial Ariel, 1970), p. 42.

2. Este documento fue localizado por Luz Ayala y Elena Petersen y se encuentra en el paquete 5 y es el expediente 14.

3. Este documento fue publicado en Guadalajara en 1856 por la Tipografía de Rodríguez y tiene 13 páginas. Corresponde a la Miscelánea 12, núm. 3 de la Biblioteca Pública de Jalisco.

4. Alma Dorantes, *Intolerancia religiosa en Jalisco* (México, D.F.: Instituto Nacional de Antropología e Historia, Dirección de Centros Regionales, Centro Regional de Occidente, 1976), p. 155.

5. Ibid., p. 156.

6. Este documento se encuentra en el Archivo Histórico de Jalisco, ramo *Instrucción Pública*, expediente 24, 1866. Véase Angélica Peregrina, "Noticia de los establecimientos para la educación de niñas en el Departamento de Jalisco en 1866," *Boletín del Archivo Histórico de Jalisco* 2 (septiembre-diciembre 1978): 17-22.

7. Este documento se encuentra en el Archivo Histórico de Jalisco, ramo *Trabajo*, asunto Legislación, año 1928.

8. Ibid., año 1927.

9. Archivo Histórico de Jalisco, ramo *Gobernación*, año 1929.

APENDICE A

Archivos Históricos de Jalisco

I. *Archivos de la Nueva Galicia*

1. Archivos de la Real Audiencia de Guadalajara: gobierno de la Audiencia, causas civiles y criminales, real hacienda, exámenes de abogados, derechos de propiedad sobre tierras y aguas y bienes de difuntos.

2. Archivo de registros notariales

3. Archivo de la Real Universidad de Guadalajara

4. Archivo del Ayuntamiento de Guadalajara

II. *Archivos del Estado de Jalisco*

1. Archivo Histórico de Jalisco (Poder Ejecutivo)

2. Archivo de la Dirección de Instrucción Pública y Archivo del Departamento de Educación Pública.

3. Archivo del Registro Civil

4. Archivo de Instrumentos Públicos (Protocolos)

5. Archivo del Registro Público de la Propiedad

6. Archivo del Congreso del Estado

7. Archivo del Poder Judicial y Archivo de la Procuraduría General

8. Archivo del Hospital Civil

9. Archivo del Hospicio Cabañas

10. Archivo de la Universidad Nacional de Guadalajara

11. Archivo del Ayuntamiento de Guadalajara

12. Archivos Municipales

III. *Archivo Eclesiásticos*

1. Archivo del Arzobispado de Guadalajara

2. Archivo del Cabildo Eclesiástico de Guadalajara

3. Archivo de los Conventos

4. Archivo del Colegio Seminario Tridentino

5. Archivos Parroquiales

EL USO DEL CUERPO FEMENINO EN LA EPOCA COLONIAL MEXICANA A TRAVES DE LOS ESTUDIOS DE DEMOGRAFIA HISTORICA

Abstract

Census records, baptismal, marriage and burial registers taken by civil and eclesiastical administrators provide an important source of data for the investigation of the function of woman's reproductive role in colonial New Spain. Mexico's colonial period spans 300 years of history, an immense territory of indefinite boundaries and diverse cultural influences. This complexity was easily overlooked in Spanish census counts when, for example, indigeneous family units were treated as if synonymous with the monogamous nuclear family of Europeans. References to categories listed as "indigeneous," "polygamous," "monogamous," "Christian" and "heathen," however, does note diverse indigeneous family formations recorded by the Spanish. Unlike their European counterparts women in prehispanic society could either enter into polygamous (restricted to the privileged sectors) or monogamous conjugal relations on a stable, trial or temporary basis with recourse to divorce.

The author argues woman's role as reproducer of the species represents an important resource which Judeo-Christian doctrine has sought to control since biblical times by confining its exercise to legitimate conjugal relations making inheritance possible and facilitating the transfer of private property. As reproducers of legitimate and illegitimate offspring women by extension reproduce class, caste and social status and this capacity is placed in check by the censure of women's participation in extramarital sex and the condemnation of their illegitimate issue.

Monogamous marriage patterns accompanied by the imposition of Christianity replaced polygamous relations among the native population requiring males to select a legitimate wife from among their many wives the result of which imposed illegitimate status on former wives and their children. Also, matrimony between

Christian converts and spouses who refused to convert were dissolved. Hence, Christians and males were provided alternatives for terminating past conjugal relationships and ridding themselves of undesirable spouses and offspring.

The inflexibility of these and other rules was compromised by the exigencies of those in control of the means of production. On the one hand, restrictions on the marriage patterns of the indigeneous population were relaxed in order to secure the reproduction of a native labor force which had been seriously depleted by disease. The bubonic plagues (Hueyecocoliztli) of 1545 and 1575 nearly wipe out the native population of the colonial period. On the other hand, the Church and *hacendados* (large estate landowners) appropriated illegitimate, abandoned and unwanted children via orphanages, the *compadrazgo* system of social relations, and the "taking in" of children to be used as a cheap source of labor. Also, poverty and the censure of women's reproductive capacities contributed to the abortion, infanticide and desertion of children. Abandoned children in urban areas were often the issue of adultery, prostitution and other illicit liaisons between *mestizos*, Indians or Spaniards. Forsaken children in rural areas were more than likely the legitimate offspring of impoverished indigeneous couples unable to care for their children.

Women who kept their children, the author argues, frequently dealt with the burden of single parenthood by assuming the status of widowhood. The designation "widow" offered women an ideal civil status beyond the immediate control of a male for women with children but no husband. Consequently, many rural and urban women without husbands presented themselves as widows in order to protect their families from the social invectives against divorced, abandoned, and unwed mothers.

The prevalence of this practice is illustrated by a census taken in Mexico City in 1811. In that year one fourth of the adult female population (over the age of 25) is single and of these a surprisingly high 33 percent refer to themselves as "widows." Recourse to the utilization of this status by so many women suggests a viable alternative to social respectibility in a society where female sexuality is rigidly controlled and where a woman without a man is indeed alone.

EL USO DEL CUERPO FEMENINO EN LA EPOCA COLONIAL MEXICANA A TRAVES DE LOS ESTUDIOS DE DEMOGRAFIA HISTORICA

by

Elsa Malvido

Definición de mujer en 1611:[1]

Mujer. Del nombre latino *mulier.* Muchas cosas se pudieran dezir en esta palabra; pero otros las dizen, y con más libertad de lo que sería razón.

Lo que yo diré aora se entiende de las que, huyendo la modesta compostura de su obligación, viven con la desahogo, afloxando las riendas a su natural, para que corra libre y desbocado hasta precipitarse; no de las cuerdas recogidas, cuyo honor es su destino, y el recogimiento, que estás han sido crédito y lustre de naciones y monarquías. Esto presupuesto, digo con San Máximo que la mala es tormento de la casa, naufragio del hombre, embarco del sossiego, cautiverio de la vida, daño contínuo, guerra voluntaria, fiera doméstica, disfrasado veneno y mal necesario.

"Somos," dixo una, "para dar consejos muy pobres, para acarrear daños y desdichas poderossimas y en la fábrica de un engaño grandes artífices."

Vio Diógenes pendientes infamemente de un olivo a unas que la justicia avía castigado con aquel suplicio y dixo: "¡Ojalá todos los árboles del mundo llevaran este fruto!"

¡Geroglifico de la muger lo es la nao combatida del Levanteo norte entre sobervias o las acosadas y ésta: A vento. En Athenas pusieron este M.M.M.M.; dieron aquellos ingenios floridas diferentes salidas y varias explicaciones sin acierto, sólo Platón le logró poniendo al pie de las letras: Mulier mala mors mariti. Casóse con una de estatura desmedrada Demócrito, siendo él de grande y crecida, y preguntándole porqué se avía casado con muger tan pequeña respondió: "Elegí del mal el menor." Finalmente, hablando Marco Aurelio de las mugeres, dize: "El amor de todas se puede dixerir con sola una píldora, y la pasión de una sola no se desopilará con todo el ruybarbo de Alexandría."

Noy dens Fol 117r

Introducción

La demografía histórica explica cómo responde el hombre animal a las leyes que le ha impuesto el control social. En general el hombre obedece a esas leyes y por excepción las viola, pero en determinadas circunstanciases más generalizada la violación que el acatamiento.

Tenemos dos fuentes históricas de la época colonial para cuantificar los fenómenos demográficos que nos interesan: los censos, padrones o recuentos parciales o totales de la población, y las actas de bautizo, matrimonios y defunciones o estadísticas vitales.

Estas fuentes, no obstante la riqueza de su información, traducidas a gráficas requieren complementarse con los datos de otros documentos, que les den vida y ayuden a situarlas en su contexto histórico. Sin que la mujer haya sido el tema de las investigaciones de demografía histórica, por medio de éstas podemos ver algunos problemas que afectaron el uso del cuerpo femenino en la época colonial. Ahora bien, el período colonial novohispano abarca 300 años y un inmenso territorio de fronteras indefenidas en cuyo interior se sucedieron distintas culturas; en consecuencia, la documentación a la que recurrimos para cuantificar el fenómeno refleja esa complejidad y falta de unidad.

Los reyes españoles tuvieron siempre la pretensión de unificar sus reinos. Se valieron de la unidad religiosa y, para implantarla, llegaron a la destrucción de los indios y secuestros de sus bienes; otros elementos de unificación impuestos fueron el idioma castellano, el sometimiento a la corona, todo lo cual produjo una patología biosocial ajena a América.[2]

El Ser Biológico de la Mujer:
La Fecundidad

El uso del cuerpo femenino ha sido legislado y controlado por la iglesia conforme a los principios de las Sagradas Escrituras y los Comentarios de los Padres de la Iglesia, no hay discrepancia entre la religión, la legislación civil y las costumbres socialmente aceptadas.

La legislación pertinente al cuerpo femenino no debe considerarse como excepcional ni como privativa de la religión católica, pues sus antecedentes se remontan al tiempo en que los grupos humanos descubrieron a la mujer como única reproductora de la especie, momento en el cual las sociedades se vieron obligadas a regular el enorme poder del cuerpo femenino. Entonces se originaron diferentes formas de transaccion sobre el cuerpo de la mujer, transacciones de las que aún hoy son objeto ella y sus productos: los hijos.

Antecedentes Teóricos: La Biblia

La Biblia relata el origen del hombre y del pecado. En el "Libro Primero de Moisés" al hablar de La Creación en los versículos siguientes:

26. Entonces dijo Dios: Hagamos al hombre a nuestra imagen, conforme a nuestra semejanza, y señóree en los peces del mar, en las aves de los cielos, en las bestias, en toda la tierra, y en todo animal que se arrastra sobre la tierra.

27. Y creó Dios al hombre a su imagen, a imagen de Dios lo creó; varón y hembra los creó.

28. Y los bendijo Dios y les dijo: Fructificad y multiplicaos, llenad la tierra, y sojuzgadla y señoread en los peces del mar, en las aves de los cielos y en todas las bestias que se mueven sobre la tierra.[3]

Esta parte se complementa con el capítulo Segundo, en los siguientes versículos:

117

7. Entonces Jehová Dios formó al hombre del polvo de la tierra, y sopló en su nariz aliento de vida, y fue el hombre un ser viviente.[4]

18. Y dijó Jehová Dios: "No es bueno que el hombre esté solo; le haré ayuda idónea para él."

21. Entonces Jehová Dios hizo caer sueño profundo sobre Adán y mientras éste dormía, tomó una de sus costillas, y cerró la carne en su lugar.

22. Y de la costilla que Jehová Dios tomó del hombre, hizo una mujer, y la trajo al hombre.

23. Dijo entonces Adán: "Esta es ahora hueso de mis huesos y carne de mi carne; ésta será llamada Varona porque del varón fue tomada."[5]

La igual procedencia de todas las especies y el varón y el origen particular de la Varona según la Biblia, marca una superioridad ideológica entre sus componentes. Dios en persona modeló en "polvo de la tierra" al hombre y como producto de segunda surge "su mujer"; Dios es masculino y creador.

En el capítulo tercero "la mujer es seducida por la serpiente" y habrá de provocar que pierdan el Paraíso, que sufran hambre, dolor, enfermedad y muerte:

12. Y el hombre respondió: "La mujer que me diste por compañera me dió del árbol y yo comí."

13. Entonces dijo la mujer: "La serpiente me engaño, y comí."[6]

En el versículo 16 Dios le dice a la mujer: "Multiplicaré en gran manera los dolores en tus preñeces, con dolor darás a luz los hijos; y tu deseo será para tu marido, *y él se enseñoreará de ti (o tu voluntad será sujeta a tu marido)*."

20. Y llamó Adán el nombre de su mujer, Eva, por cuanto ella era madre de todos los vivientes.[7]

Y Dios los lanza del Edén.

Del relato bíblico sobre el origen directamente divino del hombre y del mediatizado de la mujer, se van perfilando los siguientes datos:

1. El orígen divino del hombre y de todos los demás seres modelados en arcilla.

2. El orígen divino para costillar de la varona del varón.

3. La falta que cometió Eva fue el desdivinizar el cuerpo y acarrear penas corporales para ambos, culminando con la muerte.

4. La pena para Eva fue además poseer la capacidad de reproducir la especie, ya que Dios sólo la creó.

5. El precio que Eva debe pagar por la capacidad reproductora será el dolor y la supeditación al hombre.

6. La primera falta se cometió en el cuerpo (comieron del fruto prohibido) por lo tanto las penas son a través del cuerpo: hambre, sed, celo, sueño, trabajo, parir, sometimiento, enfermedad, y muerte.

El Nuevo Testamento

Al consolidarse el pensamiento cristiano con los Padres de la Iglesia éstos reforzaron los planteamientos anteriores expuestos en la Biblia y luego en el Nuevo Testamento, actualizada eventualmente por Jesucristo.

La doctrina cristiana, al inicio de nuestra era influyó decisivamente en los sistemas normativos del derecho y las costumbres sociales aceptadas, entre éstas se legisló sobre el cuerpo.

Los lazos del cuerpo identifican propiedad privada y bienes hereditarios, determinándose a través del matrimonio monogámico indisoluble.

La Iglesia irá adaptando su legislación a los nuevos sistemas políticos y sociales.

El trabajo de Sergio Ortega "El discurso del Nuevo Testamento sobre el matrimonio, la familia y los comportamientos sexuales" nos sirve de hilo del carrete para entrar a esta parte del estudio.[8]

Según él, en el discurso mismo San Pablo parece ser la clave y síntesis de la teoría vigente a la llegada de los españoles.

Sobre lo que Ortega llama "comportamiento sexuales rechazados" encuentra en el Nuevo Testamento las siguientes formas y frencuencias de rechazo:

Fornicación entre solteros	23 veces
Adulterio	23 veces
Prostitución	6 veces
Homosexualidad entre hombres	4 veces
Incesto	4 veces
Exhibicionismo o desnudez	3 veces
Procreación extramarital[9]	2 veces

El uso del cuerpo es cada vez más reprimido o negado y restringido exclusivamente al matrimonio. Si analizamos bien el cuadro de Ortega, encontramos que se condena la sexualidad extramarital en 4 de los puntos y que sumando las frecuencias del discurso, llegan a 58 de un total de 66 referencias, o sea, que es el punto central del discurso nuevo. Lo más interesante para nosotros resulta de que estos reglamentos pertenecieron a formas socio-económicas antiguas, que las Jerarquías de la Iglesia han ido adaptando su ideología en cada período histórico como lo han necesitado.

De la Teoría Práctica

Vuelva, vuelva caballero no sea tan descortés de las hijas que yo tengo la que querais.[10]

Veamos cómo este discurso fue aplicado en México durante la Colonia y apoyemos con padrones y recuentos de población sus nefastos efectos, basándome en trabajos elaborados a partir de documentos producidos por la administración eclesiástica y civil, como encargados del control moral, de la mentalidad y de la sexualidad.

Para la Europa cristiana, la única forma de justificación del uso del cuerpo femenino fue la fecundidad dentro del matrimonio monogámico, disoluble sólo por la muerte de uno de los cónyuges.[11] La mujer no tiene derechos por sí misma, a nada; es considerada menor de edad y deberá tener dueño: padre, esposo, Dios en el caso de las monjas, (que) es ambas cosas.

El fin social de la mujer no es solamente el de ser reproductora de la especie, sino que tiene el poder de reproducir una casta, clase o grupo en particular. Por eso la monogamia es para la mujer; el hombre puede hacer uso del cuerpo de otras mujeres, aunque en forma ilegal pagando por usarlo. En realidad lo que paga es la negación a la fecundación de esos cuerpos, porque reproducirían a "un grupo útil pero indeseable," según dice Santo Tomás: "las prostitutas"; su existencia está legislada como ilegal y viven como parásitos de la monogamia.[12] Su forma de vida es pecaminosa pero no delictiva, "un mal necesario" decía la Iglesia.

A la llegada de los españoles, los hombres americanos estaban organizados en sociedades precapitalistas diversas. Solo haré mención de documentos que dejaron constancia de esa organización entre las altas culturas mayas y mexicas, pues al tratarse de adaptarlas al nuevo orden, los religiosos tuvieron que crear un código particular de Excepciones a los Indios[13] no por su rebeldía, característica de los chichimecas más que de los grupos sedentarios, sino por la complejidad y diversidad de relaciones socio-culturales.

Los europeos, al hacer sus conteos de la población indígena a través de padrones, censos, etc. conceptualizaban la organización social como: "la familia" y "hombre casado por casa de cabeza de familia monogámica y nuclear." En los padrones se asentaron otros microcosmos: "las familias indígenas" poligámicas, monogámicas, fieles e infieles, no "la familia."[14]

Por los documentos hasta ahora estudiados, parece que en la época prehispánica no había una correlación directa entre el uso del cuerpo femenino y "el matrimonio," pues a pesar de haber sido una sociedad muy rígida, permitía hacia la sexualidad, sobre todo hacia la heterosexualidad, una mayor flexibilidad que la tolerada posteriormente por los europeos.

De los tipos de relaciones sociales que refleja la sexualidad femenina, hemos encontrado: poligámicas (uniones privativas de los grupos de poder) y monogámicas (relaciones generalizadas al pueblo). En ambos casos podría tener las siguientes opciones: a) Unión a prueba o temporal; b) Unión estable; c) Disolución de la unión estable o no, cuando no había entendimiento; y d) Viudez.

Ante esta realidad, las categorías con que los españoles calificaron a las mujeres, casadas fueron: casadas (poligámicas o monogámicas); abandonadas (puede referirse a las mujeres de matrimonio a prueba); divorciadas; y viudas.

Todas ellas fueron afectadas por el nuevo sistema: el matrimonio cristiano fue un requisito religioso y civil, por lo tanto para regularizar a las parejas no fue suficiente su monogamia, sino que además, ambos cónyuges aceptaran la nueva fe para poder así justificar el uso del cuerpo, como lo había establecido San Pablo.

De los datos que tenemos sobre los caciques polígamos; éstos, una vez que fueron bautizados, tuvieron el conflicto de decidir cuál de sus esposas sería ahora la legítima. La legislación decía que: "era la primera que habían tomado" pero como no convenía obligarlos, decidieron que se quedaran con la que ellos quisieran como excepción. El resultado inmediato de esa opción, fue la segregación social de muchas mujeres, sus hijos y sus familias de las primeras exconcubinas, ahora calificadas de ilegítimas y sus hijos denominados "fornezinos o hijos del adulterio," según lo establecían "Las Siete Partidas," legislación de Alfonso X "El Sabio."[15]

En el caso de los matrimonios monogámicos, se podría suponer que no hubo conflicto: casi todos los hombres (así quieren hacer que lo creamos), dócil y débilmente aceptaron la nueva doctrina, pero las mujeres no, y entonces San Pablo dice: "en el caso de matrimonio de fiel con infiel, si un cónyuge abraza la fe cristiana y el otro se opone, se disuelve el matrimonio."[16] Se refiere al hecho de que si el hombre ha aceptado el bautismo y la mujer prefiere permanecer infiel, se específica "no debe presionarse a la mujer sino convencerla de que debe de cambiar, pero si cae en pecado mortal (si fornica) *por tres veces* y se le requiere para que acepte el bautismo; *si ella* no quiere, entonces él podrá tomar otra."[17] En ningún caso el discurso se refiere a que sea el hombre el fonicador infiel, esto estableció diferencias no sólo entre poligamia y monogamia sino entre una monogamia de fieles o infieles y entre amancebados hombres y mujeres produciendo amancebadas y exconcubinas, pero lo menos durante los dos primeros siglos de colonización.

Los llamados contra el amancebamiento fueron frecuentes; todos los Concilios Mexicanos tienen apartados sobre el tema.[18] En consecuencia, al hombre, indio o no, se le dió una nueva arma para deshacerse de la mujer y la prole creada en su gentilidad y/o fuera de ella.

En el siglo XVI es cuando estos fenómenos de cambios se detectan más claramente, aunque el proceso de conquista física y moral duró toda la colonia.[19] Los primeros pasos del control eclesiástico organizaron a los indios en congregaciones, para así saber más sobre la forma de vida de todos y cada uno de los feligreses.

Las restricciones sobre quiénes pueden hacer uso del cuerpo de los indios, aún para el trabajo cotidiano, tienen que irse relajando después de las dos grandes pandemias de Hueyecocoliztli (la peste bubónica) de 1545 y 1575 en la que desparecen entro el 80 a 90 por ciento de la población. En 1585 el III Concilio Mexicano legisla nuevas excepciones para la población indígena; se les permite, entre otras cosas, que los indios se casen con todas las líeas, menos con parientes directos: padres, tíos, hermanos, para evitar el incesto, pero no obstante en algunos casos se legítima el incesto ya ejercido, con tal que no cause escóndalo público,[20] ¡hay que acomodar la sexualidad a la necesidad! Se requiere mano de obra, ¿quién va a sembrar, a construir, a moler el maíz y echar tortillas? Hay que relajar el uso del cuerpo de los indios, y las políticas pronatalistas llevan a los pobres a otras modalidades de ilegitimidad de la mujer y su producto; me refiero al abandono de los hijos, práctica no usual en la época prehispánica, cuando los hijos son patrimonio de la comunidad y no de los individuos ahora la familia en sí queda reducida a propiedad del padre y sólamente le pertenecen aquellos hijos que él desea reconocer como suyos, sin importar las causas que le lleven a negar o a aceptar su paternidad. Su decisión, que aparentemente es individual, recae brutalmente sobre la mujer y su reproducción, con los títulos de: ilegítimos, expósitos de padres no conocidos, huérfanos, hijos de la iglesia.[21]

La Ilegitimidad Social y Económica de la Mujer y su Producción: Los Hijos

Pobrecita huérfanita, sin su padre sin su madre, la echaremos a la calle a llorar su desventura al cajón de la basura.

Frente a este fenómeno, encontramos dos modelos diferentes de conducta: rural y urbana. En el campo los indios habían sido desposeídos de todos sus bienes y medios de producción, los habían reducido a comunidades, sólo les dejaron el uso condicionado de su reproducción y su fuerza de trabajo. "Creced y reproduciros," les dicen, pero deshabilitados para mantener a sus hijos, la iglesia los provee de un sistema socialmente válido para deshacerse de ellos. La iglesia (propiciatoria ideológica y material del problema), se convierte en receptora y redistribuidora de ese "excedente" de hijos. Los que captarán esta mano de obra, serán los dueños de los medios de producción, hacendados, rancheros, estancieros, apareciendo éstos como los padrinos de los "hijos de padres no conocidos."

Las familias indígenas no solamente tuvieron que producir un excedente de bienes para pagar el tributo en dinero o en especie al rey, sino que tuvieron que reproducir un excedente biológico que se redistribuyó entre los dueños de los medios de producción, descapitalizando a la familia indígena por haber tenido que tributar su fuerza de trabajo y desintegrarse como grupo: esta conducta no era pecaminosa. ¡Todo lo contrario! era resultado de una sexualidad conducida.

Entre el 17 y el 20 por ciento de su reproducción, uno de cada 5 nacidos vivos, será el excedente producido por las familias monogámicas, legales, fieles, e indígenas. Sus hijos abandonados no son más que ilegítimos económicos, pues son hijos de matrimonio legítimo.

Cuando inicié la investigación sobre bautismos en Tula, empecé a encontrar los términos: "hijos de padres no conocidos," "hijos de la iglesia," "expósitos," y supuse que esta tributación de la producción variaba entre un período donde el precio del maíz y la mortalidad reflejaban una estabilidad relativa, es decir con cambios, pero no muy marcados, en el cual por lo menos, había algo que comer--y aquel que se hacía en períodos de crisis--en los cuales la mortalidad rebasa a la natalidad con creces y los precios del maíz son altos. La realidad echó por tierra mi hipótesis, para concluir que el abandono de los hijos, para las clases bajas era una conducta constante y los recogedores de hijos abandonados son los españoles, caciques, dueños de los medios de producción y, tangencialmente, de la producción femenina indígena.[22]

En las ciudades el problema es distinto desde su origen; las mujeres entran en relaciones ilegítimas gracias a la monogamia y el pauperismo. Las soluciones que se ofrecen al excedente de hijos son por un lado el abandono y por otro el filicidio, fórmula esta última que, aunque penada, se ejerció. Al decir del *Diario de México* de 1805, "todos los días aparecen cuerpos de niños por las calles de las ciudades que son arrojados desde las azoteas."[23]

Los conventos de monjas con los niños emparedados también lo evidencian; pero éstos niños son diferentes, pues eran ilegítimos sociales nacidos de relaciones ilícitas o prohibidas. Por la frequencia del infanticidio--filicidio se solicitó a la iglesia y al gobierno que se hicieran cargo de hacer casas de expósitos. "En éste último siglo (XIX) se ha extendido la misericordia a remediar los infanticidios que se experimentaban en los desgraciados casos de ocultar las mujeres su fragilidad" por el interés de su vida o de su honor, estableciéndose en las cuidades populosa casas de expósitos que sirvieran para cubrir la reputación de la madre y proteger la vida del hijo inocente. Por los documentos podemos asegurar que se trata en su mayoría de hijos del adulterio y de la prostitución.[24]

Muchos de estos niños serían utilizados como "carne de cañón" para poblar la Alta California o bien se les rentaba para hacer oficios.[25] El hospicio del Señor San José se abrió en la ciudad de México sólo para proteger a mujeres españolas, casadas o no, que habían caído en pecado, y para cubrir su reputación se les recibía ocultamente, las criaturas irían a parar a la Casa de Expósitos del Señor San José.[26] Los indios y mestizos no tenían reputación que cubrir.

Había desde luego semejanzas entre los casos de las cuidades y del campo, ya que el abandono era siempre un modo de desintegración, descapitalización, marginación y explotación concreta de la sexualidad, cuyo origen era el pauperismo. No obstante, las alternativas eran distintas: las casas de expósitos o la caridad cristiana pública en la cuidad; las casas de los dueños de los medios de producción en el campo o la caridad cristiana individual. En ambos casos, se preparaba a los niños abandonados para trabajar y capitalizar la inversión a corto plazo; el tipo de actividad también variaba en la ciudad y en el campo.

De los niños de la ciudad se puede asegurar que en su mayoría eran hijos ilegítimos de india o mestiza con español o con casta, además pobres; o hijos de española con cualquiera de los grupos, y no necesariamente pobres. En cambio, los del campo eran hijos legítimos de indios, en su mayoría rechazados de sus familias no por situaciones morales, sino como única alternativa frente al infanticidio social, o sea el tener que dejar morir de hambre o enfermedad al recién nacido.

El Unico Espacio Sexual de la Mujer sin Hombre

Yo soy la viudita de Santa Isabel que quiero casarme y no se con quién.

La mortalidad preferencial de hombres sobre mujeres no es un hecho privativo de la época colonial, sino de la especie humana.

125

Aunque con sus variaciones socioeconómicas, el índice de viudez siempre ha favorecido a la mujer (favorecido es mucho decir). En este caso ninguna ley social ha podido remediar la debilidad biológica e inmunogénica del hombre frente a la mujer, a quien se la proporcionan las hormonas femeninas, elementos que hasta hace poco tiempo ha sido estudiado.

Así, un buen número de madres ex-exposas, quedan liberadas legítimamente con sus hijos. Este mismo fenómeno se ha detectado tanto en zonas rurales como urbanas; sin embargo, sobrevivir solas era difícil y en algunos casos imposible, con lo cual se ha podido observar una forma de "reintegración" a la familia a través del rematrimonio de los viudos por un lado, pero por otro hemos visto que muchas mujeres se decían viudas y no lo eran. La viudez fue una respuesta femenina al control dominante masculino, así lo demuestra el trabajo de Silvia Arrom sobre el censo de la ciudad de México en 1811.[27] En él se presenta una diferencia en la composición de la población por sexos, donde el 54 por ciento del total de la población de las grandes ciudades se componen de mujeres, cantidad numerosa de población rural y semi-urbana en busca de oportunidades las más de las veces de fantasías, esta migración aún hoy día es preferencialmente femenina.

En números concretos, una cuarta parte de la población femenina adulta (de más de 25 años) es soltera y de ellas el 33 por ciento son viudas, o sea que el 58 por ciento viven sin hombre; legalmente hablando. Sin embargo no sabemos cuántas de éstas mujeres viudas, (33%) se autonombran así, eran, o habían sido, concubinas de algún o algunos hombres casados, viudos o solteros; para saberlo con exactitud se requeriría hacer una correlación entre los libros de matrimonio y las defunciones de años cercanos a 1811 y el censo mismo de 1811, trabajo de titanes que no se ha hecho por ahora.

Lo que sí queda claro es que el uso del término "viuda" fue el único mecanismo que le permitió a la mujer liberar su cuerpo y, lo más importante, salvar a su reputación y sus hijos, gracias a la muerte real o ficticia del contrario.

La mujer sola no tiene valor en esta sociedad, y por tener a un hombre al lado con el cual valorarse socialmente, legal o ilegalmente, ha sido capaz de matar a su única fuerza reproductora, sus hijos.

Ahora bien, dentro de 33 por ciento de las viudas, los censores incluyeron a las madres solteras, pero no sabemos cuántas de ellas lo eran; lo que sí podemos pensar es que toda mujer en situación ilegal podía legitimarse autodenominándose "viuda," ya que "sólo el estado de viudez permitía la mujer gozar de su plena capacidad civil,"[28] pues de otra manera estaban sometidas a al patria potestad, al régimen tutelar, a la autoridad marital o clerical.

Desde los tiempos de la colonización americana, la ley dio a la mujer viuda una libertad que no tendría en ninguna circunstancia de su vida, pasó la prueba y sobrevivió. El caso de las viudad es comparable al censal actual. El dato de 1970 sobre estado civil da por cada dos (2.04) mujeres divorciadas un hombre divorciado. ¿La moral se ha relajado? ¡No! Hoy la mujer se dice divorciada o, casada, no viuda y el hombre contínua siendo polígamo.[29]

Sin embargo la categoría de viudas exigía que estas mujeres fueran jefes de sus familias, lo que significaba el costo económico de su "independencia" y respetabilidad, nada fácil en una sociedad de hombres (donde el promedio de vida, estado de viudez llegaba a los 20 años); no obstante, este estado dio a la mujer la posibilidad de ejercer la poliandria espaciada legal, en caso de reincidencia matrimonial o ilegal, pero como honorable viuda.

En conclusión, la viudez era el estado ideal de la mujer y el único que, como resultado de la desintegración familiar, le daba status y libertad, sin tener que recurrir al filicidio, al abandono o a la clandestinidad.

Hemos visto algunos ejemplos de la opresión que la cultura occidental ejerció con su sexualidad en México, formas básicas que todavía hoy sufrimos con algunas variantes como el divorcio, pues en esta época había divorcio de cuerpos pero no se podía rematrimoniar casi nadie, la disolución existía en casos extremos y entre gente poderosa, nunca enter pobres. Las casas de recogidas fueron una pesadilla más que una ayuda para la mujer come se ve en los libros que tocan el tema.[30]

Conclusiones

Varias cosas se desprenden de este trabajo. La primera sería que a pesar de las leyes restrictivas a la mujer, dos de sus potencialidades no han podido ser dominadas: ser Eva, la madre de todos los hombres o la reproductora de la expecie y la resistencia biológica que le permite ser la viuda de Adán.

Esto, por una lado, pero por otro le han restringido socialmente su potencialidad de instinto maternal, característica esta de los mamíferos superiores, grupo al que pertenece la especie humana, obligándola al filicidio, aborto y abandono a menos de que reproduzca lo que su dueño desee. "Honrra, con muy grande pro, viene a los hijos en ser legítimos. Serán por ende las honrras de sus padres. Y otros pueden recibir Dignidad, e Orden Sagrada de la Iglesia, y otras honrran seglares; y aun heredan a sus padres, y a sus abuelos, y a los otros sus parientes, así como dice en el Título de las herencias; lo que no pueden hacer los otros que no son legítimos."[31]

Mientras que Adán podrá fecundar a muchas mujeres, pero sólo reconocerá aquella mujer e hijos que él desee como herederos de su propiedad privada, las Evas no reconocidas como propiedad del fecundador cargarán con el efecto del pecado, el rechazo moral y la obligación de crear al producto, que Adán consideró excedente, prefiriendo Eva en muchos casos y como última solución recurrir al filicidio real o social.

Por lo tanto, algo que debe rescatar la mujer es su fuerza reproductiva en el sentido amplio y cultural, para reproducir no a la especie que el hombre quiere, sino a la especie que ella quisiera; a sus iguales, no a sus contrarios, así, la maternidad que ha sido vista como negativa, destructora y limitante de la realización de la mujer, sería la más grande de sus fuerzas.

Notas

1. Sebastián de Cobarrubias, "Definición de mujer," en *Tesoro de la Lengua Castellana Española* (Madrid y México: Turner, 1984), p. 818.
2. Patología bio-social es representativa de un conjunto de enfermedades que he dividido en biológica, sociales y biosociales. La primera incluye viruela, sarampion, tosferina, varicela, etc. La segunda se refiere al hambre, alcoholismo, prostitución, ilegitimidad de los hijos y su abandono, etc. La última tiene que ver con enfermedades como la peste bubónica. En México casi todas estas enfermedades fueron desconocidas antes de la llegada de los europeos. Para una explicación más amplia véase Elsa Malvido, "El Siglo, XVI, una nueva patología en America," en *La ciencia moderna y el Nuevo Mundo* (Madrid, 1985), pp. 367-378.
3. *Textos Bíblicos, Antología,* (México, D.F.: Origen, 1984), pp. 7-12.
4. Ibid.
5. Ibid.
6. Ibid.
7. Ibid.

8. Sergio Ortega, "El discurso del Nuevo Testamento sobre el matrimonio, la familia y los comportamientos sexuales," *Cuadernos de Trabajo* 35 (1980): 77-104.

9. Ibid.

10. Vicente T. Mendoza, *Lírica infantil de México*, Lecturas Mexicanas No. 26 (México, D.F.: Cultura Sep, 1980), pp. 55-106, 127.

11. Philippe Ariés, "Le mariage indissoluble," en *Sexualités Occidentales* (Paris: Seuil, 1982), pp. 148-168.

12. Ana María Atondo, "Algunos grupos desviantes en el México Colonial," en *Familia y Sexualidad en Nueva España* (México, D.F.: Cultura Sep, 1982), pp. 275-283.

13. Hipólito Vera Fortino, *Apuntamientos Históricos de los Concilios Provinciales Mexicanos y Privilegios de América*, 5 vols. (Amecameca, México: Imprenta del Colegio Católico, 1893).

14. Pedro Carrasco, "The Joint Family in Ancient Mexico: The Case of Molotla, in *Essays of Kinship in Mexico* (Pittsburgh: University of Pittsburgh Press, 1976), p. 48; Francisco López de Gómara, *Historia General de las Indias, Conquista de México*, Vol. 2 (Barcelona: Orbis., 1985), p. 307; Serge Gruzinsky, "Matrimonio y sexualidad en México y Texcoco en los albores de la conquista o la pluralidad de los discursos," *Cuadernos de Trabajo* 35 (1980): 19-76.

15. Códigos Españoles, "Títulos y leyes de la Quarta Partida," en *Código de las Siete Partidas*, Vol. 3 (España: Imprenta de la Publicidad, 1848), pp. 815-819.

16. Hipólito Vera Fortino, *Colección de Documentos Eclesiásticos*, Vol. 2 (Amecameca, México: Imprenta de Colegio Católico, 1887), p. 120.

17. Vera Fortino, *Colección*, 5 vols.

18. Ibid.

19. Serge Gruzinzky, "La conquista de los cuerpos," en *Familia y sexualidad en Nueva España* (México, D.F.: Cultura Sep, 1982), pp. 177-206.

20. Vera Fortino, *Colección*, vol. 2 (1887). Además dice: "Cualquier casado, que presumiere tener públicamente manceba, o el no casado o casado, que tuviéra a su pariente, o a mujer casada o infiel por manceba, así él como ella ... se les debía aplicar excomunión ... según la gravedad del delito y la calidad de las personas." Vol. 2, p. 524.

21. Elsa Malvido, "El abandono de los hijos una forma de control de la mano de obra indígena y del tamaño de la familia en

la época colonial: Tula, 1683-1780," *Historia Mexicana* 81 (1981): 251-561.

22. Ibid.

23. Ibid.

24. Ibid.

25. Ibid.

26. Biblioteca de Historia de la Medicina, *Ordenanzas del Hospicio del Señor San José de México* (México, 1797).

27. Silvia M. Arrom, "Marriage Patterns in Mexico City, 1811," *Journal of Family History* 4 (Winter 1978): 376-391.

28. J.M. Ots Capdequí, *El estado español en las Indias* (Cuba: Edición de Ciencias Sociales, 1975), pp. 117-118.

29. Secretaría de Industria y Comercio, *Censo General de Población, 1970. Resúmen General* (México, D.F.: Dirección General de Estadística, 1972), p. 101.

30. Josefina Muriel, *Los recogimientos de mujeres* (México, D.F.: Universidad Nacional Autónoma Metropolitana, 1974).

31. Códigos Españoles, *Código de las Siete Partidas*, Vol. 2, p. 485.

NOTES ON THE USE OF PARISH REGISTERS IN THE RECONSTRUCTION OF CHICANA HISTORY IN CALIFORNIA PRIOR TO 1850

by

Helen Lara-Cea

This paper is part of a larger project which attempts to reconstruct the demographic, social and economic evolution of the community of San Jose de Guadalupe, Alta California from 1777 to 1850.[1] The remarks made herein are based primarily on data contained in the five extant census reports (1790, 1792, 1799, 1833 and 1840) and the baptismal, marriage and burial registers of the Mission of Santa Clara.[2]

Books on early California fill many library shelves. Yet a review of that literature reveals little about the society or the population of the *pueblo* communities and fails to adequately explain the relationship of these communities to other institutions of colonization or to the Amerindian communities.[3] Instead, the literature conveys a superficial and stereotypical image of the inhabitants of early California. Our knowledge of *pueblo* communities is, as a result, rudimentary. Moreover, the lack of contextual framework and narrow focus of standard narrative histories reinforce the popular notion that the settlement of California was marginal. The idea that these settlements were small and remained small has influenced the portrayal of the inhabitants as a static-marginal people.

Information contained in the *Mission Santa Clara Parish Registers* refutes the notion that the population of San Jose was static. These records lay the basis for a detailed reconstruction of communities associated with the parishes. By delineating the vital statistics of the population and offering information about its social and economic relationships, the *Parish Registers* attest to the dynamism and complexity of the community of San Jose de Guadalupe.

131

Specific to women, the *Parish Registers* classify and describe the social relationships between California women, verify our notion that they assumed certain roles, elucidate some of their values and beliefs, and reveal roles not previously ascribed to them. The format and purpose of the records highlight the social relationships of women as mothers, fostermothers, daughters, wives, widows, sisters, cousins, grandmothers and aunts. Women's roles as childbearers and nurturers are reinforced by descriptions of them as mothers of newborns, brides, grooms and the deceased. They are also presented as the fostermothers of foundlings and as godmothers of adopted orphaned children. Women emerge as midwives, doctors, layministers and godmothers. Their roles and functions outside of reproduction, domestic work and religious service are also described in the records. While straightforward descriptions of them as wage earners are sparce--as are classifications to comparably equate their work activities to men's occupational activities--women are described in passing as farmers, servants and business propriatresses. In short, the *Parish Records* suggest that the role of women is complex and multi-facted.[4]

The Records

The *Parish Registers*, for the seventy-three-year period under study, contain vital statistics of the Parish of the Mission of Santa Clara. The area served by the Franciscan and Seraphic friars assigned to the Mission of Santa Clara included the mission, *pueblo* and surrounding area (roughly similar to the present-day boundaries of Santa Clara County).[5] Entries were written in ink on leather-bond books of blank paper by a succession of Franciscan and Seraphic friars, their Superiors and a number of civilian and military assistants who worked under their supervision.[6] The set of *Mission Santa Clara Parish Registers* encompasses approximately 9,750 baptisms (3 volumes), 3,067 marriages (1 volume) and 8,510 burials (2 volumes).[7] The set is not subdivided into volumes according to specific racial or ethnic categories, but such designations do accompany each entry.[8] The 1,862 baptismal, 419 marriage and 914 burial entries pertaining to individuals identified in the *Parish Registers* as residents of the town (Indian and non-Indian) and non-Indian residents of the mission and surrounding areas were transcribed from the microfilmed originals and are the subject of this study.[9]

132

All volumes share a basic format: a brief columnar summary of each entry appears on the left side of the sheet, accompanied by a more detailed narrative paragraph(s) on the right. The columnar summaries include: the number of the entry, name of the baptized, married or buried individual, and the race or ethnic identification of the individual(s) involved. The narrative passage includes: the date the sacrament was administered, the date of birth, marriage or death relative to the sacrament, names of all parties present and information about them, names of and information about parents, spouses or godparents who may not have been present, information relevant to the individual involved, a brief description of the ceremony and the friar's signature.[10] (The appendix to this paper includes samples of the three entry formats as well as a listing of information contained in the baptismal entries.)

Baptismal entries focus on the background of the child or adult baptized. For example, the marital status of the parents was listed, as was the father's occupation and the family's place of residence. Often times, the individual described in most detail was the godparent(s). Overall, the baptismal entries are the most comprehensive entries.[11]

Marriage entries were subject to more variation in length and content over time. In general, these entries were shorter than baptismal entries. They focus on the history of the bride and groom, primarily to ensure that neither had been previously committed to another individual. A lengthy residential history was included for any *soldado de cuera* (military officier) who had been stationed throughout Alta California or in other Northern Frontier settlements. Again, the names of all parties (those being wed and their witnesses, references and parents) were often included. The race or ethnic identification of the couple was entered along with the date of the ceremony. Names of the couple, their race and their references were cited as was the date of the ceremony.[12]

The burial entries, although also subject to variation in length and content, were generally brief. They included the full name of the deceased, his/her race or ethnic identification, age (in general terms, such as "adult" or "child), the relationship of the individual to the community (i.e., "soldier attached to the *pueblo*," "resident of the town," or "traveler"), the relationship of the individual to other community members (i.e., "son of," "wife of," "widow of" or "adopted son of") and the burial date. The cause of death was rarely specified. The causes most often cited for death were childbirth, fall from a horse, unspecified disease, and death at the hands of another.[13]

For members of the "non-Indian" community, the *Parish Registers* appear to offer reliable and comprehensive information for several reasons: 1) as fees for the administration of sacraments, and their filing and recording in the *Parish Registers* were not levied during this period, nobody was excluded from registration due to an inability to pay;[14] 2) baptisms were performed and recorded within three to four days of birth although performance of the sacrament and its recording are not usually specified; 3) although a preliminary comparison of the records does reveal omissions (for example, case number 1041 of the *Burial Registers* concerns the death of an infant and includes reference to the child's baptism despite the fact that no corresponding entry exists in the *Baptismal Register*) the linkage of names throughout the *Registers* along with use of the census lists does reduce the undercount; 4) although the undercount on incidence of consenual unions is presently unknown, a fairly accurate estimate should be ascertained through the linkage of census records and registers; 5) some stillbirths were recorded; and 6) gaps in the records appear restricted to two periods of civil turmoil: secularization in 1833 and the American conquest in 1846.[15]

The Community

The Mission of Santa Clara was founded on 12 January 1777. Ten months later, on 29 November 1777, the Pueblo of San Jose de Guadalupe was founded "about three quarters of a league or slightly less"[16] Further south, along the banks of the Rio de Nuestra Señora de Guadalupe. Although floods forced the mission and town to relocate five separate times, they eventually settled within a two mile distance of one another.[17] Competition and conflict between Amerindians, settlers, missionaries, administrators, soldiers and various institutions have been the focus of much of the material about this period in San Jose history. But in light of information contained in the registers, the interactions between these various groups--as well as their distinct internal dynamics--assume new dimensions.

San Jose was the first town founded in California. From a population of only 66 persons in 1777, San Jose grew to a town of over 3,000 by 1846.[18] Nevertheless, as one of only three official *pueblos* established under Spanish rule,[19] historians have pointed to its small founding population. Even more significant, they have underestimated the relative number of San Jose residents by applying a narrow definition of "settler" which excludes individuals on the basis of their race, sex, occupation, age and subsequent relationship to the institutionalized colonization process. One study states that: "Although 15 men had been brought by Moraga to establish the new *pueblo* of San Jose, only five were actually *pobladores* in the full sense of the word. They were Manuel Amestica, a mulatto and a widower with a one-year old son Joaquin Gabriel; Ignacio Archuleta, a Spaniard, with his wife Ignacia ... Manuel Gonzalez, an Apache Indian, his wife Micaela, with five children ... Only these were given land, a salary, rations and a loan of tools and animals."[20]

That the population failed to grow at a more rapid pace is often blamed on townspeople who have been labeled a "dissolute lot"--lazy, worthless, immoral and criminal.[21] Women, in particular, have been signaled out for condemnation. They have been described as women of easy virtue whose profligacy bore responsibility for the town's failure. Virtually never portrayed as vital economic and social participants in a dynamic society, these women have been seen, at best, as ornamental creatures and, at worst, as "Mexican/Indian harlots."[22]

Standard histories of early California seldom address the demographic conditions that characterized New Spain south of the Northern Frontier and they rarely examine the economic hardships imposed on relatively small groups of settlers traveling hundreds of miles to settle in a still unproductive land.[23] While the *Parish Registers* are not free of the gender and class biases which characterize literary sources,[24] they do disclose information which contradicts the pejorative image of Mexican colonists and raise questions about the implicit assumptions which underlie traditional interpretations of early California history. These records illuminate a complex evolution of the covert (and overt) patterns of socio-economic relationships which functioned within the early San Jose community. They also point to the gradual social transformation of the *pueblo's* society, reflected in changes in its concepts of social status, gender-ascribed roles, and racial identity chronicled in the *Parish Registers*. It is my contention that these address and dispel the myth of the worthless, immoral and lazy Mexican colonist.[25]

The literature has maligned the settlers as "the dregs of society," "so-called Spaniards"[26] and "a dissolute lot largely of 'worthless character.'"[27] The depiction of the town as small and marginal is not surprising, given the qualified head counts and slanderous descriptions of the population. In many traditional studies, the size of town populations have been extrapolated and calculated from numbers gleaned from the census records. Often, these figures were fabricated.[28] The census reports themselves are not definitive. Their reliability and usefulness--given the manner of their processing, transcription and manipulation--is questionable.[29] Transcriptions from the parish records also present problems, some of which are attributable to the succession of scholars who have attemptd to correct other's copies.[30]

A related problem with traditional studies is their lack of attention to population structures and their focus on personal saga and geneological investigation which is based on an uncritical use of the sources. Understandably, these studies do not address the interplay and possible correlations between economic activity and population. A multi-faceted treatment of the subject may explain certain aspects of social transformation in the records. One important exception to these studies is *Essays in Population History* by Sherbourne Cook and Woodrow Borah.[31] The last volume of this series not only estimates population in eight northern California parishes based on information in the parish registers, but compares mortality and marriage rates between the Indian and non-Indian communities. Their work suggests that further study may prove the settlers to have been a hardy lot.[32]

A study of the population of the parish of Santa Clara raises conceptual questions which are still far from resolved. These issues encompass the concepts of race and class as evidenced in the dynamics of the settler community, the relationship between California's Native American communities (mission and non-mission) and the *pueblos*, and the incorporation of California's Native Americans into those *pueblos*. Women, as the primary agents of demographic movement out of the missions and *rancherías* into the *pueblos* play a pivotal role in the examination of these issues.

The format and content of the *Parish Registers* document the incorporation of multi-racial groups into the *pueblo* population. The first settler group, (which arrived in 1777), as well as subsequent individuals and groups, was ethnically diverse and included persons described as Indian, mulatto, mestizo and Spanish.[33] The settlers, with rare exception, were described as *gente de razón* in the *Parish Registers*.[34]

Some scholars have interpreted the use of the term *gente de razón* in racial terms: "Gente de razón (literally people with (sic) reason): a term used by Spaniards in the Indies to designate non-

Indians."[35] Another defined the term thus: "Gente de razón: Literally, people of reason. Term denoting social and economic superiority. In most cases reserved for persons of European blood."[36]

Though these definitions were meant to apply to the *gente de razón* in California, the parish records indicate a broader use of the term. For example, individuals residing in the town of San Jose were rarely Spaniards, yet they were identified in the *Parish Registers* as *gente de razón*.

The coadunate format of the *Registers* encouraged the incorporation of town dwellers into the *gente de razón* category. Because only one set of *Registers* was used to record the vital statistics of the entire parish, data was not separated according to racial or ethnic characteristics and entries pertaining to California's Native Americans, Apache settlers, Spaniards, mulattos, *castas* and, later, Americans, French, Italian and English settlers were interspersed throughout the set of volumes. Racial descriptions were included in the columnar summary as well as in the narrative body of the entries.

This should not imply that San Jose was without ethnic or class distinctions. Although the term *gente de razón* became synonymous with "town dweller" and, to a certain extent, distinguished local residents from those living in the mission or on *rancherías*, the town's "non-Indian" population was far from homogenous. There was both economic and social stratification. Nevertheless, the records indicate that for a period of time, the racial connotations associated with the term *gente de razón* were suspended.[37]

The most dynamic component in the evolution of San Jose's population was the continuous incorporation of immigrants. Much has been written about the *pueblo's* incorporation of Anglo-Saxons. Yet the steady influx of persons identified as "Indians"--whether from the immediate area or from greater distances has not been studied. Prior to 1830, "Indian" immigrants who had remained in town for an as yet indeterminate period of time, were described as *gente de razón*. Then, beginning in the 1830's *pueblo* residents were more frequently described as *vecinos* (residents). The increased Indian migration of this time may have influenced the adoption of the new term.[38]

San Jose's original settlers were an ethnically diverse group and were recognized as such in their respective places of origin. Nevertheless, parish records point to a process of social transformation as indications of ethnic diversity became subsumed under the all-encompassing term *gente de razón*. This early transformation set the tone for the subsequent incorporation of California Indians residing (in the town or on the outskirts of town) with *de razón* families into the *gente de razón* category. The impact this transformation may have had on San Jose's social and economic structures has not been addressed.

Nonetheless, the rare but explicit and pithy comments written in the margins of the entries suggest that the issue of ethnic classification was controversial. For example, friars' comments such as "what is considered *de razón* in these parts" (author's translation), indicate some dissent on the matter.[39] The friars, most of whom were Spaniards and rarely from humble origins, apparently disagreed with the broader application of the term *gente de razón* and took exception to the social flexibility that it implied. This opinion may have been held by people outside the monastic community, perhaps by those most affected by the social, economic and political transformations suggested by the changing terminology.

The experience of the Apache and other "Indian" settlers--who along with their descendants were often described as *de razón*--established a framework in which local Native Americans were gradually "transformed" into *gente de razón*. The transition from *indio* to *gente de razón* was a subtle one. The settlers simply disappeared as "Indian" from the *Parish Registers*. Although the records indicate a transition, we do not know what the transition meant in socio-economic or cultural terms.[40]

Three groups of people made the transition from California Native American to *gente de razón*. These groups were: 1) Women who married *pobladores* or soldiers. The children of these Native American women were described as *de razón* in the *Baptismal Register*; 2) Family groups which moved into towns. While the first and, perhaps, the second born of these families were listed as "*indio*, but living in the town," the following children and all grandchildren were listed as *de razón*;[41] and 3) Men who married *pobladoras*. One such man is specifically identified in the parish records.

Indian women directly affected the process of transition in greater numbers than did Indian men. Overall, the process of Indian migration into the *pueblo* was small relative to the size of the mission and hinterland population. But the migration was significant, given the size of the town, continuous nature of the movement, and the economic roles that the *Parish Registers* suggest these immigrants assumed. Neither the racial hierarchy of the settlement nor the cultural impact of the transitional process have been assessed.

Women

The *Baptismal Registers* which document the continuous incorporation of "Indian" women into the *pueblo* community also highlight the unexpected roles these women assumed within the town's social strucuture. For example, the comprehensive administration and recording of baptisms (and to a lesser extent, burials) necessitated the regular use of layministers. These individuals were, with few exceptions, women. Layministers performed baptisms and last rites whenever death appeared imminent and a friar was unavailable. Such instances were frequent because: 1) only two friars were assigned to the mission and, often, one or both were away from the compound; 2) the friars' primary duty was to the mission (5,971 baptisms of local Indians between 1777 and 1810) rather than to the *pueblo*; 3) both friars took on many responsibilities and, so, had far too little time available for such ministry; (4) there was a two-to four-mile distance between the mission and the *pueblo*; (5) high infant mortality characterized the frontier; and (6) natural childbirth was a time-consuming process. For all these reasons many baptisms were performed and recorded throughout the period by persons other than the friars.[42]

Descriptions of these laity-administered baptisms are detailed in the *Baptismal Register*. Often, the entries have an inquisitorial tone. Because the eternal destiny of every soul depended upon the proper administration of the Sacrament of Baptism, the friars rigorously questioned the manner, timing and wording of the rite when performed by a layminister. What is more, they questioned and evaluated the actions of that layminister. The women, administering the sacraments were described in terms of their marital status. Rarely were they described as midwives, although the information in the entries indicated that, indeed, they were midwives. The particulars of the ritual were entered in standard format along with the friar's evaluation of the ritual and his speculation regarding the destiny of the soul of the departed. The majority of these baptisms are recorded to have been "correctly administered," but some entries do indicate that a soul died without benefit of sacramental blessing because the ritual had not been administered in the prescribed manner. This was considered a great tragedy as the eternal destination of the soul of the departed lay in jeopardy and was quite possibly doomed to eternal damnation.[43]

The baptismal entries clearly identify those who routinely administered the sacrament. The frequently cited presence of certain individuals, the skill required of them, the great responsibility they assumed and the regularity with which they reported their administration of the sacraments made each of them pivotal to the maintenance of these records.[44]

Who were these individuals who ministered the baptismal sacraments with such regularity as to constitute a vocation? They were, with few exceptions, women. The records cite the presence of men at many baptisms administered by layministers, but the entries suggest that men rarely assumed the obligation and responsibility of administering the sacrament. Women, on the other hand, often played multiple roles at births--as midwives, layministers and godmothers. Several narrative accounts described a woman who "... delivered the infant, baptized the infant because of fraility and fear of death ... the godmother is the same women who baptized the child."[45]

The godparents' duties were, in a sense, an extension of the layministry. The godparent's primary duty was to oversee the religious and moral upbringing of the godchild.[46] In addition to serving as the godmothers of *pobladores*, some women were the godmothers of literally dozens of California Indians born at the mission and surrounding area. In fact, most of the baptismal entries in the *Mission Santa Clara Baptismal Register* cite only one godparent. With few exceptions that religious guardian was a woman. In view of specific evidence of layministers assuming the duties and responsibilities of godmothership, it would seem that godmothership was ancillary to the layministry.

Despite their pivotal role within early California society, women did not receive formal recognition in the *Parish Registers*. Women were not described, for example, as "Barbara Pacheco: godmother, midwide and layminister." Instead, they were described as "Barbara Pacheco, *mujer de* ..." (wife of). The dichotomy between the services performed by women and those for which they were officially recognized is seen most clearly in the parish death records where a differential treatment of men and women prevails. For example, when a man died without benefit of the Last Sacraments, his occupation, moral character and religious devotion were described and a notation was made to the effect that his exemplary life should assure his heavenly reward. Women did not receive such obituaries. Thus, although they regularly performed services central to the religious beliefs of the community and crucial to the maintenance of the *Registers*, women's importance to the community was never officially acknowledged.

Despite the social biases of the period, the *Parish Registers* reveal the pivotal roles assumed by *pueblo* women. In so doing, they negate notions of laziness, worthlessness and criminality. In particular, the role of women as layministers speaks to their morality, honesty, sense of duty and contribution to society. If typical stereotypes about Mexican women are based on racially and culturally biased concepts of morality,[47] then these parish records belie the historical stereotype of the frivolous Mexican harlot.[48] Indeed, the *Parish Registers'* only references to immorality among the women of San Jose appear in the records of illegitimate births, of which there were few.[49]

The overwhelming majority of infants born in San Jose were described as *"hijo/hija legitimo(a) de"* (legitimate son/daughter of) followed by the father's name.[50] Illegitimacy was indicated by three phrases: *"padre no conocido"* (father unknown); the name of the father and mother followed by the word *"soltero/a"* (single); or explicit and detailed comments were made about the unmarried parent(s).[51] The linkage of marriage records with baptismal records may indicate consensual unions not explicitly indicated in the baptismal records. These relationships would have to be checked against the registers of other parishes, census reports and Northrop's data.[52] The accuracy of the low rate of illegitimacy is underscored by the documentation of illegitimate stillbirths and the listings of only two foundlings identified as *de razón* during the seventy three-year period under investigation. Based on baptismal and marriage entries, the preliminary impression is that women who bore children in San Jose were married.[53]

While the number of illegitimate births appears low, it is important to note that the rate of illegitimate to legitimate births fluctuated. The five illegitimate births prior to 1800 are clustered in the early years of settlement. In fact, one of the settlers arrived pregnant and gave birth to the first infant listed as *de razón*.[54] The rise in illegitimate births after 1820 parallels contact and trade with foreigners and was not a widespread phenomenon. The clusters of illegitimate births occurred in times of social dislocation and economic change and as the *Parish Registers* indicate, involved only a small group of women.[55]

Our knowledge of the demographic factors which influence and reflect illegitimacy are, as yet, rudimentary.[56] The linkage and assessment of information recorded in the *Parish Registers* will expand our knowledge of population, net migration, age structure, sex ratios, race and ethnic composition, occupational structure, age at marriage, birth intervals, age-specific fertility, illegitimacy and mortality in early California. Consequently, more definitive statements about the social causes and ramifications of birth outside wedlock will eventually be possible.

Conclusion

These statistical manipulations will one day enable us to ascertain precisely the context in which women lived on this frontier. Already, *Parish Registers* describe religious ceremonies and rituals which reveal the continuity of women's presence and their profound sense of social responsibility. Women acted upon their beliefs and served their communities throughout the seventy-three-period discussed in this paper. They traveled from town to mission in all seasons and weather, endured the inquisition of the friars and reported the births they attended, the baptisms they administered (including those performed on the stillborn) and the instances in which they assumed the role of godparent. Men shouldered the first two responsibilities in less than a handful of cases. With regard to the third, the sole godparent most frequently cited in the *Parish Register* was "godmother."

The mission account books and the *Parish Registers* illuminate aspects of the *pueblo* population and its relationship to the Indian and religious communities which are not addressed in the traditional histories of San Jose. They also reveal that a complex and dynamic social structure operated in and around the *pueblo*. Perhaps most important, the records belie the racist, sexist and self-limiting images embodied in more traditional historical literature. Leaving behind the stereotypes of California's colonial Mexicans, women emerge from this new analysis as "surprisingly" integral members of a most dynamic society.

142

Appendix A

Baptismal Entry

#5248
Juana
P^a de
Razon

En 18 de Diziembre de 1806 en la Yglesia de esta M^n puse los S^{tos} Oleos ÿ bautizé *sub condicione*, a un Niño de dos dias de nacido Hijo Legitimo de Bartholome Bolonges soldado de cuera de S^n Fran^{co} y de Mª Nicolassa Linares, haviendo Mª Luissa Botiller muger de Sebastian Sepulveda confessado que por haver nacido malo le echó el agua, pero ql. por hallarse perturbada no sabia si al mismo tpo pronunció la forma, al ql. puse por nombre Juan ÿ fue Madrina la misma Mª Luissa arriba dho ql. quedo instruida del Parentesco espiritual ÿ para ql. conste lo firmo.

Fr. Jose Viader

#5207
Juana
Francisca de
Garcia Parvula
d Razon

30 de Agosto 1806
El R.P. Fr. Domingo de Carranza suplio las ceremonias ÿ puso los S^{tos} Oleos a una niña hija legitima del soldado de cuera Juan Chrisistomo Galindo, y de Jacoba Bernal la ql. nacio el dia 26 del oho, ÿ por estar mala la bautizo Mª Gertrudis del Castillo, Partera del Pueblo, con nombres de Juan Francisca de Garcia, ÿ para ql. conste lo firmo.

Fr. Jose Viader

Appendix B

Marriage Entry

#2
Juan Ant^o
Amesquita
viudo
con
Josepha
Acuña
viuda
de
Razon

En 25 de Mayo de 1778 en la Yglesia de esta Mission de St Clara, haviendo precedido la debida presentacion, y Juridica informacion por testigos, q^e fueron Gabriel Peralta, Athanasio Vasquez Jp Miguel Silva, y Juan Ant^o Azenes sold.^{s} de cuera, y haviendo se leido las tres amonestacion.^{s} *intex misauna solemnia* en tres dias testinos, segun ordena el S^{to} Concilio Tridenuno, y no resultaron de impedim^{to} alguno, case en *facie eclesia* delante de testigos Valerio Mesa, Zeferino Lugo, y otras personas a Juan Ant^o Amesquita viudo de Juana Guana. e hijo legitimo de Manuel Amesquita, y Juana Sanchez difuntos, vecinos del Pueblo de Maiapa con Josepha de Acuña viuda de Jph Anto Garcia e hija legitima de Manuel de Acuña, y Petra Thadea difuntos, vecinos del Real de Minas del S^n Jph del Parral y parg.^{e} conste lo firmo en Oho dia.

Fr Thomas de la Peña

#515
Fran^{co} M^a
Castro con M^a
Gavriela
Barriyesa de
Razon

En Feb 16 1795
Fran^{co} Mª Castro sol^{to}
Gavriela Barriesa Sol^{ta}
Testigos, Ygnacio Castro y novn Jose Higuera y otros.

Fr. Manuel Fernandez

Appendix C

Burial Entry

#30
Maria de la
Luz Parvula
de Razon

En 26 de Oct.^{e} de 1779 di sepulaura eclesisatica en la Yglesia de esta Mision a una niña de tres años de edad, q^e murio el dia Anteced.^{e} llamada Maria de la Luz, hija de Joseph Manuel Valencia soldado de cuera, y de su difunta Muger, y parag.^{e} conste lo firmo.

Fr. Thomas de la Peña

#5411
Lucas
Altamirano
Adulto d
Razon

En 24 de dizi 1821 di sepultura ecle^{ca} al cuerpo de Lucas Altamirano que el dia anterior murio repentinamente, segun explican se acostó con su mug^r y haviendose levantado p^a hacer su necessida cayó, y muy poco despues espiro.

Jose Viader

#5412
Geronima
Garcia Adulta
d Razon

En 25 de diz 1821 di sepultura al cuerpo de Geronima Garcia Muger que era del ant^e Lucas Altamirano, la que de resultas de la Muerte repentina Oho quedo privada asta que fino que fue hayer 24, con la Absolucion, y extreman.

Jose Viader

145

Appendix D

Computer Statistical Analysis Index

Baptisms

Record

Year

Area

Specific Record

Unknown

Full Name

Entry Number

X Entry Number

First Name

Middle Name

Last Name

X Last Name

Titled Name

Sex

Ethnic Identity

Age Group

Changed Name

Sacrament

Sacrament Date

Event Date

Entry Date Sacrament Place Name

Event Place Name

Special Circumstances

X Special Circumstances

XX Special Circumstances

Legitimacy

Marital Status of Parents

Abandonment

Adoption

Other Circumstances

Father's Full Name

       First Name

       Middle Name

       Last Name

       X Last Name

       Title

       Occupation

       Place of Residence

       Prior Residence

       X Prior Residence

Birthplace

Legitimacy

Father's Full Name

    Information

Mother's Full Name

    Information

Ethnic Identity

Mother's Full Name

    First Name

    Middle Name

    Last Name

    X Last Name

    Title

    Occupation

    Place of Residence

    Prior Place of Residence

    X Prior Place of Residence

    Birthplace

    Legitimacy

    Father's Full Name

        Information

Mother's Full Name

Information

Ethnic Identity

Godfather's Full Name

Title

Occupation

Marital Status

Spouse's Full Name

Information

X Information

Place of Residence

Prior Place of Residence

Birthplace

Present at Ceremony

Godfather's Relationship to the Family

Other

X Other

Proxy

Administered Sacrament

Gave Testamony

Godmother's Full Name

Title

Occupation

Marital Status

Spouse's Full Name

Information

X Information

Place of Residence

Prior Residence

Birthplace

Present at Ceremony

Godmother's relationship to the Family

Other

X Other

Proxy

Administered Sacrament

Gave Testimony

Special Circumstances

Danger of Death

Death of Mother

Late Registration

Further Explanation

Presiding Lay Minister's Full Name

Sex

Experienced

Information

Midwife's Full Name

Sex

Experienced

Information

Presiding Priest

Attended

Recording Priest

Attended

Notes

1. San José was founded on 29 November 1777. However, the first *de razón* entry was entered into the of *Mission Santa Clara Baptismal Register* on 31 July 1777. The mission was founded on 12 January 1777. The *Mission Santa Clara Parish Registers* were not kept in a consistent manner after 1850.

2. *Mission Santa Clara Parish Registers.* University of Santa Clara Archives, University of Santa Clara, Santa Clara, California. Father McKevitt, S.J., Archivist of the University of Santa Clara and the library research staff at the university allowed the use of the microfilm copy of the *Registers* and showed great patience, as the project took much longer than I anticipated. Zoeth Skinner Eldrege, "Padrones y extractos de libros de missiones de California 1776-1846," Bancroft Library, University of California, Berkeley.

3. I am aware of the controversies regarding the definition of community. See Alan MacFarlane, Sarah Harrison, and Charles Jardine, *Reconstructing Historical Communities* (London: Cambridge University Press, 1977), chapter one. For the purpose of this study the distinction is geographic and restricted to persons designated as *de razón* in the *Mission Santa Clara Parish Registers*. Standard sources for the history of San Jose include Hubert Howe Bancroft, *History of California*, 6 vols. (San Francisco: The History Company, 1884-90; reprint ed., Santa Barbara, California: Wallace Hebberd, 1963); Edwin Beiharz and Donald O. Mers Jr., *San Jose California's First City* (Tulsa, Oklahoma: Continental Heritage Press, 1980); Lalla Rookh Boone, "The History of the Santa Clara Valley: The Spanish Period," (Master's thesis, University of California, Berkeley, 1922); Zoeth Skinner Eldredge, *History of California*, 2 vols. (New York: The Century History Company, 1915); Florian Guest O.F.M., "The Establishment of the Villa Branciforte," *California Historical Quarterly* 40 (March 1962): 29-50; Frederic Hall, *History of San Jose* (San Francisco: A.L. Bancroft and Co., 1871); C. Alan Hutchinson, *Frontier Settlement in Mexican California* (New Haven: Yale University Press, 1969); Oakah L. Jones Jr. *Los Paisanos: Spanish Settlers on the Northern Frontier of New Spain* (Norman: University of Oklahoma, 1979); Arthur Dunning Spearman S.J. *The Five Franciscan Churches of Mission Santa Clara 1777-1825* (Palo Alto: National Press, 1963); Frank Gilbert Tremayne, "History of the Santa Clara Valley: The Mexican Period," (Master's thesis, University of California, Berkeley, 1923); Oscar O. Winther, *The Story of San Jose: California's First*

Pueblo, 1777-1869 (San Francisco: California Historical Society, 1935).

4. *Mission Santa Clara Parish Registers*. See appendices for examples of the entries.

5. Sherbourne F. Cook and Woodrow Borah, *Essays in Population History*, 3 vols. (Berkeley: University of California Press, 1971-1979), 3: 177-311; Spearman, *Five Franciscan Churches*. The Tulares were served by the Mission, they came from the area of Stanislaus, San Joaquin and the Central Valley. Cook and Borah devote a large section of their book to the Tulares, see *Essays in Population History* 3: 194-220.

6. *Mission Santa Clara Parish Registers*. The majority of the entries are signed by the friars assigned to the mission. Some of the entries are signed by a friar, but are clearly in the hand of another. Sometimes one friar would perform the ritual and another would enter the information in the *Registers*. In other instances, a visiting superior performed the ceremonies and conveyed the information to the friar(s) assigned to the mission. There are several entries made after 1840, where the individual who entered the information and signed the entry was not a friar. In one such instance a *poblador* signed the entry, in a few other entries the author may have been a protestant minister.

7. *Mission Santa Clara Parish Registers*. There is a wide divergence of opinion regarding the number of entries in the *Registers* as there are numerous errors in the numerical sequence of the entries. In the *Baptismal Register* there are several such errors, one such error was caused by the confusion of an 8(8,000) for 9(9,000). Thus the total number of baptisms is at least a thousand less than the total indicated at the end of the Register. These problems are particular to the period which immediately preceeded and followed secularization. Although the official date of secularization is 27 December 1836, (see Spearman, *Five Franciscan Churches*, p. v), the *Parish Registers* indicate civil strife and turmoil as early as March of 1833, when the Mission was entrusted to Fr. Francisco Garcia Diego of El Colegio de Nuestra Señora de Guadalupe de Zacatecas. The *Registers* were not regularly reviewed and corrected after 1833. However, these errors (with exceptions) are clearly noticeable if not discernable. There was little duplication of *de razón* entries. The estimates of *de razón* entries and total entries are preliminary estimates.

8. *Mission Santa Clara Parish Registers*. Richard Konetzke, "Documentos para la historia y crítica de los registros parroquiales en las Indias," *Revista de Indias* 25 (1946): 581-86. Konetzke

presents an interesting discussion of the implications of multiple racially divided registers.

9. *Mission Santa Clara Parish Registers.* The microfilm copies vary in legibility. They are much in demand by local historians and geneologists. Much of the film is scratched. Some is quite difficult to decifer. The preliminary transcription of the data took approximately six months. These handwritten transcripts are being entered into a word processing system. Once the data is rechecked organized and preliminary linkages are made, it will be transfered to the Burroughs system, where more complicated statistical manipulation of the data will be attempted.

10. *Mission Santa Clara Parish Registers.* The most noticeable change in the size and format of entries was in the *Marriage Register* after secularization. These entries varied greatly in length and content from this point. Some entries included the use (which up to this point had been rare) of Don and Doña and were so lengthy as to cover a page or more (regular entries were often so short as to include five to a page). Other subtle changes in the format and content suggest increasing social stratification. One such change is in the selection of godmother, whereas, before class did not appear to be an issue in the selection of godmothers, such a shift (indicated by the use of titles and claims of Spanish heritage) is indicated after secularization.

11. *Mission Santa Clara Baptismal Registers.* The baptismal entries often times included more information about the godparent(s) than the parents.

12. *Mission Santa Clara Parish Registers.* The *Registers* indicate differences between *soldados de cuera* and *soldados* attached to the mission and town. Among the differences, were place of residence: *soldados de cuera* were often listed as residing out of town (i.e. San Francisco or Monterey). Beiharz and Mers, *San Jose, California's First City* p. 26, define *soldados de cuera* as "leather jacketed soldiers ... They were expert horsemen recruited mainly from the *rancho* country of the Mexican plateau--more cowboy than soldiers, according to Croix and indured a hard life, hunger, thirst, and the greatest inclemencies."

13. *Mission Santa Clara Burial Register.*

14. *Mission Santa Clara Parish Registers.* The *Registers* contain information about unsuccessful attempts to levy fees and do not indicate charges and their payment.

15. *Mission Santa Clara Parish Registers.* See note 7.

16. Spearman, *Five Franciscan Churches.* Spearman has a detailed account of the disputes regarding mission and *pueblo*

boundaries and the relocations after floods. Spearman, *Five Franciscan Churches*, p. 15, has a translation of the *Mission Santa Clara Informe* of 31 December 1777. He states that *informes* were the semiannual and biennial summary reports prepared by the friars and sent to the Father President of the California Missions, the Viceroy and the Archivo de las Indias. The statistics cited in the *informes* were gleened form the *Parish Registers* and the *Mission Account Books*. For a discussion on the cooperation between missions and settlements and a detailed look at the Account Books see Robert Archibald, *The Economic Aspects of the California Missions* (Washington D.C.: Academy of American Franciscan History, 1978).

17. Spearman, *Five Franciscan Missions*. This work is a reconstruction (using many primary sources) of the five Santa Clara Mission relocations.

18. Eldrege, "Padrones y extractos," and Beiharz and Mers, *California's First City*, p. 50.

19. The other *pueblos* were Los Angeles (1781) and Villa Branciforte (1797). Branciforte has been presented in the worst light. The image of criminality and decay is most apparent in the narrative histories of Branciforte. This imagery has been projected on to the other *pueblos*: "It was planned to make Branciforte a better town than San Jose and Los Angeles; the settlers were to be robust farmers from cool or temperate climates, masons, tailors, hatters, shoemakers, and even fishermen to engage in whaling. Discharged soldiers were welcome. But the results were even more disappointing than they had been for the two previous towns. Nine settlers, recruited in Guadalajara mainly from vagabonds and criminals, arrived in 1797. They were poverty-striken, poorly clad, and ill with veneral disease." See Hutchinson, *Frontier Settlement in Mexican California*, p. 63.

20. Beiharz and Mers, *California's First City*, p. 26.

21. Jones, *Los Paisanos*, p. 218. Jones quotes Bancroft, *History of California*, vol. 1, p. 601. Also see: Bancroft, *History of California*, vol. 2, p. 155; Hutchinson, *Frontier Settlement in Mexican California,* p. 63; Tremayne, "History of the Santa Clara Valley," pp. 91 and 93. Beiharz and Mers discuss the shortcomings of official correspondence: "Even so fairminded a man as Alfred Robinson, who visited San Jose in 1830, could find nothing good to say about the male portion of the population." (*California's First City*, p. 44). See Antonia Castañeda's analysis of the literature in this volume for her comments of this double standard.

22. The term 'frivolous Mexican harlots' is a distillation of the images presented in the literature in particular Tremayne who quotes William Henry Dana and Charles Wilkes, both of whom traveled in California and were involved in business ventures.

23. The Spanish Monarch's evaluation of the settlement of Alta California set the tone for subsequent descriptions of *pueblo* settlers. Emphasis on the institutions of colonization, and use of official correspondence has formed the basis of a history of the *pueblos* based on the statements and recollections of persons who viewed the settlers as competitors, adversaries, persons of inferior race, class, and social position, and persons difficult to control. The persistence of the prejorative characterizations of Mexican colonists is due in part to the uncritical use of literary sources. The reports, letters, papers, and biographies of clerics and civil officials, the memoirs of the well-to-do, and the observations of foreign business and military agents, reveal social, racial, economic, and political differences between the authors and the people they describe. The authors of these "historical documents" set themselves apart from their subjects. The ethnocentric, racist, and sexist attitudes of the authors are often readily apparent. The motives and interests of these partisan observers and participants, however, are discussed in the traditional histories, but the prejorative depiction of settlers is presented at face value.

24. See note 23.

25. *Mission Santa Clara Parish Registers.* The vital statistics which are contained in the *Registers* are essential to the demographic reconstruction of this settlement. However, the use of the *Registers* need not be limited to these readily apparent uses. The narrative passages reveal subtleties of social and economic relationships which are not readily apparent in supportive documents.

26. Jones, *Los Paisanos*, p. 216.

27. Ibid., p. 38. See note 21.

28. J.N. Bowman, "The Resident Neophytes of the California Missions (1769-1834)," *The Historical Society of Southern California Quarterly* 40 (June 1958): 138-148. See Cook and Borah, *Essays in Population History*, 3: 181 for a discussion of Bowman. Marie E. Northrop, *Spanish-Mexican Families of Early California: 1769-1850*, vol. 1 (New Orleans: Polyanthos, 1976). This is a very useful volume but it has limitations. The book contains the most comprehensive list of Mexicanos and their family ties. The author spent 15 years correcting the records which had been corrected by Temple (Thomas Workman Temple,

"Genealogical Tables of Spanish and Mexican Families," Bancroft Library, University of California, Berkeley). Temple had, in turn, corrected the work of Bancroft et. al. Northrop's work is incomplete in that she followed families for one and sometimes two generations. There are also notable ommissions (the Vasquez family is, with the exception of one brief reference, omitted from the volumne. See Sherbourne F. Cook, *The Population of the California Indians 1769-1970*, (Berkeley: University of California Press, 1976), p. 30.

29. Ibid.
30. Ibid.
31. Cook and Borah, *Essays in Population History*. See note 5.
32. Ibid., p. 311.
33. *Mission Santa Clara Parish Registers*. Beiharz and Mers, *California's First City*, pp. 26-29. Cook and Borah, *Essays in Population History*, vol. 3, pp. 177-79.
34. Hutchinson, *Frontier Settlement in Mexican California*, p. 62n. See note 33.
35. Maynard Geiger, O.F.M., *Franciscan Missionaries in Hispanic California 1769-1848* (San Marino: The Huntington Library, 1969), p. 269.
36. Thomas C. Barnes, Thomas Naylor and Charles Polzer, *Northern New Spain Research Guide* (Tucson: University of Arizona Press, 1981), p. 135.
37. *Mission Santa Clara Parish Registers*.
38. *Mission Santa Clara Parish Registers*. Cook and Borah, *Essays in Population History*, vol. 3, pp. 177-78.
39. *Mission Santa Clara Parish Registers*. *Mission Santa Clara Baptismal Register*, entry #8659 is listed as:

#8659
Mª Ysabel
Liberata
del Refugio
de los que
llaman de Razon

(Alvisu)   dated July 22, 1834

40. Cook and Borah, *Essays in Population History*, vol. 3, p. 310. Cook and Borah discuss *unión libre* and the use of *vecina* and *vecino* in terms of racial fusion.

157

We are not entitled to conclude from this data that we have the true rate of racial fusion between people of Hispanic culture and California Indians, for much of the procreation of children probably proceeded without religious marriage or any formal legal union, just as *unión libre* is an important form of sexual association in Mexico today. The children of such unions more likely would be counted as Indians, since the mother would be an Indian, and with the collapse of the mission system might never enter the white man's records. Furthermore, in the last years of our study, 1835-1854, a process was taking place that is also characteristic of Hispanic culture. Indian neophytes, who may have been Christian for as many as three generations, were settling among the *gente de razón* in San Jose and other Hispanic settlements and were winning acceptance, as is shown in the marginal entries for baptisms and marriages, which begin to use the terms *vecino* and *vecina* (also employed increasingly for the *gente de razón*) in place of *indígena*, that is to say, Indian.

41. Ibid.
42. *Mission Santa Clara Parish Registers.*
43. Ibid.
44. Ibid.
45. See Appendix A *Mission Santa Clara Baptismal Register*, example #5248.
46. *Mission Santa Clara Baptismal Register.*
47. See Antonia Castañeda in this volume.
48. Tremayne, "History of the Santa Clara Valley," pp. 91 and 93. Tremayne relies on Richard Henry Dana, *Two Years Before the Mast* (New York: Airmont Press, 1965) and Charles Wilkes, *Narrative of the United States Exploring Expedition During the Years 1838, 1839, 1840, 1841, 1842*, 5 vols. (Philadelphia, 1844) in the development of his discussion.
49. *Mission Santa Clara Baptismal Register; Mission Santa Clara Marriage Register;* Cook and Borah, *Essays in Population History*, vol. 3, p. 278.
50. *Mission Santa Clara Baptismal Register.* Cook and Borah, *Essays in Population History*, vol. 3, pp. 277-311.
51. *Mission Santa Clara Parish Registers.*
52. Northrop, *Spanish-Mexican Families of Early California.*
53. *Mission Santa Clara Parish Registers.* Cook and Borah, *Essays in Population History*, vol. 3, pp. 177-311. Cook and Borah discuss the limitations of the data throughout their volume.
54. *Mission Santa Clara Baptismal Register*, entry #57:

#57   (1777)
Antonio
Parvo° de
Razon

31 de Julio de dho año
baptize privadamente un niño
recien nacido hijo de Maria
Petra Azeves soltera
y de Joseph Ant° Gonzales
soltero soldao de cuera

En 5 de Agosto en la Yglesia
de esta Mision le puse los
S^{tos} Oleos y supli las
demandas ceremonias de N^{a}.
Sta Me Yglesia, y paraq.^{e}
conste lo firmo en esta
Mision de Sta Clara en dho
dia mes y año.

Fr. Thomas de la Peña

55. *Mission Santa Clara Baptismal Register.*
56. Peter Laslett, Karla Oosterveen and Richard Smith, *Bastardy and it Comparative History* (London: Edward Arnold, 1980).

ORAL HISTORY: CONSIDERATIONS AND PROBLEMS FOR ITS USE IN THE HISTORY OF MEXICANAS IN THE UNITED STATES

by

Raquel Rubio-Goldsmith

Doña Teodora offered me yet another cup of strong, black coffee. The aroma of the big, paper-thin, Sonoran tortillas filled the small, linoleum-covered kitchen and I knew that with the coffee I would receive a buttered tortilla straight from the round, home-made, *comal* (a flat, earthen-ware cooking pan) balanced on the gas-burning, Sear's stove. For three days, from ten in the morning until early evening, I had been sitting in the same comfortable wooden chair, taking cup after cup of black coffee and consuming hot tortillas. Doña Teodora was ninety years old and although she would take occasional breaks from patting, extending, and turning over tortillas to let her cat in or out, it appeared that I was the only one exhausted at the end of the day. But once out, as I went over the notes, filed and organized the tape cassettes, exhilaration would set in. The intellectual and emotional excitement I had previously experienced when a pertinent document would suddenly appear waned in comparision to the gestures and words, the joy and anger doña Teodora offered.

She had not written down her thoughts; but the ideas, recollections, and images evoked by her lively oral expression were jewels for anyone who wanted to know about the life of Mexicanas in booming mining towns in Chihuahua, Sonora, and Arizona. She never kept a diary. The thought of writing a memoir would have been put aside as presumptuous. But all her life doña Teodora had lived amidst the telling and retelling of family stories. Genealogies of her own family as well as complete and up-to-date information of the marriages, births, and deaths of numerous families that made up her community were all well-kept memories. These chains of generations were fleshed out with recollections of the many events and tribulations of these families. Oral history had proven to be a fertile field for my research on the history of Mexicanas.

My search had begun in libraries and archives--repositories of traditional history. The available sources were to be found in census reports, church records, directories, and other such statistical information. These, however, as important as they are cannot provide one of the essential dimensions of history, the full narrative of the human experience that defies quantification and classification. In certain social groups this gap can be filled with diaries, memories, letters, or even reports from others. In the case of Mexicanas in the United States, one of the many devastating consequences of defeat and conquest has been that the traditional institutions that preserve and transfer culture (the documentation of the past) have ignored these personal written sources. The letters, writings, and documents of Mexicans have rarely, if ever, been included in archives, special collections, or libraries. At best, some centers have attempted to collect newspapers published by Mexicans, but the effort was started late. It is constant frustration for the historian who tries to reconstruct the past from newspapers because, although titles abound, collections are scarce and often incomplete.

Having read of the use of oral history in journals (usually criticisms and attacks on its legitimacy for the historian) and remembering that my grandmother could tell countless "true" stories when she was alive, I decided to turn to oral history to investigate the past of Mexicanas.

James Hoopes explains that oral history is based on documents that are spoken: "songs, speeches, interviews and formal and informal conversation are all oral documents."[1] These documents, however, are useful to the historian only if they are preserved. Some have been preserved through memorization as in the oral traditions of many societies; more recently, spoken memory has been taped-recorded. Jan Vansina in his study, *Oral Tradition: A Study in Historical Methodology*,[2] demonstrates that oral tradition is a valuable source for the history of certain non-literate societies. However, his use of formalized methodology for the preservation of the past is not the only type of oral document that is available. Specific to the history of Mexicanas, oral interviews, their preservation, and transcription are emerging as a primary source. This paper will examine this alternative as a primary source for the investigation of the history of Mexicanas.

Although many hours of previous study and preparation had taken me to doña Teodora's kitchen, I soon realized that the richness and depth of the spoken work challenges the comforting social science theories and models. Should it be a structured questionnaire or an open-ended interview? Was I really an insider or were the experiences that had made the lives of my interviewees such that although I could speak Spanish and am Mexicana I was still an outsider? With these and many more questions, I plunged ahead. Time was running out for some of the women: it was then or never. Later, when the interviews were completed and I was able to study them I found the oral interview useful for several different reasons. I attempted an evaluation of their worth. My analysis of the interviews of doña Teodora and those of several other Mexicanas made it clear to me that the oral histories of Mexicanas can be used in at least three ways by historians: first, as the primary source material necessary for the analytical development of a conceptual framework that represents the experiences and culture of Mexicanas; second, as a self-standing oral document that preserves recollections and spoken memories providing the counterpoint to one-voiced history; third, as the creation of a new historical document that views the interview as a totality including the interviewer.

Paradigms: Old and New

Due to social and political movements of the twentieth century as well as the influence exercised by the growth of the social sciences, subjects considered legitimate areas of historical inquiry have expanded. History had primarily been concerned with selective, important events; now recurring experiences and patterns are also studied. French historiography has shown us that history can also broaden our knowledge of past consciousness not immediately evident to the unaware contemporaries.[3] History has moved from the singular event structural reality; from short to long views; from the individual to the collective. It is precisely in this expanded consciousness of history that we find the history of women. For Mexicanas in the U.S., an even larger sphere of consciousness must be developed. Mexicanas as cultural entity in the United States have evolved under the shadow of conquest. Despite the fact that Mexican migration into the Southwest reached its highest levels long after the North American defeat of Mexico in 1848, the social, economic and political patterns of a defeated peoples persist.[4] The history of such peoples defies not only traditional sources, but also challenges social science models derived from victorious imperialistic experiences. Historians have ignored us and folklorists have barely heard us. Shirley Ardener would include us in the "mute" groups.[5] If the above is true for Mexicans as a group, the subordinate position of women in the society at large means that it is even more difficult to reconstruct the past of Mexicanas.

Our history cannot be written without new sources. Those sources will then determine which concepts are needed to illuminate and interpret the past, but these must emerge from the "mute" groups themselves. This will permit the events and structures to be described to assume a culturally relevant perspective, thus, emphasizing the point of the culture being studied. The use of theoretical constructs must follow the voices of the people who live the reality, consciously, or not. For too long the experience of women has been studied according to male-oriented sources and constructs. These must be questioned. Jensen expresses this when she writes: "Oral history has quite another function--to explore meanings of behaviors heretofore ignored as trivial; to suggest new conceptual categories, to get behind the ostensible patterns of women's life choices."[6]

For the history of Mexicans the sources primarily exist in our own worlds. And it is here where we must begin. I often found that as the memory awakened, other sources would emerge. Boxes of letters, photographs, and even manuscripts and diaries would appear. Long-standing assumptions of illiteracy were shattered and had to be re-examined. I saw that constant reevaluation became the rule rather than the exception. I entered women's worlds created on the margin--not only of Anglo life--but of, and outside of, the lives of their own fathers, husbands, sons, brothers, or priests, bosses, and bureaucrats.

The history of Mexicanas, as that of other women, promises to enrich traditional categories while demanding a reexamination of the interrelationships between various disciplines.[7] If oral interviews are to be accorded their full potential as a historical source, it behooves social scientists and historians to reconsider their techniques.

Words: Spoken Memories

Examination of the oral interview uncovers four basic integrating relationships.[8] The content of the interview must be evaluated in light of these relationships: one, the relationship between the interviewer and interviewee; two, the relationship between the interviewer and the historical phenomena; three, the relationship between the interviewee and the historical phenomena; and four, the relationship between the interviewer, the interviewee and the historical phenomena. These relationships do not exist at different times but rather are simultaneous. The oral interview must be seen as an integrated event that takes place at one particular moment in time. Each of these relationships brings to the fore certain possibilities and certain problems and issues that concern the history of Mexicanas.

1. *The Relationship Between the Interviewer and the Interviewee.*

According to Clark, Hydes and McMahan, this relationship is synchronic in nature. "That is, the communication occurring between the interviewer and the interviewee is situation bound; it takes place at a specific moment in time."[9] Through this relationship other relationships emerge. There are at least two basic issues to consider at this point: one, the insider/outsider situation and two, the responsibilities of the researcher to the interviewee. Anthropologists have studied the insider/outsider issue extensively. Topics, approaches, and attitudes can differ greatly from the insider view of the culture to the outsider view. Patricia Zavella in her article, "Doing Chicana Life Histories: Refining the Insider's Perspective," concludes that,

> First we should remember that rapport is not automatic even if its been reached once before. Instead, there are levels of rapport, and it is a continual process to achieve intimacy not only with the same informant through successive interviews, but also throughout each encounter ... We also need to anticipate that our status as insiders will only allow an entrance. From there, because we are also outsiders, we must be prepared for reticence, political differences and various social distances.[10]

Zevella's conclusions require that we reconsider whether because a Mexican woman interviews another Mexican woman it necessarily means that the interview will provide more or better information. The insider/outsider issue is much more complex than simply speaking the same language or having names of the same ethnic background. At this point in our history, what does it mean to be an "insider"? For Mexicanas in the United States, it means to be Mexicana; to speak Spanish probably; to have lived in a barrio, maybe; to be Catholic, maybe. But delving further, in all probability the interviewer will be fluent in English; will have done graduate work in the social sciences in the United States (possibly in Mexico); and, even if she has come from a working-class family, by the time of the interview it is possible that she belongs to the professional class. The interviewee, meanwhile, possibly still lives in a barrio; may only speak Spanish; and, even if her family has entered a different socio-economic group, her life probably has been more a part of the marginal barrio than that of the industrialized, Anglo society. The insider/outsider paradigm has many facets and if the historian is to pretend to be an insider he or she must be aware of the incredible differences with his/her own group. In many cases young Mexicanas, with college degrees who are part of the post-industrial world, interview grandmothers whose world views are centered in a marginal, developing society. This is the mere tip of the structural iceberg. In the United States, Mexicana society suffers from an acute case of disjunctive development. The rising economic levels may far outpace socialization mechanisms within the culture.

To be an insider, can be important but it can also be important to be an outsider. As Zavella points out, a certain reticence by the interviewee to discuss private topics precisely because she was an insider was a problem she had to overcome.[11] In contrast, for Joyce Griffin, also an anthropologist, it was precisely because she was an outsider that she had established a good relationship with Navajo women. Because she was not threatening, she was given private information.[12] I do not mean to imply that the outsider can get more information than the insider. I am trying to demonstrate how difficult it is to unravel the insider/outsider issue. The interview will be colored by this relationship and the historian must consider who the interviewer is in his/her analysis of what the interviewee has to say. Possibly the insider/outsider issue should not be seen as a clearly marked polarity, but rather as a continuum. When the historical oral document is interpreted, the historian can evaluate where on the continuum the interviewer can be placed.

Some anthropologists have addressed this problem by publishing their experiences in the field. This way both documents stand, the field work itself and the field work process. Of course, the historian must use both documents. A similar problem is addressed by methodology developed by anthropologists such as Barbara Myerhoff in her study, *Number Our Days*.[13] Having studied other cultures as an outsider, refining tools of observation and participation, the anthropologist returns to study his or her own culture. The skills learned as an outsider can be well used as an insider.[14]

In recent years both anthropologists and sociologists have discussed ethical considerations surrounding the relationships between interviewee and interviewer. Is it fair to pry into the affairs and secrets (this is particularly possible when discussing family matters and sexuality) of others if the interviewer offers nothing in return? Baca Zinn, a sociologist, speaks to the social-political responsibilities as she analyzes the roles and responsibilities of the outsider researcher and concludes that,

> The creation of a social science which has liberating rather than oppressive ramifications will require fundamental alterations in the relationships between minority peoples and conditions of research. Gestures of reciprocity do not, by themselves, alter the unequal nature of research relationships. Nor is having research conducted by insiders sufficient to alter the past research. Field research conducted by committed minority scholars may provide a corrective to past empirical distortions in that we are better able to get at some truths. However, our minority identity and commitment to be accountable to the people we study may also pose unique problems. These problems should serve to remind us of our political responsibility and compel us to carry out our research with ethical and intellectual integrity.[15]

Not only does history have a role in the redefinitions of the collective visions of a people, it also opens horizons of understanding for the individual. Historians must address both responsibilities if they are to meet acceptable standards of ethical and intellectual integrity. Possibly a central question for the historian can be posed by asking why the study of the history of Mexicanas/Chicanas is an important endeavor at this time? Is it to reinforce a body of knowledge constructed through words and interpretations of "all-knowing" men? Of course not. The study of the history of Mexicanas in the United States and Chicanas must be a contribution towards reaffirmation as a people and liberation as women. These words are not written as political rhetoric. They are put forth as a proposition for historians to consider as we formulate our ethical codes.

Precisely because of these responsibilities, traditional practices of historical research should not be discarded. The search for historical truth will always demand intellectual integrity and accountability. The oral historian must make all necessary provisions for the preservation and public availability of all oral documents. Libraries and archives readily accept the charge, but the oral historian must assume the responsibility of putting the documents there. While necessary for professional accountability, this act also implies an individual responsibility to the interviewee. The customary legal releases are not always sufficient. As rapport and intimacy grow during the interviews, often the tape-recorder is left on and important personal and private information is divulged. The interviewee owns her voice, her life, her attitudes, her ideas, and her reflections. If she does not want certain information to be public, she has a right to keep it private. What can the oral historian do? First, the historian can respect the wishes of the interviewee, possibly arriving at a solution that allows the information to remain private if possible damage or harm can result. The historian need not study every single topic now. Future scholars will uncover what has been left unexamined.

The individual aspect of the ethical issue clearly shows through the experiences described by Elizabeth Jameson ("May and Me: A Working Paper on Relationships with Informants and Communities") Joyce Griffin ("Inside and Outside: The Moebius Strip of Oral History") and Patricia Zavella ("Doing Chicana Life Histories: Refining the Insider's Perspective"). Jameson concludes,

> Relationships with informants are richer and more complex than relationships with documents because they are human relationships. A person's life is being shared, and that fact raises into sharp relief the special obligations of feminist history, which I

think are informed by the desire to present women as subjects of our own history.[16]

Individual responsibility for Elizabeth Jameson included going to the funeral of her informant May. Jameson tells us that, "on Tuesday we went to Cripple Creek and Salida for the funeral and burial. I was not so moved at my grandmothers' deaths--they had never been able to share with me as adult women. And the trust remains. Much of what I have to say is May's story, and I write partly because I promised her it wouldn't be lost."[17] Undoubtedly, the interviewer needs to respond personally with even stricter codes of decency and responsibility than when he or she is concerned with written documents.

2. *The Relationship Between the Interviewer and the Historical Phenomena to be Interpreted.*

In this, a diachronic relationship, the historian should feel at ease. Here possibly, the insider can establish a privileged position. This relationship can be described as follows:

> What the oral historian knows about the historical phenomenon in the present presupposes the existence of an historical tradition, evolving from the phenomenon that has developed *through time.* The evolution of this historical tradition is, in essence, a succession of synchronic moments. These synochronic moments of understanding, interpreting and giving meaning to the historical phenomenon are such that its meaning is conveyed to the present.[18]

But can this construct be realistically applied to the situation of Mexicanas? On one hand, historiography at best has igonored our past with the occasional stereotype with little or no basis in historical investigation. Also, the perpetual problem that faces groups whose history is unknown arises; that is, often the past is considered a replica of the cultural present.[19] This problem is particularly true for Mexicanas because the existing bibliography primarily includes research by sociologists and educators describing the cultural present. How much history of Mexicanas is it possible for the interviewer to know? Does this mean that the historian should be frightened away from doing oral history because we know so little? No, but it should tell us that, the historian must go to the interviewee with humility and an open mind to all that she has to say. Precisely herein lies the tremendous importance of oral history for Mexicanas. If our past is not readily accessible and living memories from Mexicanas themselves are one of the few sources from Mexicanas themselves, then these memories must be preserved and used with care. There are many "emic" views of the culture, not just one. The oral historian can make an important contribution by preserving as many histories as possible. Only then can responsible interpretations ensue. Let us consider also the possibility of using basic interview frameworks, as proposed by sociologist Katherine Jensen in order, "to gather consistent kinds of information, to allow coding and content analysis at varying levels of complexity. Our work can then be replicated by others in different times."[20]

3. *The Relationship between the Interviewee and the Historical Phenomenon.*

In this case the relationship is seen through time, that is, it is diachronic. But the interviewee knows about the past in a different way than the interviewer because she has actually lived and experienced the event or events.

> Since any lived experience can acquire meaning only to the extent that it is "reflected upon" after it occurs, the interviewee's knowledge of the event develops diachronically. What the interviewee knows about his/her lived-through experience in the present, is dependent on how he/she understood, interpreted, and gave meaning to the experience in various synchronic moments occuring through time.[21]

Here is the core of the interview. The historian can utilize all the skills of interpretation that are used for written sources. Oral expression and listening to the tape-recorded interviews, however, adds dimensions not available in written documents. For example, the telling pause communicates maybe more than the words that follow. Oral interviews must be heard by the historian. That is to say, reading the transcript is not enough for a full knowledge of their content.

4. *The Interdependent Relationship Between the Interviewer, the Interviewee, and the Historical Phenomenon.*

This portion of the oral document can provide an excellent source for future research. A new historical source is created in this relationship. Not only is there the spoken memory of the historical event, but the dynamic interaction between two human beings around a particular topic or topics is added. Each person, coming from a different world enters into discourse. Unless the interviewer is a total nonentity, the interaction preserved on tape will provide fascinating possibilities for future research. One example of their potential would be the linguistic analysis of selected interviews. Mexicanas have lived in worlds of two (sometimes three) languages. Our Spanish vocabulary has increased with new technology and different relationships. At times the lexicon has implied political and collective assertion, at times it has been the vehicle to assert individual existence. When a non-Spanish speaker interviews a Spanish-speaking Mexicana, even if the latter is fluent in English, the oral historian ignores an integral portion of that woman's experience. Much may be left out. On the other hand, the research potential in a comparative study using interviews between Mexicanas and English-speaking males and interviews between Mexicanas may provide illuminating data for the study of gender and race. Future historians will find rich sources if the oral historian recognizes the importance of the interrelationship described here. It is not useless to consider the inclusion of the experiences and impressions of the interviewer as an appendix to the main interview.

Conclusions

The historical development of Mexicanas in the United States, following patterns of oppression and discrimination by Anglo society, has precluded the preservation of traditional sources for the historian. This places the oral historian at a disadvantage because it precludes thorough historical preparation. Yet precisely because of this lack of formal sources the memories of Mexicanas become all the more important. Therefore, oral history emerges as a peculiarly apt source because it is the only one that not only provides a forum for the voice of Mexicanas amidst the records compiled by men, but also can uncover hidden written sources.

Analysis of the oral interview demonstrates that the relationships of the interview can create several other dimensions for use by the historian. Therefore, oral historians must examine their own participation in the interview process and integrate it in their analysis creating a new historical document.

Notes

1. James Hoopes, *Oral History: An Introduction for Students* (Chapel Hill: The University of North Carolina Press, 1979).
2. Jan Vansina, *Oral Tradition: A Study of Historical Methodology* (Chicago: Aldine Publishing Co., 1965).
3. Ciro F.S. Cardoso, *Los Métodos de la Historia* (México, D.F.: Editorial Grijalbo, 1977). p. 27.
4. Juan Gómez-Quiñones and Antonio Ríos Bustamante, "La Comunidad al Norte del Rio Bravo," en *La otra cara de México: el pueblo chicano*, ed. David R. Maciel (México, D.F.: Ediciones "El Caballito," 1977), p. 42.
5. Shirley Ardener, ed., *Perceiving Women* (New York: Wiley, 1975).
6. Katherine Jensen, "Oral History: Can it Contribute to Quantitative Studies?" Southwest Institute for Research on Women Working Paper No. 11, University of Arizona, 1982, p. 4.
7. Linda K. Kerver and Jane DeHart Mathews, *Women's America: Refocusing the Past* (New York and Oxford: Oxford University Press, 1982). p. 4.
8. E. Culpeper Clark, Michael J. Hyde, and Eva M. McMahan, "Communication in the Oral History Interview: Investigating Problems of Interpreting Oral Data," *International Journal of Oral History* 1 (1980): 31-32.
9. Ibid., p. 32.
10. Patricia Zavella, "Doing Chicana Life Histories: Refining the Insider's Perspective," Southwest Institute for Research on Women Working Paper No. 13, University of Arizona, 1982, pp. 9-10.
11. Ibid.
12. Joyce Griffen, "Inside and Outside: the Moebius Strip of Oral History" Southwest Institute for Research on Women Working Paper No. 13, University of Arizona, 1982, pp. 5-6.
13. Barbara Myerhoff, *Number Our Days* (New York: Simon and Schuster, 1978).

14. After reading on the insider/outsider issue I had several discussions with a colleague, anthropologist Angela Zerdavis. Thanks to her patience and insight I have a better understanding of its complexity.

15. Maxine Baca Zinn, "Field Research in Minority Communities: Ethical, Methodological and Political Observations by an Insider," *Social Problems* 1 (1979): 217-18.

16. Elizabeth Jameson, "May and Me": A Working Paper on Relationships with Informants and Communities," Southwest Institute for Research on Women, Working Paper No. 13, University of Arizona, 1982, p. 1.

17. Ibid., p. 11

18. Clark, Hyde and McMahan, "Oral History Interview," p. 32.

19. Margaret T. Hogden, *Anthropology, History and Cultural Change* (Tuscon: Wenner-Gren Foundation for Anthropological Research, 1979), p. 17; and Jan Vansina, "How the Kingdom of the Great Makako and Certain Clapperless Bells Become Topics for Research," in *The Historian's Workshop*, ed. M. Curtis, pp. 224-39.

20. Katherine Jensen, "Oral History," p. 8.

21. Clark, Hyde and McMahon, "Oral History Interview," p. 32.

MEXICAN WOMEN ON STRIKE: MEMORY, HISTORY AND ORAL NARRATIVES*

by

Devra Anne Weber

> *"This I remember. Some people put this out of their minds and forget it. I don't. I don't want to forget it. I don't want it to take the best of me, but I want it to be there because this is what happened. This is the truth, you know. History."*[1]

Introduction

Oral histories, more than any other historical source, pivot around the central if complex relationship between memory and history. Flowing from this relationship is the source of the richness, immediacy and unique value of oral histories. But it is just this relation to memory which can be both frustrating and challenging to historians and readers of history.

Oral histories are shaped by two simultaneous dialogues. One occurs between the individual and his or her own memory. The other occurs with the interviewer. The relationship with the interviewer determines how much will be shared or what will be shared or, perhaps, altered or fabricated. This is shaped by the questions asked, the class, ethnicity and gender of the two people, and the subjective elements of sensitivity and compatibility which may bridge or accentuate differences between them. The individual's dialogue with his or her own memory determines the internal structuring of the individual consciousness and the oral history created by this. Yet memory, reflecting the complexity of human beings, can be contradictory and contentious, as well as reflective, insightful, articulate, and perceptive. Most importantly, memory is ultimately faithful only to an internal logic of consciousness.

---

* I would like to thank Michael Frisch, Ron Grele, Teresa McKenna and the members of the Los Angeles Labor History group for comments on earlier drafts of this paper. My special gratitude to the women of the 1933 cotton strike.

Oral histories are a crucial source for exploring the history of Mexican women.[2] Oral histories provide some answers to fundamental questions about life and work, culture and cultural change, women's perceptions, values and consciousness which are unavailable from more traditional sources. Yet there are problems with oral sources. One is the problem of memory: a frequent lament is that oral histories are factually inaccurate and thus a poor historical source. Another problem arises from how oral sources are used. In our enthusiasm over these sources which carry us out of dusty archives and into the world, oral histories are often used without critical analysis. They are often used in historical reassessments which aim, in part, to reconnect people with their own history. Yet we all act within a framework of institutional relations, struggles and divisions, change and process. As a result, using oral histories uncritically and without reevaluating the overall historical framework may ultimately reinforce what we are trying to change--peoples' alienation from their own past--by including them in a written history only to relegate them to anecdotal and colorful bystanders watching the traditionally conceived parade of historical process march by in front of them.[3]

This paper will explore how oral histories can be used, with their strengths and their weaknesses. This will touch upon the obvious--of how oral narratives can yield information about daily life and work. It will also address how oral histories can help in understanding the consciousness of these women and how, in this case, factual inaccuracies, frustrating as they are, follow an inherent logic which can be revealing of the internal meaning of these narratives and lead us to a greater understanding of peoples' interpretation of these events. This paper draw on a series of oral histories with Mexican women who were cotton pickers in California's San Joaquin Valley during the 1930s and participated in the 1933 cotton strike by over 18,000 workers. The paper focuses on the oral narrative of Rosaura Valdez.[4]

Mrs. Valdez and the 1933 Cotton Strike

Mrs. Valdez, born near Torreon, Mexico, was not atypical of women who were in the strike. She came from Mexico, where her father had been a *sembrador*, a small farmer or sharecropper, eking out a livable but bleak existence. She had barely reached adolescence when the Mexican revolution broke out in 1910. With the exception of a rebellious sister-in-law, neither she nor her immediate family participated in the revolution.[5] As with many non combatants, her memories of the revolution were not of the opposing ideologies nor issues, but of hunger, fear and death.[6] Fleeing the revolution, the family crossed the border into Texas and three years later settled in the Los Angeles *colonia* of Maravilla. By 1933, she was 24, married, with two children and lived in a small San Joaquin Valley town.[7]

The agricultural industry in which she worked was, by 1933, California's major industry and cotton the most rapidly expanding crop in the states cornucopia. Cotton depended on Mexican labor, and highly capitalized, large cotton ranches of over 300 acres dominated the industry and hired the largest number of agricultural workers in the state. Approximately 20,000 workers picked the 208,000 acres of San Joaquin Valley cotton. Social relations were shaped by the size and the managerial structure on the ranches.[8] Mexican workers migrated annually to the San Joaquin Valley to live on private labor camps which were rural versions of company towns.[9] Here they lived in company owned housing, bought from company stores to which many remained in perpetual debt, and on the larger ranches sent their children to company schools. Their work and daily lives were supervised by a racially structured hierarchy dominated by Anglo managers and foremen: below them were Mexican contractors who recruited the workers, supervised work and acted as the intermediary between workers and their English speaking employers.

With the onslaught of the depression, agricultural prices fell and growers slashed wages. Workers, who had received $1.25 per a hundred pounds of cotton in 1926, were now receiving only 60 cents for the same amount in 1933. In response--and despite the threat of deportation--Mexican farm workers went on strike in crop after crop in California, convulsing the agricultural industry and sending tremors through the San Joaquin Valley. Encouraged by the erroneous belief that they were included in section 7A of the National Recovery Act of the New Deal which guaranteed the right of workers to bargain collectively, they shut down the agricultural heartland of the biggest industry of California. The wave of strikes began in May in southern California, around Los Angeles, and by August spread north into the San Joaquin Valley. While under the banner of the Cannery and Agricultural Workers Industrial Union (CAWIU), the strikes were conducted largely by Mexican workers and Mexican organizers.[10] Extensive familial and social networks among the workers acted as conduits in spreading the strike and galvanizing workers to walk out. Thus the spread and success of the strikes depended as much, if not more, on the family and social networks of the Mexican workers as it did on the small but effective and ambitious union.

In October the strike wave crested in the cotton fields of the San Joaquin Valley when 18,000 cotton pickers went on strike. The strike brought picking to a standstill over one hundred miles of the California cotton belt. Growers evicted strikers from their ranch homes and the evicted strikers formed ad hoc camps on empty land. The largest camp was near the town of Corcoran where 3500 strikers congregated. Strikers formed mobile picket lines which paraded in front of selected ranches where some workers still picked. Growers, panicked by the realization that anticipated new workers would not be forthcoming to pick their crop, retaliated by organizing groups of armed vigilantes who worked with local law enforcement to stop picketing and intimidate strikers. Workers were beaten and within two weeks growers had shot and killed three strikers.

As the intensity of the conflict escalated, the strike became the unintentional testing ground for the New Deal's as yet unclear agricultural policy. The federal government sent in food to starving strikers. George Creel, an arbitrator with the National Recovery Administration was sent in to settle the strike. But the strikers held out for over a month before a negotiated settlement between growers, and the California, United States and Mexican governments reached a compromised wage of 75 cents per one hundred pounds.[11]

Mexicanas were a vital part of the strike, and about half of the strikers at Corcoran were women. They ran the camp kitchen, cared for the children and marched on picket lines. They distributed food and clothing. Some attended strike meetings and a few spoke at the meetings. And it was the women who confronted Mexican strikebreakers. In short, women were an essential element to this strike, but have been basically obscured from its history. Mrs. Valdez went on strike and was on the picket lines. She was not a leader, but one of the many women who made the strike possible.

Voice and Community

Before launching into the content of the oral histories, a word is in order about the voice, the tone of oral histories. How information is conveyed is often as important as what is said, and can emphasize or contradict the verbal message. Conversation and social interaction are a major part of women's lives and gesture and voice are crucial to these communications. The verbal message, the "song" of a story, is especially important for people with a strong oral tradition. As Jan Vansina has pointed out, oral traditions are often also an art form, drama and literature. Oral histories are often dramatic and move with a grace and continuity which embodies analytical reflections to communicate an understanding of social relations and the complexities of human existence.

Mrs. Valdez structured her oral history in the form of stories or vignettes. Most sections had distinct beginnings and endings, interrupted only if I interjected a question. She developed characters, villains and heroes, hardship and tragedy (but little comedy). How this story was constructed and its characters developed embodied her assessment of the conflict.

As she told her story, the characters developed voices of their own, each with separate and distinct tones and cadence which reflected, perhaps to some extent, their personalities but moreover her assessment of them and their role in the drama. Strike breakers, for example, spoke in high pitched and pleading voices: the listener understood immediately that they were measly cowards. The strikers voices were a clear contrast, as they spoke in sonorous, deep and steady tones: they had the voice of authority, seemed to represent a communal voice and verbalized what Mrs. Valdez considered community values.

Mrs. Valdez's sense of collective values, later expressed in the collective action, either by strikers as a whole or by women, was expressed in a collective voice. At times individuals spoke in her stories: the grower, Mr. Peterson; her contractor, "Chicho" Vidaurri; and the woman leader "la Lourdes." But more often people spoke in one collective voice which transcended the individual. This sense of community as told through the voices became a central feature of her narrative and permeated everything she said about the strike. Thus, in effect, a sense of unanimity permeated her story: an analysis of solidarity and clear cut division.[12] In short, how she told the story underlined, accentuated and modified the meaning of the story itself.

The "story" she told conveyed not only the "facts" as she remembered them but also conveyed non-verbal analysis. Mrs. Valdez's voice, gestures and inflections conveyed both implications and meanings. She gestured with her arms and hands ... a flat palm hard down on the table to make a point, both hands help up as she began again. Her "stories" had clear beginnings and often ended with verbal punctuations such as "and that's the way it was." She switched tenses around as in the heat of the story the past became the present and then receded again into the past. Vocal inflections carried a tonal counterpoint to her words as they jumped, vibrated, climbed and then descended on the tone of her voice.

Mrs. Valdez' memories of the 1933 strike focused on two major concerns: providing and caring for her family and her role as a striker. How she structured these memories reveals something about her perceptions and her consciousness as a woman, a Mexican, and a worker. Her memories of the strike focused on the collectivity of Mexicans and, within this, the collectivity of Mexican women.

Mrs. Valdez' narrative suggests a sense of national identity which is an important underpinning to her narrative and reflects the importance of national cohesion against an historic background of Anglo-Mexican hostility.[13] Mrs. Valdez vividly recounted the story of the United States' appropriation of Mexican land in 1848 and the Treaty of Guadalupe Hidalgo which ceded the area to the United States. She drew from stories of Mexican rebellion against U.S. rule in California and the nineteenth century California guerrillas, Tiburcio Vasquez and Joaquin Murietta: the knowledge that Mexicans were working on the land which once belonged to Mexico increased her antagonism towards Anglo bosses. Mrs. Valdez may well have felt like Mrs. Martinez who, upon arriving at the valley, pointed out to her son and told him "Mira lo que nos arrebataron los bárbaros."[14]

The Mexican revolution of 1910 to 1920 influenced strikers in several ways. Only a few years away from the revolution, most Mexicans on strike had lived through the revolution and, some, the reverberations and conflicts which rocked Mexico in its wake. For many, such as Mrs. Valdez, their memories of the revolution were of hunger, death and disruption. Yet the legacy of the revolution was important in several respects. The military experience was crucial in protecting the camp: often led by ex-military officers, Mexican veterans at the Corcoran camp formed a formidable armed security system which even the gun-happy growers shrank from attacking, and organized groups patrolled the roads to deter potential strikebreakers. Yet Mrs. Valdez remembers that the strike encouraged the recounting of stories of the revolution which were told, retold, and debated in the camp, punctuated by arguments between various factions of the revolution.[15] The extent to which Mexicans employed the images and slogans of the revolution helped solidify a sense of community, Workers named the rough roads in the camp after revolutionary heroes and Mexican towns which suggested their common roots. Even Mrs. Valdez, whose individual memories of the revolution were primarily of the terror it held for her, shared in a collective memory of a national struggle and its symbols: Mrs.Valdez disdainfully compared the strikebreakers with the traitors who had "sold the head of Pancho Villa."[16]

In the oral histories Mrs. Valdez expressed a sense of collectivity among Mexicans. It needs to be pointed out that there were, in fact, many divisions among Mexicans: between different workers; between strikers and strikebreakers; between contractors and workers; between people from different areas of Mexico; and between people who had fought with different factions of the revolution or the Cristero movement in the 1920s. Yet working for Anglo bosses and the conflict of the strike emphasized an identification as Mexicans which overshadowed other divisions. This no doubt contributed to the recollection of many interviewed of an overall collectivity of Mexican strikers.

Mrs. Valdez' memories of the beginnings of the strike and the ensuing conflict with the grower suggest a sense of a collectivity as workers. On the Peterson ranch where Mrs. Valdez worked with her husband, the grower refused to meet strikers' demands for $1 for picking 100 pounds of cotton and workers walked out. The 150 workers who left the fields confronted their labor contractor Narciso Vidaurri. Mrs. Valdez recounted the confrontation between the interests of the workers, the grower and the contractor. All are represented with one voice.

Chicho said, "You'd better go and work because if you don't go they're going to throw you out of the camp!

"So they throw us out! We're not afraid. But we won't pick any more unless they pay us to pick."

Then he said, "He's (the grower, Peterson) not going to pay more and he wants the cabins vacated immediately in order to house other people who will pick."

[Mrs. Valdez leaned forward and interjected her own comment into the dialogue:]

181

But you think they could have gotten other people?! ...
When *everybody* was on strike? ... Who would have picked?

Then Chicho said, "Do what you think ... If you want to
work it's up to you. If you don't want to work, its up to
you. The point is that those who won't work will be
thrown out ...

And the people said, "NONE OF US WILL WORK!!" Yes,
that is what they said, "NONE OF US!!"

Then old man Peterson asked him. "What did they say?"
And he [Chicho] said, "They said no. That if one goes,
they all go. That if one stays, they all stay. But they want
more pay." ... Peterson said, "No. No. They aren't going to
be paid more."[17]

Within minutes, Peterson's men loaded the strikers' belongings
onto trucks and dumped them onto the highway adjoining the
ranch. The evicted strikers joined those evicted from other
ranches on a plot of land on the outskirts of town. Within a week
3500 strikers were camped at what became known as the Corcoran
camp. The camp resembled a small town, larger than the adjacent
town of Corcoran itself. Rows of cars attached to lean-tos formed
rough roads in the camp, each corresponding to workers from a
particular ranch. Workers formed a camp security force. The Circo
Azteca, a small traveling circus unexpectedly stranded on the land,
stayed through the strike and provided nightly entertainment and
diversion. The camp became the hub of strike activity, the center
for the CAWIU office on the west side of the San Joaquin Valley,
the base for picket lines, a meeting place for daily strike meetings,
and a visiting point, later, for government officials and the press.

The Community of Mexican Women

Mrs. Valdez also remembered a collectivity of Mexican
women. By 1933, Mexican women worked alongside men in the
fields. They, as the men, were paid piece rates, 60 cents for each
one hundred pounds of cotton picked. It required skill and
experience to choose which bolls to pick and which to leave, to
adroitly pick the bolls while avoiding twigs and dirt, and to pick
rapidly enough to make money. Women picked, on the average,

two hundred pounds per ten hour day. Picking in the mile long rows of cotton required strength, skill and stamina:

> But let me describe to you what we had to go through. I'd have a twelve foot sack, about this wide. I'd tie the sack around my waist and the sack would go between my legs and I'd go on the cotton row, picking cotton and just putting it in there ... So when we finally got it filled real good then we would pick up the [hundred pound] sack, toss [sic] it up on our shoulders, and then I would walk, put it up there on the scale and have it weighed, put it back on my shoulder, climb up a ladder up on a wagon and empty that sack in.[18]

Mrs. Valdez recounted the hardships which women faced in caring for their families: the houses without heat which contributed to disease; preparing food for her family without stoves and cooking over fires in oil barrels. The issue of food played a central role in her memory. Getting enough food to eat could be a problem when wages were low, and the depression forced some women to forage for berries to eat. Others subsisted at times on flour and water. Food was an issue of survival. As in almost all societies, women were in charge of preparing the food and Mrs. Valdez' concern about food was repeated in oral histories with other women. While men recounted the depression and strike in terms of wages and conditions in general, women remembered these events in terms of food. This is not to say that men were oblivious or unconcerned. Rather it suggests that the woman's role in preparing food made this a central aspect of their consciousness and affected the way they both perceived, remembered and articulated the events of the strike.

Who Mrs. Valdez remembered as leaders is reflective of this sense of a community of women. When initially asked about leaders, Mrs. Valdez replied there were none. Later she named two, her labor contractor Chicho Vidaurri and Lourdes Castillo. Chicho she considered a leader, in the sense of someone you go to resolve problems, get help from, and use as a resource. This indeed fits, in many respects, the role that contractors played on the camps. But within the strike, Chicho was replaced in her memory by Lourdes Castillo. Lourdes is an interesting choice for several reasons.

Most obviously, Lourdes was a woman. But beyond that, Lourdes represented the transition which many Mexican women were undergoing during the process of the revolution, migration, and change in work. The Mexican revolution had convulsed Mexican families and, with it, the role of women. Women left alone to fend for themselves took care of farming, the family, often migrated and women sometimes fought on their own. The "soldaderas" were camp followers who went with men of all factions into battle. Most cooked, nursed, and provided sexual and emotional comfort. But some fought and were even executed in the course of battle. This image of "la soldadera," the woman fighting on behalf of the Mexican community as a whole, was praised as a national symbol of strength and resistance. Yet it was an ambivalent precedent. For while soldaderas may have fought in the revolution, in so doing they broke with traditional values. Thus while people praised the *image* of the *soldadera* within the context of an often mythified revolution, they were critical of the relative sexual freedom and independence which accompanied it. The term "soldadera" became double edged and, when used against individual women, was at times synonymous with "whore."

Ambivalence about independent women followed Mexicanas to the United States. The gender mores of the United States differed in some respects from rural Mexico. Some of these changes were cosmetic. Women bobbed their hair, adopted new dress, wore make up. But such changes reflected a changing gender division of labor. In the United States women began to work for wages. Often these were the younger, unmarried women who worked in canneries or garment factories unobserved by watchful male relatives.[19]

Some moved out of their family houses. And some women became financially independent, running bars and *cantinas*, often to support their children. Financial independence and a changing gender division of labor outside the house altered expectations of women's responsibilities and obligations. Women who adopted these new ways, either in appearance or through financial or social independence still risked the approbation of segments of the community, male and female.

Lourdes Castillo was an attractive, single woman who lived in the town of Corcoran. She wore make up, bobbed her hair and wore stylish dresses. Financially independent, she owned and ran the local bar. Lourdes became involved with the strike when union organizers asked her to store food for the camp in her *cantina*. Mrs. Valdez remembers that Lourdes was in charge of keeping a log of who entered and left the camp and spoke at meetings. She was also in charge of distributing food.[20] Thus Lourdes reflects women's concern about food. At the same time she epitomized the cultural transition of Mexican women and the changing gender roles from pre-revolutionary Mexico to the more fluid wage society of California. Within the context of the strike, it was precisely her financial independence which enabled her to perform this function of storing and distributing the food. Mrs. Valdez' enthusiastic memories of Lourdes perhaps suggest Mrs. Valdez' changing values for women, even if not directly expressed in her own life.[21]

While Mrs. Valdez described the abysmal conditions under which women labored, the women were active, not passive, participants in the strike. Women joined the daily picket lines which paraded in front of the cotton fields where strikebreakers picked. Older women still sporting the long hair and rebozos of rural Mexico, younger women who had adapted the flapper styles of the United States, and young girls barely into their teens rode together in trucks to the picket lines where they badgered strikebreakers into leaving the fields. Their activities on the picket line led women to set up make shift child care centers to care for children and they established a camp kitchen which fed men without families.

As the weeks wore on women expanded their role. When, after three weeks growers still refused to settle, the women organized and led confrontations with Mexican strikebreakers which resulted in pitched battles. Mrs. Valdez remembers that the women decided that they, not the men, would enter the fields to confront strikebreakers.[22] They reasoned that strikebreakers would be less likely to physically hurt the women.

In organized groups, the women entered the field to talk to strikebreakers. The women appealed to strikebreakers on the grounds of the community good to leave the fields and join the strike. They appealed on class and national grounds--as "poor people" and "Mexicanos" to join the strike. Those from the same regions or villages in Mexico sought out compatriots to appeal to them on the basis of more localized, and usually stronger, loyalties. Those who refused to join the strike were denounced as a disgrace. Mrs. Valdez disdainfully compared the strikebreakers with the national traitors who had "sold the head of Pancho Villa."

Few strikebreakers left the fields, and exhortations turned to threats. A strikebreaker who had the audacity to work after being fed by the striking women in the camp was threatened with a painful poisoning if he tried to touch the food again. Talking turned to armed conflict. Women who had come armed with lead pipes and knives, in expectation of using these more persuasive methods if verbal appeals were unheeded, went after the strikebreakers. One ripped a cotton sack with a knife, emptying its contents onto the ground. Others began to hit the strikebreakers with the pipes, their fists or whatever was handy.

Although strikers had felt that the women would not be hurt, the male strikebreakers retaliated, and at least one woman was brutally beaten.

> The same women who were in the trucks, who were in the ... picket line ... these women went in and beat up all those that were inside (the fields) picking cotton ... They tore their clothes. They ripped their hats and the [picking] sacks ... And bad. Ohhh! It was ugly! It was an ugly sight. I was just looking and said "No. No." I watched the blood flowing from them.

> [She imitated the strikebreakers' voice in a high pitched, pleading tone.] "Don't hit us. Leave them [other strikebreakers] alone. Don't hit them."

> [Her voice drops as the collective voice of the strikers speak.] "Let them be set upon," she says. "If we are going cold and hungry then you should too," she says. "They're cowards ... sell outs. Scum," she said.

> [Her voice rises as the strikebreakers continue their plea.] "Because we live far away, we come from Los Angeles ... We need to have money to leave ..."

> "Yes," she says [her voice lowers and slows as it again becomes the voice of the strikers] "We also have to eat and we also have family," she says. "But we are not sell outs!"[23]

Several points in this passage underline the importance of the collectivity of women in Mrs. Valdez' memory. Mrs. Valdez' statement that the women went in because, at least in this instance, it was more women's business, suggests a sense that women were acting on behalf of the community. For Mrs. Valdez, it also carried a suggestion that it was the role of women to do this and that the men had little to do with the decision or even opposed it. "Because women take more chances. The men always hold back because they are men and all. But the women, no. The men couldn't make us do anything. They couldn't make us do anything (to prevent us from going) and so we all went off in a flash."[24] She also focuses, again, on food: the confrontation between the women and strikebreakers focused on feeding their families. At this juncture, the two strands of her narration come together. Her memories of the need for strikers to stay together, the collectivity, is presented in relationship to the availability of food.[25] Of course this underlines a harsh reality: strikebreakers chose to continue to work in order to feed their families in the face of the depression; and without food strikers would eventually be forced back to work. In any case, her recollection suggests not only the reality of this confrontation, but what Mrs. Valdez understood as the central strike issues and the strength of her support of the strike. In her account, when strikebreakers appeal to the women, this is expressed in terms of understanding that the strikebreakers have to feed their families; when the women rebuke them, they reply with "Yes ... We also have to eat and we also have family. *But we are not sellouts!*[26] Discussions about staying on strike, discussions about negotiations were all couched in relation to food or the lack of food. Thus her concerns as a woman are underscored by her concerns in the strike. Her interests as a Mexican worker were considered, weighed and expressed within the context of her interest as a woman, mother and wife.

For Mrs. Valdez, food remained central in her memory of the strike. As the strike wore on, conditions grew harsher in the Corcoran camp. Growers lobbed incendiaries over the fence at night. Food became hard to get and at least one child died of malnutrition.[27] About two weeks into the strike, partially in response to growing public concern about the killing of several strikers, California Governor Rolph overrode NRA regulations which stipulated that relief was not to be given to strikers not under arbitration, and, over the protestations of local boards of supervisors, sent in trucks of milk and other food to the embattled camp. Mrs. Valdez remembers nothing about the role of federal, state or local relief agencies, but she remembered the foods brought in "... rice, beans, milk, everything they sent in." At a meeting where Lourdes was talking to strikers the issue of food, or the lack of food, was juxtaposed against their stance in the strike.

She [Lourdes] was telling them that they might have to go hungry for awhile.

"But look," she said, "... they are bringing us food. We'll
each get just a little, but we're not going to starve," she
says. "But don't leave. But don't ANYBODY go to work.
Even if a rancher comes and tells you 'come on, lets go,'
don't anybody go," she says. "Look, even if its a little bit,
we're eating. But we aren't starving. They're bringing us
food."

[Mrs. Valdez interjected.] They brought us milk and
everything. Yes everybody that was working [in the
strikers camp] were told not to go with any rancher. They
were told not to believe any rancher. But everyone had to
stand together as one. Everyone had an equal vote [in what
was decided] ... equal.[28]

Mrs. Valdez was clear about the effects of a united front on
both sides, that if one grower broke with the others the rest would
follow.

[The collective voice speaks.] "No. And no. [they said] No.
No. If you pay us this much, then we go. And if one
[rancher] pays [the demand] then all the ranchers have to
pay the same. They had to, you see.[29]

The themes of unit and the importance of women was carried
over into her recollection of the final negotiations.

The Portuguese [a growers' representative] told [the strikers
representative] that the ranchers ... were going to have a
meeting at [the strikers' camp] with 'la Lourdes.'

"Yes," he says, ... "We're going to pay you so much. All of
us are going to sign so that then all of you can return to
your camps to work."

"Yes," said [the strikers' representative] "But not a cent less.
No. We won't go until we have a set wage. Then all of us
go. But if there is something more [if there is more
trouble] NONE of us go. Not even ONE of us leave the
camp."

[Mrs. Valdez leaned back and summed it up] And all that ... And that's the way it was. That's the way it was.[30]

The strike was settled, the ranchers had been beaten, and wages went up. Mrs. Valdez continued:

They paid $2.50 per hundred pounds .. Yes. Yes ... Look, they were paid well. They were paid well for the hundred pounds. Forty cents wasn't money. Forty cents for the hundred pounds wasn't money. But $2.50, I believe that is ... And then the following year, three dollars, and then after three and a half. And then four.[31]

The Structure of Memory

Mrs. Valdez' account of the strike and the role of women in it was revealing. What she remembered, how she structured her memories, and the meaning she gave to them, in short, her consciousness and perception of events, tell us more about why Mexicanas supported the strike than interviews with leaders might have. Without the perceptions of women such as Mrs. Valdez it would be more difficult to understand the dynamics of the strike and why people supported it for over a month. Rosaura Valdez remembered her life as a farmworker, life in the Corcoran, daily activities on the picket lines, and strike leaders unrecorded in written accounts.

Even more to the point, she remembers (or recounts) a collectivity of spirit and action among the Mexican striking community. In her telling of the story workers speak in a collective voice and act as a united group. She remembers little or no dissent. In her account, *all* the workers on the Peterson ranch walked out together to join the strike, *all* the women were on the picket lines, and *all* the strikers voted unanimously to stay on strike. Growers were also a united group, spoke with one voice and were presented as a collective opposition. The lines between worker and grower were clearly drawn. Mrs. Valdez credits the solidarity of the strikers for the strike's success and exhortations for workers to stick together were laced throughout her narrative: workers "had to stand together as one"; everybody voted as a collective voice not to go back to work until the ranchers met their demands. In the final meeting with growers, the solid phalanx of workers seemed to be in control and, in the face of this united opposition, the growers gave in. For Mrs. Valdez, it was this solidarity which had won the strike.

Mrs. Valdez also focused on a largely female collectivity. She remembered the hardships of Mexican women. For Mrs. Valdez, as other women, getting enough food for her family was a constant theme. Perhaps this is why, in part, Lourdes stands out so clearly in her memories, for Lourdes was a leader around the issue of food which concerned women. Women also stand out most vividly in her memories of the strike and picket lines. In her description of the women's decision to enter the fields she also implies a judgment about men and women, and she praised the women's cohesion as a group.

Women's participation in the strike also changed their self perception and aspects of their relations with their husbands and the community. A large part of this was implicit. Mrs. Valdez praised women for their role in the confrontation and described them as "brave," "tough," and "mean."[32] Even some men admiringly remembered women who were brave and, in a denial that this was a female role at all, who "could fight like a man." Yet this admiration was evidently short lived or at best ambivalent. All of the women interviewed admiringly described the actions of *other* women, but denied that they had taken part in the beatings. This included one woman who, according to all other informants, had beaten strikebreakers with a lead pipe.

For Mrs. Valdez, her active participation in the strike provided some compensation for the hurts of a philandering and abusive husband. She was contemptuous of her husband who, while a striker, did not go on picket lines and thus was not, by her estimation, a "real striker." By implication it was the people on the picket line, picket lines composed largely of women, who were the real strikers. She also remembered the strikebreakers as being males. Thus the confrontations between strikebreakers and strikers was, in her memory, also a confrontation between men and women. In her memory, she pictures these conflicts as between authoritative and strong women representing the community, and simpering, pleading men who were betraying the women and the community as a whole.[33] Mrs. Valdez stated flatly that the women were braver than the men and men played little part in her narrative. She remembered female leadership, female participation, female concerns and a largely female victory. While other interviews and sources may disagree, her narrative suggests something about Mrs. Valdez' reality of the strike of 1933.

What Mrs. Valdez didn't say was both revealing and suggestive of the limitations of oral narratives in writing history. Mrs. Valdez either did not know about or did not recount several crucial factors in the strike. Mrs. Valdez, as many other strikers interviewed, knew nothing of the CAWIU per se, despite daily strike meetings and the small CAWIU office, marked by a handwritten sign in Spanish hung loosely over a wooden table in the middle of the camp.[34] This was not confined to the women, as several men also knew nothing of the union. Perhaps the union didn't reach the strikers, or seemed irrelevant. Understandably, she also didn't recognize the names of Anglo strike leaders mentioned in accounts.

The role of the New Deal and the negotiations of the governments--Mexican, United States and Californian--play no part in her narrative. She didn't know about or didn't remember that the Mexican consul, Enrique Bravo, visited the camp and talked to an assembly of strikers. She didn't recount visits by government officials nor threats to deport strikers. And she recounted nothing about the negotiations which led to the eventual settlement of the strike. Her memory of the strike was, in looking at the entire history, thus limited. Her memory of the strike settlement was also factually inaccurate. The wage at the beginning of the season had been set at 60 cents per one hundred pounds. The final settlement of the strike resulted in a compromise wage of 75 cents per hundred pounds. Yet Mrs. Valdez remembers the original pay as 40 cents and the settlement wage as $2.50.

Thus her narrative could be criticized as both incomplete and inaccurate. Yet her narrative has an underlying logic which is faithful to the overall structure of her memory, of her reality. Why is her memory inaccurate? In part she may have simply not known of some of the events, an interesting point in itself. But, as in the case of the wages, there are points she would have known but which she remembers, or recounts, inaccurately. Perhaps she confuses the 1933 wage increase with the wage increases of the 1940s. Perhaps it was a lapse of memory and a confusion with other events which we don't have sufficient information to fully understand. Or perhaps she wanted to make it clear how successful the strike had been. This would have been in keeping with other parts of her interview. A main theme throughout the narrative, for instance, is her emphasis on the complete unity of the Mexican workers. Yet there is clear evidence of tension and discord: the confrontations with the strikebreakers, the initial dispute with her contractor, her own marital battles with her husband. Yet although Mrs. Valdez may even remember this discord, what she either remembered or at least told me--as the history of the strike--was an overwhelming unity. Her narration of the high wages make the same point: that the strike was successful. It was her *interpretation* of the strike which ultimately structured how she remembered the strike, organized her facts and recounted the outcome to me. Her factual inaccuracies may say as much if not more about what the strike *meant* to her than a careful rendition of the facts.

Mrs. Valdez' memories of the strike were similar to those of other women I spoke with. Like her, the women did not know about or recall the union, conventional strike leadership, or the role of the governments in ending the strike. Yet they expressed similar assumptions about the collective nature of the strike.

For example, Lydia Ramos' memories were similar in emphasis and interpretation. In 1933 she had worked in the fields for three years, migrating with her family from their hometown in Anaheim in southern California to work in the San Joaquin Valley. Although work was hard to find in this depression year, the Ramos family found work picking cotton near Delano. A few days after they began, workers went on strike. Despite the acute shortage of food, money, and gas to get home, the Ramos family walked out because, as Lydia Ramos recalls,

> This was in '33 ... We didn't know what union it was or who was organizing or nothing. We just knew that there a strike and that WE were not going to break a strike. That's all we knew.

Her unhesitating support for a strike about which she knew so little was remarkable, especially after the discussion about the shortage of food and money. Hadn't they at least discussed the pros and cons about going out on strike? I asked her why they wouldn't break a strike. There was a long pause. Her look and the length of the pause gave me the impression that she thought the question strange. She spoke slowly and carefully.

> Well, we believe in justice. So I want everything that's good for me and I want everything that's good for somebody else. Not just for them ... but equality and justice. If you're going to break somebody's strike, that's just going against your beliefs.

An interview with Mrs. Ramos' uncle, Braulio Garcia, suggests how later events may have affected her memory of the strike. Mr. Garcia, head of the family after the grandfather's death, was 24 in 1933. He said that not only did the family not walk out in Delano, but that they had never worked near Delano. Because of the age difference and his clarity of memory about other events, his memory may have been more factually accurate. If Mrs. Ramos' memory was inaccurate, what does this inaccuracy tell us?

Information about her later life may shed light on this. In 1965 Mrs. Ramos went on strike near Delano and helped develop the United Farm Workers union. She became deeply involved with the union and the strike had a major impact on her adult life. The 1965 strike began in Delano: perhaps this is why she remembers Delano as the site of the 1933 strike as well. If so, this suggests that she may have transposed the *meaning* of her experience in Delano in 1965 onto that of the 1933 strike. How much did her experience with the UFW in the 1960s reshape her memories of the 1933 strike and influence the reasons she gave for walking out? Did the idea of justice and equality come out of the 1933 strike, or was it the product of the 1965 strike which emphasized civil rights? Mrs. Ramos links the two events in her mind because the meaning of the events are similar to her and, whether the examples are gleaned from a strike in 1933 or 1965, the importance of unions and solidarity are the same.

Conclusion

Oral narratives thus reflect peoples' memory of the past: they can be inaccurate, contradictory and show the influence of the passage of time and the effects of alienation. As people become more alienated from the meaning of their history, they tend to individualize their lives and experiences. For example, Michael Frisch points out that in Studs Terkel's book *Hard Times*, many of the people interviewed perceived the devastating effects of the depression not as evidence of systemic collapse but as a manifestation of personal failure.[35] Certainly there are exceptions, people who have developed an historical perspective on their own lives, work and society.

We confront the same problem of alienation when using oral narratives. How oral narratives are understood reflects the consciousness of the reader. Used uncritically, they are open to misinterpretation and may reinforce rather than alleviate the separation from a meaningful past. This is especially true of people who have been ignored by written history. Readers may have no concept of the history of Mexican working women, for example, and lack an historical framework within which to situate and understand their narratives. The filters of cultural and class differences and chauvinism may also be obstacles. And some may embrace these narratives as colorful and emotional personal statements while ignoring Mexican women as reflective and conscious participants in history.

As valuable as oral testimonies are, they are not a complete history nor can they, by themselves, address the problems of historical amnesia. To do this, oral narratives need to be interpreted and placed within an historical framework encompassing institutional and social relations, struggle and change. Yet within this they provide a unique and invaluable historical source. Used critically, oral narratives can reveal the transformations in consciousness and culture over time. They can be used to place self conscious and reflective people in the front of the parade of the historical process. And, perhaps, they can help return to us all a greater understanding of our lives by reuniting us with the meaning of our past.

Notes

1. Cesar Chavez, quoted in Studs Terkel, *Hard Times* (New York: Avon Books, 1970) p. 75.

2. All but one of the women I spoke with had been born and partially raised in Mexico. Although all have lived in the United States over fifty years, all but one identified themselves as Mexicanas by birth, culture and ethnicity. The one woman born and raised in the United States referred to herself interchangeably as Mexicana and Chicana.

3. For intriguing discussions of these questions see: Michael Frisch, "The Memory of History," *Radical History Review* 25 (October 1981); Michael Frisch, "Oral History and *Hard Times*: A Review Essay," *Red Buffalo*, vols. 1 and 2, n.d.; Ronald J. Grele, *Envelopes of Sound: The Art of Oral History*, 2nd. edition, (Chicago: Precedent Publishing, 1981).

4. All of the names used are pseudonyms. Interview by author with Rosaura Valdez, Hanford, California, January 1982.

5. The sister-in-law is an interesting, if fragmentary, part of Mrs. Valdez' memory. From Mrs. Valdez' account, the sister-in-

194

law left her husband (Mrs. Valdez' brother) to join a group of revolutionaries, as a *compañera* of one of them. When she returned to see her children, she threatened to have the entire family killed by her new lover. It was in the wake of this threat that the family fled to the United States.

6. That these were the main concerns of many Mexicans does not undermine the importance of the revolution in their lives nor the extent to which the images and symbols of the revolution *later* became symbols of collective resistance, on both a class and national scale.

7. She and her husband migrated every year to pick grapes with their labor contractor, Narciso "Chicho" Vidaurri, and then returned to the town of Corcoran where they lived and worked on the Peterson ranch for around six months of every year. Their limited migration pattern was not atypical, but they were slightly more stable than many of the workers who migrated from southern California and worked in more crops.

8. In California, any piece of cultivated land over a few acres is consistently called a ranch.

9. By 1933, the overwhelming majority of Mexican workers in cotton did not migrate annually from Mexico. Most had settled in neighborhoods in the Los Angeles area or in the Imperial Valley, adjacent to the Mexican border. Others migrated from Texas. Workers were not the "homing pigeons" which growers described as descending on the fields at harvest and afterwards cheerfully departing for Mexico. They were residents and some of the younger pickers were citizens.

10. Caroline Decker, one of the CAWIU organizers, said the group was "a union in name, a rallying point, but as far as organization ... it was actually non-existant." She explained: "It was in our heads, and in our ideals. But it wasn't a reality. It was when strikes began popping out all over the state that the union began to take on an identity." Interview by author with Caroline Decker, San Raphael, California, June 1982.

11. The most thorough account of the cotton strike is by Paul S. Taylor and Clark Kerr. "Documentary History of the Cotton Strike," in United States Congress, Senate, Subcommittee of the Committee on Education and Labor, *Hearings on S. Res. 266, Violations of Free Speech and the Rights of Labor*, Report no. 1150, 77th Cong., 2nd Sess. (Washington, D.C.: Government Printing Office, 1942) pt. 4. An interesting account of both the strike and government participation can be found in Cletus Daniel,

Bitter Harvest: A History of California Farmworkers, 1870-1941 (Ithaca: Cornell University Press, 1981).

12. For those of you who are pausing to question her analysis, I want to emphasize that this is her analysis. I would disagree with her analysis of solidarity, and the disputes among strikers would I think bear this out. Nevertheless, what is exactly the point here is that even if her historical analysis is questionable, it tells us a great deal about her conception of the strike and perhaps her conception of what I should be told about it.

13. In Mexico, Mexicans tended to have a greater sense of identity with the town or state they came from than with the country as a whole. These identities are still strong in the 1980s, as are the rivalries which exist between them. It has been argued that the Mexican revolution helped create a sense of national consciousness. One of the primary reasons was its opposition to foreign interests. For those who migrated north, across the Rio Bravo, the sense of opposition to Anglo Americans was even greater. It was on the border areas, after all, where the *corridos* of resistance developed, and where many have argued the sense of Mexican nationalism was strongest. For how this contributed to the sense of a separate consciousness as Mexicans living north of Mexico, see Juan Gómez-Quiñones, *On Culture*.

14. "Look at what the barbarians have stolen from us." Interview by author with Guillermo Martinez, Los Angeles, April 1982.

15. The open disagreements were probably limited. If I can extrapolate from rural Mexico, large numbers of people do not clearly remember the factions of the revolution and their respective positions. The experience of the revolution varied from area to area, and people's perception of it differed from one town to another. In several areas of Michoacan, and the birthplace of some of the strikers, including the town of San Francisco Angumacutiro and the neighboring rancho Anchihuacaro, people lumped together everybody who opposed the government as "villistas," or members of the troops belonging to Francisco Villa. This could include either supporters of Zapata, Carranza or a legendary and unpopular bandit in Michoacan named Inez Chavez Garcia. Omar Fonseca and Lilia Moreno found the same to be true in Jaripo, Michoacan in their book *Jaripo: Pueblo de Migrantes* (Jiquilpan, Michoacan: Centro de Estudios de la Revolución Mexicana "Lázaro Cárdenas" A.C., 1984). The rather fuzzy definitions of alliances can also be seen in Paul Friedrich's *Agrarian Revolt in a Mexican Village* (Chicago: University of

Chicago Press, 1970). Stronger lines might have been drawn over the Cristero battles, but here again alliances depended more on local familial and class alliances than on national positions.

16. After his death, Villa's corpse was disinterred and decapitated. In the 1920s the head was stolen and the incident became a legend.

17. Chicho dijo, "Ustedes es mejor que salgan a trabajar porque si no los van a hechar fuera del campo."

"Pos que nos hechan!" dijo, "No tenemos miedo. Pero no las pizcamos mas si no nos paga."

Pos él dice que "No que no les va ha pagar y que quiere las casas imediatamente disocupadas para traer otra gente que le pizque."

[Mrs. Valdez leaned forward and interjected her own comment into the dialogue:] ¿Tu piensas que iba a traer otra gente, si cuando *todo* estaba en huelga? Quien les pizcaba?

Entonces Chicho dijo, "Entonces ustedes piénsenlo, Yo no quiero meterme" dijo. Ustedes saben ... si quieren trabajar queda en ustedes si no quieren trabajar, lo mismo queda de ustedes. La cuestión es que él los va aventar pa' fuera si no van a trabajar ..."

Dijeron ellos, "NINGUNO TRABAJAMOS." Si, dijeron, "NINGUNO."

Entonces dijo el viejo Peterson, "Que dijo?" Y [Chicho] dijo "Dicen que no. Que si salen unos, salen todos. Si se queden unos se quedan todos. Pero si les voy a pagar más." Dijo [Peterson] "No, no les voy a pagar más." Entonces, "Dice que no que entonces no."

18. Interview by author with Lydia Ramos, Fresno, California, June 1981.

19. Mrs. Valdez, in describing her brother who kept an eye on her during a dance in Maravilla, near Los Angeles, said that he watched her "in the style of those on the other side." In other words, she was aware that this 'watchful' behavior had its roots in the other side, in Mexico, and was different from the mores in the United States.

20. It is unclear whether Lourdes did keep the log. In a brief interview, Lourdes confirmed that she spoke at meetings and distributed food.

21. Other women were mixed about Lourdes. Talking to a couple in Corcoran the husband remembered the attractive *cantina* owner with obvious affection. His wife countered with saying that she was nothing but a *soldadera*.

22. It is unclear exactly who made this decision. Roberto Castro, a member of the central strike committee, said the strike

committee made the decision that women should enter the fields to confront strikebreakers because the women would be less likely to be hurt. The women remembered no such decision and said that the women made the decision. It is hard to ferret out the origins of the idea.

Even is the strike committee made the decision, the action was in keeping with spontaneous decisions by women which both antedated and followed this strike. Mexican women in Mexico City and other parts of the republic had taken part in bread riots in the colonial period. They had fought in the revolution. And in California, later strikes, both in the 1930s, but also as recently as the 1980s, were punctuated by groups of Mexican women invading the fields to confront strikebreakers both verbally and physically. In short, it was a female form of protest women had used both before and after the strike.

23. Las mismas mujeres que iban en los troques ... que iban en el picoteo. Adentro, les pegaron. Les rompieron su ropa. Les partieron los sombreros y los sacos y se los hicieron asina y todo. Y malos! Ohh! Se mira feo! Feo se miraba. Y nomas miraba y decia "no, no." Yo miraba la sangre que les escurría.

[She imitates the strikebearers in high-pitched, pleading tones:] "No les peguen, déjenlos, no les peguen."

[Her voice drops as the voice of the strikers speak:] "Que se los lleve el esto ... Si a nosotros nos esta llevando de frio y de hambre pos que a ellos también. No tienen [huevos] ... vendidos, muertos de hambre!

[Her voice rises as the strikebreakers continue their plea:] "Pos nosotros vivimos muy lejos, venimos de Los Angeles ... tienes que saber de donde, que tenemos que tener dinero pa' irnos."

[Her voice lowers and slows as it again becomes the voice of the strikers:] "Si ... nosotros también tenemos que comer; y también tenemos familia. *Pero no somos vendidos!*

24. "Porque las mujeres tenemos más chanza. Siempre los hombres se detienen más porque son hombres y todo. Y las mujeres no. Los hombres no nos pueden hacer nada. No nos podian hacer nada pos ahí vamos en zumba."

25. This is not arguing that these were the only arguments actually expressed in the conflict, simply saying that this is how she remembered the confrontation.

26. "Sí ... Nosotros también tenemos que comer y también tenemos familia. *Pero no somos vendidos!*"

27. As the local district attorney admitted after the strike, conditions in the strikers' camp were no worse than those of the

cotton labor camps. Growers did use the bad conditions, however, to pressure the health department to close the strikers' camp as a menace to public health.

28. Pa' [Lourdes] decirles que pasaran hambre.

"Mira" dice ... "aunque alcanzemos poquito pero no nos estamos muriendo de hambre," dice. "Pero no salga. Pero NINGUNO a trabajar ... aunque venga el ranchero y les diga que, que vamos y que pa' ca. No vaya ninguno!" dice.

"Miren, aunque sea poquito estamos comiendo ... pero no nos hemos muerto de hambre. 'Ta viniendo comida ... nos estan trayendo comida."

[Mrs. Valdez interjected:] Leche y todo nos daban ... Sí. Y a todos ahí los que trabajaban diciendo que no fueran con ningún ranchero. Que no se creeran de ningún ranchero. Que todos se agarraban de un solo modo que nadien, todos parejos tuvieran su voto, parejos ...

29. [The collective voice speaks:] No. Y no que no. No. Si nos paga tanto vamos. Y al pagar un ranchero tenían que pagar todos lo mismo. Tenían, ves.

30. El portuguese [a growers' representative] ... le dijera que ahí iban los rancheros ... a tener un mitin en el campo donde estaban todos ahí campados con la Lourdes Castillo y todo.

"Sí," dice. "Ahí vamos a juntarnos todos los rancheros. Y vamos a firmar. Les vamos a pagar tanto. Y vamos a firmar todos para que entonces, sí, y vayan cada quien a sus campos a trabajar."

"Sí," dice [the strikers' representative], "pero no un centavo menos. No. No salimos hasta que tengan un ... sueldo fijo. Todos vamos. Pero de ahí en más, ni uno vamos. *Ni uno* salimos del campo." Y todo.

31. Ellos pagaron $2.50 por la *hundred pounds* ... Sí. Sí. Les pagaron bien. Ves, que les pagaron bien. Les pagaran bien los cien libros. Cuarenta centavos no era dinero. Cuarenta centavos por *the hundred* no era dinero. Pos $2.50, yo lo creo ... Y ya el siguiente año, *three dollars*, y luego después *three and a half*. Y luego *four*.

32. The latter two descriptions can be used to describe "unfeminine" women, or women who step outside their prescribed boundaries. Within this context Mrs. Valdez's connotation was positive.

33. It is not clear if this was correct or not. Given the tensions of the strike, it is possible that only the men went out to pick.

34. This may have been due to several factors. The union was small and had few organizers in the Valley. These were English

speaking and relied on Mexicans, some of whom did join the union, to contact workers. This should not discount the role of the CAWIU, however. The union was crucial as a rallying point, and linked the disparate groups together, helped organize picket lines, wrote leaflets and played a role in publicizing the strike and in the final negotiations.

35. Michael Frisch, "Oral History and *Hard Times*," p. 231.

ALTERNATIVE SOURCES TO WOMEN'S HISTORY: LITERATURE

by

Carmen Ramos Escandon

Introduction

A reawakened consciousness has rescued the Chicano experience in the the United States from oblivion primarily through the works of Chicano scholars. The increasing availability of their contributions on the history and literature of Mexican people gives a broader perspective on Chicano culture and lifestyles. While this development is valuable and significant, the historical experience of Mexican Americans in the United States has often been assessed from the dominant Anglo Protestant culture's point of view. A distorted picture tends to emerge, depicting Chicanos as alien and deviant from mainstream North American and western historical experience. Measuring the Chicano experience against the predominant Anglo norms and values assumes that this way of life lacks validity and legitimacy, and that it is an aberration from the dominant culture's acceptable behavior. In particular, early sociological studies of the Mexican American community's structure clearly depicted family life and culture as deviant,[1] and contrasted and compared Chicano culture with the culture of poverty, as though they were closely, if not completely, related. Despite important differences, Chicano cultural values are often regarded as products of the culture of poverty and are characterized as opposed and inferior to those of the dominant culture.[2] It is also believed that elements in the Anglo culture such as independence, wealth, success, family detachment, and so forth do not apply to Chicanos.

201

The phenomenon is not new. The Chicano community's experience reflects how a foreign culture imposes itself as a dominating force, dismissing that community's culture as illegitimate. Historically, the dominant group in any given society posits the social, economic, political and cultural superiority of its values. Because Chicanos have been traditionally accused of being "different" and have had their historical experiences systematically misinterpreted, it is necessary to return to the sources of their own voices and self-interpretations, sources liberated from the influences imposed on them by the dominant culture.

The uniqueness of the Chicano historical experience as analyzed and studied by Chicano historians has been generally ignored, ridiculed, or devalued in the standard texts on United States history. Such stances can be traced to the belief, mentioned above, that because the Chicano experience does not mirror the cultural characteristics of a white Protestant majority, it cannot be considered an integral part of the American historical experience. These textbooks have excised from American history objective descriptions of the important and meaningful roles played by American minorities.[3] Similarly, crucial contributions by workers, women, and Blacks have been equally mishandled. Consequently, a "double consciousness" has developed among many Chicanos who are "forced to look at (themselves) through the eyes of others."[4]

The result is a false consciousness, through which the dominant Anglo society, by creating and promulgating a distorted image of Chicanos, prevents them from taking pride in their own identity and culture, and pressures them instead *to whiten by whatever means necessary*. Gilberto López y Rivas, for instance, cites the case of Mexican Americans who so strongly identified as Whites that their pro-U.S. loyalties led them to oppose Chicano anti-Vietnam War protests because they considered these unpatriotic.[5]

In the extreme, such behavior reflects the kinds of attitudes that can emerge from the dominant culture's constant bombardment (especially through mass media) of Chicanos with distorted images of Mexican Americans and their culture. This bias has not been limited to mass communication but has characterized academic work as well, especially prior to the formation of Chicano Studies centers at leading universities. Academics have described people of Mexican descent as picturesque, yet peculiar while their culture has been referred to as backward and traditional. That is to say, Chicanos have not been analyzed or understood in the context of their own values and historical experience. It is not surprising that many Chicanos have assimilated the dominant norms devaluing and rejecting their own cultural traditions.

The attempt to deprive a people of their history, language, culture, and other critical forms of human interaction and experience is symptomatic of cultural imperialism, to be exposed and resisted as the first step to true self-awareness. For Chicanos the search for the sources of an authentic history and culture is complex, often occurring within a void.

Stereotypes of the Chicana

The problem of searching for historical contributions by Chicanas is enormous because though they are half of the Chicano population, their roles and influence are rarely described. Most studies have been conducted by "Anglo writers, who have lacked sufficient understanding of Mexican Americans to portray the Chicana accurately."[6] Chicanas have not only been exploited because they belong to an oppressed minority, but also because they are victims of sexual discrimination. Some authors have pointed out a threefold oppression: as Chicanas, as members of the working class, and as women. Others argue that the Chicana's struggle is no different from that of Chicano men.[7]

This debate, however, does not substantially change the fact that the search for an authentic history and experience of Chicanas is difficult unless we can develop alternative sources for analysis. Looking for Chicana contributions in standard history textbooks presents us with the first frustrating problem of, quite simply, not finding any. Such texts focus on dates, names, battles and events in political history where the political actors are mainly men. These texts make the following assumptions: a) historical development is equated with political events; b) politics is the affairs of men; c) the public domain is the only legitimate arena for political activity, decision making, important business, and the *real world*; d) only those events taking place in the public domain are worthy of historical chronicle. From this, we are led to believe that the private domestic domain is the appropriate world for women. It is only here, in seclusion and isolation, that women's activities take on meaning and legitimacy. Here, women can properly advance and develop through housekeeping, child rearing, gardening, and so forth. According to these stereotypes,

203

women's primary concerns are home and family, and are not involved in much else.

The pervasive delimitation of women's activities to the domestic domain is simultaneously the cause and effect of women's isolation from the public arena and seclusion at home. This traditional view of the sexual division of labor has been tested and increasingly questioned as women become integrated into professions. This testing and questioning is a recent phenomenon and the world of women's activities, interests, and points of view remain to be adequately researched. How do we gather, evaluate and preserve information on women when data are neither recorded nor available?

With respect to Chicanas, do we escape myths depicting them as weak, submissive, overly respectful wives who completely lack initiative and critical intellectual attitudes?[8] Stereotypes of the Chicana avoid examining the nature and source of her oppression, her reaction to it, and her ambitions. The attempt to demythologize the Chicana becomes more complex because her role is crucial to the socialization of children. The Chicana mother is the vehicle through which the new generation learns the group's norms and values. As the center of family life, she is expected to play a supportive, but not necessarily stereotypic, role to husband and family. This complex balance is particularly difficult to examine and evaluate by those researchers unaware of the value ascribed to her function in Chicano culture.

For example, according to traditional norms, a Mexican woman is supposed to marry early. Sometimes marriage is considered to be her only life option, "the only possible vehicle by which she can improve herself as a human being."[9] The importance assigned to marriage among Chicanas sharply contrasts with that of North America's feminist movement. Chicanos consider the roles of married men and women complementary, not contradictory. Moreover, contrary to the belief that North American feminism made Chicanas aware of their rights and strengths, Chicanas have consistently argued that the model for their role in the community and the source of pride in their own sex has come from their mothers and grandmothers, whose courage set examples for them to follow with their own children.

The new generation of Chicanas realizes that it is their responsibility to shed illegitimate myths and to improve their lives by exposing and asserting themselves against racism, sexism, and class oppression. Such consciousness-raising and activism have resulted in confrontations with machismo, social and educational discrimination, the double standard, the confining roles ascribed to women by the Catholic Church, and ideologies that keep women subjugated.[10] Yet, only an active, comprehensive reassessment of Chicanas' everyday experiences within their families, communities, organizations, work places, and educational institutions will produce a new and enduring awareness.

The path to awareness is made more difficult by the preocuupation of traditional texts with political life, making little or no room for women. The realm of Chicanas' traditional domestic roles are also often hard to trace, particularly when they are obscured by their historical experiences as an oppressed group. In explaining a problem in Chicana studies, historiographic research would have to outline the specific period in which testimony and documentation appear as well as identify the special characteristics of the event. Furthermore, evaluating the historical experience of Chicanas, or any group or individual, requires a thorough understanding of their values, lifestyles, socioeconomic origins, and varied aspects of their social and family lives. Sources adopting such approaches have yet to be found.

The social mores that determine conduct and confine women to the home must be examined in their historical context through whatever sources and documents are available. Historically, men have determined women's standards of conduct, but little or nothing is known about how women felt about these norms. To find out these attitudes, diaries, memoirs, and oral traditions, although limited, are invaluable and revealing personal sources. Literature provides another alternative, for it reveals the complexities of their protrayal and the society in which women live.

Literature as an Historical Source

Traditionally, literature has been recognized as an important tool in sharpening social analysis and pointing to its internal contradictions.[11] In the eighteenth century, Voltaire, Madame de Stael, Tocqueville and others stressed that through literature society asserted and assessed itself. During the late eighteenth century, when modern bourgeois society consolidated itself, assertion and self-analysis acquired certain characteristics. One was the increase in audience, which contributed to the influence of literature.[12] Another was social morality. The novel was used as a vehicle for setting a good example, for convincing people of the importance of moral values.[13] To the writer, the moral impact on the reader was of paramount importance. Moreover, writers were concerned with the truthfulness of their stories: Novels should not be mere imagery, nor should they distort the truth. No clear distinction between fact and fiction had been established yet.[14]

Late in the nineteenth century, literature and history developed different points of emphasis: The novel became more concerned with imagination while history with truth. The relationship between the two disciplines, however, was still complex. For example, novelists often wrote stories based on history, using erudite studies and sophisticated research material to establish the historical facts. This material served as the core of their fictional characters and events, which can also be clearly inspired by the writers' friends and acquaintances as well as themselves. Hence, both settings and characters were based on reality. However, the writers' intentions were not to write history nor to reproduce reality in details.[15] Nevertheless, an element of historical fact had to remain; otherwise, the novelist might not be able to hold the reader's interest. Dickens, Scott, Balzac, and Dostoevski owed much of their success to their ability to weave historical events into the plots of their stories. To construct a given period in narrative, particularly in historical novels, writers frequently used historical documents such as reports on the conditions of the working class.

Historians faced a different problem. To what extent could they use novels in their historical analysis? As with other documents, historians evaluated and judged documents depending on when, by whom, under what circumstances, and with what aim they were written.

In the case of literature, the writer's motivation in producing the work must be taken into consideration. In fiction, novelists give a personal interpretations of events and expose their feelings. Their points of view are admittedly, and often pointedly, not objective. Through language and imagination, situation, characters, events, moods are created, and by so doing, the author is consciously interpreting reality. But despite the element of imagination, the writers' visions are completely independent because they result from their particular historic, geographic, and socioeconomic situations as much as they are the products of personal creativity. Fact and fiction thus become closely related. It is precisely in attempting to unravel each element in a particular piece of work, that historians confront one of their most challenging tasks. While literature can and should be used as a valid source, its utility and value as historical testimony should be carefully considered.

From this perspective, for example, the nineteenth century realist and naturalist novels of Balzac and Zola are invaluable sources of perspectives of life, aesthetic values, class, and inter-class relations among that century's French society, confirming the view that literature serves as a tool for social analysis in a given period. There may be agreement that literature reflects the social and historical conditions in terms of the product (literary work) and the producer (writer). Yet what determines the recognition and acceptance of literary work as representative of a particular culture, period, and social group?[16]

Chicano Literature

This question is especially relevant in the case of Chicano literature. Because of ethnocentrism, some of the earliest references made to Mexicans in North American literature describe them as lazy, cowardly barbarians completely lacking in any kind of sophistication.[17] It is important to note that the image of the Mexican as inferior appears in American literature during the period prior to and during the 1848 Mexican-American War. One is led to conclude that such derogatory attitudes stem from propaganda favoring United States involvement in that war. By contrast, Anglo Americans are depicted as patriotic, intelligent, and above all, brave.[18] This propagandistic function of literature should not be ignored--it is precisely because of their role as vehicles for the diffusion of these and other sentiments that literary works have been acknowledged and considered representative of given periods. According to at least one Chicano writer, ideas conveyed through literature can penetrate the intellect and stimulate the emotions, senses, and imagination.[19]

Analyzing and evaluating the influence of literature on the social life of a given group is requisite to a proper assessment of literary works as historical sources.[20] With respect to Chicano literature, Chicanos themselves have been extremely conscious of how literary works may convey concepts and commentary on social conditions, work, family life and, above all, between their culture and that of Anglos.[21] Chicano writers readily acknowledge the potential of literary work to convey self-awareness and transmit cultural values. These two considerations have come to characterize the Chicano novel.[22] Moreover, Chicano novelists make concerted efforts to portray life in Chicano communities as accurately and realistically as possible. Does this explicit intention in the Chicano novel permit us to use it as an authentic alternative source in historical research?

The answer to this question leads us to the problem of historical objectivity. To claim that the Chicano novel tries to depict the conditions of Chicano communities faithfully does not necessarily mean that it succeeds. Claims of faithful representation are common to realistic and naturalistic novels and cannot be taken at face value. Nevertheless, such assertions cannot be dismissed on the grounds that fictional literature has no relation to history, since, we have seen, this is not so.

The historiographic use of literary works must take into account that while literature (even in its most realistic examples) makes no claim to total objectivity or truthfulness in the same way that an historical piece of work does, neither is it only a product of the imagination. Chicano writers often use personal experiences and real events as a basis for constructing the world in their novels. One must assume that the outcome is a literary product in which fact and fiction are so mixed as to become practically indistinguishable.[23] While the historian cannot cite a novel as if it were an historical document (for the intention in the two cases is different), the novel is historically valuable because it reflects a writer's view of society and culture, and provides useful insights into the conditions it describes. Thus, writers portray Chicano communities to give us their views of this life; these views reflect reality as the author sees it. Insofar as they are capable of communicating their vision to their audience, writers bear witness to their times and societies.[24]

The problem becomes more complex when the image of women in literature is involved, since most writers are males and few examples of women's writings are available. The difference in the gender of the author of a literary work is important. Women generally possess a more intimate vision of women's problems and a keener understanding of their own thought processes.[25] In spite of this difference, a literary work written by a man on women should not be summarily dismissed, since the author is trying to make a statement that can be subjected to interpretation and historiographic analysis.

The value of Chicano literature as a tool for historians does not end there. Through its portrayal of cultural conditions, traditions, mores, traits, and their effects on individuals, the Chicano novel becomes another source of information and insight into the prevalent moral beliefs of a culture. This point is important to women's history. Chicanas are the major transmitters of culture in their communities; writers can give us considerable information about their lives, domestic activities, their roles in society, and the way society views them. Enlightening information can be conveyed by a male writer's treatment of women's problems and thoughts, though he may also convey misconceptions. While limitations attributable to the writer's sex must be considered, the historical value of this type of novel should not be overlooked. Inaccuracies, inconsistencies, and contradictions concerning women are part of their complex, unexplored, and interesting history, and one may conclude that the search to unveil women's history can and should lead us to the use of literature as an alternative and complementary source.

Notes

1.   For a discussion of Mexican American stereotypes in the social science literature see Edward Casavantes, "Pride and Prejudice: A Mexican American Dilemma," in *Chicanos: Social and Psychological Perspectives*, edited by Carrol A. Hernandez, Marsha J. Haug, and Nathaniel N. Wagner (St. Louis: The C.V. Mosby Company, 1976), pp. 9-14. For research on value assimilation and behavior change among Mexican Americans see Lyle and Magdaline Shanon, *Minority Migrants in the Urban Community* (Beverly Hills: Sage Publications, 1973). For the media's caricature of Mexican Americans see Mario Obledo, "Mexican Americans and the Media," in *La Causa Chicana*, edited by Margaret M. Mangold (New York: Family Service Association of America, 1971), pp. 6-16.

2.   Associating Chicano culture with the culture of poverty is misleading and ignores complex sociocultural and economic relations between the Mexican American community and the predominant capitalist structure under which it exists.

3.   See Feliciano Rivera, "The Teaching of Chicano History," in *The Chicanos: Mexican American Voices*, edited by E. Ludwig and James Santibanez (Baltimore: Penguin Books, 1971), pp. 199-204. For a critique of cultural biases as reflected in the written works of California historians see Raymond V. Padilla, "A Critique of Pittian History," in *Voices*, edited by Octavio I. Romano-V (Berkeley: Quinto Sol Publications, 1971), pp. 65-106.

4.   Raul Guzman cited in Richard Vasquez, "Chicano Studies: Sensitivity for Two Cultures," in Ludwig and Santibanez, *The Chicanos*, p. 207. For a refutation by Mexican American social scientists of the Mexican American image projected by the social sciences see Reyes Ramos and Martha Ramos, "The Mexican American: Am I Who They Say I Am?" in *The Chicanos: As We See Ourselves*, edited by Arnulfo D. Trejo (Tucson: The University of Arizona Press, 1979), pp. 49-66.

5.   Gilberto López y Rivas, *Los chicanos: una minoría nacional explotada* (Mexico, D.F.: Editorial Nuestro Tiempo, 1971), p. 88.

6.   Sylvia Alicia Gonzales, "The Chicana Perspective: A Design for Self-Awareness," in *The Chicanos: As We See Ourselves*, p. 83.

7.   "La Chicana: The Brown Woman and Today's Struggle," in *The Chicanos: Life and Struggles of the Mexican Minority in the United States*, edited by Gilberto López y Rivas (New York: Monthly Review Press, 1973), pp. 168-174; and "On the Brown Women's Struggle!: Statement from the Brown Women's Venceremos Collective," in *The Chicanos: Life and Struggles*, pp. 171-174.

8.   See William Madsen, *The Mexican-Americans of South Texas* (New York: Holt, Rhinehart, and Winston, 1964). Misconceptions resulting from the portrayal of Chicanas as passive and submissive have influenced the work of educational, service-oriented, and law enforcement institutions which according to Sylvia Gonzales "have many times utilized these distorted pictures in developing programs to respond to the needs of the Chicana," see Gonzales, "The Chicana Perspective," p. 83.

9.   Ibid., p. 88.

10.   Mirta Vidal, *Chicanas Speak Out: Women, New Voice of La Raza* (New York: Pathfinder Press, 1971), p. 3.

11.   Despite the fact that some structuralist schools of literary analysis argue that literary work should only be analyzed in terms of its own internal structure, the relationship between literature and the society in which it is produced has been widely acknowledged.

12.   See Rafael Gutiérrez Girardot, "Teoría social de la literatura, esbozo de sus problemas," *Escritura: Teoría y crítica literaria* 1 (enero, junio 1976): 42.

13.   Though criticism of the time alledged that literary fiction served no real purpose because of its lack of realism, authors were concerned with reality and infused their work with

relevant facts whenever these would add credibility to their writings. Monroe Berger, *La novela y las ciencias sociales* (Mexico, D.F.: Fondo de Cultura Económica, 1979), pp. 285, 304-309.

14. For instance, though Henry Fielding, the author of *Tom Jones*, often used his work to make social and political comments in the prologues and notes of his works, these were clearly separated from the main text. Prologues were often used to make the reader participate in the novel's process of creation, but at the same time, continuously kept him/her informed of the author's opinions. Fielding considered these to be an indispensable part of his work, see Berger, *La novela*, pp. 211, 217, 307.

15. "El novelista al mezclar los datos con su imaginación, busca información para enterarse de una comunidad, un modo de vida o un individuo, pero inventa algo no obstante, para cambiar lo que ha aprendido o añadirle algo," see Berger, *La novela*, pp. 289, 293.

16. For a discussion on the methodological problems of the social theory of literature see Guitiérrez Girardot, *Escritura*, p. 42.

17. Cecil Robinson discusses the contempt of American writers toward the alledged Mexican indifference toward technological progress in *With the Ears of Strangers: The Mexican in American Literature* (Tucson: University of Arizona Press, 1969), p. 31.

18. Marcienne Rocard, *Les Fils du Soleil* (Paris: Maisonneuve et Larose, 1980), pp. 4-35.

19. In his discussion of the development of the Chicano novel, Trejo identifies *Pocho* as the precursor of the Chicano novel *sui generis* because it gives "insights into the social, economic and political conflicts that confront the Mexican American." See Trejo, "As We See Ourselves in Chicano Literature," in *The Chicanos: As We See Ourselves*, p. 200.

20. This, of course, is not an easy task. Careful consideration must be given to the author's literary intentions, accuracy, and the representativeness of his work in comparison to other similar works. For such purposes, anthropological studies could be very useful.

21. See Trejo, *The Chicanos: As We See Ourselves*, p. 199. Also see Jesús Rodriguez, "La busqueda de identidad y sus motivos en la literatura chicana," in *Chicanos: Antología, histórica y literaria*, comp. Tino Villanueva (Mexico, D.F.: Fondo de Cultura Económica, Colección Tierra Firme, 1980), pp. 200-208. When asked to identify the most outstanding qualities of Chicano

literature José Antonio Villareal commented: "There is really only one outstanding quality of Chicano literature and that is that it is informing the vast majority of Americans that there are Americans who look differently, live differently and who are lost to the rest of America, except the great agrarian corporations." See Juan Bruce Novoa, "Interview with José Antonio Villareal," *Revista Chicano-Riqueña* 4 (Spring 1976): 47.

22.   See, for instance, Juan Bruce Novoa, *Chicano Authors: Inquiry by Interview* (Austin: University of Texas Press, 1980).

23.   Though Mario Vargas Llosa has utilized in *La guerra del fin del mundo* elements and characters from the history of Canudos, he does not consider that novel to be an historical work. See Ignacio Solares, "Entrevista con Mario Vargas Llosa," *Vuelta* 1 (junio 1982): 26-29.

24.   Octavio Paz believes that the relation between literature and society is not a casual but a dialectical one in which literature expresses society and, thereby, changes it. See Octavio Paz, "América Latina y la democracia," *Vuelta* 1 (junio 1982): 38.

25. Harry Levin believes that the novel, as a genre, was always considered to be the domain of women. See his *El realismo francés: Stendhal, Zola, Proust* (Barcelona: Editorial Iliad, 1974), p. 48. With respect to Chicana literary writers, Arthur Ramírez makes a similar observation in "Estella Portillo: The Dialectic of Oppression and Liberation," *Revista Chicano-Riqueña* 8 (Summer 1980): 106-114. For treatment on the oversimplified images of women in Chicano literature see Judy Salinas, "The Image of Women in Chicano Literature," *Revista Chicano-Riqueña* 4 (Fall 1976):139-148. Salinas argues that "good" women are patterned after the Virgin Mary whereas "bad" women are patterned after Eve. For sources on Chicana women see Roberto Cabello-Argandoña, Juan Gómez-Quiñones, and Patricia Herrera Duran, *The Chicana: A Comprehensive Bibliographic Study* (Los Angeles: Chicano Studies Center Publications, University of California, 1975).

THE POLITICAL ECONOMY OF NINETEENTH CENTURY STEREOTYPES OF CALIFORNIANAS

by

Antonia I. Castañeda

Recent scholarship in Chicano and women's history has challenged the limited, stereotypic images of Mexicanos and women prevalent in the contemporary and historical literature of nineteenth century California and the American west.[1] In studying North American imperial expansion, Chicano and other scholars have concluded that perjorative, racist stereotypes of Mexicanos, in particular, were an integral part of an ideology that helped justify the Mexican-American War as well as subsequent repression in the conquered territory. One scholar persuasively argues that the notion of Manifest Destiny, which *a priori* assumed the inferiority of Mexicanos, was "the product of a campaign of ideological manipulation."[2]

In addition, studies in women's history, which tend to focus on the changing material reality and developing ideology of the United States, conclude that the constrictive, stereotypic molds into which women have been cast in the literature are sex and class based. The literature of the period was generally written by middle class, Anglo males who interpreted women's experience from their own gender and class perspective of women's proper roles. In this way, these authors created sexist and unidimensional protrayals of women. Recent work has shown that even in the literature of the American West--where greater sexual equality allegedly existed--women are stereotyped into four sexually

213

defined roles: gentle tamers, sunbonneted helpmates, hell-raisers and bad women.[3]

According to these studies, sexually defined stereotypes of women are rooted in the material changes which occurred in the nineteenth century when the United States was moving from an agricultural economy to mercantile capitalism. This transition from a pre-industrial economy physically removed the workplace from the household. In the process, many of women's traditional economic functions disappeared and the social relations of production were transformed. Women began to be defined primarily by their sexual function as reproducers of the species, and by the social roles ascribed to wife and mother. During the nineteenth century the view that women's proper place was in the home formed a central part of the ideology of an industrializing America--an ideology which came to enshrine women in the cult of true womanhood.[4]

However, these studies have not yet examined the portrayal of Mexican women and the relationship between stereotypes and ideology. Furthermore, these discussions have altogether ignored the intersection of sex, race and class in the development of America's ideology in the nineteenth century. Although Mexican women in California--Californianas--have never been the subject of any major historical work, they do appear in three kinds of North American literature which presents them in a contradictory, but nevertheless, stereotypic light. This literature--which spans both the nineteenth and twentieth centuries--includes contemporary travel, journalistic and biographical works; nineteenth and twentieth century novels; and general histories, both academic and popular, of California.[5]

This paper examines contemporary North American literature on early California and the stereotypes it presents of Mexican women.[6] The effort here is to examine the literature within the framework of mid-nineteenth century America's system of beliefs and ideas, and to suggest how the images of Mexicanas fit into that system. The discussion focuses on Richard Henry Dana's *Two Years Before the Mast* (1840), Thomas Jefferson Farnham's *Travels in California and Scenes in the Pacific Ocean* (1844) and Alfred Robinson's *Life in California* (1846). As an integral part of nineteenth century American, but particularly Californian, literary culture, these works have served as primary sources for historical, novelistic and popular accounts of provincial California. Dana and Robinson's works in particular have long influenced perceptions and interpretations of Mexicanos in California.

214

While the contemporary and historical literature purports to present accurate descriptions of Mexican women's experience and condition, it actually constructs stereotypic images which serve ideological purposes. The stereotypes manifest the polarities of "good" and "bad" women applied to women generally. This simplistic dichotomous portrayal is further complicated by stereotypical notions of gender, race and class. While these prejudices are evident in most accounts of Mexicanas, and while all the descriptions purport to present transhistorical or timeless images, the descriptions do, in fact, vary considerably across time in terms of the particular aspects of these stereotypes which are emphasized. These variations correlate with the changing needs of the capitalist and imperialist system, its shifting relations to Mexicano culture and economy in California and the evolving ideology of the nature of women.[7]

The earliest images of Mexican women in North American literature appeared in contemporary travel, journalistic and biographical accounts written in the 1830s and 1840s.[8] The authors were Anglo men--merchants, sailors and adventurers--engaged in the hide and tallow trade and/or America's westward expansion. Some arrived in the early 1820s when the newly independent Mexico opened its borders to foreign trade. They brought their wares from Boston to Valpariso to California. In this remote province, recently freed from the grasp of Spain's stringent regulations and mercantilist economic policies, Yankee and English traders found a ready market for the Chinese, European and American goods crammed into the holds of their ships. They soon established a brisk, lucrative trade, exchanging their cargo for hides and tallow, often at a 200 percent profit.[9]

The next two decades--the 1830s and 1840s were years of escalating conflict between the young Mexican Republic and an expanding United States. The conflict, which culminated in the Mexican-American War, raged hot and cold in California prior to the actual outbreak of war in 1846.[10] The three narratives discussed in this paper appeared during the height of this rising conflict.

Richard Henry Dana in *Two Years Before the Mast*, (published anonymously in 1840), presented the first major image of Mexican women in California. Dana, the scion of a cultivated patrician family in Cambridge, Massachussetts, sailed to California on the Pilgrim, a ship belonging to Bryant, Sturgis, and Company, the major American firm engaged in the hide and tallow trade. In this work, Dana recorded his experiences as a sailor as well as his

215

impressions of the country, the land and the people he saw on his journey during his two years aboard ship.

Dana has little to say of a positive nature about Mexican people in general. His views of Mexican women, which center on virtue, are moralistic and judgmental. According to Dana, "The fondness for dress among the women is excessive, and is sometimes their ruin. A present of a fine mantel, or a necklace or pair of earrings gains the favor of a greater part. Nothing is more common than to see a woman living in a house of only two rooms, with the ground for a floor, dressed in spangled satin shoes, silk gown, high comb, gilt if not gold, earrings and necklace. If their husbands do not dress them well enough, they will soon receive presents from others."[11] Therefore, Dana points out, "the women have but little virtue," and "their morality is, of course, none of the best." Although the "instances of infidelity are much less frequent than one would at first suppose," Dana attributes this to "the extreme jealousy and deadly revenge of their husbands."[12] To this Yankee patrician, Mexican women are profligate, without virtue and morals, whose excesses are only kept in check by a husband's vengeful wrath. In this narrative Mexican women are seen as purely sexual creatures.

Dana's work, which had immediate success in the United States and England, set the precedent for negative images of Mexican women in California. He created the image of Mexicanas as "bad" women. This condemnation of Mexican women's virtue appears again and again in subsequent works. The view of Mexicanas as women of easy virtue and latent infidelity easily led to the stereotype of the Mexicana as prostitute in the literature of the gold rush.

While Dana's writing attempted to convey the impression of an interested but rather detached objective observer of California's people and life, Thomas Jefferson Farnham's *Travels in California and Scenes in the Pacific Ocean*, published in 1844-45, was sensationalistic and vituperative. Farnham, a lawyer, came to California from Illinois by way of Oregon. He arrived in Monterey in 1841 and immediately took up the cause of Issac Graham and his band of sixty foreigners. Governor Alvarado had shipped the group to jail in Mexico on charges of conspiracy to overthrow the government.[13] Farnham described his travels on the Pacific Coast and detailed the Graham side of the political affair. Throughout his account Farnham consistently derided the Californianos. In his words, "the Californians are an imbecile, pusillanimous race of men, and unfit to control the destinies of that beautiful country."[14] In clear, direct and hostile terms, Farnham echoed the same sentiment that Dana and others had expressed with more subtlety, replacing passionate partisanship for the previous pretense of objectivity.

The Californiano's mixed racial background is a constant theme in Farnham's narrative. It is also the focus of his blunt comment on women, of whom he states "The ladies, dear creatures, I wish they were whiter, and that their cheekbones did not in their great condescension assimilate their manners and customs so remarkably to their Indian neighbors."[15] Unlike Dana, who was, at times, ambivalent about the racial characteristics and beauty of the elite Californianas, Farnham was clear about their racial origins and his own racial views.

Like Dana, Farnham was also concerned with the Californiana's dress and appearance. While Dana focused on the extravagance of dress, Farnham centered on the looseness of the clothing and the women's "indelicate" form. "A pity it is," notes Farnham, "that they have not stay and corset makers' signs among them, for they allow their waists to grow as God designed they should, like Venus de Medici, that ill-bred statue that had no kind mother to lash its vitals into delicate form."[16] Since Californian women do not lash their own or their daughter's "vitals into delicate form," they obviously are neither proper themselves nor are raising proper daughters for California. Farnham would have women's dress hide their form in the multiple layers of clothing that simultaneously hid the bodies of middle-class women in the United States and severely limited their physical mobility. Although Farnham made few additional direct statements about women, he did relate the woeful tale of a Southern lad's romance with a Californiana. The young man, who was ready to bequeath her all his worldly goods, was left bereft by the infidelity of his Californiana sweetheart.[17] For Farnham, whose work justified the fillibustering efforts of foreigners in California, Mexican women had no redeeming qualities.

Alfred Robinson, while no less concerned than Dana or Farnham with Californiana's virtue, morality, race and appearance, countered his countrymen's negative image by presenting the polar opposite view--albeit only of upper-class women--in his work, *Life in California*, published in 1846. Unlike Dana, who spent only a short time in California, or Farnham, who came in 1841, Robinson had been in California since 1829 and was on intimate terms with the Californianos. As resident agent for Bryant, Sturgis, and Company he had extensive business dealings with the province's largest landowners.[18]

In 1837, at the age of thirty, Robinson converted to Catholicism and married fourteen-year-old Ana Maria de la Guerra of the elite de la Guerra y Noriega family of Santa Barbara. The de la Guerras were one of the very few families in California who could truthfully claim Spanish ancestry. Life in California was written from the viewpoint of an observer who "sought to refute the inaccuracies of itinerant travelers like Dana."[19]

Robinson interspersed descriptions of women's physical appearance, dress, manners, conduct and spiritual qualities throughout his work.[20] In this book, Californianas are universally chaste, modest, virtuous, beautiful, industrious, wellbred aristocratic Spanish ladies. "With vice so prevalent amongst the men," Robinson states in his most explicit passage, "the female portion of the community, it is worthy of remark, do not seem to have felt its influence, and perhaps there are few places in the world where, in proportion to the number of inhabitants, can be found more chastity, industrious habits, and correct deportment, than among the women of this place."[21] Robinson defended the morals, virtue and racial purity of elite Californianas. By making racial and class distinctions among Californianas he transformed the image of immoral, bad and sexual women into the image of the sexually pure, good Californiana.

Dana and Farnham cast Mexican women into molds of the women of easy virtue, no morals and racial inferiority. Robinson cast elite Californianas into the stereotype of a genteel, well bred Spanish aristocrat with virtue and morals intact. Her European ancestry and aristocratic background, to say nothing of her economic value, made her worthy of marriage. Dana and Farnham, in their concern with the Californiana's race, virtue and morals set the parameters of the stereotype. Robinson accepted the parameters and addressed the same issues.

Recently, these nineteenth century narratives have attracted the attention of scholars and others working in Chicano, Women's, California and Southwestern history and culture. While Chicano historians and other scholars have noted the existence of contradictory stereotypes of women, few have examined the nature of these dual images. Generally, these scholars have attributed Mexicano stereotypes to historical Hispanophobia, anti-Catholicism, racial prejudice and to the economic and political issues involved in the Mexican-American War. More recently,

David Langum and Janet LeCompte have specifically addressed the image of Californianas and Nuevo Mexicanas in nineteenth century works written by Anglos.[22]

Langum, who recognizes the existence of contradictory views and their focus on the issues of morality and virtue, argues that the negative image was the minority view. And this image, he further argues, was class-based. That is, it not only derived from upper-class Yankees like Dana, but more importantly, the subjects of the image were lower-class Mexican women, the only group of Californianas with whom Dana, as a sailor, had any contact. According to Langum, Dana had neither access to nor interaction with upper-class women. He could not, like Robinson, form an opposite view, and therefore generalized his observations of lower-class Californianas to all women. Ignoring the sexist bias in these works, Langum not only attributes the dichotomous images of Californianas to the class prejudice of the writers and the class origin of the subjects, he further assumes that the stereotypes were accurate for lower-class women.[23]

While class was most certainly an issue in the development of dichotomous stereotypes of women, Langum's argument does not entirely hold up. Although Dana was not, like Robinson, on intimate terms with the Californiano elite, he did have the opportunity to observe them at close hand, and on occasion, he attended their social functions. In fact, he attended the festivities and dance celebrating Robinson's marriage to Ana Maria de la Guerra. As he develops it, Langum's class explanation is merely an extension of Cecil Robinson's earlier interpretation of pejorative Mexicano stereotypes in American travel literature immediately preceding the Mexican-American War.[24] Robinson argued that Anglos formed a mistaken perception of all Mexicanos on the basis of contact with relatively few Mexicans in the border area. This interpretation has been challenged and refuted as the basis for the development of stereotypes of the Mexicanos.[25]

LeCompte, whose main interest is the independence of Nuevo Mexicanas during Mexico's Republican period, also notes Anglo writers' comments about the dark skin of New Mexican women, their idleness, boldness of demeanor, revealing clothing and deplorably low standards of female chastity. She attributes Anglos' negative views of the Nuevo Mexicana's morality to the sexism inherent in Anglo norms for proper female behavior. And these norms, LeCompte continues, were conditioned by the more constrictive position of women in North American society and culture, and by the corollary view of womanhood as the upholder and symbol of American morality. Unfortunately, LeCompte does not develop the argument. The article is devoted to an exposition of the economic and social independence of New Mexican women; it generalizes about the nature of their independence without substantive research.[26]

Despite the limitations of Langum and LeCompte's work, both essays are suggestive and raise the issue of class, women's economic dislocation and sexism as relevant to American stereotyping of Mexican women.[27] However, for the historian attemtping to reconstruct the history of Mexican women in nineteenth century California, the ideological and historical significance of these particular dichotomous stereotypes remains to be clearly confronted.

My research leads me to concur with the conclusions of earlier studies that nineteenth century North American literature on California expressed an ideological perspective reflecting an economic interest in California, that the stereotypes of Mexicanos, including those of women, functioned as instruments of conquest, and thus served the political and economic interests of an expanding United States.[28] However, I would further argue that the stereotypes of women were not static; they changed across time--from the pre-War period, through the War, the gold rush and the late Victorian era.[29] The changing images of Mexicanas in California, I further assert, were consistent with the economic and socio-political needs of a changing U.S. capitalist and imperialist system.

Initially, the pejorative images of Mexican people, which derived from the authors' firm belief in Anglo America's racial, moral, economic and political superiority, served to devalue the people occupying a land base the United States wanted to acquire--through purchase if possible, by war if necessary. The values of supremacy, including male supremacy, expressed in the creation of negative stereotypes and embedded in the notion of Manifest Destiny, were central to America's ideology--an ideology based on the exclusion of non-whites from the rights and privileges of American democratic principles and institutions. Thus, the early negative stereotypes of Mexican people focused on their racial characteristics and alleged debased condition. These stereotypes appeared regardless of class or circumstance of the writers. Their writings uniformly portrayed the same image of Mexicanos whether the latter were encountered in the Mexican interior or in Mexico's northernmost provinces.[30]

The material basis of nineteenth century racist ideology and stereotypes of Mexicanos has been addressed by other scholars. However, these stereotypes have not been examined specifically within the framework of an ideology in transition.[31] Nor have these studies examined ideas about women in America's ideological structure, or the stereotypes of women in relation to war, conquest and ideology. In short, the dimension of sex, as well as the interaction of sex, race and class have been ignored. In this regard I would argue the following four points: (1) nineteenth century stereotypes of Mexican women revolved around the issue of women's virtue and morality; (2) these stereotypes were both sexually and racially defined; (3) judgments of Mexicanas' morality were one of the indices used to judge the moral fiber of the Mexican people; and (4) women's economic value and class position in California were pivotal to the dichotomous stereotypes cast in the 1840s and varied across time.

In addition to its racial bias, American ideology of the mid-nineteenth century reflected the economic, social and cultural changes attendant in the transition from commercial to industrial capitalism and the nation's concomitant movement towards continental imperialism. Certain aspects of America's ideology were in process of reformulation as values consistent with changing economic and social relationships increasingly being shaped by the entrepreneurial and rising industrial classes. Among the most important ideological reformulations accompanying the economic transformation was the redefinition of the role and position of women in American society.[32]

The changing image of Mexican women, I contend, derived from America's unfolding system of beliefs and ideas about sex and race, as well as about economic and political expansion. With reference to Mexicanas, these images functioned on two levels: first, as rationalization for war and conquest and, second, as rationalization for the subordination of women.

In the mid-nineteenth century, capitalist ideology was defining womenhood in terms of specific gender roles that excluded the dimension of economic production. Women's social worth was increasingly constricted within proscribed norms around her home, her only power base. A women's value and power were determined by possession and exhibition of certain cardinal virtues: piety, purity, submissiveness and domesticity. All four virtues were central to a woman's moral strength and character that were largely judged by her sexual conduct. With sexual purity her only form of power and the home her only sphere of

221

influence, womankind was now only supposed to produce children and a moral, virtuous culture, a culture she inculcated in her progeny along with the appropriate gender roles.[33] Thus, in the developing bourgeois ideology, the American woman held her country's morality in her hands. By the mid 1840s, when Anglo Americans were publishing their impressions of California, ideas and definitions of women's role derived from the ethos of the bourgeois class whose hegemony extended to the definition and production of culture. Within that culture, women were expected to act within the proscribed norms of what one scholar has called "the cult of true womanhood.[34]

Although the image of woman sheltered from the competition of the marketplace was generally appropriate only for middle-class women, by the mid-nineteenth century the notion of woman as the purveyor of a people's morality was being applied to all women in general. The American woman became the symbol of the country's innocence, morality, and virtue; she was held almost solely responsible for the morality and virtue of the nation. Thus, in the 1840s, women's value was not only determined by her newly defined gender-specific roles, but she represented the moral strength of her country.[35] This view of women was part of the ideological framework within which North American authors, most of whom were from the middle class, perceived, interpreted and judged the Mexican female in California.

Anglo American male writers assigned to Mexican women the same social value based on gender specific norms and roles they assigned to white womanhood in the United States. However, for Mexican women, the dimension of race was also integral to the judgment of their virtue and morality. Nineteenth century Anglo Americans' views of Mexican people as racially inferior are well-documented and need not be elaborated here.[36] What does need to be understood is that in terms of women, America's racial bias against Mexicanos coalesced with the moral judgment of women and hardened into a stereotype of Mexicanas as both racially and morally inferior, with one reinforcing the other in a most pernicious way. In her study of Nuevo Mexicanas, Le Compte further underscores this point by arguing that Anglo "... visitors from the land of the double standard, blamed New Mexicans' sexual freedom entirely on women."[37] Thus, the most salient stereotype of Mexicanas in the pre-War literature is that of the racially inferior sexual creature--the "bad" woman of easy virtue and no morality.[38] In America's ideological framework, racially inferior people found wanting in moral strength deserved to lose their country. Stereotypes of Mexican women's morality not only encompassed both the sexual and racial dimensions, but were also the basis for moral judgments about Mexican people as a whole.

While Anglo women in industrializing North America were being economically displaced and entombed in the virtues of domesticity, Mexican women in agro-pastoral California were an economic asset. Hispanic law protected women's property rights and gave them equal inheritance rights with males. Mexicanas held an economic power their North American sisters were rapidly losing.[39] Mexican women's economic significance did not escape the Anglos' perception or appropriation; and it clearly affected the creation of a new image--a counter to the pejorative stereotype of the "bad" woman.

From the mid 1820s to the end of Mexican rule, a number of intermarriages between elite Californianas and Anglo males were celebrated in California.[40] Most of the Anglos who married Californianas prior to the North American occupation acquired land through their marriage. The land grants often became the basis for vast wealth.

Californiana-Anglo marriages were occurring at the moment that commercial capitalism of international proportions was penetrating the developing agro-pastoral economy of Alta California.[41] The nascent economy, based on the rise of private property and the corollary rise of an elite *ranchero* class of large landowners, was tied through the hide and tallow trade to European, Latin American and North American markets. Manufactured goods and products from these markets were being rapidly introduced into this remote Mexican province.[42] At the same time, Mexican women, particularly elite women, held significant economic power as large property owners in their own right, as conveyors of property to others, and as consumers in a nascent but expanding market.[43] Most of the Anglos who married Californianas were merchants and traders who were directly related to the development of commerce in California. Marriage to an elite Californiana, in addition to landed wealth, also established family and kinship ties with the largest Californiano landowners.[44] Marriage solidified class alliances between Anglo merchants and the Californiano elite, who were jointly establishing control of California's economy. The image of Californianas as "good" women emerged from these marriages and economic alliances on the eve of the Mexican-American War.

The positive image portraying Mexican women as aristocratic, virtuous Spanish ladies directly contradicted the negative view of

Californianas--but it did so by singling out elite Californianas, denying their racial identity, and treating them as racially superior to Californiano males and the rest of their people. Further, the new, positive image was no less a stereotype than the negative portrayal. With few exceptions, women in California, including women of the elite *ranchero* class, were neither Spanish nor aristocratic by birth. They, like their male counterparts, were of mixed-blood or *mestizo* origin. Whether of military or *poblador* (settler) families, their grandparents or parents migrated to California from the impoverished classes of Mexico's Northern frontier provinces.[45] Further, the positive portrayal of these elite women in the literature of the 1840s did not extend to the Californiano male, including the male members of the women's families. In this literature, while the women were transformed into Spanish ladies the men remained Mexicans.[46]

While the accounts written by Anglo husbands of elite Californianas attempted to refute the pejorative images of Californiana womanhood, both sets of writing treated Californiano males in equally contemptuous, racist terms.[47] Thus, although the corrective image made racial and class distinctions in its treatment of women, it did not make the same distinctions in its treatment of males.[48] In the corrective literature, elite and non-elite Californiano males were viewed as racially inferior, and the *rancheros'* class aspirations (*hidalgismo*) were ridiculed. In Europeanizing Californiana *mestizas* and *mulatas* and proclaiming them industrious, moral and chaste, the corrective image justified and rationalized the union of a racially, morally superior Anglo man to a woman of an inferior racial and moral stock. Robinson's Europeanization of Californianas fulfilled Thomas Jefferson Farnham's racist wish that: "the ladies, dear creatures," be made whiter. Finally, the new image transformed elite Californianas into the epitome of the ideal woman enshrined in the cult of True Womanhood. Once the conquest was at hand, the portrayal of Californianas shifted from a negative to a positive image and severed her from her racial, cultural and historical reality.

In this paper I have tried to outline the sexual, racial and economic dimensions of the dichotomous images of Mexican women by focusing on three narratives which defined the stereotypes. I have suggested that this literature and the stereotypes it presents reflected an ideology which not only excluded non-whites from American principles and institutions, but that the stereotypes of women, which represent the intersection of sex, race and class, functioned as instruments of

224

imperialism, conquest and subordination. I will conclude this paper by discussing more precisely how the literary images of Mexican women in California derived from and served the ideological interests of the changing political economy in the United States.

The stereotypes of Californianas cast in the early 1840s, coincident with the period leading to and encompassing the Mexican-American War, presented the polarities of the "bad" and "good" stereotypes of Mexicanas in California.[49] The former set the precedent for pejorative stereotypes of Mexicanas in the North American mind. The latter effectively separated elite women from their history, gave them a new history, and thus made them acceptable to Americans. Both stereotypes revolved around sexual definitions of women's virtue and morality. Both dealt with race but with a crucial difference. The elite Californianas were deemed European and superior while the mass of Mexican women were viewed as Indian and inferior. On the other hand, the contemporary literature, which other scholars have concluded played an ideological role in the justification of war, contained negative images of Mexican women who were seen as caretakers of their own and their peoples' morality.[50] These images formed part of the belief and idea system that rationalized the war and dispossession of the land base. On the other hand, the positive image of Californianas, who were also considered caretakers of morality, legitimized Anglos' marriage to them and provided the necessary validity for their new roles as American wives and mothers. The positive image facilitated the assimilation of these upper-class women into American society.[51]

As the United States consolidated its conquest of California and the Southwest in the post-War period, the negative and positive images of Mexicanas and Californianas hardened into stereotypes of the Mexican prostitute and the romantic, but fading Spanish beauty that still plague us today. In the literature of the gold rush the negative views of women's morality were generalized to Mexicanas and Latinas who migrated to California during the period. These views found continued expression in the almost singular depiction of Mexicanas/Latinas as fandango dancers, prostitutes and consorts of Mexican bandits.[52] The pejorative stereotype of Mexicanas as women of easy virtue was cemented into the image of the volatile, sensuous, Mexican prostitute. It is significant that Juanita (Josefa) of Downieville, the only woman hanged during the gold rush era, was Mexicana. For her, the image, the beliefs and the ideas that manufactured them, had dire consequences.[53]

The commonly advanced notion that women, due to their scarcity in the Mother Lode, were afforded moral, emotional and physical protection and respect by Anglo miners, does not hold for Mexican women.[54] Mexicanas, as part of the conquered nation, and as part of the group of more knowledgeable, experienced and initially successful miners competing with Anglos in the Placers, became one object of the violence and lawlessness directed against Mexicanos/Latinos. Mexican women's gender did not protect them from the brutality of racism or the rapacity attendant in the competition for gold. Virulent anti-Mexican sentiment combined with economic interest led to the First Foreign Miners' Tax of 1849, which technically levied a tax on all foreign miners but was inspired by the desire to eliminate Mexican competition from the mines.[55] For Mexicanas in the gold rush era, the combined force of sexism, racism and economic interest resulted in a hardening of pejorative stereotypes which further impugned their sex and their race.

The image of the woman of easy virtue, firmly fixed in the literature in the years preceeding the war, easily transformed into the Mexican prostitute. It further helped to justify the exclusion of Mexicanos/Latinos from the mines and rationalized their subordination in California. With specific reference to women but also inclusive of men, the literature of the post-War/gold rush era further cemented the earlier shift that divided Mexican women along racial and class lines.

Negative stereotypes of women from the post-War period to the end of the nineteenth century were specifically applied to Mexicanas and Latinas who migrated to California from Mexico and Latin America. Newspaper accounts make a distinction between Mexicanas/Latinas and Californianas. Mexicanas are prostitutes and would remain so for the rest of the century-- Californianas are not.

In the literature of the late nineteenth century, Robinson's positive image of Californianas as aristocratic Spanish ladies was picked up, further elaborated and generalized to women living in California prior to the Mexican-American War. And in the pre-War period, now romanticized as the "splendid idle forties," and the "halcyon days of long ago," Californianas are depicted as gentle reposing souls sweetly attending to the sublime domestic duties of ministering to large households of family and Indian servants on their *caballero* husband's baronial estate. If single, these gay and beautiful Spanish *senoritas* are in a constant flurry

226

of girlish activity and preparation for the next *fiesta* and the next beau--a dashing American, of course.[56]

The important point here is that this image not only negates Californianas' *mestizo* racial origins, ignores or denies the existence of any kind of work and assigns them all the attributes of "True Womanhood," it also locates their existence in a remote, bygone past. They were, but they no longer are. In this representation, the Mexican prostitute and the Spanish Californiana are totally unrelated by race, culture, class, history or circumstance. In the former there is immorality, racial impurity, degradation and contemporary presence. In the latter there is European racial origins, morality, cultural refinement and historical distance.

Irrespective of the view, the end result was the same. Mexicana or Californiana, both representations rended women in California ignorant, vacuous and powerless. In both cases, her Catholicism and culture made her priest-ridden, male dominated, superstitious and passive. Undemocratic Spanish and Mexican governance made her ignorant. If Mexicana, however, her immorality and racial impurity established her lack of value and exacerbated her ignorance. As part of the conquered Mexican nation, the War confirmed her powerlessness. If Californiana, on the other hand, her racial pruity, morality and economic worth elevated her status, making her worthy of marrying an Anglo while dispossessing her of her racial, historical, cultural and class roots. With marriage and a husband's possession of her property, elite Californianas forefeited their economic power. Finally, the Californiana's presence was abstracted to an era long past, her person romanticized. In either case, Mexicana or Californiana, the conquest was complete.

In removing Californianas and their existence from the present, North American writers and their public could rationalize the violence perpetrated against Mexicanos throughout the post-War period to the end of the nineteenth century. One scholar attributes the romanticization of the Californianos--for the romantic, nostalgic view now reincoporated males--to the sympathy the victor has for the vanquished.[57] I would argue that the nostalgic, romantic stereotype of the Californianos projected in late nineteenth century literature served specifically to rationalize the dispossession of the elite *ranchero* class.

Finally, the early narratives which set the parameters for the dichotomous images of Mexican women were written during the brief Republican period of Mexican California. Yet, these dual images have become the standard view of Californianas for the entire nineteenth century in the historical, as well as the novelistic, poetic and popular literature. The dichotomous stereotypes cast in the 1840s have not only frozen Mexican women into a specific, exceedingly narrow time frame and effectively obscured her historical reality for the nineteenth century, they have also exacerbated the notion of discontinuity between nineteenth and twentieth century Mexican women and their history.[58]

In view of the consistency of the stereotypes, Mexican women appear not to have an historical presence prior to the 1840s, and to exist only as romantic, but fading Spanish beauties after the Mexican-American War. By the turn of the century, Californianas, like their brethren, cease to exist historically. Within this perspective there is no continuity with women prior to the 1840s, nor any room for continuity between Mexicanas who were here during the 1840s and those who migrated from Mexico during the gold rush or who were part of the Mexican migration in the latter part of the century. In the literature, Mexican women's historical existence is defined out of all but a few short years of the nineteenth century. Her historical presence is confined to the 1840s and left to the assumptions, perceptions and interests of Anglo-American entrepreneurs and filibusters who wrote about California in a period of American continental imperialism that resulted in the Mexican-American War.

Notes

1. For an important historiographical essay see Juan Gómez-Quiñones and Luis L. Arroyo, "On the State of Chicano History: Observations on its Development, Interpretations and Theory, 1970-1974," *Western Historical Quarterly* 7 (April 1976): 155-185. For a general survey of Chicano history see Rodolfo Acuña, *Occupied America: A History of Chicanos*, 2nd ed. (New York: Harper & Row, 1981). For theoretical interpretations see Tomas Almaguer, *Interpreting Chicano History: The "World-System" Approach to 19th Century California* (Berkeley: Institute for the Study of Social Change, Working Paper Series, no. 101, University of California, 1977) and Mario Barrera, *Race and Class in the Southwest* (Notre Dame: University of Notre Dame Press, 1979). For a discussion of the economic motives behind the Mexican-American War see Glen W. Price, *Origins of the War with Mexico:*

The Polk-Stockton Intrigue (Austin: University of Texas Press, 1967). For a description of the Mexican-American War in California and subsequent displacement of Mexicanos see Leonard Pitt, *The Decline of the Californios: A Social History of the Spanish-Speaking Californians, 1846-1890* (Berkeley: University of California Press, 1970). For a discussion of post-war displacement in a specific California community see Albert Camarillo, *Chicanos in a Changing Society: From Mexican Pueblos to American Barrios in Santa Barbara and Southern California, 1848-1930* (Cambridge: Harvard University Press, 1979). For specific discussion and varied analysis of stereotypes of Mexicanos in North American literature see James H. Lacy, "New Mexico Women in Early American Writings," *New Mexico Historical Review* 34 (1959); James Hart, *American Images of Spanish California* (Berkeley: Friends of the Bancroft Library, 1960); Cecil Robinson, *With the Ears of Strangers: The Mexican in American Literature* (Tucson: University of Arizona Press, 1963); Beverly Trulio, "Anglo American Attitudes Toward New Mexican Women," *Journal of the West* 12 (1973): 229-239; Harry Clark, "Their Pride, Their Manners, and Their Voices: Sources of the Traditional Portrait of Early Californians," *California Historical Review* 52 (Spring 1974): 71-82; Raymond A. Paredes, "The Mexican Image in American Travel Literature, 1831-1869," *New Mexico Historical Review* 52 (January 1977): 5-59; Raymond Paredes, "The Origins of Anti-Mexican Sentiment in the United States," *New Scholar* 6 (1977): 139-165; Doris L. Meyer, "Early Mexican American Responses to Negative Stereotyping," *New Mexico Historical Review* 53 (January 1978) 75-91; David Langum, "California Women and the Image of Virtue," *Southern California Quarterly* 59 (Fall 1977): 245-250; David J. Weber, "'Scarce More than Apes': Historical Roots of Anglo-American Stereotypes of Mexicans," in *New Spain's Far Northern Frontier*, ed. David J. Weber (Albuquerque: University of New Mexico Press, 1979), pp. 293-304; Janet LeCompte, "The Independent Women of Hispanic New Mexico, 1821-1846," *Western Historical Quarterly* 12 (January 1981): 17-35.

2. Barrera, in *Race and Class in the Southwest*, p. 12, is one of the few scholars who discusses manifest destiny specifically in terms of ideology. Hart, Paredes and Clark discuss American attitudes and the literature in terms of justification and rationalization for war and dispossession but do not fully develop an ideological interpretation. See also Ronald Takaki, *Iron Cages:*

Race and Culture in 19th-Century America (New York: Alfred A. Knopf, 1979).

3. For an excellent series of historiographical essays see Part I: Historiography on Women, in *Liberating Women's History: Theoretical and Critical Essays*, ed. Berenice A. Carroll (Urbana: University of Chicago Press, 1976), pp. 1-92. See also Ann D. Gordon, Mari Jo Buhle, and Nancy Schrom Dye, *Women in American History* (Somerville: New England Free Press) an undated pamphlet of an article first published in *Radical America* 5 (July-August 1971); Barbara Sicherman, "Review Essay: American History," *Signs: Journal of Women in Culture and Society* 5 (1975): 461-485; Joan M. Jensen and Darlis A. Miller, "The Gentle Tamers Revisited: New Approaches to the History of Women in the American West," *Pacific Historical Review* 44 (May 1980): 173-213. For treatment of specific themes see Julie Roy Jeffrey, *Frontier Women: The Trans-Mississippi West, 1840-1880* (New York: Hill & Wang, 1979); Angela Y. Davis, *Women, Race, and Class* (New York: Random House, 1981); Alice Kessler-Harris, *Women Have Always Worked* (New York: The Feminist Press, 1981), pp. 2-101; Carolyn Ware, "Introduction" in *Class, Sex and the Woman Worker*, eds. Milton Cantor and Bruce Laurie (Westport, Conn.: Greenwood Press, 1979), pp. 3-19.

4. Ann D. Gordon et. al., *Women in American History*; Ann D. Gordon and Mari Jo Buhle, "Sex and Class in Colonial and Mid 19th-Century America," in *Liberating Women's History*, pp. 278-300; Barbara Welter, "The Cult of True Womanhood," *The American Quarterly* 18 (1966): 151-174; Barbara Welter, *Dimity Convictions* (Athens: Ohio University Press, 1976).

5. While there is as yet no major historical study of Mexican women in California several conference papers have made important contributions to the developing scholarship. See Anita Abascal, "Parteras, Llaveras y Maestras: Women in Provincial California," paper presented at the Conference of the West Coast Association of Women Historians, Los Angeles, California, May, 1976; Helen Lara Cea, "Preliminary Conclusions in the Reconstruction of Chicana History in San Jose, 1777-1850," (revised version in this volume); and Cynthia Orozco, "Mexican Elite Women in the 19th-Century: Work, Social Life, and Intermarriage," paper presented at "Mexicana/Chicana Women's History Symposium," Santa Monica, California, March 1982; Gloria E. Miranda, "Family Patterns and the Social Order in Hispanic Santa Barbara, 1784-1848" (Ph.D. diss., University of

Southern California, 1978); and Langum "Image of Virtue," pp. 245-250.

6. The three nineteenth century works treated in this paper are Richard Henry Dana, Jr., *Two Years Before the Mast* (New York: Harper & Brothers, 1840; reprint ed., New York: Airmont Publishing Company, Inc., 1965); Thomas Jefferson Farnham, *Travelers in California and Scenes in the Pacific Ocean* (New York: Saxton & Miles, 1844; reprint ed., Oakland: Biobooks, 1947); and Alfred Robinson, *Life in California* (New York: Wiley & Putnam, 1846; reprint ed., Santa Barbara: Peregrine Press, Inc., 1970).

7. While this analysis is largely based on my close reading of the contemporary literature, I also drew upon the theoretical analysis in Davis, *Women, Race, and Class*; Gordon et. al., *Women in American History*; Gordon and Buhle, "Sex and Class in Colonial and Mid 19th-Century America"; and Marion S. Goldman *Gold Diggers and Silver Miners: Prostitution and Social Life in the Comstock Lode* (Ann Arbor: University of Michigan Press, 1981).

8. See note 6.

9. Pitt, *Decline of the Californios*, p. 12. For the development of commerce in California see Hubert Howe Bancroft, *History of California* (San Francisco: H.H. Bancroft & Company, 1885), vol. 2, chapters 13 and 19; vol. 3, chapters 5 and 13. For private *ranchos* to 1830 see Bancroft, *History of California*, vol. 2, p. 63 and footnote 24, p. 63. For development of the hide and tallow trade see Bancroft, *History of California*, vol. 2, p. 668. For presence of foreign residents in California, see Bancroft *History of California*, vol. 3, chapter 6. For land and private *ranchos* see W.W. Robinson, *Land in California* (Berkeley: University of California Press, 1949; paperback edition, 1979), chapters 4-6.

10. Pitt, *Decline of the Californios*, pp. 26-27.

11. Dana, *Two Years Before the Mast*, p. 66.

12. Ibid., p. 136.

13. Pitt, *Decline of the Californios*, p. 20.

14. Farnham, *Travels in California*, p. 148.

15. Ibid.

16. Ibid.

17. Ibid., p. 23-24.

18. A. Robinson, *Life in California*, pp. v-xii.

19. Ibid., p. vii; See also Langum, "Image of Virtue," p. 246.

20. A. Robinson, *Life in California*, pp. 13, 30, 32, 37, 41, 50, 51, 62.

21. Ibid., p. 51.

22. See note 3 for citation of studies dealing with nineteenth century narratives and their portrayal of Mexicanos including articles that focus on women. See note 5 for citations of articles specifically treating Mexican women in nineteenth century California.

23. Langum, "Image of Virtue," pp. 245-250.

24. Cecil Robinson, *With the Ears of Strangers.*

25. See Paredes, "Origins of Anti-Mexican Sentiment"; Paredes, "The Mexican Image"; and Weber, "'Scarce More than Apes.'"

26. LeCompte, "Independent Women," pp. 17-35.

27. See also Trulio, "Attitudes Towards Mexican Women," pp. 229-239.

28. Almaguer, *Interpreting Chicano History*, pp. 10-16; Barrera, *Race and Class in the Southwest*, pp. 7-33; and Weber, "'Scarce More than Apes,'" pp. 293-304.

29. The statement is based on my close reading of the contemporary literature.

30. For a discussion of racial stereotypes see Paredes, "The Mexican Image"; Paredes, "Origins of Anti-Mexican Sentiment"; and Weber, "'Scarce More than Apes.'"

31. See Barrera, *Race and Class in the Southwest*; and Acuña, *Occupied America.* Both works address the material basis of racism.

32. Gordon and Buhle, "Sex and Class"; Gordon et.al., *Women in American History*; Kessler-Harris, *Women Have Always Worked*, pp. 22-51.

33. Gordon and Buhle, "Sex and Class," pp. 283-288; Welter, "The Cult of True Womanhood," pp. 151-174; and Welter, *Dimity Convictions.*

34. Welter, "The Cult of True Womanhood."

35. Ibid.

36. Paredes, "Origins of Anti-Mexican Sentiment," pp. 139-165; Weber, "'Scarce More Than Apes'"; and Hart, *American Images of Spanish California.*

37. LeCompte, "Independent Women," p. 22.

38. This portrayal of Mexicanas is typical of Dana's *Two Years Before the Mast*, and Farnham's *Travels in California.*

39. E. N. Van Kleffens, *Hispanic Law* (Edinburgh: Edinburgh University Press, 1968).

40. My research on intermarriage is in the early stages. From the secondary literature we only know about a few of the more

publicized marriages between Californianas and Anglos, including the following:

1820 - Maria Lugarda Castro to Thomas Doak
1822 - Guadalupe Ortega to Joseph Chapman
1825 - Teresa de la Guerra y Noriega to William Edward Petty Hartnell
1825 - Josefa Carrillo (San Diego) elopement and marriage to Captain Henry Delano Fitch
1827 - Marcelina Estudillo to Captain William A. Gale
1829 - Josefa Carrillo (Santa Barbara) to Captain William Goodwin Dana
1831 - Maria Francisca Butron to William Robert Garner
1837 - Ana Maria de la Guerra y Noriega to Alfred Robinson
1847 - Maria Estudillo to William Heath Davis, Jr.

Also married before the North American occupation were:
Arcadia Bandini to Abel Stearns
Rosalia Vallejo to Jacob Leese
Adelaida Estrada to David Spence
Encarnacion Vallejo to John Rodgers Cooper.

41. Almaguer, "Interpreting Chicano History," pp. 10-16; Andrew Rolle, "Introduction" to Robinson, *Life in California*, pp. vi-ix, p. xi, he notes that "Robinson's generation helped to provide the precedents for Americanizing California," p. xi.

42. See note 9.

43. Mexican Archives, Civil Records, 1821-1848, Office of the Monterey County Clerk, Salinas, California, Volumes 6-16. My research in these archives reveals that Mexican women were engaged in various kinds of property transactions in the Monterey District. Preliminary research reveals that these transactions included 25 petitions for and awards of land; 6 suits for rights of succession; 5 civil suits regarding property; 3 sales of houses; 2 transactions regarding ownership of herds of horses; one woman used property as a dowery; and 3 petitioned for and received cattle/horse brands. I have not calculated the acreage involved.

My research of probate records in Monterey County has yielded few wills left by women in Spanish/Mexican California. However, in the three wills that I have located, the women all left property to family members. Bowman, who defines prominence for women as property ownership, uses the records of the private land grant cases before the Board of Land Commissioners to discuss women property owners in provincial California. He located sixty-six women grantees who were directly or indirectly connected with the provincial land grants and listed twenty-two women who "carried the operation through from concession to patent for over 355,000 acres of land, or over 41 percent of the patented land grants to women." See J.N. Bowman, "Prominent Women of Provincial California," *Historical Quarterly of Southern California* 39 (June 1957): 149-166.

44. Rolle, "Introduction," to Robinson, *Life in California*, p. vii refers specifically to Robinson, but the same generalization applies to Anglos marrying into the Bandini, Carrillo, Castro, Estudillo, Pico, and Vallejo families, who along with the de la Guerras, were large landowners and politically powerful. See also Henry Lynch, "Six Families: A Study of the Power and Influence of the Alvarado, Carrillo, Castro, de la Guerra, Pico, and Vallejo Families in California, 1769-1846," (Master's thesis, California State University, Sacramento, 1977).

45. The census and mission registers recording population, births, marriages and deaths during the Spanish period clearly indicate the racial (for both men and women) and class (occupations, for men only) origins of the people who came as military personnel or as settlers. While people often elevated their racial status in these records by designating themselves "Español" even though it was physically evident that they were of mixed blood, the records nevertheless reveal the population was largely *mestizo*, which included various racial mixtures. The following list of census records includes only those censuses which listed race and/or occupation for the Monterey District. Unless otherwise indicated these records are all in the Bancroft Library, Provincial State Papers, Benicia Military: Real Presidio de Monterey, Lista de la compañía del referido presidio, 30 julio de 1782, Vol. IV, pp. 663-694; Lista de la compañía, 23 mayo de 1791, Vol. XV, pp. 10-12; Lista de los individuos de esta jurisdicción que se consideran aptos para el servicio en la compañía de milicia ... que se hallen en este presidio, 1805, Monterey; Padrón del Real Presidio de Monterey, 1816, vol. 49, p. 894; Mission of San Carlos Borromeo, *Book of Marriages*, Vol. 1, 1772-1855 (Monterey: Archdiocese of Monterey). The Book of Marriages that researchers work with at the Archdiocese is a photocopy of the original *Libro de matrimonios*.

46. Hart, *American Images of Spanish California*, pp. 21-22.

47. Langum, "Image of Virtue," p. 246.

48. Robinson, *Life in California*. A dichotomized view of Californianos and Californianas runs throughout Robinson's book. See also, Clark, "Their Pride, Their Manners and Their Voices," who states "... many writers commented on the cruelty of the

Spanish spurs. The tradition has had to allow the Californians a streak of cruelty, so that a picture of an oddly dichotomized society of tender-hearted women and bestial men has sometimes appeared in the Californians created by later writers, and this dichotomy may be inferred from the passages on each sex in *Life in California*"; and Pitt, *Decline of the Californios*, pp. 15, 17.

49. Dana, *Two Years Before the Mast*; Farnham, *Travels in California*; Robinson, *Life in California*.

50. See Barrera, *Race and Class in the Southwest*, p. 12; Paredes, "Origins of Anti-Mexican Sentiment"; Paredes, "The Mexican Image"; and Clark, "Their Pride, Their Manners, and Their Voices."

51. Historically, through intermarriage, common law marriage or concubinage, women have been central to the process of assimilation and acculturation of the conquered group. Often the first level of this process occurs among the elite of both societies, or at least between the elite of the conquered society and the earliest arrivals of the conquering group. The issue of Californianas and assimilation will be treated more extensively in an expanded version of this paper.*

52. For a relatively recent scholarly work that recognizes the significance of the issue of sex and Mexicanas in the gold rush era but which accepts, and thus maintains the standard, stereotypic view of Mexicanas as prostitutes, see Pitt, *Decline of the Californios*, pp. 71-73.

53. William B. Secrest, *Juanita: The Only Woman Lynched During Gold Rush Days* (Fresno: Saga-West Publishing Company, 1967); Pitt, in *Decline of the Californios*, p. 73, accepts the standard view that Juanita (Josefa) of Downieville was a prostitute even though extensive documentation does not prove her prostitution.

54. Julie Roy Jeffrey, *Frontier Women*, pp. 107-146, presents a well-balanced description and discussion of women on the mining frontier. For an excellent analysis of prostitution in the mining frontier and the issue of "respectable" and "non-respectable" women, see Marion Goldman, *Gold Diggers and Silver Miners*. For a discussion of the literature describing the elevated status of women due to their scarcity in the Mother Lode see Jensen and Miller, "The Gentle Tamers Revisited."

55. Pitt, *Decline of the Californios*, pp. 60-65.

56. See Hart, *American Images of Spanish California*, p. 33; Hunt Jackson, *Ramona: A Story* (Boston: Roberts Brothers, 1892).

57. Clark, "Their Pride, Their Manners, and Their Voices," pp. 72, 81.

58. Most of the historical literature on California directly or indirectly reflects an interpretation of discontinuity between Californianos and Mexicanos. The most succinct statement is by Moses Rischin, "Continuities and Discontinuities in Spanish-Speaking California," in *Ethnic Conflict in California History*, ed. Charles Wollenberg (Los Angeles: Tinnon-Brown Publishers, 1969), pp. 43-60; see also John Womack, Jr., "Who Are the Chicanos?" *The New York Review of Books*, 19 (August 1972): 12-18; and Arthur Corwin, "Mexican American History: An Assessment," *Pacific Historical Review* 42 (August 1973): 269-308.

EL EMBRION NACIONALISTA VISTO A TRAVES DE LA OBRA DE SOR JUANA INES DE LA CRUZ

Abstract

There are those who argue the work of the poet-savant of colonial New Spain, Sor Juana Inés de la Cruz (1651-1695), is exclusively the work of the Golden Age. Any reference in her work to local events or expressive styles is merely a reflection of popular inspiration, certainly never of nationalist sentiments.

In response, María R. González argues the contrary: the popular literary forms, lyric poetry, encomia and comedies, by Sor Juana unmistakenly reveal aspects of nascent Mexican nationalism. This nationalism is expressed through references to a homeland, a social consciousness and critique, awareness of racial distinctiveness and inequalities, and subtle political statements. Sor Juana's new citizen is the descendant of two cultures, one far off and unknown and the other familiar and close to the heart. Mexico is her inspiration and being the homeland of an indigenous population and native-born Criollos, a source of American pride. Her "Loa al auto del Cetro de Jose" conveys an ideological struggle between Indian and Spanish worldviews. The Church, handmaiden of the Spanish conquest, does not escape criticism by the learned nun when resentment is expressed against the Christian faith for having been violently imposed on the New World. Her songs are critical of the misery and pain to which the downtrodden of colonial New Spain are subjected. In one of these, she uses Black idiom to express racial discrimination. Her comedies reveal Criollo annoyance with the Spanish oppressor who she derogatorily refers to as "gachupines." Desire for liberty is subtlely expressed by asking the Mexican Eagle, symbol of liberty for the motherland, to take flight.

Sor Juana's national, political and social sensitivities and inquietude, however, are disguised and implicit. The colonial regime of her times force Sor Juana to mask national sentiments in the popular style of baroque ornateness. It is argued her dissimulation contributes to the formation of the Mexican character to which Octavio Paz refers in the *Labyrinth of Solitude*. These characteristics paradoxically affect dissimulation and courtesy, profound modesty and racial pride, seriousness and intimate sensitivity.

EL EMBRION NACIONALISTA
VISTO A TRAVES DE LA OBRA
DE SOR JUANA INES DE LA CRUZ *

by

María R. González

Dedico este trabajo a mi entrañable
amiga Patricia Wilson y a mi querida
compañera de seminario Sonia Zuñiga Lomelí.

Ya pasada la primera época de la conquista militar en tierras de la Nueva España, en los primeros años del siglo diecisiete, se inicia casi en las postrimerías del mismo una segunda etapa de conquista, que de hecho será la más importante; nos ereferimos a la conquista social, política y económica que sufrió la Nueva España. Era inevitable que al ocurrir esta segunda etapa se dieran transformaciones sociales que repercutirían tanto entre los conquistadores como entre los conquistados. Estos cambios dieron lugar al nacimiento de nuevas clases sociales marcadas cada una dentro de los diferentes estratos socio-económicos del grupo racial al que cada uno pertenecía. Asi los peninsulares fueron los que sin discusión alguna gozaron de todos los beneficios materiales consecuentes a la conquista militar. Inferiores a los peninsulares se encontraban los criollos; en lo más bajo de la escala social se hallaban los mestizos, indios, negros y zambos. En esta época la colonia escolástica sólo se manifestaba a los ojos de los pobladores novo-hispanos, como un palacio lleno de lujos y vanidades en cuyas entrañas el poder central se iba debilitando por la ineptitud administrativa de quienes regían el gobierno virreinal:

La riqueza y poder del clero y de sus instituticones originó numerosos y frecuentes conflictos que produjeron

---

* This is a revised version of an article which first appeared in Aztlan: International Journal of Chicano Studies Research 12 (Spring 1981): 23-37.

un estado de agitación e intranquilidad casi permanente. Los choques más violentos y dramáticos se sucitaron entre el clero y el poder civil, provocando disturbios y motines. El más célebre de estos choques entre la Iglesia y el Estado se produjo en 1622 al desarrollarse el grave conflicto entre el arzobispo Pérez de la Serna y el entonces virrey Gelves, que culminó con el incendio del palacio virreinal por el populacho de la capital.[1]

Parecía a simple vista que los diversos componentes sociales de la colonia se encontraban conformes con lo que habían logrado cada uno dentro de los diversos niveles económicos; y aunque no manifestaran un sentimiento bélico real, dentro de ellos se estaba gestando una lucha ideológica que no mostraría su perfil sino hasta finales del siglo diecisiete y principios del dieciocho con las guerras de Independencia. Durante los últimos años del siglo diecisiete la clase criolla ya empezaba a reaccionar abiertamente contra la tiranía de la Corona española, al igual que algunos sectores de la clase baja; entre ella, obviamente la de los indios. En estos años postreros se registran algunos levantamientos indígenas en diferentes áreas geográficas del país, pero no logran intimidar a la clase dominante. Esta no veía aún como una amenaza sería a estos pobres indios que empezaban a protestar por su situación social tan precaria dentro de la sociedad novohispana. Don Carlos de Sigüenza y Góngora apunta estos hechos en su libro *Relaciones históricas*.[2]

Es a mediados de este siglo cuando emerge Sor Juana Inés de la Cruz (1651?-1695), figura de extraordinario talento artístico e intelectual que vendría a iluminar con su pensamiento el cielo de la Nueva España. Sería ella quien con su exquisita creación literaria marcaría la pauta dentro de los ambientes literarios de su tiempo.

Es particularmente curioso ver como aún a trescientos años de distancia su obra sigue siendo objeto de acaloradas discusiones. Una de las más recientes polémicas que se han suscitado en los ámbitos literarios, es la posible existencia de un nacionalismo en Sor Juana. Es pertinente aclarar que hay críticos que afirman categóricamente que no existe ningún rasgo de nacionalismo en su obra, y que si se manifiesta algún resquicio, es mera coincidencia. Tal es el caso del reconocido crítico chileno Arturo Torres Ríoseco, quien se expresa de la siguiente manera:

Toda la obra de Sor Juana--comedias, sonetos, romances, villancicos, crítica--obedece a la mejor inspiración poética del Siglo de Oro. Sería inútil pretender en su obra rasgos mexicanos; no los hay ni en su temática. Las referencias que hace a veces a acontecimento locales y el uso de palabras indígenas no bastan para darle carácter de poeta mexicano y únicamente dan un donaire de inspiración popular a su poesía.[3]

Después de haber leído lo anterior sería tal vez un tanto presuntuoso de nuestra parte insistir en la idea de un nacionalismo embrionario en la obra de Sor Juana. Pero, apoyándo en todos esos elementos enumerados por Ríoseco, difícil es pensar que la poetisa haya incluido en su obra esas presencias mexicanas sólo con el fin de presumir de conocedora de la realidad social y cultural del aborígen mexicano. No creemos que esta presencia de elementos populares obedecieran al simple afán de adornar las páginas de su obra. Opinamos que esas menciones folklóricas obedecían a una conciencia histórica muy clara en Sor Juana Inés.

Para poder presentar una argumentación clara y en términos más concretos sobre este tema, se hace necesario estudiar no la obra en su totalidad, sino simplemente parte de ella que nos sirva de testimonio irrevocable para dejar bien constada la existencia de ese nacionalismo embrionario que presentimos en la obra de Sor Juana. Utilizaremos con tal propósito dentro de la lírica, romances, sonetos, y villancicos. Y en el terreno del teatro se verá "Loa al auto del Cetro de José," "Los Empeños de una casa," en donde se encuentra insertado un sainete (importante para nuestro trabajo), y finalmente, se verá el sarao que se encuentra al final de la comedia, "Llamando a cuatro naciones."

Lírica

En la lírica de Sor Juana Inés de la Cruz se encuentran dos romances en los que se hallan indicios de un orgullo nacional que indudablemente poesía. En el romance que aparece con el número 24, Sor Juana reconoce que América, aunque conquistada, tiene derecho a ser llamada "ufana" y el "Aguila Mexicana"; de levantar su "imperial vuelo," que aquí se presenta como símbolo de la libertad y de la patria, tanto para los aborígenes mexicanos como para los criollos, ya que para los primeros representa la antigua patria y para los segundos la recién erguida nación, con la cual ya se identificaban plenamente:

Levanta América ufana
la coronada cabeza,
y el Aguila Mexicana
el imperial vuelo tienda

Aquí sí que se ha de ver
una maravilla nueva
de añadir más a lo más
de que el Mexicano crezca.[4]

En el segundo romance que es el número 36, Sor Juana habla por boca de una señora del palacio del virrey, para aclarar en tono irónico que también en Mexico hay su "poquita de etiqueta." Indudablemente que este romance iba dirigido hacia las damas de la alta sociedad colonial española que buscaban imitar en todas las costumbres a la corte española:

Y que de la Damería
se ajaban las preeminencias
(que en México también hay
su poquita de etiqueta) ... [5]

Más tarde aparece un soneto con una imagen que indiscutiblemente representa la nación mexicana en el mundo cristiano. Nos referimos a la "Virgen Morena" que es vista como patrona muy especial de los indios cristianos."[6] La estrofa que a continuación presentamos es la que incluye la dicha imagen:

La compuesta de flores Maravilla,
divina Protectora Americana,
que a ser se pasa Rosa Mexicana
apareciendo Rosa de Castilla.[7]

Este trozo de la estrofa mencionada claramente nos da la relación histórica de cuando la Virgen de Guadalupe quedó estampada en el ayate del indio Juan Diego, pasando a ser de esta manera símbolo mexicano. Sor Juana logra atinadamente enaltecer la sublime imagen que fungió como sintetizadora de la conquista espiritual que sufrió el indio mexicano a consecuencia de la conquista militar.

En sus villancicos borbotean elementos autóctonos: indígenas, negros, mestizos, y criollos, que exaltan el sabor popular nacional. Estos elementos populares dentro de su obra la identifican como mujer consciente de la realidad étnicosocial de su patria; ademas, como dice Ermilo Abreau Gomez:

> Recibe las influencias de la vida rústica en los solares de Nepantla y de Amecameca. Se entrega a su interpretación, aprovechando sus recursos populares. Recoge el espíritu de humildad, el hálito de dolor, la idea de patria primaria o incompleta--y el resentimiento de las clases aborígenes. De los esclavos, indios, negros y mulatos, toma modismos, refranes y formas de expresión lírica. El hablar de estas gentes la vierte en sus Villancicos y Letras Sagradas Profanas.[8]

Ejemplos claves--en donde se revelan elementos autóctonos-- son los que se hallan en el villancico número 224 casi al final en donde se da la "Ensaladilla." En esta sección del villancico al inicio de la ensaladilla interpone Sor Juana el dialecto del negro en tono muy vivo y musical terminando con un "Tocotín escrito en la lengua del indio mexicano, el náhuatl":

> --Tla ya timohuica,
> totlazo Zuapilli,
> maca ammo, Tonantzin,
> titechmoilcahuíliz.
>
> Ma nel in Ilhuícac
> huel timomaquítiz
> ¿amo nozo quenman
> timotlalnamíctiz?
>
> In moayo que mochtin
> huel motilinzque;
> tlaca amo, tehuatzin
> ticmomatlaníliz.
>
> Ma mopampantizinco
> in moayolcatintin,
> in itla poholtin,
> tictomac huizque.

Totlatlácol mochtin
fiololquiztizque;
ilhuícac fiazaue,
timitzittalizque:

Ca mitztlacamati
motlazo Piltzintli,
mac tel, in tempampa
xicomotlatlauhtili.

Tlaca ammo quinequi,
xicomoilnamiquili
ca monacayotzin
oticmomaquiti.

Mochichhualayo
oquimomitili,
tla motemictia
ihuan Tetepitzin.

in campa cemícac
timonemitíliz,
cemícac mochíhuaz
in monahuatiltzin.[9]

En este tocotín a través del mismo lenguaje del antiguo
mexicano, Sor Juana recogió la imagen autóctona del mundo
pagano indígena; tal es el caso de Tonantzin (Nuestra Madre), que
equivale al símbolo de la Virgen de Guadalupe (Madre de los
mexicanos). Logra perfectamente armonizar el mundo cristiano con
el mundo pagano del indio mexicano, mostrándonos con ésto un
gran reconocimiento equitativo a ambas imágenes religiosas, que
después de todo sirvieron a un sólo propósito: cristianizar al indio.

En el tercer nocturno del villancico número 232, Sor Juana se
vale de la expresión verbal del negro americano, para dejarnos ver
un problema social muy característico del período colonial: la
discriminación racial. Sor Juana la expresa en una forma muy
delicada que difícilmente se pudiera decir que está haciendo una
crítica. En el villancico el negro quiere cantarle a la Virgen, pero
el blanco lo echa fuera:

--¿Quién es? - Un Neglyo
--¡Vaya, vaya fuera,
que en Fiesta de luces,
toda de purezas,
no es bien se permita
haya cosa negra!

A lo que contesta el negro:

Aunque negro, blanco
Somo, lela, lela,
que il alma rivota
blanca sá no prieta

--¡Diga, diga, diga!
¡Zambio, lela, lela!^{10}

Al final de la "Ensaladilla" del villancico 233 dedicado en honor de San Pedro Nolasco "redentor de los esclavos,"[11] se ve una mezcla de dos entidades linguísticas: el náhuatl y el español mexicano, creando así Sor Juana su "Tocotín Mestizo"[12] que le da originalidad a su villancico. El tocotín es un baile o danza que se conocía muy bien en la época colonial y que sigue siendo tradicional, ejectándose especialmente en los días de grandes festividades religiosas. En tales fechas los indígenas en grupos acuden a las puertas de los templos católicos a danzar en honor del santo o santa de su devoción. Esta mezcla, que se da de todos los componentes folklóricos de la joven patria, sirve para corroborar que Sor Juana se sentía muy cercana a la realidad socio-cultural de su patria.

Teatro

Sor Juana, en su "Loa al auto del Divino Narcisco," deja la huella imborrable de la batalla espiritual que libraron los antiguos pobladores de América en contienda con el hombre español al tratar de implantarle éste una religión ajena a su cultura. Hay en la loa una gran conciencia histórica que manifiesta el interés que tuvo la poetisa en legarnos un trozo de historia mexicana en su auto. María Esther Pérez nos dice que "Sor Juana quiso escribir esta pequeña pieza con el propósito de presentarnos la realidad de la conquista y la colonización que en alguna forma le tocó vivir" y

que la poetisa buscó compartir esa experiencia histórica vivida
indirectamente por ella.[13]

También en la "Loa al auto del Cetro de José" encontramos
indicios de esa conciencia histórica de la que hablábamos en la
"Loa al Divino Narciso." Sor Juana se vale de los personajes
alegóricos "Idolotría" y "Fe" para presentarnos una vez más la lucha
ideológica religiosa entre América y España. En la primera parte
de la escena segunda de la loa hay manifestaciones muy claras de
esa lid ideológica entre ambas América y España. En la loa se
produce un resentimiento hacia la fe cristiana por haberse
introducido ésta de un modo tan violento en el imperio de
Idolatría:

> ¡No, mientras viva mi rabia,
> Fe, conseguirás tu intento,
> que aunque (a pesar de mis ansias)
> privándome la Corona,
> que por edades tan largas
> pacífica poesía,
> introdujiste tirana
> tu dominio en mis Imperios,
> predicando la Cristiana
> Ley, a cuyo fin te abrieron
> violenta senda las armas;
> y aunque la Ley Natural
> que en estos Reinos estaba
> como violenta conmigo,
> se haya puesto de tus banda;
> y aunque casi todas ya
> mis gentes, avasalladas
> de tu activa persuasión,
> todos tus Dogmas abrazan;
> con todo (vuelvo a decir),
> no ha de ser tu fuerza tanta,
> que pueda de una vez sola
> quitar las tan radicadas
> reliquias de mis costumbres!
> Y así, aunque me ves postrada,
> no es tanto que no te impida
> el que demuelas las Aras
> adonde los Sacrificios
> son las Víctimas Humanas.

Soy, por más que tú me ultrajes,
la que sabrá defender
fueros de edades tan largas,
pues Alegórica Idea,
Consideración abstracta
soy, que colectivamente
casi todo el Reino abraza.

Y así, con la voz de todos,
como Plenipotenciaria
de todos los Indios, vengo
a decirte que, aunque ufana
estés de que convertidos
sigan tus Banderas sacras,
no intentes con la violencia
inmutar la antigua usanza
que en sacrificios tienen,
pues para tu intento basta
el que a un solo Dios adoren,
destruyendo las estatuas
de sus Dioses; supuesto
que adorar Deidad hagan
los mejores sacrificios,
que son los de sangre humana.

Antes hay mayor razón,
porque si a Deidad más alta
se debe mejor ofrenda,
¿por qué tú quieres privarla
de ese culto? Pues el yerro,
no en el Sacrificio estaba,
sino en el objeto, pues
se ofreció a Deidades falsas;
y si ahora al verdadero
Dios quieren sacrificarla,
pues el error fue el objeto,
mudar el objeto basta.[14]

Paulatinamente en el desarrollo de la loa se va dando la reconciliación entre la Fe e Idolatría, hasta que finalmente la primera vence sobre la segunda. Esta conversión que se da en el auto de una manera alegórica reconcilia a América con el

Occidente. Entre juego de palabras netamente barroquistas muy bien seleccionadas, sor Juana recoge la queja sometida del nativo mexicano; que aunque bárbaro a los ojos del español, dado su afán por los sacrificios humanos para honor de sus dioses no dejaba de tener su sensibilidad original. Esto no es sino una evidencia más de la gran conciencia histórica cultural que Sor Juana manifestaba hacia la verdad indígena.

Comedia

En la comedia de capa y espada "Los empeños de una casa" nos dice Arturo Torres Ríoseco "que no existe ninguna característica mexicana y se creería estar en presencia de un escritor peninsular."[15] Por otro lado, Ezequiel Chávez opina que "es una comedia típicamente mexicana, especialmente en el carácter de Castaño, gracioso, que él cree distinto a los españoles."[16] Añadiremos que sí existe en la comedia un aire de mexicanidad en el sentido irónico y hasta pícaro que se percibe en en la comedia a través de Castaño, un personaje de comedia. La picardía encerrada en el lenguaje de doble sentido y populista de Castaño, nos va dibujando esquemáticamente a ese nuevo humor local de la comedia novo-hispana. Esta forma de humor tan matizado en Sor Juana a través de su personaje cómico nos subyuga por su manera tan peculiar de hacer resaltar una situación de enredos llena de un nuevo sabor de la comedia disfrazada americana. En el "Sainete Segundo" que se halla intercalado en la comedia, Sor Juana hace la crítica en tal modo festivo, que impide que el público se enfade con ella. Este detalle nos hace pensar que indudablemente en la sociedad novo-hispana de su tiempo se sentía en el ambiente un cierto resquemor contra los opresores. Y Sor Juana, como mujer sensible, recoge en su obra ese resentimiento que empieza a florecer en las conciencias criollas mexicanas. La palabra "gachupines" o cachupines utilizada en el sainete es la que nos da la clave de este sentimiento, pues está dicha en un sentido peyorativo. Aunque la palabra en sí no encierra un tono despectivo, ya que simplemente significaba, según el *Diccionario de la real academia Española*, "una persona que emigraba de España a América," en la época de la colonia se usaba con hondo significado derrogativo:

> Gachupines parecen
> recién venidos
> porque todo el teatro
> se hunde a silbos.[17]

Además en este mismo sainete Sor Juana hace una señalización refinadamente crítica de la comedia española a través de Muñiz su personaje de comedia:

> Amigo, mejor Celestina,
> en cuanto a ser comedia ultramarina:
> que siempre las de España son mejores,
> y para digerirles los humores,
> son ligeras; que nunca son pesadas
> las cosas que por agua están pasadas.[18]

Aquí, Sor Juana reconoce que la comedia americana, aunque pasada por agua es buena, claro aunque con algunos defectos. Nos aclara que la comedia local aunque mestiza tiene también su sabor y que puede ser tan buena como la española. Aquí una vez más Sor Juana embozada bajo la sombra barroquista hace resaltar lo local. Inmediatamente, después de hacer esta breve observación Sor Juana pasa inteligentemente a una auto-crítica cuando pronuncia al final del trozo:

> Pero la Celestina que esta risa
> os causó, era mestiza
> y acabada a retazos,
> y si le faltó traza, tuvo trazos,
> y con diverso genio
> se formó de un trapiche y de un ingenio.
> Y en fin, en su poesía,
> por lo bueno, lo malo se suplía;
> pero aquí, ¡vive Cristo, que no puedo
> sufrir los disparates de Acevedo![19]

Sor Juana cierra la comedia con broche de oro, al presentar su sarao "Llamado a cuatro naciones" en el que aparecen españoles, negros, italianos y mexicanos. Aquí no encontramos menciones de elementos mexicanos, a excepción del uso del vocablo "Mexicanos," que aplica para hacer el llamado.

249

Vistas todas las partes en donde se presentan indicios de mexicanidad en la obra de Sor Juana Inés de la Cruz, es difícil que dejemos de percibir una susceptibilidad nacionalista en ella. Puede ser que nunca lleguemos a aceptar de una manera contundente esta sensibilidad, dado el carácter social y político que revistió la Colonia en su época. Por otro lado, se hace necesario enfatizar que fue precisamente la Colonia la que la obligó a esconder esa sensibilidad nacional bajo la máscara del barroco. En las postrimerías de su vida cuando se le pide que deje de escribir Sor Juana se encierra en un mutismo de creatividad mortal cincelando con ésto, un aspecto de la formación del carácter del mexicano, que tanto discute Octavio Paz en su *Laberinto de la soledad.*

A Sor Juana se le ha dado una orden cortante, y ella ha obedecido. Al ser se le ha dominado con la palabra dicha con intención despiadada por aquellos que jamás pudieron aceptar la capacidad intelectual de esta mujer. Debemos ver que se ha logrado doblegar al ser exterior, pero no al ser interior en donde sigue bullendo la inquietud creadora. Después de la prohibición siempre se le notará ocupada en los quehaceres religiosos y humanitarios, pero en su interior la mente ésta lejos y ausente porque en su silencio se encierra y se preserva. Plantada en su arisca soledad espinosa y cortés, Sor Juana se protege de los necios ataques de sus enemigos. El silencio y la palabra, la cortesía y el desprecio, la ironía y la resignación todos juntos son parte de su personalidad de mujer doblegada a los caprichos de sus superiores:

Por eso su estilo vital y su estilo literario tiene que ser estilos sordinos, de sútiles disimulos, de juegos conceptuales; esmeros de la astucia para no herir susceptibilidades; alardes de la inteligencia para decir y no decir al mismo tiempo; para revelar cosas y a la vez dejarlas discretamente encubiertas; para amonestar sin soliviantar; para aconsejar sin razonar la unidad del soberano; para profetizar sin asustar; para expresarse, con una palabra, sin atrevimiento. En este difícil juego, muy mexicano por cierto, de la sinceridad frente a la manera, se revela no sólo la forma necesaria de reaccionar frente a una época absolutista e intolerante, sino también la típica, compleja y sútil sensibilidad del mexicano, mezcla de disimulo y de cortesía; de modestia profunda y de orgullo racial; seriedad un poco impresionante y de íntima sensibilidad.[20]

250

Su silencio fue el arma adecuada usada en contra de la orden eclesiástica colonial que jamás supo aceptar la sensibilidad intelectual de Sor Juana, pero ella pese a estas imposiciones absurdas, su espíritu de genio anduvo siempre en busca de la verdadera esencia del ser.

Vemos pues, Sor Juana nunca fue ajena a su realidad histórica ni a su condición de criolla, aunque las circunstancias la hayan obligado a esconder su verdadero sentir. Ella reconoció en su momento la existencia de esta nueva tierra mexicana que enalteció el espíritu nacional mexicano. Si ella no hubiese tenido una conciencia social de lo que significaba el ser mexicano, probablemente no gozaríamos de ningún elemento indígena, criollo, o negro de los que logramos apreciar en su obra. Hubiese sido más fácil para la monja ignorar todos los acontecimientos del pasado y del presente mexicano y vivir la vida conventual sin ninguna preocupación que nublara su pensamiento. Hubiese sido más cómodo para ella ignorar esta realidad mexicana y dedicarse simplemente a escribir versos para halagar el oído y la vanidad de los miembros del virreinato. Pero quiso asomarse a través de la ventana social y ver el mundo de dolor y miseria que se escondía tras el telón colonial: "Por detrás de su orgullo nacional se esconde un reproche a la voracidad europea y al carácter discriminatorio del trato de los pueblos esclavos"[21] y como ser consciente, sufría por la forma en que eran tratados los indios y negros de su patria:

A Sor Juana le duelen las vejaciones de que son víctimas indios y negros por igual. Sus padecimientos, su explotación constante, la afrenta que significa la confinación en que se les tiene, el desprecio con que el blanco mira a los seres de piel más oscura que la suya, hacen sentir a la monja jerónima el mundo de dolor en que se debaten los pueblos miserables bajo la fuerza del que se considera superior a ellos.[22]

Así pues la obra de Sor Juana Inés de la Cruz nos sirve como prueba histórica e irrevocable para constatar este nacionalismo embrionario. Su obra, su pensamiento, nos han quedado como llama reveladora de una naciente conciencia nacionalista: "Su obra significa el momento en que la conciencia criolla empieza a perfilarse en una dirección auténticamente revolucionaria.[23] En su obra ha logrado dejar plasmada toda la esencia de una nueva sensibilidad arrolladora surgida dentro de su momento histórico.

Indiscutiblemente ella supo captar el nuevo sentir mexicanista que se empezaba a respirar en el aire colonial de su época. En ese nuevo ser nacional, Sor Juana sintió una plena identificación y una comunión con su patria; hacia esa tierra criolla y mestiza que, después de todo, fue la única tierra que le sirvió de inspiración. Y ese reconocimiento a lo nacional va mucho más allá de un simple folklorismo intelectual de su parte sino buscó, por el contrario, manifestar la nueva inquietud que iba proyectándose hacia una auténtica ideología mexicana que intentaba desligarse del proteccionismo colonial.

Algunos se obstinan en empañar el pensamiento y la obra de Sor Juana Inés de la Cruz con observaciones necias y superficiales, y no siempre dichas con las mejores intenciones, además llevan el propósito de subestimar la integridad creadora e intelectual de ella. Al contrario, se debe admirar a esta mujer en cuyo carácter se sintetiza toda una nueva sensibilidad refinadamente intelectual, pero a la vez audaz.

Su despliegue como poetisa, prosista y pensadora fue marcando intuitivamente el camino que debería seguir el nuevo ser nacional, al que se le iba incrustando en su piel y en su espíritu el sabor de una futura independencia que le llegaría un siglo más tarde. En Sor Juana debemos ver a la artista que supo pintarnos el panorama colonial a través de su obra literaria y que nos dio las primeras cinceladas del retrato y el perfil del nuevo ciudadano que se bullía entre dos patrias: la una lejana y desconocida; y la otra muy cerca a los ojos y al corazón.

Aún, aunque se quiera acallar o minimizar la obra de esta ilustre mexicana, se le debe de reconocer la gran contribución que hizo en su tiempo y que continúa haciendo a las letras y al pensamiento intelectual moderno de nuestra historia nacional.

Notas

1. Agustín Cue Cánovas, *Historia social y económica de México: 1521-1854* (México, D.F.: Editorial Trillas, 1980), p. 163.
2. Carlos de Sigüenza y Góngora, *Relaciones históricas* (México, D.F.: Universidad Nacional Autónoma de México, 1940), p. xviii.
3. Arturo Torres Ríoseco, "Sor Juana Inés de la Cruz," *Revista Iberoamericana* 12 (1947): 31-38.
4. Sor Juana Inés de la Cruz, *Obras Completas* (México, D.F.: Porrúa, 1975).

5. Ibid., p. 33.

6. José Gutiérrez Casillas, *Historia de la iglesia en México* (México, D.F.: Editorial Porrúa, 1974), p. 67.

7. de la Cruz, *Obras Completas*, p. 164.

8. Ermilo Abreu Gómez, "Prólogo a *Poesías de Sor Juana Inés de la Cruz* (México, D.F.: Botas, 1940), p. 75.

9. de la Cruz, *Obras Completas*, p. 212.

10. Ibid., p. 217.

11. Luis Leal, "Tocotín Mestizo," *Abside* 18 (1954): 57.

12. Ibid., p. 52.

13. María Esther Pérez, "Elementos folklóricos indígenas en las loas introducidas al teatro religioso de Sor Juana," en *Lo americano en el teatro de Sor Juana Inés de la Cruz* (New York: Eliseo Torres e Hijos, 1975), p. 223.

14. de la Cruz, *Obras Completas*, pp. 464-70.

15. Arturo Torres Ríoseco, "Tres dramaturgos mexicanos del período colonial (Eslava, Alarcón, Sor Juana)," *Ensayos de literatura latinoamericana* (México, D.F.: Fundo de Cultura Económica, Colección Tezontle, 1954), p. 45.

16. Ezequiel Chávez citado por Ríoseco, "Tres dramaturgos," p. 45.

17. de la Cruz, *Obras Completas*, p. 679.

18. Ibid., p. 675.

19. Ibid., p. 676.

20. Anita Arroyo, "La mexicanidad en el estilo de Sor Juana," *Revista Iberoamericana* 17 (1952): 64. Anita Arroyo se vale del ensayo escrito por Octavio Paz en *El laberinto de la soledad* para resaltar la importancia que tiene el disimulo en la formación del carácter del mexicano, que hace distinguir a Sor Juana como mexicana.

21. Francisco López Cámara, "La conciencia criolla en Sor Juana y Sigüenza," *Historia Mexicana* 6 (1957): 362.

22. Ibid., p. 362.

23. Ibid.

Work Experience and
Labor Activism

Part III

Work Experience
and
Labor Activism

CHICANAS IN
THE GREAT DEPRESSION

by

Louise Año Nuevo Kerr

The purpose of this essay is to place the experience of Chicanas living in Chicago during the Great Depression of the 1930s in the context of three recent historiographic foci and to align that urban experience with the general, contemporaneous fabric of U.S. social history. The three contexts to which this discussion refers are, logically enough, Chicano history, ethnic history and women's history. Analyzed within the confines of these distinct disciplines (and perhaps only because the depression was an aberrant time), the history of Chicanas in Chicago contradicts many generalizations which have been made about Chicanos, immigrants and working-class women.

The Economic Allure of Chicago

Those who have dealt with Chicano history--and they number only a few more than those who have dealt with Chicana history-- maintain that in geographical, generational and occupational terms, the Chicano experience was undergoing tremendous change around 1920. Until that time, Chicanos were found almost exclusively in the Southwest: in Texas, Arizona, New Mexico, Colorado and California. Some were the descendants of people who had lived in the former northwestern section of Mexico at the conclusion of the Mexican War in 1848. Yet a large and increasing number of Mexicans living in the United States were immigrants. They had migrated to the United States at various times since the 1880s, but most arrived in the decade between 1910 and 1920--following the outset of the 1910 Mexican Revolution.

Most immigrants settled in the southwestern states, where there were sizeable and often well established Chicano communities. These communities had already developed relationships (usually negative) with the dominant Anglo society which surrounded them. These communities, included not only newly arrived immigrants, but older immigrants and their children as well as some descendants of the original Mexican land-grant holders or their workers. Although there were indications that Chicanos in the Southwest were beginning to enter non-agricultural work, few were employed by industry in 1920.[1]

After 1910, Mexicans fleeing revolution began to realize that the railroads which linked Mexico to the Southwest also extended north, into the eastern and northwestern United States and into midwestern cities such as Chicago. At the same time, northern industrial and agricultural interests were faced with a need to find a new source of labor. The flow of European immigrant labor upon which they depended had been halted with the onset of World War I. As a result, both industry and agriculture actively sought to inform Mexicans in the Southwest and northern Mexico (as well as rural southern Blacks) that work opportunities were available further north.

Throughout the 1920s, Mexicans living in various parts of the United States (as well as those contemplating a move north from Mexico) were recruited for unskilled and low-paying jobs in Chicago industry, especially in the steel, meat-packing and railroad industries. The movement of Mexicans northward proceeded so rapidly that by 1930 almost 20,000 lived in Chicago.[2]

A study done in 1924 of "Small Wage-Earners in Chicago" shows that 65 percent of Mexicans surveyed were unmarried men or men living in the city without their wives. Of the 35 percent who were women, most were married but not all had children. By 1930 only three out of every ten Mexicans in the city were children under the age of sixteen.[3] Thus, by the end of the 1920s, Chicago's population was distinct from that of the Southwest: it consisted primarily of young males and, except for the youngsters born during the decade, was first-generation immigrant.

Chicanos who arrived in Chicago during the 1920s were part of a new phase of Chicano history. They found themselves compared as often to other local immigrants who had been coming to the city over 75 years as to the Chicanos of the Southwest. For the Mexicans, as the Irish, Italians, Jews and Poles who had preceded them (often to the same neighborhoods where they were settling) had come as young adults from peasant rural backgrounds to work in urban industry. As the most recent arrivals, however, they were struggling to survive in a hostile, nativistic environment which would reach its nadir in 1924 with the pasage of quota acts designed to restrict further European immigration and confine established ethnic communities.

Although Mexicans in Chicago followed patterns established by Mexicans in the Southwest and other European immigrants in Chicago. Chicanos in this period faced specific circumstances which distinguished them from both these groups. Similarly, although Chicanas arriving after World War I seemed to replicate the experiences of other Mexicanas and immigrant women, they also devised their own unique responses.

Two Views of the Chicana Experience

Histories of working-class and ethnic women have usually fallen into one of two broad (often mutually exclusive) categories. The history of Chicanas, in particular, is confined to this dichotomy of interpretation. One school of historical interpretation maintains that, uprooted from their traditional culture, Mexican women established families as part of a cultural milieu in which they were (1) discouraged from working outside the home at any occupation except those in the home or those which demanded skills similar to those they used in the home; 2) isolated from each other and from the larger society by their husbands and by their lack of language facility; 3) often rejected by their children who were usually thrust into the larger society via school attendance or early work experience.

Another historical interpretation portrays immigrant women as part of the labor force--an integral part of the organization of workers and of the ethnic community. It portrays radical women whose consciousness is raised and whose energies are channeled into changing those conditions which the industrial system induced and imposed on the ethnic group as a whole. This immigrant woman is usually thought to have come to the United States when she was young, and her rebelliousness is considered a product of her own experiences with "the system."

At first, Chicanas seem to fit neatly into the former, more traditional interpretation. Nearly half (47 percent) of all Mexican women who arrived in Chicago during the 1920s had to find work immediately. Most worked in the home as boarding housekeepers, yet a significant number (23 percent) worked outside the home in such "female" occupations as lampshade-makers, laundresses, waitresses and small manufacturing operatives. Mexicanas had to find work because so many Mexican families could not adequately subsist on the earnings of the male head of household. The seasonal, usually unskilled employment and under-employment of Mexican men forced many families to depend almost as much on women's earnings as on that of the men. Yet even taking the woman's salary into account, two-thirds of all Mexican families made less than $100 a month--a figure which, even during the 1920s, signified poverty.[4]

When Mexican women moved to the city (whether from Mexico or the agricultural Midwest), their family life was disrupted. The injury or death of Mexican men, even more than desertion, left many women alone as single parents. Women were forced to become more self reliant at a time when the city offered fewer economic options. Social service records indicate that family members (fathers and brothers, especially) often tried to help, partly to maintain traditional relationships. Often however, their own low income hampered their efforts.[5] In effect, women had to find alternative means of providing for themselves and, if necessary, for their families.

Some women turned to the church for assistance. During the 1920's two Chicago parishes began attending to the needs of the Spanish-speaking. Protestant missionaries also actively doled out social services and were surprisingly effective in converting Mexican women to their church: by the end of the decade, 25 percent of Mexican churchgoers (most of them women) were Protestant. Still, even in the largest Catholic parish--Our Lady of Guadalupe in the South Chicago neighborhood--church attendance rarely exceeded 100 on any given Sunday. Put simply, church outreach was limited. As for the extended family, this traditional form of support was faltering and, so, women were forced to seek other, less traditional means of support.

Records indicate, for example, that social service contact with Mexicans was disproportionately initiated by women--often through their children. Schools began to monitor illness, settlement houses sought mothers who might provide training in nutrition and child care, social workers investigated living conditions in the home. At first, the effects of such contact were limited. The help they offered could not replace wages. Even where circumstances were less desperate, Mexican immigrants (especially women) continued to have a difficult time adjusting to their new environment. As one report stated:

> There seems to be little or no time set aside for recreation for adults in this family and equipment for it is very inadequate in the home. Mr. G. seems mildly interested in the children's recreation and does not object to their belonging to the clubs at the settlement (house) and the parks. The parents have never gone to picnics or parties together since coming to Chicago and an occasional visit to a friend's home seems to be the chief diversion. Mr. G. has gone to the movies three times since coming to Chicago ...

> Mrs. G. has attended only one party since coming to Chicago, this being a farewell party for a family which was leaving for Mexico. When asked what recreation the family had on Sundays, she replied, "I make all day eat, only eat ..." Asked what the big event of the year for the family was, she replied, "every time was the same for me."[6]

Because this description is somewhat biased by the middle-class sensibilities of the female social worker who wrote it, Mrs. G. should not be viewed as the prototype of the recently-arrived Mexican women. Still, the portrait does coincide with and contributes to the traditional interpretation of first-generation immigrant (and migrant) women in the city, including Chicanas in the Southwest. According to all available sources, most Mexican women in Chicago during the 1920s did not work outside the home. Those who did were limited to "female" jobs. Their low or non-existent income, as well as their unfamiliarity with the English language and U.S. culture, isolated them from the larger community. It also seems they inhabited a world different and often separate from that of their husbands and children.

Without disputing the accuracy or completeness of the data which has contributed to this traditional view of Chicana history, scholarly investigation has yet to come to terms with the entire story. They fail to explain how--less than a decade later--many of these first generation women faced the same (if not more difficult) circumstances but collectively identified and took advantage of broader lifestyle options.

The Great Depression

As the Great Depression began, Mexican women were forced to adjust to the grim economic reality that had hit the nation. One of the first and most painful consequences was the end to open immigration and the implementation of a formal and informal policy of repatriation of Mexicans. For Mexican women as well as men, repatriation had an immediate demographic effect.

Between 1930 and 1933 the Mexican population in Chicago fell by 30 percent--from 20,000 to 14,000. In 1934, it fell another ten percent.[7] The population decline equally affected all three neighborhoods in which Mexicans had begun to establish communities. There were, of course, instances in which entire families (including American-born children) were sent back to Mexico. The net result was a rise in the proportion of Mexican women and children among Chicago's Spanish-speaking residents.

Aside from this demographic shift, Mexicanas were forced to become more independent than they had been during the 1920s. In 1935, a survey of *Illinois Persons on Relief* revealed that among the 7,000 Mexicans studied, 1,340 were family households. Of these, 63 percent were complete nuclear families, 13 percent were childless and 24 percent were single-parent households--most of which (313 out of 390) were headed by widowed, divorced or separated women. Over half (52 percent) of all persons counted were under the age of 16 years. This figure was a jump from 30 percent in 1930.[8]

The consequences of the Depression forced many Mexicans to leave Chicago and had a devastating economic impact. Proportionately, more Mexicanas lost their jobs than did any other group except Blacks. In 1935 thirty-two percent of all Mexicans in the city were unemployed as compared to 47 percent of the Black population and 11 percent of all other foreign-born residents. Among the female heads of household who reported that they had worked at some point in the past, only 25 percent were actively seeking work and almost none were employed.[9]

Despite the Depression's severe economic constraints, the adjustment of Mexicans in Chicago generally seemed to improve rather than deteriorate throughout the 1930s. With some variation among neighborhoods, there was evidence of increasing residential and social stability within the community which stemmed from and contributed to a greater sense of permanence and belonging.

By 1935, the average length of residence had reached ten years for Mexicans who remained in the area.[10] One manifestation of Mexican commitment to life in Illinois was a rise in the number of English speakers. Sixty percent of all Mexican female heads of household surveyed in 1935 spoke English. This figure is lower than that for men, yet surprisingly high for first-generation immigrant women.[11] These women were not learning English on or for the job. So, where were they learning it? And what were they learning along with it?

Many young Mexican women were attending school. Chicanas as a local group, enrolled in public school (up to the age of 16) in higher proportions than ever before (and in higher proportions than they are today in some neighborhoods). In fact, more women than men attended classes.[12] Older women were enrolling in adult school especially in the two neighborhoods which had active settlement house programs: the Packingtown Settlement in Back of the Yards and Hull House in the Near West Side. Spanish-speaking women were attending school. Even in South Chicago, where steelworkers and their families were isolated from other ethnic groups and not as well-served by social service settlements, a number of adults became involved in continuing education programs, which encouraged interaction with other people in the neighborhoods.

There is evidence that throughout the 1930s, Mexican women, as well as men, increasingly involved themselves in worker activities. At first, they seemed to limit their energies to Mexican mutual aid societies but, gradually, they joined multi-ethnic unemployed worker groups as well as craft and industrial organizations. Eventually, they joined inter-ethnic unions which had been encouraged by the Wagner Act of 1935 to seek Mexican, European ethnic and Black participation in industries such as meat-packing and steel. Women, particularly young women, were active in the evolution of unionizing activities. Although each of these labor organizations reflected intra-ethnic and neighborhood schisms which fragmented the local Mexican community, they also represented the Chicano population's embryonic moves toward inter-ethnic cooperation.

One union, *El Frente Popular* (The Popular Front) was especially active in its efforts to include women. Although the organization had its roots in Mexico and was originally organized with the intention of maintaining ties to the homeland, El Frente gradually shifted its focus from events in Mexico to events in Chicago. It began to concentrate less on tradition and more on the changing roles and needs of local Mexican residents. A series of lectures held in 1937 shows this change in direction: "The Way the Mexican Worker Must Follow," "The Woman's Place in Modern Society," and "What Must Be the Road that Mexican Youth Must Follow in Chicago" all reflect the intensity with which union members debated the social issues of the day. With varying success, El Frente held meetings in all Chicago neighborhoods. That fact alone suggests some agreement on the relevance of the topics discussed.[13]

Local Chicana Lifestyles

Life within the city varied a great deal from one neighborhood to another. Among the differences between neighborhoods which affected women and how they viewed options open to them were: the size of the Chicano population within the neighborhood (i.e., the proportion of Mexicans); their concentration within the neighborhood (especially if that concentration was imposed); and inter-ethnic contact within the neighborhood. Although these differences were also influenced by the economic stability of the industry upon which each neighborhood depended, economic stability in itself does not seem to have significantly affected how women responded to the urban world.

The Near West Side, for example, was nearest the central part of the city and not economically dependent upon any one industry. It was home to the largest number of Chicanos in Chicago. Except for the economic limitations imposed by low income, Mexicans could move freely in the Near West Side. Perhaps as a result, Chicanos in the Near West Side were the most transient in the city. Many Chicanas from the Near West Side participated in adult education programs, craft classes, social clubs and church functions. Proportionately, however, they seemed less inclined to become involved in outside activities than were Chicanas in other local neighborhoods. Throughout the 1930s, Mexican women in the Near West Side remained more "Mexican" in their outlook than did their counterparts in other neighborhoods. In this, they were very much like their ethnic neighbors, especially Italians who were the predominant group in the area. Women of all ethnic groups living here tended to keep company with their compatriots. Still Mexicans remained the most traditional of all--albeit, not quite as traditional as they had been during the 1920s.

South Chicago was, however, quite a different environment. There, at the extreme southeastern edge of the city, the large number of Poles (the largest ethnic group) and other European immigrants restricted the fairly small Chicano population to one portion of the neighborhood. Economically, South Chicago's future was bound to industry. Chicanos placed emphasis on local and contemporary needs and had English as well as Spanish-speaking organizations and Mexican-American as well as Mexican activities. Although social integration, with other ethnic groups in general, was not encouraged, men were urged to join the new inter-ethnic unions. For their part, women were not inclined (nor were they always allowed) to join in activities with other ethnic women. The continued viability of ethnic parishes indicates that Mexicans, like other distinct cultural groups in the area, sought to maintain and adapt their tradition to the local setting. In general, South Chicago was a community in transition from Mexican to Mexican-American.

Back of the Yards, the smallest of the major Chicano settlements in Chicago was dominated by the nearby meat-packing plants. Although it had historically been ethnically divided into a hodge podge of sub units in which no one group dominated, the neighborhood had come under the influence of Saul Alinsky and his neighborhood organizers in the thirties. As a result of organizing it had become a place of greater inter-ethnic organization than either of the other neighborhoods in which Chicanos lived. No less vulnerable to the economic stress of the Depression than other parts of the city, Back of the Yards gradually became a place in which neighborhood cooperation led to greater participation of all ethnic groups in neighborhood organizations. Among Chicanos this could be seen not only in their increased participation in strictly Chicano activities, but an increased participation in inter-ethnic activities.

The slow but steady transformation of the Mexican Mothers' Club perhaps best illustrates Chicanas from Back of the Yards adapted to an inter-ethnic environment. Sponsored by and headquartered in the Packingtown settlement house, the club met for at least six years, during which time its purpose changed and developed. In 1934, as noted in the settlement house report, Mexican women met to take courses in "basketry, knitting, and other handicrafts." By 1936 the club had added more members. While most of them were still Spanish-speaking, they were urging their members to "speak English." Their outings included a field trip to the NBC radio studios in downtown Chicago, from which many of the most popular soap operas emanated. In 1937, the women sponsored a series of discussions covering various local Chicago issues such as public education, local government, and even the possible benefits of a new city manager plan.

Reorganizing in 1939 (and with a special emphasis on English), the Mexican Mothers' Club "changed its name to the Mexican Women's English Club." Evidently membership was successfully opened to a wider local constituency. When the settlement house's inter-ethnic knitting group discovered that one Mexican member did not know why Thanksgiving was celebrated, a Jewish member offered to explain the meaning and origins of the holiday "as she had found a book in the library about Pilgrims."[14]

Chicago Chicanas: A Unique Constituency

The description of differences among the three neighborhoods provides a guide to the spectrum of experiences which characterized life for Mexicans in Chicago during the Depression. Taken together, they show that within a decade and a half of their arrival in the city, these immigrant women found, and created for themselves opportunities to become involved in emerging inter-ethnic unions, community, and neighborhood activities as well as those of the ethnic group. They took advantage of educational opportunities unavailable to them prior to their arrival in Chicago and which would not be accessible to many immigrants who would arrive in Illinois later.

On the verge of World War II, Chicanas in Chicago were outside the mainstream of Chicano, immigrant and working class women's history. Clearly, they behaved and adapted to city life in ways that defy standard interpretations of Chicano history. Specifically, their participation in the broader community (especially the inter-ethnic community) came earlier and was proportionately greater than has yet been retrospectively observed in any other southwestern urban setting.

Chicanas must also be analyzed as a group distinct from the mainstream of immigrant history. Although women of other ethnic groups responded to life in Chicago in much the same ways as did Mexican women, these women had been in the city for at least a full generation and a half by the end of the Depression. Thus, the responses of Mexican women were more similar to second-generation ethnic women.

Finally, this particular group of women falls outside the parameters of conventional working-class women's history in that their experiences fall into a spectrum which is neither traditional nor radical. In other words, while relatively few Mexican women at the end of the 1930s remained isolated from each other or from the outside world, almost none were involved in "changing the system."

Despite pressures to repatriate, and over and above the exigencies of economic distress, Chicanas who remained in Chicago during the Depression attained a degree of personal and collective independence. Although this may not strike the reader as surprising, such independence is rarely ascribed to immigrant women, especially Mexicanas. Whether this should be ascribed to the time in which they lived or to some special qualities of the group itself is a question that has yet to be fully answered.

Notes

1. See especially Paul S. Taylor, *Mexican Labor in the United States*, vol. 6, nos. 1-5, vol. 7, nos. 1-2 (Berkeley: University of California Press, 1928-32); and Manuel Gamio, *Mexican Immigration to the United States: A Study of Human Migration and Adjustment* (1930; reprint ed., New York: Dove, 1971).

2. U.S. Bureau of the Census, *Abstract of the Fifteenth Census of the United States* (Washington: U.S. Government Printing Office, 1933), p. 98.

3. Ernest W. Burgess and Charles Newcomb, ed. *Census Data of the City of Chicago, 1930* (Chicago: University of Chicago Press, 1933), pp. 83-91, 135-137, 159-161.

4. Elizabeth Ann Hughes, *Living Conditions of Small Wage-Earners in Chicago* (Chicago: City of Chicago, Department of Public Welfare, 1925), p. 45-46.

5. See Robert Redfield, "Mexicans in Chicago: 1924-25," Robert Redfield Papers, Special Collections, University of Chicago.

6. "Placida and Severna Gonzalez," Robert Redfield Papers, Special Collections, University of Chicago.

7. U.S. Bureau of the Census, *Abstract of the Fifteenth Census*, p. 98; see also *Social Service Directory and Yearbook* (Chicago: Chicago Council of Social Agencies, 1933), pp. 199-229; and Charles Newcomb and Richard O. Lang, eds. *Census Data of*

the City of Chicago, 1934 (Chicago: University of Chicago Press, 1934), pp. 295-483.

8.   Elizabeth Ann Hughes, *Illinois Persons on Relief in 1935*, Works Project Administration Project No. 165-54-6018 (Chicago: Works Progress Administration, 1937), p. 93.

9.   Ibid.

10.   Edward Jackson Baur, "Mexican Migration to Chicago" Record Group 69, Records of the Works Progress Administration, National Archives, Washington, 1930, p. 7.

11.   Hughes, *Illinois Persons on Relief in 1935*, pp. 68-69.

12.   Ibid.

13.   La Defensa (Chicago), 10 Oct. 1937; 20 June 1937; 11 April 1937, as translated in *Chicago Foreign Language Press Survey*, Microfilm Reel 62.

14. "Annual Report: 1934"; "Annual Report: 1936"; "Annual Report: 1937"; "Annual Report: 1939," University of Chicago Settlement House Papers, Chicago Historical Society.

MANUELA SOLIS SAGER AND EMMA B. TENAYUCA: A TRIBUTE[1]

by

Roberto R. Calderón and Emilio Zamora

One of the most memorable highlights of the annual conferences of the National Association for Chicano Studies (NACS) has been the formal recognition of the work of Américo Paredes, Ernesto Galarza, Carey McWilliams and Julian Samora. In recognizing and honoring the accomplishments and contributions of these scholars to our history and culture, NACS paid tribute to the purpose and will that guided their scholarly and political contributions to Mexican people.

In 1984 the NACS conference extended this tradition by honoring Manuela Solis Sager and Emma B. Tenayuca, two labor activists who organized and led Mexican workers' movements in Texas during the 1930s.[2] In doing so, NACS acknowledged the key role of women in our history of struggle and underscored the need to bring this knowledge to the classroom and explore it in our research. This event like many others which have honored Manuela and Emma gave recognition to the commitment, courage and dedication these women displayed during a turbulent period in this country's history. They were also the first women to be thus honored and recognized by NACS since its inception twelve years ago.

We wish to acknowledge the valuable assistance of Leticia López, Oscar R. Martí and María Ortiz. We also appreciate the support given by the Chicano Studies Center, UCLA, the sponsor of this effort. Most importantly, we are grateful to Manuela Solis Sager and Emma B. Tenayuca for sharing with us those distant yet inspiring moments in the struggle.

Manuela's and Emma's intellectual formation was strongly impacted by social and political developments they had experienced while growing up in South Texas, many of these experiences they shared in common with other inhabitants of Mexican communities of the Southwest. Their families had nurtured the pride, love and concern which conditioned their personal experiences as individuals and as Mexicans during the early decades of the century.

Both women credit their families for giving them a sense of compassion for their neighbors and respect for fairness which would later play an important role in their fight for the rights of Mexican workers. Theirs was a community in which self-help, cooperation and protest activities were part of the cultural milieu and political environment of their childhood. All too familiar with conditions of social inequality and discrimination against people of color, their strong ties to their Mexican origins and their early exposure to Mexican political and cultural events reinforced in them a nationalist and working class identity. Their memories are clear on this.

Profile of Mexican Workers

A short note on the conditions that gave rise to Mexican labor activity during the 1930s is in order. The first three decades of the twentieth century registered the dramatic rise and urbanization of Mexicans in the United States, in part, this was the result of an increase in immigration from Mexico. By 1930, approximately 40 percent of this country's total Mexican population resided in Texas and 30 percent in California. The significant expansion of the U.S. national economy, particularly evident in the industrial development of the Southwest, stimulated this growth and concentration. Discrimination against Mexican workers, however, denied them fair wages and relegated them to unskilled occupations. In 1930 this condition is revealed by the following statistics: 41 percent of all employed Mexicans worked in agriculture; 11 percent in transportation; 3 percent in mining; 23 percent in manufacturing; and 10 percent in domestic and personal services. That is, 88 percent of all Mexican workers in the United States were employed in low-paying, unskilled occupations.

Also, the participation of Mexican women in wage labor increased noticeably. They worked at even lower-paying, segregated jobs representative of extensions of housework. In 1930, twenty percent of Mexicana workers were farm workers; 45 percent were domestic and personal service workers; some 5 percent were saleswomen; with the remainder employed in textiles, food processing and packing industries.

As in earlier periods, opposition to discrimination and inequality gave rise to increased labor organizing and strike activity among Mexicans throughout the United States. Independent Mexican workers' organizations sought affiliation with national labor unions. And they were welcomed by the more progressive labor federations such as the Workers Alliance of America and the United Cannery, Agricultural, Packing and Allied Workers of America (UCAPAWA). Membership figures suggest the participation of Mexican workers registered greater numbers for these progressive labor unions than for the American Federation of Labor (AFL). These figures also indicate Mexican workers' organizations were an important part of the unionization strategies of the Congress of Industrial Organization (CIO) in contrast to that of the exclusive, craft-oriented AFL. Importantly, the activism of Mexicans in the labor movement of the 1930s was enhanced as never before by the growing number of female Mexican workers. Women such as Manuela Solis Sager and Emma B. Tenayuca played crucial roles in the leadership of these historic labor struggles.

Leadership Activity

Manuela's history as an activist began in Laredo, Texas between 1932 and 1933 when she helped organize unions and strikes among garment and agricultural workers. By 1934 she had gained the respect and admiration of fellow agricultural workers and was awarded by La Asociación de Jornaleros a year-long scholarship to attend the highly respected Universidad Obrera, a leftist labor school in Mexico City. Upon her return to Laredo, she joined her husband, James Sager, and other Laredo unionists in consolidating local efforts into a statewide Mexican labor movement. This resulted in a statewide conference held in 1935 at Corpus Christi which attracted delegates representing numerous Mexican community organizations including labor unions and other community collectivities.

The Corpus Christi conference established the South Texas Agricultural Workers Union (STAWU) which was to coordinate organizing work among Mexican workers, particularly field and packing shed workers. Manuela and James were appointed official organizers for the STAWU. The STAWU's decision to give them the responsibility of organizing the entire Rio Grande Valley is indicative of the confidence their ability and dedication had earned them. Indeed, the area was known as one of the most difficult places to organize, principally because of strong anti-Mexican and anti-union sentiments held by growers, packing shed owners and law enforcement officials.

Despite strong opposition and violent union busting tactics, Manuela and James managed to assist workers in organizing several Mexican unions totaling a membership of over 1,000 field and packing shed workers. Recalcitrant bosses, however, made it almost impossible to translate labor organizing success into gains at the workplace. After serious deliberation, Manuela and James decided to leave for San Antonio to meet with organizers from throughout the state. In San Antonio the possibility of bringing to fruition a major Mexican labor victory seemed tenable.

Once there, both husband and wife became an integral part of a formidable labor strike by Mexican pecan shellers, the majority of whom were women. They joined with union members and union leadership such as Emma Tenayuca with whom they had been in contact since the early 1930s. Since Emma was so intimately tied to the events of these early labor struggles, it is impossible to speak of one without the other.

Emma began her involvement in the labor movement at the age of sixteen when she read of the 1932 and 1933 strikes against the Finck Cigar Company in San Antonio. She walked the picket line and subsequently joined the strikers in jail. During 1934 and 1935, Emma was also prominent in the formation of two locals of the International Ladies Garment Workers Union. By 1937, she had become a member of the Executive Committee of the Workers Alliance of America, a national federation of unemployed workers' organizations. She had also assumed the position of general secretary of some ten Alliance chapters in San Antonio. Many of the Alliance members were affiliated with local unions of cigar, garment and pecan shelling workers.

When at the end of January, 1938, approximately 2,000 pecan shellers went out on strike against the local industry, they asked Emma to act as their strike spokesperson and this she did enthusiastically. Her speeches were passionately arousing and her popularity soared making her one of the most respected and

dedicated union leaders in San Antonio. It was during this time
that she became known as " La Pasionaria."

Strikers were teargassed on at least six occasions, as some 150
San Antonio city police officers were deployed to prevent the
strike from spreading. Over a thousand strikers were jailed and
sent to both the city and county penal facilities. Trivial and even
ludicrous charges such as obstructing the sidewalk were trumped
up to arrest strikers. Repression and intimidation were used to
instill fear in workers and keep them from joining the strike.
These tactics were only partially successful: six to eight thousand
pecan shellers, most of them women, did heed the call to strike.
Soup kitchens were established and thousands received their meals
there. The Texas Women's International League for Peace and
Freedom assisted in the operation of the soup kitchens and
extended additional help in other areas. Had it not been for
threats, numerous Mexican-owned and operated businesses would
have given their help to strikers, but city politicos promised they
would find cause to shut down establishments known to render
assistance to the strikers.

The leadership and membership of the strike and pecan
shellers' unions was comprised primarily of women. The Comisión
Pro-Conferencia had three members, two of them women,
Manuela Solis Sager and Juana Sánchez. And two of the three
members of the Strike Committee were women, Emma Tenayuca
and Minnie Rendón. Thus, four out of six major strike leaders
were women in the front lines working directly with the rank and
file.

The strike helped to call attention to the deplorable working
conditions of Mexican laborers and the Texas Industrial
Commission began a series of hearings into the strikers'
grievances. The governor of the state intervened and attempted to
persuade the pecan shelling industry to arbitrate. The industry
finally joined the bargaining table and agreed on a settlement
favoring the workers' demands.

The strike, while restoring wages to pre-strike levels,
regrettably, saw its nominal gains whittled away a few months
later when the industry remechanized.[3] Thousands of pecan
shellers were displaced leaving approximately a thousand youthful
employees in the city's entire pecan shelling industry. In the
meantime, just as the Depression seemed to be easing up on
Mexican workers, war loomed large on the horizon portending a
hiatus for Mexican participation in the Texas labor movement.

After the victorious strike and abrogated settlement, both Emma and Manuela maintained a political course that awaits a more detailed examination than this short note can accommodate. Some observations, however, should be made. In 1939, Emma assumed the position of chair of the Texas Communist Party. In that same year, she also co-authored what is still the most lucid and accurate analysis of the Mexican working class ever produced by a member of the Communist Party. Emma's effectiveness and popularity as a Mexican labor leader often made her the focal point of anti-union and anti-Mexican hysteria which eventually forced her to leave Texas to ensure her personal safety. Years later she would return to San Antonio as a certified teacher and teach until her recent retirement. She still teaches occasionally.

Manuela, on the other hand, remained with her husband in San Antonio where she has continued her involvement in progressive causes related to the Chicano movement, the women's movement, immigrant rights, electoral politics, and opposition to U.S. interventionist foreign policy. She feels strongly about these issues as evidenced in her acceptance speech at the NACS conference.

Both women are an inspiration and no doubt will continue to provide examples of courage, dedication, and purpose. As Mexicans, their history of involvement and accomplishment underscores the struggle and search for justice and equality among our people.

The following is the text of the acceptance presentations Manuela Solis Sager and Emma B. Tenayuca delivered at the 1984 NACS conference.

Manuela Solis Sager

"Voy a leerles algo en español porque ... es la lengua mía y quisiera dejar un mensaje a ustedes y les voy a tener que leer porque estoy muy nerviosa y *excited* con todos esto.

"El mensaje que debemos dejar con los educadores es muy simple. Al investigar la clase obrera mexicana hay que estudiarnos como lo que somos, *obreros*, y al estudiar a los obreros hay que entender nuestras luchas contra el imperialismo, nuestras luchas contra las industrias, nuestras luchas contra las universidades y en las áreas agrícolas. Pero al estudiar también hay que participar en esas luchas--no se debe estudiarlas solamente.

"Fuera con Reagan en el '84! Abajo con la intervención imperialista en Centroamérica! Y empleos para todos nosotros y paz.

"También quiero decirle algo a la mujer mexicana y a la mujer en general. Esto no lo escribí, lo estoy diciendo de mi corazón. Esto quiero decirles a ustedes--que así como nosotros luchamos, ustedes tienen que seguir esta lucha y seguir adelante y ayudarnos ... Yo ya ... voy a cumplir 73 años el 29 de abril y estoy en la lucha desde hace más de cincuenta años y quisiera que cada uno de nosotros, siguiéramos adelante sobre ese mismo tema y ayudar a la clase trabajadora, a las luchas del pueblo trabajador!"

Emma B. Tenayuca

"The first thing I would like to do is thank you very, very much. During the thirties when I was working in San Antonio I never attached any importance to my work. I never kept newspaper clippings. Actually, I was too busy organizing and working.

"I was born in San Antonio ... on my mother's side of the family, I am a descendant of Spaniards who came to Texas and settled in one of the colonies on the Louisiana border. There was a mission established there. On my father's side, we never claimed anything but Indian blood, and so throughout my life I didn't have a fashionable Spanish name like García or Sánchez, I carried an Indian name. And I was very, very conscious of that. It was this historical background and my grandparents' attitude which formed my ideas and actually gave me the courage later to undertake the type of work I did in San Antonio. I had wonderful parents and wonderful grandparents.

"I remember since I was about five watching the Battle of Flowers parade in front of Santa Rosa Hospital right in front of the Plaza del Zacate. I also remember, and I was quite young, the election of Ma Ferguson. Here was the occasion for quite a discussion in my family between my grandfather and my mother's uncle. My father had voted for Jim Ferguson, even though Ferguson had been forced out ... for having taken some money from the University of Texas. My parents, my grandfather, and his family voted for Ma Ferguson and the reason for that was because she had stood up against the Ku Klux Klan in Texas.

"A memory comes back to me of hooded figures. I also remember one particular circular, and it read "one hundred percent White Protestant Americans." That left me out. I was a Catholic and also ... a mestiza, a mixture of Indian and Spanish. During the time I was growing up, it was very difficult to ignore ... conditions in San Antonio. Ours was a close-knit family, and I didn't remember any discrimination, actually, until I started school. A lot of people found out that it was hard to push me around.

"But during the time that I was growing up here in San Antonio, my home, I had deep roots there and I felt a strong attachment with the past. I went to the mission when I was quite young. I remember we used to hold confessions on the eighth of December, which is the day of Our Immaculate Conception. I remember kicking up the dust and discovering my first Indian arrow, and that of course excited my imagination. My father taught me to fish in the San Antonio River, and it was that river that almost brought about my drowning. I was pulled out of that river with water rushing out of my nose and my mouth. I never learned to swim after that.

"I witnessed a lot of discussion on topics such as Carranza and the Cristero Movement. I could not help but be impressed by the discussions ... of my family, my family circle. Also, the Plaza del Zacate was the type of place where everyone went on Saturdays and Sundays to hold discussions. If you went there you could find a minister preaching. You could also find revolutionists from Mexico holding discussions. I was exposed to all of this. I was also exposed to the nature of politics and to ... form[s] of corruption. I remember as a youngster attending a political rally with my father. Sandwiches were distributed and inside the sandwich was a five-dollar bill. I didn't get one, neither did my father.

"Let me give you an idea of what it meant to be a Mexican in San Antonio. There were no bus drivers that were Mexicans when I was growing up. The only Mexican workers employed by the City Public Service and the Water Board were laborers, ditch diggers. I remember they used to take the leaves from the pecan trees and they would put them on their heads in order to go out and dig ditches. I came into contact with many, many families who had grievances, who had not been paid. I was perhaps eight or nine years old at the time. On one occasion while at the Plaza with my grandfather there was a family of poor migrant workers who came and a collection was made for them. I learned that while the family had harvested a crop, the farm owner who lived somewhere in the Rio Grande Valley had awakened the family at two or three in the morning, and he and his son ran the family from the land with shotguns. I remember this discussion at the Plaza on a Saturday and they decided to go down to the Mexican Consul and [raise] charges against the farmer. People from the Plaza accompanied the family to the Mexican Consul. It turned out that the family was Texas-born. This made quite an impression on me as a seventeen-year-old, a recent graduate from high school.

"One of the first groups of organized workers that I remember were women and it is with them that we saw the beginning of the breakup of the type of political organization that existed in San Antonio. And I saw those women herded and taken to jail. The second time that happened, I went to jail with them. These were the Finck Cigar workers on strike. In both the Finck Cigar and pecan shelling strikes there was a desire to keep ... Mexican workers as a reserve labor pool which could be used in case of strikes. There was poverty everywhere.

"My city enjoyed the dubious reputation of having one of the highest tuberculosis rates in the country. My San Antonio also had the reputation of having one of the highest infant mortality rates. It was these things and ... the fact that I had a grandfather who lost his money when the banks were closed in 1932 that made a deep impression on me. I think it was the combination of being a Texan, being a Mexican, and being more Indian than Spanish that propelled me to take action. I don't think I ever thought in terms of fear. If I had, I think I would have stayed home.

"We had demonstrations of 10,000 unemployed workers demanding employment. We visited the mayor's office. We staged a strike at City Hall, and it was there that I was arrested. I went to jail many times. A nun friend used to write to me and tell me, 'Emma, I have to read the papers to see whether you are in or out of jail.'

"I believe that what was done there and what had to be done was confronting the power structure. It was the struggles of the Workers' Alliance, ... bringing in ... people of mutual aid organizations, some of whom had been anarchists. I read all about the Wobblies and in my mind I also became an anarchist.

"I had the idea of actually beginning with the Finck Cigar strike, of actually attacking the power structure, but at the same time doing it in such a manner that we did not get beaten up. We didn't go to jail too often you see. It was much easier for twenty or thirty of us to go to jail for three days or seventy-two hours. It was easier doing that than to fight. And we had many demonstrations in San Antonio. We have now a COPS (Citizens Organized for Public Service) organization, and I assure you that it is one of the most democratic and progressive organizations. And a very active organization, too!

"So in giving thanks I am thinking of the Finck Cigar strikers. I'm also thinking of the garment workers who went to jail and whose strikes were broken. I'm thinking also of men such as Maury Maverick, Sr. of San Antonio. I'm also thinking of the then Texas assistant attorney general, Everett Looney, who came to San Antonio and defended me on a charge of inciting to riot and, therefore, I was able to spend my twentieth, twenty-first, and twenty-third birthdays out of jail. I thank you very much."

NOTES

1. This paper is a revised version of an article of the same title published in *Chicana Voices: Intersections of Class, Race and Gender*, eds. Teresa Cordova, Norma Cantú, Gilberto Cardenas, Juan García, and Christine M. Sierra. (Austin: National Association for Chicano Studies, Center for Mexican American Studies, University of Texas at Austin, 1986), pp. 30-41.

2. The NACS conference program honoring Manuela and Emma was sponsored by the Chicano Studies Research Center at UCLA and organized by the authors. The accompanying reception was sponsored by the Center for Mexican American Studies, The University of Texas, Austin, and the Mexican American Chamber of Commerce, Austin, Texas. The program included a slide presentation on the condition of Mexican workers and the history

of Mexican labor activity in Texas during the 1930s as well as introductory remarks by Calderón and Zamora. The slide presentation and accompanying materials have been deposited at the Chicano Studies Research Library, UCLA, for public use.

3. Prior to the beginning of the Depression in the early 1930s, the San Antonio pecan shelling industry had been mechanized. But the Depression made manual labor more profitable than mechanization during most of the 1930s.

A PROMISE FULFILLED:
MEXICAN CANNERY WORKERS
IN SOUTHERN CALIFORNIA*

by

Vicki L. Ruiz

Since 1930 approximately one-quarter of all Mexican women wage earners in the Southwest have found employment as blue collar industrial workers (25.3% (1930), 25.6% (1980)).[1] These women have been overwhelmingly segregated into semi-skilled, assembly line positions. Garment and food processing firms historically have hired Mexicanas for seasonal line tasks. Whether sewing slacks or canning peaches, these workers have generally been separated from the year-round, higher paid male employees. This ghettoization by job and gender has in many instances facilitated labor activism among Mexican women. An examination of a rank and file union within a Los Angeles cannery from 1939 to 1945 illuminates the transformation of women's networks into channels for change.

On August 31, 1939, during a record-breaking heat wave, nearly all of the four hundred and thirty workers at the California Sanitary Canning Company (popularly known as Cal San), one of the largest food processing plants in Los Angeles, staged a massive walk-out and established a twenty-four hour picket line in front of the plant. The primary goals of these employees, mostly Mexican women, concerned not only higher wages and better working conditions, but also recognition of their union--The United Cannery, Agricultural, Packing and Allied Workers of America, Local 75--and a closed shop.

---

*Reprinted from The Pacific Historian: A Quarterly of Western History and Ideas 2 (Summer 1986): 50-61. This article is taken from Cannery Women, Cannery Lives: Mexican Women, Unionization and the California Food Processing Industry, 1930-1950 (New Mexico, 1987).

The Cal San strike marked the beginning of labor activism by Mexicana cannery and packing workers in Los Angeles. This essay steps beyond a straight narrative, chronicling the rise and fall of UCAPAWA locals in California. It provides a glimpse of cannery life--the formal, as well as the informal, social structures governing the shop floor. An awareness of the varying lifestyles and attitudes of women food processing workers will be developed in these pages. No single model representing either the typical female or typical Mexicana industrial worker exists. Contrary to the stereotype of the Hispanic woman tied to the kitchen, most Mexican women, at some point in their lives, have been wage laborers. Since 1880, food processing has meant employment for Spanish-speaking women living in California, attracted to the industry because of seasonal schedules and extended family networks within the plants.[2]

During the 1930s, the canning labor force included young daughters, newly-married women, middle-aged wives, and widows. Occasionally, three generations worked at a particular cannery--daughter, mother, and grandmother. These Mexicanas entered the job market as members of a family wage economy. They pooled their resources to put food on the table. "My father was a busboy," one former Cal San employee recalled, "and to keep the family going ... in order to bring in a little more money ... my mother, my grandmother, my mother's brother, my sister and I all worked together at Cal San."[3]

Some Mexicanas, who had worked initially out of economic necessity, stayed in the canneries in order to buy the "extras"--a radio, a phonograph, jazz records, fashionable clothes. These consumers often had middle-class aspirations, and at times, entire families labored to achieve material advancement (and in some cases, assimilation), while in others, only the wives or daughters expressed interest in acquiring an American lifestyle. One woman defied her husband by working outside the home. Justifying her action, she asserted that she wanted to move to a "better" neighborhood because she didn't want her children growing up with "Italians and Mexicans."[4]

Some teenagers had no specific, goal-oriented rationale for laboring in the food processing industry. They simply "drifted" into cannery life; they wanted to join their friends at work or were bored at home. Like the first women factory workers in the United States, the New England mill hands of the 1830s, Mexican women entered the labor force for every conceivable reason and for no reason at all. Work added variety and opened new avenues of choices.[5]

In one sense, cannery labor for the unmarried daughter represented a break from the traditional family. While most young Mexicanas maintained their cultural identity, many yearned for more independence, particularly after noticing the more liberal lifestyles of self-supporting Anglo co-workers. Sometimes young Mexican women would meet at work, become friends, and decide to room together. Although their families lived in the Los Angeles area and disapproved of their daughters living away from home, these women defied parental authority by renting an apartment.[6]

Kin networks, however, remained an integral part of cannery life. These extended family structures fostered the development of a "cannery culture." A collective identity among food processing workers emerged as a result of family ties, job segregation by gender, and working conditions. Although women comprised seventy-five percent of the labor force in California canneries and packing houses, they were clustered into specific departments-- washing, grading, cutting, canning, and packing--and their earnings varied with production levels. They engaged in piece work while male employees, conversely, as warehousemen and cooks, received hourly wages.[7]

Mexicana family and work networks resembled those found by historian Thomas Dublin in the Lowell, Massachusetts, mills in the ante-bellum era. California canneries and New England cotton mills, though a century apart, contained similar intricate kin and friendship networks. Dublin's statement that women "recruited one another ... secured jobs for each other, and helped newcomers make the numerous adjustments called for in a very new and different setting" can be applied directly to the Mexican experience. Mexican women, too, not only assisted their relatives and friends in obtaining employment but also initiated neophytes into the rigor of cannery routines. For instance, in the sorting department of the California Sanitary Canning Company, seasoned workers taught new arrivals the techniques of grading peaches. "Fancies" went into one bin; those considered "choice" into another; those destined for fruit cocktail into a third box; and finally the rots had to be discarded. Since peach fuzz irritated bare skin, women shared their cold cream with the initiates, encouraging them to coat their hands and arms in order to relieve the itching and to protect their skin from further inflammation.[8] Thus, as Dublin notes for the Lowell mills, one can find "clear evidence of the maintenance of traditional kinds of social relationships in a new setting and serving new purposes."[9]

Standing in the same spot week after week, month after month, women workers often developed friendships crossing family and ethnic lines. While Mexicanas constituted the largest number of workers, many Russian Jewish women also found employment in southern California food processing firms.[10] Their day-to-day problems (slippery floors, peach fuzz, production speeds-ups, arbitrary supervisors, and even sexual harassment) cemented feelings of solidarity among these women, as well as nurturing an "us against them" mentality in relation to management. They also shared common concerns, such as seniority status, quotas, wages, and child care.

Child care was a key issue for married women who at times organized themselves to secure suitable babysitting arrangements. In one cannery, the workers established an off-plant nursery, hired and paid an elderly woman who found it "darn hard ... taking care of 25 to 30 little ones." During World War II, some Orange County cannery workers, stranded without any day care alternatives, resorted to locking their small children in their cars. These particular workers, as UCAPAWA members, fought for and won management-financed day care on the firm's premises, which lasted for the duration of World War II.[11] Cooperation among women food processing workers was an expression of their collective identity within the plants.

At Cal San many Mexican and Jewish workers shared another bond--neighborhood. Both groups lived in Boyle Heights, an East Los Angeles working-class community. Although Mexican and Jewish women lived on different blocks, they congregated at street car stops during the early morning hours. Sometimes friendships developed across ethnic lines. These women, if not friends, were at least passing acquaintances. Later, as UCAPAWA members, they would become mutual allies.[12]

Cannery workers employed a special jargon when conversing among themselves. Speaking in terms of when an event took place by referring to the fruit or vegetable being processed, workers knew immediately when the incident occurred, for different crops arrived on the premises during particular months. For instance, the phrase "We met in spinach, fell in love in peaches, and married in tomatoes" indicates that the couple met in March, fell in love in August, and married in October.[13]

Historians Leslie Tentler and Susan Porter Benson, studying women workers on the east coast, have also documented the existence of female work cultures. However, unlike the women Tentler studied, Spanish-speaking cannery workers were not waiting for Prince Charming to marry them and take them away from factory labor. Mexican women realized that they probably would continue their seasonal labor after marriage. Also in contrast, Benson, delineating cooperative work patterns among department store clerks from 1890 to 1940, asserted that women experienced peer sanctions if they exceeded their "stint" or standard sales quota.[14] Mexican cannery workers differed from eastern clerks in that they did not receive a set salary, but were paid according to their production level. Collaboration and unity among piece rate employees attested to the strength of the cannery culture. Although increasing managerial control at one level, gender-determined job segmentation did facilitate the development of a collective identity among women in varying occupations and of diverse ethnic backgrounds.

Of these work related networks, the cannery culture appeared unique in that it also included men. Comprising twenty-five percent of the labor force, men also felt a sense of identity as food processing workers. Familial and ethnic bonds served to integrate male employees into the cannery culture. Mexicans, particularly, were often related to women workers by birth or marriage. In fact, it was not unusual for young people to meet their future spouses inside the plants. Cannery romances and courtships provided fertile *chisme* which traveled from one kin or peer network to the next.[15]

The cannery culture was a curious blend of Mexican extended families and a general women's work culture, nurtured by assembly line segregation and common interests. Networks within the plants cut across generation, gender, and ethnicity. A detailed examination of the California Sanitary Canning Company further illuminates the unique collective identity among food processing workers. Cal San, a one plant operation, handled a variety of crops--apricots and peaches in the summer, tomatoes and pimentoes in the fall, spinach in the winter and early spring. This diversity enabled the facility, which employed approximately four hundred people, to remain open at least seven months a year.[16]

Female workers received relatively little for their labors due to the seasonal nature of their work and the piece rate scale. In the Cal San warehouse and kitchen departments, exclusively male areas, workers received an hourly wage ranging from fifty-eight to seventy cents an hour. On the other hand, in the washing, grading, cutting and canning divisions, exclusively female areas, employees earned according to their production level.[17] In order to make a respectable wage, a woman had to secure a favorable position on the line, a spot near the chutes or gates where the produce first entered the department. Carmen Bernal Escobar, a former Cal San employee, recalled:

> There were two long tables with sinks that you find in old-fashioned houses and fruit would come down out of the chutes and we would wash them and put them out on a belt. I had the first place so I could work for as long as I wanted. Women in the middle hoarded fruit because the work wouldn't last forever and the women at the end really suffered. Sometimes they would stand there for hours before any fruit would come down for them to wash. They just got the leftovers. Those at the end of the line hardly made nothing.[18]

Although an efficient employee positioned in a favorable spot on the line could earn as much as one dollar an hour, most women workers averaged thirty to thirty-five cents. Their male counterparts, however, earned from $5.25 to $6.25 per day.[19]

Though wages were low, there was no dearth of owner paternalism. Cal San's owners, George and Joseph Shapiro, took personal interest in the firm's operations. Both brothers made daily tours of each department, inspecting machinery, opening cans, and chatting with personnel. Sometimes a favored employee--especially if young, female, and attractive--would receive a pat on the cheek or a friendly hug; or as one informant stated, "a good pinch on the butt."[20]

While the Shapiros kept close watch on the activities within the cannery, the foremen and floor ladies exercised a great deal of autonomous authority over workers. They assigned them positions on the line, punched their time cards and even determined where they could buy lunch. Of course, these supervisors could fire an employee at their discretion. One floor lady earned the unflattering sobriquet "San Quentin." Some workers, in order to make a livable wage, cultivated the friendship of their supervisors. One favored employee even had the luxury of taking an afternoon nap. Forepersons also hosted wedding and baby showers for "their girls." While the "pets" enjoyed preferential treatment, they also acquired the animosity of their co-workers.[21]

The supervisors (all Anglo) neither spoke nor understood Spanish. The language barrier contributed to increasing tensions inside the plant, especially when management had the authority to discharge an employee for speaking Spanish. Foremen also took advantage of the situation by altering productions cards of workers who spoke only Spanish. One foreman, for example, was noted for routinely cheating his Mexicana mother-in-law out of her hard-earned wages. Some women sensed something was wrong but either could not express their suspicions or were afraid to do so. Bilingual employees, cognizant of management's indiscretions, were threatened with dismissal.[22] In general, low wages, tyrannical forepersons, and the "pet" system prompted attempts at unionization. In 1937 a group of workers tried to establish an American Federation of Labor union, but a stable local failed to develop. Two years later Cal San employees renewed their trade union efforts, this time under the banner of UCAPAWA-CIO.[23]

The United Cannery, Agricultural, Packing and Allied Workers of America has long been an orphan of twentieth-century labor history even though it was the seventh largest CIO affiliate in its day. Probable reasons for this neglect include the union's relatively short life--1937-1950--and its eventual expulsion from the CIO on the grounds of alleged communist domination. UCAPAWA's leadership was left-oriented, although not directly connected to the Communist Party. Many of the executive officers and organizers identified themselves as Marxists, but others could be labeled New Deal liberals. As one UCAPAWA national vice-president, Luisa Moreno, stated, "UCAPAWA was a left union not a communist union." Union leaders shared a vision of a national, decentralized labor union, one in which power flowed from below. Local members controlled their own meetings and elected their own officers and business agents. National and state offices helped coordinate the individual needs and endeavors of each local. Moreover, UCAPAWA's deliberate recruitment of Black, Mexican, and female labor organizers and subsequent unionizing campaigns aimed at minority workers reflected its leaders' commitment to those sectors of the working-class generally ignored by traditional craft unions.[24]

This CIO affiliate, in its policies and practices, closely resembled the nineteenth-century Knights of Labor. Like the Knights, UCAPAWA leaders publicly boasted that their organization welcomed all persons regardless of race, nationality, creed, or gender. Both groups fostered grass roots participation as well as local leadership. Perhaps it was no coincidence that the official UCAPAWA motto "An Injury To One Is An Injury To All" paraphrased the Knights' "An Injury To One Is The Concern Of All."[25]

In California UCAPAWA initially concentrated on organizing agricultural workers, but with limited success. The union, however, began to make inroads among food processing workers in the Northeast and in Texas. Because of its successes in organizing canneries and packing houses, as well as the inability of maintaining viable dues-paying unions among farm workers, union policy shifted. After 1939, union leaders emphasized the establishment of strong, solvent cannery and packing house locals, hoping to use them as bases of operations for future farm labor campaigns.[26] One of the first plants to experience this new wave of activity was the California Sanitary Canning Company.

In July 1939, Dorothy Ray Healey, a national vice-president of UCAPAWA, began to recruit Cal San workers. Healey, a vivacious young woman of twenty-four, already had eight years of labor organizing experience. At the age of sixteen, she participated in the San Jose, California, cannery strike as a representative of the Cannery and Agricultural Workers Industrial Union (C&AWIU). Healey had assumed leadership positions in both the C&AWIU and the Young Communist League.[27]

Dorothy Healey's primary task involved organizing as many employees as possible. She distributed leaflets and membership cards outside the cannery gates. Healey talked with workers before and after work, and visited their homes. She also encouraged new recruits who proselytized inside the plants during lunch time. As former Cal San employee Julia Luna Mount remembered, "Enthusiastic people like myself would take the literature and bring it into the plant. We would hand it to everybody, explain it, and encourage everybody to pay attention." Workers organizing other workers was a common trade union strategy, and within three weeks four hundred (out of 430) employees had joined UCAPAWA. This phenomenal membership drive indicates not only worker receptiveness and Healey's prowess as an activist but also the existence of a cannery culture. Membership cards traveled from one kin or peer network to the next. Meetings were held in workers' homes so that entire families could listen to Healey and her recruits.[28]

The Shapiros refused to recognize the union or negotiate with its representatives. On August 31, 1939, at the height of the peach season, the vast majority of Cal San employees left their stations and staged a dramatic walk-out. Only thirty workers stayed behind and sixteen of these stragglers joined the picket lines outside the plant the next day. Although the strike occurred at the peak of the company's most profitable season and elicited the support of most line personnel, management refused to bargain with the local. In fact, the owners issued press statements to the effect that the union did not represent a majority of the workers.[29]

In anticipation of a protracted strike, Healey immediately organized workers into a number of committees. A negotiating committee, picket details, and food committees were formed. The strikers' demands included union recognition, a closed shop, elimination of the piece rate system, minimal wage increases, and the dismissal of nearly every supervisor. Healey persuaded the workers to assign top priority to the closed shop demand. The striking employees realized the risk they were taking, for only one UCAPAWA local had secured a closed shop contract.[30]

The food committee persuaded East Los Angeles grocers to donate various staples such as flour, sugar, and baby food to the Cal San strikers. Many business people obviously considered their donations to be advertisements and gestures of goodwill toward their customers. Some undoubtedly acted out of a political consciousness since earlier in the year East Los Angeles merchants had financed El Congreso De Pueblos Que Hablan Español, the first national civil rights assembly among Latinos in the United States.[31] Whatever the roots of its success, the food committee sparked new strategies among the rank and file.

Early in the strike, the unionists extended their activities beyond their twenty-four hour, seven days a week picket line outside the plant. They discovered a supplementary tactic--the secondary boycott. Encouraged by their success in obtaining food donations from local markets, workers took the initiative themselves and formed boycott teams. The team leaders approached the managers of various retail and wholesale groceries in the Los Angeles area urging them to refuse Cal San products and to remove current stocks from their shelves. If a manager was unsympathetic, a small band of women picketed the establishment during business hours. In addition, the International Brotherhood of Teamsters officially vowed to honor the strike. It proved to be only a verbal commitment, for many of its members crossed the picket lines in order to pick up and deliver Cal San goods. At one point Mexicana unions members became so incensed by the sight of several Teamsters unloading their trucks that they climbed onto the loading platform and quickly "depantsed" a group of surprised and embarrassed Teamsters. The secondary boycott was an effective tactic--forty retail and wholesale grocers abided by the strikers' request.[32]

Action by National Labor Relations Board further raised the morale of the striking employees. The NLRB formally reprimanded the Shapiros for refusing to bargain with the UCAPAWA affiliate. However, the timing of the strike, the successful boycott, and favorable governmental decisions failed to bring management to the bargaining table. After a two and a half month stalemate, the workers initiated an innovative technique that became, as Healey recalled, "the straw that broke the Shapiros' back."[33]

Both George and Joseph Shapiro lived in affluent sections of Los Angeles, and their wealthy neighbors were as surprised as the brothers to discover one morning a small group of children conducting orderly picket lines on the Shapiros' front lawns. These malnourished waifs carried signs with such slogans as "Shapiro is starving my Mama" and "I'm underfed because my Mama is underpaid." Many of the neighbors became so moved by the sight of these children conducting what became a twenty-four hour vigil that they offered their support, usually by distributing food and beverages. And if this was not enough, the owners were reproached by several members of their synagogue. After several days of community pressures, the Shapiros finally agreed to meet with Local 75's negotiating team.[34] The strike had ended.

A settlement was quickly reached. Although the workers failed to win the elimination of the piece rate system, they did receive a five cent wage increase, and many forepersons found themselves unemployed. More importantly, Local 75 had become the second UCAPAWA affiliate (and the first on the west coast) to negotiate successfully a closed shop contract.[35]

The consolidation of the union became the most important task facing Cal San employees. At post-strike meetings, Dorothy Healey outlined election procedures and general operating by-laws. Male and female workers who had assumed leadership positions during the confrontation captured every major post. For example, Carmen Bernal Escobar, head of the secondary boycott committee, became "head shop steward of the women."[36] Soon UCAPAWA organizers Luke Hinman and Ted Rasmussen replaced Dorothy Healey at Cal San. These two men, however, concentrated their organizing energies on a nearby walnut packing plant and, thus, devoted little time to Cal San workers. In late 1940, Luisa Moreno, an UCAPAWA representative, took charge of consolidating Local 75. Like Dorothy Healey, Moreno had a long history of labor activism prior to her tenure with UCAPAWA. As a professional organizer for the AF of L and later for the CIO, Moreno had unionized workers in cigar making plants in Florida and Pennsylvania.[37]

Luisa Moreno helped insure the vitality of Local 75. She vigorously enforced government regulations and contract stipulations. She also encouraged members to air any grievances immediately. On a number of occasions, her fluency in Spanish and English allayed misunderstandings between Mexicana workers and Anglo supervisors. Participation in civic events, such as the annual Labor Day parade, fostered worker solidarity and union pride. The employees also banded together to break certain hiring policies. With one very light-skinned exception, the brothers had refused to hire Blacks. With union pressure, however, in early 1942, the Shapiros relented and hired approximately thirty Blacks. By mid-1941, Local 75 had developed into a strong, united democratic trade union and its members soon embarked on a campaign to organize their counterparts in nearby packing plants.[38]

In 1941, Luisa Moreno, recently elected vice-president of UCAPAWA, was placed in charge of organizing other food processing plants in southern California. She enlisted the aid of Cal San workers in consolidating Local 92 at the California Walnut Growers' Association plant, and Elmo Parra, president of Local 75, headed the Organizing Committee. Cal San workers also participated in the initial union drive at nearby Royal Packing, a plant which processed Ortega Chile products. Since ninety-five percent of Royal Packing employees were Mexican, the Spanish-speaking members of Local 75 played a crucial role in the UCAPAWA effort. They also organized workers at the Glaser Nut Company and Mission Pack. The result of this spate of union activism was the formation of Local 3. By 1942, this local had become the second largest UCAPAWA union.[39]

Mexican women played instrumental roles in the operation of Local 3. In 1943, for example, they filled eight of the fifteen elected positions of the local. They served as major officers and as executive board members. Local 3 effectively enforced contract stipulations and protective legislation, and its members proved able negotiators during annual contract renewals. In July, 1942, for example, *UCAPAWA News* proclaimed the newly-signed Cal San contract to be "the best in the state." Also, in 1943, workers at the

Walnut plant successfully negotiated an incentive plan provision in their contract. The local also provided benefits that few industrial unions could match--free legal advice and a hospitalization plan.[40]

Union members also played active roles in the war effort. At Cal San, a joint labor-management production committee worked to devise more efficient processing methods. As part of the "Food for Victory" campaign, Cal San employees increased their production of spinach to unprecedented levels. In 1942 and 1943, workers at the California Walnut plant donated one day's wages to the American Red Cross. Local 3 also sponsored a successful blood drive. Throughout this period, worker solidarity remained strong. When Cal San closed its doors in 1945, the union arranged jobs for the former employees at the California Walnut plant.[41]

The success of UCAPAWA at the California Sanitary Canning Company can be explained by a number of factors. Prevailing work conditions heightened the union's attractiveness. Elements outside the plant also prompted receptivity among employees. These workers were undoubtedly influenced by the wave of CIO organizing drives being conducted in the Los Angeles area. One woman, for example, joined Local 75 primarily because her husband was a member of the CIO Furniture Workers Union.[42] Along with the Wagner Act, passage of favorable legislation, such as the Fair Labor Standards Act, the Public Contracts Act, and the California minimum wage laws (which set wage and hour levels for cannery personnel), led to the rise of a strong UCAPAWA affiliate.[43] Workers decided that the only way they could benefit from recent protective legislation was to form a union with enough clout to force management to honor these regulations.

World War II also contributed to the development of potent UCAPAWA food processing locals, not only in southern California, but nationwide. To feed U.S. troops at home and abroad, as well as the military and civilian population of America's allies, the federal government issued thousands of contracts to canneries and packing houses.[44] Because of this increased demand for canned goods and related products, management required a plentiful supply of content, hard-working employees. Meanwhile the higher-paying defense industries began to compete for the labor of food processing personnel. Accordingly, canners and packers became more amenable to worker demands than at any other time in the history of food processing. Thus, during the early 1940s, cannery workers, usually at the bottom end of the socio-economic scale, had become "labor aristocrats" due to wartime exigencies.[45]

They were in an atypical position to gain important concessions from their employers in terms of higher wages, better conditions, and greater benefits. As UCAPAWA members, women food processing workers utilized their temporary status to achieve an improved standard of living.[46]

Of course, the dedication and organizing skills of UCAPAWA professionals Dorothy Ray Healey and Luisa Moreno must not be minimized. While Healey played a critical role in the local's initial successes, it was under Moreno's leadership that workers consolidated these gains and branched out to help organize employees in neighboring food processing facilities. The recruitment of minority workers by Healey and Moreno and their stress on local leadership reflect the feasibility and vitality of a democratic trade unionism.

Finally, the most significant ingredient accounting for Local 75's success was the phenomenal degree of worker involvement in the building and nurturing of the union. Deriving strength from their networks within the plant, Cal San workers built an effective local. The cannery culture had, in effect, become translated into unionization. Furthermore, UCAPAWA locals provided women cannery workers with the crucial "social space"[47] necessary to assert their independence and display their talents. They were not rote employees numbed by repetition, but women with dreams, goals, tenacity, and intellect. Unionization became an opportunity to demonstrate their shrewdness and dedication to a common cause. Mexicanas not only followed the organizers' leads but also developed strategies of their own. A fierce loyalty developed as the result of rank and file participation and leadership. Forty years after the strike, Carmen Bernal Escobar emphatically declared, "UCAPAWA was the greatest thing that ever happened to the workers at Cal San. It changed everything and everybody."[48]

This pattern of labor activism is not unique. Laurie Coyle, Gail Hershatter, and Emily Honig in their study of the Farah Strike documented the close bonds that developed among Mexican women garment workers in El Paso, Texas. Anthropologist Patricia Zavella has also explored similar networks among female electronics workers in Albuquerque, New Mexico, and food processing workers in San Jose.[49] But while kin and friendship networks remain part of cannery life, UCAPAWA did not last beyond 1950. After World War II, red-baiting, the disintegration of the national union, Teamster sweetheart contracts and an indifferent NLRB spelled the defeat of democratic trade unionism among Mexican food processing workers. Those employees who refused to join the Teamsters were fired and blacklisted. The Immigration and Naturalization Service, moreover, deported several UCAPAWA activists, including Luisa Moreno.[50] In the face of such concerted opposition, Local 3 could not survive. Yet, the UCAPAWA movement demonstrated that Mexican women, given sufficient opportunity and encouragement, could exercise control over their work lives, and their family ties and exchanges on the line became the channels for unionization.

Notes

1. Vicki Ruiz, "Working for Wages: Mexican Women in the American Southwest, 1930-1980," Southwest Institute for Research on Women, Working Paper No. 19 (1984): 2.

2. Albert Camarillo, *Chicanos in a Changing Society* (Cambridge, Mass: Harvard University Press, 1979), pp. 92, 137, 157, 221; Pedro Castillo, "The Making of a Mexican Barrio: Los Angeles, 1890-1920," (Ph.D. diss., University of California Santa Barbara, 1979), p. 154; Ruiz, "Working for Wages" p. 17.

3. Paul S. Taylor, "Women in Industry," field notes for his book, *Mexican Labor in the United States, 1927-1930*, Paul S. Taylor Collection, Bancroft Library, Berkeley; Heller Committee for Research in Social Economics of the University of California; and Constantine Panuzio, *How Mexicans Earn and Live*, University of California Publication in Economics, 13, No. 1, Cost of Living Studies V (Berkeley: University of California, 1933), pp. 12, 15. Interview with Julia Luna Mount, November 17, 1983, by the author. The term *family wage economy* first appeared in Louise Tilly and Joan Scott, *Women, Work and Family* (New York: Holt, Rinehart and Winston, 1978).

4. Taylor, field notes.

5. Taylor, field notes; Caroline F. Ware, *The Early New England Cotton Manufacturer* (Boston: Houghton Mifflin Company, 1931; rpt. ed., New York, NY: Johnson Reprint Corporation, 1966), pp. 217-219.

6. Douglas Monroy, "An Essay on Understanding the Work Experience of Mexicans in Southern California, 1900-1939," *Aztlan: International Journal of Chicano Studies Research*, 12 (Spring 1981): 70; Taylor, field notes.

7. U.S. National Youth Administration, State of California, *An Occupational Study of the Fruit and Vegetable Canning Industry in California.* Prepared by Edward G. Stoy and Frances W. Strong, State of California (1938), pp. 15-39. My thoughts on the development of a cannery culture derive from oral interviews with former cannery and packing house workers and organizers, and from the works of Patricia Zavella, Thomas Dublin, and Louise Lamphere.

8. Thomas Dublin, *Women at Work: The Transformation of Work and Community in Lowell, Massachussetts, 1826-1860* (New York: Columbia University Press, 1979), pp. 41-48; interview with Carmen Bernal Escobar, February 11, 1979 by the author; Mount interview; letter from Luisa Moreno dated March 22, 1983, to the author.

9. Dublin, p. 48.

10. Mount interview; Escobar interview.

11. "Interview with Elizabeth Nicholas" by Ann Baxandall Krooth and Jaclyn Greenberg published in *Harvest Quarterly*, Nos. 3-4 (September-December 1976): 15-16; interview with Luisa Moreno, August 5, 1976, by Albert Camarillo.

12. Howard Shorr, "Boyle Heights Population Estimates: 1940" (unpublished materials); David Weissman, "Boyle Heights--A Study in Ghettos," *The Reflex* 6 (July 1935): 32; Mount interview; interview with María Rodriguez, April 26, 1984, by the author. Note: María Rodriguez is a pseudonym used at the person's request.

13. Interview with Luisa Moreno, July 27, 1978, by the author.

14. Leslie Woodcock Tentler, *Wage Earning Women: Industrial Work and Family Life in the United States, 1900-1930* (New York: Oxford University Press, 1979), pp. 71-75; Escobar interview; Susan Porter Benson, "'The Customers Ain't God': The Work Culture of Department Store Saleswomen, 1890-1940," in *Working Class America*, eds. Michael H. Frisch and Daniel J. Walkowitz (Urbana: University of Illinois Press, 1983), pp. 197-198.

15. *N.Y.A. Study*, pp. 15-39; Castillo, p. 154; Moreno interview, July 1978; Rodriguez interview, April 1984. Note *Chisme* means gossip.

16. California Canners' Directory (July 1936), p. 2; Escobar interview; *UCAPAWA News*, September 1939; *Economic Material on the California Cannery Industry*, prepared by Research Department, California CIO Council (February 1946), p. 18; California Governor C.C. Young, Mexican Fact-Finding Committee, *Mexicans in California* (San Francisco: California State

295

Printing Office, 1930; reprinted by R and E Research Associates, San Francisco, 1970), pp. 49-54, 89; interview with Dorothy Ray Healey, January 21, 1979, by the author; Escobar interview; letter fron Luisa Moreno dated July 28, 1979, to the author.

17. U.S., Department of Labor, Women's Bureau, *Application of Labor Legislation to the Fruit and Vegetable Preserving Industries*, Bulletin of the Women's Bureau, No. 176 (Washington, D.C.: Government Printing Office, 1940), p. 90; Escobar interview, *N.Y.A. Study*, pp. 15-39.

18. Escobar interview; Rodriguez interview.

19. Escobar interview; *N.Y.A. Study*; pp. 15-39.

20. Escobar interview; Mount interview.

21. Escobar interview; Healey interview.

22. Escobar interview.

23. Victor B. Nelson-Cisneros, "UCAPAWA and Chicanos in California: The Farm Worker Period," *Aztlán: International Journal of Chicano Studies Research* 6 (Fall 1976): 463.

24. Interview with Luisa Moreno, September 6, 1979, by the author; Healey interview; Moreno interview, August 1976; Moreno interview, July 1978; *Report of Donald Henderson, General President to the Second Annual Convention of the United Cannery, Agricultural, Packing and Allied Workers of America* (San Francisco, December 12-16, 1938), pp. 14, 22, 32-33; *Proceedings, First National Convention of the United Cannery, Agricultural, Packing and Allied Workers of America* (Denver, July 9-12, 1937), p. 21; *New York Times*, November 24, 1938; *Proceedings, Third National Convention of the United Cannery, Agricultural, Packing and Allied Workers of America* (Chicago, December 3-7, 1940), pp. 60-66.

25. Philip S. Foner, *Women and the American Labor Movement* (New York: The Free Press, 1979), pp. 190-94, 197-98, 211-12; Susan Levine, "Labor's True Woman: Domesticity and Equal Rights in the Knights of Labor," *Journal of American History* 70 (September 1983): 323-339; Sidney Lens, *The Labor Wars* (Garden City, New York: Anchor Books, 1974), p. 65; *Constitution and By-Laws*, as amended by the Second National Convention of the United Cannery, Agriculural, Packing and Allied Workers of America. Effective December 17, 1938, pp. 2, 26-7.

26. Sam Kushner, *Long Road to Delano* (New York: International Publishers, 1975), pp. 90-91; Nelson-Cisneros, pp. 460-67, 473; *Proceedings, Third UCAPAWA Convention*, p. 10; *Executive Officers' Report*, pp. 9-10.

27. Nelson-Cisneros, p. 463; Healey interview; *UCAPAWA News*, October 1939.

28. Healey interview; Escobar interview; *UCAPAWA News*, September 1939; Mount interview.

29. Escobar interview; Healey interview; *UCAPAWA News*, September 1939; *Los Angeles Times*, September 1, 1939.

30. Healey interview; Escobar interview.

31. Escobar interview; Moreno interview, August 1976; Albert Camarillo, *Chicanos in California* (San Francisco: Boyd & Fraser, 1984), pp. 61-63.

32. *UCAPAWA News*, September 1939; *UCAPAWA News*, December 1939; Escobar interview.

33. *UCAPAWA News*, September 1939; Healey interview.

34. Healey interview; *UCAPAWA News*, September 1939; *UCAPAWA News*, December 1939.

35. Healey interview; Escobar interview; *UCAPAWA News*, December 1939.

36. Escobar interview; Healey interview; Moreno letter, July 1979.

37. Moreno interview, September 1979; Moreno interview August 12-13, 1977 with Albert Camarillo; Escobar interview; Moreno interview, July 1978.

38. Escobar interview; Moreno interview, September 1979; Moreno letter, July 1979.

39. *UCAPAWA News*, August 25, 1941; Moreno interview, September 1979; Moreno letter, July 1979; *UCAPAWA News*, November 17, 1941; *UCAPAWA News*, December 1, 1941.

40. *UCAPAWA News*, February 1, 1943; *UCAPAWA News*, July 15, 1942; *UCAPAWA News*, December 15, 1943; *UCAPAWA News*, June 15, 1942; *UCAPAWA News*, July 1, 1944.

41. *UCAPAWA News*, April 10, 1942; *UCAPAWA News*, April 1, 1943; *UCAPAWA News*, March 11, 1942; *UCAPAWA News*, May 15, 1943; *FTA News*, January 1, 1945; Moreno interview, September 1979; Moreno letter, July 1979.

42. Escobar interview; for more information concerning other CIO campaigns, see Luis Leobardo Arroyo, "Chicano Participation in Organized Labor: The CIO in Los Angeles, 1938-1950," *Aztlán: International Journal of Chicano Studies Research* 6 (Summer 1975): 277-303.

43. *Women's Bureau Bulletin*, pp. 3-8, 102-03.

44. Vicki L. Ruiz, "UCAPAWA, Chicanas, and the California Food Processing Industry, 1937-1950," (Ph.D. diss., Stanford University, 1982), pp. 164, 194.

45. The term *labor aristrocracy* first appeared in E.J. Hobsbawn's *Labouring Men: Studies in the History of Labour* (New York: Basic Books, Inc., 1964). Other historians have refined the applicability and criteria for the term.

46. Ruiz, "UCAPAWA, Chicanas," pp. 151-176.

47. Sara Evans has defined "social space" as an area "within which members of an oppressed group can develop an independent sense of worth in contrast to their received definitions as second-class or inferior citizens." *Personal Politics* (New York: Vintage Books, 1980), p. 219.

48. Escobar interview.

49. Laurie Coyle, Gail Hershatter, and Emily Honig, "Women at Farah: An Unfinished Story," in *Mexican Women in the United States: Struggles Past and Present*, eds. Magdalena Mora and Adelaida R. Del Castillo (Los Angeles: Chicano Studies Research Publications, University of California, 1980); Patricia Zavella, "Support Networks of Young Chicana Workers," paper presented at the Western Social Science Association Meeting, Albuquerque, New Mexico, April 29, 1983; Patricia Zavella, "Women, Work and Family in the Chicano Community: Cannery Workers of the Santa Clara Valley," (Ph.D. diss., University of California, Berkeley, 1982).

50. For more information on the Teamster take-over, see Ruiz, "UCAPAWA, Chicanas," pp. 206-243.

UNDOCUMENTED FEMALE LABOR IN THE UNITED STATES SOUTHWEST: AN ESSAY ON MIGRATION, CONSCIOUSNESS, OPPRESSION AND STRUGGLE

by

Lourdes Arguelles

> *"... the historic role of capitalism is to destroy history, to sever the link with the past and to orientate all effort and imagination to that which is about to occur ... Destroying the peasants could be a final act of historical elimination."*
>
> John Berger, *Pig Earth*

Despite statements to the contrary, migration and resettlement theorizing in academic circles in the United States continues to rely primarily on individual motivational constructs deemed operative primarily in a male-oriented context. This perspective assumes that it is predominantly male migrants who move in search of occupational and/or welfare opportunities presumably available in the receiving nations.[1] This male traffic is conceived to be a result of individual responses to the pull of more affluent economies as well as conditions of stagnation and underdevelopment in their home countries.[2] Within this analytical framework women migrants tend to be conceptualized as personal dependents following male-initiated migratory streams.[3] In a similar vein, the structuring and management of immigrant everyday life and enclaves are construed as individual and male tasks.[4]

This theorizing and the empirical work it has generated are problematic in three respects. First, this conceptual schema disregards the obvious, that is, data showing that for masses of peoples who cross international borders, personal motives tend to be epiphenomenal to a global political economy. Individual border crossings in fact are almost always preceded by profound changes in the relationships between capital and labor in the capitalist world economy. Second, a rediscovered history of women-initiated migratory waves and of an international tradition of immigrant women struggles in workplaces and communities makes the implicit sexual bias of this empirico-theoretic approach conspicuous. Third, this mechanistic approach presents a crude analysis of areas of life recognized as critical to an understanding of any human process (e.g., emotions, levels of consciousness, etc.); an approach clearly out of place in a time of sustained effort to transcend the positivistic paradigm in the social sciences.[5]

Recent Marxist, neo-marxist, and feminist critiques of this migration/resettlement paradigm have highlighted its theoretical biases and the shortcomings of the empirical work it has yielded. However, they have failed to generate a body of scholarship on immigrant men and women which fuses the macro and individual perspectives and elucidates the multi-dimensional connections between the two. In short, these critiques have not led to a scholarship capable of critically apprehending the changing nature of immigrant experiences and conceptualizing, or facilitating emancipatory praxis with or at the behest of immigrants. The reasons for this failure are many and are beyond the scope of this paper. One of the most important, however, deserves to be mentioned if only in passing: the creation of career opportunities in immigrant research controlled by academic, state, and private philanthropic bureaucrats who determine what is fundable and publishable. This has systematically discouraged in-depth, qualitative, longitudinal, and committed research efforts by investigators who are most responsive to the collective interests of working class immigrants.

This essay is based on material drawn from an on-going investigation and conceived of as a partial response to the theoretical, empirical and funding situation alluded to above. It was designed to identify and make explicit key organizing principles of the daily experience of immigrant women workers in the United States Southwest during the initial stages of their resettlement in the 1980's. It was also designed to suggest possible directions for organizing and providing educational assistance to these women. The paper is divided into four parts which discuss the women's background, the methods of inquiry, the key organizing principles of immigrant women's daily lives in the United States, and a proposal for action.

300

The Women's Background

Historically, Latina immigrants to the United States Southwest have come mostly from Mexico. Survey and field studies data, however, clearly shows that these women do not come from among the poorest and the landless: the Mexican rural proletariat tends to migrate within the country and come to the United States as part of Bracero and Bracero-style programs. Undocumented labor migration streams usually are composed of landholders. Further, these women rarely come alone but are part of kin and kin-related networks. This pattern of migration stems from the difficulties that rural proletariats and single women have in gathering the resources needed to cross over.[6]

Thus, a good number of Mexican immigrant women belong to the small land-owning class (minifundistas) and travel to the United States as part of a collective strategy to keep their embattled landholdings (minifundios) afloat. The world view they bring with them is firmly rooted in the peasantry. Hence, to understand it one has to realize how the peasant manifests himself/herself in Mexico.[7]

Unlike in Western Europe, the peasantry in capitalist peripheral and semi-peripheral economies is not a mere holdover of precapitalist times which will tend to disappear with more development. Mexican peasants in particular for the most part, regional variations nothwithstanding, are integrated, into the capitalist economy where they fulfill important economic functions. They retain, however, a distinctively peasant way of life and thought. For example, for these women the household (differentiated but not exclusive of the family, co-resident dwelling groups, and kinship structures) is the basic unit of production and consumption. Many studies have documented the rich variety of sustenance strategies which these peasant households have engaged in to meet their own needs within a changing social structure such as the one resulting from the accelerating capitalization of agriculture. These strategies have included share-cropping, craft production and sale, and internal changes in the division of labor. They have also consisted of armed rebellion, banditry, and sabotage.[8] The words of one collaborator to this investigation vividly portrays life and struggle in one such household: "Since I was a little girl I knew what it was to survive. We tried everything, my mother, my father, my brothers and sisters, and even my grandfather who was quite old.

First we tried to make ends meet by selling crafts. But this was impossible because everyday we made less and less from the land, having no water most of the time. Then there were times when my mother and my father had to fight the federales at gun point because they were trying to evict us. I helped all along."[9]

There are indications, however, that many of these resistance strategies are dying out in Mexico. Improvements in the State coercive mechanisms, such as the modernization of law and of the enforcement apparatuses have led to a decline of the most extreme forms of resistance available to peasants.[10] Currently, most peasant households survive by partially allocating their work force, including the women, to wage labor. The women appear to be involved in this re-allocation and consider this process to be one of the more egalitarian practices of household decision making. Lucia explains: "The men are almost ashamed and they defer to us again and again."[11]

This collectivistic ethos of peasant households initially provide a degree of protection for female peasants from the alienation endemic to wage labor. Lupe, a campesina from Michoacan, expressed it this way: "Well, one has to do it. We must all four share to see if we can make it together as we did in the past. I do my part and others do their part."[12]

Assignment to wage labor eventually means emigration to the United States. Not surprisingly, it does not mean they abandon either their peasant way of life nor the consciousness derived from it. John Berger has incisively described this consciousness as "... a sequence of repeated acts of survival. One where each act is pushed as a thread through the eye of a needle and the thread is tradition ...."[13] It is in this context that the attitudes and behavior of women migrants from Mexico can best be understood. For a majority of these women migration does not signify the opening of new vistas and new possibilities. Rather, it is a transitory time to be endured so as to re-become.[14] *Transitory* because the goal of these women is to go back to Mexico: in fact a high proportion eventually do return. *Endure* because the peasant woman thinks of her imposed obligations as part of her natural duties and of a much larger whole. *Re-become* because unlike the female proletarian who will dream of transforming everything which has condemned her to being a worker, the peasant women refuses to contemplate the disappearance of all that which gives meaning to her life.

Methods of Inquiry

The investigation into the organizing principles of these women's daily life in the United States began in 1979. Throughout the women have been collaborators, not objects of research. Samples of approximately thirty collaborators between the ages of 18 and 54 were selected for each of the four different politico-economic and ethno-national settings of Tucson, Albuquerque, San Diego, and Los Angeles. Snowball and non-random procedures were used in sample development and selection given the undocumented status of most of these women which made the use of more standard sampling techniques impossible. As the principles of everyday life began to be identified, new collaborators were found whose own experiences raised questions about these principles. This was done to allow a dialectical interaction between the investigative process and sample selection. Three major methods of inquiry were used: in-depth interviews, oral histories, and ethnographies. Data from these were triangulated with survey data from other studies.[15] Finally, the resultant data were syncretized using a tacking procedure.[16]

Female Labor From Mexico: Organizing Principles of Their Everyday Life in the United States

When Mexican women enter the United States their first task is to find employment. Their wages are to be remitted back home. Shelter is almost always available to them through relatives and/or friends and the women interpret this as an extension of conditions back home. Maria, a recent arrival from Michoacan explains: "I've never had problems in finding a house to live in. There is always someone who will take you in. That is the way it is back home. The problem is getting a job so you can contribute to the house and send money back."[17] Berta, a factory worker originally from Guerrero in whose house Maria lives adds: "We always have two or three people who have just arrived living with us. They stay as long as they need to .... The women stay longer and I'm happy because they get a lot of company and help."[18] Few women in the initial stages of their stay feel the need to have their own house. Many in fact see it as a potential drawback. Maria commented: "I don't want a house for myself now or even when Tomas (her husband) crosses. It is too much for us. I like living with Berta and the kids."[19]

A good number of these women enter the United States labor market as domestic workers in private homes. Their employers are Anglos and ethnic minorities in the professional-managerial strata. It is here that the women encounter a major difficulty associated with wage labor: the assignment of value to labor time. Only those who have been directly involved in petty commodity production and sale before migrating appear to have a basic understanding of this mechanism. Ramona, a domestic in Los Angeles explains: "I made tortillas in La Caja for many years. So I knew what time it took to make them and how much they sold for. So I know what to ask for my work."[20] For the most part, these women rely on the advice of male relatives to put a price on their labor. The men, in turn, tend to undervalue female labor and as a consequence wage demands by recent women migrants tend to be characteristically low.

Though an initial lack of expertise in assessing the market value for labor time conditions these women's lives, it is the anxiety-ridden existence of the "sin papeles" (being without legal resident documents) that sets its tone.[21] Thus, the threat of deportation is another critical principle organizing the United States experience of undocumented female labor. The fear of it is all encompassing and paradoxically seems to increase the longer the women stay. It is not uncommon to find recent migrants more confident than those who have been in the country for years. There is apparently no significant relationship between this increasing fear and negative experiences with the Immigration and Naturalization Service (INS) nor with feelings of having more to lose (in the form of personal property, friends, and jobs). This growing fear appears to be connected with the women's cyclic conceptualization of time; a conceptualization which interprets key aspects in their lives as constantly changing yet eventually returning to their source. Hence, with the passing months and years of residence in this country, the women rather than feeling secure begin to feel that the time when they will be returned home is rapidly approaching; an event they will accept as fate and even welcome. The fear derives mostly from dents in their peasant identity and from an apprehensiveness of supernatural retribution for having transgressed. To begin to understand at least partially how these feelings of transgressions appear in these women's consciousness, it is important to probe further into the dynamics of their experiences as workers in the United States. One good place to start is with the realization that in Latin America, particularly in non urban areas, domestic workers become part of the family. Here, however, undocumented women are unable to integrate into their employer's family structure and vicariously partake in its emotional dynamics. In a nutshell, they are alienated. Furthermore, domestic work in the United States has been largely mechanized.[22] The women's first months of domestic employment are basically an apprenticeship in tending machines in assembly-line fashion. Their timid efforts at demonstrating worth through expertise in baking, sewing, cooking, etc. are discouraged. Ramona explains: "The lady of the house tells me what I want to do takes a lot of time and doesn't pay. She brings in fresh baked bread and throws away shoes and clothing that just need to be fixed a little."[23] The process of de-skilling and then re-skilling peasant women starts here. As a result very different principles begin to structure their everyday life. Let us look at some of these.

Tending machines leaves the operative's mind free to wander. The Mexicana quickly fills the time with television and radio programs. Undocumented domestics spend approximately four hours a day watching television. Four more hours are spent listening to the radio. Undoubtedly, as in most contemporary societies including rural Mexico, the mass media has assumed an increasing role in filling up surplus consciousness[24] and in the creation and socialization of desire and behavior. However, the uniqueness of a high intensity market setting such as the United States lies in the rapidity by which the media teaches us to identify states of feeling with types of commodities. In this setting the vast number and variety of material objects enjoins the person to break down states of feelings into progressively smaller components and instructs him or her in the delicate art of recombining the pieces. A major outcome of all this is simple to understand: the fragmentation of needs requires a steadily more intensive effort by the individual to hold together her identity and personal integrity. More concretely, this means spending more time in consumption activities. The impact of media on the consumption patterns of the Mexicana domestic worker is compounded by the emphasis on appearance and display in their upper-middle class home/workplaces. Adela, a domestic worker in Los Angeles comments: "It seems we are always like in a store window. One has to dress right, smell right ...."[25]

Gradually, the Mexican becomes intensely conscious of each and every one of her body parts and of the complex consumption tasks involved in adequately taking care of them. In time, the consumerism to which this leads begins to take its toll. The women report high states of anxiety and feelings of having transgressed. Juana, a domestic from Guerrero, suffering from deep depression states: "I was never aware of me that much and that makes me nervous. I feel I am thinking something bad and God is going to punish me and that something terrible is going to happen to me and my family."[26]

Increased consumption conflicts with the duty to remit money back home. Dolores, a domestic from Sonora explains it this way: "I feel bad because I have many needs and now I cannot send as much as I should back home. I have had fights with Jose' (her brother) many times about this. But he too is sending little back home and wants me to make up for it."[27]

These conflicts often lead to physical violence and an increase in male abuse of woman relatives. Our data documents the high incidence of physical abuse by males in this population. It also lays bare the control these men have over the externalities of women's existence--control over income, expenditures, and work time. On the other hand, through talking with the women we were able to grasp the powerlessness of the men and, more important, the emergence within these women's consciousness of a pattern of yielding which in the United States is less a result of fear and tradition, than the need to compensate for the male's lack of power. La China explained it: "Chon has it so bad that I can feel it. It makes me want to let him take care of things. He was never that bad back home."[28] In addition to the alienation and repetition intrinsic of mechanized domestic work and the control over lives excercised by male relatives, other oppressive conditions in the domestic workplace have major impacts in the lives of these women. These include not only low pay, lack of social security and fringe benefits, and a high incidence of verbal abuse by employers, but also the attempts by employers to increase these women's productivity through drugs. Many of these women reported becoming hooked on stimulants at their place of employment. In an interview a New Mexico employer--a Chicano engineer--discussed the reasons why his wife had procured amphetamines for Rosa, their domestic: "She was always so sad, so down, I guess it's the Indian in her, that she could barely do what she was told. Now she is much happier."[29]

Passivity is however not the norm among these women. Rebelliousness, strategies of non-compliance, and hatred of their employers are not uncommon. Aggression however, is frequently displaced and often directed toward self. The women also manage to systematically immerse themselves in still another escape route--the Mexican movie subculture. Unlike Latino TV and radio stations which exacerbate consumer needs, the Mexican movie targeted to working class groups offers vicarious satisfaction and an easy entry into fantasy which allows the women to forget their everyday existence. "I leave the movies thinking I have lived the whole thing," says Isabel a domestic from Guerrero. "I don't feel lonely," claims Maria, a domestic from Sonora.[30]

Loneliness is another principle that organizes the life of the female undocumented worker, particularly the domestic who spends a good number of her days isolated or in their words: "Estando encerrada."[31] These women have many strategies to combat loneliness which sometimes are only partially effective. They involve trips back home, frequently planned by the male relative when he finds "his woman" pulling away from the cultural bond. They also include the establishment of social networks with other undocumented where a substantial barter of goods and services takes place. But for the most part, the everyday existence of the undocumented woman domestic is isolated. Farm work where available is often sought to alleviate loneliness as well as to augment earnings.

Women in the non-border areas of Arizona and New Mexico have, until recently, found employment in the secondary or the non-personal service sector less of an alternative than for women in other parts of the Southwest and California. Yet when, undocumented women enter these jobs they bring into the factory their peasant outlook and a plethora of escape strategies which emanate from her socialization in the United States. A factory organizer in Yuma, Arizona summarizes the argument of those who see the latter as dominant in the behavior of these women at the workplace. "They think they are here temporarily and are looking for ways to improve what is back home not what is here. They always think they are well paid because they think so little of what they do. And then all they want to do is watch TV or a movie. I guess they truly want to forget they are here and what is more they can."[32] A closer look at undocumented women's labor realities however yields a very different scenario, in which women engage in formal and informal resistance and struggle and readily forget or put temporarily aside escape strategies. In the words of Carmela: "I know how to fight and I do it in many ways at whatever cost."[33]

A Proposal

For organizers and progressive helpers (e.g., teachers, social workers, etc.) the apprehension of the background, migration motivations, and critical principles of everyday existence of Mexican undocumented women in terms of both consciousness and behavior underscores the need to enable the women to recapture and refine past modes of resistance and to assist them in developing effective strategies of empowerment. It must be recognized that many of these women are temporarily subproletarians who after years of oppression and exploitation in the United States, return to their meager landholdings in Mexico. Paradoxically, in spite of their vulnerability and well-known functions within capitalist economies, these peasant households indeed retard the viability of advanced capitalist production as they continue to underbid the capitalist entrepreneur totally dependent on wage labor.

Hence an initial focus on conditions back home in conscientization work with these women seems appropriate. An organizer in El Mirage commented: "You need to let them talk and not think that what happened to them back there is past and must be forgotten. Slowly they'll make the connections. Like the best political science class in college between the horrors of capital here and there."[34]

Listening however is not sufficient. Enabling critical reflection is needed if resistance to capital is to be encouraged among these women. In the words of a Tucson activist: "I did not realize what was being done to me in the United States until I recalled what was done to me in Guerrero and by whom. Then I realized they were one and the same. Then I knew I had to fight back. It was easier for me to start thinking of fighting in Mexico because I have a base there, but most important because that is where it all started for me. When I realized what I had to do I started fighting here too. I guess I became what I'm now ... a fighter.[35]

These women need specific tools to deepen their consciousness to recognize the newer multiple forms of oppression and exploitation to which they are subjected in United States consumption and work place sites. In a nutshell, the development of comprehensive programs to enable critical consciousness, empowerment and resistance effective in a transnational context is an urgent necessity; programs capable of impacting positively on both a short-term and a long-term basis in the women's everyday lives both in Mexico and in the United States.

A modified and woman-centered version of the unionization, education, and economic development project of the Arizona Farmworkers Union (AFW) may be one among many transition-type answers.[36] Several years in existence, the AFW project has unionized male undocumented agricultural workers in Arizona, improved their working and living conditions, and increased their consciousness of oppression. Further, it has financed economic development projects to humanize life in the Mexican rural areas from where the majority of its members tend to come from. The funds for these projects were obtained from employers as part of the union-contract.

A women's version of the AFW project could begin by recruiting women into discussion circles. To insure membership of both recent and older migrants, recruitment for the circles could be done partially through male relatives who are known to worker organizations given the male control of early undocumented everyday life and the isolation of many of the women. These circles would highlight the importance of women's historical roles and struggles, a kind of compensatory history. But unlike the recent public phenomena in the United States they will build on the strong sense of historical interconnectedness in these women. The circles would also be arenas for discussion of these women's everyday life problems both in Mexico and the United States. This exploration of what it means to remember the past is intended to yield strategies on what to do with memories to make them active and alive, as opposed to mere objects of collection. The analysis of alternatives would be the evaluation of different strategies and tactics would be a portion of the totality of the circle experience. Because of the women's traditionally low literacy levels and the impact of mass media, a creative use of audiovisual technology would be mandatory. Part of the task would be to expedite the end of visual innocence, and facilitation of the critique of consumerism and the activation of traditional and non-traditional workplace organizing activity appropriate to the various sectors these women are inserted in (e.g., service, garment, electronics, etc.). Eventually, a program to assist the women's households and community and their position within Mexico could be enabled. Producers and consumer cooperatives and clinics initiated and staffed by the women could be organized in geographical areas from where a large proportion of these women migrants come. These projects should be as much import-replacing in nature as possible and geared to encourage flexibility and a modicum of development in the "peasant" economy.[37] Funds for these projects could be obtained, as the AFW has already successfully done, from the women's employers in some sectors as part and parcel of well-negotiated contracts. The proposed project can allow organizers and helpers to build on the women's own resources particularly on the remnants of a collectivistic mutual aid ethos and on the experience of resistance to capitalist encroachment. In doing so, the helpers themselves might benefit from exposure to traditional skills which may assist in certain conjuntures in retarding the de-skilling processes endemic to capitalism. It can also expose those in helpers' roles to an alternative view of life and therefore of helping.[38]

This organizing and empowerment approach is not aimed at detracting from the long term goal of enabling the incorporation of immigrant women to participate in a transnational proletarian strategy of struggle. On the contrary, programs enabling a higher level of organization, political consciousness and positive action among these women cannot but help insure that their historical experience of oppression and resistance becomes integral in the actual formulation of both the vision and the practice of struggle.

Notes

1. This androcentric approach to research constructs the actor as male and tends to consider females as acted upon rather than as co-actors. See M. Eichler, *Nonsexist Research Methods* (Boston: Allen and Unwin, 1983), pp. 22-27.

2. See T. Weaver and T. Downing, *Mexican Migration* (Tucson: University of Arizona Bureau of Ethnic Research, 1976); United Nations, *The Determinants and Consequences of Population Trends*, Vol. 1 (New York: United Nations, 1973).

3. Also, G. De Jong and F. Ahmad, "Motivation for Migration of Welfare Clients," in *Internal Migration: The New World and The Third World*, A.H. Richmond and D. Kubat, eds. (Beverly Hills: Sage Publications, 1976).

4. For a more detailed discussion of this approach see L. Arguelles and G. Romero, "The Communication Networks of Mexican Women Workers in Los Angeles," in *Communication and Class Struggle: 3 New Historical Subjects*, A. Mattelart, ed. (Paris: International General, 1990).

5.   S. Harding, *The Science Question in Feminism* (Ithaca: Cornell University Press, 1986), pp. 42-43.

6.   See J. Bustamante, "Undocumented Migration from Mexico: A Research Report," *International Migration Review* 11 (1977): 149-178; L. Arizpe, "The Rural Exodus in Mexico and Mexican Migration to the United States," *International Migration Review* 15 (1981): 626-649.

7.   See, for example, I. Dinnerman, "Patterns of Adaptation Among Households of U.S. Bound Migrants from Michoacan, Mexico," *International Migration Review* 12 (1978): 620-644.

8.   For a discussion of various factors contributing to the decline of resistance strategies available to the peasantry see P. O'Malley, "Social Bandits, Modern Capitalism, and the Traditional Peasantry: A Critique of Hobsbawn," *Journal of Peasant Studies* 6 (1979): 489-501.

9.   Personal interview, Tucson, January 7, 1982.

10.   See note 4.

11.   Personal interview, Los Mochis, February 25, 1982.

12.   Personal interview, Albuquerque, New Mexico, January 7, 1979.

13.   J. Berger, "Towards Understanding Peasant Experiences," *Race and Class* 19 (1975): 352.

14.   Marta Lopez-Garza, Estevan Flores, and Wayne Cornelius among others share a different perspective. For these investigators most of these migrant women come here to stay. The subjects of their investigations were mostly women who can be characterized as "socially linked" with children and community for some of these differences. Marta Lopez-Garza, personal communication, May 19, 1987.

15.   For example, L. Arizpe, "Mujeres migrantes y economía campesina: análisis de una cohorte migratoria a la ciudad de México, 1940-1970, *América Indígena* 38 (abril-junio, 1978): 303-326; T. de Barbieri, "Notas para el estudio del trabajo doméstico," *Demografía y Economía* 34 (1977); K. Young "Economía campesina, unidad domestica y migración" *América Indígena* 2 (abril-junio, 1978): 279-302 among others.

16.   A "tacking procedure" is an approach to synchretic research involving engagement by the investigator with the person or group which is the focus of investigation. The researcher next distances herself from the situation by analyzing what has been experienced. Then the researcher returns to the situation as participant with the understanding she has gained from the

distancing perspective. This movement from participation to analysis is done at several stages of the investigation.

17.   Personal interview, San Diego, February 2, 1985.

18.   Personal interview, San Diego, February 2, 1985.

19.   Personal interview, Los Angeles, February 6, 1984.

20.   Personal interview, Los Angeles, February 6, 1984.

21.   For the impact of the amnesty program on these women see note 4.

22.   For an excellent discussion of the impact of conventional mechanization see L. Hirschhorn, *Beyond Mechanization: Work and Technology in a Post-industrial Age* (Cambridge: MIT Press), p. 58.

23.   Personal interview, Los Angeles, February 8, 1984.

24.   Surplus consciousness refers to mind-spaces free from thoughts derived from the routine of everyday life.

25.   Personal interview, Los Angeles, February 9, 1984.

26.   Personal interview, Albuquerque, January 7, 1979.

27.   Personal interview, Tucson, October 6, 1981.

28.   Personal interview, Phoenix, October 6, 1981.

29.   Personal interview, Albuquerque, January 9, 1979.

30.   Personal interview, Las Cruces, November 6, 1982.

31.   Locked in.

32.   Key Informant interview, El Mirage, Arizona, November 1, 1981.

33.   Personal interview, Tucson, November 5, 1981.

34.   Key informant interview, Yuma, November 18, 1981.

35.   Ibid.

36.   Other programs such as C.O.M.O. in Juarez, Mexico are also worthwhile models to be investigated.

37.   For a lucid discussion of improvements needed in deteriorating economies see J. Jacobs, *Cities and the Wealth of Nature* (New York: Vintage Books, 1985), pp. 72-78.

38.   A model program utilizing Latino women's traditional roles and strengths as teachers and healers is currently in place in Long Beach, California as part of the AIDS Education Project. See N.A. Pino and L. Arguelles, *Entrenos: Pláticas About AIDS* (Long Beach: AIDS Education Project, 1988).

IMPACTO SOCIAL DEL SISMO, MEXICO 1985: LAS COSTURERAS

Abstract

On 20 October 1985 Mexico's Sindicato Nacional 19 de Septiembre was created representing 5,000 garment workers from the State of Mexico, Morelos, Coahuila and Guanajuato; a month before the plight of their working conditions had been virtually unknown. A month before on September 19 Mexico City was hit by a powerful earthquake which nearly obliterated its downtown area; the center of Mexico City's clandestine garment industry. Weeks later the bodies of garment workers were pulled from the rubble while their co-workers stood in vigil; their presence among the remnants of factory sites called public attention to the working conditions of garment workers.

The history of Mexico City's garment industry goes back to the nineteenth century, but the industry did not expand significantly until the 1940s. This industry, competitive and dynamic, is an important source of employment for lower-income women. According to government figures the industry employed approximately 300,000 workers (mostly women) in 1982 a significant rise from the 175,000 employed in 1975. However, less than half of those employed in 1982 were paid minimum wages or provided benefits as required by Mexico's labor laws. Recourse to illegal strategies by the industry is evidenced by the fact that in 1982 more than 2,000 businesses in the city's garment district were operating without official permits. Moreover, buildings used as factories were old, in ill repair (some structures having visible fractures), and were never meant to sustain the heavy weight of the machinery, materials and personnel utilized by the industry. These buildings easily gave way under the impact of the earthquake.

Garment workers commonly refered to as *costureras* work an average of ten hours daily, are paid minimum wages often less, given no medical coverage, social security benefits or workers' compensation, and are subject to dismissal without notice. Many *costureras* are single heads of household with families to support and must depend on female kinship and neighborhood social networks (mothers, sisters, daughters and neighbors) to help them care for their families while they work. Most *costureras* are poorly educated and have learned their sewing skills from other women who are familiar with the industry and its work. It takes them approximately one to three hours daily to commute to and from work on public transportation.

Though grievances against the industry had been filed in the past by workers these had been generally ignored by official union representation. But the tragedy of the earthquake incited renewed efforts on behalf of the *costureras* and by October 10, government agencies, official unions and Mexico's equivalent of the House of Representatives offered their help as did independent unions (not affiliated with official unions), and leftist political parties such as the PSUM and the PRT. Groups of activist lawyers assisted in the filing of grievances and depositions. The women formed the Garment Workers' Front (Frente de Costureras) through which they coordinated efforts to return to work and collect wages owed them by employers who stealthily removed machinery from the rubble and closed shop without informing their employees. These events culminated in a meeting between the *costureras* and President De la Madrid with whom they discussed their grievances. Most important, the formation of the Sindicato Nacional 19 de Septiembre could now begin to more effectively address the working class interests of Mexico's garment workers.

IMPACTO SOCIAL DEL SISMO, MEXICO 1985: LAS COSTURERAS

by

Marisol Arbeláez A.

Contexto Social

Los sismos del 19 y 20 de septiembre no sólo abatieron a la ciudad de México por una inesperada tragedia sino que expusieron a la sociedad en su conjunto las dramáticas condiciones de trabajo en que se desempeñaban las costureras.

Muchas de las trabajadoras de la industria del vestido fueron víctimas al perecer azotadas por los derrumbes de las fábricas de Topeka, Dedal y Amal, entre otras. Después de cuatro semanas las misiones de rescate aún continuaban recuperando los cuerpos de las costureras muertas por el desplome de los edificios.

A la denominada "Area Topeka"--perímetro de la industria de la confección--correspondió a la VI Zona Militar del DN-II-E. Aquí la ayuda vino tarde ante la magnitud de la tragedia y no por el número de voluntarios particulares--familiares, amigos, vecinos y transeuntes--que acudieron en cantidades abrumadoras, sino por la falta de maquinaria pesada indispensable para remover las grandes lozas y vigas de concreto que atraparon a un número indeterminado de trabajadoras. Por otra parte, tampoco se sabrá el número de costureras muertas o heridas con certeza.

Muchos días pasaron antes de que se tuvieran las primeras informaciones sobre el impacto de los sismos en las fábricas y talleres de la confección. La confusión del desorden era sobrecogedora. El cúmulo de las noticias se centraba en los derrumbes de los hoteles, lo edificios de gobierno y los multifamiliares. Las notas periodísticas se dispersaban por los acontecimientos de las zonas afectadas y sólo una semana después del impacto la vorágine noticiosa sobre las costureras empezó a ser motivo de primera plana.

Las costureras que habían salido ese jueves 19 de septiembre hacia sus trabajos sufrieron diferentes destinos. Las que iniciaban la jornada a las 7 de la mañana, el desplome de los edificios las atrapó inmisericordemente. Las demás vivieron el terremoto en el camino, al taller o al almacen. Estas últimas no pudieron llegar por la interrupción del transporte o se regresaron a sus hogares angustiadas por la suerte de sus familiares. Ante muchas que habían llegado en ese momento a las puertas, los edificios se vinieron abajo. Poco tiempo paso para que estas mujeres acudieran al auxilio de los gritos de sus compañeras bajo el escombro.

Al día siguiente, las costureras, en pequeños grupos, ocuparon las calles en las inmediaciones de los derrumbes. Los cuerpos de seguridad del ejército las habían retirado de los edificios destruidos. Sin embargo, ellas no se alejaron de sus antiguas fábricas, se situaron en las aceras del frente o en las esquinas más cercanas. Con su presencia física--ante los escombros--las costureras empezaron poco a poco a ser sujetos visibles para la sociedad.

Las costureras invadieron las calles del centro, la colonia Obrera, la Moderna y la Tránsito pues allí estaban la mayoría de las fábricas de la industria de la confección. Grupos pequeños y medianos se destacaron en puestos de vigilia permanente y se confundían con los observadores, los voluntarios prestos a intervenir y los familiares de los atrapados.

En los edificios donde había costureras bajo los derrumbes--en las calles de San Antonio Abad, José María Othón y Avenida del Taller--las trabajadoras ilesas colaboraron en las tareas de rescate junto a los familiares, amigos y voluntarios supervisados por el ejército. Todos ellos formaron una organización con una funcionalidad extraordinaria e impecable división de las tareas de ayuda.

En el destrozado edificio de Dedal--Annabel--las costureras reconstruyeron de memoria la distribución del piso y al detalle la disposición de los cuartos, la posición de las máquinas, mesas de corte y planchado, anaqueles y los accesos desde las escaleras. Ellas colaboraron una y otra vez en la elaboración de los planos con que se asistieron para el rescate los voluntarios, constructoras y ejército. Reconstruían las ubicaciones de las trabajadoras en el momento del terremoto y los lugares hacia donde corrieron cuando empezaron a caer las lozas. Por esta precisa reconstrucción de la memoria se pudo rescatar a muchos de sus compañeros aún con vida y sacar los cuerpos de los muertos sin recurrir a la búsqueda azarosa.

El lunes 23 de septiembre los grupos de costureras eran más nutridos. Ellas estaban día y noche. Hacían guardia permanente y vigilaban atentas la movilización general de los rescatistas. Las costureras esperaban. Esperaban a los dueños o a los encargados de los talleres derruidos o en vías de serlo. Las costureras estaban a la expectativa de cualquier informe. En el caso de las atrapadas sobre su suerte última y sobre la evacuación de las máquinas, de materias primas y prendas. Cuando aparecían algunos dueños todas corrían y arremolinaban alrededor. Hablaban todas y demandaban. Querían saber dónde iba a estar la nueva instalación, querían la continuidad de su empleo, querían el pago del salario de la semana del terremoto, querían recuperar sus herramientas, documentos y prendas de labor. Querían seguir. Querían trabajar.

Muchos de los dueños aparecieron sólo para trasladar la maquinaria y mercancía, otros--los más--no aseguraban ni pago ni continuidad, unos pagaron la semana vencida y desaparecieron, otros jamás se hicieron presentes.

Desde este momento, las costureras decidieron permanecer frente a la incertidumbre. Fue desde esta espera incierta que las costureras hicieron posible el conocimiento de su historia y desde la calle denunciaron, levantaron el reclamo y exigieron la reparación de los años de injusticia a los que el terremoto puso su límite.

La Industria del Vestido en la Gran Ciudad

La ubicación de las fábricas y talleres de la confección concentradas en la Ciudad de México se proyecta con la historia misma de la metrópoli. La centralización de esta actividad en el perímetro del desastre no tiene una fecha precisa aunque existen datos que mencionan la localización de la costura en esta área desde el siglo XIX.

La expansión de los conglomerados de la industria parte desde la década de los años cuarenta, al igual que la configuración industrial misma del país. La dinámica de concentración espacial de la actividad no es ajena a la agrupación comercial y de los servicios en el mismo lugar de la ciudad.

La ocupación de talleres, fábricas y almacenes del vestido desde el centro y hacia las colonias vecinas alude a la facilidad de los accesos entre la ciudad, la rápida ocupación de edificios de rentas bajas, la distribución concentrada, el despliegue de talleres

317

en espacios reducidos, la disponibilidad de mano de obra barata, abundante y con cierto nivel de calificación, lo inmediato de materias e insumos básicos a menor costo, al igual que lo contiguo de los servicios y ninguna necesidad de esperar o fundar infraestructuras básicas.

La industria del vestido cuenta con varias ramas: confección de ropa interior y exterior para hombres y mujeres y niños; ropa de trabajo, medias y calcetines, fajas y lencería en general, camisas y trajes, faldas pantalones y vestidos; pañuelos, corbatas, ropa tejida de punto, deportiva, uniformes escolares y demás similares. De igual manera están las dedicadas a la elaboración de manteles, colchas, sábanas y artículos para mesa, cocina y baño.

En los talleres, por lo general se llevaba todo el proceso de diseño, corte, elaboración de los modelos y producción en serie, terminados, empaque y distribución. La actividad en cada taller variaba: estaban los dedicados unicamente al diseño y corte como las maquiladoras donde se ensamblaba, cosía, se revisaba calidad y se empacaba de regreso a la fábrica que contrataba maquila y manejaba la marca.

Es usual el uso diferencial de las marcas de conformidad con la prenda elaborada. Unos talleres se dedicaban a la elaboración de la línea masculina o deportiva de una marca particular y otros a las líneas femeninas, de maternidad o juvenil. También están las maquilas que trabajan para diferentes marcas y las que sólo etiquetan y distribuyen.

La industria del vestido es reconocida como una de las más dinámicas, de mayor crecimiento, expansión y generadora importante de empleo. La industria entre 1960 y 1978 tuvo una expansión del 5.7 por ciento anual y el promedio calculado para los siguientes seis años era alrededor del 7 por ciento. La ocupación de las fuerza de trabajo femenina en la actividad, según los datos del censo industrial de 1975, era aproximadamente de 175,000 mujeres. De acuerdo a las cifras proporcionadas por la Secretaría de Programación y Presupuesto, (SPP) para 1982 los empleados en forma directa en la rama textil y del vestido son cerca de 300,000. Sin embargo, los obreros en las actividades de la confección de prendas de vestir, de punto, interior, exterior y similares, los que tenían salario y prestaciones de ley eran unicamente 125,000. Este recuento numérico de la Ciudad de México y su área metropolitana es por supuesto para las empresas que cuentan con algún tipo de registro como IMSS, SPP, SHCP, etc. Sin embargo, como quedó ampliamente demostrado en el curso del mes de septiembre a octubre de 1985 la mayoría de estas industrias del vestido estaban fuera del empadronamiento oficial. Un número grande de las empresas de la confección eran clandestina--su número estimado es de más de 2,000. Sin embargo, aún para las empresas que contaban con el reconocimiento oficial y empleados y papeles en regla tenían un número incalculable de trabajadores fuera de las nominas.

Las fábricas, talleres y maquilas de la industria textil y del vestido en el perímetro céntrico de la ciudad de México configuran una gran confusión a la hora de establecer los rangos y diferencias entre los tipos de negociaciones que representan. Las fábricas donominadas como tales son talleres grandes, los talleres reconocidos, maquilas y los talleres, fábricas.

La industria ocupaba por los general uno o más de los pisos de los edificios de la zona en que se concentraba. Así, los edificios albergaban según el número de plantas a igual número de empresas de la rama. También estaban aquí las bodegas, oficinas administrativas y representaciones comerciales. En cada planta se almacenaba la materia prima, las prendas elaboradas y todo lo relacionado con el negocio y también de sus dueños. En la planta baja de los edificios se encontraban las tiendas que igual vendían al mayoreo que al menudeo.

Es desde este nucleo vital ubicado, en el centro del Distrito Federal que se controlaba la producción y venta del vestido a la propia ciudad, al valle de México y al país.

Los edificios que fueron ocupados y destinados para albergar a la industria nunca fueron proyectados para tal uso--al igual que lo mayoritario de los bienes inmobiliarios de la Ciudad--puesto que cuando más habían sido calculados para alojar oficinas o departamentos de habitación.

De acuerdo a algunos de los ingenieros que realizaron los peritajes de los edificios derrumbados, los daños ocasionados en los inmuebles por el terremoto se debieron no sólo a la fuerza del impacto de este sino también a las excesivas cargas que soportaban. La maquinaria, los materiales y el número fluctuante de personas que transitaban diariamente en cada piso afectaron sin duda a las instalaciones. Estos daños ya eran visibles previamente al sismo. Por cierto, el edificio colapsado de Annabel tenía hace muchos años una enorme fractura visible en la escalera y no obstante las llamadas de atención jamás se le dio reparación alguna.

El Trabajo de la Confección

Jornadas de 10 o más horas; salario mínimo, mínimo profesional o menos del mínimo; ausencia de seguro social, Infonavit, y prestaciones. Despidos masivos y sin previo aviso, ninguna indemnización o liquidación conforme a la ley. Estas son normas y características de las condiciones de trabajo de la industria. El sistema de trabajo en la actividad tenía dos vertientes: el destajo y la fracción. En el primero, el salario se pagaba conforme al número de prendas completas elaboradas o secciones de la misma realizadas durante la jornada de trabajo. Así entre más hicieran las costureras más ganaban. Dependiendo de la temporada--invierno o primavera--variaban los montos pagados por falda, saco, sastre o conjunto. Por esta indumentaria se pagaban 70, 90, 130 o 250 pesos por cada uno. No había cuotas fijas y las cantidades variaban de negocio a negocio. Las costureras trabajan por este sistema más horas y más intensamente porque para tener un ingreso similar al mínimo o superior a este, como era lo usual bajo este modo de trabajar, tenían que acelerar el ritmo y extender el horario.

Para cobrar el salario al destajo se llevaba un control por medio de cupones en los cuales se imprimía el nombre de la costurera y las expecificaciones de la prenda, talla y trabajo efectuado. Cuando se cortaba la raya semanal se recogían los cupones y les entregaban una cantidad fijada por los patrones, pero sin que la trabajadora nunca supiera con seguridad cuanto iba a recibir por la labor realizada.

El sistema de la fracción fue introducido en cada fábrica o taller sin previo aviso. Este sistema significaba que cada costurera hiciera una parte de la prenda. Así en la confección de un saco, una cosía espaldas y delanteros, otra las mangas, las demás aplicaciones, hacían dobladillos y ponían botones. La prenda daba varias vueltas entre las costureras hasta llegar a planchado y empaque. Al trabajar por fracción se les asignaba a las trabajadoras un salario mínimo semanal y trabajaban las mismas horas que bajo el destajo.

El cambio introducido irritó a las costureras de la Fábrica La Jacobina, pues estas realizaron un estudio comparativo de los dos sistemas y llegaron la conclusión de que ahora continuaban realizando el mismo trabajo pero sus ingresos habían disminuido notablemente. Tres de las costureras levantaron demandas en Conciliación y Arbitraje a principio del año de 1985 por lo que consideraban una arbitrariedad.

Las costureras de esta fábricas, en su conjunto, solicitaron al encargado regresar al sistema del destajo puesto que ellas no obstante que se les exigía la misma productividad y dedicación con el sistema de fracción recibían el salario que habían logrado obtener al destajo.

Ocasionalmente las costureras laboraban tiempos extraordinarios--más allá de las jornadas de 10 horas--y se les entregaba una cantidad adicional por el trabajo realizado y no conforme a las estipulaciones de ley.

Los salarios variaban por empresa, no obstante su relativa cercanía. A algunas costureras les pagaban 8,500 a la semana, a otras 10,755 y a algunas 14,000 por el mismo trabajo. Había diferencias internas en los sueldos conforme a la experiencia y a la aplicación y rapidez.

Las costureras llevaban al trabajo las tijeras, las escuadras, los denominados patos y otros utensilios útiles a la confección. Era usual que estos instrumentos fueran propiedad de las costureras. La herramienta la habían adquirido a lo largo de los años de trabajo y les era útil no sólo en la fábrica, sino también en sus casas ya que hacían trabajos de costura para los hijos, familiares y vecinos y eventualmente como ingresos adicionales.

Con el sistema de trabajo que fuera, las costureras sufrían y eran atacadas por enfermedades profesionales que agredían inicialmente sus ojos. Teniendo que estar con la mirada fija en la costura por largas horas o las prendas eran muy complicadas en su elaboración o lo que las costureras llaman "muy entretenidas," bajo una luz de neón, resulta en una tensión insoportable para los ojos. Las consecuencias son las enfermedades como cataratas, conjuntivitis crónica, la pérdida parcial de la visión por la vía de la miopía creciente y los ojos que ellas dicen "llorosos." La consulta a los oftalmologos les significa no solamente gastos incosteables sino el uso de lentes permanentes y con ellos la posibilidad de pérdida del empleo. Este deterioro físico no sólo es para los ojos sino también los pulmones y el sistema respiratorio en general. Respirar frecuentemente la pelusa y el polvo de las telas menoscaba la buena salud y la resistencia de los bronquios. Las condiciones de ventilación de los pisos no era adecuada ni suficiente, máxime si se considera que la instalaciones se encontraban enzonas de la ciudad altamente contaminadas.

Las largas jornadas de trabajo sentadas antes las máquinas-- cuando se ven obligadas a acentuar la intensidad y rapidez con las que cosen, hacen que la tensión muscular se resiente sobre las espaldas y es frecuente la queja del dolor en los riñones. El ruido de las máquinas también ataca al sistema auditivo. Los altos decibles que producen estas máquinas de costura afectan también a la buena audición y al sistema nervioso.

Las costureras--como ahora es suficientemente conocido--en su mayoría no se encontraban afiliadas al seguro social. Por ello cualquier quebranto en su salud debería ser atendido por los médicos particulares, automedicados o desatendidos. De igual manera es esto cierto para hijos y familiares en línea directa.

En caso de que cualquier padecimiento las inhabilitara para asistir puntualmente al trabajo o en el dado caso de que alguno de los hijos enfermara y necesitara de la reclusión en el hogar bajo sus cuidados, ese día era rigurosamente, descontado de sus percepciones semanales. Tampoco podían pedir permisos excepcionales para realizar trámites escolares o asistir a alguna emergencia.

La salud era vista como un problema personal y su ausencia atribuida a la responsibilidad individual. Cuando las trabajadoras se embarazaban y según lo estipula la ley deberían contar con las licencias correspondientes al parto y crianza, las costureras renunciaban o sencillamente se iban a tener a sus hijos y con posterioridad regresaban al mismo empleo o a otro similar, ante la ausencia de la cobertura legal.

Hacerse vieja en la industria significaba el riesgo creciente del desempleo y la angustia de la supervivencia. Acusación constante para las trabajadoras en edad madura era el aparecer cansadas, agotadas y viejas como sinónimo de inservibles. Permanecer muchos años en el mismo centro de trabajo aumenta las posibilidades de ir a la calle en cualquier momento aunque se mantenga por parte de las costureras la secreta esperanza del reconocimento a los años de trabajo, la constancia y la lealtad. Las trabajadoras que contaban con 15 o 20 años de antigüedad estaban conscientes y temerosas del riesgo de los años acumulados. Jubilaciones o primas de antigüedad son derechos desconocidos en las fábricas y almacenes del ramo.

La disciplina recta en las horas de trabajo era requisito indispensable para la continuidad del empleo. Separadas por filas, rigurosamente alineadas, visualizando un sólo frente, las costureras eran vigiladas por supervisores o supervisoras. La conversación era distracción y baja del rendimiento. Cuando se les permitía dialogar tenían que tener las manos en movimiento sobre la costura, la tijera o la plancha.

La inactividad era fuertemente sancionada al igual, que los intentos de cuestionamiento a los malos tratos y agresiones. La costurera que osaba a enfrentar era inmediatamente despedida y sin contemplaciones.

En algunos talleres las trabajadoras eran revisadas a la hora de la salida, por otros de sus propios compañeros, con el fin de verificar que no se llevaban ninguna prenda. Continuamente se les reiteraba que no deberían extraer ningún artículo ya que esto sería automaticamente considerado como robo, y por tanto sujeto de sanción.

Los casos excepcionales de buenas relaciones--cordiales y afables--entre patrones, supervisoras y costureras existen. Algunas refirieron la suave convivencia cotidiana y la amabilidad compartida en las fiestas navideñas y la despedida del año.

Pago de aguinaldos--cuando existía--era una semana rigurosa, no contaban con prima vacacional y los pagos por reparto de utilidades eran cantidades que iban entre 500 y 1000 pesos.

Las anteriores son algunas de las características de las condiciones de trabajo que denunciaron las costureras y que eran parte de su vida diaria hasta que el terremoto destruyó a las fábricas. Estas condiciones eran lo normal y al romperse esta habitual y natural relación laboral las consecuencias no se hicieron esperar.

Los Empresarios de la Confección ante los Derrumbes

Muy pocas y parcas fueron las declaraciones de los empresarios de la confección ante la calamidad del acontecimiento. Los comunicados provenían en su parte sustancial de los voceros oficiales del gremio, la Cámara de la Industria del Vestido.

Los informes vertidos por esta asociación a veces contradictorios pero las más de justificaciones y declaraciones defensivas indicaron en todo momento no sólo el deseo de protegerse ante la cantidad de acusaciones de que eran objeto sino de ampararse ante las acciones legales emprendidas por las autoridades laborales en contra de algunos de sus afiliados.

En las colonias céntricas se habla de por lo menos 2,000 industrias del ramo y de ellas se mencionan 500 dañadas, 200 totalmente destruidas, 150 parcialmente inhabilitadas y las restantes en posibilidad de recuperación.

Los números en todo momento oscilaron y se reconoció que muchas empresas estaban fuera de cualquier cuantificación ya que operaban al margen de los registros.

Durante los primeros días la Cámara de la Industria no sólo no reconocía que hubiera trabajadoras muertas por los derrumbes de los edificios sino que aseguraban la continuidad de las relaciones laborales, el pago de los salarios y de la actividad. Estas declaraciones contundente del 6 de octubre rapidamente fueron impugnadas por los rescates de San Antonio Abad, con las denuncias de desaparición de las fuentes de trabajo y la negativa de los dueños a pagar cantidad alguna por indemnizaciones o salarios vencidos.

De igual manera, ante la avalancha de los acontecimientos desatados por las revelaciones de las costureras ante los medios de comunicación, los empresarios recurrieron a la estrategia de la suspensión de labores por casos fortuitos no atribuibles al patrón. Bajo el rubro de "conflictos especiales " de la Ley Federal del Trabajo los industriales buscaban proteger sus intereses y la no procedencia de acciones de incautación y embargo.

Sin embargo, días mediaron para que algunos empresarios desocuparan prontamente las instalaciones de los negocios dañados, aun antes de las diligencias legales entre las partes. Los visitantes a las diligencias legales entre las partes. Los visitantes a la zona afectada podían observar como se efectuaban las maniobras de desocupación de los inmuebles. Los dueños de las industrias mediante permiso previo de la zona militar entraron con camiones de mudanzas y asistidos por algunos de sus trabajadores trasladaban maquinas, telas, prendas y todo cuanto era posible llevarse. También querían las cajas fuertes donde se encontraban valores y documentos cobrales. Los patrones dirigían las maniobras desde abajo de los trabajadores que subían a los diferentes pisos y que con gran riesgo de su seguridad personal descolgaban desde las ventanas las prendas y las telas. Los que apresuradamente desalojaron las fábricas también se llevaron consigo a los empleados de confianza, a los que antiguamente habían adquirido esta categoría, que ahora ayudaron a desalojar. Dejaron atrás a un número grande de trabajadores sin que estos supieran donde estaban las nuevas instalaciones y mucho menos haber recibido pago alguno por liquidación.

Trabajadoras que no habían asistido al lugar, colaborado o intentado hablar con los empresarios de pronto llegaron y se encontraron con que sus centros de trabajo eran ahora lugares vacíos. En las aceras polvosas estaban las antiguas trabajadoras perplejas ante la única evidencia de los letreros de las vidireras.

Excepcionalmente algún empresario quiso declarar y exponer a la opinión pública su posición. Manifestó pérdidas millonarias y planteó la necesidad de la intervención gubernamental para reconstruir a la derruida industria. Pidió créditos blandos, infraestructura y excepciones fiscales para descentralizar, facilidades y liberación de las franquicias a la importación de las materias primas.

Las costureras proporcionaron algunos de los nombres de los dueños de las fábricas y ellos eran de origen judio del medio oriente al igual que de procedencia sirio-libanesa. Algunos estudios señalan a estos grupos acaparando la industria desde la década de los años treinta. Los negocios han pasado por generaciones completas y otros de incorporación reciente en la actividad.

No obstante, muchas de las declaraciones que atribuyeron a la pertenencia étnica de los propietarios la operación de la industria al margen de la legislación laboral y la explotación extraordinaria de la mano de obra femenina, estas son difíciles de probar y sustentar. La situación precaria de las costureras y la existencia de empresarios esquilmadores en la industria se ramifican en el tiempo histórico y de ello da cuenta el testimonio de las obreras mexicanas durante el siglo XIX:

EL NUEVO ESQUILMO
A LAS COSTURERAS DE LA MUNICION

"¡Que sea por muchos años!" Así esclamaban nuestros antepasados cada vez que un nuevo virrey llegaba de la Metrópoli española.

Tal exclamación implicaba un deseo: que el nuevo gobernante durara mucho tiempo en el poder, para que otros no vinieran a imponer nuevas exacciones y gabelas al entonces deprimido pueblo mexicano.

Es que en la conciencia de aquellos afligidos seres había la convicción de que la infatuación del nuevo virrey había de hacerles más difícil su condición económica.

Tal cual entonces, está pasando hoy con el vellocino de oro, o sea la contrata del vestuario para el ejército por otro nombre: munición.

Cada contratista que se va deja a su sucesor una lección, mejor dicho una ruta de explotación que éste aprovecha mejor para sí, con detrimento del interesante gremio de costureras.

Hace algunos años una costurera de munición sin contar con máquina, ganaba al día, trabajando ocho horas, de un peso a doce reales.

Entonces el señor De la Barrera era el contratista.

Después de este señor, vino otro, que hizo bajar el precio de la manufactura en un 25%; más tarde otro, siguiendo la rutina, lo hizo bajar al 50% y después otro y otro más, con iguales propensiones, hasta hacer imposible la vida, por el bajísimo precio a que ha llegado la munición, sin embargo del auxilio de la máquina de coser, pues trabajando 12 horas al día una desventurada costurera apenas si alcanza una ganancia de 50 centavos.

Pues bien, todavía a este miserable tipo se le ha bajado un 12.5%, por una combinación ingeniosa.

El contratista paga al tipo corriente; pero sus empleados, convirtiéndose en subcontratista, toman para sí arbitrariamente, lo que más les conviene, y es por eso que hoy una costurera, con todo y el auxilio de la máquina, se considera feliz si gana en 12 horas de trabajo, la miserable suma de 30 a 40 centavos.

Cualquiera dirá que todo el mundo tiene derecho para especular en terreno no vedado.

Mas si la ley escrita no restringe las especulaciones, cuando de ellas resulta un beneficio general, cual es la extensión del monopolio, la conciencia las condena, porque ellas originan un mal directo para determinado gremio.

En este caso está el de las costureras de la munición.

Este desventurado gremio, cuyo trabajo está monopolizado por un contratista y sus secuaces, es el único en el país que sufre el monopolio.

En consecuencias, creemos que está en las facultades del Supremo Gobierno hacerlo cesar, mucho más existiendo una cláusula obligatoria para el contratista de pagar por una tarifa especial la manufactura de la munición.

Nos seguiremos ocupando de este asunto.

Anónimo [1]

Ellas, Las Costureras

Muchas de las costureras son madres solteras, viudas, abandonadas o separadas y en virtud del patriarcalismo prevaleciente constituidas en cabezas de familia. Aquí lo usual es la desaparición de los padres de los hijos y la absoluta indiferencia e irresponsabilidad de la aportación económica.

Ellas tienen entre 2 y 7 hijos en promedio. A estos hay que proporcionar habitación, alimento, vestido, salud y educación. Ellas no se debaten en tribunales familiares ni solicitan, simplemente enfrentan los problemas de la supervivencia. Las costureras jovenes que no tienen hijos, son miembros de familias numerosas donde hay que aportar dinero para la sobrevivencia de todos.

Muchas no sólo se encargan de los hijos sino también de sus padres y hermanos menores. Son raras las que cuentan con un compañero que comparta el gasto familiar.

Ellas se apoyan en las otras mujeres de sus familias, madres y hermanas o hijas mayores que son las que cuidan de los niños pequeños cuando ellas estan en el taller. Recurren con las vecinas cuando no hay mujeres de la familia en la cercania. También suelen pagar a mujeres para que cuiden y alimenten a los hijos.

Las costureras tienen sólo la primaria o algunos años de ella y las hay las que nunca fueron a la escuela y que no saben leer ni escribir. Ellas quieren sin embargo que sus hijos estudien pues confian en los beneficios de la escuela para que no vivan lo que ellas han tenido que pasar.

Ellas viven por todos los rumbos populares de la gran ciudad: Netza, Ejército de Oriente, Iztapalapa, Aragón. Habitan vecindades, cuartos y departamentos arrendados. Diariamente consumen de 1 a 3 horas de transporte--metro, camiones y peseros--entre el trabajo y sus hogares.

Las costureras comen en las cocinas económicas cercanas a la fábrica o llevan sus alimentos que ingieren junto a la máquina o en los pasillos.

En la noche y los fines de semana atienden las tareas domésticas y los problemas de los hijos.

Aprendieron el oficio en las propias fábricas, en talleres pequeños o lo hicieron en sus casas a partir de la enseñanza de sus madres o alguna tía. Durante los años de trabajo se fueron especializando y entre las propias trabajadoras se transmitieron las minucias, las artes de la excelencia y el cuidado de los detalles. Algunas de las costureras más antiguas en la labor empezaron en la fábrica como casi todas inician el aprendizaje, por deshebrar. Aquí, les quitan los hilos sobrantes a la prenda y revisan la buena costura. Después aprender a planchar y a empacar cuidadosamente.

El manejo de la máquina sencilla (la de una sóla aguja) lo aprendieron--por lo general--en la práctica misma y de sus mas avezadas compañeras. Las otras máquinas, las más complejas por el

327

número de agujas, adminiculos y rapidez fueron experimentadas en el uso del oficio.

Camino de la Sindicalización

Asombro e indignación causó el conocimiento público de las condiciones laborales en que vivían cotidianamente las trabajadoras de la confección. Sin embargo, aunque nunca difundido con la amplitud de otras condiciones de trabajo, su situación de explotación y de indefensión sindical era conocida por autoridades y sindicatos. Estos últimos cuando las agruparon lo hicieron en los denominados por las propias costureras "sindicatos blancos" y las primeras tampoco atendieron al conjunto laboral aunque en sus archivos constaban las denuncias de trabajadoras que a título individual presentaban querellas contra los patrones en la Junta de Conciliación y Arbitraje.

Las costureras apostadas en la calle levantaron su voz y frente a una sociedad sensible por las lesiones recibidas del macrosismo construyeron su espacio y su presencia.

Los sindicatos en la rama de la confección no era una practica usual dentro del gremio. Cuando lo estaban nunca hicieron nada en la defensa de sus intereses. COR, CROC, CTM alegaban la titularidad pero no la salvaguarda.

Desconfianza, asombro y enojo causaron las declaraciones de los líderes obreros que manifestaron desconocimiento, ignorancia y aun la complacencia y apoyo de las costureras a su situación de explotación e indefensión.

En múltiples ocasiones y a lo largo de muchos años las costureras acudieron a las organizaciones sindicales en demanda de apoyo y ayuda. También existen (o existían antes del desplome del edificio de la Secretaría del Trabajo) las constancias de las demandas levantadas por muchas de las trabajadoras ante los tribunales de Conciliación y Arbitraje por arbitrariedades y despidos injustificados y sin liquidación.

La adscripción a los sindicatos era en muchos de los casos nominal y en otros ignorado por las propias costureras ante el pago millonario de los sobornos y las cuotas por parte de los patrones.

Las condiciones de clandestinaje de muchos de los talleres que eran detectadas por inspectores y líderes obreros eran mantenidas en la sombra previo pago disuasivo o la amenaza del cierre de la fuente de trabajo.

El reclamo constante y creciente de las costureras damnificadas por el terremoto empieza a tener respuesta a partir del 10 de octubre. Asociaciones y organismos civiles y gubernamentales reconocen publicamente el "problema de las costureras". La Confederación de Trabajadores de México (CTM), el Congreso del Trabajo (CT), la Cámara de Diputados a través de sus sectores obreros, la junta local de Conciliación y Arbitraje y todo el andamiaje de la Secretaría del Trabajo empiezan a actuar.

Paralelamente han intervenido organizaciones de izquierda como el Partido Socialista Unificado de México (PSUM) y el Partido Revolucionario de los Trabajadores (PRT), sindicatos independientes como el Sindicato de Trabajadores de la Universidad Nacional Autónoma de México (STUNAM) y el Sindicato Independiente de Trabajadores de la Universidad Autónoma Metropolitana (SITUAM), asociaciones profesionales como el Frente de Abogados Democráticos y se forma un Comité de Apoyo integrado por académicas con el objeto depresionar en la búsqueda de una solución favorable y expedita para las trabajadoras de la confección.

Antes de la intervención de estas organizaciones, las costureras habían sido visitadas en las diferentes áreas donde se encontraban por licenciados hábiles en el litigio laboral pidiéndole la cantidad de 5,000 pesos por trabajadora a fin de llevar el caso ante las autoridades laborales por indemnización a los deudos, pago de los sueldos caidos y acuerdos sobre reubicación o liquidación. Otros pedían el 35 por ciento del valor de lo rescatado de entre los escombros más los gastos por llevar el litigio y que sumaba prácticamente el 50 por ciento de lo que se pudiera lograr en tribuanales.

Mientras las costureras permanecían en la expectativa aparecieron otros personajes por el área. Eran las enviadas de fábricas ubicadas en zonas distintas de la cuidad que les ofrecían trabajo inmediato y sueldos bajos. En las secciones de los anuncios clasificados de los periódicos proliferaron las solicitudes de empleos en la confección por distintos rumbos de la ciudad.

De igual manera no faltaron los líderes sindicales que la conminaron a tomar pago entre 5,000 y 7,000 pesos por la semana laboral del sismo, dejar de hacer barullo y buscar empleo donde fuera.

Empresarios cuyos locales sufrieron danos menores o apenas visibles continuaron laborando junto a los derrumbes y los rescates de cadáveres. Algunos aprovecharon la gran cantidad de mano de obra cesante para renovar por completo su planta de trabajadores y otros pagaban la mitad de los salarios anteriores con el fin de recuperar pérdidas supuestas.

Las costureras de la zona Topeka levantaron un campamento y a partir de allí los hasta entonces grupos dispersos empezaron a configurarse en una unidad. Así tomó cuerpo el Frente de Costureras en lucha y se inició la coordinación de las acciones orientadas a solucionar el problema de la interrupción del trabajo, las indemnizaciones, el pago de los salarios y las liquidaciones.

El 11 de octubre la Secretaría del Trabajo instaló un modulo de información y asesoría en el cruce de las calles de San Antonio Abad y Avenida del Taller. Esta acción, sin precentes en la historia de los conflictos laborales, tuvo por objeto el levantamiento de las actas en contra de los patrones por el incumplimiento de los pagos de sueldos atrasados y la falta de respuesta ante la demanda de indemnización a los familiares de las costureras muertas. La agilidad en los trámites fue asombrosa ya que rápidamente se turnaban las actas para pronta resolución en la Procuraduría de la Defensa del Trabajo del DDF.

Los primeros resultados fueron inusitadamente prontos. Se lograron arreglos expeditos entre costureras y patrones al igual que se dictaminaron embargos precautorios de maquinarias y materiales de las empresas afectadas, con el fin de asegurar el pago de salarios caidos.

Las consecuencias de la movilización generalizada, la presencia física de las costureras en la calle y el apoyo de organizaciones suscitaron reacciones más profundas y no se limitaron a unos cuantos acuerdos obrero patronales o a los embargos y promesas de pago.

La denuncia como ejercicio diario y la presión constante a través de la prensa escrita y hablada al igual que la permanencia indefinida en la calle de las costureras movieron a la negociación y al arreglo.

El develamiento de un historia de explotación de años desencadenó conmociones en las cúpulas sindicales y en las de las autoridades del trabajo. Las renuncias se presentan en cascada en la Secretaría del Trabajo y se anuncian las averiguaciones y juicios a las conductas de líderes obreros.

El 15 de octubre, Arsenio Farell Cubillas, Secretario del Trabajo reconoce la colusión de autoridades laborales y sindicales en perjuicio de las costureras. Sus declaraciones contundentes amenazan con procedimientos penales contra empresarios, funcionarios públicos y líderes obreros. A partir de ese momento se desata entre los tres sectores involucrados una guerra de comunicados y la orquestación de acusaciones mutuas, defensas y justificaciones.

Ante las discrepancias en la cumbre las costureras no ceden y tres días más tarde marchan hacia Los Pinos donde son recibidas por el Presidente y el Secretario del Trabajo. En este recinto se reiteran denuncias y levantan demandas de pronta solución. El arreglo al conflicto se plantea desde la organización de las costureras en una asociación sindical única y la formulación de un contrato colectivo de trabajo para la rama de la confección.

El 20 de octubre se anuncia formalmente la formación del Sindicato Nacional 19 de Septiembre con una membresía de 5,000 costureras del Distrito Federal, Estado de México, Morelos, Coahuila y Guanajuato. Ese mismo día se procedió al registro y a la formación de comisiones mixtas para resolver de inmediato el problema del empleo por la vía de la creación de una cooperativa y la negociación con los patrones para la reapertura de las fuentes de trabajo.

Desde este momento se inicia una nueva historia para las mujeres que trabajan en la costura. Visibles al fin, pusieron al descubierto una vida de ilegalidad y de agravios y sobre todo, con su lucha, demostraron una indomable voluntad de victoria, dignidad y autonomía.

Notas

1. Anónimo, "El nuevo esquilmo a la costureras de la munición," *La Convención Radical Obrera*, a. XV, núm. 683, 24 de febrero de 1901, p. 1. Este testimonio además se encuentra en *La Mujer y el Movimiento Obrero Mexicano en el Siglo XIX. Antología de la Prensa Obrera* (México, D.F.: Centro de Estudios Históricos del Movimiento Obrero Mexicano, 1975), pp. 145-146.

PANORAMA DE LAS LUCHAS DE LA MUJER MEXICANA EN EL SIGLO XX

Abstract

Historically the women's movement in Mexico has made its most dynamic contributions to social struggle when its goals have been affiliated with those of progressive political and labor struggles. The country's revolutionary period, the Cárdenas administration, and the labor strife of the last twenty years, thus, provide a vantage point from which to view women's activism in twentieth century Mexico.

By 1913 scores of Mexican women participate in revolutionary activism, first, as helpmates and, later, as journalists and working women promoting progressive changes in the status of women. By 1916 the First Feminist Congress of Yucatán (Primer Congreso Feminista de Yucatán) is organized under the aegis of the state's progressive governor, Salvador Alvarado, and results in the formation of the Leagues of Feminine Orientation (Ligas de Orientación Femenina) of Yucatán, Chiapas, and Tabasco. These leagues make demands for land, equal pay, education and birth control on behalf of working-class and peasant women. Soon after the Mexican Communist Party (PCM) is founded in 1919 and it also takes an assertive stance on the equality and rights of women in its platform. For the most part, however, postrevolutionary Mexican society relegates women to traditional roles.

Despite this, in 1923 the First Feminist National Congress (Primer Congreso Nacional Feminista) makes a call for the rights and equality of women. Five years later, the country's Civil Code is reformed providing greater advantages for women. But it is not until 1931 during the First National Congress of Working Class and Peasant Women (Primer Congreso Nacional de Mujeres Obreras y Campesinas) held in Mexico City that illiterate and educated women, Catholics and communists come together to discuss fundamental women's issues establishing the most important achievement for Mexican women since the women's movement is initiated. Its participants discuss the development of a national campaign for the rights of women. In 1933 and 1934 the Second and Third sequels to the Congress follow respectively and although no real gains are made the cumulative effect of the three congresses prepare the ground for the formation of the country's most important women's organization: the United Front for the Rights of Women (Frente Unido Pro Derechos de la Mujer).

The formation of the Front is initiated by the PCM during the liberal administration of Lázaro Cárdenas (1934-1940) through which the women's movement in Mexico expands and wins government support. Its program calls for women to be given equal rights, the right to vote, and greater educational opportunities. It also calls for the reform of the Civil Code, Federal Work Law, and the Agrarian Code. Dependency on government support, however, weakens the organization and results in its eventual demise.

By the 1940s the women's movement erodes to a few small groups while capitalist development relegates working-class women to low-paying jobs and absorbs middle-class feminists into the system. When Mexico finally grants women formal citizenship rights in 1953 there are no longer groups capable of making demands on behalf of women's rights. It is not until 1970 that women once again begin organizational struggle and emerge as politically active groups.

Groups such as the National Front in Struggle for the Liberation and Rights of Women (Frente Nacional de Lucha por la Liberación y los Derechos de las Mujeres) are led by young university women of middle-class background and reflect ideological directions taken from North American, French, and Italian feminists. Women activists also organize to bring national and international attention to political repression in Mexico. They form the Committee on Political Prisoners, Persecuted, Exiled and Missing Persons (Comité de Presos, Perseguidos, Exiliados y Desaparecidos Políticos) headed by the mother of one of the missing, Rosario Ibarra Piedra.

In 1980 the Second National Meeting of Peasant Oganizations (Segundo Encuentro Nacional de Organizaciones Campesinas) is held and peasant women, representative of 45 percent of Mexico's female population, take an active part in it. Their objectives include ending repression in the countryside, liberating imprisoned men and women, and securing public services, potable water, healthcare, and education for the peasant population.

In 1970 Luis Echeverría becomes president of Mexico and having to compensate for the harsh political repression of the previous administration which culminates in the infamous Massacre of Tlatelolco his administration assumes a liberal, politically tolerant facade. In this context an independent (not officially recognized) union movement known as Insurgencia Obrera emerges and successfully organizes electrical workers and university employees into the STERM (1971-72) and SUTERM (1972-75) and effectively challenges the corruption of traditional unions until the movement is suppressed by government forces aided by the Confederación de Trabajadores Mexicanos (CTM), Mexico's largest confederation of officially recognized unions.

The formation of the Coordinadora de Mujeres Trabajadoras (the Working Women's Coordinator) in 1981 is the outcome of a new strategy by the independent workers' movement which must now work within the structure of official unions with the objective of winning over sectors of the nation's largest unions. The Coordinadora attempts to raise the consciousness of Mexican women not only as members of an exploited working class but as members of an exploited sex. It provides a national basis of support for peasant and working class women.

Within the past ten years, progress in the working conditions of women has come at the expense of long and difficult battles by groups of women among them the country's telephone operators, Mexico City's subway attendants, and women employed in the manufacture of shoes. Until recently, however, women's struggles in Mexico have not developed in conjunction with nor been equally supported by progressive movements dominated by males. On the contrary, women find that one of their major obstacles is male chauvinism which, for Mexicans, is rooted in a history of conquerers, colonizers, and, now, national bourgeoisie.

335

PANORAMA DE LAS LUCHAS DE LA MUJER MEXICANA EN EL SIGLO XX

by

Concepción Ruiz Funes y Enriqueta Tuñón

Las luchas de la mujer en México se manifestarán a lo largo de este siglo de diferentes maneras. Por un lado el contexto histórico y social en el que se dan es complejo y contradictorio, lo cual es lógicamente un factor determinante que hace que la lucha sea más difícil y los logros sean pocos. Por otro lado, hay que tener presente para comprender y analizar estas luchas que la sociedad mexicana--tradicionalmente machista y paternalista--ha relegado a la mujer a un papel secundario y subordinado y la ha constituido en propiedad exclusiva del hombre, convirtiéndola al mismo tiempo en la responsable única y absoluta de la crianza y educación de los hijos. Todo lo anterior: sociedad y núcleo familiar nos debe llevar a realizar un análisis de la familia mexicana.

Si hacemos un recorrido de las luchas emprendidas por la mujer observamos que éstas han sido relevantes, combativas y en muchos momentos amplias, cuando a lo largo de la historia de México han coincidido con situaciones de auge de las luchas sociales.

Si bien el objetivo de nuestro trabajo es presentar un panorama de los movimientos y luchas de la mujer que surgen en la última década, consideramos importante presentar como antecedentes un breve panorama histórico.

Ricardo Flores Magón, en *Regeneración*, (24 de septiembre de 1910) pública un manifiesto dedicado a la mujer en donde hace un análisis del papel que ésta tiene en la sociedad desde sus orígenes; para concluir: "La condición de la mujer en este siglo varía según su categoría social, pero a pesar de la dulcificación de las costumbres, a pesar de los progresos de la filosofía, la mujer sigue subordinada al hombre por la tradición y por la ley. En todos los tiempos la mujer ha sido considerada como un ser inferior al hombre, no sólo por la ley, sino también por la costumbre, y a ese erróneo e injusto concepto se debe el infortunio que sufre desde que la humanidad se diferenciaba apenas de la fauna primitiva por el uso del fuego y el hacha de sílex...totalmente ignorante de los problemas de la tierra, la mujer se encuentra de improviso envuelta en el torbellino de la actividad industrial que necesita brazos, brazos baratos sobre todo, para hacer frente a la competencia provocada por la voracidad de los príncipes del dinero y echa garra de ella, aprovechando la circunstancia de que no está organizada con las de su clase para luchar con sus hermanos los trabajadores contra la rapacidad del capital. A esto se debe que la mujer, aún trabajando más que el hombre gana menos y que la miseria y el maltrato y el desprecio son hoy, como lo fueron ayer, los frutos amargos que recoge por toda una existencia de sacrificio... Compañeras: hombres y mujeres sufren por igual la tiranía de un ambiente político y social que está en completo desacuerdo con los progresos de la civilización y las conquistas de la filosofía... Haced que nuestros esposos, nuestros hermanos, nuestros padres, nuestros hijos y nuestros amigos tomen el fusil. A quien se niegue a empuñar una arma contra la opresión, escupidle el rostro."[1] Este es el llamado magonista a que la mujer haga conciencia y participe en la lucha contra la opresión.

Cuando se inicia la lucha revolucionaria, la incorporación de las mujeres es masiva a partir de 1913. En el principio su participación se limita a acompañar al hombre a donde éste vaya para, a su lado, seguir ejerciendo su papel tradicional: hacerle la comida, parir a los hijos, cargar utensilios y armamento. Más tarde surgieron grupos organizados de mujeres trabajadoras, maestras, estudiantes y empleadas que, en las condiciones más adversas, crean periódicos y programas que proponen cambios en la situación de la mujer dentro de los principios planteados por la lucha revolucionaria, y al mismo tiempo atienden hospitales de campana, ayudan a la población civil, realizan labores de enlace y algunas de ellas participan como combatientes.[2]

En 1916, al llegar Salvador Alvarado a Yucatán impulsa el desarrollo de las organizaciones sindicales con el fin de garantizarse una amplia base social de apoyo. En esta coyuntura se desarrolla el Primer Congreso Feminista de Yucatán. La iniciativa de la organización del Congreso parte de un grupo de maestras, y más que aportar ideas a la causa de las mujeres, refleja que existen mujeres dispuestas a luchar por su propia causa, enmarcada fundamentalmente en el problema magisterial y haciendo énfasis en que la liberación de la mujer debe darse sin que se dejen de cumplir los deberes del hogar. No obstante el Congreso tiene una trascendencia importante, porque a partir de su realización surgen las Ligas de Orientación Femenina en Yucatán, Chiapas y Tabasco, las cuales ya plantean demandas concretas de la mujer obrera y campesina: dotación de parcelas e instrumentos de labranza, igualdad de salarios y participación sindical, ampliación de la educación popular, protección a la maternidad, abolición de la clasificación 'hijo natural' y, ya entonces, facilidades para el control de la natalidad.

En la Constitución de Querétaro de 1917, aparecen algunas disposiciones de carácter protector, en relación al trabajo de las mujeres, dentro de un espíritu paternalista que considera a la mujer una menor de edad: 1) A trabajo igual salario igual. (Este principio de justicia ha sido interpretado como una posición tomada en favor de las mujeres, pero en realidad los constituyentes pensaron en los trabajadores extranjeros y particularmente norteamericanos, que recibían salarios superiores a los mexicanos; 2) Derecho a la educación; 3) Salario mínimo obligatorio; 4) Reducción de la jornada laboral; 5) Prohibición del trabajo nocturno e insalubre; y 6) No desempeñar trabajos que exijan esfuerzo durante los tres meses anteriores al parto, un mes de descano obligatorio después del parto con salario íntegro y conservación del empleo y derechos contractuales, así como dos descanos extraordinarios al día durante la lactancia. Estos artículos tan avanzados, de hecho se quedan en el papel. A partir de estos años, las luchas continúan, pero a la nueva sociedad postrevolucionaria no le interesa el desarrollo de la mujer, insistiendo en mantenerla en su papel tradicional.

En 1919 se funda el Partido Comunista Mexicano (PCM). Su plataforma incluye la lucha por los derechos y la igualdad de la mujer.

En 1923 se realiza el Primer Congreso Nacional Feminista, sus objectivos: obtener la igualdad civil y política y todos aquellos derechos que son específicos de la mujer. Se publican diferentes revistas, la más importante aparece en 1926, *Mujer*, la cual tiene una gran difución y realiza una buena labor de concientización. Así en 1928 se plantean una serie de reformas al Código Civil que redundarán en beneficio de la mujer.

El Primer Congreso Nacional de Mujeres Obreras y
Campesinas se realiza en la ciudad de México en octubre de 1931.
Este es probablemente el logro más importante que se obtiene
desde que se inician las luchas femeniles. Acuden al Congreso
mujeres analfabetas e instruidas, católicas y comunistas y discuten
aspectos fundamentales de la mujer. La temática abarcó los
siguientes aspectos: 1) Implantación del cooperativismo entre las
mujeres obreras y campesinas; 2) Organización de la mujer para
los cultivos campesinos; 3) Desarrollo de una campaña nacionalista
para la reivindicación de los derechos de la mujer; 4)
Establecimiento de un banco familiar campesino; 5) Definición de
la situación civil y política de la mujer; y 6) Establecimiento de un
cuerpo protector del nino que orientará la educación y velará por
sus derechos.

A pesar de que los temas eran de interes general,
independientemente de la ideología de los grupos que asistieron,
durante el desarrollo del Congreso se desata una lucha entre las
delegadas del Partido Nacional Revolucionario (oficial y en el
poder) y las delegadas de organizaciones o partidos de izquierda.
Las delegadas comunistas forman un Bloque de Izquierda que
denuncia el carácter oficialista del Congreso y presenta una serie
de tesis sobre la situación de obreras y campesinas, haciendo un
llamado a las mujeres para que luchen desde organizaciones
clasistas y se centren en defender sus intereses específicos de clase.

En 1933 y 1934 se realizan el Segundo y Tercer Congreso
Nacional de Mujeres Obreras y Campesinas. El contenido del
temario fue similar al del Primero; pero se acentúan las diferencias
entre las posturas oficiales y las de organizaciones de izquierda, sin
que se llegue a ningún logro efectivo. No obstante, esta serie de
congresos preparan el terreno para lo que María Antonieta Rascón
nos dice será la organización femenil más importante del país: el
Frente Unico Pro Derechos de la Mujer (FUPDM). Hay que
considerar que esta organización se crea por iniciativa del PCM y
durante el gobierno de Lázaro Cárdenas (1934-1940), en el que los
postulados de la Revolución cobran de nuevo vigencia y la política
nacional se centra en dar solución a toda la problemática que
presentan las clases desposeídas. En este marco el movimiento
femenil se amplía, profundiza y adquiere fuerza y apoyo
gubernamental. En su ensayo, "La mujer y la lucha social," María
Antonieta Rascón nos informa que el programa que presenta el
Frente se resume en los siguientes puntos:

1) Derecho sin limitación a votar y ser votadas.

2) Modificaciones a los códigos civiles del país para tener igualdad de derechos con el hombre.

3) Modificaciones a la Ley Federal del Trabajo a fin de hacer compatible el trabajo femenino con la maternidad.

4) Modificaciones al Código Agrario para que puedan ser dotadas de tierras todas las mujeres que reúnan los mismos requisitos que actualmente tienen que llenar los hombres.

5) Estatuto jurídico para las trabajadoras del Estado.

6) Incorporación de la mujer indígena al movimiento social y político del país.

7) Establecimiento de centros de trabajo para mujeres desocupadas.

8) Mejoramiento integral del niño y protección efectiva a la infancia.

9) Amplía cultura para la mujer.[3]

Es indudable que el gobierno de Cárdenas apoya las demandas surgidas del Frente, pero quizá esto contribuye a que a lo largo de este periódo presidencial la fuerza que adquiere el Frente desde su fundación vaya decayendo debido a que hace recaer en el Estado una tarea que sólo las mujeres podrían llevar a cabo hasta sus últimas consecuencias; esto da pie para que el Frente se desintegre con la política posterior al sexenio cardenista, por no haber analizado en su debido momento la importancia de que las luchas femeniles debían darse con el apoyo estatal y de organizaciones y partidos de izquierda, pero como una acción independiente de las mujeres, en la cual la lucha debe ser colectiva.

A partir de 1940, las necesidades del desarrollo capitalista obligan a la mujer a incorporarse al trabajo asalariado, en los empleos peor remunerados. En esta forma, el impulso que habían logrado los movimientos femeniles y las organizaciones obreras, campesinas y magisteriales de mujeres, van desapareciendo y quedan sólo algunos núcleos reducidos.

En este contexto, posiblemente las mujeres pertenecientes a algunos sectores de la clase media hubieran podido continuar la lucha; pero absorbidas por el sistema, aceptan la política oficial y por lo tanto aceptan las reglas del juego impuestas por el hombre. Su actividad de luchadoras feministas se reduce a organizaciones internacionales de mujeres, congresos, encuentros, seminarios, periodismo o docencia; pero sin perspectivas de acciones concretas y organizadas que reivindiquen sus derechos, no sólo de ciudadanas y asalariadas, sino también sus derechos como mujer.

En 1953, oficialmente la mujer entra a formar parte de la vida pública mexicana: se le reconoce su carácter de ciudadana otorgándole el derecho de voto y la posibilidad de ocupar cargos políticos. Sin embargo ya no existían grupos, ni siquiera voces que masivamente demandaran reivindicaciones específicas de la mujer.

En 1962, el PCM publica su tesis sobre el trabajo femenil; sus objetivos: ganar grandes sectores de mujeres trabajadoras para formar una organización autónoma de mujeres que impulse la lucha por sus derechos y reivindicaciones específicas. Por primera vez en México se plantea la tesis de que la emancipación de la mujer sólo se conquistará aboliendo la explotación del hombre por el hombre.

En 1964, promovido por la Unión Nacional de Mujeres Mexicanas se realiza el Congreso de Unificación de Mujeres Mexicanas, al que asisten varias organizaciones de izquierda. Las demandas que surgen del Congreso son laborales y políticas: 1) Derecho al trabajo; 2) A trabajo igual salario igual; 3) Control de precios; 4) Lucha contra la represión política; y 5) Libertad de presos políticos.

De hecho, nuevamente se piden reivindicaciones que no son especificamente de la situación de explotación y opresión que vive la mujer, por otro lado no se obtiene nada, pues la situación política que vive el país es crítica y el grado de movilización de las organizaciones de izquierda esta limitada por este contexto.

El año 1968 es crucial en la historia contemporánea de México. No sólo surge el movimiento estudiantil que culminaría el 2 de octubre con la matanza de Tlatelolco, surgen también movimientos campesinos independientes, sindicatos democráticos, etc. Todo lo cual presenta nuevamente una situación coyuntural favorable y propicia para que se reinicien las luchas de la mujer. Aunque la historia oficial presenta esta etapa del desarrollo nacional como el momento en que la sociedad mexicana ha alcanzado un alto grado de desarrollo, civilización y libertad, es fácil darse cuenta que esta modernización del país (que se inicia a partir del periódo alemanista) se logra a costa de la miseria creciente de las masas y de la concentración desproporcionada de la riqueza en manos de unos cuantos.

Tlatelolco constituyó un punto de ruptura en la evolución ideológica del país, acentuando los enfrentamientos politicos. El Estado perdió su hegemonía ideológica a un grado sin precedente. Los símbolos de la revolución mexicana fueron usados para justificar la represión. Acabaron vaciados de contenido.

En este contexto, en 1970, entra Luis Echeverría al poder, quien desarrolla una política populista y una aparente apertura democrática. A partir de ese año en México la lucha de las mujeres se reinicia en forma organizada. Sus diversas demandas se manifiestan a través de diferentes organizaciones y están relacionadas con su posición de clase. Las organizaciones que surgen en este momento están compuestas de grupos feministas, organizaciones de mujeres contra la represión política, organizaciones campesinas independientes de las oficiales, y sindicatos independientes de los oficiales.

Grupos Feministas

Se crea un movimiento feminista importante, compuesto por muy diversos grupos con influencia del feminismo norteamericano, francés e italiano fundamentalmente. Sus militantes son, en su mayoría, jóvenes universitarias de clase media. Los distintos grupos feministas posiblemente han planteado divergencias en sus puntos de vista sobre la problemática de la mujer mexicana, algunos más radicalizados que otros; pero sus metas y procedimientos no difieren mucho. Su trabajo se ha venido realizando, en general, entre mujeres de clase media y en algunos casos se han acercado a obreras, campesinas y amas de casa. Pero sus metas fundamentales son similares a las de los movimientos feministas de Europa y Estados Unidos, estas piden: 1) Terminar con la discriminación legal de la mujer; 2) Luchar por el aborto libre y gratuito, elaborando un proyecto de ley de gran trascendencia; 3) Apoyar a mujeres violadas, creando un centro de ayuda médica, psicológica y asesoría legal; y 4) Defender a mujeres golpeadas.

En 1978, estos grupos feministas hacen un llamado a los partidos de izquierda y sindicatos independientes para crear un frente amplio que promueva la autorganización de las mujeres. Así, el 8 de marzo de 1979 se constituye el Frente Nacional de Lucha por la Liberación y los Derechos de las Mujeres (FNALIDM). Al principio el trabajo se desarrolla con cierta uniformidad, pero en 1980 empiezan a surgir diferencias provocadas fundamentalmente por la doble militancia (en un partido y en un grupo feminista), lo cual debilita la organización. Es pronto para hacer un balance, no obstante se puede decir que su mayor logro ha sido la elaboración de la Ley de Maternidad

Responsable, que defienden en la Cámara los diputados de la Coalición de Izquierda.

Organizaciones de Mujeres contra la Represión Política

La situación de represión política que vive hoy América Latina, hace que se formen diversas organizaciones de mujeres que enfrentan esta agresión y luchan a favor de los miles de desaparecidos, torturados o asesinados por motivos políticos.

El 28 de agosto de 1978, tras una huelga de hambre llevada a cabo por ochenta y tres madres de desaparecidos políticos, se crea en México el Comité de Presos, Perseguidos, Exiliados y Desaparecidos Políticos; su lider y organizadora es Rosario Ibarra de Piedra. A partir de entonces, esta mujer seguida por madres, esposas, hermanas, hijas, organiza manifestaciones, viaja y da a conocer el caso de los desaparecidos ante el mundo. Hoy en México se sabe que hay 481 desaparecidos políticos, entre ellos los hijos de las ochenta y tres madres que iniciaron su protesta en 1978. Elena Poniatowska nos dice en *Fuerte es el Silencio*: "lo que está haciendo Rosario Ibarra de Piedra es darle una conciencia a este país tan olvidadizo, tan valemadrista, tan barrido de noticias, lleno de hombres y mujeres de ancianos y de niños que viven en el más absoluto desamparo. Rosario solita, esta mujer que fue rica y protegida y amada por sus hijos, consentida por su esposo, ahora se para en todos los juzgados, exigiendo justicia. Rosario se ha hecho a si misma con los materiales recibidos en los últimos años: La indiferencia, el silencio, el engaño, los "no" que le dan en cada antesala, y como ha sido fuerte, estos materiales: la dura arcilla humana, el concreto, la varilla, han cambiado su vida. Para bien. Muchachos que salen después de tres, cuatro, cinco años de cárcel, ahora levantan un acta, sin importarles la persecución posterior, el hecho de que puedan desaparecerlos nuevamente, torturarlos y hasta matarlos, alegando que fueron muertos en un enfrentamiento armado con la policía. Un país gana mucho cuando sus ciudadanos aprenden a defenderse, y las actas son un primer paso."[4]

Movimientos como este, organizados por mujeres, no sólo se dan en México, de dan en toda América Latina. La desaparición es el arma más terrible que emplea el enemigo: destruye al sujeto e incide en forma directa en las personas cercanas. Este tipo de organizaciones formadas fundamentalmente por mujeres, realizan una lucha diaria, a veces silenciosa, que dadas las condiciones dictatoriales de nuestro continente son duras y son un ejemplo de la capacidad de lucha política que tiene la mujer.

Organizaciones Campesinas Independientes

Las mujeres campesinas en México siembran, barbechan y cosechan maíz al lado del hombre; cortan legumbres, fruta, algodón y café; se emplean como peones de campo con salarios inferiores a los del hombre; tejen y confeccionan ropa; ahuman carne y pescado; fabrican artesanías. Cerca del cuarenta y cinco porciento de la población femenina en México realiza estas labores, recibiendo salarios inferiores a los del hombre; además de desempeñar todo el trabajo doméstico, económicamente inactivo y tener toda la crianza de los hijos.

En abril de 1980 se realiza el Segundo Encuentro Nacional de Organizaciones Campesinas. En él ya participan algunas mujeres, con el objetivo principal de exponer sus experiencias en la lucha, como mujeres y como campesinas. Plantean que su lucha es a la par con el hombre como explotados. Sus metas son: 1) Alto a la represión en el campo y libertad a esposos, hijos y compañeras presas; 2) Servicios públicos y agua potable; 3) Educación extensiva, gratuita y popular; y 4) Centros de salud, médicos, y medicinas. Sus alternativas incluyen la creación de una organización de mujeres campesinas a nivel nacional al interior de la Coordinadora Nacional Plan de Ayala (CNPA, organización campesina independiente de la Confederación Nacional Campesina, oficial), la formación de comités de mujeres campesinas en todas las organizaciones de CNPA, y la participación de la mujer en todas las instancias.

No se puede hablar todavía de hechos y resultados, pero es claro que la campesina mexicana todavía no puede realizar una lucha por obtener logros más deseados, debe centrarse antes en lucha para ganar reivindicaciones, no sólo como campesina asalariada ante el patrón, sino como ser humano ante el hombre y la sociedad.

Sindicatos Independientes

Por ser éste el tema concreto del trabajo, consideramos importante hacer ciertas reflexiones sobre las condiciones políticas en las que surge el sindicalismo independiente en México.

Luis Echeverría llega al poder en 1970. El país enfrenta, por un lado, una franca crisis económica debido a la política de supuesto "desarrollo estabilizador" de los gobiernos anteriores. En 1973 se da un estancamiento del salario real que para 1977 será de absoluta caida; por otro lado, se enfrenta a una crisis política seria, motivada por la falta de consenso expresada en 1968. La necesidad de contar con base de apoyo popular, más la necesidad de superar las contradiciones propias del modelo estabilizador, llevarán a Echeverría a adoptar una política discursiva, de claro tono populista, sobre todo en sus primeros cuatro años de gobierno, que terminó en una franca política de represión.

Para el movimiento obrero fueron claras las declaraciones del presidente, cuando afirmó que durante su mandato sí se respetaría la voluntad de los trabajadores y la ley. Esta nueva postura del ejecutivo respondía a la necesidad de suavizar las diferencias sociales, provocadas por el modelo anterior, y aumentar el mercado interno, para lo cual había que modernizar el sistema de control sindical, que había basado la paz social en la total antidemocracia de los años anteriores.

En este sentido, Echeverría propició pugnas internas entre los sindicatos oficiales y la política "abierta" de las autoridades laborales permitió, en algunos casos, el surgimiento de un nuevo sindicalismo, básicamente economicista y ubicado en empresas modernas de alta composición de capital. La respuesta de la burocracia sindical tradicional no se hizo esperar. En 1971, Fidel Velázquez, lider eterno de la Confederación de Trabajadores Mexicanos (CTM), declaraba que en el movimiento obrero se encontraría siempre todo un ejército dispuesto a la lucha abierta, constitucional o no. Paralelamente a esta declaración, se daba la noticia de que grupos de desempleados recibían instrucción paramilitar.

Al lado de esta pugna real entre burocracia política y burocracia sindical, a partir de 1972 empezó a desarrollarse otro fenómeno que sería el fundamental en el sexenio y que obligó a que se realizaran nuevas alianzas entre el gobierno y los sindicatos oficiales. Fue la llamada Insurgencia Obrera. Para entender su surgimiento no basta hablar de la crisis económica ni de la política abierta de carácter laboral durante este regimen, aunque estos sean elementos claves. Es importante reconocer el papel del sindicalismo en México, como un sindicalismo oficial, alejado de las necesidades reales de los trabajadores y casi exclusivamente fuente de empleos y de poder político para los líderes.

Con esta tradición, los obreros veían, y muy agudamente en este período, que los sindicatos no eran verdaderos instrumentos de defensa de sus intereses y que, para recuperar el sentido clasista del sindicato había que negar el sindicalismo oficial y crear nuevos sindicatos democráticos formados por los propios obreros, que sí hacían asambleas y respetaban los estatutos.

La Insurgencia Obrera entonces, más que democratizar los sindicatos oficiales, afiliados a las centrales, reivindicaba la demanda de sindicatos independientes. Se partía de la imposibilidad de recuperar algo que nunca había sido de los trabajadores, de ahí que sólo los viejos sindicatos nacionales de industria (ferrocarrileros, mineros, petroleros) se plantearon democratizar y los sindicatos de empresa quitarse la tutela de las centrales y crear sindicatos únicos.

Los sindicatos en lucha por su independencia se concentraron en las tareas legales de su registro y se agruparon en torno a despachos laborales más que a organizaciones políticas, aunque también se dio el caso. El momento de auge de Insurgencia Obrera se dio en 1974-75, y obligó a un reacomodo tanto de los sindicatos oficiales como del gobierno que se trasluce en emplazamiento a huelgas por parte de los oficialistas y por parte del Estado a negar registros y a acusar las huelgas de ilegales. Los movimientos independientes, como consecuencia de los anterior se radicalizan y adoptan formas de lucha extralegales, paros, marchas, mítines, manifestaciones independientes el Primero de Mayo, y poder obrero.

Paulatinamente, a partir de 1973, se intentan crear formas de coordinación entre los movimientos. Surgen el Frente Popular de Chihuahua, la Coordinadora de Huelgas de Naucalpan, el Frente Sindical Independiente de Yucatán, la Intersindical del Valle de México, la Coordinadora Sindical de Cuernavaca, etc. Sin embargo son sindicatos de empresa, cada uno con problemas específicos, con revisiones de contrato en fechas distintas, que enfrenten cada uno y solos a su patrón. Excepto la creación de sindicatos independientes en las universidades, el único intento aglutinador serio a nivel nacional y con planteamientos amplios fue el Sindicato de Trabajadores Electricistas de la República Mexicana (STERM), 1971-72 y la Tendencia Democrática del Sindicato Unico de Trabajadores Electricistas de la República Mexicana (SUTERM) en 1972-75, hasta que es expulsada la dirección democrática de su lider Galván, despedidos cientos de sus simpatizantes y la Tendencia deja de ser su centro aglutinador, que por experiencia y recursos había sido en casi todas las ciudades del país.

La represión a la Tendencia Democrática no fue así solamente el apoyo por parte del gobierno a los sindicatos oficiales (CTM), sino también la defensa total de éste. El golpe final fue negar los registros y los patrones despedir masivamente a los obreros, obligándolos a largos juicios legales de desgaste.

Ante esta perspectiva, a partir de 1976 y ya durante el gobierno de José López Portillo, el movimiento obrero independiente adopta otro tipo de lucha: *democratizar desde dentro a los sindicatos oficiales e ir ganando secciones en las grandes centrales.*

Dentro de la lucha independiente ha habido movimientos importantes de sindicatos con mayoría de mujeres, principalmente en las ramas textil y de la confección. Las mujeres en estas luchas lograron llegar a participar como cualquier otro trabajador, lo cual ya significa un gran avance, pero nunca se plantearon ni ellas ni los sindicatos, demandar beligerantemente demandas propias. De aquí, surge la Coordinadora de Mujeres Trabajadoras, que agrupa viejos sindicatos independientes de la época de Echeverría y secciones recientemente democratizadas pero que son parte formal de las centrales oficiales y que intenta definir demandas generales de las mujeres trabajadoras, intercambiar experiencias e implementar instancias de coordinación y apoyo mutuo.

La Coordinadora de Mujeres Trabajadoras

El tema de la mujer obrera ha sido abordado a través de un enfoque económico o estadístico en el que se resalta la participación femenina en la mano de obra industrial, el porcentaje de oferta y demanda que representa, la posibilidad de su incorporación masiva al ejército industrial de reserva y sus repercusiones en la percepción salarial.

Se le ha estudiado como parte, y como parte secundaria, del movimiento obrero organizado y únicamente bajo el aspecto de obrera asalariada. Esto ha llevado a que la categoría mujer obrera se haya aplicado solamente a aquellas mujeres asalariadas en una fábrica.

Sin embargo hay que considerar que la mujer ama de casa, esposa de trabajador, pertenece también a la clase obrera pues comparte su forma de vida, su sistema de valores, y es igualmente explotada indirectamente por el comprador de la fuerza de trabajo del hombre, y directamente por su propio hombre. Los censos oficiales aportan datos que muestran que aumenta el número de mujeres incorporadas al mundo industrial; pero ¿cuál es su situación, cuál es la realidad de su vida cotidiana?

Jornada de trabajo industrial y jornada de trabajo doméstico, incapacidad para incorporarse a la vida sindical inclusive en los sindicatos democráticos independientes, por la doble jornada que tiene que realizar, lo cual hace sumamente difícil que una mujer pueda asistir a actos o reuniones por las noches o fuera de la ciudad. En este sentido, la mujer obrera se ve impedida no sólo para establecer demandas de carácter laboral sino para incorporar demandas específicas de su condición de mujer tales como: guarderías, tiempos de lactancia, alto al abuso sexual para conseguir la planta, aumento de salario, escalafón, opciones de capacitación, y más.

El caso de las trabajadoras domésticas asalariadas es todavía peor, ni siquiera tienen una instancia desde donde puedan hacerse oir. En 1970 había medio millión de mujeres incorporadas a este servicio. En las mismas condiciones inhumanas se encuentran las obreras maquiladoras.

No obstante, se empieza ya a haber algunos logros, nuevamente aislados en estos últimos 10 años. En empresas de la confección y el calzado, después de largas huelgas de mujeres se ha logrado evitar despidos e irregularidades en los salarios.

Las tacquilleras del Metro consideradas empleadas de confianza, con salario mínimo, sin escalafón, ni prestaciones, responsables del dinero, sufren robos, violaciones y trabajan ocho horas diarias, sin poder tomar alimentos, sin permiso de ir al baño y en muchas ocasiones teniendo que doblar turno por ausencia de otra compañera; encarcadas en un sindicato charro emprenden su lucha (650 mujeres) que dura 5 años, logran su base, nuevas condiciones de trabajo que se cumplen en parte, pero por lo menos realizan un papel importante dentro del sindicato, aunque sus logros no son ni muchísimo menos los deseables.

En otra empresa estatal, Teléfonos de México, donde el sesenta porciento de los trabajadores son mujeres, con un sindicato democrático pero fragmentado, también las mujeres emprenden su batalla, pues sus condiciones de trabajo son infrahumanas, logrando mejorarlas al cabo de tres años de lucha. Como éstos, podríamos mencionar varios intentos más, aislados, pero que aportan granito de arena.

Lo que sí es un hecho importante y que vemos en todos estos movimientos, es que todas las luchas tienen un doble frente, no se desarrollan, hasta ahora, apoyadas y hombro con hombro con las luchas del hombre, por el contrario, encuentran uno de sus principales obstáculos en la mentalidad, machista del mexicano, inculcada y fomentada a través de su historia por conquistadores, colonizadores y finalmente por la burguesía nacional. De tal manera, la mujer en el campo es mercancía y existe como objeto sexual en la class obrera y en la burguesía. Creemos por esto que La Coordinadora de Mujeres Trabajadoras es importante, porque como veremos, abarca la problemática de la mujer trabajadora en su sentido más amplio.

Es un hecho, entonces, que la mujer asalariada va a formar parte en la vida sindical (siempre limitada por falta de tiempo libre ya que sufre la doble jornada). Se integra pero como un trabajador más y si se llegan a plantear demandas netamente femeninas, éstas, hasta el momento, se terminan relegando por asuntos prioritarios.

Es importante que la mujer tome conciencia de sus problemas, no sólo como trabajador explotado sino como mujer. Con este fin se ha creado la Coordinadora de Mujeres Trabajadoras, para concientizar a las mujeres para presionar que su sindicato las tome en cuenta como tales y luche por sus demandas femeninas. También lucha la Coordinadora para que la mujer tome conciencia de que para mejorar su situación no sólo debe obtener logros a nivel sindical, sino que al mismo tiempo debe luchar en su hogar, la lucha debe darse conjunta para acabar así con la doble explotación.

Para hablar del surgimiento de la Coordinadora nos remontaremos a octubre de 1980 en que se organizó el Primer Encuentro Nacional de Mujeres al que asistieron campesinas, colonas y obreras de diversas partes del país. El Encuentro agrupó a las mujeres en 2 grupos: obreras y colonas; y campesinas.

El primer día de la reunión se repartieron questionarios entre las asistentes relacionados con la problemática general de cada uno de los grupos. El primer grupo (obreras y colonas) concluyó haciendo notar la doble jornada de la mujer trabajadora (centro de trabajo y hogar), explotada no sólo por el patrón sino también por el marido quien no participa en el trabajo doméstico y con quien su relación no es de compañerismo.

Para solucionar estos problemas se decidió que la mujer debe luchar en su hugar, a nivel individual para evitar esta explotación, pero que también es fundamental la unión para organizarse, y trabajar en conjunto para acabar con esa situación.

Las campesinas, por su parte, hicieron notar su papel de "objeto" frente al marido, el que jámas le ayuda, al igual que los hijos varones, en las faenas del hogar ya que éste es un trabajo que "humilla" al hombre. Plantearon otro problema grave del campo y es la educación que se le da a los niños, en sentido de que deben de respetar al hombre y al *rico*. Como posible solución, al igual que al primer grupo, se vio la necesidad de no luchar aisladas en casa para concientizar al marido sino también unirse y organizarse para tener más fuerza.

El segundo tema se centró en el trabajo de la mujer. Por un lado, obreras y colonas expusieron sus problemas: menos sueldo que el hombre por trabajo igual; abuso sexual de los jefes; contratos cortos para tenerlas más controladas (si hay embarazo se les rescinde el contrato); y el ama de casa tiene un trabajo no remunerado por lo tanto no se le da la importancia que tiene aunque constituye la infraestructura necesaria para que el marido pueda producir pues le permite ir a su centro de trabajo descansado, elimentado y limpio.

En la discusión de este tema, se concluyó en el Primer Encuentro Nacional de Mujeres que debemos luchar por obtener el mismo salario que el hombre, prestaciones, buen trato y lograr que el sindicato apoye demandas femeninas como guarderías y comedores comunitarios.

Para lograr lo anterior hay que unirse, organizarse creando grupos de reflexión para analizar los problemas y ver el modo de solucionarlos. Hay que hacer notar cómo hasta ahora la solución que dan las mujeres en el Primer Encuentro Nacional es "unirse" y "organizarse" de ahí que surje la idea de formar la Coordinadora de Mujeres Trabajadoras que como veremos más adelante intentan unir y organizar a las mujeres.

Al referirse las campesinas a su trabajo hicieron notar que cuando trabajan fuera de casa ocupan de 6 a 10 horas diarias, les pagan poquísimo (30 pesos diarios por lavar, 100 a 150 pesos en un taller de artesanía), no las protege la ley, no tienen seguro social, trabajan en condiciones de esclavas.

Después de hablar de la situación general de la mujer en México, de su trabajo y los problemas que se presentan en este sentido, hubo representantes de colonias populares como Colonia Progresista de Ixtapalapa, del Ajusco, Unidad Vicente Guerrero de Ixtapalapa, Ciudad Netzahualcoyotl entre otros, quienes dieron a conocer sus problemas fundamentales, su forma de organización, de lucha y los logros obtenidos.

En el mismo sentido hubo también representantes de sindicatos como de la Refrigeradora Tapepan, y la Universidad Nacional Autónoma de México (UNAM), también esposas de obreros de Mexicana de Envases, S.A. (MESA) y mujeres que vinieron representando comunidades de diversas partes del país, como por ejemplo de: Oteapan, Veracruz; Venustiano Carranza, Chiapas; Zapotlán del Río, Jalisco; Coatetelco, Morelos; Aquila, Michoacán; Minzapán, Veracruz; Benito Juárez, Oaxaca; Sanctorum, Tlaxcala; y Luis Pérez Gil, Tabasco.

Con lo anterior nos damos cuenta que hubo muchos grupos representados en este Primer Encuentro, grupos no sólo del Distrito Federal, sino de diversas entidades del país, es más, todo finalizó con la exposición dada por representantes de mujeres de Raymondville, Texas, de Guatemala, El Salvador y Nicaragua sobre la situación femenina en dichos países.

Como conclusión del Primer Encuentro Nacional las mujeres vieron la necesidad de unirse y organizarse para encontrar la mejor manera de lucha. El primer paso a dar es dividirse por zonas y sectores creándose así 3 sectores compuestas de obreras, campesinas y colonas; 2 zonas de obreras y 2 de campesinas. Las zonas obreras son la del norte (Nuevo León, Durango y Zacatecas) y la del valle de México (Distrito Federal, estado de México, y Morelos) y las zonas campesinas son las del Sureste (Chiapas, Veracruz y Tabasco) y la del Norte (Nuevo León, Durango y Zacatecas). Las colonas no se han organizado.

Después de este Primer Encuentro Nacional de Mujeres, el grupo de trabajadoras y esposas de trabajadores vio la necesidad de organizar su propio encuentro para: descubrir los problemas de la gran mayoría de las mujeres trabajadoras con el fin de encontrar demandas comunes a mujeres de distintos centros de trabajo; y buscar mecanismos para enfrentar los problemas conjuntamente, formas para resolverlos y crear canales de apoyo mutuo.

Este Primer Encuentro de Mujeres Trabajadoras se realizó el 23 y 24 de mayo de 1981, en el alberque del CREA, en la ciudad de México y estuvo organizado por el Centro Integral de Desarrollo Humano de America Latina (CIDHAL) y algunos sindicatos independientes que habían asistido al Primer Encuentro Nacional de Mujeres de octubre de 1980. Los temas tratados fueron: problemas de la mujer en el centro de trabajo, en el hogar, y en la organización sindical o gremial.[5] Para discutir los temas se organizaron grupos de trabajo formados por mujeres se distintos centros de trabajo con una coordinadora para moderar la discusión.

El Encuentro comenzó con una película que motivaba al análisis de la situación de la mujer en la sociedad y a continuación se discutieron los temas anteriormente mencionados. Una vez discutidos las moderadoras y redactoras resumieron y sistematizaron las discusiones que se fueron dando, de tal manera que al finalizar el primer día ya estaban listas las síntasis de las discusiones desarrolladas ese día por cada grupo. Con estas síntesis se inició la discusión al segundo día que consistió en decidir las formas de organización y lucha para lograr las demandas femeninas. El Encuentro terminó con una reunión plenaria en la que se expusieron las demandas y las formas de organización y lucha propuestas. Así pues el planteamiento hecho de cada uno de los temas a tratar fue el siguiente:

Planteamiento de Temas

Condición de la mujer asalariada:

1. Tienen los trabajos más monótanos y en general una extensión del trabajo doméstico (limpieza).
2. Cuando hay una oportunidad de promoción o capacitación son los hombres quienes la aprovechan, entre otras cosas, porque estas astividades quedan fuera de las horas de trabajo y la mujer tiene la doble jornada.
3. Contratos eventuales, si se embaraza o se casa, no les renuevan el contrato.
4. En general sus puestos son de menos responsabilidad que los de los hombres.
5. Es víctima de abuso sexual por parte de los jefes.
6. Existen rivalidades con sus companeros a causa del "machismo."

Condición de la mujer en el hogar:

1. La mujer realiza el trabajo en el hogar aparte del laboral lo que tiene por resultado que no tiene tiempo libre para capacitarse o para descansar.
2. El hombre no le ayuda y cuando lo hace es siempre una concesión negociada.

3.   Si la mujer trabaja fuera del hogar es una concesión del marido.
4.   La mujer trabajadora carece de facilidades como guarderías suficientes o comedores colectivas.
5.   El "macho" le hace sentirse culpable por "abandonar el hogar" para ir a trabajar y además al ver que ellas trabajan fuera del hogar en muchas ocasiones dejan ellos de aportar.

Participación sindical de la mujer:

1.   El trabajo del hogar (doble jornada) le impide participar en asambleas sindicales.
2.   Ellas mismas no se sienten capaces de participar activamente.
3.   Si participan es como base casi nunca en puestos directivos.
4.   Los sindicatos "charros" a veces nombran delegadas porque creen que es más fácil controlarlas.
5.   Si participan activamente en la vida sindical son criticadas por compañeros y compañeras.

Demandas

Trabajo Asalariado:

1.   Que se cumpla la Ley Federal del Trabajo.
2.   Que no se haga examen médico come requisito para ser empleados.
3.   Que no haya topes en las categorías.
4.   Que les permitan faltar al trabajo a hombres y mujeres cuando los hijos estén enfermos.
5.   Que se instalen suficientes guarderías, comedores, lavanderías o que se den ayudas económicas para estos servicios.
6.   Que realmente se le de a la mujer la misma preparación que al hombre y que se les capacite a las horas de trabajo.
7.   Que se implante el horario de cuarenta horas de trabajo en todos los centros.

Trabajo Doméstico:

1.   Que se reconozca el trabajo doméstico como necesario en la sociedad.

2.   Que los hombres reconozcan su obligación de asumir en igualdad de condiciones las tareas de la casa y el cuidado de los hijos.

Lucha Sindical:

1.   Que se impulse la mayor participación de las mujeres incluso la de las esposas de trabajadores exigiendo el apoyo de los compañeros.
2.   Que los sindicatos promuevan sistemas de guarderías durante la realización de actividades sindicales.
3.   Que se reconozca la capacidad de las mujeres para desempeñar cualquier cargo sindical.
4.   Que se incluye en los contratos colectivos de trabajo que el respeto y buen trato a las mujeres por parte de las autoridades.

Una vez expuestos los problemas y las demandas de las mujeres trabajadoras se propusieron las siguientes formas de lucha: 1) Promover la formación de grupos de mujeres solidarias cuyo fin sea dirigir una labor de concientización entre las mujeres; 2) Difundir las demandas de este primer encuentro; 3) Incluir en las demandas sindicales estas demandas femeninas; y 4) Crear centros de apoyo para difundir la problemática de la mujer. Es así como a raíz del Primer Encuentro de Mujeres Trabajadoras se crea la *Coordinadora de Mujeres Trabajadoras.*

La Coordinadora entonces es un organismo recién creado (mayo 1981) y dedicado a concientizar a la mujer sobre su probemática como tal y a luchar por acabar con su situación de explotación; es también un organismo de apoyo a las luchas sindicales y demandas de mujeres, además de dar formación política a las compañeras de la Coordinadora, ellas parten del problema de clase pero después pasan a hablar del problema de la mujer.

Es todavía un grupo pequeño de empleadas y obreras de diversos sindicatos y esposas de trabajadores. Aún no podemos hablar de resultados dado su recién creación, pero sí de sus objetivos, anteriormente mencionados, y de su organización que se ha dividido por sectores y zonas, que son hasta ahora: 1) zona norte (agrupa sindicatos del norte de la ciudad de México que incluye Azcapotzalco, Vallejo, Tlalnepantla); 2) zona sur (Tlalpan y Ixtapalapa); 3) zona centro (agrupa sindicatos que no son de fábricas, como el de Tepepan, Pesca, Instituto Nacional de

Antropología e Historia (INAH); y 4) universitarios (STUNAM). Las zonas tienen sus características específicas y sus propias tareas y se reunen periódicamente, de acuerdo a sus necesidades. Cada quince días hay una reunión con las representantes de cada uno de los sindicatos, en donde se informa de las actividades realizadas de cara a la Coordinadora.

Este tipo de organización, por sus características y el contexto actual de nuestro país, es posible que logre una lucha más concreta y por lo tanto objetivos más específicos que lleven a mejorar las condiciones de las mujeres trabajadoras en México.

Conclusiones

Nos interesa el tema de la mujer como trabajadora, ama de casa, esposa de trabajador, trabajadora doméstica asalariada, como responsable de la educación de sus hijos y en fin, como trabajador que realiza una doble jornada y que se incorpora a las luchas sindicales y políticas.

Hasta la creación de la Coordinadora de Mujeres Trabajadoras no se había abordado el tema de la mujer tan ampliamente, es por eso que pensamos que seguir el desarrollo y realizar un estudio amplio de este organismo reviste una gran importancia, no solamente por los objetivos que se propone, sino por que se da en una crítica coyuntura histórica de México y se presenta como una alternativa interesante para resolver la problemática de la mujer.

Como investigadores conscientes y comprometidos con nuestra realidad social, nuestra obligación es colaborar lo más ampliamente con la lucha emprendida por este tipo de organizaciones.

Apendice A

Algunos Sindicatos y Organizaciones Representados en la Coordinadora de Mujeres Trabajadoras

Sindicato del Instituto Mexicano de Rehabilitación

Sindicato Unico de Trabajadores de la Industria Nuclear (SUTIN)

Sindicato de Trabajadores de la Universidad Nacional Autónoma de México (STUNAM)

Sindicato Independiente de Trabajadores de la Universidad Autónoma Metropolitana (SITUAM)

Delegación D-III-24, Sec 11 del INAH (Sección de Técnicos, Manuales y Adminstrativos)

Mexicana de Envases S.A. (MESA, esposas de los trabajadores)

Sindicato de Trabajadores de DINA

Sindicato de Trabajadores del Metro

Sindicato de Trabajadores de Creaciones Maribi

Sindicato de Trabajadores de la Secretaría de la Reforma Agraria

Sindicato de Trabajadores de SIEMENS

Sindicato de Trabajores de La Azteca

Sindicato Unico de Trabajadores de Calzado SANDAC

Sindicato de Trabajadores de ARMUZ

Sindicato de Trabajadores y Empleados de PESCA

Sindicato de Trabajadores de YALE

Sindicato de Trabajadores y Empleados de la Secretaría de Programación y Presupuesto

RIVETEX

Comité Central de Lucha del Magisterio de Morelos

Centro Integral de Desarrollo Humano de América Latina (CIDHAL)

Sindicato de Trabajadores de Uranis de México (UROMEX, seccional de SUTIN)

Sindicato Independiente Nacional de Trabajadores y Empleados del
Colegio Bachilleres (SINTCS)

Participan también mujeres desempleadas e independientes.

Notas

1.   Ricardo Flores Magón, *Artículos Políticos, 1917*
(México, D.F.: Ediciones Antorcha, 1981).
2.   Vease María Antonieta Rascón, "La mujer y la lucha
social", en *Imagen y realidad de la mujer*, comp. por Elena
Urrutia (México, D.F.: SepSetentas/Diana, 1979), pp. 139-174.
3.   Ibid., p. 161.
4.   Elena Poniatowska, *Fuerte es el Silencio* (México, D.F.:
Editorial Era, 1980).
5.   Las tareas de las organizadoras fueron: 1) elaborar un
programa y un método de discusión; 2) procurarse recursos
económicos para llevarlo a cabo; 3) buscar un local para el
Encuentro; 4) organizar una guardería para los hijos de las
participantes; 5) buscar participantes; 6) elaborar un cuestionario
inicial con los primeros temas a discutir; 7) buscar materiales de
apoyo; 8) formar los grupos de discusión; 9) coordinar el
Encuentro; y 10) recopilar y sistematizar el material.

Gender, Patriarchy
and Feminism

Part IV

Gender, Patriarchy and Feminism

EL SEXO Y SU CONDICIONAMIENTO CULTURAL EN EL MUNDO PREHISPANICO

Abstract

The social conditioning of the sexes and avenues for mobility in prehispanic society is examined based on the controversial chronicles of Don Fernando de Alva Ixtlixochitl. His material makes reference to the nobility of Texcoco in the Valley of Mexico as it was believed to have existed approximately one hundred years before the conquest of Mexico.

Warfare provided males from all sectors of society a means of social advancement through their exploits in war. The honor, rights, and privileges of the warrior hierarchy and nobility exempted these individuals from having to pay taxes, entitled them to receive tribute and personal services, and granted them the privilege of polygamy. Nobles, unlike *macehuales* (commoners), were allowed as many women as they could afford to keep.

Avenues for female social mobility prevailed through the institution of concubinage and the practice of exchanging women. It was commonplace to express gratitude and respect through the giving and receiving of women and maidens. Less socially-ranked families gave their daughters to nobles of high rank to provide them the advantages of a better social position. That polygamy was practiced only among the upper classes suggests this was once a monogamous society as were their Chichimec and Toltec ancestors. The latter prohibited their nobility from remarrying upon the death of a spouse although commoners were allowed to remarry under similar circumstances; they, nonetheless, distinguished between legitimate and illegitimate wives and progeny.

Fifteenth century society in the Valley of Mexico sought to maintain the community's well being through compliance with a moral system of warrior ethics, austerity, and ascetism. Much was expected of the nobility and transgressions by them were more severely punished than were those committed by commoners. Rank and sex determined appropriate punishment.

Rank also determined rights and privileges. During festive events nobles, unlike warriors, moved freely and could pick and choose among women attending the event. Nocturnal rendezvous between these women and nobles were mediated by older female go-betweens known as "matronas" (matrons). Warriors, too, were accorded privileges with the opposite sex. A professional class of women known as "alegradoras" (those who delight) were companions to warriors during festivals. Little is known about *alegradoras*, their origin or education.

Generally, males were admonished to approach sexual relations with temperance and moderation; females were sexually repressed. Young women were to remain virgins until married and after marriage they were to devote themselves to the gods, their husbands, motherhood, and hard work. Women who died in childbirth were revered and elevated to the status of goddess.

Social ideals and actual behavior did not, however, always coincide. A case involving adultery was once brought before King Netzahaulcoyotzin in which the accused, two elderly, gray-haired women, defended themselves by declaring that women, unlike men, never loose their sexual potency and, therefore, through no fault of their own, are most susceptible to carnal pleasures.

EL SEXO Y
SU CONDICIONAMIENTO CULTURAL
EN EL MUNDO PREHISPANICO

by

Iris A. Blanco

Este breve ensayo es el resultado de una relectura de las obras de Don Fernando de Alva Ixtlixochitl (1568-1648), cronista sobre el que se han emitido juicios negativos y que algunos investigadores del pasado prehispánico no consideran muy idóneo para sacar conclusiones exactas.

Sin embargo, volver a leerlo después del estudio de otras fuentes es entrar de nuevo en una historia llena de vida y datos valiosos. Describe como fue la vida en la ciudad y reino de Texcoco, recreando el mundo de sus antepasados indígenas del cual si ya no fue testigo, se siente depositario fiel de su historia, costumbres y tradiciones.

Su prosa puede ser ampulosa, el relato inflado y orgulloso, como corresponde a su tradición hispánica e indígena tan entrelazadas en los escritos de los descendientes de nobles indígenas y "conquistadores"; pero su relación deja una sensación diferente a la de otras escritas por cronistas españoles.

Personifica la ambigüedad del cronista mestizo. Cristiano por un lado y gran conocedor de códices y cantos en lenguas indias, por otro. Su imaginación y fantasía corren por el relato idealizado de aquel mundo que se había ido para siempre. Trató de ser veraz y se indignaba con las falsedades como la del viejo indígena que gustaba en especial de contar a los españoles que el rey Ixtlixochitl había nacido de un huevo de águila.

Es crítico de la época de la gentilidad pero la penetra y la entiende; describe sus crueldades pero las atenúa (era la ley y la costumbre de la tierra afirma). Tiene la distancia del que ya no está por completo dentro ni por época o lazos de sangre, pero no acaba de estar por completo enteramente fuera.

Resintió por otra parte, verse reducido a los trabajos de campo o manuales, como tantos otros nobles indígenas después de la Conquista, sobre todo cuando sus ancestros indios habían luchado a brazo partido junto a los españoles en la toma de Tenochtitlán, y habían sido de los primeros en convertirse al catolicismo. Vivían en espera constante de que la corona española les devolviera sus viejos privilegios, a los que se sentían acreedores, como herederos de casa real.

Quizás sea por estas razones que Don Fernando informa como otros cronistas mestizos tanto sobre la vida de la corte, en especial de las casas reales y de sus innumerables mujeres; de los distintos rangos y categorías de las mismas. Relata como el primer Ixtlixochitl no quiso aceptar una mujer legítima que le ofreció el entonces señor más poderoso del Valle de México, añadiendo que sólo la aceptó de concubina. Sin embargo, enfatiza que concubinas o no, una vez que las mujeres entraban en aquellas casas, y si tenían descendencia, los hijos podían llegar a ocupar posiciones de importancia; el origen modesto por parte de la madre, no era lo definitivo, la guerra en última instancia era lo que hacía y deshacía posiciones, honores y privilegios.

Lamentablemente, como siempre, la mayoría de los datos son sobre las mujeres nobles, pero se puede inferir que si los nobles pudieron tener, primeras y segundas mujeres, concubinas, mancebas pedidas y no pedidas, esclavas, y más, es lógico suponer que no todas provenían de los estamentos más altos de la sociedad.

Fue común y general entre los señores a manera de agrado, de rendir respeto o mostrar reciprocidad, el ofrecer y tomar mujeres y doncellas.

Los nobles tuvieron derecho, como premio a sus hazañas, a tener todas las mujeres que podían mantener. Las mujeres podían adquirir así una protección ventajosa, según la casa a que pertenecían. Ninguno de los señores creía perder nada porque: "siendo costumbre de reyes y señores pedir a sus sobrinas y deudas hasta de segundo grado en adelante para casarse con ellas y tenerlas por sus damas y concubinas, con que quedaban honradas y amparadas, y en puesto que a falta de los legítimos herederos sus hijos el reino y cuando menos señores de pueblos y lugares."[1]

No es, pues, de extrañar que las familias menos encumbradas encontraran natural ofrecer a sus hijas y doncellas a señores de más rango. Incluso doncellas de alto linaje, como en el caso legendario de la bella Xochitl, se ven obligadas a cumplir los deseos del gran señor, en este caso el de Tula: "la hizo llevar a un lugarcito pequeño fuera de la ciudad poniéndole muchas guardias

364

... avisando a sus padres que no tuvieran cuidado ... que hicieran cuenta que la tenían en casa ... sus padres aunque lo sintieron mucho lo disimularon."[2]

Se ve aquí con claridad cómo funcionaba desde aquellos tiempos del imperio tolteca la dinámica de tomar mujeres y de aceptar que se las tomen, sin poder evitarlo; y vemos que cuando el padre de la doncella se queja o reclama, se le dice que no ha habido ofensa por "haber sido cosa del rey."

"Donde hay fuerza, derecho se pierde." Esta simple y llana aceptación a que les pidan y tomen doncellas debió chocar tanto a los misioneros, que les hizo decir que las familias las ofrecían y regalaban como fruta madura.

Si así fue el proceder entre los nobles en el intercambio de mujeres de cierta posición, bastara una cita para ver cuál fue su relación con los hombres y mujeres del pueblo. La cita no corresponde a la ciudad de Texcoco, pero ejemplifica la condición de los llamados macehuales o populares, en el siglo quince en todo el Valle de México. Se dice que fue desde entonces cuando la aristocracia guerrera quedó en control de los estamentos más bajos de la sociedad, los cuales prometieron: "os servir y tributar y ser vuestros terrasgueros y de edificar vuestras casas y de os servir como verdaderos señores nuestros, y de dar nuestras hijas y hermanas para que os sirváis de ellas ... y finalmente vendemos y subjetamos nuestras personas a vuestro servicio para siempre."[3]

Hubo vez que una mujer modestísima fue madre de un gran monarca, como en el caso de Izcoatl, hijo de esclava de Azcapotzalco. Pero debió ser el origen social de la mujer lo que determinó el rango con que entraba en la casa grande.

Pedro Carrasco en sus estudios ha demostrado ampliamente que aquella sociedad no fue una sociedad totalmente cerrada como la sociedad de castas, sino que sus miembros gozaron de relativa movilidad social, gracias a los honores y dignidades que se adquirían en el ejercicio de la guerra.

La poliginia, como el estar libres de impuestos, recibir tributos y servicios personales fueron derechos y atributos de la nobleza; y a su vez la poliginia fue un medio y posibilidad de escalar a mejores posiciones de rango y prestigio social; no hay duda que fue factor de movilidad derivado en última instancia también de la guerra, y totalmente sujeto a la misma. Las familias colocaban a las mujeres lo más ventajosamente que se podía. A esto se había llegado en la época a la que nos referimos en este trabajo, que es aproximadamente los cien años anteriores a la conquista; pero me interesa saber si la situación fue siempre igual, o como evolución hasta llegar a esta poliginia tan extendida en las capas altas de la sociedad.

Si nos remontamos con Ixtlixochitl a los primeros habitantes, a los llamados chichimecas, cepa y origen del reino de Texcoco, descubrimos que bajo este nombre se englobaban a todos los grupos de guerreros cazadores que bajaban de las regiones áridas del norte de México. Ixtlixochitl, nos los describe como monógamos, desplazándose en nucleos pequeños, "andaban en familias," no todos parecían tener el mismo nivel cultural. Había unos con ciertos conocimientos de agricultura, mientras otros eran eminentemente cazadores y recolectores.

Fray Bernardino de Sahagún, siempre última autoridad en estos temas, nos dice que los que eran del todo bárbaros: "cada uno andaba y vivía de por sí con su mujer sola, buscando lo necesario para su sustentación de la vida ... estos tales no cometían adulterio unos a otros, y tarde o casi nunca se hallaba algun adulterio."[4] Pero, si esto sucedía, se les hacía un juicio público y "estando vivos los flechaban."[5]

Al hablar de los toltecas, estos ya se distinguen como pueblos agricultores, social y políticamente organizados, además de su fama como consumados artistas. En lo referente a sus costumbres matrimoniales, Ixtlixochitl dice: "no tenían más que una mujer, y era legítima, y en muríendose no se podían casar y guardaban castidad hasta que morían, y las mujeres si morían los maridos antes que ellas heredaban el reino, y en muríendose ellas sus hijos legítimos, y ni más ni menos no podían casarse otra vez así como sus maridos y la gente común lo mismo en lo de tener una sola mujer legítima, pero podían casarse segunda y tercera vez."[6]

Se encuentra aquí una supuesta monogamia entre los señores y los populares, y una obligatoria castidad para los dos sexos entre la nobleza; se introduce, sin embargo, el concepto de mujer legítima, o sea que obviamente debieron existir otras mujeres además de la legítima. Mientras los intereses hereditarios no permitieron a los nobles volver a casarse, los del pueblo siempre lo pudieron hacer.

Otro dato sobre los toltecas, muy significativo, fue el del voto de castidad que tuvieron que hacer al salir huyendo de su ciudad: "que en veintitrés años no habían de conocer a sus mujeres ni ellas a sus maridos, y los que quebrantasen este voto habían de ser castigados cruelmente."[7]

Es obviamente exageración en cuanto a la duración, pero revela que en situaciones difíciles como la del destierro, se imponen controles drásticos de natalidad por medio de abstinencias y tabúes de tipo antiguo. Es una vuelta a la existencia insegura y asediada como la de la vida de la chichimecas, donde lo único que cuenta es la sobre-vivencia del grupo como tal; los controles sexuales son a nombre de la colectividad que huye y que debe perdurar.

En el caso de Mesoamerica, la guerra fue la gran constante histórica. Oleadas tras oleadas irrumpieron en el Valle de México, manteniendo el espíritu bélico y las costumbres de los pueblos guerreros, mientras los grupos ya asentados iban poco a poco adaptándose a las maneras urbanas y sedentarias de las gentes del Valle.

Las comunidades eran por excelencia agrícolas, sin embargo la guerra nunca dejó de motivar e impulsar a los jefes guerreros. A pesar de los cultivos, y los años de abundancia, los hombres siempre vivieron inseguros y atemorizados de lo que las fuerzas de la naturaleza podían desencadenas. Las tormentas, sequías, heladas, plagas, hambres, todo era motivo para consultar y pedir la clemencia a los dioses. Sus sacerdotes, desde siempre guías y oraculos, fueron además jefes guerreros. Los guerreros fueron los conductores religiosos del pueblo, en otras palabras, no hay modo de separar guerra y religión; son una y la misma cosa. Ella reclamó desde las más humildes exigencias de ayunos, abstinencias, ofrendas, castigos corporales, hasta los masivos sacrificios humanos de los últimos tiempos.

La vieja moral guerrera y cazadora, se transformó en preceptos y consejos morales de austeridad y ascetismo, que se transmitían por medio de la tradición oral, de una generación a otra.

Y no eran simples palabras o ideales abstractos, a los que los miembros de la sociedad debían aspirar, sino obligaciones que se debían abedecer o correr el riesgo de ser castigado con dureza, pues de su cumplimiento dependía el bien común.

Los castigos en materia sexual fueron más rígidos para los miembros de la nobleza que para el pueblo, aunque veremos que el rango contó mucho; los castigos serán pregonados para todos los infractores, pero el rango y el sexo hará que sean juzgados de manera diferente. Ixtlixochitl nos cuenta con lujo de detalles algunos de los castigos, increíblemente duros cuando se trata de que pueda caer la más mínima sombra de deshonor sobre el gran monarca.

A Netzahualcoyotl, el rey poeta que gobernó en Texcoco (1418-1472), se le atribuye un código cuyo primer artículo va dirigido a los adúlteros y sus castigos. Increíble parece desde hoy imaginar que con tales castigos, que incluían no solo a los adúlteros, sino a sirvientes y allegados, alguien desafiara las normas y se atreviera a desafiar las iras de los poderosos.

Lapidación, estrangulamiento, incineración, esparcimiento de cenizas en las afueras de la ciudad: de manera implacable se trataba de borrar el delito para que no quedara el más mínimo rastro de lo sucedido. Esta era la ley y la costumbre de la tierra, dice Ixtlixochitl, y en verdad fue parte del orden y concierto que admiraron los misioneros españoles, aunque lamentaran los métodos tiránicos que se empleaban para mantenerlo.

Este orden "natural" venía de muy lejos, lo que parecen diferencias esenciales entre hombres y mujeres, eran para ellos las dos caras de una moneda ya que no era posible la honra sin tacha del guerrero sin la intachable castidad de la mujer. Tal parece que la estructura y organización de la sociedad favorece totalmente al hombre.

Entre los hombres mismos, hubo enormes diferencias; los de arriba siempre tuvieron más derechos; los de igual condición se respetaron y se temieron entre sí, y se cuidaban mucho de traspasar los territorios prohibidos, que eran como cotos de caza cerrados; los de más abajo disimularon y los de hasta abajo aguantaron. Como las decisiones nunca fueron individuales sino colectivas o familiares, el intercambio o los arreglos matrimoniales traían toda una serie de derechos y obligaciones, las cuales desaparecen casi de golpe con la Conquista; los españoles simplemente toman las mujeres sin respetar aquellos arreglos interfamiliares, no entienden el tejido de todas estas relaciones dentro de la comunidad.

Los grandes señores de Texcoco a pesar de sus inmensas ventajas, rompieron muchas veces los códigos del honor. Tomaron mujeres ya pedidas o dadas a otros señores. La crónica de Ixtlixochitl es fuente inagotable de amores repentinos, deseos violentos, trampas, engaños, traiciones y muertes. Los grandes señores fueron capaces de actos reprobables dentro de su sistema de honor por quedarse con alguna doncella.

Tuvieron, por ser figuras públicas, que sacrificar algún hijo por los simples rumores de que había mirado a alguna de sus concubinas.

Ixtlixochitl critica estas actitudes, y critica aquel ambiente de concubinas y mujeres dispuestas a promover diferencias y a beneficiar sus intereses y los de sus hijos. Curiosamente en todas las crónicas siempre hay referencias a líos de mujeres y a la decadencia de las ciudades, como si lo uno trajera lo otro; lo más probable es que haya un momento en que se abandonan las reglas de austeridad y rígida moral en las ciudades, cuando sus capas superiores llegan a olvidarse de la sublime misión de la guerra y simplemente se dedican a disfrutar de sus beneficios, y la buena vida significa el gozar de las mujeres, el beber, el uso de ropas y alhajas de lujo. Todo era producto de una educación recibida desde niños. Ixtlixochitl nos relata cómo un pequeño noble mata a su nana al encontrarla acompañada de varón. Al explicar por qué lo había hecho replicó: "dijo que en la sala donde le leían las ochenta leyes, se mandaba que nadie recuestase a las damas y criadas de su palacio, ni ellas diesen ocasión, pena de vida, y así la mató por cumplir con la ley."[8]

Si los niños nobles podían ser así, y si los soberanos son tales señores de horca y cuchillo, ¿cual sería la suerte de la mujer del soberano que transgredía las normas? Sorprende el atrevimiento cuando se sabe que muchas mujeres vivían en casa del señor desde niñas y estaban educadas de manera tal que el cronista Torquemada nos las describe como "viejas de muchos años," dado su silencio y modales como de ancianas. Algunas mujeres pudieron transgredir las normas y llegar muy lejos, y el castigo no se hizo esperar.

El castigo a Chalchiuhnenetzin, mujer de Netzahualpilli (1472-1515), hermana del gran monarca de Tenochtitlán, fue extraordinario. Se suspendió la guerra para que todo el mundo pudiera acudir, tanto aliados como enemigos. Fue un llamado general: "para que trajesen a sus mujeres, las hijas, aunque fuesen muy pequeñas porque hallasen en este ejemplar castigo que se había de hacer."[9]

Aquella mujer principal y parienta en primer grado del gran soberano tenochca, era la mujer legítima de un gran señor que tenía cientos de mujeres y de hijos. El castigo debió ser un gran suceso que suspendió el sublime oficio de la guerra.

Este fenomenal escarmiento no debe hacernos pensar que esto sólo sucedía a una mujer principal que cometía adulterio. El código del honor del soberano era tal, que entre las versiones sobre la muerte del gran señor de Tenochtitlán, Chimalpopoca, se piensa que sus propios familiares pudieron haberle dado muerte, por razones políticas, por considerarle debil y pusilánime. Entre las razones para demostrar su debilidad, se cuenta que sufrió con cobardía, los ultrajes de otro gran señor de Azcapotzalco que llegó incluso a exhibirse públicamente con las damas y concubinas de Chimalpopoca.

Se trata de aclarar o iluminar un tema tan trillado e incluso tan distorsionado como el del sexismo, partiendo de que aquella sociedad trató de condicionar a todos sus miembros, hombres y mujeres, y desde pequeños. Los consejos relativos al comportamiento sexual se les repetían desde que entraban en la pubertad.

La diferencia entre los hombres y las mujeres, es que mientras a los varones se les recomienda moderación y templanza, es decir se da por hecho que empiezan a tener relación con mujeres desde jóvenes, las jóvenes nobles son celosamente guardadas y se espera de ellas castidad total antes del matrimonio.[10]

A los demasiado jovenes, solteros se les recomienda: "no te arrojes a la mujer como un perro se arroja a lo que ha de comer." Una vez casado se le recomienda: "no te des demasiado a ella porque te echarás a perder ... si frecuentares la delectación carnal, aunque sea con tu mujer solamente, te secarás."[11]

Antes de casada, virgen. Y de casada debe dirigir toda su actividad al trabajo, la devoción a los dioses, y los cuidados extremos hacia su familia.

La guerra fué la función esencial de los guerreros nobles. La de la mujer fue la maternidad. El hombre fue condicionado a morir en el guerra, como sublimación última de su vida. La mujer fué la fuerza vital, la reproducción de las huestes guerreras. De ahí su sacralización o transformación en diosa al morir en el parto, considerado como lucha, hazaña de guerra, para capturar al guerrero que se lleva en el vietre. La vida producida por la mujer terminaría en los campos de batalla. La muerte de esos guerreros era como la savia de la nueva vida que se renovaba cada año en las cosechas y la abundancia del grano divino: el maíz. Los dioses alimentados con la guerra devolvían al hombre el bienestar y la alimentación de sus comunidades.

La mujer fué condicionada para la guerra, la aceptó casi sin lamentarse. Poquísimas quejas encontramos en las crónicas, alguna en "la fiesta de la diosa Toci" y en "el terror de la soberana de Tlaltelolco" hacia la violencia y las violaciones que ocurren en la guerra.

Ya hemos mencionado que se era muy estricto con los jóvenes nobles puesto que ellos serán los representantes de los estamentos sacerdotales y guerreros y modelo ideal de los grandes señores. La conducta esperada es de temperancia y moderación. Los castigos son hacia ellos de máxima dureza; parecería una contradicción, pues son los del mayor acceso a las mujeres; quizás sea esta la razón.

Se les repite una y otra vez cómo debe ser el comportamiento con las mujeres, cómo deben tratar de mantener el equilibrio, dentro de las fricciones que surgían entre las distintas categorías de guerreros, en cuanto al trato y manera de acercarse a sus hijas y doncellas. Se trataba de lograr el equilibrio entre los diferentes estratos de la sociedad.

Esto está magistralmente descrito en Fray Bernardino de Sahagún en "la fiesta de los grandes señores" o Huey Tecuilhuitl. Mientras todos los guerreros ocupaban su lugar exacto de acuerdo a su jerarquía militar, los nobles eran los únicos que no tenían lugar fijo, se movían a su antojo. Paseando, mirando, escogiendo a su gusto entre las doncellas que asisten a la ceremonia.[12] Los nobles con la máxima discreción y por medio de las amas o matronas que las cuidan y acompañan, conciertan con ellas citas nocturnas, después de las cuales, en la misma noche, son devueltas a sus barrios con dádivas y regalos de los señores. Las viejas amas también recibían lo que les correspondía como mediadoras.

Estas viejas matronas, eran las grandes conocedoras de todo lo que pasaba en sus comunidades, incluso las aficiones ocultas o no conocidas por todos; los deseos secretos de nobles y guerreros. Si algo salía mal siempre se les podía culpar y fueron instrumentalizadas para llevar a cabo estos menesteres tan impropios de hombres y menos de esforzados varones.

El condicionamiento de los hombres iba más allá de las formas de comportamiento público, en que todo quedaba como bajo una máscara, por dentro de una coraza de frialdad que impresionó tanto a los españoles, que llegaron a decir que entre los indios no existía el amor, la afición como el que ellos sentían hacia el otro sexo. Pocos como el padre Durán, que se había criado desde niño entre aquellos indios, supieron que los jóvenes se tenían cariño, y desde jóvenes muchas veces se comprometían en silencio el uno para el otro, mientras ensayaban los bailes para las grandes festividades.[13]

Con los varones se trató ante todo de mantener el fervor guerrero, la dureza, la austeridad, evitar el sentimentalismo, los lazos afectivos que les reblandecieran, esto era lo imperdonable.

Le sucedió esto a un gran guerrero tlaxcalteca, Tlahuicole, valiente entre valientes. Los mexicanos no sólo le ofrecieron el perdón sino quedarse con ellos para siempre, porque se decía que con su sola presencia hacía temblar la tierra. Hecho prisionero, se le rindieron todos los respetos, hasta que lo encontraron "cada día llorando y suspirando por sus hijos y mujeres."[14] Perdió todo el respeto, le retiraron la comida y los guardianes que le vigilaban. Fue esto tal deshonor que lo condujo al suicidio despeñándose desde las alturas. El condicionamiento va más allá de lo físico, es una actitud frente a la vida, inculcada desde pequeños.

Los guerreros de menos categoría tuvieron, o se les permitió, una actitud más liberal, y en cuanto acudían y hacían algo en la guerra podían amancebarse. Los guerreros afamados tuvieron además mujeres educadas en el arte de agradar y divertir, sobre todo en las temporadas de ocio. Se dice que los patios de ciertos templos se llenaban de estas mujeres que curiosamente los indígenas llamaron "alegradoras" y los españoles peyorativamente "rameras." Según algunos estudios del pasado prehispánico está todavía por saberse quiénes fueron, cuál era su origen y cómo eran educadas. Consideradas como verdaderas profesionales, su existencia es todavía aparentemente una contradicción en una sociedad en que la poliginia fue tan extendida entre la nobleza y ciertas capas de los guerreros, los pardos por ejemplo, que no eran nobles.

Si se aconsejó la temperancia a los nobles, la mujer debió estar más reprimidas en el orden sexual. Ella pudo ser una más entre las múltiples mujeres que el senor almacenaba en casa; pudo quedar a veces con su capacidad genésica neutralizada o desaprovechada. Llenó su tiempo con devociones, constantes ayunos, abstinencias. Gran parte de su vida la pasó frente al telar combatiendo, como se decía, su ociosidad o malos pensamientos.

En aquellas casas llenas de mujeres, de distinta condición como ya hemos visto, hubo que mantener un máximo de orden y de cuidadosa intimidad sexual. De las mujeres se esperó lo contrario de los hombres, lo afectivo, lo cariñoso, un estado constante de preocupación y ansiedad por el bienestar de todos los suyos. Esto era el modelo ideal.

Ixtlixochitl a pesar de ser crítico de aquella época, la embellece de manera que casi nos hace olvidar todo el rigor y la dureza de la misma. En una anécdota en que nos quiere mostrar la magnanimidad del gran señor Netzahualcoyotl, relata cómo un viudo cuya mujer ha sido ejecutada por adulterio, se lamenta con el rey diciendo que la ejecución había sido innecesaria, pues confiesa que no solo la amaba, sino que ya la había perdonado de todo corazón. El señor asombrado dice que no ha hecho más que cumplir con la ley y la costumbre. Para el cronista, la historia tiene un final feliz, pues el rey en un gran gesto a la manera de los reyes españoles que aparecen en las obras de teatro del Siglo de Oro, le regala en este caso una joven y bella mujer. Nos parece de momento ver reunidas aquí la tradición hispánica con la indígena como corresponde a un cronista mestizo que escribe a principios del siglo diecisiete. Todo de momento parece bello y verdadero si no fuera por el hecho de que dentro de las dos culturas era casi insólito el perdón del adulterio.

El adulterio es algo que hay que evitar a todo costo en estas sociedades guerreras y más que nada en sus capas más altas. El temor al adulterio es tal, que los consejos de templanza en lo sexual van dirigidos con el propósito de que el hombre conserve su fortaleza hasta el final, hasta su vejez. Terminaremos con otra anécdota, que en este caso es más que eso porque ha pasado a ser parte de los consejos tradicionales que se dirigen de generación en generación. Pondremos la cita entera, que muestra con claridad las diferencias en materia sexual que existieron entre las clases nobles y gente de alcurnia y los resentimientos y problemas que esto, lógicamente, creaba entre los sexos:

> Quiérote dar otro ejemplo y notale muy bien, para que te sea todo como mochila, para que vivas castamente en este mundo: Siendo vivo el señor de Tezcuco [sic] llamado Nezahualcoyotzin, fueron presas dos viejas, que tenían los cabellos blancos como la nieve de viejas, y fueron presas porque adulteraron e hicieron traición a sus maridos, que eran viejos como ellas, y unos mancebillos sacristanejos tuvieron acceso a ellas.
>
> El señor Nezahualcoyotzin, cuando las llevaron a su presencia para que las sentenciase, preguntólas diciendo: Abuelas nuestras, ¿es verdad que todavía tenéis deseo de deleite carnal? ¿Aún no estáis hartas siendo tan viejas como sois? ¿Qué sentíades cuando erades mozas? Decídmelo, pues estáis en mi presencia, por este caso.
>
> Ellas respondieron: Señor nuestro rey, oiga vuestra alteza: Vosotros los hombres, cesáis de viejos de querer la deleitación carnal, por haber frecuentádola en la juventud, porque se acaba la potencia y la simiente humana; pero nosotras las mujeres nunca nos hartamos, ni nos enfadamos de esta obra, porque es nuestro cuerpo como una sima y como una barranca honda que nunca se hinche, recibe todo cuanto le echan y desea más y demanda más, y si esto no hacemos no tenemos vida. Esto te digo hijo mío, para que vivas recatado y con discreción, y que vayas poco a poco, y no te des prisa en este negocio tan feo y perjudicial."[15]

Notas

1. Fernando de Alva Ixtlixochitl, *Obras Históricas*, Vol. 2 (México, D.F.: Secretaría de Fomento, 1892), p. 298.

2. Ibid., Vol. 1, p. 44.

3. Diego de Durán, *Historia de Las Indias de Nueva España e Islas de la Tierra Firme*, Vol. 2 (México, D.F.: Editorial Porrúa, 1967), p. 80.

4. Fray Bernardino de Sahagún, *Historia General de las Cosas de Nueva España*, Vol. 3, Libro 10 (México, D.F.: Editorial Porrúa, 1956), p. 191.

5. Ibid.

6. Ixtlixochitl, *Obras Históricas*, Vol. 1, p. 41.

7. Ibid., p. 25.

8. Ibid., Vol. 2, p. 302.

9. Ibid., p. 287.

10. Juan Bautista Pomar, *Relaciones de Texcoco y de la Nueva España* (México, D.F.: Salvador Chavez Hayhoe, 1941), p. 35.

11. Sahagún, *Historia General*, Vol. 2, Libro 1, p. 146.

12. Ibid., Vol. 1, Libro 2, p. 125.

13. Durán, *Historia de las Indias*, Vol. 2, p. 256.

14. Ibid., p. 456.

15. Sahagún, *Historia General*, Vol. 1, Libro 2, p. 178.

EDUCACION Y PAPEL
DE LA MUJER EN MEXICO

Abstract

Major cultural and socio-political events alter the direction of Mexican women's social participation and educational status from Pre-Columbian times to the present. Mesoamerican culture, in particular Mexica society, designated women's primary social role as one of wife and mother. Religiosity, austerity, chastity (before and after marriage) sacrifice, and hard work were expected of and admired in women. Educational institutions--the Calmécac for noble girls and the Ipochcalli for commoners--taught young girls domestic skills and duties. Parents instilled in girls a sense of moral and social responsiblity toward their roles as wives and mothers. Common women had also to work outside the home and did so as agricultural laborers, artesans, and merchants.

The Spanish conquest of Mesoamerica brought with it a medieval conception of conflicting feminine ideals comprised of the ancient Greek belief in the inferiority of women, the Roman institution of civil equality between the sexes, and the ambivalent Judeo-Christian concept of the spiritual superiority of women. The Church was instrumental in the remoulding of women's roles through indoctrination in the Catholic faith and internship in convents. The social behavior of women, nonetheless, appears to have been more flexible than ideology or written accounts would have us believe. The intellectual prodigy, Sor Juana Inés de la Cruz, breached traditional norms by serving in the viceroyal court and entering the nunnery despite her illigitimate birth. She wrote Latin America's first feminist statement by responding to criticism of her intellectual pursuits by members of the church hierarchy.

The Age of Enlightment and the French bourbons influenced Mexican education through its emphasis on the importance of education as an instrument of progress. Carlos III's decree of 1784 abolished certain prohibitions against the employment of women, defended the admission of women to professional institutions, and incited state and church interest in the education of girls. The education of women in the seventeenth and eighteenth centuries, nonetheless, emphasized curricula which encouraged domesticity and motherhood. Women remained excluded from institutions of higher education for most of the 19th century. After 1861, Benito Juárez closed Mexico's convents and introduced the reform of Mexico's educational system. His Minister of Justice and Education, Ignacio Ramírez, defended the education of women and advocated their admittance to and enrollment in institutions of higher education.

The Revolution of 1910 involved the participation of women *en masse* and their activism faciliated the passing of Mexico's divorce law in 1915. A year later, Yucatan's governor, Salvador Alvarado, encouraged and supported Mexico's first feminist congress. Two decades later, the country's most important feminist group, Frente Unido Pro Derechos de la Mujer, was organized in 1935 by politically progressive women. By the 1920s there was already a small sector of professional women aware of the inequality and exploitation of women. Their influence in the V, VI, and VII Interamerican Conferences held in Latin America helped to inform and agitate for the civil and juridical rights of women. In 1953 Mexico gave women the vote. In another twenty years Mexico would initiate a birth control campaign and reform its work laws giving women more employment opportunities. In 1974 the country revised its Civil Code and gave equal rights and obligations to both sexes in marriage and divorce.

Generally, however, Mexican women's progress has been uneven and social class inequalities persist. Today, there are more 17-year-old girls with children than there are 17-year-old girls in school and two out of every five women in Mexico's urban areas are domestic servants. The lack of male psychological adjustment to women's changing roles also is resulting in an increased divorce rate equal to that of developed countries. Overall, the educational and political progress of Mexican women must be seen within the context of Mexico's underdevelopment.

EDUCACION Y PAPEL
DE LA MUJER EN MEXICO

by

Josefina Zoraida Vasquez

Apenas hace unos años que ha empezado a escribirse sobre la historia de la mujer y por lo tanto todo lo que pueda decirse resulta provisional y tendrá que revisarse con nuevas investigaciones. Realmente se ha escrito poco para despejar las dudas existentes. Y el tema no es fácil, pues dado que la cultura mexicana se constituyó por la confluencia de por lo menos dos raíces: la cultura mesoamericana y la española, tan difíciles de definir por su propia heterogeneidad, es difícil aprehender lo que ha caracterizado a la historia de la mujer, en cada una de las etapas de la historia mexicana. En general, del lado mesoamericano, se subraya siempre el legado de la cultura mexica por ser la del pueblo hegemónico a la llegada de los españoles. La cultura mexica procedía, por lo demás, del tronco común mesoamericano, con los mismos valores y las mismas creencias, aunque la actitud guerrera y el espíritu de sacrificio fueran peculiares de los mexicas. Parece ser que todas las culturas mesomericanas asignaron a la mujer el papel principal de ser madre y esposa, lo cual no obstó para que desempeñara un papel en el trabajo agrícola, artesanal y comercial. La imagen ideal de la mexica requería devoción a los dioses, castidad antes y después del matrimonio, generosidad, si era principal y trabajadora, si era plebeya. Parecía que todo lo requerido para formar mujeres que se ajustaran a los fines de las sociedad podría trasmitirse en el hogar y en la comunidad, pero el Estado mexica, tan cuidadoso de su proyecto social de dominio guerrero, no pudo dejar de ocuparse de la formación de las jóvenes. Dos instituciones, el Calmécac para nobles y el Ipochcalli para plebeyas, se ocuparon de educarlas.

Desde su nacimiento, a las niñas parecia indicarseles como camino único el hogar y se les presentaban los objetos que indicaban su destino doméstico. Desde pequeñas empezaban a aprender con su madre las labores propias de su sexo: hilar, tejer, labrar, moler el maíz y barrer la casa. La familia se ocupaba también de la educación moral y social de sus hijos; desarrollaba las virtudes que preciaba y evitaba los defectos que aborrecía, como la mentira, la desobediencia y el descuido, que eran castigados con dureza. Tanto a los niños, como a las niñas, se les acostumbraba a una vida muy austera y a un sacrificio continuo.

En cuanto podían caminar, las niñas llevaban las ofrendas al templo en sustitución de sus madres. No sabemos a qué edad ingresaban en los colegios pero sí que el Calmécac, a diferencia del Ipochcalli, era internado. En este último las mayores se hacían cargo de las menores, mientras en el internado la enseñanza estaba a cargo de unas viejas. Bernal Díaz nos describe esta institución: "muchas hijas de vecinos mexicanos ... estaban como a manera de recogimientos que querían parecer monjas; también tejían y todo en pluma. Estas monjas tenían sus casas cerca del gran Cu del Huichilobos. Las metían sus padres en aquella religión hasta que se casaban." Todo parece indicar que era un medio de preparar a las jóvenes para el matrimonio, al tiempo que se les protegía del peligro de cualquier deshonra.

El concepto que se tenía del destino de las mujeres era un tanto trágico. En *Literatura del México Antiguo*, Miguel Leon nos permite oír la voz de alguno de los discursos que los padres solían decir a las niñas en momentos importantes, veremos que denotan una concepción terrible:

> Aquí estás, mi hijita, mi collar de piedras finas, mi plumaje, mi hechura humana, la nacida de mí ... Ahora que ya miras por tí, date cuenta. Aquí es de este modo: no hay alegría, no hay felicidad. Hay angustia, preocupación, cansancio ... Mira, escucha, advierte, así es en la tierra: no seas vana, no andes como quiera, no andes sin rumbo ... Sé cuidadosa, porque vienes de gente principal, desciendes de ella ... Mira no te deshonres a tí misma, a nuestros señores, a los príncipes, a los gobernantes que nos precedieron. No te hagas como la gente del pueblo, no vengas a salir plebeya ... He aquí tu oficio, lo que tendrás que hacer: durante la noche y durante el día conságrate a las cosas de Dios ... Hazle súplicas, invócalo, llámalo, ruégale mucho cuando estés en el lugar donde duermes. Así se te hará gustoso el sueño ... Y durante la noche está vigilante, levántate aprisa, extiende tus manos ... Abre bien los ojos

para ver como es el arte tolteca ... Pon atención, aplícate,
no seas vana, deja de ser negliente contigo misma ... Que
nunca sea vano el corazón de alguien, nadie diga de tí, te
señale con el dedo, hable de tí ... No los afrentes con algo,
no como quiera desees las cosas de la tierra, no como
quiera pretendas gustarlas, aquello que se llama las cosas
sexuales ... No como si fuera en un mercado busques al que
será tu compañero, no lo llames, no andes con apetito de
él. Pero si tú desdeñas al que puede ser tu compañero, no
vaya a ser de tí se burle y te conviertas en mujer pública
... Quien quiera que sea tu compañero, vosotros, juntos,
tendréis que acabar la vida. No lo dejes, agárrate a él,
cuélgate de él, aunque sea un pobre hombre.

A este idea de que la vida es difícil y triste, se suma la
obligación de sacrificarse por su familia, por su marido, legado
que parece ser el más persistente del mundo mesoamericano a la
mujer mexicana.

La llegada de los españoles dio origen a una nueva sociedad,
constituida por diversos grupos sociales, con una compleja red de
relaciones derivadas de una situación de conquista. Sin duda, el
proceso de conformación de esa nueva sociedad, con sus valores y
creencias, fue lento y es difícil caracterizar sus etapas y
tipificarlas, pues no sabemos suficiente de ninguna de ellas. Lo
que sí es indiscutible es que con los españoles llegó el
contradictorio concepto medieval hispánico sobre la mujer, en el
cual se mezclaban la concepción griega de la inferioridad, la
romana de la igualdad civil de los sexos y ambivalente visión
judeo-cristiana de una cierta superioridad espiritual de la mujer,
con uno que otro tinte musulmán.

La mujer española había logrado a través de la larga guerra de
reconquista una situación que le daba gran independencia de
acción tanto en el hogar como en sociedad en general. Tal vez
porque la guerra de reconquista obligó a los hombres a estar por
largos periodos ausentes del hogar, la mujer tuvo oportunidad de
ejercer roles que le eran vedados en otras sociedades del Viejo
Mundo. Esto explica la presencia de mujeres decididas y fuertes
como Isabel la Católica o la Leona de Castilla, de eruditas como
Beatriz Galindo, la Latina o Francisca de Nebrija, catedrática de
la Universidad Complutense a la muerte de su famoso padre. Por
ello no es raro que en el Nuevo Mundo hubiera encomenderas y
colonizadoras, y que las mujeres pelearan ante la Corona de
privilegios para ellas, para sus maridos o para sus hijos, a pesar de

que, al no haber cambiado los conceptos básicos, a medida que se asentaba la vida se ponía en vigor una inferioridad jurídica. No obstante, la situación de la mujer hispánica aventajaba con mucho la contemporánea de sus hermanas de otras partes del mundo, pues tenía acceso a los gremios, heredaba propiedades y títulos y los manejaba, aunque como ha afirmado José María Ots, "sólo el estado de viudez permitía a la mujer gozar de su plena capacidad civil."

Esto no obsta para que la visión de la naturaleza y del destino femenino fuera la estrecha idea expresada por Luis Vives en *La instrucción de la mujer cristiana* o Fray Luis de León en *La perfecta casada*, todavía expresada por Fray Alonso de Herrera en 1637 en el *Espejo de la perfecta casada*. Y hubo un divorcio entre la prática y la teoría vigentes, aunque no fue violento: la imagen ideal de la mujer se mantuvo, pero la práctica no fue tan rígida. Y es bueno tener esto presente, pues los estudios se hacen a menudo a base de análisis de leyes y doctrinas y hace falta enfrentarlas a usos e idearios. Vives concedía que la mujer era "animal de razón, como el hombre" pero existía para ser madre y esposa, por lo que había que educarla para liberarla de los vicios que "hijos son de la ignorancia"; debía enseñársele "sólo aquellas letras que forman las costumbres a la virtud" y sólo excepcionalmente dejarla ir más allá, para no contaminarla, alejándola de su único pero verdadero cuidado: guardar su castidad. Sin duda, la expansión imperial y la Contrarreforma hicieron que España perdiera el dinamismo del siglo quince y principios del siglo dieciseis. Junto con muchas innovaciones, se perdió la posibilidad de las mujeres de tener acceso a la universidad y para el siglo diecisiete quedarían al margen de la vida intelectual y Sor Juana sólo podía soñar en asistir a la Universidad, disfrazada de hombre.

Ahora bien, en el Nuevo Mundo los horizontes se estrecharon en muchos campos en el empeño evangelizador de poner en ejercicio un cristianismo primitivo. Los frailes encontraron que el espíritu indígena estaba cerca de las virtudes cristianas más preciadas y subrayaron el idealismo en sus prédicas. Y fue a través de la evangelización que los españoles trasmitieron su imagen ideal de mujer, la influencia más poderosa en la modelación de gran parte de la nueva sociedad novohispana, ya que como pasaron pocas españolas a las India, la posibilidad de la influencia de su presencia fuerte y decidida fue menor que la de las ideas trasmitidas por los frailes.

En la sociedad colonial, la mujer quedó en situación de dependencia familiar y social en los diversos estratos sociales. A la española, sin embargo, se le concedió el paso a las Indias cuando podía hacerlo sin obstáculos familiares, e incluso se le dieron alugnos privilegios. A las indias se les consideró seres libres y quedaron exentas de la calidad de esclavas y del pago de tributo. Estas situaciones bien podían considerarse privilegiadas pero, en la prática, las indígenas fueron utilizadas como objectos, de los cuales cualquier hombre de mayor *status* podía disponer.

Sin duda la educación improvisada para cristianizar a los indios, aún antes de afirmarse el dominio español, influiría en mayor o menos medida en la vida de las mujeres indígenas. Además, el obispo Zumárraga tomó en cuenta la influencia decisiva de la mujer en la sociedad y se empeñó en reeducarlas. En 1530 se abrió un colegio de niñas en Texcoco y más tarde otros con beatas enviadas por la emperatriz Isabel para instruirlas "en las cosas de nuestra santa fe católica." El propio Zumárraga trajo de España seglares para lograr el mismo fin: convertir a las niñas en buenas cristianas para que, una vez casada, "enseñasen a sus maridos las cosas de nuestra santa fe y alguna policía honesta y buen modo de vivir." La educación de las niñas, sin embargo, no prosperó, tanto por la resistencia de los padres que se negaban a entregarlas a los colegios, como porque "los indios, ni los que se crían en los conventos, rehusaban de casar con las doctrinadas en las casas de niñas, diciendo que se criaban ociosas y los maridos las tendrían en poco, ni los querrían servir según la costumbre suya ... por haber sido criadas de mujer de Castilla." Zumárraga mismo se quejaba de que las mismas españolas enviadas a educarlas "la mayor parte no se aplican, ni se humillan ... ni tienen el recogimiento y honestidad que tendrían las religiosas", por ello el obispo pedía la apertura de conventos de monjas, pero la Corona se resistió. Hay que subrayar, sin embargo, que el rechazo no era a la religión, sino más bien a un modo de vida que violentaba las costumbres indígenas. Lo que es cierto es que a partir de 1544 cesó todo intento de educación integral de las niñas indígenas. Hasta bien entrado el siglo dieciocho sólo aprenderían labores propias del hogar y doctrina en la parroquia, aunque no hay que olvidar que de cualquier manera la labor catequística modificaba parte de su conducta. En diversas ocasiones la Corona determinó que abrieran escuelas de castellanización y las niñas fueron incluidas y, a partir de 1680, las huérfanas indias fueron admitidas en recogimientos especiales.

El gobierno español resistió mucho la fundación de conventos femeninos. Pero la evidente necesidad de proteger a las criollas que permanecieran solteras condujo a su establecimiento a partir de 1542, año en que se fundó el primer convento de concepcionistas en México, seguido de otro en Oaxaca en 1577. En estos conventos además de las profesas, se admitían pequeños grupos de niñas que aprendían con ellas doctrina y labores y, según afirman algunos autores, muchas veces lectura y escritura. Sabemos que la mayor parte de las criollas que aprendían doctrina, labores, lectura y escritura lo hacían en las Amigas o Migas, pequeñas escuelas organizadas por mujeres necesitadas, que no pasaban en los exámenes del gremio de maestros y que cobraban por enseñar lo que sabían, que no era mucho.

La estrechez de miras con que se veía el papel de la mujer en el siglo diecisiete lo ilustra el caso de Sor Juana Inés de la Cruz, cuya sorprendente inteligencia y vocación decidida la obligó a recluirse en un convento. El caso de Sor Juana resulta interesante illustración de las contradicciones de la mentalidad novohispana. Juana era hija ilegítima, lo que no obstó para que sirviera en la corte de los virreyes, donde llegó a brillar por sus conocimientos y poesía. La novohispana era, después de todo, una sociedad católica donde el pecado resultaba perdonable. Cuando Juana tuvo que pensar en decidir su vida, tuvo que considerar que carecía de un peculio personal que le permitiera continuar con su vocación, sin tener que casarse. El matrimonio hubiera resuelto el problema económico, pero hubiera sido el fin de su vocación, pues no era fácil encontrar un marido adecuado a su sensibilidad y sabiduría. Además necesitaba protección, por lo que el convento "era lo menos desproporcionado y lo más decente," según ella misma confesaría. Hecha la resolución principal, en el convento Juana se rodeó de instrumentos científicos y de libros y trató de cumplir sus obligaciones religiosas, robando algo de tiempo para cultivar sus conocimientos universalistas y escribir teatro y poesía. Pero su vida, además de las molestias de la vida comunitaria que sin duda la molestaban, no dejó de tener sobresaltos. Bajo el seudónimo de Sor Filotea, el obispo de Puebla la acusó de falta de piedad y de afanes mundanos por proseguir con su vocación intelectual. Sor Juana contestó a Sor Filotea en una brillante carta que es el único planteamiento colonial que nos queda sobre los problemas femeninos. A pesar de su resistencia, Sor Juana se vería a la postre precisada a renunciar su biblioteca e instrumentos más tarde y, por fortuna, una muerte temprana la liberaría de toda su desesperanza.

El ejemplo de la madre de Sor Juana, quien a pesar de haber tenido hijos ilegítimos se mantuvo en contacto con la misma corte virreinal, muestra lo absurdo de pensar que las mujeres limitaran su actividad a "tomar estado" (en el matrimonio o en el convento) y se rigieran por los estrechos conceptos que Fray Alonso de Herrera deducía de los proverbios bíblicos en su *Espejo de la perfecta casada*. En todas las clases hubo "desviaciones", de otra forma no habría habido necesidad de fundar recogimientos que no sólo albergaban a huérfanas, solteras, viudas y abandonadas, sino también a prostitutas, para su corrección. Como Edith Couturier y Asunción Lavrín han mostrado ya, la misma élite, más sujetas a las normas vigentes que otras clases, ingresó a menudo en estos recogimientos. Y no sólo eso, también abundaron las mujeres que manejaban haciendas y prósperas minas, manipulaban a sus familias para mejorar el *status* social y económico de sus hijos, se casaban múltiples veces e incluso, cuando les venía en gana, fuera de su grupo racial, disponían de primogenituras, herencia y títulos, a su buen saber y entender. Parece cierto que las más libres en aquella sociedad eran las viudas pero, en general, la sociedad era más permisiva de lo que podría pensarse. En las capas populares la situación siempre ha sido más flexible, pues el número de familias presididas por mujeres era muy grande y su situación exigía éstas se ganaran la vida de cualquier manera.

Hasta 1683 las criollas pobres no tenían oportunidad de educarse fuera del hogar, pero en ese año se fundó la primera institución para niñas pobres: el Colegio de Belem. El colegio estaba organizado en departamentos, donde las niñas vivían en grupos presididos por una mujer. La disciplina era conventual y se les enseñaban labores de aguja, música de órgano o canto y, por supuesto, doctrina. A esta primera institución le seguirían otras muchas en el siglo dieciocho, como el Colegio de Niñas (1725), el Colegio de San Ignacio o las Vizcaínas (1767) y otros semejantes en Oaxaca, Guadalajara, Puebla e Irapuato. Los años no pasaron en balde y para principios del siglo dieciocho se había generado también un gran cambio en los prejuicios españoles y se abría, en 1724, el primer convento para niñas indígenas: el convento de Corpus Christi. Para que esto fuera posible, hubo que reunir una gran acumulación de pruebas de la religiosidad que habían desplegado las indígenas en beaterías, recogimientos y conventos, en donde a menudo servían o se amparaban, pues era muy fuerte la convicción de que los indígenas, por ser nuevos cristianos, eran incapaces de verdadera religiosidad.

Pero a esta transformación de mentalidad, producida por la madurez de la sociedad criolla novohispana, se sumaría la influencia del exterior. Por un lado llegó la mundaneidad que importaban al imperio español los borbones franceses; por el otro, la ideología que aparejó la Ilustración con su intento de regeneración de la vida social y económica. Esta daría mucha importancia a la educación como instrumento de progreso. Y este proyecto social ilustrado, que preparaba la hegemonía burguesa, sería utilizado por la élite novohispana para independizar a la colonia.

La Ilustración trajo un cambio profundo que no pudo menos que influir en la concepción de la mujer. Benito Feijoó en su *Teatro crítico universal* escribió una "Defensa de las Mujeres," en donde rebatía hasta argumentos derivados de la *Biblia*. E incluía una lista de mujeres notables para probar cómo, cuando éstas tenían oportunidad de ejercitar sus ingenios, destacaban. "Sepan las mujeres, decía, que no son en el conocimiento inferiores a los hombres: con eso entrarán confiadamente a rebatir su sofisma, donde se disfraza con capa de razón, las sinrazones."

El Conde de Campomanes también defendió la igualdad intelectual de los dos sexos y abogó por probarlo dando la misma educación a ambos pues, según él, por experiencia se sabía "que el ingenio no distingue de sexos y que la mujer bien educada no cede en luces, ni en disposiciones a los hombres, pero en las operaciones manuales es mucho más ágil que ellos." Campomanes creía que parte del estancamiento económico español tenía su origen en la lastimosa ociosidad en que permanecían las mujeres y, para superar ese estado, aconsejaba se les educara y se eliminara toda reglamentación contra su trabajo. Seguramente fueron sus ideas las que inspiraron el decreto expedido en 1784 por Carlos III, que abolía la prohibición para que las mujeres desempeñaran algunos trabajos. Este decreto se hizo extensivo a la Nueva España en 1798. Para entonces las mujeres eran hilanderas, tejedoras, confiteras, azotadoras de sombreros, agujeteras, zurradoras, zapateras, encuadernadoras, tabaqueras, etc. y sabemos que los gremios las admitieron, aunque casi siempre como aprendices y oficiales, aunque hay pruebas de que alguna, como Francisca Villaseñor, vecina de Orizaba pasara su examen y lograra ser Maestra. En algunos trabajos, las novohispanas laboraron al lado de hombres, tal el caso de las fábricas de tabaco que empleaban cientos de trabajadoras, lo que ocasionaba la "desviación de las buenas costumbres," pues aunque se separaba a los dos sexos y salían por distintas puertas, afuera se juntaban.

Carlos III defendió también la admisión de mujeres a las sociedades económicas y una mujer fue admitida como miembro de la Real Academia de la Lengua. Ese clima favoreció que tanto el Estado, como la Iglesia y los particulares se empeñaran en multiplicar las escuelas y que, ya en forma regular, se enseñara a las niñas por lo menos a leer. A esto contribuyó también el que durante la segunda mitad del siglo dieciocho hubiera hecho su entrada a la Nueva España la orden francesa de la Compañía de María, consagrada a la educación de las niñas. El Colegio de la Enseñanza, como se le conoció, había sido fundado gracias al sostenimiento y esfuerzos de María Ignacia Azlor y Echeverri y de inmediato influyó en otras instituciones; así, el convento de Corpus Christi estableció un colegio de religiosas de esa orden y en 1760 se fundó el Colegio de Nuestra Señora de Guadalupe para niñas indígenas.

Lo que es indudable es que la educación fue uno de los temas fundamentales de la política, antes y después de la independencia. Desde 1754 se había pasado un decreto que exigía a las parroquias sostener escuelas que enseñaran doctrina y lectura en lengua española y que el virrey Galvez se encargaría de insistir en exigir su cumplimiento.

Los ayuntamientos en México y Guadalajara se mostraron también activos en la fundación de escuelas públicas, aunque no siempre se preocuparan por su mantenimiento. Y el cambio fue grande, por lo memos en las grandes ciudades como México y Guadalajara, en cuyas escuelas públicas se instruían tantas niñas como niños. Algunos internados, como los Colegios de San Ignacio y de Niñas, abrirían también escuelas externas para niñas pobres, lo que contribuiría a la alfabetización femenina. Los intendentes no quisieron quedarse atrás y la mayoría se preocuparon también por impulsar la educación. El intendente de Guadalajara fue más allá y "para evitar los continuos males que la falta de parteras o comadres instruidas, produce a la humanidad," pensó en la conveniencia de que se adiestraran a las que ya ejercían y ordenó al cirujano mayor del hospital real que lo hiciera.

En realidad, durante la segunda mitad del siglo dieciocho se sentaron los lineamientos generales de lo que constituirían las metas de la educación liberal. Los primeros años del siglo diecinueve presenciaron la expansión de estas ideas y la multiplicación de fundaciones educativas en donde lectura, escritura y cuentas se enseñaban con regularidad. Poco a poco se fueron agregando otras materias: historia sagrada, dibujo, geografía y geometría. Aún en colegios para niñas indias pobres, se insistiría en que las alumnas "adelantarán ... si se les estimula a pensar y a discurrir." Muchos pensadores políticos como Fernández de Lizardi, acervo crítico de la educación de las niñas, en su novela *La quijotita y su prima* (1818-1819), Wenceslao Barquera y Carlos María de Bustamante, articulistas del *Diario de México*,

escribieron en forma constante sobre la educación del sexo "débil,"
aunque dentro de la concepción tradicional de la mujer, que la
concebía como cera blanda que los hombres modelaban. En gran
medida el tema de la mujer se manejaría en la línea establecida a
fines del dieciocho, por la española Josefa Amar y Borbón en su
discurso sobre *La educación física y moral de las mujeres* (1790).
Doña Josefa atacaba el condicionamiento que se daba a las niñas
para crecer bellas y agradables al sexo opuesto, que les impedía
convertirse en verdaderos seres humanos, en detrimento de su
marido y de sus hijos. Para ella, la educación de las niñas debía
prepararlas para el papel de madres.

De todas maneras, la independencia no trajo cambios drásticos
en la vida, pues toda transformación social es siempre lenta. No
obstante, como las mujeres desempenaron un papel en la lucha y,
aunque no siempre fuera reconocido del todo, se les permitió
traspasar los límites tradicionales de su actuación. De manera que
al inaugurarse la vida nacional, mujeres como doña Petra Tornel
de Velasco, la "Güera" Rodríguez y su hija Josefa Villamil,
Condesa de Regla, se convirtieron en influyentes de la nueva
sociedad, pues en sus tertulias se reunían todos los importantes. Y
las mujeres se hicieron oír también por escrito. En 1817, en una
publicación periódica, Dalmira Regurviasa abogaba por una
educación más amplia para las mujeres y, en 1823, Ana Josefa
Caballero de Borda publicaba su *Necesidad de un establecimiento
de educación para jóvenes mexicanas*. La Academia no llegó a
fundarse, pero abrió paso a la idea de que las mujeres podían
aprender algo más que lectura, labores "propias de su sexo" y
doctrina, y un buen número de los nuevos colegios femeninos
ampliaron sus enseñanzas.

En verdad todos estaban de acuerdo en que la educación era el
camino único hacia el progreso y no se excluía de tal ambición a
las mujeres, pues como afirmaba *El Aguila Mexicana* en 1828, una
mujer sin educación era un parásito. Pero la bancarrota económica
y las guerras extranjeras conspiraron para impedir que se hicieran
realidad los sueños de educación popular. No teniendo medios la
gran tarea quedó en manos de la Compañía Lancasteriana que algo
logró.

La instrucción de las niñas se fue ampliando y algunos
establecimientos, como el de la señora Desmotier, según anuncio
en la *Lima de Vulcano* del 2 febrero de 1836, ofrecían enseñanza
de inglés y francés, letra inglesa, ortografía, doctrina, gramática,
aritmética, historia sagrada, historia de los pueblos antiguous,
música instrumental sobre piano forte, dibujo y costura. No

sabemos cuantas mujeres llegaron a educarse con esos adornos, pero sí que el ideal de educación femenina llegó a hacer que se aprendiera a leer y escribir, gramática y aritmética (para defenderse si se queda sola) un oficio, mejor remunerado que el de costurera (platera o relojera), religión, urbanidad y, tal vez, música (para hacerse agradable a su familia). Todo sin tomar en cuenta su potencial, ni sus preferencias. Se opinaba como la cita neoyorkina que transcribía la revista *El amigo de la religión*: "... leer, escribir, saber aritmética, bordar, música ¡qué adornos tan propios de una señorita!"

Las mujeres quedaron excluidas de las instituciones de educación superior durante tres cuartos de siglos. Por nuevo decreto de 1842, se les instruyó para ser comadronas con información ... nada más. Lo logrado hasta la década de 1820 fue lo máximo que pudieron alcanzar. Se impuso, por desgracia, el pensamiento expresado por Lizardi, "la posición de la mujer es inferior al hombre según la ley natural, la ley civil y la ley divina." Su argumento derivaba de la debilidad física que según muchos la preparaba para la maternidad. Este pensamiento reaccionario impidió que se consumara la progresista meta del Conde de Campomanes "la mujer tiene el mismo uso de razón que el hombre ... sólo el descuido que padece en su enseñanza, la diferencia, sin culpa suya."

Tal vez, a corto plazo, más efectiva que la educación iba a ser la apertura al mundo que trajo la independencia. No sólo hubo un mejoramiento de las comunicaciones con el interior y el exterior gracias a diligencias y paquebotes que permitieron que las mujeres se movieran de un lado para otro, sino que el establecimiento de extranjeros influyó en un cambio de costumbres y permitió que la secularización de vida, iniciada con los borbones, se extendiera considerablemente. Las mujeres se veían en casinos y tertulias, en teatros y fiestas cívicas y como participantes de toda novedad que llegara al país, ya fuera un predistigitador famoso, un microscopio o un alumbrado de gas. Y la esfera en que se movía la mujer se ampliaba sin que nadie lo notara. Así por ejemplo Eugenio Robertson después de haber hecho varios viajes en su globo aerostático, logró convencer a una agraciada jovencita mexicana para que lo acompañara en su ascenso por los aires, y aunque no dejó de haber quien lo considerara un descato, la muchedumbre enloqueció de gusto al ver a su paisana compartir la gloria de la singular aventura.

Por desgracia es difícil reconstruir la vida de las mujeres de esa época, pues carecemos de documentos femeninos que nos cuenten de sus sueños y frustraciones, deseos y problemas, goces y éxitos. La Marquesa Calderón, con todo y la parcialidad que implica su condición de extranjera protestante, y Manuel Payno parecen ser las fuentes más ricas. Pero aprehender cualquier aspecto de una sociedad de transición es de por sí tema escurridizo y mucho más en el caso de una heterogeneidad tal como la mexicana de los albores independientes.

Gracias a la Marquesa Calderón tenemos un cuadro de la vida de las mujeres ricas mexicanas: su inutilidad, ignorancia y tontería, rodeadas de sus criados y criadas, causa, como hoy en día, de la mayor parte de sus dolores de cabeza, y su vida de visitas, teatro y paseos. "En términos generales--dice--las señoras y señoritas mexicanas escriben, leen y tocan un poco, cosen, cuidan de su casa y de sus hijos. Cuando digo que leen, quiero decir que saben leer, cuando digo que escriben, no quiero decir que lo hagan siempre con buena ortografía." Su relato sobre la profesión de algunas monjas es tan impresionista que ha conducido a la idea errónea de que la vida conventual fuera una alternativa al matrimonio. La imposibilidad del hecho es total porque en esa época quedaban pocas monjas y es bueno recordar que según Mariano Cuevas en su *Historia de la Iglesia en México*, aún en el periodo en que más hubo en los 157 conventos existentes, ascendieron sólo a 1700 monjas. De manera que entonces, como ahora, la verdadera alternativa al matrimonio era la soltería, ya que ser monja bastante excepcional, para los 3,000,000 de mujeres que por entonces había.

Guillermo Prieto en sus *Memorias* nos pinta la vida de lo que se llamaba entonces clase media, es decir, el pequeño grupo de profesionistas y burócratas, que tenían un pasar mediocre con grandes altibajos ocasionados por los cambios de gobierno, las bolas y la bancarrota hacendaria. En esa clase, la formación de la niña la determinaba una educación religiosa que producía curiosas polaridades: "tenía su muñeca vestida de monja, su perrito faldero y su bastidor para bordar. A todas se permitía la escritura y el maestro de baile y la maestra de piano ... El ocio más completo, el desden mas absoluto a la gente baja, la idea mas arraigada de que la mujer, al casarse, era la víctima, perdía su libertad y renunciaba al estado perfecto de virgen que la llevaba al cielo ...." Producía, eso sí, esposas devotas que mantenían un primor de hogar y estaban dispuestas a sacrificarlo todo por su familia.

Gracia a las novelas de Payno e Inclán podemos atisbar un poco la vida de las mujeres de otros grupos sociales. En el campo o en la ciudad, en pobres accesorias o vecindades, en ranchos grandes o pequeños, en cuevas o chiqueros, desfilan una variedad infinita de tipos femeninos. Ahí está la pobre vieja pepenadora que no tiene otro medio de sobrevivir que buscar en la basura en donde encuentra al niño abandonado en "la viña"; las miserables indígenas "descendientes de los orgullosos aztecas"; que habitan tan cerca de la capital y se dedican a recoger "tequesquite y mosquitos de la orilla del lago, que cambian en la ciudad por mendrugos de pan y venas de chile." En contraste, encontramos a la comodina doña Pascuala, la hija de cura español casada con un indio ranchero de buen pasar, que se permite el lujo del chocolate, comer carne y beber leche dos o tres veces a la semana. Y que llevaba una vida por "lo demás sosegada y monótona. Se levantaba con la luz ... se ocupaba de barrer la casa, de echar ramas en el brasero ... de dar de comer a las gallinas, limpiar las jaulas de los pájaros, regar macetas ... preparar la comida ... y el tiempo libre lo consagraba la lectura." También está la próspera frutera Cecilia, vestida de "tela fina," rebozos de Tenancingo, cuyos buenos negocios no eran obstaculizados por sus cuentas que, por desconocer la aritmética, hacía con los dedos de la mano y ayudada con frijoles de colores. Honesta y sencilla, no se había casado "porque persuadida de que la solicitaban o por la mala o por su dinero, con ninguno guiso buen trato más que de puro comercio." Aparecen también, por supuesto, las chinas alegres, con su corpiño rojo y falda rabona que nunca tienen buen fin. Abundan las sirvientas leales y también desleales, las solteronas arrimadas que se ven obligadas a ofrecer su trabajo, a cambio de un rincón y un taco. Las mujeres son víctimas o simples espectadoras; hasta la hija del Conde, caída en pecado, renuncia a su hijo y a su amante por imposición paterna y sobrevive sólo gracias al cuidado de su nana y de sus criados. Y el cuadro se completa con la historia de los abusos de maridos y amantes, sobre todo en las clases populares.

Todo este cuadro parecía diferir poco, en lo fundamental, de la vida femenina novohispana y, sin embargo, los pequeños matices de modas, posibilidad de hacer carrera de maestra, entrar a trabajar en las fábricas textiles--que a partir de 1840 se fueron multiplicando--hacían una diferencia para mediados de siglo. Para 1850 las voces secularizadoras iban ganando ya la partida y habían disminuido grandemente "las vocaciones religiosas." Después del triunfo liberal de 1861 se aseguraba esta tendencia, pues se clausuraron los conventos y se devolvió las dotes a las monjas con la venta de los bienes eclesiásticos. Sólo, temporalmente, Juárez hizo excepción de las monjas de la Caridad. El establecimiento del Segundo Imperio fue el último intento reaccionario por revivir la sociedad estratificada colonial y fracasó por completo pues los conservadores eligieron un monarca liberal. Entre los sueños fugaces de Maximiliano para su flamante imperio estuvieron una reforma educativa y una agraria, y dentro de las preocupaciones de la Emperatriz estuvo la educación de las niñas. Gracias a su interés, se ordenó un informe sobre la situación de la misma, que en general era mala y desigual, pues si bien en estados ricos como Jalisco habían varias instituciones, en otros como Tamaulipas no existía una sola escuela.

El triunfo de Juárez en 1867 significó además de la elección definitiva del republicanismo como solución política, la posibilidad de planear integralmente una reforma educativa. La multiplicación de escuelas fue notable y el cambio de mentalidad empezó a hacerse aparente. Uno de los Ministros de Justicia e Instrucción, don Ignacio Ramírez, defendería que se diera la misma educación a hombres y mujeres, aunque todavía con base a la influencia que tendrían como madres de futuros ciudadanos. "¡Cuánta diferencia resultará entre la niñez pasada entre mujeres instruidas y nuestra actual infancia que sigue amamantándose de miserables consejas!" Insistía en que la mujer tenía ya "personalidad religiosa y civil y sólo le falta la política" lo cual le parecía curiosa anomalía, porque sin duda no dejaba de ejercer su influencia en esa esfera y, "¡Cosa rara! La mujer que no puede ser elector, ni alcalde, puede ser reina!" Para Ramírez ya no había duda que las mujeres debían tener derechos políticos plenos y que el adquirirlos permitiría que prestaran su colaboración al perfeccionamiento de la sociedad.

En todo el mundo, la segundo mitad del siglo diecinueve vería ampliarse el horizonte educativo y laboral de las mujeres. En Estados Unidos se habían graduado ya las primeras universitarias y en todas partes se reconocía la necesidad de que las mujeres tuvieran mayores oportunidades educativas y aunque con grandes reservas, se empezaron a eliminar las trabas existentes en muchos países. En México, sería el esfuerzo de Ignacio Ramírez el que se cancelaran las limitaciones formales para que las mujeres fueran admitidas en escuelas superiorses. Hasta ese momento, la única carrera apropiada para las jóvenes era la de maestra, aunque las nuevas escuelas técnicas les ofrecían la oportunidad de estudiar telegrafía, taquigrafía, mecanografía, corte y confección. La secretarial se consideró otro tarea apropiada para las mujeres, aunque la sociedad mexicana vio con prevención su trabajo en oficinas, al lado de los hombres. Y el obstáculo de la tradición y la familia mostró ser poderoso, pues las profesionistas lucharon mucho sin mayor éxito casi medio siglo. De todas maneras para

1886 se graduó la primera dentista y en 1887 se graduó la primera médica cirujana y antes de fin de siglo había ya una abogada. Algunas de las graduadas no llegaron a ejercer, pues padres, hermanos y maridos de clases medias y altas verían hasta bien entrado el siglo veinte como un golpe a su honor y a su capacidad de mantener a su familia el que sus hijas, hermanas o esposas trabajaran.

La estabilización que trajo dictadura porfirista y el orden neocolonial que conllevó, dio por resultado la construcción de una red ferrocarrilera que unía por vez primera gran parte de la república, llevando y trayendo toda clase de influencias, modas y problemas. El país empezó a industrializarse y la urbanización se extendió. El número de mujeres que entraron a la fuerza de trabajo empezó a crecer y con ello su participación en sindicatos y huelgas. Como a las mexicanas se les pagaba menos que a los hombres en las fábricas, ya el Manifiesto del Primer Congreso Obrero Mexicano de 1876 planteó la necesidad de mejorar las condiciones de trabajo de las obreras. Y a pesar de que las mujeres económicamente activas en 1910 apenas representaron el 8.8 porciento, y en 1880 una mujer, Carmen Huerta, había presidido el Segundo Congreso Obrero, se había constituido asociaciones feministas que planteaban reivindicaciones y Juana Belén Guitiérrez de Mendoza publicaba la revista *Vesper*. Pero fueron las pésimas condiciones laborales las que obligarían a las mujeres a desempeñar un papel más activo. En 1904 se vieron involucradas en las huelgas textiles de Río Blanco y cayeron en la lucha. En 1906 formaron parte del Partido Liberal Mexicano que incluía, entre sus pronunciamientos, varios referentes al *status* de las trabajadoras. Pero la situación de la mexicana no era una excepción, en todo el mundo continuaba bajo la tutela paternal o conyugal y carecía de derechos políticos. Las mexicanas habían entrado en oficinas, escuelas, talleres y fábricas, pero la presión social en contra de su trabajo a veces la obligaba a preferir el hambre, a la marginación a que la condenaba su medio cuando elegía un puesto de secretaria. En la novela de Julio Sesto, *La Tortola de Ajusco*, escrita en 1914 se ve claramente esto; Fémina, la protagonista, decide entrar a trabajar para ayudar a su madre, pero lucha contra la opinión de sus amigos, que piensan que: "en los ejercicios intelectuales, en las funciones oficinescas de macho, los órganos de la mujer se transforman, toda ella se transforma, moral y físicamante; en las labores mentales, el cerebro de la mujer se desarrolla en demasía, con menoscabo de los demás órganos y esas mujeres así, se anulan para sentir y desear el amor y se atrofían para ser fecundadas."

La Revolución Mexicana iniciada en 1910 dio oportunidad para que las mujeres participaran masivamente en la lucha. Unas se sumaron a los partidos políticos, pero las más partieron a los campos de batalla, solas o para acompañar a sus hombres o sirvieron de espías, recaderas, animadoras, informantes. La urgencia de la lucha impidió que se aplicaran los prejuicios vigentes, que suspendieron su validez en medio del caos. La visibilidad de su lucha hizo que el 29 de diciembre de 1915 se aprobara la ley de divorcio y se reconociera la necesidad de reformas legislativas de importancia. Pero las aspiraciones rebasaban las posibilidades. Las ideas que abogaban abiertamente por un cambio total en la situación de la mujer en la sociedad se habían extendido y en algunas regiones las condiciones revolucionarias permitieron que los intentos se radicalizaran. En 1915 el gobernador de Yucatán, Salvador Alvarado, convocaba el primer Congreso Feminista de Yucatán con estas palabras:

Es un error social educar a la mujer para un sociedad que ya no existe, habituándola a que, como en la antigüedad, permanezca recluida en el hogar ... pues la vida activa de la evolución exige su concurso en una mayoría de las actividades humanas ... Para que puedan formarse generaciones libres y fuertes es necesario que la mujer obtenga un estado jurídico que la ennoblezca, una educación que le permita vivir con independencia.

Alvarado se empeñó en abrir las puertas de los puestos públicos a las mujeres, proporcionar oportunidades de educación vocacional y otorgarles el derecho de abandonar la casa paterna a los 21 años, si así lo deseaban. Felipe Carillo Puerto, su sucesor en el gobierno, también simpatizó con la causa feminista y no sólo propuso en 1921 la ley que concedía el voto a las mujeres yucatecas, sino que patrocinó la elección de una mujer como presidente del Consejo Municipal de Mérida y de tres diputadas a la legislatura estatal. Otra de las contribuciones de Carrillo Puerto a las luchas feministas fue la publicación, en 1922 de la traducción del folleto de Margaret Sanger titulado *La regulación de la natalidad o la brújula del hogar*. Todos estos acontecimientos explican que la Constitución de 1917 consagrara en su artículo 123 una serie de protecciones laborales para las mujeres mexicanas, que en otros países se conquistarían más tarde: jornada de 8 horas, descanso obligatorio, permiso de gravidez y permiso para amamantar a sus hijos durante la jornada de trabajo.

Con el estrecho contacto entre las latinoamericanas y las sufragistas inglesas y norteamericanas, aparecieron diversas organizaciones feministas y en 1919 se realizó un Congreso de Obreras y Campesinas y en 1921 uno Femenino, que convocaría a la reunión del Congreso Nacional Feminista de 1922.

El hecho es que para la década de 1920 existía un pequeño grupo de profesionistas conscientes de su desigualdad humana y cívica y una fuerza de trabajo femenina explotada. Gracias al impulso de las reuniones celebradas en todo el continente, las organizaciones americanas lograron que el problema de los derechos femeninos se presentara ante la V Conferencia Interamericana, que se celebraría en Chile en 1923 y se aprobara la resolución de recomendar "el estudio de los medios de abolir las incapacidades constitucionales y legales en razón de sexo." Poco después se formó la Liga de Mujeres Ibéricas e Hispanoamericanas que continuó una lucha para ampliar la presencia política femenina aunque con poco resultado. En la VI Conferencia Interamericana de la Habana se presionó para que los acuerdos de Santiago entraran en vigor. Esta presión llevó a establecer la Comisión Interamericana de Mujeres que prepararía la información jurídica necesaria para que la VII Conferencia pudiera "abordar el estudio de la igualdad civil y política de la mujer del Continente." Poco después, Ecuador concedía el voto a las mujeres, pero en México lo único que se logró fue que el nuevo Partido Nacional Revolucionario (antecedente del PRI) fundara una sección femenina y a pesar de la radicalización que trajo la depresión económica de los años treinta, las mujeres no lograron dar un paso adelante en sus aspiraciones. Por el contrario, el hecho de que varias de las asociaciones feministas se comprometieron con un movimiento en favor de la educación sexual resultó en un desprestigio al fracasar rotundamente.

El caso fue tal que cuando se presentó un estudio comparativo de los derechos del hombre y la mujer en la VII Conferencia Interamericana de Montevideo, México no lo suscribió, como tampoco el proyecto de convención en la Sociedad de Naciones para impedir toda distinción de sexo "en materia de nacionalidad." La legislación mexicana, como la de otros países latinoamericanos, condenaba a la mujer casada con extranjero a perder su nacionalidad y le negaba el derecho de trasmitir la nacionalidad a sus hijos. De todas maneras se aprobaron las modificaciones de 1934 y 1939 que eliminaban la cláusula que condenaba a las mujeres casadas con extranjeros a perder su nacionalidad, pero las mujeres, ya que la madre no tenía los mismos derechos que el padre en la trasmisión de nacionalidad a los hijos. Discriminación que se borró hasta la década de los setentas.

A pesar de muchos reveses, la nueva efervescencia revolucionaria de los años treinta permitió que un grupo reducido, pero capaz y hábil, lograra movilizar obreras y campesinas y fundar, en 1935, la organización femenina más importante que ha existido en el país: el Frente Unido Pro Derechos de la Mujer. No se trataba de un grupo solamente sufragista, sus dirigentes tenían conciencia de las múltiples limitaciones legales y pretendían lograr la modificación de los códigos civiles estatales, la Ley Federal del Trabajo y el Código Agrario, este último, de manera que las campesinas fueran elegibles para obtener tierras ejidales. Este y otro grupo femenino del Partido Communista se constituyeron en voceros de los diversos puntos de vista sobre las aspiraciones femeninas. Y, a pesar de que la oposición dentro del Partido Nacional Revolucionario era muy fuerte, las manifestaciones y mítines femeninos ejercieron tal presión que pareció que la obtención del sufragio era inminente. El presidente Cárdenas envió una iniciativa de ley para reformar la Constitución, el 13 de septiembre de 1937. En julio del año siguiente fue aprobada por el Congreso y después ratificada por muchos estados; sin embargo, nunca se publicó en el *Diario Oficial* para entrar en vigor. Todo hace pensar que en los círculos políticos oficialistas se temió que el voto femenino favoreciera al candidato de oposición, Juan Andrew Almazán, que contaba con las simpatías del clero. Sea como fuere, las mexicanas fracasaron en su esfuerzo, justo al tiempo que la VIII Conferencia Interamericana de 1938 hacía la Declaración de Lima que reconocía a la mujer derecho: a) a igual tratamiento político que el hombre; b) a gozar de igualdad en el orden civil; c) a las más amplias oportunidades y protección en el trabajo; y d) al más amplio amparo como madre.

La Conferencia urgía a los gobiernos de las repúblicas americanas a adoptar "con la urgencia posible, la legislación consiguiente para la realización integral de los principios contenidos en la presente Declaración."

Para entonces, la idea del derecho a la igualdad ante la ley era firme y aún los más inseguros varones no se atrevían a negar que las mujeres tenían derecho a votar, aunque expresaban escrúpulos de que participara activamente en la vida política, por temor de que perdieran sus maravillosas virtudes hogareñas. El grupo consagrado a lograr el sufragio era pequeño pero tan decidido a lograr su objectivo que se multiplicó para presionar por todos los conductos.

La Segunda Guerra Mundial sirvió para probar las múltiples capacidades femeninas: en la producción, en los servicios hospitalarios, en el frente de batalla y las privó a menudo de las protecciones tradicionales. De manera que era natural que al inaugurarse la Organización de Naciones Unidas (ONU), la igualdad de derechos humanos fuera fundamento de su existencia y que la Organización de Estados Americanos institucionalizara en 1945 un Comité Interamericano de Mujeres.

Para 1948, la ONU definía claramente los derechos políticos en la "Declaración Universal de Derechos Humanos" y la Comisión presentaba su *Informe ante la IX Conferencia Internacional Americana sobre derechos civiles y políticos de la mujer* en Washington. El informe y la situación en los nuevos países asiáticos y africanos hicieron necesaria una convención especial de la ONU sobre los derechos políticos de la mujer. En ella se especificaba que los Estados miembros adquirían el compromiso de que las mujeres votaran y fueran elegidas en igualdad de términos que los hombres. En México se había adicionado el artículo 115 constitucional para que la mujer participara en igualdad de condiciones en las elecciones municipales y en algunos estados como Yucatán, Chiapas, Puebla, Guanajuato y Michoacán se había dejado en sus manos no sólo las tareas agrícolas, sino también los asuntos de la comunidad. Fue, pues, el reconocimiento de una situación de hecho. Pero el voto federal no se logró hasta 1953.

En el campo educativo, el avance fue más constante. En las áreas urbanas la niñas entraron a las escuelas primarias casi en iguales números que los niños y hasta 1942 asistieron a escuelas oficiales coeducativas. La enseñanza secundaria, establecida en 1926 creció lentamente hasta la década de 1950 y sólo con la urbanización e industrialización que tuvo lugar a partir de la Segunda Guerra Mundial, empezó a crecer a un ritmo acelerado. Las escuelas secretariales y técnicas fueron los más seguros recursos de educación de las mujeres hasta la década de 1950, en que empezaron a entrar en grandes números en las universidades. A excepción de las humanidades y las carreras administrativas, números menores de mujeres entraron en otras profesiones, pero empezaron a figurar en todos los campos, aunque lidiando todavía con la desconfianza del público hacia su capacidad. El ambiente académico ha dado a la mujer amplias posibilidades, sin embargo, todavía no ha habido una rectora de universidad.

Pero fueron las transformaciones mundiales y la industrialización las que influyeron en los cambios más importantes en el *status* de la mujer. A partir de la década de 1950 las mujeres entraron en números importantes en la fuerza de trabajo y muchas industrias las empezaron a entrenar preferentemente, por el grado de cuidado y cumplimiento que demostraron. En algunas de las plantas maquiladoras de industrias norteamericanas en la frontera, las mujeres también han llegado a ocupar cifras importantes en el empleo.

Los medios de comunicación masiva también tuvieron una influencia importante para diseminar modas e ideas. El radio y el cine, primero, y la televisión después, llevaron mensajes hasta los más recónditos rincones del territorio. Estos muchas veces han sido contradictorios, pero de todas formas, radionovelas, máquinas del hogar, anticonceptivos, bluejeans, y más hicieron surgir la aspiración de un lugar más digno en la sociedad. En las capas sociales más privilegiadas se sintió también la influencia del movimiento feminista norteamericano y algunas de las revistas de amplia circulación, dirigidas a la clase media, como *Vanidades, Buenhogar, Claudia* y *Kena* se han convertido en voceros de actitudes renovantes. En realidad, las dos primeras han acusado un cambio de opinión, pues por largos años fueron portadoras de ideas tradicionales.

En grandes capas de la sociedad todavía existe hostilidad a cualquier idea que signifique cualquier transformación de la familia; se acepta que la mujer se eduque, que trabaje y ejerza sus derechos políticos, pero sólo por excepción se reconoce la necesidad de cambiar la educación y socialización de las mujeres; se las sigue formando sólo para ser esposas y madres, lo cual limita el desarrollo de su potencial como seres humanos.

El cambio legal operado en México no deja de ser sorprendente. Se ha tratado de detectar toda discriminación para derogarla. El carácter proteccionista de la Ley Federal del Trabajo de 1961 que prohibía ocupar a las mujeres en labores peligrosas e insalubres y servicios extraodinarios, desapareció en la nueva Ley del Trabajo de 1970 y la reforma del artículo 123 constitucional ahora prohibe dichas labores sólo a la mujer embarazada. En 1974 se reformó también el Código Civil para establecer igualdad de derechos y obligaciones para ambos cónyuges, tanto en el matrimonio como en el devorcio.

El progresso no ha sido homogéneo para todos los grupos sociales. Muchas contradicciones se han mantenido y la igualdad de derechos políticos existe sobre todo en el papel. El alto porcentaje de madres solteras y esposas abandonadas, que siempre han existido en México en las clases populares, hace que el papel de proveedora no sea nuevo para la mujer mexicana. Su supuesta religiosidad y reaccionarismo que sirvieron para negarle el voto en los años treinta, por temor a que votara a favor del candidato de derecha, también sirvió para retrasar la difusión sobre el control de la natalidad, y a pesar del monstruoso crecimiento demográfico no fue sino hasta la década de 1970 que se inició una tímida campaña con el *slogan* "vámomos haciendo menos, para vivir mejor."

Las conquistas son en cierta medida impresionantes: la ley concede a la mujer igualdad de derechos, le protege su maternidad, le ha abierto oportunidades de educación y trabajo y hasta puestos de responsabilidad. No obstante, la situación deja mucho que desear. En primer lugar, la sociedad aún las condiciona para pensar que sólo puede realizarse a través de sus hijos. Las nuevas circunstancias permiten a un grupo cada vez más amplio, un proyecto de vida personal más plena, pero con resultados a menudo negativos. Como no se ha logrado el ajuste psicológico masculino al nuevo papel femenino, el resultado ha sido desastroso para la familia, pues el porcentaje de divorcios empieza a competir con el de los países desarrollados. Por otra parte, en gran medida, las conquistas benefician principalmente a un pequeño grupo de mujeres educadas, puesto que la mayoría de las trabajadoras se emplean en servicios, oficios y tareas menores. En la ciudad, de cada cinco trabajadoras, dos son sirvientas y en el campo son nulas las oportunidades de trabajo remunerado para la mujer, lo que las condena a una gran dependencia. Esto, sin embargo, está en camino de cambio pues en los últimos años las mujeres han entrado en grandes números en los servicios policiales, aduaneros y sorprendentemente, en la industria de la construcción. Ya hay un buen número de ingenieras, albañilas, plomeras, y electricistas. La principal compañía mexicana de construcción utiliza buenos números de albañilas para trabajos cuidadosos y un punto a su favor es que no hacen el famoso San Lunes.

El que existan secciones femeninas en partidos y sindicatos demuestra que en la política las mujeres se encuentran en situación de dependencia. Desde luego, todavía hay pocas mujeres en puestos importantes, aunque hay que reconocer que no han sabido aprovechar el oportunismo político de los últimos tiempos que ha andado en busca de candidatas. Desde 1977 hay una gobernadora y desde 1980 una secretaria de Estado y, por supuesto, hay y ha habido diputadas, senadoras y ministras de la Supreme Corte.

Sin duda la situación es compleja y difícil de apreciar, pues a todo ese contradictorio proceso se le suma el subdesarrollo. Gran parte de la problemática actual tiene que ver con la educación, tanto formal como informal. A pesar de la apertura educativa, todavía hay más muchachas de 17 años con hijos, que en la escuela. Pero es la educación informal la que tiene más peso en la situación de inferioridad de las mujeres. La familia, las instituciones religiosas, el radio, la televisión, los comerciales, el cine, los monitos y los libros de texto continúan enviando mensajes tradicionales sobre el papel de la mujer, su conducta, sus posibilidades, etc. Viejas ideas y creencias se agazapan detrás de las reformas que otorgan derechos y amplían oportunidades de educación y de trabajo, y sirven de freno efectivo del desenvolvimiento exitoso de la mayoría de las vidas femeninas. Por eso la lucha importante que resta por hacer está en vencer muchas sutilezas del vocabulario, de las imágenes y estereotipos que parecen inofensivos, pero que son efectivos instrumentos de domino. Claro que en la medida que se amplíen las oportunidades de educación, las mujeres podrán elegir la maternidad con responsabilidad y no sufrirla como algo accidental e inevitable, como ha sido el caso de nuestras clases populares.

El estado de transición social con dos sistemas de valores dificultan el proceso de liberación femenina, pero parece ser por hoy un paso indispensable para lograr una sociedad más justa y la oportunidad para que la mujer contribuya en todos los campos de la vida, con el potencial que hasta ahora ha permanecido inerte.

LA LLORONA,
THE THIRD LEGEND OF GREATER MEXICO:
CULTURAL SYMBOLS, WOMEN,
AND THE POLITICAL UNCONSCIOUS

by

José E. Limón

> *must be the season of the witch*
> *the witch*
> *la llorona*

As any student of Greater Mexican culture knows, two legendary female figures dominate this culture, lending structure to its early history and exercising their influence unto the present day.[1] The first is the figure of Doña Marina, as she was known to the conquering Spaniards, or *La Malinche*, as she became even more widely known to post-conquest Mexico. She is, of course, the Indian woman who, according to legend, politically and sexually betrayed indigenous Mexico by becoming Cortés' mistress on the eve of the Spanish conquest, and by helping to make that conquest possible. The second dominant legendary figure is *La Virgen de Guadalupe* who enters the Mexican consciousness with her appearance to the Indian Juan Diego in 1531, but does not fully emerge in that consciousness until the events of 1810. Both have been the subjects of sustained and serious intellectual inquiry and reflection. I shall review this literature in formulating the argument of this paper which focused on a third Mexican female figure but in relationship to La Malinche and La Virgen.

My thanks to Suzanne Seriff for her research assistance and my deep gratitude to Joan Lidoff for sharing her stimulating work with me. As always, my continuous appreciation to Marianna for her critical counsel and her careful reading of the manuscript. Finally, in memory of mi abuelita, Doña Margarita Garza de Araiza, who started this paper many years ago with her telling of La Llorona and her recollection of social injustice on both sides of the Rio Grande, where, she said, La Llorona walks at night.

I refer to *La Llorona* or the Weeping Woman, a distinct relative of the Medea story and now a syncretism of European and indigenous cultural forms firmly grounded in the Greater Mexican cultural experience. The depth and breadth of this grounding have remained relatively unexplored in comparison to that of the other two female symbols. She has also been the subject of some scholarly analyses, but these have been of a limited character as I will argue later in more detail. In contrast to the broader, historically dialectical, and, I think, more provocative interpretation that have been offered for the first two figures, the meanings of La Llorona have been more confined by functionalist and localized interpretations.

It is, therefore, the primary purpose of this essay to interrogate the symbolic structure of La Llorona in relationship to a wider context of meaning, which is nothing less than the social history of Greater Mexico. If successful, my analysis will propose La Llorona as the third, comparatively unacknowledged, major female symbol of Greater Mexican socio-cultural life. If articulated with this history and not merely with local contexts, she may be understood at two levels: first, as a positive, contestative symbol for the women of Greater Mexico and second as a critical symbolic reproduction of a socially unfulfilled utopian longing within the Mexican folk masses who tell her story. She speaks to the social and psychological needs of both Greater Mexican sectors, needs left unmet by the hegemonic, hierarchical, masculinized, and increasingly capitalistic social order imposed on the Mexican folk masses since their beginning.

Yet, to fully understand this signification, it is necessary to reacknowledge a now conventional perspective, namely that signs or structures of signs such as these legends, take meaning only in relation of difference to other signs. In this cultural instance, we can interpretively grasp the weeping woman only in relationship to her sister signs and then only when all are grounded in concrete historical experience. I do not propose here a pure, idealized structuralism. Indeed, my interpretation will ultimately be formed by the theoretical work of the Marxist cultural critic, Fredric Jameson, although along the interpretive way, I cannot fail to draw on recent advances in feminist cultural theory, given the nature of my subject. It is my hope that this analysis will open the way for a more global and profound feminist understanding of this symbolic triad, because until feminist analyses fully speak to the totality of oppression, they will have done only half their task.

Mistress and Virgin: Early Mexican History

Let us begin by returning to our first two key symbols, La Malinche and La Virgen de Guadalupe. We have already recounted the essential core of both legends, but it remains to be specified how and why they became key Mexican symbols and thereby structured early Mexican history, at least according to their analyst. We should first consider the foremost of these analysts, Octavio Paz, who, in his *The Labyrinth of Solitude*, gave us an authoritative and validating analysis of a widespread cultural understanding of these two symbols in Mexican life.[2] For Paz, Doña Marina, is the personification of a stigmatized female category--*la chingada*--"the mother who has suffered-- metaphorically or actually--the corrosive and defaming action implicit in the verb that gives her her name."[3] (The root infinitive is of course, *chingar*--to sexually violate.) Paz continues by way of a comparison central to our immediate interest.

> In contrast to Guadalupe, who is the Virgin Mother, the Chingada is the violated mother ... Both of them are passive figures. Guadalupe is pure, receptive, and the benefits she bestows are of the same order: she consoles quiets, dries tears, calms passions. The Chingada is even more passive. Her passivity is abject: she does not resist violence, but is an inert heap of bones, blood, and dust. Her taint is constitutional and resides, as we said earlier, in her sex.[4]

Paz says little else about La Virgen, but he does historicize the latter figure: "the Chingada is a representation of the violated Mother" and therefore, "it is appropriate to associate her with the Conquest," which he considers to be "a violation, not only in the historical sense but also in the very flesh of Indian women." La Malinche becomes a "symbol of this violation," a "figure representing the Indian women who were fascinated, violated, or seduced by the Spaniards." And, in the same way that "a small boy will not forgive his mother if she abandons him to search for his father, the Mexican people have not forgiven La Malinche for her betrayal."[5] I will want to return to Paz's contrast between mistress and virgin, but first it is useful to have a parallel historical understanding of La Virgen de Guadalupe. For such an understanding we have still no better authority than the distinguished anthropologist Eric Wolf.

In a now classic article, Wolf argues that La Virgin de Guadalupe is a master symbol of and for national Mexico.[6] As a symbol having both European and Indian features, she is able to represent the collective aspirations of Mexico because she is symbolically related to both indigenous and mestizo sex roles and familial patterns. For the Indian, she reproduces the mother who provides love, warmth and nourishment, while in the more patriarchal authoritarian mestizo family, she comes to represent a counter-principle. In this second "context of adult male dominance and sexual assertion, discharged against submissive females and children ... the Guadalupe symbol is charged with the energy of rebellion against the father."[7] But, for Wolf, La Virgen de Guadalupe "is important to Mexicans not only because she is a supernatural mother, but also because she embodies their major political and religious aspirations."[8] Appearing as she does to an Indian ten years after the conquest and becoming increasingly important through the seventeenth century, the symbol affords the Indians at least some legitimization of their religious cultural heritage; perhaps more importantly, even as Guadalupe.

> ... guaranteed a rightful place to the Indians in the new social system of New Spain the myth also held appeal to the large group of disinherited who arose in New Spain as illegitimate offsprings of Spanish fathers and Indian mothers, or through impoverishment, acculturation, or loss of status within the Indian and Spanish group."[9]

Wolf implies that for all these subordinated groups, but particularly for the growing numbers of mestizos, "the Guadalupe myth came to represent not merely the guarantee of their assured place in heaven, but the guarantee of their place in society here and now." Politically, this symbolic guarantee meant that the inspired longings for a maternally fulfilled paradise eventually "gave rise to a political wish for a Mexican paradise, in which the illegitimate sons would possess the country, and the irresponsible Spanish overlords, who never acknowledged the social responsibilities of their paternity, would be driven from the land."[10] Finally,

> In this perspective, the Mexican War of Independence marks the final realization of the apocalyptic promise ...

the promise of life held out by the supernatural mother has become the promise of an independent Mexico, liberated from the irrational authority of the Spanish father-oppressors and restored to the chosen nation whose election had been manifest in the apparition of the Virgin at Tepeyac ... Mother; food, hope, health, life; supernatural salvation from oppression; chosen people and national independence--all find expression in a single symbol.[11]

Thus far I have tried only to provide you with a general exegesis of two Mexican female national symbols in relationship to early Mexican history. There is, however, another exegetical dimension which by now is possibly bordering on the obvious. I refer to the historical structuring principle clearly implicit in Paz's earlier comparative remarks and surprisingly absent in Wolf's assessment. When Paz tells us that La Malinche, as the personification of the Chingada, stands in contrast to La Virgen de Guadalupe, he is also implying that, concretely and historically, the Virgin is a redemptive symbol for both indigenous and *mestizo* Mexicans allowing them to regain both social status and moral certainty after the degradation of the Conquest symbolically expressed through Doña Marina's "betrayal." Such a redemptive function is, of course, precisely what Wolf attributes to the Virgin myth except that he inexplicably does not mention Doña Marina as the earlier contrastive symbol of Mexico's disinheritance and loss of status.

At this point it may not be amiss to wonder why such a strongly patriarchal society as Mexico articulates its early history in the symbols of femininity. I shall approach this complex issue at a later point, and in this next section, take up the relationship of Mexican femaleness to these symbols by considering feminist analyses of these two key symbols. However, let me remind you of my primary enterprise by noting an event that according to legend occurred in the still early years of the colonial period, after both Doña Marina's "betrayal" and the emergence of La Virgen de Guadalupe ten years later. Luis González Obregón tells us that at mid-sixteenth century, the residents of Mexico City "would awaken in fright to hear the sad and prolonged crying of a woman in the streets no doubt in deep moral and physical pain."[12]

Mexican Female Symbols
and Feminist Perspective

As in most of the rest of the world, a feminist intellectual discourse has been re-emerging within the Greater Mexican community at least since the mid 1960s.[13] In the specific interest and defense of Mexican women, this discourse has necessarily devoted a good deal of its attention to the critical analysis of the dominating socio-cultural structures of patriarchy. Given what we have already seen of the first two national symbols, it should come as no major surprise that they and their previous interpreters have come under such feminist critical scrutiny. In Mexico, for example, Juana Armanda Alegría has focused on the "madonna/whore" ideological implications of La Virgen de Guadalupe and La Malinche.[14] In the latter case, the alleged betrayal to Mexico by a morally weak woman has been and continues to be used to ratify the Mexican male domination of women, while in the former, a pure, maternal yet virginal figure sets the ideological standard by which real ordinary women are judged and controlled. Extending Alegría's argument across the U.S.-Mexico border, Mirandé and Enríquez tell us that "a polarized perspective of women thus emerges, whereby only La Malinche as supreme evil and La Virgen as supreme good are possible." For them, "Chicanas inherit this polarity; the ideal of virginity until marriage and saintly docility thereafter are general cultural norms, and deviations from this ideal are viewed as moral lapses."[15]

In an effort to critically counter the obvious repressive ideological effects of La Malinche, Alegría in Mexico and Adelaida Del Castillo in the United States have offered revisionist interpretations of Doña Marina's biography to show that she was a real, sensitive, intelligent woman who had to deal with Cortés under specific personal and political constraints.[16] However, as Mirandé and Enríquez conclude, "Revelations of historical data on the role of La Malinche in the Conquest will probably not temper the severity with which she continues to be treated in Mexican and Chicano culture," and one might suspect, the severity which at times, can be transferred to real women.[17]

Mirandé and Enríquez can cite no similar revisionist effort on behalf of La Virgen de Guadalupe, and I suspect that this absence is due to the richer, more complex, multi-vocalic character of this symbol, as Eric Wolf has already demonstrated for us. That is, even while she does represent idealized and possibly repressive standards of purity, she also has functioned as a symbol of popular resistance for Mexicans in general not only in 1810 but in 1910 and, in the United States, in 1965 as well. Further, she undoubtedly continues to play a complex and not entirely passive role for the marginalized women of Greater Mexico.[18] As such, it is much easier to critically pin point La Malinche as a symbolic source of repression for Mexican women, than it is to argue a parallel case for La Virgen. Nevertheless, I think it possible and necessary to argue just such a case even while recognizing the symbol's continuing potency among women, and remaining open to the restoration of the symbol's resistive powers as happened in 1965 in Delano, California during the farmworker's strike. To take this more critical view of La Virgen de Guadalupe and thus to begin to open my case for La Llorona, it is necessary to trace the historical masculinization of the Lady of Tepeyac and her subsequent incorporation into what Michel Foulcault would call the sites and discourses of power.[19]

We may begin with one of Professor Américo Paredes' subtle but important observations. "In modern Mexico," he tells us, "the Virgin of Guadalupe is not the all embracing symbol she once was ..."[20] to which we can add Victor and Edith Turner's more extended analysis. Comparing her to *nuestra Señora de los Remedios* (a lesser symbol), they tell us "that the Guadalupe pilgrimage today is far more coherently systematized and structured," and that "two major causes exist" for this systematization and structuring." On the one hand, there has been almost an excess of ecclesiastical approbation for the cultus, from the time of Bishop Zumárraga onward. On the other hand, they continue (and, I, for one, believe it is fundamentally the same patriarchal hand), because Guadalupe has served as a rallying point for Mexican nationalism, systematization of the pilgrimage has parallelled the ever-stricter organization and articulation of the republic under the Partido Revolucionario Institucional"(PRI)[21] They conclude:

> Undoubtedly the support from the Mexican hierarchy and papacy has contributed both to the popularity of the devotion among the vast majority of ordinary Mexicans and to its use as a legitimating device for the various types of Mexican nationalism.[22]

The Turners wisely recognized that such nationalism is never simple and "always alloyed with ethnic, class, and local considerations"; that there are several regional and ethnic Mexicos as well as "rich and poor Mexicos." However, from this insight they draw a too socially optimistic conclusion, namely that all of these Mexicos, particularly the last two, "find their point of convergence, their common perspective in our Lady of Guadalupe."[23] Undoubtedly they have such a convergence, but whether they have a "common perspective" that is, a common ideological interest, is quite another matter. If ideology and ideological symbolic forms are involved in the production and reproduction of social power, then in a sharply divided society such as Mexico, different class and gender interests are probably making different and contradictory symbolic uses of La Virgin at best. At worst, in the hands of a masculinized official church and the PRI, her pilgrimage at least has become almost wholly incorporated into a hegemonic ideological symbol to produce a false, pacifying maternal sense of "national unity" for those who are clearly marginalized. When powerful masculinized interests such as the Mexican Catholic Church and PRI find much to admire in a national symbol, or practice, one has to wonder whose interests are ultimately served by that symbol or practice. From a social power perspective, La Virgen de Guadalupe, it turns out, may be less "pure" and "maternal" than we thought. Further, given that the Virgen is officially sanctioned by the Church in the United States, the pacifying effect of this symbol may also play into the power relationships between Mexican-Americans and U.S. institutions.

From the preceding it should be clear that the symbol of La Malinche has played a repressive role with particular regard to women in Greater Mexican society, a role which I might now add is also more generally repressive to the extent that both women and men also find in her an easy "explanation," a scapegoat, for the ills and misfortunes of Mexico, when the real causes lie elsewhere. It should therefore come as no surprise that from the beginning, it has been principally men-in-authority who have promulgated this now highly official legend. I have already cited the authoritative Octavio Paz who discusses but does not critically deconstruct the legend, and we can also note Adelaida Del Castillo's absolutely correct attack on the equally authoritative Carlos Fuentes for his more explicit and uncritical participation in this promulgation.[24] However, in spite of this feminist critical exposure and efforts to rewrite her biography, "Social (negative) judgements of La Malinche will undoubtedly persist ..." according to Mirandé and Enríquez.[25] The case for La Virgen de Guadalupe is more complex, for even while feminist criticism has pointed to the idealized repression she represents, nonetheless, I emphasize, she has been a constant source both for women's as well as general popular resistance. With such a contradiction clearly present, her ideological uses are at best mixed, particularly in the twentieth century, and are perhaps more clearly serving the interests of social domination, given what appears to be her increased incorporation into the structures of masculinized authority on both sides of the United States-Mexico border. Such incorporations, however, are never complete and they vary historically.

We are left, then, with an irony and an empty space in the popular discourse of Greater Mexican women and of Greater Mexico in general. Ironically, these two major female symbols do not clearly serve female interests. Further, at another level they may ideologically ratify, not only the particular domination of women, but also the continuing exploitation of the Greater Mexican folk masses by a bi-national structure of power. Is there no major, popular female symbolic discourse that clearly speaks to interests of these folk masses at both of these levels? I submit there is, and we may find it in the legend of the woman whom we left cryingin the streets of Mexico City some few pages and centuries ago.

La Llorona: A Legend of Greater Mexico

La Llorona has not been accorded such a contestative and critical national purpose by her previous interpreters, although some do take us a few steps in the direction of this larger view. Later, I shall critically take up these localized interpretations; for the moment, I want to treat the more prosaic, though by no means unimportant, issues surrounding the genesis and formal definition of this legend.

The first of these concerns the origins of the legend--whether Indian or European--although most Mexicanist folklorists believe the matter to besettled. As with so much that is Mexican, we are dealing with a syncretic production. Citing Bacil F. Kirtley[26] and Robert A. Barakat,[27] Paredes, the most distinguished scholar of Mexican folklore, tell us "that it is basically a European narrative ... emphasizing a Europeanized milieu and European values." Further, and a point I shall return to later, Paredes argues that as such, La Llorona was a literary legend. Nevertheless, Professor Paredes continues, La Llorona struck deep roots in Mexican tradition because it was grafted on an Indian legend cycle about a "supernatural woman who seduces men when they are alone on the roads or working in the fields, often killing them.[28] We might also add as Kirtley does, that she was also grafted unto another distinctive Indian legend, that of Ciuacoatl, the Aztec goddess, who according to Fray Bernardino de Sahagún, appeared in the night crying out for dead children.[29] What the Europeans add are the motifs of (1) a woman with children (2) betrayed by an adulterous husband, their father, (3) a revengeful infanticide, and (4) anguished repentance during which she cries for her children. Drawing on the two previously noted traditions, the indigenous peoples add an *Indian* woman, sometimes in a flowing white dress, crying *in the night*, near a body of water (an important element in Aztec mythology), and confronting people, mostly men who are terrified when they see her.[30] After an extensive study of 120 narratives collected in Mexico City from a variety of informants representing different parts of Mexico, Fernando Horcasitas and Douglas Butterworth, employing the methods of the historic-geographic school, generate three predominant types of narratives of La Llorona, types which fit well with the European and the Indian versions and a third type representing a fusion of the two.[31] It is this third version which I take as my working ideal narrative, even while recognizing the continuation of other variants and the fluidity of narration, as I shall note later.

For even as we offer this as the full narrative, we should note that informants have not always related it as such. What they often offer are partial fragmented renditions. My examination of most of the collected narratives or summations clearly implies this composite. Bess Lomax-Hawes has pointed to this problem, even while confirming the various motifs that are often implied if not actually uttered at each narration.

> One begins to wonder, indeed, if there is a central legend; perhaps, we are dealing, rather, with a cluster of traditional elements of which the most stable may be the name of La Llorona itself, the associated act of weeping, and her appearance as a ghost in the form of a woman, almost always dangerous. Closely associated additional elements include white clothing, walking at night, appearance near water or during a rainfall, continuous searching, betrayal (sometimes *by* and sometimes *of* the central figure) and, what is the most emotionally

impressive attribute, the loss or murder of the child who is the object of the search.[32]

The result is, as Barakat correctly notes, "Mexico's most popular and diverse legend."[33] Having taken account of its origins and diverse character, it is to its popularity and its diverse character that I shall now extend my inquiry. Let us first specifically and geographically affirm Barakat's claim of popularity even while amplifying it. We know of La Llorona's narrative presence in Zacatecas, Jalisco, Sinaloa, Guanajuato, Oaxaca and Mexico City, among other places in Mexico, but we also know of her in New Mexico, Texas, Los Angeles and in southern Arizona.[34] While we know of her through a good amount of scholarly work, most of this work has been either one of collecting and identifying texts or of dealing with the aforementioned problems of origins. Ironically and contravening La Llorona's intense international popularity, she has received precious little close analytical, interpretive attention in relationship to Greater Mexican society and culture.

La Llorona: Feminist Misunderstanding and Localized Interpretations

What is available can be mostly placed into two groups of studies which I shall call historical/feminist and contextual/functionalist. The first has the virtue of offering broad understanding of La Llorona in relationship to feminist concerns paralleling those we have already seen for our first two symbols. Unfortunately these interpreters do not see a distinctive third role for La Llorona preferring instead to see her as still another version of La Malinche or in some cases, La Malinche combined with aspects of La Virgen de Guadalupe, but nonetheless, a female symbol which sanctions the domination of Mexican women. First among these is, again, Octavio Paz, for whom "The Chingada is one of the Mexican representations of maternity like La Llorona ..."[35] Other more contemporary commentators have also expanded upon this brief interpretation. Thus, in a recent general review of Mexican-American women's folklore, Rosan A. Jordan reads La Llorona as a ratification of an oppressive motherhood, an interpretation which is not only wrong in its passive understanding, but also rests on a now quite dated 1967 study based in turn on 1960 census data of Mexican-American fertility.

This dated data leads her into an historically unwarranted stereotype for the 1980s.

> It is likely that the La Llorona tradition serves as an expression of some of the fears and apprehensions they feel about being mothers and caring for children. The unresolved nature of La Llorona's plight makes her a pathetic figure even when her evil nature is stressed. And perhaps there is parallel between the eternal nature of La Llorona's fate and the seemingly unending years of motherhood the Mexican American woman undergoes. At the same time, however, the frightening figure is obviously intended as a cultural reinforcement to encourage conscientious maternal behavior in Mexican-American mothers.[36]

Similarly, though on a larger scale, Mirandé and Enríquez offer an equally passive reading, thus depriving the Chicana of a most potent symbol of resistance. For them La Llorona is

> ... a female who strayed from her proper role as mother, wife, mistress, lover, or patriot ... a woman who regrets her transgression or bemoans having been denied the fulfillment of her role ... La Llorona persists as an image of a woman who willingly or unwillingly fails to comply with feminine imperatives. As such, a moral light is cast on her, and she again reflects a cultural heritage that is relentless in its expectations of feminine role.[37]

The second group of studies--really two--are tightly contextual, ethnographically informed analyses of La Llorona in specific cultural geographic settings. While they gain some specific interpretive sense of the symbolic uses of La Llorona in particular communities, by definition they do not offer any larger interpretation for this widely popular legend. I refer to the work of Michael Kearney and Lomax-Hawes on La Llorona among Zapotec-mestizo peasants in Oaxaca and among Mexican-American delinquent girls in Los Angeles, respectively.[38]

Kearney's analysis is based on field observation and data collected in Ixtepeji, Oaxaca. His interpretive strategy is to use the full composite narrative cited earlier and to argue that it constitutes a shared symbolic projection of certain Ixtepejano cultural values which, in turn, are seen as responses to a "perceived social and geographic environment, which Ixtepejanos view as inherently hostile and constantly menacing the individual." Chief among these values is *aire* (wind) for the wind is perceived to carry evil, and *muina*, "an internalized anger, usually resulting from envy which causes people and spirits to want to harm others." Deception and treachery; (*engaño*) are the chief means of harming, and the result seems to be a pervasive sense of abandonment, suffering and fatalism although Kearney leaves this whole casual relationship unclear.[39]

From this cultural perspective, Kearney understands La Llorona to be a testament to the values of deception, treachery, abandonment (of the woman and then the children) with the entire symbolic structure as the embodiment of *aire* and motivated by *muina*. Kearney also finds a more particular function for the legend, namely as a projection of female hostility and a desire for revenge toward men. The *muina* it turns out, has a gender focus and is not sexually undifferentiated because another value *venganza* (vengeance) intervenes and focuses the projection toward a particular target. However, these men are often said to be *parranderos* (drunkards) so that Kearney also attributes a more general function to the story--to instruct in the problem of moral deviancy.

Kearney's study has a number of problems which Paredes has pointed out in the past.[40] If a narrative like La Llorona is going to carry so much interpretive weight for understanding the culture of one community, it is rather strange that Kearney was not able to collect a single local example and relies instead on the composite form. Second, Kearney clearly needed a more fluent command of Spanish to successfully carry out this fieldwork; Professor Paredes has pointed to Kearney's total misunderstanding of gender forms in Spanish, and in this particular study, Kearney tells us that she kills only male children because his informants say *hijos* and *niños*. Because they never say *hijas*, Kearney concludes they therefore must be talking about males only, not clearly understanding that *hijos* applies both to males and females unless one is speaking *only* of women. In this context *hijos* means children.[41] I stress this point, because it will prove crucial to my own interpretation.

Finally, as a member of that particular anthropological genre of peasant studies inspired by George Foster, Kearney's analysis almost wholly divorces society and history from culture. In this particular study we are told that culture is a response to "a perceived social and geographical environment ..." viewed as

411

inherently hostile" (*emphasis mine*) clearly implying that the Ixtepejanos have no evaluative, rational, historical or sociological basis for their perception. Yet, in his longer study of which La Llorona is a part, Kearney tells us that the "Ixtepejanos will readily tell you how the hard times came to them and have continued to the present day." What follows is nothing less than the repressive history of Mexico as it has forced itself upon these people to the present day, when an impersonal international market economy threatens their day-to-day living. Yet, incredibly, Kearney concludes this one page account of history and political economy with this sentence: "Apart from their historical misfortune, the Ixtepejanos perceive their current life condition in a negative light."[42] Since they themselves readily testify to the casual meaning of an oppressive history in their lives, it is difficult to see how they can perceive their conditions in a negative light "apart" from history and present economic circumstance. History and economy, I propose, form what Kearney takes as "culture," and it is intimately related to La Llorona though not in the representational, reproductive way he proposes. Later, I shall argue just the opposite, namely that La Llorona is reproductive of a counter-ideology through which women and men struggle with their life condition.

On the other hand, Lomax-Hawes implicitly acknowledges history and political economy in her fine analysis of La Llorona in a juvenile hall. Also, unlike Kearney, she relies on field collected narratives for her interpretations which, in the most tentative of ways, points us in the interpretive direction of the present paper. The girls in this juvenile hall are Black and Anglo as well as Mexican-American, although it is clear that the latter are the active bearers of the weeping woman tradition. Rather than basing her claims on a reified notion of culture as does Kearney, Lomax-Hawes offers an intriguing though limited socio-psychological reading of La Llorona's symbolic meaning for these girls. By applying a Proppian analysis to the legend, she is able to show that unlike the "traditional" tale in Propp's corpus, La Llorona does not move from a state of disequilibrium to one of equilibrium. "The state of disequilibrium" created by the woman's abandonment and the infanticide "is never corrected" as the woman spends the rest of her days crying for her children. Then, in a perceptive interpretive move, Lomax-Hawes understands this narrative's open ended structure as a symbolic means by which these girls "are signalling the basic realities of their situation"; they are producing "a rational, though disguised, reaction to a state of disequilibrium." Given their social background and the indefinite incarceration they spend in juvenile hall, these girls are "children of loss, children of need, children of lack, and tragically, it would seem that their tales are quite accurate prognoses of their probable futures ... and ... the girls of Las Palmas continue to signal the essential unwholeness of their condition."[43]

For all of its perceptiveness and acuteness of interpretation, Lomax-Hawes' essay, as I said, only implicitly addresses the sources and causes of "the essential unwholeness" of the girls' condition. Further she does not specify feminine, and for that matter the feminist relationship of La Llorona to these girls, although there is an intriguing hint of such a relationship in her conclusion when she relates a legend variant in which a ghostly mother rescues one of these girls. That is a lead I will pursue in the next section. Finally, and it is not really within her purview, Lomax-Hawes does not attempt to move beyond the confines of the juvenile hall to locate La Llorona in any wider historical context, even as she offers a brief suggestion along these lines by way of a footnote reference to a colleague who suggested to her "that La Llorona figure in Mexico might symbolize the loss of identity suffered by the native Indian population during and after the European conquest."[44] He is right, although I would and will speak of the total Mexican folk population and extend his chronology to the present day.

La Llorona: A Critical Female Legend of Greater Mexico

In the preceding I have pointed to two groups of studies which evaluate La Llorona in socio-cultural terms, and which fall short of a contestative and critical understanding and offer only historically limited, localized interpretations.[45] Neither group fully attempts to develop an interpretation which either would locate La Llorona as a more active female symbol than La Virgen and La Malinche, or locate this symbol in the social process of Mexican history as Wolf and Paz did for La Virgen and La Malinche, respectively. In this final section I will develop such a larger analysis which will argue for La Llorona as a symbol that speaks to the course of Greater Mexican history and does so for women in particular, but through the idiom of women also symbolizes the utopian longing of the Greater Mexican folk masses.

We are not entirely without precedent in this analysis, although these precedents need greater, particularly theoretical, development. I have already pointed to Kearney's negative precedent, stimulating for what it does *not* do, and to Lomax-Hawes for their intriguing, implicit leads. We also need to acknowledge other. Horcasitas and Butterworth, for example, point to an unfilled research agenda similar to that applied by Lomax-Hawes' footnoted colleague.

> The social upheavel brought about by the Spanish conquest was undoubtedly another factor which kept La Llorona alive. There seems to have been a definite place for the Weeping Woman in the troubled centuries during which the European and the native populations struggled to adapt to one another in a painful cultural, social, and racial accomodation.[46]

This points to but does not explain Ixtepeji or a juvenile hall in Los Angeles. Finally, in an anticipatory perception that comes closest to the interests of this paper, the Mexican feminist Alegría offers provocative questions and partial answers. "Why," she asks, "has this womanly phantasm prevailed in our tradition in such a salient manner?" Because "women cry," some will say. "Possibly, but this is rationalization, not explanation."

> What is the reason that the Mexican people have continued to move through their imagination the idea of a woman dressed in white? What are the mechanisms that sustain this legend?

For Alegría, the answer lies in social reality, in victimization, in vengeance, in justice; for women, yes, but as the previous quote suggests, for the "Mexican people."

> La Llorona, even before she becomes a phantasm, is a real woman, harshly mistreated, hurt, a victim; in losing her children, in her husband's betrayal, or for a thousand other reasons. As a consequence her pain knows no limits, and later endowed with "supernatural" powers, she seeks justice through vengeance, even as she makes evident the guilt of the others in her never ending cry.[47]

I want to pursue and extend these anticipatory precedents as I now come to my own interpretive analysis of this legendary figure. In response to the legend's immense popularity throughout historical and contemporary Greater Mexico, I wish to offer an analysis consonant with that popularity, one that takes us beyond localized explanations and indeed, incorporates them. I wish to consider what peasants in Oaxaca and girls in Los Angeles have in common. In response to the legend's resonance in the Mexican folk consciousness--male and female--I wish to offer an analysis that extends beyond women even while recognizing the full force of the symbol as a critical and powerful discourse on women's lives. I shall begin with this latter point and then move to a wider though no less feminist analysis.

Who is La Llorona as a critical symbol for women? Who is this female phantasm who narratively appears and reappears throughout Greater Mexico, including my own field world of south Texas? *"Pos, era esta pobre girl,"* (Well, there was this poor girl) says one of my informants in conversation with two other women and myself:

> *y mató a sus kids ... Dicen que los echó en* Lake Casablanca, and you can hear her there *en las noches*, crying and crying ... (and she killed her kids ... they say that she threw them in Lake Casablanca, and you can hear her there at night crying and crying.

"¿Por qué los mató?" (Why did she kill them?) I ask. Another woman replies: *"Pos, su* husband *la dejó por una vieja."* (Well, her husband left her for "another woman.") To which still the third woman immediately comments *"¡Qué cabrón!"* Roughly equivalent to but not synonymous with, "that bastard!"[48]

Who is La Llorona? We can easily and by contrast see what she is not. She is not consonant with Greater Mexico's "official" female legends. Here, we have, as Alegría suggests, a real woman --a lover, wife, mother and a social contradiction--whose sexual being and reproductive powers are not mystified and obscured through an officially sanctioned paradox of virgin maternity. In this respect she offers no super-human ideal which, by its very existence as a male-sponsored image, sets an oppressive standard for the evaluation of women's conduct. La Llorona is explicitly the counter-hegemonic denial of the first pole in the "madonna/whore" symbolic, ideological configuration of women.

She does kill the children and wanders the night, and not usually as a result of God's punishment although some versions do include this motif. Is this act not a basis for claiming, as Mirandé and Enríquez do, that she therefore becomes a constraining articulation of patriarchal norms for what women should do, namely take care of their children and preserve the nuclear family? I take a different view. The infanticide is not the articulation of a repressed resentment against child caring as Jordan implies, but rather the humanly understandable, if extreme and morally incorrect, reaction of a woman to sexual and familial betrayal by a man in a Mexican cultural context where such betrayal was a common and recurrent experience for women. In this act La Llorona is violating patriarchal norms, but not in any obvious superficial way which would make her a "moral" example to women. She kills because she is also living out the most extreme articulation of the everyday social and psychological contradictions created by those norms for Mexican women. To this extent, it is here that the legend poses a more fundamental oppositional threat to men because by her act she symbolically destroys the familial basis for patriarchy. However, this too may be too simple a reading because it suggests that she and women are mechanically following through Fredriech Engel's analysis of the bourgeois family. The story and the women are more complex. We must remember the most often neglected motif in this legend, namely that she also continues to search for her children near a body of water which, if I may take Freud as my authority in this feminist analysis is, in folklore, intimately associated with birth.[49] As such, I submit that La Llorona offers us a fascinating paradox: the symbolic destruction of the nuclear family at one stage, and the later possible restoration of her maternal bonds from the waters of rebirth as a second stage. One must conclude that waters will also heal her patriarchally induced insanity. I would also add that it points to the interesting image of restored world of love in which men--at least men as she experienced them--are absent.

This absence, this symbolic exclusion of men, structurally resolves the problem created by men, in the initial betrayal by the husband or the lover. It is on these grounds, therefore, that we must also object to the understanding of La Llorona, as a reinforcement of La Malinche and thereby an articulation of the other ideological pole in the "madonna/whore" complex. I have never understood this kind of interpretation offered by Paz, Mirandé and Enríquez. If anything, this story, in most of its versions, absolutely denies and reverses this most oppressive categorization of women. It is exactly an oppositional narrative to La Malinche. It is the husband who is the "whore" in this case! And, it is as a consequence of his prostitution that events are set in motion. Further, and ironically, this symbolization of men as prostitutes may, in fact, speak to a more pervasive social reality for Greater Mexico than its counter view of females. We can elaborate this point in another direction, if we take account of the often included Indian legend which has been added to the European narrative. I refer to those instances in the legend's narration when La Llorona is said to encounter men as she walks along looking for her children. We can be reminded here of Luis González-Obregón's literary account of La Llorona's effect on men in the colonial period. When the Spanish conquerors would encounter her "they became ... pale, mute and frozen like marble."[50] In various other folkloric accounts, as Kearney has noted, her effect on the men she meets is even more terrifying, at times causing their death. One of my South Texas female informants reports: *"Sí, dicen que de eso murió el Sr. Tapia; le dió un ataque cuando la vió."* (Yes, they say that's why Mr. Tapia died, he had an attack when he saw her.) It is in these encounters when La Llorona passes from betrayed grieving mother to frightening phantasm that we see what Silvia Bonvenschen calls the return of the witch, as a powerful, repressed female symbol that periodically returns in women's consciousness to "speak" for their interests against male domination.[51]

Thus far I have argued for La Llorona's critical efficacy as a powerful, contestative female symbol, basing my argument on the legend's narrative motifs. We can reinforce this argument by noting an important difference in the performers and performance contexts of this legend in comparison to the other two female symbols. In contrast to the male dominated promotion and circulation of these "official" legends, La Llorona remains largely *in the hands of women* (emphasis mine). That is, based on the available data, it is clear that it is usually women who narrate this story, although they narrate it to both male and female children primarily. I stress this point because it demonstrates that women control this expressive resource, and it therefore speaks to the greater possibility that it is articulating their own symbolic perceptions of the world.

There is still another interesting possibility that emerges from this female context of performance. La Llorona's various scholarly commentators have often noted the formal fluidity--the shifts and changes--of this narrative, often with exasperation (see Lomax-Hawes, p. 11). While this fluidity may exasperate folklorists who want a well bounded "text," it may be at the ideological center of women's lives and their organizational aesthetics. As my own South Texas fieldwork suggests, there may never be a single dominant narrator and narrative but rather a collective experience in which women seem to cooperate in developing a single story line. In a fine paper on the aesthetics of women's fiction and criticism, my colleague Joan Lidoff traces this aesthetic to a "female sensibility" which she suggests is grounded in the particular psychological development of girls, at least in Western culture.[52] Drawing on psychologist Nancy Chodorow's work, Lidoff proposes "that girls, never having to establish an opposite gender identity, never sever their original attachment to the mother as do boys." As a result, there is "a subsequent prolonged and ambivalent struggle for separation between mothers and daughters," which possibly creates a female to female paradigm of experience.

> The complexities and ambiguities of this process of differentiation remain in women's adult identities: women do not tend to see themselves as firmly delimited and discretely autonomous. More closely determined by their relations to others, maintaining a closer and less defensive relation to primitive emotional states and to feelings of dependence and vulnerability, women experience their ego boundaries as more fluid or flexible to men. This suggests that fluid conceptions of relationship between self and other, inner and outer, may be intrinsic to female sensibility. I suggest that both the relationship with mother and the sense of self and reality that develop from it are formative for women's literary style.[53]

I think that this formulation precisely describes the literary performance style of La Llorona as it has become known to folklorists, although more fieldwork remains to be done on such ethnoaesthetic issues. I am also intrigued by the replication of what Lidoff calls "fluid boundaries" in the story content itself. Here I wish to wholly exploit the notion of fluidity in its most literal and at the same time most metaphorical sense. For a female sensibility of *fluid* boundaries is precisely what is articulated in La Llorona's initial denial of her children through water; her fluid crying of tears for them and finally her implied hope of their restoration from the water-of-birth even as she herself becomes fluidity itself walking at the boundaries of the water in her flowing gown.

I propose then that in terms of its symbolism, social context and organizational aesthetics, La Llorona is an important, critical contestative performance in the everyday lives of the ordinary women of Greater Mexico. In my argument, she stands in sharp contrast to those two other symbols whose efficacy on behalf of women is at best unclear and contradictory. I could end my essay here with at least a plausible argument having been made for thinking of her as an important part of Greater Mexican women's symbolic repertoire for responding to domination rather than thinking of her as a silly fairy tale, or worse still, as a symbol through which women are further dominated. However, periodically throughout this essay, I have been promising a broader, more global analysis namely, La Llorona's relationship to all of the folk masses of Greater Mexico. If only on a demographic basis, this strikes me as a broader charter, although I now re-submit a paradoxical thesis, namely that it is through the symbolic idiom of women, particularly this woman, that men and women keep before them an unfilled and therefore potent longing for an historically denied social justice, a political unconscious.

La Llorona:
History and the Political Unconscious

The latter phrase, is not my own. I owe it and this final analysis to Fredric Jameson who in his book by the title has given us important and new ways to think about the political role of narrative in social life from a Marxist perspective.[54] For Jameson, the largest critical project is to understand how any given narrative--*Don Quixote, Heart of Darkness,* or *La Llorona* becomes a part of what he takes to be the master narrative of world history. These symbolic acts

> can recover their original urgency for us only if they are retold within the unity of a single great collective story; only if, in however disguised and symbolic a form, they are seen as sharing a single fundamental theme--for Marxism, the collective struggle to wrest a realm of Freedom from a realm of Necessity; only if they are grasped as vital episodes in a single vast unfinished plot ...

"It is," he continues, "in detecting the traces of that uninterrupted narrative, in restoring to the surface of the text the repressed and buried reality of this fundamental history, that the doctrine of a political unconscious finds its function and necessity."[55]

For Jameson each narrative (and for that matter any symbolic production) is open to an analysis which will restore its "repressed and buried reality," its "traces," into a relationship of meaning with the master narrative. To this analytical end he proposes a three fold model of analysis which demonstrates a narrative's meaning in increasingly wider social contexts of "horizons," although in this discussion I shall take up only the first two.[56] These are, first that of "political history, in the narrow sense of punctual event and a chronicle-like sequence of happenings in time." By this slightly pejorative formulation, Jameson does not mean to diminish the importance of this interpretive level where symbolic acts may offer imaginary resolutions of real and localized social contradictions. For Jameson such resolutions are provided both through the formal aesthetic organization of such acts and their symbolic contents.[57]

The social contradictions presented at this level are relatively manifest to those who experience them. Correspondingly, these contradictions are rendered and resolved at a fairly conscious level in the symbolic act. We can illustrate and use this first interpretive horizon with our materials, for I would argue that the emergence of La Llorona in the colonial period and her persistence today presents just such an enduring and clear imaginary resolution to the immediate, concrete, social contradiction presented to women by Greater Mexico's patriarchal history. This imposed contradiction, itself articulated through the iconic signs of madonna and whore, is addressed and resolved through the historically continuous mythic projection of a "real" woman who, as I suggested earlier, experiences the effects of this contradiction and resolves it through the narrative's formal structure. We begin with the presence of patriarchy and conclude with its exclusion in favor of an implied, utopian female centered community of real maternity and love. As such the narrative initially reproduces but ultimately negates the political history of women in Greater Mexico--"the chronicle-like sequence of happenings in time" as written by males is the history of women's domination. As Jameson further suggests, "the literary work or cultural object, as though for the first time, brings into being that very situation to which it is also, at one and the same time, a reaction. It articulates its own situation and textualizes it ..."[58]

Such a resolution, however, while terribly important as part of the political unconscious, speaks only to the political unconscious of women and to the obvious and compelling social contradiction posed for women. But, I remain intrigued as I once was haunted by La Llorona when, as a child, I listened to my grandmother's and aunts' recounting of her story. For, notwithstanding Kearney's mistaken comments on male children, and my own earlier commentary on the female definition of La Llorona, it is clear that, as children, both females and males constitute the usual audience for these performances, and, it seems reasonable to assume they keep the story in their collective consciousness. As my anthropologist colleague, Carlos Vélez, reports from his own childhood in southern Arizona, "Listening to the sounds of heavy breathing outside in the yard at night, covered by clean white sheets, we children whispered stories of La Llorona ..."[59] These children, I will remind you, are generally the Greater Mexican folk masses. I suggest we have a more global participation in this narrative, one, that, in Mexico, is constituted and defined by class, and the other in the United States by class and ethnicity. In this class context I would argue that La Llorona also speaks to these at least demographically wider interest in a Greater Mexican context. How is it possible, for this decidedly female legend to also articulate such class interest? We can see this interpretive possibility if we now take up Jameson's second horizon of meaning for narrative as a socially symbolic act, together with what careful students of Mexican society have told us about gender, class and power. As I have already begun suggesting, this second interpretive horizon which Jameson calls the "social" becomes operative "only at the moment in which the organizing categories of analysis become those of social class," more particularly the antagonistic and active relationship between "a dominant and a laboring class" whose ideologies and symbolic acts are also involved in an active, dialectical and antagonistic relationship.

> A ruling class ideology will explore various strategies for the legitimation of its own power position, while an oppositional culture or ideology will, often in covert and disguised strategies, seek to contest and to undermine the dominant "value system."

Following Bakhtin, Jameson stresses the dialogical character of this relationship and its articulation through "the general unity of a shared code," shared that is by the active, antagonistic contestants although rendered in distinct *paroles* of conflicting symbolic, ideological interests.[60]

In this kind of class-based analysis "the individual utterance or text is grasped as a symbolic move in an essentially polemic and strategic ideological confrontation between classes ..." It is, however, an uneven symbolic confrontation from the perspective of global power. Because of the class nature and authority of writing, Jameson implies (echoing Foucault) that "the cultural monuments and masterworks that have survived tend necessarily to perpetuate only a single voice in this class dialogue, the voice of a hegemonic class ..." What is required at this level of analysis is the interpretive reconstruction of the voice of the dominated, "a voice for the most part stifled and reduced to silence, marginalized, its own utterances scattered to the winds, or reappropriated in their turn by hegemonic culture."[61] (We are forced immediately to think here of La Llorona, "marginalized, its own utterances scattered to the winds" and of the reappropriation of the once wholly subservient Virgin of Guadalupe). At this interesting juncture in his exposition, Jameson sub-consciously recognizes the power of what so many of us call *folklore* although he cannot name it, an interesting historical repression in itself. It is in this "framework" he tells us,

> in which the reconstruction of so-called popular cultures must properly take place--most notably, form the fragments of essentially peasant cultures: folksongs, fairy tales, popular festivals, occult or oppositional systems of belief such as magic and witchcraft ... only an ultimate rewriting of these utterances in these terms of their essentially polemic and subversive strategies restores them to their proper place in the dialogic system of social class.[62]

Let me attempt such a rewriting of La Llorona even while objecting, as Jane Marcus has also done,[63] to Jameson's own patriarchal tendency, a tendency which implicitly devalues that which is stifled, silenced and scattered until it is reconstructed, clearly rewritten and allowed to speak. (It is also, by the way, an impulse in much contemporary systematizing intellectual discourse.) With a more fluid approach, La Llorona has a polemic and subversive place in the dialogic system of social classes in Greater Mexico, although as Jameson recognizes, at this level of analysis, symbolic practices such as La Llorona are often, "covert and disguised strategies," addressing social class contradictions in more indirect and therefore more richly symbolic and multi-vocal fashion than at the first level.

We can begin our analysis with the late Victor Turner's observation derived directly from his understanding of Mexican history. He tells us that "at a deeper structural level," when social power is sharply mal-distributed between two groups and where, such as in Mexico, both groups

> regard masculinity and patriliny as the sources of authority, legitimacy, office, economic wealth, and every kind of structural continuity, the unity, continuity, and countervailing "power of the weak", the sentiment of ultimate wholeness of the total community, is often assigned to female, especially to maternal symbols ...[64]

As Turner correctly argued and Wolf before him, in colonial Mexico, this countervailing sentiment was assigned initially to La Virgen de Guadalupe by those not in power, principally Indians but also mestizos. However, I have already pointed to the problematic character of this assignment into our own time. In comparison to the increasingly compromised and official role of La Virgen, La Llorona has remained folkloric, as she was in the beginning, a maternal female symbol that speaks from and to the "wholeness of the total community" and articulates the countervailing power of those masses who on a class basis are rendered "weak" in Greater Mexican society. How does she articulate this disguised subversive mission to those who continue to disempower the weak of Greater Mexico not only structurally but culturally as well? We may continue our interpretive rewriting not initially with the "text" but by first grasping the symbolic class implications of the social production and context of the narrative. In this production, no masculine pope, PRI, or president intervenes at an ideological distance. As I suggested earlier, the shaping of this story is fundamentally guided by a woman's sensibility that encourages fluid boundaries. However, read at the second level of class relations, this folkloric mode of production also offers for all of its participants the social reality and symbol of collective democratic action for all manner of production "according to the laws of beauty" as Marx once said.[65] Even as the first words of the story emerge, it becomes a collective birth which in its gradual disclosures speaks to a different principle of social organization inherently antagonistic to the alienating, individualistic and hierarchical principals of capitalist commodity production, (a continuing tension in Greater Mexican cultural life).

But, of course, finally we do have a narrative "text" which begins usually with the betrayal of the woman by her adulterous husband which can be understood at the level of class relations. If Turner is right in his correlation of patriarchy and political/class power, then we cannot help but also understand this motif of sexual betrayal as a masculinized/feminized symbolic reproduction of class and power distinctions extant since the colonial period. In the early phase of this period, as La Llorona emerges, sexuality and social power are almost too painfully and intimately correlated. (There is no need for a Michel Foucault here to interpret this awful literality.) The Spanish male colonials forced themselves upon Indian women in a series of adulterous relationships, which, in addition to their terrible trauma for women, also had the class effect of reproducing a new mestizo labor force to continuously replace the devoured by mines and consumed on plantations. This, while infecting all with disease and the debilitating ideological "knowledge" that they were all "hijos de la chingada" (children of whores). And, indeed, one early colonial version of La Llorona reported by Frances Toor specifically correlates class and women. A woman of lower class origins, (Indian?) "a pretty but humble maiden named Luisa" is betrayed by a lover "of high society" who has fathered her children. In this more European version she kills the children with a dagger and then walks crying in the night in insane torment.[66]

By the eighteenth century when, according to Jaime E. Rodríguez O., social relations had become clearly capitalistic,[67] masculinized authority and class power remained intimately correlated; and the identification of the socially weak with the maternal femininity of La Virgen de Guadalupe, begun in 1531 had, according to Wolf, taken increasing hold. Indeed, in 1810, as we have seen, she contributed to Mexico's momentary effort to find herself, an effort soon thwarted.

The nineteenth century offered little change in social relations. There are two moments of hope: 1810, and the brief ascendancy of liberalism from 1858 to 1876. In both cases it is interesting to note, the efforts are led by, first Miguel Hidalgo, a priest, and therefore not a "full" man in the narrow patriarchal sense of the term; second, in 1861 we see a liberalism led by Benito Juárez, a Zapotec Indian who as governor of Oaxaca supported the education of women. However, both of these efforts are relatively brief; another kind of man, patriarchal and authoritarian dominated Mexico in the nineteenth century as she continued her increasingly capitalistic course. Of these the most patriarchal and authoritarian is Santa Anna who, for a bribe, abandoned the Mexicans to their fateful encounter with the United States. He also managed to plunge his own country into a social degradation exceeded perhaps only by that created by the second such figure, Don Porfirio Diaz. Ruling autocratically in the late nineteenth century, Diaz made necessary the Revolution of 1910 that forced many impoverished Mexicans across the border, while many others died in Mexico crying *tierra y libertad* (land and liberty) and waving the banner of La Virgen de Guadalupe. And even as they still honored the female symbol, the folk masses, those who left and those who stayed, continued to tell another story of a woman who is betrayed by an immoral man. As the masses waited for *tierra y libertad* after the Revolution, Mexico continued its patriarchal politics as it plunged ahead into advanced capitalism and mass poverty. In the twentieth century, according to Paredes, we can also note the mass media sponsored emergence of the cult of the macho in Greater Mexico.[68] More Mexicans continued to come into the United States even as the Mexican-Americans experienced their own poverty and the new trauma of racism. Today, amidst presidential proclamations of "the year of the Hispanic" and the immense popularity of Mexican food, malnutrition and health in general continue to be severe problems in many parts of Mexican America, along with bad education, and limited social representation. Unfortunately, we can also see some elements of the newly emerging masculinized "Hispanic" leadership applying the politics of betrayal of the Anglo patriarchs, a politics that the urban masses and the *campesinos* of Mexico know only too well.[69] As my informant said, "Pos, su husband la dejó por una vieja." (Well, her husband left her for another woman.)

But our story doesn't stop with betrayal. Why, as a consequence of this betrayal, does this Mexican "woman" commit insane infanticide? What is the social meaning of this awesome, compelling murder, especially when taken in the cultural context of Mexican motherhood? If we pursue the logic of my symbolic social class reading, we can only conclude that woman (Mexico) has engaged in a form of social infanticide. This "infanticide," projected in awe onto La Llorona is as a consequence, a now pervasive but induced national malaise, a perhaps temporary insanity *produced historically by those who socially dominate.*

From the beginning when Cortés persuaded the other Indian tribes to help bring down the Aztecs (only to betray them also), to periodic blood lettings called "revolutions," dominated by powerful interests, the Greater Mexican folk masses, in displaced response to domination and scarcity, have inflicted great injury to themselves and to their future social interests. They have hurt themselves not only in these periodic paroxysms of misled "revolutionary" violence but also in less dramatic, more enduring ways synonymous with alienation in a capitalist culture. I refer to the everyday masculinized ethic of *chingar* in which, according to Eric Wolf, "men expect hostility and aggression from others, so they rise to defend themselves with hostility and aggression" and "personal encounters thus become daily dramas in which the participants transcend the limits of the workday world through gestures of potency or submission."[70] In critical retrospect we can now also see how *muina*, the "internalized anger ... which causes people ... to want to harm others" in Kearney's Ixtepeji may also be this sort of violence produced, not "inherently" or from "envy," but rather by history. Mexico experienced history, "y mató a sus kids" (and she killed her kids).

We hasten to re-emphasize that all of this tendency toward violence is no culturalist Mexican "fascination with death" as an Octavio Paz might have it. Perhaps it is more like an Ilongot headhunter of Northern Luzon. When anthropologist Renato Rosaldo asked him why he took heads, he replied that rage born of grief impells him to kill his fellow human beings. Rosaldo continues: "The act of severing and tossing away the victim's head enables him, he says, to vent and hopefully throw away the anger of his bereavement."[71] The headhunter recovers from his grief through ritualized killing, but in the case of Greater Mexico that also grieves, it would strain the comparison to claim that its "killing" has meant ritual recovery. I leave that kind of masculine poetic understanding for Paz who thinks of bloody revolutions as "fiestas of bullets."[72]

Yet there is a possible, implied, an utopian recovery from insanity in our symbolic social narrative. The feminine Mexico of the weak is not left in a state of mindless, unritualized violence and insanity, but Kearney, interested only in the symbolic reproduction of violence, says little about this next step in the narrative. La Llorona grieves and searches for her children whose recovery is made tantalizingly possible because their death by water is ambiguous, for it is also the water of rebirth. I will remind you that this crucial water motif was added to the basic European narrative by the first weak ones in Mexican history, the subjugated indigenous people. It is not enough to grieve--too many Virgin Marys do that; a subversive symbolic strategy must hold out some possibility of recovery, and it is through the vital insertion of this motif that the indigenous peoples seemed to articulate their own possibilities; later these possibilities are transferred to the rest of Mexico's subjugated who are left in possession of few things among them this story. This Mexico of the weak, after infanticide, recognizes its plight and continues to walk near the waters of its own social rebirth, although this resolution is left open, utopian, and therefore artistically compelling as a symbolic ideological charter. We can now also sense the social resonance of Bess Lomax-Hawes' unconsciously haunting language. Like the girls of Las Palmas, the Greater Mexican folk masses are "children of loss, children of need, children of lack" who, through their narrative, "signal the essential unwholeness of their condition." Potentially, they are also grieving, haunting mothers reaching for their children across fluid boundaries. But, let us finish our story; *dice la gente* (the people say) that men often meet this woman who terrifies and sometimes kills them. This is still another motif, the Ciuacoatl legend, added by the indigenous peoples and illustrating, as does the water motif, Jameson's observation on the way ideological struggles occur within "the general unity of a shared code." In this instance, conceptions of the female and of legend (literature vs. folklore, in the latter case). Symbolically, this motif seems to suggest that the utopian renewal of a recovered Mexico with her children pointedly excludes the reappearance of a masculinized, hierarchical, treacherous class authority. Power as patriarchy must be destroyed if a new social order is to re-emerge and survive in Greater Mexico, one that, in the most powerful kind of feminism, speaks not only of women but through the power of women for *all* of the socially weak.

La Llorona. Her story and ours come to an end, and it is not clear that Greater Mexico will ever find her children; only the compelling utopian possibility is held out at the end of the day's work, night after dark night, in each retelling of the flowing white gown and the unanswered lament, a story whispered in a thousand vital places along the many arteries from Michoacán to Michigan, from Oaxaca to the Yakima, from Tlaxcala to Tucson; "*pos, era esta pobre girl*" and, I have interpretively suggested, "*era esta pobre gente*" (there were these poor people). No virgin or whore was she or they; only--and this is enough--socially produced and betrayed historical subjects in search of their community through their own symbolic idiom of women. Should this reunion in rejection of patriarchal class power ever take place, well ... I too will leave my story open except to complete my initial poetic epigraph by that most bardic and prophetic of our Chicano poets, the Mexican born Alurista, who, in his far better poetic art, anticipated this prosaic paper many years ago.

MUST BE THE SEASON OF THE WITCH

must be the season of the witch
the witch
la llorona
she lost her children
and she cries
in the ravines of industry
her children
devoured by computers
and the gears
must be the season of the witch
i hear bones crack
in pain
and sobbing
the witch pangs
her children have forgotten
the magic of *durango*
and that of *moctezuma*
--the *huiclamina*
must be the season of the witch
the witch cries
her children suffer: without her[73]

Notes

1. I shall use the phrase "Greater Mexico" and "Greater Mexican" to refer to the peoples of Mexican descent on both sides of the Mexico-United States border. It is intended to highlight those common cultural elements such as the symbols discussed in this paper and common socio-historical experiences such as the Mexican Revolution and immigration. It does not assume an absolutely homogeneous culture. As with so much else in my intellectual and political formation, I take the concept from Américo Paredes.

2. Octavio Paz, *The Labyrinth of Solitude: Life and Thought in Mexico* (New York: Grove Press, 1961).

3. Ibid., p. 75.

4. Ibid., p. 85.

5. Ibid., p. 86.

6. Eric R. Wolf, "The Virgen de Guadalupe: A Mexican National Symbol," *Journal of American Folklore* 71 (1958): 34-39.

7. Ibid., p. 36.

8. Ibid., p. 37.

9. Ibid.

10. Ibid., pp. 37-38.

11. Ibid., p. 38.

12. Luis González-Obregón, *Las Calles de Mexico* (Mexico D.F.: Botas, 1936), p. 18. The translation is my own.

13. For an example of early feminist politics within the Mexican American community, see my "El Primer Congreso Mexicanista de 1911: A Precursor to Contemporary Chicanismo," *Aztlán: International Journal of Chicano Studies Research* (Summer 1974): 85-117. See also references 14-15 below.

14. Juana Armanda Alegría, *Sicología de las Mexicanas* (Mexico D.F.: Editorial Diana).

15. Alfredo Mirandé and Evangelina Enríquez, *La Chicana: The Mexican American Woman* (Chicago: The University of Chicago Press, 1979), p. 28.

16. Adelaida R. Del Castillo, "Malintzín Tenépal: A Preliminary Look into a New Perspective" in *Essays on La Mujer*, eds. Rosaura Sánchez and Rosa Martínez Cruz, Anthology No. 1 (Los Angeles: UCLA Chicano Studies Center Publications, 1977), pp. 124-149.

17. Mirandé and Enríquez, p. 29.

18. Victor Turner, "Hidalgo: History as Social Drama" in his *Dramas, Fields, and Metaphors: Symbolic Action in Human Society* (Ithaca: Cornell University Press); Kay Turner, "Mexican American Home Altars: Towards Their Interpretation," *Aztlán: International Journal of Chicano Studies Research* 13 (1982): 309-326.

19. Michel Foulcault, *Power/Knowledge: Selected Interviews and Other Writings, 1972-1977*, ed. Colin Gordon (New York: Pantheon Books), pp. 78-108.

20. Américo Paredes, "Mexican Legendry and the Rise of the Mestizo" in *American Folk Legend: A Symposium*, ed. Wayland D. Hand (Berkeley and Los Angeles: University of California Press), p. 101.

21. Victor Turner, and Edith Turner, *Image and Pilgrimage in Christian Culture* (Oxford: Basil Blackwell), p. 93.

22. Ibid., p. 94.

23. Ibid.

24. Del Castillo, p. 140.

25. Mirandé and Enríquez, p. 31.

26. Bacil F. Kirtley, "La Llorona and Related Themes," *Western Folklore* 19 (1960): 155-168.

27. Robert A. Barakat, "Aztec Motifs in La Llorona," *Southern Folklore Quarterly* 29 (1965): 288-296.

28. Paredes, p. 103.

29. Fray Bernardino de Sahagún, *Historia general de las cosas de Nueva España*, Vol. 3 (México, D.F.: Nueva España), p. 25.

30. Barakat, see note 27.

31. Fernando Horcasitas and Douglas Butterworth, "La Llorona," *Tlalocan: Revista de Fuentes para el Conociento de las Culturas Indígenas de México* 4 (1963): 204-224.

32. Bess Lomax-Hawes, "La Llorona in Juvenile Hall," *Western Folklore* 27 (1968): 153-170.

33. Barakat, p. 288.

34. Elaine K. Miller, *Mexican Folk Narrative from the Los Angeles Area* (Austin: University of Texas Press, 1973); Betty Leddy, "La Llorona in Southern Arizona," *Western Folklore* 7 (1948): 272-277.

35. Paz, p. 75.

36. Rosan A. Jordan, "The Vaginal Serpent and Other Themes from Mexican-American Women's Role" in *Women's Folklore, Women's Culture*, eds. Rosan A. Jordan and Susan J. Kalcik (Philadelphia: University of Pennsylvania Press, 1985), pp. 26-44.

37. Ibid., p. 33.

38. Lomax-Hawes, pp. 153-190; Michael Kearney, "La Llorona as a Social Symbol," *Western Folklore* 27 (1968): 199-206.

39. Kearney, p. 20.

40. Américo Paredes, "On Ethnographic Work Among Minority Groups: A Folklorist's Perspective," in *New Directions in Chicano Scholarship*, eds. Raymund A. Paredes and Ricardo Romo (La Jolla: Chicano Studies Center University of California at San Diego), pp. 1-32.

41. Kearney, p. 204.

42. Michael Kearney, *The Winds of Ixtepeji: World View and Society in a Mexican Town* (New York: Holt, Rinehart, and Winston, 1972), p. 6.

43. Lomax-Hawes, p. 170.

44. Ibid., p. 165.

45. Generally I suggest, as I do here particularly, that we do not have to abandon these local interpretations; rather, we have to reincorporate them at other meaningful levels of context and information. In this respect I am influenced by Richard Bauman, "The Field Study of Folklore in Context," in *Handbook of American Folklore*, ed. Richard M. Dorson (Bloomington: Indiana University Press, 1983), pp. 362-368, and Victor W. Turner, "Forms of Symbolic Action," *Proceedings of the 1969 Annual Spring Meeting of the American Ethnological Society*, ed. Robert F. Spencer (Seattle: University of Washington Press, 1969), pp. 3-25.

46. Horcasitas and Butterworth, p. 223.

47. Alegría, p. 120-121.

48. Field notes: Three Adult Mexican American Women, Lower Middle Class (Laredo, Texas), June 18, 1981.

49. Sigmund Freud, *A General Introduction to Psychoanalysis* (New York: Washington Square Press, 1964), p. 168.

50. González-Obregón, p. 18.

51. Silvia Bovenschen, "The Contemporary Witch, the Historical Witch, and the Witch Myth: The Witch Subject of the Appropriation of Nature and Object of the Domination of Nature," *New German Critique* 15 (1978): 83-119.

52. Joan Lidoff, "Her Mother's Voice: Reading Towards a Feminist Poetics, Tillie Olsen and Grace Paley" Unpublished Ms. To appear as part of Joan Lidoff, *Fluid Boundaries: The Origins of a Distinctive Women's Voice in Literature* (Chicago: University of Chicago Press, forthcoming).

53. Ibid., p. 5.

54. Fredric Jameson, *The Political Unconscious: Narrative as a Socially Symbolic Act* (Ithaca: Cornell University Press, 1981).

55. Ibid., pp. 19-20.

56. At the third horizon Jameson would have us understand narrative in terms of its contribution to the course of universal class history defined as a dialectical contestation between different mode of production. Here, however, for the sake of argumentative coherence and specificity, I wish to address only Greater Mexican history in sexual and class terms.

57. Ibid., p. 79.

58. Ibid., p. 82.

59. Carlos G. Vélez-Ibáñez "Ourselves Through the Eyes of an Anthropologist," in *The Chicanos as We See Ourselves*, ed. Arnulfo D. Trejo (Tucson: University of Arizona Press, 1979), p. 41.

60. Jameson, p. 84.

61. Ibid., p. 85.

62. Ibid., pp. 85-86.

63. Jane Marcus, "Storming the Toolshed," in *Feminist Theory: A Critique of Ideology*, eds. Nannerl O. Keohane, Michelle, Z. Rosaldo and Barbara C. Gelpi (Chicago: University of Chicago Press, 1982) p. 220.

64. Turner, "Hidalgo: History as Social Drama," p. 152.

65. Karl Marx, from *The Economic and Philosophic Manuscripts in The Marx-Engels Reader*, ed. Robert C. Tucker (New York: Norton), p. 76.

66. Frances Toot, *A Treasury of Mexican Folkways* (New York: Crown Publishers, 1947), p. 532.

67. Jaime E. Rodríguez O., *Down From Colonialism: Mexico's Nineteenth Century Crisis* (Los Angeles: UCLA Chicano Studies Research Publications, 1983).

68. Américo Paredes, "Estados Unidos, México y el machismo," *Journal of Inter-American Studies* 9 (1967): 65-84.

69. The section from pages 28 to 30 draws from and combines these sources: Michael C. Meyer and William L. Sherman, *The Course of Mexican History* (New York: Oxford University Press, 1979); James D. Cockcroft, *Mexico: Class Formation, Capital Accumulation and the State* (New York: Monthly Review Press, 1983); Roger D. Hansen, *The Politics of Mexican Development* (Baltimore: John Hopkins University Press, 1971); Carlos G. Vélez-Ibáñez, *Rituals of Marginality: Politics, Process, and Cultural Change in Urban Central Mexico* (Berkeley: University of California Press, 1983); Rodolfo Acuña, *Occupied America: A History of Chicanos*, 2nd. Ed. (New York: Harper and Row, 1981).

70. Eric R. Wolf, *Sons of the Shaking Earth* (Chicago: The University of Chicago Press, 1959).

71. Renato Rosaldo, "Grief and a Headhunter's Rage: On the Cultural Force of Emotions" in *Text, Play, and Story: The Construction of Self and Society*, ed. Edward M. Bruner, 1983 Proceedings of the American Ethnological Society (Washington, D.C.: American Ethnological Society, 1984), p. 178.

72. Octavio Paz, p. 148.

73. Alurista, "must be the season of the witch" in *Fiesta in Aztlan: Anthology of Chicano Poetry* (Santa Barbara: Capra Press, 1981), p. 83. This poem was first published in 1971.

"THEY DIDN'T CALL THEM 'PADRE' FOR NOTHING": PATRIARCHY IN HISPANIC CALIFORNIA

by

Douglas Monroy

Introduction

It is clear the sexual substratum of society influences history. Social historians, though, will probably never agree about precisely how this sexual dialectic compels history nor how history transformed specific aspects of sexual power relations. We know the emergence of capitalism and liberal social relations altered women's relationship to production, as the family economy on the private or communally owned farm became the husband's business, or when both husband and wife became wage workers. Yet, all the while, women's relationship neither to reproduction nor to their patriarchs changed fundamentally. Certainly the domination of women predates private property and the labor market. How this father-rule influenced class, caste, and racial hierarchies is an increasingly debated question of theoretical and political significance.

For social history this challenging issue has practical value as well. An exploration of the specifics of the patriarchal relations of Spanish and Mexican California contribute at once to our understanding of Mexican women in the United States and to our understanding of patriarchy, the most universal set of power relations. This study attests to how broader patterns of subjugation, in which various forms of sexual dominance figure substantially, emerge, at least in good part, form the rule of men. By viewing patriarchy in its historical context, we begin to define and understand more precisely the nature of this institution.

Patriarchy, the vise which has constricted the development of women in history, is rendered by men without much regard for color of skin, economic position, or historical period in which it takes place. As the white European slave-owner profoundly influenced the history of the African slave in America, so too have men substantially generated the weighty historical circumstances in which the history of all women has evolved. While resistance to male despotism and degree of autonomy women have created for themselves vary from culture to culture and historical epoch to historical epoch, an understanding of women's roles calls for not only an investigation into how women impelled history for themselves and society in general, but also a critical history of men as the creators of patriarchy. By no means, however, should such inquiry further the impression that men are the primary subjects of history and women the objects. Indeed the tension between the desires and activities of women and patriarchal stricture seems to provide as much fuel for the engine of history as class or race.

As much fuel or more fuel? To what extent do the omnipresent racial and economic dominations emerge from patriarchy? Capitalists, lords, *hacendados*, and slave-holders, *indio caciques* and Spanish priests, Californio *rancheros* and Anglo ranchers were, after all, men. To what extent did priests, *conquistadores*, and capitalist ranchers dominate Indians as economic exploiters and to what extent did they do so as men? To what extent is the racially-organized economic domination of Mexicans and Indians sexual as well? Are sexual and economic forms of domination part of the same male cultural construct? The evidence presented in this paper about Spanish and Mexican California suggests that domination was significantly patriarchal and that specific forms of this domination proceeded largely from the model of the power relations which prevailed between men and women. While the exigencies of Yankee capitalism and Spanish feudalism produced expansion into California, the conquerors' maleness figures fundamentally in the form and content of that conquest.

Weaponry and physical force are only one element of conquest. Historically, one nation conquers another not only through military force but by the domination of a people's most intimate activity as in the conquest of women by men through coerced sex. La Malinche (Cortez's Indian consort and translator) was hardly the only one to so succumb. The sexual exploitation of slave women by their Southern gentlemen masters is also well known. In war it is generally assumed victorious soldiers will rape and pillage. But is this a reward or an integral part of the conquest? The modern-day United States effort to subjugate Vietnam entailed the sexual conquest of Vietnamese women. White, Black and Latino soldiers dehumanized them and saw these women as theirs for the taking. When has sexual terror not accompanied military conquest? Surely it seems to be an ancillary aspect of conquest because such terror conveys a message of total powerlessness to the vanquished.[1]

Domination, of course, is more than military force; the vanquished internalize the power relations. The conquest of intimacy most effectively creates the despair of resistance which enables the conquerors to continue to dominate and exploit after the guns are put away. It is harder for conquered men to pound their chests in defiance if they have been rendered powerless by losing their control over "their" women. Spain's conquest of California proved no different. Particular men controlled native sexuality.

Sex and Sin

The Spanish colonialization of California began in earnest in 1769. Fearful of encroachment from other powers, especially Russia, Spain sought to transform the native population into loyal subjects of His Catholic Majesty, the King of Spain. To this end, the Indians were converted to Christianity, taught Spanish and farming in a "civilized," sedentary manner, and expected to adopt Christian sexual mores. Gifts and soldiers induced the semi-nomadic Indians to come to the missions. While the priests continually pleaded for moral men to replace the reckless adventurers, the governor pleaded for civility on the part of the soldiers towards Indian women. It was not uncommon for soldiers to be severely punished for transgressions against women for it is clear that in Spanish California soldiers exerted their power over women. The priests constantly complained about how such license countered their efforts. Bancroft tells how the Spanish acquired converts at Mission San Gabriel: the soldiers "pursued them to their *rancherías*, where they lassoed women for their lust and killed such males as dared to interfere." Syphilis, introduced by soldiers, seems to have caused more Indian deaths than any other disease.

All was not rape and pillage. Many soldiers married Indian women, who undoubtedly gained personal prestige from such marriages. Yet civilization for many Indians meant men were killed in raids, women raped, and their children brought up in the missions, where they were hispanicized.[2]

Priests were concerned with restraining sexuality and controlled it forcefully. In California, they confronted their antithesis. Priests were sexually restrained, punctual, monotheistic, sedentary, and bent on accumulating wealth for the missions. What they did was, of course, virtuous. What the Indians did, largely the opposite, was, of course, sinful. The Indians were everything the Europeans had been trying to transcend and/or repress. The padres, like most European fathers, already knew how to treat people whose sexuality and general lack of control threatened their "civilized" state. They had conquered "carnal lust" in Europe by terrorizing and persecuting women who realized Satan's will through their "insatiable" desire. Clearly, sexuality was a fearful, if not a satanic issue for these fathers. In New Spain they confronted primitive and apparently uncontrolled, infantile beings who represented that over which their civilization thought it had triumphed. Any ambivalence on their part about their own victory over instinct could be submerged in the rigorous control of someone else--the Indian "children." Transgressions, including sexual ones, were punished "with the authority which Almighty God concedes to parents for the education of their children," said Friar Tapis of Mission Santa Barbara. All "children," both biological and spiritual, became desexualized in European culture. Said Father Abella, "The Indians did not care for their health, but like every son of Adam, pined for freedom and women." Subsequently, civilization for the Indians according to these priests meant, among other things, Indians would have to be restrained sexually.[3]

If fathers enforced sexual restraint with lock and key friars secured the chastity of Indian maidens by also locking them up. Class tensions do not seem to have produced sufficient anxiety among property holders that they felt the need to make fast their private property. There seems to have been enough material goods in bounteous early California for all. The padres perceived, instead, too much sex and, thus, felt the need to lock Indian maidens in the *monjero*, "secure against any insult." The young women could not come out except during daylight.[4] While such "protection" certainly saved many women from the outrage of soldiers, its primary intent is clear. These fathers dominated Native Americans by controlling what padres feared to be unrestrained, satanic sexuality.

In response *indios* expressed resentment at this policy and rebelled on occasion. One incident at Mission Santa Cruz is particularly illustrative of the extent of their dissatisfaction. In October 1812, the neophytes, fearing that Padre Quintana had ordered an iron strap to punish fornication and theft, apprehended the padre, castrated him and left him for dead. And, as if to add insult to injury, while Padre Quintana expired his attackers unlocked the *monjero*, let out the women "y se juntaron jovenes de los dos sexos y tuvieron su diversión," recalled an eyewitness to the orgy which followed.[5] Needless to say, this kind of reaction by the Indians was not common; Padre Quintana died and those responsible were severely punished. Generally, the enforcement of European sexual mores was successful, although victims were not willing participants.

The psycho-sexual dynamics of the usually celibate, sometimes profligate, ever tortured fathers and their relatively promiscuous charges are something bewildering to unravel. It is unlikely that the Franciscans simply and naively sought to elevate the Indians to their civilized level. Human motivation is inevitably more complex. Punishing Indians for sex, Satan's nefariousness, undoubtedly enhanced the fathers' righteousness. They also gained status in Heaven by purifying society of people whose actions affronted the Europeans' God; ideally, if not actually, restraining the Indians appeased His wrath. These men not infrequently punished Indians with a severity which bordered on sadism. While perhaps merely justifying the righteousness of their civilizing mission, whipping *indios* with a wire-flecked cat-o'-nine-tails for sexual transgressions conjures up an image of a powerfully ambivalent sexuality expressed as pious, paternal, corporal punishment.

In the same manner that the European fathers made the youngest people as dependent as women with the invention of childhood, so too the California padres made Indians into dependent children.[6] By converting Indians to Christianity and settled agricultural ways, the padres undermined their economic and cultural foundations. The California Indians now depended upon the mission system for physical and emotional sustenance and interaction. They were children not only in the worldview of the European Franciscans but in their actual dependency. While trying to sever Indians from the bosom of Mother Nature so they might "grow up" to civilization, the padres succeeded only in making them infantile.

The Patriarchal Don

Growing alongside the mission system of populating Alta California were the *ranchos* and the *pueblos*. In both its economic and social relations, the *rancho* mirrored the feudal manor. A system of reciprocal obligations, protections, and privileges prevailed throughout society.[7] The *ranchero*, or Don, ruled his family and Indian laborers firmly, personally, and often benevolently. The *ranchero* patriarch exacted thoroughgoing submission from his wife, children, and *indios*. In exchange, he was to rule benignly and provide for his underlings. In the same manner that Indians allegedly submitted to the padres in exchange for security, tutelage, and salvation, women also received protection. Civil authorities could, and often did, severely punish rape and desertion. And on the *ranchos*, fathers locked up their unmarried daughters at night. The relationship between fathers and children was rigid but affectionate. Men ruled their Indians similarly. After the government secularized the missions in the 1830s, the homeless Indians labored for the *ranchos* in exchange for food, some clothing, and a place to live. They were now the Don's children.

What did the *rancheros* do with their various children? The Indian ones they worked. Even before they were freed from the missions, *indios* produced the cattle whose hides and tallow enabled the *rancheros*--who actually rented Indians from the padres--to live a life of relative leisure. The *rancheros* thoroughly controlled production after secularization, because the *rancho* contained all production, carpentry, cooking, herding, washing, sewing, and viniculture, within its crude boundaries. Observers agreed that Indians did the work, but certainly not all of it. The rest of the production seems to have been undertaken by the *rancheros'* women. Said one old Don, "The largest part of the tasks was entrusted to the women; they busied themselves with their domestic duties, cut the wood necessary for the meal, sowed in their gardens the seeds indispensable to the household." The patriarchs, on the other hand, "spent their lives on horseback, riding through fields, lassoing or killing cattle."[8] Men controlled production by virtue of their position in the social hierarchy which the culture assigned not only by class and nationality but by sex.

Their biological children the Dons gave away. Thus, men controlled reproduction too. Marriage agreements among the upper class seems to have taken place "only between the fathers of the children," as one *ranchero* remembered. While it is possible that fathers considered the desires and flirtations of their children in the dispositions of their lives, they still controlled who would eventually inherit their property and the mantle of patriarchy when they unlocked their daughters and delivered them away.[9] Other factors, however, entered the formula and botched their attempts at control.

While generally he may or may not have done an effective job for his daughter's material and emotional satisfaction in his choice of a husband, the California Don unintentionally undermined his people and culture by his selection. In the several decades before the formal Anglo-American conquest of California, many Anglos from the United States and England and some Europeans settled in the territory. Armed with cash and the skill of effective market calculation, these people quickly dominated Hispanic California's commerce. Eager to have their daughters marry well and to forge alliances with these ascendent men, the Californios bestowed their daughters on them. As the Indian *caciques* who gave their daughters to the Spanish *conquistadores* quickly discovered, when one cedes one's daughters, much more is actually exchanged. The Californios, intent on maintaining their economic and social position by drawing the new, financially-minded men into their kinship network, gave up their line of descent and their source of wealth and power, which was land. They relinquished their culture's whole future. Abel Stearns, one of the largest landowners in the history of California, started his 200,000-acre empire, which extended from the Santa Ana Mountains near present-day La Habra to the ocean, by marrying Don Juan Bandini's 14-year-old daughter in 1841 when he was forty. Downtown businessman John Temple, through his marriage, came to possess the huge Rancho Los Cerritos, which is now Long Beach. Englishman John Foster married one of Pio Pico's daughters and, by loaning his non-business-minded father-in-law money, wound up with most of the ex-governor's land. In the north, most land was alienated to lawyers and other men who, discouraged in the goldfields, swarmed over the Mexicans' *ranchos* after 1849. Such examples are not isolated, especially in Southern California.[10]

While California's allegiance changed in 1848, life and work on the southern *ranchos* did not. Indians and *cholos* continued to supply the necessary labor. Trapped by the new and foreign phenomenon of the labor market and alcohol, or both, and paid half the wages of white workers, the same people who supported the Dons in their leisurely lives now built capitalist agriculture in

Southern California. Both cultures saw these actual producers as lazy, sinful, uncontrolled, and stupid. But while the Spanish sought to elevate them to their own level and retain them as Hispanicized, tithe- and tax-paying subjects of His Catholic Majesty, Anglo-Americans rationalized or even advocated their destruction. "They are lazy, idle to the last degree," said a United States government agent in 1850, adding they "will disappear from the face of the earth as the settlements of the whites extend over the country." They also called them "women," revealing the lowly disdain in which the female sex was held. "Even though they use the bow and arrow," the same agent reported to the Secretary of State, "they are too lazy and effeminate to make successful hunters." A traveler in 1876 noted that "the women are very much like the men, almost wholly given to a vagabond life," and then wondered, "why, then, make such an outcry about ejecting a lot of worthless Indians from land which they never owned and never intended to own?"[11]

Although Yankees disparaged the California Indians, they sexually exploited their women. They too dominated by sexual conquest. In the northern counties in the thirty years after United States occupation, Yankee men appropriated an astounding 30 percent, some twelve thousand of the native women, either by prostitution, forced cohabitation, common law marriage, or rape. In some counties, the figure exceeded 50 percent. Again, some of these women undoubtedly benefited, if only briefly, from the material benefits of white society. From reports of Indian agents, we know also that the Indian women gained some bargaining power with Indian men due to the threatening, new possibility of acquiring a white "spouse." Yet, as the Indian agent at Eureka reported in 1871, the "women prostituted themselves ... from sheer necessity." Certainly the removal of so many Indian women from their tribes wreaked havoc with their traditional ways and helped generate the demoralization and dissolution of their culture.[12]

How much change did the Treaty of Guadalupe Hidalgo bring to Southern California? In terms of the colors of the flags, access to the mineral and land wealth for Anglo-American settlers to the exclusion of Mexicans, and the political power of Californios, indeed much changed. But from the perspective of the Indians, both those who labored on the *ranchos* and those still in their own communities, the domination by European fathers simply continued, albeit with even more brutality. The United States' conquest of California only brought new fathers. Under the domination of these new rulers, the history of Anglo California would now unfold. They would use a lopsided labor market instead of the old caste system to control production and gloriously profit, but the liberal patriarchs still conquered and ruled as men. They compared those they conquered to women, and men disparaged women who opposed the results of the expansion enterprise.

The male enterprise of the United States conquest of the people and the land of the West alienated many Anglo women. Even though, once they got there, they certainly supported the pacification (that is, the conquest and massacre of Indians), women more often than not lamented the harsh, lonely trip to the isolated West and occasionally revolted against their men. A woman, Helen Hunt Jackson, also commanded the moral and propaganda assault against the United States destruction of the California Indians. Patriarchy consistently closed ranks against its opposition. Theodore Roosevelt saw Jackson as spiteful and abusive, and in the 1940s historian Allan Nevins saw her as sentimental and intuitive. However reluctantly, Anglo women were loaded on the wagons for the trip West. Since then historians' gentlemanly point of view has obscured the social history of the migration.[13]

Future Research

Clearly, patriarchy in Hispanic California has broader implications than previous historians have indicated. Hopefully this paper will contribute not only to a better understanding of the status of the Mexican woman in the United States but also to recognition of the way in which patriarchy extends its influence over the evolution of history. For our purposes here, it now appears that the traditional ideas about civilizing and conquering inadequately explain the relationship between Spaniards and their institutions and what transpired in California. The centrality of sexual domination by men to Spain's domination cannot be denied. The reproduction of economic hierarchy has much to do with sexual attitudes as well. Moreover, the United States conquest, having much to do with "Manifest Destiny," the expansiveness of Yankee capitalism, and masculine adventurousness, of course, was achieved in large part by the transfer of women between culturally distinct men. When we study the Chicana we must also consider the broader implications of patriarchal relations, both Hispanic and Anglo. She is not alone in her subjugation by the various fathers. We must also come to understand how such power relations changed over time. What did the new liberal world which the Yankee men brought mean for Mexican woman? She still worked hard both inside and outside the home. Race and class continued to delimit her role and status. But did the erosion of the traditional external restraints and reciprocal relationships also erode the protections for which women exchanged submission? In other words, has the evolution of liberal society and its reliance on individual discipline freed Hispanic males to treat women as they desire without anything to replace the protections she had in Old California? An understanding of Hispanic and Anglo patriarchy, it should now be clear, is central to understanding the history of Mexican women in the United States in relation to both the dominant culture and their own. Furthermore, what she has encountered in history she also encounters (and accommodates and defies) in her current, daily life.

It is to these areas that the study of Mexican women in the United States must now turn. What have they carved from male-dominated history? What did daughters talk about behind locked doors at night? What female collectivities emerged when women of all castes went to bathe and wash clothes at the river? Was there a distinctive women's art represented in their stitchery and in the dances women performed without men? Did those elite *hijas del país* who married the business-minded newcomers serve merely as real estate brokers? Or did they gain higher status and influence through their marriages by positioning themselves at a crucial spot between the two cultures? To what extent did women join unions, particularly large female ones, as workers, as Mexicans, and as women?

Until recently, men almost exclusively have retold history and they dealt only with themselves. When they had the opportunity to interview members of past generations, they asked only men. It is now our task to uncover what they could not even imagine existed.

Notes

1.   Frances Fitzgerald, *Fire in the Lake: The Vietnamese and the Americans in Vietnam* (New York: Randon House, 1973), pp. 490-500; Michael Herr, *Dispatches* (New York: Alfred A. Knopf, 1977), p. 138; Susan Brownmiller, *Against Our Will: Men,*

Women and Rape (New York: Simon and Schuster, 1975), pp. 23-34.

2.   Nellie Van de Grift Sanchez, *The Spanish Period* (Chicago and New York: The Lewis Publishing Company, 1930); Hubert Howe Bancroft, *History of California* (San Francisco: The History Book Company, 1884) vol. 1, pp. 182-2, 381, 640; vol. 2, p. 575; Robert Archibald, *The Economic Aspects of the California Missions* (Washington, D.C.: Academy of American Franciscan History, 1978), p.157; Florian F. Guest, O.F.M., "The Indian Policy Under Fermin Francisco de Lasuen, California's Second Father President," *California Historical Quarterly* 45: 195-224; Alfred L. Kroeber, *Handbook of the Indians of California* (Washington, D.C.: Government Printing Office, 1925), pp. 633, 839.

3.   Sanchez, *The Spanish Period*, p. 300; Bancroft, *History of California*, (1884) vol. 1, p. 217; Hubert Howe Bancroft, *California Pastoral, 1789-1848* (San Francisco: The History Book Company, 1884), p. 626; and E.B. Webb, *Indian Life at the Old Missions* (Los Angeles: W.F. Lewis, 1952), p. 149.

4.   Carlos N. Hijar, "California in 1834: Recollections," Bancroft Library, MS, 1877; Sanchez, *The Spanish Period*, p. 306; Webb, *Indian Life*, (1952), pp. 27-28; Bancroft, *California Pastoral*, p. 232. Married women lived with their husbands in the *ranchería* on the outskirts of the mission.

5.   José María Amador, "Memorias sobre la historia de California," Bancroft Library, MS, 1877, pp. 73-77; Fr. Zephyrin Engelhardt, *The Franciscans in California* (Harbor Springs, Michigan: Holy Childhood Indian School, 1897), p. 376; Bancroft, *California Pastoral* (1888), p. 596; and Irving Berdine Richman, *California Under Spain and Mexico, 1535-1847* (Boston and New York: Cooper Square Publishers, 1965), p. 465.

6.   Patriarchy exists not only in relation to women but to children as well. As the concept and role of children emerged towards the end of the Middle Ages, the youngest of the species took on a new function. As simply "little people," only their economic dependence distinguished them from other producers. "Childhood" emerged when children became the basis for the new nuclear family. Like women, who lost their productive role, children now too became "respected" and elevated. The fathers made them psychologically dependent, "innocent" and asexual. Children were now lumped with women, apparently elevated but actually demoted to a common dependent status. See Philippe

Ariès, *Centuries of Childhood: A Social History of Family Life* (New York: Alfred A. Knopf, 1962).

7.   Capitaine A. Duhaut-Cilly, *Voyage autour du Monde, principalment a la California et Iles Sandwich, pendant les annees 1826, 1827, 1828 et 1829*, 2 vols. (Paris 1834-5) edited and translated by Charles Franklin Carter as "Duhaut-Cilly's Account of California in the Years 1827-28," *California Historical Society Quarterly* 8 (1929): 311; Sanchez, *The Spanish Period*, pp. 355, 433-34; Robert Glass Cleland, *The Cattle on a Thousand Hills: Southern California, 1850-1880* (San Marino: Huntington Library, 1941), pp. 30-1, 53; Amador, "Memorias," pp. 113, 228; Bancroft, *California Pastoral*, p. 588; Bancroft, *History of California*, vol. 2: 42-53, 552-3; vol. 6: 563; George Harwood Philips, "Indians in Los Angeles, 1781-1875: Economic Integration, Social Disintegration," *Pacific Historical Review* 49 (August 1980): 427-451; and Webb, *Indian Life*, p. 30.

8.   Cleland, *Cattle on a Thousand Hills*, p. 53; C. Allen Hutchinson, *Frontier Settlements in Mexican California: The Hijar-Padres Colony and Its Origins, 1769-1835* (New Haven: Yale University Press, 1969), pp. 81, 138; Hijar, *California in 1834*, p. 9; Bancroft, *California Pastoral*, pp. 312, 333; and Sheldon G. Jackson, *A British Ranchero in Old California: Life and Times of Henry Dalton and the Rancho Azusa* (Azusa: A.H. Clark Co., 1977).

9.   Hijar, *California in 1834*, p. 22. See Gayle Rubin, "The Traffic in Women: Notes on the 'Political Economy' of Sex," in *Toward An Anthropology of Women* ed. Rayna R. Reiter (New York: Monthly Review Press, 1975), pp. 170-184, on the effects and function of "gifts of women."

10.   Lilian Charlotte Lederer, "A Study of Anglo-American Settlers in Los Angeles County Previous to the Admission of California to the Union," (Master's thesis, University of Southern California, 1927), pp. 2-5, 24-28; Cleland, *Cattle on a Thousand Hills*, pp. 34, 113, 184-207; and Security-First National Bank of Los Angeles, *El Pueblo: Los Angeles Before the Railroads* (Los Angeles: Equitable Branch of the Security Trust & Savings Bank, 1928), p. 21.

11.   T. Butler King, *Report of Hon. T. Butler King on California* (Washington, D.C.: Gideon and Co., 1850), pp. 16-17; and D.L. Phillips, *Letters From California: Its Mountains, Valleys, Plains, Lakes, Rivers, Climate and Production* (Springfield, 1877), p. 98.

12.   Sherbourne F. Cook, *The Conflict Between the California Indian and White Civilization* (Berkeley and Los Angeles: University of California Press, 1976), pp. 329-343.

13.   John Mack Faragher, *Women and Men on the Overland Trail* (New Haven: Yale University Press, 1979), pp. 88-143; Helen Hunt Jackson, *A Century of Dishonor: The Early Crusade for Indian Reform* (New York: Harper and Row, 1965), editor's introduction by Andrew F. Rolle, pp. xii-xix.

MARRIAGE AND SEDUCTION IN COLONIAL NEW MEXICO

by

Ramón A. Gutiérrez

Early on the spring morning of 15 April 1702, Bentura de Esquibel appeared before the local parish priest in Sante Fe, New Mexico to begin the necessary procedures so that he could be joined in holy wedlock with Doña Bernardina Rosa Lucero de Godoy. The announcement of the marriage had hardly been read in church to the Sunday faithful when a short note reached the hands of Fray Manuel Moreno.

> Most Reverend Father. Would your reverence impede the marriage of Bentura de Esquibel. It has come to my attention that he wants to contract matrimony with the daughter of Lucero. I have very urgent reasons for impeding the marriage.

> Signed: Juana Lujan

The following day Juana Lujan appeared before Fray Moreno and explained that Bentura could not take Doña Bernardina as his wife because he had given her a previous promise of marriage. Juana complained to the priest that Bentura had tarnished her honor; snatched the flower of her virginity; had impregnated her; and, now, refused to make good on the promises by which he had had his pleasure. Weeks of litigation followed. In the end, Juana did not get the marriage that she desired. She was left dissolute and with a child "that would know no father."[1]

The major issues involved in this 1702 Santa Fe case of seduction and marital impediment due to a previous promise of betrothal elucidate some of the cultural values surrounding social reproduction and, more specifically, the relationship between the sexes, in colonial New Mexico. What follows is a detailed examination of this marital case as the focal point for a discussion of the social order in colonial New Mexico as revealed through sexual ideals, norms, and practice.

* * *

Marriage in colonial New Mexico was under the exclusive jurisdiction of the Catholic Church until 1778. Before nuptials could be celebrated, it was the responsibility of the local friar to undertake a thorough investigation to determine whether any impediments to the proposed union existed. The formulary for the *diligencia matrimonial*, as the investigation was known, had been established at the Council of Trent and required that the potential bride and groom, as well as two witnesses on behalf of each candidate, appear to answer a litany of questions. The intent of this procedure was to enforce the ecclesiastical concern over the definition of appropriate and inappropriate conjugal partners. The church fathers held that matrimony could not occur between persons found to have a canonic impediment.

Impediments fell into two categories: dire impediments, which prohibited marriage, required papal or episcopal dispensation, and annulled a nuptial if discovered after the ceremony; and preventative impediments, which were of lesser severity, could be dispensed by the lower clergy, and infrequently undermined the legitimacy of the contract. The dire impediments of most importance were consanguinity, affinity, a solemn vow of chastity, religious orders, differences in religion, bigamy, polygamy, male impotence, crime, misrepresentation, coercion, and previous promise of bethrothal.

It was to fulfill the requirements stipulated in canon law that Bentura de Esquibel appeared before Fray Manuel Moreno on 15 April 1702, declaring that he was a Spaniard, the legitimate son of Antonio de Araña and María Esquivel, a servant in the household of the governor of New Mexico, and eager to enter into the state of holy matrimony with Doña Bernardina Lucero de Godoy, the legitimate daughter of two Spaniards, Antonio Lucero de Godoy and Antonia Barela. During the investigation no hidden impediments surfaced. As Bentura signed the document, he jotted that he was nineteen years old; Bernardina noted her age as sixteen. Both were slightly younger than the mean age at which males and females first married in New Mexico between 1700 and 1709 (22.3 years and 17.8 years, respectively).[2]

Once the matrimonial investigation was complete, and before the nuptial could be celebrated, the officiating priest was required to announce the proposed union from the church pulpit on three consecutive Sundays. If members of the congregation knew of any reason for inhibiting the marriage, they were required to communicate their disquietudes or knowledge to the priest.

Sitting there in the pews at Santa Fe's San Miguel Church on Sunday, 17 April 1702, the visibly pregnant Juana Lujan heard the news. The announcement took her totally by surprise. How could Bentura be contracting marriage with Bernardina, she wondered? Bentura had given her a promise of marriage. Fray Moreno received Juana's note concerning the hidden impediment and immediately abrogated the matrimonial plan pending further investigation of the allegations. Juana, Bentura, and a variety of witnesses appeared before the ecclesiastical tribunal to present their version of the disputed events.

While the court docket is conspiciously silent on the origins of Juana and Bentura's friendship, their courtship was largely clandestine. Since a family's public reputation, or its honor-status (the source of one's right to precedence in a community), was based on the honor-virtue or the proper sexual conduct of one's children, it was common to segregate the sexes and confine the women to limited social spaces. Because women were considered the weaker sex, frail to the pleasures of the flesh and the desires of men, they had to be isolated. Petronila de las Cuebas had thus appropriately warned Juana Lujan's mother that if she wanted to protect her daughter's virginity, "she should keep her always behind locked doors, lest she experience some grave difficulty."

Since the aristocracy's power and wealth could be more seriously threatened by an inappropriate marriage, they wielded more guidance in the socialization of their children to deter undesirable behavior. Obviously, they had the most to lose--their honor, their blood lines, their patrimonies--by a son or daughter succumbing to personal desires over family considerations. The difference between the aristocracy and popular classes in sexual segregation and female seclusion was one of degree rather than kind. Only in upper-class households--where servants and retainers abounded and productive activities did not consume all familial resources--could time and energy be expended to see that a daughter was properly restrained. If a parent had been widowed or the family was particularly large, the chances of being constantly attentive to a daughter's activities were made more difficult.

Every male household head had a sacred space and adytum of physical territoriality that surrounded him and his various forms of property. The profanity of the external world was ritually set apart from the sanctity within by crucifixes and icons that marked doorposts and windows and protected the inhabitants from evil invasions. The groom lifting his new bride over the threshold symbolized both the creation of a new household and passage into a man's sacrosanct domain. Things that promised existence over time, that provided shelter from the hositilities of the environment, had to be jealously guarded within. Among those things to be protected from defilement was a female's sexual purity. Since it was through a woman's childbearing capacity that the labor force was reproduced, and since maternity was undeniable while paternity was not, lust and any misalliance that might stem from it could only be precluded through female seclusion and the high symbolic value placed on virginity.

It was thus no coincidence that Bentura's initial intrusion into the Lujan household to gain the affections of Juana occurred during the darkness of the night, when most heinous and sinister acts were usually accomplished. Antonia de Sandoval, whose house was located near Juana's, reported that "through the roof Bentura would enter the house at night" to spend time with Juana.

Seduction in eighteenth century New Mexico followed a fairly regular pattern. A young man would begin the process of courtship by gaining the attention of a woman. After she was sufficiently knowledgeable of his attractions and had reciprocated with trust, he would take advantage of the confidence established and, by promising marriage, would attain his sexual desires. The discovery of the illicit act was likely only if pregnancy resulted. Then, a whole range of actions were possible depending on the circumstances and the social class of the individuals involved.

The burden of proof in seduction was always placed on the woman and her family. She had to produce witnesses who would testify to her betrothal, to her good conduct, and to her virginity. If witnesses to the betrothal did not exist, which was precisely Juana Lujan's predicament (for as she lamented "the only witness I have to the promise is God Almighty and His Son Jesus Christ, for our meeting, occurred in such solitude that even though my father and mother were in the same house, they were in a different room and could not hear, see, or note what was happening"), then the woman had to produce the *prenda*, the gift which was ritually exchanged between lovers as an outward sign of their intention to marry. Thus, Juana Lujan told the ecclesiastical judge, "I lost my honor and as proof that Bentura de Esquibel truly gave me his word of marriage I have a silver medal of Our Lady of Guadalupe, the weight of a large silver coin." *Prendas* were given great importance by the courts as evidence, for after such a gift was bestowed, a maiden felt secure in submitting to the sexual desires of her husband-to-be. For if pregnancy from pre-marital contact resulted, the proposed marriage would redeem the woman's dishonor and free her from any public scandal.

That Bentura initially wanted to marry Juana Lujan and free her from her "damnification" was attested to by several witnesses. Mateo Marquez testified that when he had told Bentura that he (Mateo) was interested in courting Juana, Bentura had responded "do not do any such thing for I have already given her my promise of marriage and she will be my wife because of that promise." Antonia de Sandoval, a cook in the governor's household, said that her coworker, Ana Lujan, had told her that Bentura de Esquibel had publicly given Juana Lujan a promise of marriage.

Because Juana's honor had been sullied through seduction, Bentura now felt confident that any parental aversion to their marriage would be easily overcome. A nuptial was one way of restoring a deflowered maiden's personal and familial honor. Hoping to accomplish this, Bentura called at Juana's parents' home. Juana's mother flatly rejected the matrimonial bid. "It is not my wish, nor the wish of Juana's kin, for I want to marry my daughter to a man that knows how to work." Parents in New Mexico often objected to a suitor because he was thought to lack enterprise and industry. Economic opportunities on the frontier of Christendom required that if a man was going to transcend his ascribed status, potential for personal achievement was necessary. A man who lacked a profession might not be able to provide the sort of existence parents might want for their daughter. Frequently, this excuse was also a thinly veiled guise for inequalities based on class.[3]

Bentura's family and employer also stymied his marriage desires. Antonio de Esquibel, Bentura's brother, threatened that he would "shame Bentura publicly with curses and make him bite the dust" if he tried to marry Juana Lujan. Bentura retorted that he would enter the state of grace with whomever he chose "for first comes my soul, and I do not want the devil to take me."

451

Unfortunately for Bentura's soul, more powerful individuals were constraining his behavior. Bentura's father felt that "Juana Lujan is not Bentura's equal in honor or racial status," and such disparity made marriage repulsive. While it is not clear exactly what Juana Lujan's race was, social inequality--be it due to birth, race, lineage, family name, wealth, or occupation--was cause for parental opposition to marriage.

The Spanish Crown made it very clear to the Catholic Church, in numerous directives through most of the eighteenth century, that the social class pretensions of New Spain's aristocracy and elite would be buttressed by the state. The authority of a father, rooted in natural law, justified the rejection of a spouse for a child that was deemed unequal. The belief in New Mexico was that equality in status should exist between marital candidates. In cases where disparity in social status existed between the marital candidates, and marriage was being contracted solely as a way of restoring the honor of a seduced maiden, the Crown ordered in 1753 that:

> If the maiden seduced under promise of marriage is inferior in status, [be it in race, wealth or occupation] so that she would cause greater dishonor to his lineage if he married her than the dishonor that would fall on her by remaining seduced ... he must not marry her because of injury to himself and his entire lineage would be greater than that incurred by the maiden remaining unredeemed, and at any rate one must choose the lesser evil ... The latter is an offense of an individual and does no harm to the Republic, while the former is an offense of such gravity that it will denigrate an entire family, dishonor a person of pre-eminence, defame and stain an entire lineage and destroy a thing which gives spendour and honor to the Republic. But if the seduced maiden is only slightly inferior, of not very marked inequality, so that her inferiority does not cause marked dishonor to the family, he must be compelled to marry her; because in this case her dishonor would be greater if she remained unredeemed than the dishonor that could befall the seducer's family through the marriage.[4]

Thus, in colonial New Mexico, if the social inequality between proposed conjugal partners was excessive, familial status took precedence over the redemption of a seduced woman's moral integrity. The Catholic Church frequently clashed with the state over this issue. Clerics were much more concerned with the community's morality and placed such temporal issues as family prestige in a secondary position. To thwart Bentura's subversive desires for Juana, the governor of New Mexico sent him to Parral for a few months. There, it was hoped, Bentura would forget his love. Before leaving for Parral, Pedro Montes Oca carried a secret message to Juana in which Bentura told her:

> That he kissed her hands, and how was she, and that he was about to ask his confessor to tell the governor, his master, that he wanted to enter the holy state of matrimony with her, to let him know her thoughts and desires ... Juana told [Pedro] to tell Bentura that she kissed his hands, and how was he, and that even if he went to Mexico City, or elsewhere, she would wait for him up to four years, and if after that, something happened or there was some other mishap, that he should not blame her.

The months passed. Time finally displayed Juana's dishonor-- her pregnancy. When news reached her that Bentura had returned to Santa Fe, she thought that her honor would at last be redeemed from the village gossip through marriage. But Bentura's heart had hardened in Parral; he no longer desired matrimony with Juana and, as she would sadly discover while sitting in church on Sunday, 17 April 1702, now wanted Doña Bernardina Lucero de Godoy to be his wife.

The canonic impediment of previous promise of betrothal, which Juana Lujan claimed existed, required that Bentura appear before the church tribunal to contest the charges against him. The most common tactic employed by New Mexican men who wanted to shirk their responsibility for the seduction of a maiden they no longer wished to marry (or when they never had any intention of marrying in the first place but had promised marriage only to obtain sex) was to impugn the woman's reputation and virtue. By discrediting her, the fundamental requisite for marriage, which was the woman's respectability, was done away with. In such cases, the male frequently would admit his promise and sexual conquest, but would claim that refusal to marry was based on the fact that he had not found the woman a virgin. The law only punished the seduction of a virgin; all others, particularly widows and abandoned women, were considered sport for the prowess of men.

Bentura Esquibel employed this strategy before the court. Explaining why he no longer wanted to marry Juana, he said:

I had a change of heart and the woman I now truly desire is Bernardina Lucero de Godoy for she is a young maiden of whose person there is no gossip ... Bernardina is my equal for she is Spanish while [Juana] is not ... And besides, I gave Juana a promise of marriage presuming that she was a virgin; but she was not ... she is not chaste, she lacks sexual integrity and does not conduct herself as an honorable woman ... there are witnesses who have told me that she has bad habits ... she has no shame. It is known that Mateo Marques frequents her home; so it can only be presumed that he must have snatched that flower of her body, her virginity. She has also been seen cuddling with Salvador Olgín ... There is ample evidence that she has not led an honest life.

Juana retorted to all of this acidly:

How can Bentura say that I was not a virgin when he himself saw the evident sign of my virginity which was the blood that was left stamped on his shirt from our act. That same blood which I tried to wash out of the shirt because of my great remorse. And while washing the shirt at the river my cousin Phelipa Mansanares saw me and asked what blood that was, and I told her what happened the night before. She saw me burn it so that it would not serve as a testament and reminder of my frailty ... To the second charge that Mateo Marques deflowered me, it is a lie. He is my cousin and that is why he frequents our household. The other man, Salvador Olgín, I do not even know. That Bentura has had a change of heart and now wants to marry Bernardina Lucero saying that she is honorable and Spanish, I only say that I cannot dispute that Bernardina is indeed from a very honorable family; but that she is better than me in racial status is disputable, for I am as good as she. And finally, Reverend Father, I am forced, and will drop my impediment so that Bentura can marry whomever he wishes. For what kind of life would I have to endure if you forced him to marry me? And besides, the governor has threatened me, saying that he will stymie my request by whatever means are necessary. I am helpless against the sinister violence of such a formidable adversary.

Juana was finally intimidated into lifting her impediment of previous betrothal. Bentural Esquibel and Bernardina Lucero married. The ecclesiastical court ruled that because Bentura indeed owed Juana Lujan her honor, and seeing that she rejected its redemption through marriage, Bentura must still indemnify it in some way. Bentura was ordered to pay Juana Lujan 200 pesos for her dishonor. Thus the case ends.

* * *

This 1702 case of Bentura de Esquibel and Juana Lujan presented here illustrates some of the dominant cultural concerns surrounding marriage in colonial New Mexico. My attempt has been to let the historical subjects express the complexities of their own value system, actions, and emotions. As Chicanos seek out their roots, we run the risk of falsifying history if we facilely approach it with *a priori* categories and assumptions. The imposition of ideological and epistemological frameworks, created in the nineteenth and twentieth centuries to explain and understand the eighteenth, can be nothing more than a distortion of the past for the needs of the present. We must remind ourselves, after all, that history is not theory in search of empirical validation.

The most useful approach for the study of the history of women--for an understanding of how sexual, racial, and generational hierarchies have structured the past--is to examine in depth the system of symbols embedded in our language and culture relating to gender, color, and age in their own context. Next, we must attempt to unravel how those symbols were ordered ideally and in practice, their interrelations, and, finally, how they were employed to structure inequalities.[5]

I have tried to do this very briefly here. The concept of honor in colonial New Mexico displayed in seduction and marriage, reveals the concern over gender specific forms of behavior and their relation to the perpetuation of social status. An approach of pure economism would relegate the New Mexicans' concern for their females' virginity to the cultural sphere or to the ideological superstructure. Because such cultural acts are not apparently of the economic base and do not conform to strict rules of economic interest, then they are simply irrational manifestations or epiphenomena. Yet, if we examine the concern over Juana Lujan's virginity discussed above, her moral integrity most certainly conformed to rational rules of symbolic calculation. For, if a family wanted to marry their daughters to maximize social status, then their virginity had to be protected. In that society a daughter considered spoiled was a major liability. If a father was going to secure such a daughter an adequate mate, enough hard economic assets would have to be employed to compensate for her symbolic devaluation. It is in this light that the 200 peso payment by Bentura Esquibel to Juana Lujan can be understood: who would want to marry a woman who was not a virgin and whose reputation was known by all the village? Two hundred pesos-- which would buy three hundred sheep--might make such a prospect more palatable.[6]

Finally, no historian would ever dream of studying labor history or the working class without a thorough understanding of how that experience was shaped by, responded to, and resisted the power of the appropriating class. Just as there can be no master without a slave, no lord without a serf, there can be no males without females. I tried to illustrate in this work how the history of the sexes in New Mexico was interactional, relational and process-related. Only through such an approach can we hope someday to fully understand sexual power and gender ideologies.[7]

Notes

1. This case is taken from the Archives of the Archdiocese of Sante Fe, *Diligencias Matrimoniales*, Reel 60, frames 260-282. The microfilm is deposited at the New Mexico State Records Center and Archives in Santa Fe, New Mexico.

2. A fuller discussion of marriage in colonial New Mexico is found in my dissertation, "Marriage, Sex and the Family: Social Change in Colonial New Mexico, 1690-1846" (University of Wisconsin, 1980).

3. Marriage and social inequality has been brilliantly studied by Verena Martinez-Alier, *Marriage, Class and Colour in Nineteenth-Century Cuba* (Cambridge: Cambridge University Press, 1974). See also Brigid Brophy, "The Rococo Seducer," *The London Magazine*, 2 (May, 1962): 54-71.

4. "Dictamen del Dr. Tembra acerca de la consulta que se hizo sobre si el Cura o cualquier juez eclesiastico puede o debe impedir los matrimonios entre consortes desiguales, celebrados ya

esposales con juramento de complirlos, sin consentimiento paterno," Mexico, 1752. Quoted in Martinez-Alier, p. 101.

5. For more details on the techniques of cultural analysis, see Clifford Geertz, *The Interpretation of Cultures* (New York, Basic Books, 1973). See also David Schneider, *American Kinship: A Cultural Account* (Chicago: University of Chicago Press, 1968).

6. The concept of "symbolic capital" which is implicit in this work has been greatly influenced by Pierre Bourdieu, *Outline of a Theory of Practice* (Cambridge: Cambridge University Press, 1977).

7. Joan Kelly-Gadol, "The Social Relation of the Sexes: Methodological Implications of Women's History," *SIGNS* 1 (Summer 1976): 809-823. See also Colin Bell and Howard Newby, "Husbands and Wives: The Dynamics of the Deferential Dialectic," in *Dependence and Exploitation in Work and Marriage*, Baker and Allen, eds., (New York: Longman, 1976), pp. 152-168; Carroll Smith-Rosenberg, "The Female World of Love and Ritual: Relations Between Women in Nineteenth-Century America," *SIGNS* 1 (Autumn 1975): 1-30; John M. Faragher, *Women and Men on the Overland Trail* (New Haven: Yale University Press, 1979).

"A LA MUJER": A CRITIQUE OF THE PARTIDO LIBERAL MEXICANO'S GENDER IDEOLOGY ON WOMEN

by

Emma M. Pérez

> *Throughout history women have been considered inferior to men, not only by law but also by custom.*[1]

"A La Mujer"
Ricardo Flores Magón, 1910

Introduction

The essay "A La Mujer" first appeared on 24 September 1910 in *Regeneración*, the Partido Liberal Mexicano's (PLM) newspaper. Since then, it has been reprinted in books and journals that recognize the Party's significance in Chicano and Chicana history.[2] "A La Mujer" typifies the ideology of the PLM toward women. To the male-dominated organization, women's subjugation resulted from an exploitative social structure where capitalism condemned working class women and men to the bottom of a socioeconomic hierarchy. The PLM strove to overthrow capitalism believing that only then would women and men achieve equality.

In several articles, *Regeneración* revealed the ideology of the Party and its expectations of women as revolutionaries. Two aspects of the ideology require explanation. The first is its relationship to the organization's larger political goals and ideals. *Regeneración* helped to politicize Mexican women in the Southwest, but women were politicized to serve a nationalist cause--the Mexican revolution. In essence, the male leaders relegated feminism to the back burner while nationalism, in the name of revolution, took priority. They failed to grasp that women's issues went beyond class exploitation. Gender analysis, after all, unmasks social relations between the sexes exposing patriarchal privileges and contradictions for both women and men.

459

The second aspect of ideology which demands explanation is its relationship to the women's activities in the organization and in the revolution. This was dialectical: the ideology altered the activities of the women as they interacted and changed ideology itself, if only minimally. The group's ideology on women was challenged as women's participation in the Mexican revolution tranformed them. The women of the PLM asserted themselves and challenged the men's traditional ideas about them. When women organize along with men, they are often forced to be more creative about asserting their rights and interests. In this case, PLM male members persistently harangued women to be a part of the nationalist movement. Women were limited by that domineering, male-identified ideology, yet the female members performed activities their own way.[3] They too, however, were not without contradictions. While some mimicked the men's ideas, others expressed their feminism.

Sources

Little is known about the women of the organization, from the highly visible companions of the *junta* members to the less well known women who appear only in the pages of *Regeneración*. A few studies focus on Mexican women of the revolutionary era, many more on the PLM and its leading male members--but only one biography of a Mexican woman associated with the Party exists. Ines Tovar devoted her dissertation to the life of poet and teacher Sara Estella Ramírez, who migrated to Laredo, Texas in 1898. Tovar's study provides more than the usual sketchy information on PLM women.[4] More information appears in *Sembradores, Ricardo Flores Magón y El_Partido Liberal Mexicano*, in which Juan Gómez-Quiñones discusses some of the women influenced by the PLM in the Southwest and in Mexico.[5] Shirlene Soto's dissertation, "The Mexican Woman: A Study of Her Participation in the Revolution, 1910-1940," also refers to women of the Party.[6] Many of the women came from Mexico to the United States during the revolution; in *Revoltosos*, W. Dirk Raat cites Mexican archives with additional material on PLM women.[7] Raat further acknowledges the importance of some of these women to the Party and to the revolution when he argues that "the *compañeras* of the PLM *junta* members played more than supporting roles..."[8]

Despite women's central importance, the Partido Liberal Mexicano failed to accomplish its radical goals for them. Evidence demonstrates that while women actively participated in all arenas of the revolution, they gained little from their contributions.[9] Women's revolutionary activities were understood as extentions of the home, and despite their contributions to the revolution, they remained bound to the home. As a result, they performed dual roles. The weakness of the PLM's ideology lay in its failure to acknowledge fully the implications of these dual roles and their contradictions for women. Such contradictions can only be exposed by examining gender ideology. But, the Mexican revolution created a nationalist sentiment that obscured gender oppression making ideology notably difficult to break through.

Gender and Ideology

A word about the concept of ideology and its use in this study is necessary. Ideology is not defined here as a system of values and beliefs alone. These values and beliefs are linked to material reality in a specific way. Ideology arises out of the reality of a given moment at the same time that it masks its contradictions and falsehoods.[10] An analysis of ideology, then, is not exclusively an analysis of ideas. It is also an exploration of the material reality from which ideas arise and the social relations they embody.[11] Social relations constitute not only the relations of production, or the economic sphere; they also embrace the social relations between the sexes, or patriarchal sphere. Ideology has often been confined to the economic sphere because of the connection between them.[12] But gender, too, has an ideology. While gender oppression is materially rooted, it is--like issues of race, culture, and ethnicity--intricately bound to social mores and attitudes. In analyses of oppression, gender has been subsumed by class precisely because of the social relations that create and are created by gender ideology. Specifically, gender is an assigned status to which behavior adapts, and the ideology claims that learned behavior is natural. Socialization, therefore, constructs gender identity.[13]

The Partido Liberal Mexicano's analysis of women's position in society addressed the economic sphere when it recognized that women, along with men, endured class domination. The PLM did not prove the social relations between women and men; or, the ideology that promotes and condones distinctive sex roles. Yet, the

461

Party framed an analysis that embodied gender relations, both real and imagined.

Literature on Chicanas analyzes class more fully than gender or race. For example, *Essays on La Mujer* (1977) and *Mexican Women in the United States* (1980), two anthologies on Chicanas scrutinize class, race, and more implicitly, gender, but they argue strongly that class dictates the subjugation that women of color experience.[14] The studies dissect women's status in the work place--the exploitative social relations of production under capitalism--and show how a capitalist social structure contributes to race and gender hierarchies in the labor market. In a well-known essay the authors reiterate a popular argument regarding the division of labor in the family and its relation to the division of labor in the work force. In essence, when housewives serve husbands in the home, they reproduce men's labor power. The market exploits women, along with their husbands in the factories, because housewives also create surplus value, albeit indirectly. The link is tenuous, but it is argued nonetheless. The problem is that the argument hardly addresses the full nature of women's exploitation in the home within the family.[15]

Although these critiques of capitalism disclose how the economy detrimentally affects workers according to race and gender, the studies do not pursue the implications of race and gender outside the labor market. Nor do they question women's ideological oppression, which is linked not only to the economy, but also to the patriarchy and, more specifically, the family. The family ideologically binds women to their roles as wives, mothers, and nurturers. Even in preclass societies, women were bound to a sphere that was dictated by some form of patriarchy. Rape, for instance, existed long before the rise of capitalism. Before industrialization, a woman's political and economic status in western societies was determined by her relationship to a father or a husband. Industrialization in the nineteenth century presented laws that moderately transformed this relationship, but, more importantly, industry broke up the family as an economic unit and forced low income women and all men to become wage laborers. But, only women were now held absolutely responsible for the care of the family.[16]

Class analyses are viable because one can explain surplus value and observe its results materially. When racism and sexism are observed in the market, divisions of labor and unequal wage distribution based upon race and gender can be traced. Because the ideological effects of racism and sexism cannot be measured, the assumption is that they are nonexistant. But, such conditions do not require quantitative measure to exist. Women of color experience every aspect of racism and sexism throughout their lives. Social attitudes, values, and beliefs, all elusive and immeasureable, also define their status at home and at work.

This study attempts to clarify the Partido Liberal Mexicano's gender ideology as elaborated in *Regeneración* to understand its implications for women. The intention is not to discredit the PLM and its efforts, nor to punish the past with present-mindedness. Instead, it attempts to unmask the contradictions within a leftist group's ideology that did not fully emancipate its female members.

This investigation employs a socialist feminist analysis but with the caveat that European and North American theorists did not consider Third World women when devising their paradigms. From Frederick Engels and August Bebel to the contemporary British women's school of marxist feminist thought, these theorists delved deeply into European women's working conditions.[17] Race and its cultural manifestations for women of color have yet to be resolved. But even as we learn from such thinkers, Chicana scholars must retain a sense of the grass-roots movements that make up our community. These grass-roots movements, like the Partido Liberal Mexicano, most clearly confront issues of culture, class, gender, and sexuality in our community.

A Woman's Place

The PLM, leftist with anarchist convictions, originated in Mexico City in 1900 when Ricardo Flores Magón and his brother, Jesus, published the first issue of *Regeneración*. In 1904, the central figures of the group--Ricardo Flores Magón, his brother Enrique, Camilo Arriaga, Juan Sarabia, and Santiago de la Hoz-- sought refuge in the United States. For six years, the *junta* moved from Texas, Missouri, Canada, Arizona, and California, publishing *Revolución* intermittantly with *Regeneración* while they escaped Pinkerton agents, imprisonment and Porfirio Díaz's loyalists. By this time Jesus had abandoned the revolutionary cause and later betrayed his brothers.[18]

In 1910, amid social and political turmoil, most of the group settled in Los Angeles. Through their newspaper, the PLM reached an audience throughout the Southwest. Its circulation, which rose to thirty thousand, reflected a growing influence in the Mexican community on both sides of the border. *Regeneración* earned its success in the face of fierce opposition. Often smuggled from the United States into Mexico, the paper sometimes cost the lives of those distributing it; among the casualties was a young boy shot by federal soldiers in Mexicalli.[19]

To aggravate anti-Mexican sentiments, *Los Angeles Times* owner, Harrison Gray Otis, encouraged ridiculous cartoons and scathing editorials against the revolutionists. Having purchased land at ten cents an acre from Díaz's government, Otis used the daily to protect his Mexican investment. When the *Times* was bombed in 1 October 1910, Otis and his supporters accused labor leaders, leftists, and anarchists of the terrorism. The city was clearly unwilling to welcome the Party when it already harbored undesirable socialists, anarchists, and militant laborers.[20]

The Mexican government, too, feared the rising militancy of the organization and its newspaper. Initially, the anti-Díaz publication had favored reforms for Mexico instead of revolution but on 3 September 1910, Ricardo Flores Magón declared the Party anarchist and announced a radical platform. Influenced by the writings of Pierre Proudhon, Peter Kropotkin, and especially Francisco Ferrer Guardia, the Spanish anarchist, the leading members also read works by Karl Marx and Frederick Engels to unfurl their own style of anarcho-syndicalism. Their platform demanded violent revolution, called for workers' rights, and professed equal regard for land and liberty.[21]

In addition, Flores Magón committed the Party and the newspaper to women's social equality. In its first month, *Regeneración* published Ricardo Flores Magón's celebrated essay, "A La Mujer." The author confirmed the PLM's commitment to women's issues and, more importantly, delineated the organization's ideology about women. More than any other essay, "A La Mujer" elucidates the PLM's ideological contradictions. Flores Magón's most frequently quoted work illustrates his perceptive, yet flawed, examination of women's issues. He begins the essay:

You constitute one-half of the human species and what affects humanity affects you as an integral part of it. If men are slaves, you are too. Bondage does not recognize sex; the infamy that degrades men equally degrades you. You cannot escape the shame of oppression. The same forces which conquer men strangle you.[22]

He persuaded his female audience that their suffering was equal to men's and, therefore, equally important. Warning them of the upcoming battle, he ordered: "Your duty is to help men; to be there when he suffers; to lighten his sorrow; to laugh and to sing with him when victory smiles."[23] To Flores Magón, women's task in the revolution was a traditional one--to nurture men.

His understanding of women's "bondage" was also inconsistent. For example, he defended and assaulted love and marriage in the same essay. He noted that many women succumbed to prostitution when they lacked a husband's financial support, but he proceeded to equate marriage itself with prostitution.

> When it is motivated by economic security instead of love, marriage is but another form of prostitution ... That is, a wife sells her body for food exactly as does a prostitute; this occurs in the majority of marriages.

> And what could be said of the vast army of women who do not succeed in finding a husband?[24]

Romanticism overwhelmed his logic. For Flores Magón, love justified a woman's economic dependence upon a man. He failed to recognize that between marriage and prostitution, her choices were few.

Anarchists generally denounced marriage, yet held certain ideas about women's natural duties and desires. A leading theoretician, Peter Kropotkin, attributed to women an instinctive desire to nurture and to remain in the home. Influenced by Kropotkin, Flores Magón accepted the home as woman's destined sphere, but once again, he faced a dilemma. He realized the need to expand her duties beyond the private sphere if the revolution was to be won:[25] "Demand that your husbands, brothers, fathers, sons and friends pick up the gun. Spit in the face of those who refuse to pick up a weapon against oppression."[26]

In November, only two months after the publication of "A La Mujer," the Mexican revolution erupted. After a decade of agitating for revolution and informing the public about Díaz's horrible crimes in Mexico, the PLM's influence heightened. During the revolution, women's strengths were recognized if not always rewarded. Still more articles asking women to champion the cause appeared in *Regeneración*. The editorial staff wrote most of the essays. Housed at 512 1/2 Towne Street, its writers included the Flores Magón brothers, Librado Rivera, Antonio I. Villareal,

Anselmo Figueroa, and Praxedis Guerrero. Ethel Duffy Turner, the only woman and Anglo American on staff, edited the English section for six months, but did not seem to share the other writers' interest in women's issues. Turner, who adamantly supported the Party, often reiterated themes raised in *Barbarous Mexico*, by her husband, John Turner. Excerpts from the book revealed slave-like labor in Yucatan, for example.[27] The staff at Fourth and Towne printed an essay on women, their rights, or their subjugation in every issue. Each essay does not require scrutiny since they all echoed the maxim in "A La Mujer." Some examples suffice to demonstrate the PLM's ideology on women.

Regeneración printed "La Mujer" (Woman) and "Las Revolucionarias" (Women Revolutionaries) by Praxedis Guerrero, the PLM field commander who died in 1911 while in combat. Initially, Guerrero delivered "La Mujer" before a Los Angeles audience. It closely resembles Flores Magón's essay in format, content, and ideology. Sketching PLM policy, Guerrero discussed and denounced feminism, a controversial topic in 1910. In his opinion, feminists wanted not to equal men, but to be men: "Because she cannot be a woman, she wants to be a man; and in the name of rational feminism she wants to embark upon the ugly duties that are only for men."[28] He pursued this reasoning:

> Feminism is the fundamental antagonism to women's emancipation. (Furthermore,) there is nothing attractive about a masculine female who is divorced from her sweet mission as a woman; there is nothing desirable about a woman who prefers to be manly instead of womanly. [29]

By making a distinction between feminism and women's emancipation, Guerrero persuaded those who resisted equality between the sexes to accept the Party's stance on women. To reinforce his position, he argued in the last paragraph of "La Mujer":

> Equality between the sexes will not make men out of women; instead it will enforce equal opportunities without disturbing the natural order between the sexes. Women and men must both fight for this kind of rational equality because without it there will only be tyranny and misery.[30]

To Guerrero, equality between women and men could be achieved without disturbing the natural order between them. He did not define the natural place for each gender, nor did he explain women's sweet mission. But he revealed enough. Guerrero's rhetoric defined gender ideology, the way women were conditioned and encouraged to behave in their social relations with men. Woman's behavior was believed to be intrinsic to their gender. Her sweet mission was universal language for such an ideology--it required no definition. Like Flores Magón, Guerrero summoned women to inspire their husbands, lovers, and sons to join the battle. He concluded "Las Revolucionarias" with the same demand in "A La Mujer": "Revolutionaries, the day you see us hesitate to fight, spit in our faces."[31]

Ricardo Flores Magón shared Guerrero's fascination with sex roles. In an angry commentary, the leader denigrated a former Party member for unnatural and unmanly behavior. Antonio I. Villarreal, an activist and writer who had once shared a prison cell with Flores Magón, abandoned the PLM and enlisted in Francisco Madero's growing army shortly before the wealthy landowner assumed the presidency. Intentionally humiliating Villarreal, the Party leader reproached him in "Que Hable el Maricon" (May the Fag Speak):

> I have made serious charges against Antonio I. Villarreal. I have called him a pederast, an assassin and many other things, yet he stays so calm. Why doesn't he answer?... Silence does not exculpate; and in his case silence accuses him... Everyone knows that he is silent because the accusations ring true. He is not a man but a ... pederast. Villarreal does not have a right to face any man. Villarreal should be spit upon by every man and woman.[32]

Whether or not he was a pederast is not important. More important is Flores Magón's underlying assumption. He presumed that the most incriminating charges made against any man were those that debased his masculinity, and he was probably right. Just as Guerrero impugned unwomanly women, Flores Magón assailed unmanly men. These anarchists sanctioned free and spiritual love but Flores Magón's expressed homophobia restricted his vision of love.

The PLM's interpretation of assigned sex roles was not unique to the organization. The larger and better known Socialist Party and International Workers of the World (I.W.W.) understood women in the same way. They glorified working class heroines yet commanded them at home and at work. As the Socialist Party leader, Eugene Debs, explained: "If the hand of man is magical with accomplishment, the small white hand of woman has even greater magic in that it soothes and blesses ever."[33] Even the I.W.W. song, "Rebel Girl," modeled after labor organizer, Elizabeth Gurley Flynn, honored women's courage, yet minimized their strength by insisting that women serve men.[34] This romanticism typfied the era.

Female membership in the PLM is impossible to calculate. Equally difficult to estimate are the number of women who read *Regeneración*. But statistics are not necessary to examine the group's expectations or the women's responses to them. Like socialist and anarchist women in the United States, the *magonistas* were trapped between the rhetoric that declared their freedom and the reality that ignored it. Although they subscribed to worker solidarity manifested in *Regeneración*, they did not stay at home to do so. The women stretched their functions beyond an alleged natural sphere to join a public one; but even in the public arena, work was categorized by gender. The following examples show the central female figures and the problems they faced in the organization. These *magonistas* included journalists, soldiers, organizers, and companions to the male Party members.

PLM Women's Experiences

Two soldiers from Baja California, Margarita Ortega and her daughter, Rosaura Gortari, often smuggled supplies hidden under their skirts to revolutionaries across the border. Gortari died in 1911 while she and her mother were escaping federalists. Two years later, General Victoriano Huerta's regime gained power after Madero's assassination. His militia captured, tortured, and murdered Ortega in Mexicalli.[35] Companions to Ricardo and Enrique, María Talavera and Teresa Arteaga remained PLM loyalists throughout their lives. Arteaga joined the *junta* in 1905 after leaving her home in San Pedro, California.[36]

María Talavera, frequently arrested and imprisoned by United States federal agents, was harassed not only because of her activities, but also because of her intimate involvement with Ricardo Flores Magón. The *Los Angeles Times* publicized the relationship in an article entitled "Murder-Plotting Letters Found on the Mexican Revolutionists." The article warned that Talavera was a "brilliant and bold woman anarchist who dared more than any of the men."[37] In an illustration, she resembled an upper class woman. Ricardo's mug shot appeared on the same front page. A letter, which connects the images, specified María's willingness to "kill a tyrant," if necessary. The *Times* cited this as proof that she was an "expert assassin" who plotted to kill President Roosevelt and Díaz. Love letters from María to Ricardo confessing her love demonstrate that her commitment to the PLM was both political and personal. She was an activist and a *compañera*. This contrast between lover and activist further appears in a description of Talavera as "a quiet housewife, intent on cooking *frijoles*. But in her fry pans she was seeing men fighting; hearing in the sizzle of the grease the crash of arms, the pound of horse's feet and the din and commotion of a nation's government overthrown."[38] Despite its exaggeration, the *Los Angeles Times* shows Talavera's dedication to the PLM and dual roles in the revolution. As a housewife, she risked her life for the cause. María did, in fact, endanger her life for the Party. Ethel Duffy Turner recalled when she and María visited Ricardo in a Los Angeles jail, Talavera smuggled from the cell Ricardo's plans for an uprising. Federal agents subsequently retrieved the scheme and the *Times* circulated it on the front page of the paper.[39]

In 1914, Talavera, along with Ricardo, Enrique, and Teresa settled in a communal farm near Los Angeles. Although they lived there only until 1916 with other members, the group practiced their ideals for the first time. Once again the male leaders stuck to their principles only in theory and expected more from their companions than of themselves. Women and men shared field work but not housework, and as the men generated articles for *Regeneración*, the women cooked, cleaned, and rolled newspapers for distribution.[40] When they moved to the commune, the editorial staff temporarily halted the newspaper's publication because they lacked funding. To help the journal, PLM chapter "Luz y Vida" (Light and Life) organized fundraisers. Exclusively a women's group, "Luz y Vida" was founded in November 1915 by María Juarez, Macaela Grijalva, Elisa Martinez, Carmen Mendrano, and Benita and Carmen Talavera. The women agreed that they had a responsibility to the revolution, so they served it in the only way they knew. The chapter planned benefits and dances where they sold "tamales, refrescos, and sandwiches," then donated the proceeds to *Regeneración*.[41]

Women's Essays

During the revolution, essays appeared in *Regeneración* that reaffirmed the PLM's intent to politicize women. Examples of articles written by women and men who shared similar views on women's issues are: "La Mujer Obrera Bajo el Burgués" (The Working Class Woman Under the Bourgeosie), "La Mujer Esclava" (The Enslaved Woman), "Que Luchen" (May They Struggle), "La Mujer Pide Guerra" (Women Demand War), and "Para Ti, Mujer" (For You, Woman).[42] The essays by women are critical because they demonstrate how a few women were affected by--and, in turn affected--the Party's ideology. The female journalists associated with the organization included writers living in Mexico, Texas, and California. Teresa and Andrea Villarreal, Blanca de Moncaleano, and Paula Carmona de Flores Magón, wrote for the group based in Los Angeles. Juana Gutiérrez de Mendoza, Elisa Acuña y Rosetti and Sara Estela Ramírez were writers involved with the early *junta*. Sara Estela, who died at twenty-nine, taught in Laredo, Texas where she met Ricardo and Enrique. Accompanied by Juana, Elisa, and other supporters, the brothers crossed the border for the first time and stayed with Sara Estela. In Laredo, the women grew disillusioned with the group's bickering; this led Juana and Elisa to return to Guanajuato where they resumed publication of their own newspaper, *Vesper*. The two also joined Emiliano Zapata'a agrarian movement. Unforgiving of the women's disloyality, the *junta* spread rumors to discredit Juana and Elisa, naming them "indignant women--one of whom abandoned her husband and the other engaged in obscene practices frequently." A Party member from the south squelched the lies in a letter to Ricardo and reminded him that the women were valuable and influential revolutionaries.[43]

In their essays, the women took another approach from the men's and challenged, although implicitly, the PLM's ideology of women. In "Que Luchen," for instance, Paula Carmona de Flores Magón, formerly Enrique's wife, expressed her own expectations of women:

Comrades, Mexican mothers: Push your husbands to fight ... We should all fight, men and women. Many times a woman is at fault when a man abstains from taking part in the great struggles for liberty, but she too is degraded along with men. Slavery does not dignify us, nor does misery improve our status.[44]

Identically, the Villarreal sisters responded to Flores Magón's and Guerrero's messages to women when they challenged men to revolt. In the headlines of *Regeneración* they asked, "Que Hacéis Aquí Hombres?" (Men, Why Are You Here?) and ordered: "Go, go to Mexico to conquer for us and for our children: LAND AND LIBERTY."[45] And of themselves, the Villarreals announced:

> We are women; but we are not so weak that we will abandon the struggle ... We have the right to demand strength from those who hesitate to fight.[46]

Besieging men, Teresa and Andrea emphasized their strengths over their weaknesses, perhaps to threaten or humiliate reluctant revolutionaries.

Based in San Antonio, Texas, the journalists published *El Obrero* (The Worker) and *La Mujer Moderna*, (The Modern Woman) edited by Teresa and Andrea, respectively. In the "combat" newspapers they embraced the Party's fundamental tenet--worker solidarity.[47] Originally from Coahuila, the sisters fled to Texas avoiding Porfirio Díaz's persecution. Their denunciation of Diaz caused Teresa's mistaken kidnapping and arrest in Mexico. Releasing her almost immediately, Mexican officials reported that they had intended to capture Andrea, the more outspoken of the two. Her rebellious speeches fueled her reputation. She, however, protested her notoriety: "It is not good to call me the Mexican Joan of Arc because I cannot go to Mexico on a horse at the head of my soldiers and I cannot fire a gun, my hands are too small."[48]

Blanca de Moncaleano, a journalist from Mexico, ardently supported the revolution and women's rights. Her articles exhibited a unique sensitivity, one which understood women's oppression more intimately than the male writers on staff. Formerly a journalist for *Tierra*, a leftist Mexican weekly, she arrived in the United States after her husband, Juan Moncaleano, pleaded with *Regeneración*'s readers for donations to bring Blanca and their children from Mexico.[49] Blanca de Moncaleano published her first essays for *Regeneración* in 1913. In an article printed that year, she defied woman's subjugation in the family: "Do not forget that a woman has rights equal to those of a man. She is not on this earth only to procreate, to wash dishes and to wash clothes."[50] By acknowledging women's confinement in the family, de Moncaleano went a step further than Flores Magón or

Guerrero, both of whom wanted women to extend their feminine duties beyond the home and into battle. Blanca de Moncaleano, by contrast, ordered women from their prescribed functions entirely.

She also encouraged mothers, in "Para Ti, Mujer," to send their children to *La Escuela Racionalista* located in La Casa del Obrero Internacional (The International Workers' Home). Along with her husband, an educator from Colombia, Blanca promoted the Home they helped to establish in Los Angeles in 1913 as the PLM headquarters. At the school, instructors lectured daughters against the "bonds of female slavery" and sons against the "fetters of imperialist wars."[51] The school itself mirrored the principles developed by the Catalan anarchist, Francisco Ferrer Guardia, who realized that education was the key to working class emancipation. La Casa del Obrero Mundial (The Home of Workers of the World) the anarchist quarters in Mexico City, followed Ferrer Guardia's doctrine and served as a model for the Home in Los Angeles.[52] Located at 809 Yale Street near Alpine in downtown Los Angeles, La Casa formerly housed the Orphan's Home. The *Times* sensationalized the group's arrival by reporting: "Mexican Revolutionists Establish Armed Camp in Los Angeles."[53] In fact, the armed camp was a spacious house where workers and their children could seek free housing, cultural activities, and lectures. An application submitted to the Department of Buildings in March 1914 shows that the house was subdivided into thirteen, two and three room apartments to accommodate the growing number of inhabitants.[54]

Blanca's feminism challenged *Regeneración*'s audience, as did other women's issues. Birth control, for example, appeared as the topic of an article published in 1917, shortly before the newspaper's demise. The essay showed the Partido Liberal Mexicano modifying its ideology to a degree. Its author summarized:

While a social and economic redemption cannot be expected from the practice of birth control, the annihilation of the pernicious and brutish idea that a woman is not the sole owner of her body, to do with it as she pleases, is refreshing enough while we are on our way to bigger things.[55]

Although the anonymous author admitted the importance of reproductive rights, she or he minimized its importance by suggesting that "we are on our way to bigger things." The writer implied that women's issues, like birth control, were separate form more profound world affairs and failed to grasp that women and the world are inseparable.

Conclusion

From 1910 to 1918, *Regeneración* echoed images about women that were consistent with the Party's stated ideology yet inconsistent with reality. One of many leftist journals that endorsed specific values on women, this weekly is an excellent vehicle for analyzing gender. Unlike other controversial newspapers, this one endured two decades. And, in spite of the social upheaval, *Regeneración* retained most of its original editorial staff. Ricardo Flores Magón, the Partido Liberal Mexicano's guiding visionary, sustained his romantic ideals about the revolution and envisioned gains for working men and women. Both the United States and Mexican governments considered Flores Magón an international threat until he died in Fort Leavenworth in 1922. Ricardo was serving a twenty-one year sentence for violating the Espionage Act. Choke marks on his throat led many to believe that he was strangled.[56]

For all their radicalism the PLM male leaders did not move entirely beyond their traditional views of women. Their nationalism, as expressed in the Mexican revolution, was male-identified and consequently suffocated any possibility of women shaping their own socialist-feminist agenda. The PLM women, however, manipulated and expanded the Party's platform to fit their own needs. Caught between idealism and reality, the women survived the revolution by performing double duties. To a degree, they met Party expectations as catering wives and companions. But, *las magonistas* also extended their duties beyond the home and the family, and beyond nurturing male fighters, when they moved into the public sphere. Ultimately, the PLM prescribed an ideology that promised equality to women. What the women achieved had more to do with their own interpretation of that ideology.

To place gender in the forefront of a revolutionary movement places value on women. Birth control, child-care, and shared housework, for example, are as pertinent as nationalism and worker solidarity. Until present day movements learn from our historical predecessors like the PLM, then the dilemmas that inhibit women's true liberation will be wrought with

473

contradictions and revolution will remain a dream.

Notes

1. *Regeneración*, 24 September 1910: "En todos los tiempos la
mujer ha sido considerada como un ser inferior al hombre, no sólo
por la ley, sino también por la costumbre, y a ese erróneo e
injusto concepto se debe el infortunio que sufre desde que la
humanidad se diferenciaba apenas de la fauna primitiva por el uso
del fuego y el hacha de sílex." The English translation used here is
by Prensa Sembradora and it can be found in *Mexican Women in
the United States: Struggles Past and Present*, ed. Magdalena Mora
and Adelaida R. Del Castillo (Los Angeles: Chicano Studies
Research Center Publications, University of California, 1980), p.
161.

The first issues of *Regeneración*, 1900-1901, are housed at the
Hemeroteca Nacional de México, the country's newspaper archive.
Issues from 1914-1917 are also located at the Hemeroteca. For a
complete collection of the issues published in Los Angeles from
1910-1918, refer to the Chicano Studies Research Center Library,
University of California, Los Angeles.

2. The Mexican research group, Centro de Estudios Históricos
del Movimiento Obrero Mexicano (CEHSMO), reprinted a series
of texts on Flores Magón and other PLM members. The essay "A
La Mujer" can also be found in Juan Gómez-Quiñones,
*Sembradores, Ricardo Flores Magón y El Partido Liberal
Mexicano: A Eulogy and Critique* (Los Angeles: Chicano Studies
Center Publications, University of California, 1973), pp. 114-116.

3. Radical feminists coined the terms *woman-identified* and
male-identified to discern between feminist and patriarchal ideas,
politics, and institutions. A *male-identified* person, whether male
or female, accepts the patriarchy, benefits from it and chooses to
perpetuate it. A *woman-identified* woman challenges the
patriarchy to change a social-political system which ultimately
inhibits women. Male-identified women are insipidly anti-feminist
and accept patriarchal ways to gain individual benefits. While men
are not termed woman-identified, they can, however, challenge
their sexism.

4. Ines Hernandez Tovar, "Sara Estela Ramirez: The Early
Twentieth Century Texas-Mexican Poet," (Ph.D. diss., University
of Houston, 1984). Also see Emilio Zamora, "Sara Estela Ramírez:

Una Rosa Roja en el Movimiento," in *Mexican Women in the United States*, pp. 163-69.

5. Gómez-Quiñones, *Sembradores*, p. 31 and throughout the text.

6. Shirlene Soto, "The Mexican Woman: A Study of Her Participation in the Revolution, 1910-40," (Ph.D. diss., University of New Mexico, 1977).

7. W. Dirk Raat argues the PLM would not have had an ideology without *Regeneración*. He also points out that the PLM set the stage for Porfirio Díaz's self-imposed exile. See his book, *Revoltosos: Mexico's Rebels in the United States, 1903-1923* (College Station: Texas A&M University Press, 1981), pp. 18, 37.

8. Raat, p. 32.

9. Anna Macías, *Against All Odds: The Feminist Movement in Mexico to 1940* (Westport, Conn.: Greenwood Press, 1982). See especially chapter two, "Women and the Mexican Revolution, 1910-1920."

10. Karl Marx and Frederick Engels, *The German Ideology* (Moscow: Progressive Publishers, 1976). Refer specifically to volume one which includes the criticism of Feuerbach.

11. Roisin McDonough and Rachel Harrison, "Patriarchy and Relations of Production," in *Feminism and Materialism: Women and Modes of Production*, ed. Annette Kuhn and Ann Marie Wolpe (Boston: Routledge and Kegan Paul, 1978), pp. 15-18; Louis Althusser, *Lenin and Philosophy and Other Essays* (New York: Monthly Review Press, 1971). Refer to his essay "Ideology and Ideological Apparatuses."

12. Juliet Mitchell, *Psychoanalysis and Feminism* (New York: Vintage Books, 1974), pp. 411-416. Mitchell notes that in "analysing contemporary Western society we are (as elsewhere) dealing with two autonomous areas: the economic mode of capitalism and the ideological mode of patriarchy," p. 412. Note her use of the term "patriarchal" ideology rather than "gender" ideology which addresses women more specifically. The term is derived from Michele Barrett's book, *Women's Oppression Today: Problems in Marxist Feminist Analysis* (London: Verso Editions and NLB, 1980).

13. Catherine A. Mackinnon, "Feminism, Marxism, Method and the State: An Agenda for Theory," *Signs: Journal of Women in Culture and Society* 7 (Spring 1982): 515-544. She also points out: "Gender socialization is the process through which women come to identify themselves as sexual beings, as beings that exist for men," p. 531.

14. Rosaura Sánchez and Rosa Martinez Cruz, eds. *Essays on La Mujer* (Los Angeles: Chicano Studies Research Center Publications, University of California, 1977); Mora and Del Castillo, eds. *Mexican Women in the United States.* Also expressed in these anthologies are arguments against "bourgeois" feminism, racist and classist. Current literature examines race, class, and gender without subsuming gender. Anthropologist Patricia Zavella, in her superb study on Chicana cannery workers, employs a socialist-feminist analysis to place class, race, and gender at the center of her analysis. See Patricia Zavella, *Women's Work and Chicano Families: Cannery Workers of the Santa Clara Valley* (Ithaca: Cornell University Press, 1987). Historian Vicki Ruiz also places gender at the center of her excellent study on Chicana cannery workers. See Vicki L. Ruiz, *Cannery Women, Cannery Lives: Mexican Women, Unionization, and the California Food Processing Industry, 1930-1950* (Albuquerque: University of New Mexico Press, 1987).

15. Isabel Larguía and John Dumoulin, "Toward a Science of Women's Liberation," in *Mexican Women in the United States*, pp. 45-61. To argue that women's condition in the home is oppressive because women are exploited by the rate of surplus value only addresses their ppression as laborers. Surplus value, "the value over and above that which is necessary to cover a worker's means of subsistence," says nothing of sexual exploitation. See Paul M. Sweezy, *The Theory of Capitalist Development* (New York: Monthly Review Press, 1970), pp. 56-66 for a discussion of Marx's theory of surplus value.

16. Juliet Mitchell, *Woman's Estate* (New York: Vintage Books, 1971). In chapters eight and nine, Mitchell discusses the ideology of the family to explain how the housewife and mother in a capitalist society is the backbone and preserver of the family unit which oppresses her. She is forced to uphold an institution built upon individuality and equality yet it denies her those very rights when it binds her to the home. See Nancy Cott, *The Bonds of Womanhood: Women's Sphere in New England, 1780-1835* (New Haven: Yale University Press, 1977) for a discussion of the transition to industrialization and its impact on women in New England and their status in the home.

17. Works by Sheila Rowbotham, Juliet Mitchell, Michele Barrett, and Sally Alexander, for example, provide superb Marxist-feminist analyses despite their blatant neglect of race. They cannot be faulted for the ommission, however, inasmuch as they reveal a sincere, though limited understanding of racism.

18. Ethel Duffy Turner, *Revolution in Baja California: Ricardo Flores Magón's High Noon* (Detroit: Blaine Ethridge Books, 1981), p. 109. Jesus Flores Magón became an agent for Madero who by 1911 was no longer allied with the *magonistas*.
19. Duffy Turner, *Revolution in Baja California*, pp. 3, 103; see also Armando Bartra, *Regeneración, 1900-1918* (Mexico, D.F.: ERA, 1977) for an excellent chronology of *Regeneración*'s publication.
20. *Los Angeles Times*, 2 October 1910; see Duffy Turner, *Revolution in Baja California*, p. 13 for a discussion of Harrison Gray Otis's land grab in Mexico; the bombing of the *Times* building is discussed more fully in chapters twenty-one and twenty-two of Grace Stimson's *Rise of the Labor Movement in Los Angeles* (Los Angeles: University of California Press, 1955), pp. 366-419.
21. Juan Gómez-Quiñonez, "Social Change and Intellectual Discontent: The Growth of Mexican Nationalism, 1890-1911" (Ph.D. diss., University of California, Los Angeles, 1972), pp. 149-150; Soto, "The Mexican Woman," p. 28. In July of 1906 the PLM issued its reform program where they listed provisions for the protection of women. By 1910 the PLM's anarchist views were known. I will not discuss the organization's anarchist ideology in any depth. Many studies have defined it as a mixture of unorthodox anarchism, syndicalism, and communism. See Gómez-Quiñones, *Sembradores*; Raat, *Revoltosos*; and John Hart, *Anarchism and the Mexican Working Class, 1860-1913* (Austin: University of Texas Press, 1978). John Hart argues that Mexican anarchism had a European influence and he cites the intellectuals who migrated to Mexico taking with them anarchist perspectives. Also see David Poole, *Land and Liberty: Anarchist Influences in the Mexican Revolution: Ricardo Flores Magón* (Sanday, U.K.: Cienfuegos Press, LTD., 1977).
22. *Regeneración*, 24 September 1910: "Vosotras constituís la mitad de la especie humana, y, lo que afecta a ésta, afecta a vosotras como parte integrante de la humanidad. Si el hombre es esclavo, vosotras los sois también. La cadena no reconoce sexos; la infamia que averguenza al hombre os infama de igual modo a vosotras. No podéis sustraeros a la verguenza de la opresión: la misma garra que acogota al hombre os estrangula a vosotras."
23. Ibid.: "Vuestro deber es ayudar al hombre; estar con él cuando vacila, para animarlo; volar a su lado cuando sufre para endulzar su pena y reir y cantar con él cuando el triunfo sonríe."

24. Ibid.: "prostitución es y no otra cosa, el matrimonio, cuando la mujer se casa sin que intervenga para nada el amor, sino sólo el propósito de encontrar un hombre que la mantenga, esto es, vende su cuerpo por la comida, exactamente como lo practica la mujer perdida, siendo esto lo que ocurre en la mayoría de los matrimonios.

"Y qué podría decirse del inmenso ejército de mujeres que no encuentran esposo?"

25. Hart, *Anarchism and the Mexican Working Class*, p. 17; Ricardo Flores Magón, *Artículos Políticos, 1917* (México, D.F.: Ediciones Antorcha, 1981), pp. 186-188; Gómez-Quiñones, *Sembradores*, p. 20; Margaret S. Marsh, *Anarchist Women, 1870-1920* (Philadelphia: Temple University Press, 1981), pp. 19-20. Peter Kropotkin and Pierre Joseph Proudhon were anarchist theoreticians who believed in women's instinctive bond to the domestic sphere. Interestingly, the precursors to anarchism also held similar ideas on women. As early as the thirteenth century in France, the Amalrikites "preached not only a community of goods, but also a community of women" along with perfect equality--so to speak. Amalrikite principles surfaced in the sixteenth century in the Zurich Highlands where men also held "wives and property in common," refer to E.V. Zenker, *Anarchism* (London: Methuen & Co., 1898), pp. 9-11.

26. *Regeneración*, 24 September 1910: "Haced que vuestros esposos, vuestros hermanos, vuestros padres, vuestros hijos y vuestros amigos tomen el fusil. A quien se niegue a empuñar un arma contra la opresión, escupidle el rostro."

27. Duffy Turner, *Revolution in Baja California*, p. 2; Ethel Duffy Turner, "Writings and Revolutionists," p. 22, an oral interview conducted by Ruth Teiser at the University of California Bancroft Library, Berkeley, Regional Oral History Office, 1967; *Regeneración*, 24 December 1910; John Turner, *Barbarous Mexico* (Chicago: Charles H. Kerr and Campany, 1910).

28. *Regeneración*, 6 November 1910: "No pudiendo ser mujer, la mujer quiere ser hombre; se lanza con un entusiasmo digno de un feminismo más racional en pos de todas las cosas feas que un hombre puede ser y hacer..."

29. Ibid.: El 'feminismo' sirve de base a la oposición, de los enemigos de la emancipación de la mujer. Ciertamente no hay nada atractivo en una mujer alejada de la dulce misión de su sexo para empuñar el látigo de la opresión en una mujer huyendo de su graciosa individualidad femenina para vestir la hibridez del 'honbrunamiento.'"

30. Ibid.: "La igualidad libertaria no trata de hacer *hombre* de la mujer; de las mismas oportunidades a las fracciones de la especie humana para que ambas se desarrollen sin obstáculos...sin estorbarse en el lugar que cada uno tiene en una naturaleza. Mujeres y hombres hemos de luchar por esta igualidad racional...porque sin ella habrá perpetuamente en el hogar la simiente de la tiranía, el retoño de la desdicha social."

31. "Revolucionarias: el día que nos veáis vacilar, escupidnos el rostro!" "Las Revolucionarias" was published in *Regeneración*, 14 January 1911 in the same issue that announced Guerrero's death, a blow to the PLM. In that issue Ricardo Flores Magón wrote an article in which he eulogized Guerrero and his importance to the PLM.

32. *Regeneración*, 11 September 1911: "He venido haciendo cargos concretos contra Antonio I. Villarreal. Le he llamado pederasta y asesino y otras cosas mas, y él, tan 'fresco.' Porque no contesta? El silencio no disculpa; antes, mejor, en el caso de Villarreal, acusa. Por todas partes se dice puesto que Villarreal se calla ante el tremendo cargo de que no es hombre, sino un... pederasta... Villarreal no tiene derecho a ver a ningún hombre de frente; Villarreal debe ser escupido por todos los hombres y por todas las mujeres."

33. Eugene V. Debs, "Women" in *American Appeal*, 30 October 1926. The Socialist Party weekly published the Debs memorial edition in which his essays were reprinted. In "Man," "Woman," and "Child" Debs outlined his ideas on the socialist family.

34. Elizabeth Gurley Flynn, *I Speak My Own Piece* (New York, 1955). Ann Schofield, "Rebel Girls and Union Maids: The Woman Question in Journals of the AFL and IWW, 1905-1920," *Feminist Studies* 9 (Summer 1983): 335-355. Schofield has written an excellent analysis showing how these leftist organizations fostered gender ideology in their writings on women.

35. *Regeneración*, 13 June 1914 and Duffy Turner, *Revolution in Baja California*, pp. 66-67. In an oral interview conducted on 17 April 1982 in Madera, California, *la magonista* Josephina Arancibia informed me that she had known Margarita Ortega and confirmed Ortega'a murder by the Huertistas in Mexicali.

36. Angeles Mendieta Alatorre, *La mujer en la revolución mexicana* (México, D.F.: Talleres Gráficos de la Nación, 1961), p. 39.

37. *Los Angeles Times*, 19 September 1907; Duffy Turner, *Writings and Revolutionists*. Duffy Turner tells of Talavera's

activities in the PLM. Her harassment by United States federal agents is cited in *Regeneración*, 14 October 1916.

38. *Los Angeles Times*, 19 September 1907.

39. Ibid. The newspaper printed a front page story indicting María Talavera as Magón's accomplice based on a letter she smuggled out of jail for him. The headline read: "Murder-Plotting Letters Found on the Mexican Revolutionists." Ethel Duffy Turner, a more reliable source than the *Times*, noted in an interview that while she and María Talavera visited Ricardo in a Los Angeles jail, "Maria picked up a paper from the floor of the jail cell where Ricardo had dropped it. The paper had plans for the 1908 revolution. María sent it to the border, but it was captured." See Duffy Turner, *Writings and Revolutionists*, p. 11.

40. In an interview with *magonista* Josephina Arancibia on 17 April 1982, she informed me that she and her younger sister visited the farm during summers. She remembered that while some women helped to fold newspapers and worked in the fields planting and harvesting, the women also did the cooking and the cleaning in the house. There are conflicting reports about the location of the farm, however, Señora Arancibia recalls that it was in the Silver Lake/Echo Park area of Los Angeles.

41. *Regeneración*, 6 December 1915.

42. "La Mujer Obrera Bajo el Burgués," by Antonio de Pio in *Regeneración*, 14 December 1912; "La Mujer Esclava," by René Chaughl in *Regeneración*, 20 January 1912; "Que Luchen," by Paula Carmona de Flores Magón in *Regeneración*, 8 October 1910; "La Mujer Pide Guerra," by Antonio I. Villarreal in *Regeneración*, 1 October 1910; and "Para Ti, Mujer," by Blanca de Moncaleano in *Regeneración*, 22 March 1913.

43. A. Gravioto to Ricardo Flores Magón, Mexico, 16 May 1904 in the Silvestre Terrazas Collection, University of California, Berkeley, Bancroft Library. The letter from Gravioto warns Flores Magón that he must stop the rumors scandalizing Juana Mendoza and Elisa Rosetti. The letter reveals that the two women did not leave the PLM on congenial terms, the reasons why are uncertain. The Hemeroteca Nacional houses the only two surviving issues of *Vesper*, the newspaper edited by Juana Mendoza and Elisa Rosetti.

44. *Regeneración*, 8 October 1910: "Compañeras, madres mexicanas: empujad a vuestros maridos a la lucha... Debemos luchar todos, hombres y mujeres. La mujer tiene muchas veces la culpa de que se abstenga el hombre de tomar parte en las grandes luchas por la libertad, sin pensar que con eso no hace sino

degradar al hombre y degradarse ella misma, porque la esclavitud no dignifica, la miseria no eleva el caracter."
45. *Regeneración*, 21 January 1911.
46. Ibid.: "Mujeres somos; pero no hemos sentido flaquezas que nos empujen a abandonar la pelea... Derecho tenemos a demandar entereza de los que vacilan."
47. The newspapers edited by the Villarreal sisters were advertised as such in *Regeneración*, 17 September 1910; 3 September 1910; 10 September 1910; and in many more issues. W. Dirk Raat offers a few paragraphs on the Villarreals in *Revoltosos*.
48. *El Paso Record*, 5 November 1909; also see the *San Antonio Light*, 18 August 1909; and *Woman's National Daily*, 2 November 1909 for more information on the Villarreals. These newspaper clippings can be located in the John Murray Collection, University of California, Berkeley, Bancroft Library.
49. Secretaría de Relaciones Exteriores, Archivo, México, D.F., Asunto Flores Magón, Colección L-E-918-954, sobre Juan Moncaleano. Also see *Regeneración*, 12 October 1912 and 22 February 1913.
50. *Regeneración*, 22 February 1913: "No olvidéis que la mujer tiene derechos al igual que los hombres, que no habéis llegado al mundo tan sólo para multiplicar la humanidad, soplar el fagón, lavar ropa, y fregar platos..."
51. *Regeneración*, 22 March 1913.
52. Juan Moncaleano was instrumental in founding La Casa del Obrero Mundial in Mexico City and the newspaper *Luz* in Monterrey. Essays in *Luz* supported the PLM and glorified Ferrer Guardia. See especially the 10 October and 21 November 1917 and 23 January 1918 issues. This newspaper was similar to *Regeneración* in format and in its ideology. It is fascinating to see how many anarchist newspapers were published in Mexico in the early twentieth century. *Tribuna Roja, Trabajo, Aurora Social, Nueva Solidaridad Obrera* and *Avanté* all held views on women's liberation similar to those in *Regeneración*. Consult *Regeneración*, 1, 8, 22, 29 March 1913 for news items on La Casa del Obrero Internacional and *Regeneración* 10 September, 8 October 1910, 14 December 1912 and 17 November 1917 for essays commending Ferrer Guardia and the worker's schools.
53. *Los Angeles Times*, March 1913; La Casa del Obrero Internacional in Los Angeles, California no longer stands. See the Second Annual Report of the Municipal Charities Commission, City of Los Angeles, July 1914-July 1915, p. 64 for a brief report

on the Los Angeles Orphan's Home which was situated on Yale and Alpine in 1880 and moved in 1911.
54. City Hall Land Records, Los Angeles, Department of Buildings, Application to Alter, 10 March 1914.
55. *Regeneración*, 10 February 1917 by R.G. Cox.
56. Duffy Turner, *Revolution in Baja California*, pp. 82-83.

THE WOMEN'S MOVEMENT IN MEXICO: THE FIRST AND SECOND FEMINIST CONGRESSES IN YUCATAN, 1916

by

Shirlene Soto

During the first decades of the twentieth century, the state of Yucatan became the lodestar of Mexico's women's rights movement. It was the site of Mexico's first two feminist congresses and the center of the nation's most extensive political and social participation by Mexican women. There were four principal reasons that led to Yucatan's leadership role: the active support of socialist Governor Salvador Alvarado (1915-18), the progressive ideals and leadership of Yucatecan women, the considerable wealth Yucatan derived from henequen production, and Yucatan's open encouragement of education for women.[1]

Yucatan reached the apex of its social reform during the revolutionary period while under the governorship of General Alvarado. During his administration, women played an important role in his reform programs. Unlike many Mexican revolutionaries, Alvarado considered women's emancipation an essential element of Mexico's revolutionary goal of elevating all oppressed people.

As the newly-appointed governor and military commander of the state, Alvarado arrived in early 1915 armed with orders from President Venustiano Carranza to bring the state under Constitutionalist control. After a decisive military victory in March, Alvarado set out to impose his authority, establish order, organize a government, and begin the important work of reconstruction. His brief three-year term brought many significant socio-economic changes to the state. His efforts to create a better society were influenced by his socialist philosophy and included redistribution of income, educational reform, and expansion of his political base to include unorganized labor, *campesinos*, and women.

Alvarado had an advantage few visionaries ever enjoy-- money. By the time of · the revolutionary period, henequen revenues had made Yucatan the wealthiest state in Mexico. Alvarado was in power during Yucatan's biggest henequen boom, created by the demand for twine during World War I.

Alvarado designed his programs as a means to alter radically the political, social, and economic structure of Yucatan's society. He actively promoted education for women because he believed that it was "a social error to educate women for a society that didn't exist."[2] One of his first official acts as governor was to increase the types and numbers of schools available to women from all economic levels.[3]

To win support for his educational initiatives, the governor convened Mexico's First Pedagogical Congress in September of 1915. More than six hundred teachers, most of them women, attended the Congress at state expense. Several of these teachers later provided leadership at the First and Second Feminist Congresses held in January and November of 1916. The delegates at the First Pedagogical Congress reached a consensus that co- educational and rationalist (socialist) programs should be promoted in every school, rather than the traditional religious programs. Support for this secular approach was reaffirmed at the Second Pedagogical Congress held in August of the following year.[4]

The improvement of women's working conditions was a central tenet of Alvarado's program for the reform of Yucatan's social structure. New opportunities for women were created by a progressive labor law, the formation of women's cooperatives, and the hiring of women in government offices. Several of Alvarado's labor reforms were aimed specifically at women at the lower end of the economic scale. Special laws were enacted to improve the conditions of domestic servants and prostitutes. For servants, who were mainly Mayan women and children, the decrees specified minimum wages, maximum hours, and halted the insidious practice of "adopting" orphans and retaining them as domestics. To fight the widespread corruption practiced by brothel owners and police, as well as to combat venereal disease, Alvarado eliminated bordellos (but not prostitution). He also required prostitutes to undergo periodic physical examinations and he made it an offense for men with venereal disease to patronize prostitutes.[5]

Alvarado's boldest political move during his three-year administration was to summon the first feminist congress in Mexico's history. In late October of 1915, the general announced that a women's congress would convene for three days in Merida. It was convened on 13 January 1916. Four basic themes were considered: (1) freeing women from their traditional yokes; (2) the role of primary education in the lives of women; (3) participation of women in public life; and (4) public and social functions to help women gain their rightful place in society.[6]

Following extensive preparation by an organizing committee, the Congress convened at 9:00 a.m. at the Peón Contreras Theatre in downtown Merida. Over seven hundred delegates, mostly teachers from Yucatan, attended.[7] Although most of the delegates were mainly from the middle-class, they expressed vastly differing views on women. These differences surfaced quickly as a result of a speech written by Hermila Galindo, a staunch supporter of the Carranza government. Galindo, one of Mexico's most prominent feminists and Constitutionalists, had been invited to participate in the Congress by the Department of Public Education. Unable to attend, she sent a paper to be read. In "La mujer en el porvenir" ("Women in the Future"), Galindo adamantly defended the view that women are the intellectual equal of men and should, therefore, be included in the revolutionary ranks. The most shocking part of her message, however, was her demand that women should have the same sexual freedom as men. Galindo insisted that women needed to understand their sexuality and that schools should teach sex education.[8] She was later forced to defend her position in the magazine La Mujer Moderna (which she helped to found) and in a statement sent to the Second Feminist Congress.[9]

Galindo's views sharply divided the delegates. Although it was agreed that her work should not be published by the Congress, the conservative faction did not even want her ideas discussed. Conservatives dismissed her message as immoral. Other delegates affirmed that Galindo had addressed key issues for women which should be debated. Galindo's controversial viewpoints received a thorough airing in the vigorous dialogue generated by both factions.[10]

Three basic positions emerged from the First Feminist Congress: conservative, radical, and moderate. The conservative Catholic faction condemned Galindo's paper. Especially concerned with keeping women in their traditional roles of wife and mother, the Catholic faction fought against any proposals that would threaten the status quo. They were afraid that too much education and experience would make women unattrative to the opposite sex. Francisca García Ortiz voiced this fear when she commented that "women don't need as much education" as men. She concluded her comments by declaring "women teachers don't marry!" and "encyclopedic knowledge seems to be an obstacle to happiness."[11]

The arguments of Catholic conservatives were totally unacceptable to women at the other end of the ideological spectrum. The radicals shared the socialist government's conviction that women should take an active role in society by voting and running for office. They considered women the equals of men in every sense. In their opinion, it was the government's duty to halt sexual injustices and to ensure equal opportunity to deserving and competent women.

The moderates supported education for women, especially laical and rationalist programs. They viewed education as a way of loosening the shackles that had bound women traditionally. They also argued that women should receive a practical education that would help them to be better wives and mothers. While they supported women's participation in civic affairs, they addressed the issue of suffrage more cautiously than the radicals. The moderates argued that, for the present, political rights should be exercised by men only. But women should receive the right to vote after they were adequately prepared.[12]

Moderates and radicals did agree on the need to reform the Civil Code of 1884 that so blatantly discriminated against women. Some of the areas of the outdated code that they agreed needed immediate revision included guardianship, matrimony, inheritance, and freedom for single women after the age of twenty-one. In addition, both factions agreed to support the following: laical education; the primary school reforms recommended by the First Pedagogical Congress; new school curricula; new art academies; and more public conferences.[13]

The most important proposal passed by the Congress concerned suffrage. During the final session of the Congress, on the afternoon of January 16, a suffrage petition was submitted for consideration. This petition, initiated and signed by more than 30 of the most radical women, called for the state government to take active leadership in changing the national constitution so that women would be allowed to vote in all municipal elections. It was also proposed that Yucatan's state constitution be revised to allow women, 21 and over, to vote and to run for office in municipal elections. The petition was passed unanimously by a group of exhausted women at the close of the session.[14]

While Mexico's First Feminist Congress was a landmark in the women's struggle, its immediate results were limited. The Congress did not produce a women's organization nor were its two major proposals acted upon immediately--revision of the Civil Code of

1884 and municipal suffrage. However, influenced by these two proposals, President Carranza's Law of Family Relations (April, 1917) corrected many of the faults contained in the outdated Civil Code.[15] The municipal and state vote was granted to women in Yucatan in the early 1920s under the governorship of Felipe Carrillo Puerto (1922-24). By contrast, Mexican women in most other states had to wait until 1946 before they could vote in state and municipal elections.

The most important accomplishment of the First Congress was that, for the first time, women gathered together to discuss issues vital to their struggle for equality. The Congress captured the enthusiastic spirit of the times and encouraged women to persevere in their demands for reform. General Alvarado was both pleased and troubled by the First Feminist Congress. Extensive coverage in the official newspaper, *La Voz de la Revolución*, and a telegram that General Alvarado sent to President Carranza in Mexico City on January 15, while the Congress was in session, are indicative of the deep satisfaction the General felt. With obvious pride Alvarado reported to the president: "The audience discussed in a vehement manner the most adequate ways for making women less religiously fanatic and improving their social conditions. Vibrant speeches were given with grand enthusiasm. Permit me to express to you that this is a new triumph for the revolution. A year ago, when I arrived, there were few women seen alone in public."[16] However, General Alvarado had hoped for a stronger mandate from the delegates. In an attempt to win wider support for his programs and to further clarify the issues, he announced that a Second Feminist Congress would convene in Merida in November.[17]

Held eleven months after the First Feminist Congress, the Second Feminist Congress drew less than half the attendance of the first and included many of the same delegates, mainly middle class teachers from the state of Yucatan. The tone of the second meeting was more practical and circumspect, perhaps due to its extended length (from November 23 to December 2) and to the support given to the moderate faction. Discussions paralleled those of the First Congress and included primary school education, marriage, rights of divorced parents and their offspring, women's suffrage, and office-holding. Like the first meeting, there were heated debates and protests, especially over the roles women should assume in society.

This second congress convened in the Escuela Vocacional de Artes Domésticas in Merida at 4:00 p.m. on 23 November 1916. On the first day, Mercedes Betancourt de Albertos and Candelaria

Ruz Patrón delivered strongly feminist speeches. Both speakers emphasized that women must have equality under the law. Mercedes Betancourt pointed to the contradiction between the ideals of equality--stressed by the leaders of the Mexican Revolution--and the practiced exclusion of women. As a reminder to Mexican revolutionaries, she quoted the writer and feminist Emilia Pardo Bazán, "For women to advance, it would be necessary, in the first place, that she want to and second, that she find some ground prepared, [and] some help from man also." Both speakers ended by proclaiming that, under the circumstances, emancipation was within reach if the women present would put all their souls into it. Mercedes Betancourt concluded dramatically by exclaiming, "Let us unite into an heroic phalanx and struggle until we win the inalienable rights of our sex!"[18]

After such an auspicious beginning, the Second Feminist Congress bogged down in disagreements and bickering. As in the First Congress, the suffrage issue divided the delegates. When the Suffrage Committee recommended that women over 21 be allowed to vote in municipal elections but not to run for office, there were several objections. Lucrecia Vadillo, who served on the committee, immediately took issue with its recommendations. Representing the traditional, conservative viewpoint, she explained her dissent by stating that women's mission should be one of "sweetness and peace." Women in the future should vote, she conceded, but not at present because they are unprepared. Besides, she said, suffrage "is the element that will destroy conjugal peace, wives' happiness, and family life" and Vadillo concluded by recommending that women neither vote nor run for municipal office.[19]

After the committee members completed their presentations, the suffrage question was opened to the floor for debate. Led by Mercedes Betancourt, several delegates spoke in favor of the committee's recommendations. Conservatives, under the leadership of Evelia Marrufo, who had led the conservative faction in the First Congress, opposed the committee's recommendations. To the outspoken Evelia Marrufo, women's participation in civic affairs presented a direct threat to their home life. Betancourt countered Marrufo sharply by declaring that voting hardly meant abandoning the home. The debate was so lengthy and so bitter that it carried over into Monday's business, with Betancourt and Marrufo continuing to spar on center stage. Finally, in exasperation, Betancourt reminded her audience that this was a feminist congress and that women were asking only for the right to vote. No one, she continued, would be obliged to vote if she preferred not to exercise that right. At the end of the discussion, the delegates approved suffrage for women on the municipal level (147-87), but rejected the right of women to seek municipal office (60-30).[20]

The acrimonious debate of previous days was a sharp contrast to the gaiety of the closing session. Governor Alvarado was present at the ceremonies, along with many other dignitaries. The closing ceremonies included a poetry reading, speeches and numerous praises for the delegates and their accomplishments.[21]

In comparing the two Congresses, the accomplishments of the First were more substantial. The First Congress delegates had passed resolutions supporting both the right to vote and the right to run for municipal office. While these two issues were hotly debated at the Second Congress, only the municipal suffrage resolution passed. The Second Congress did not have to contend with Galindo's radical feminist ideas. Though published and distributed in Merida, her speech to the Second Congress was never delivered.[22]

Although neither the First nor Second Feminist Congresses reached the accord that Alvarado had hoped for, they did provide a forum for Mexican women to gather and discuss their goals and aspirations. The meetings revealed the deep divisions between the position of the radical feminists (who sought equality on all levels) and the conservative faction (who strove to improve women's roles only as they related to that of wife and mother). These divisions characterized the women's movement until 1953, when national suffrage was achieved. In the context of the times, the Congresses kept the women's issue before the public and constituted an enormous step forward for the women's movement in Mexico.

Yucatan's leadership in reforms for women was halted temporarily by the passage of a bill at Mexico's Constitutional Convention in Queretaro in December, 1916 that disqualified Salvador Alvarado from running for governor of Yucatan because he had neither been born there nor had he resided there for five years.[23] Without Alvarado's leadership, plagued by a renewed outbreak of violence over the Mexican presidential succession in 1920, and caught in the economic squeeze resulting from falling henequen prices, social reforms slowed in Yucatan. However, because General Salvador Alvarado and the women of the First and Second Feminist Congresses had prepared the groundwork for the women's movement, the fire of reform was not extinguished by these adverse circumstances. The fire smoldered until it was rekindled in the early 1920s, under the leadership of socialist Governor Felipe Carrillo Puerto and his sister Elvia.

Notes

1. *La Voz de la Revolución*, 28 March 1917, p. 3; Laureana Wright de Kleinhans, *Mujeres Notables Mexicanas* (México, D.F.: Tipografía Económica, 1910), p. 403. Henequen is a fibrous plant used to make twine.
2. *La Voz de la Revolución*, 28 October 1915, p. 1.
3. Anna Macías, "Mexican Women in the Social Revolution." Paper delivered at the 86th meeting of the American Historical Association, New York City, December 1971, p. 19, quoting Salvador Alvarado, *Informe que el General Salvador Alvarado ... rinde al Primer Jefe del Ejercito Constitucionalista ... C. Venustiano Carranza. Comprende su Gestión Administrativa desde el 19 de Marzo 1915 al 28 de Febrero de 1917* (Mérida: Imprenta del Gobierno Constitucionalista, 1917), pp. 38, 52. The Macías paper was published later in *History of Latin American Civilization: Sources and Interpretations*, edited by Lewis Hanke, 2 vols. (Boston: Little, Brown and Co., 1973), 2: 459-469.
4. For a discussion of the Congress, see Antonio Bustillos Carrillo, *Yucatán al Servicio de la Patria y de la Revolución* (México, D.F.: Casa Ramírez Editores, 1959), p. 169; *La Voz de la Revolución*, 7 August 1916, pp. 1, 2.
5. Bustillos Carrillo, *Yucatán al Servicio*, p. 159; Alvaro Gamboa Ricalde, *Yucatán desde 1910*, vol. 2 (Veracruz: Imprenta "Standard," 1943-1955), pp. 370-387.
6. *La Voz de la Revolución*, 29 October 1915, pp. 1, 2.
7. Most of the delegates to the First Feminist Congress were from Yucatan because fighting had not yet ceased in many parts of Mexico and because Yucatan was geographically inaccessible and remote.
8. Sex education in public schools did not become part of the Mexican educational program until the presidency of Lázaro Cárdenas in the 1930s.
9. The complete text of Hermila Galindo's speech to the First Feminist Congress is printed in Congreso Feminista de Yucatán, *Anales de Esa Memorable Asamblea* (Mérida: Talleres Tipográficos del "Ateneo Peninsular," 1916), pp. 195-202; Artemisa Sáenz Royo [Xóchitl], *Historia Política - Social - Cultural del Movimiento Feminino en México, 1914-1950* (México, D.F.: M. León Sánchez, 1954), p. 68.
10. *Anales de Esa Memorable Asamblea*, pp. 70, 71, 77, 118. Reactions to Galindo's speech can be found also in *La Voz de la Revolución*, 14 January 1916, pp. 1-3.
11. *Anales de Esa Memorable Asamblea*, p. 72.

12. Ibid., pp. 100-109.

13. Ibid., pp. 111, 129; Adaíde Foppa, "The First Feminist Congress in Mexico, 1916," *Signs: Journal of Women in Culture and Society* 5 (August 1979): 194-195.

14. *Anales de Esa Memorable Asamblea*, pp. 126-127.

15. The Law of Family Relations, issued to supplement the 1914 law that legalized divorce, guaranteed married women guardianship and child custody rights, participation in legal suits, and the right to draw up contracts.

16. *Anales de Esa Memorable Asamblea*, p. xii.

17. *La Voz de la Revolución*, 16 November 1916, p. 1.

18. Ibid., 24 November 1916, p. 3.

19. Ibid., 28 November 1916, pp. 1, 2.

20. Ibid., 30 November 1916, pp. 1, 5. Delegates were cautious on the question of women holding municipal office. Only ninety of over two hundred delegates voted and only thirty voted in the affirmative.

21. Ibid., 3 December 1916, p. 2.

22. Hermila Galindo, *Estudio de la Srita. Hermila Galindo con motivo de los temas que han de absolverse en el Segundo Congreso Feminista de Yucatán* (Mérida: Imprenta del Gobierno Constitucionalista, 1916), p. 4. Galindo could not attend because she was ill. Elena Torres, who represented Guanajuato and held ideas similar to those of Galindo, was to deliver Galindo's message to the Congress. It is not clear why Elena Torres did not attend the meeting.

23. *Diario de los Debates del Congreso Constituyente, 1916-1917*, Comisión Nacional Para la Celebración del Sesquicentenario de la Proclamación de la Independencia Nacional y del Cincuentenario de la Revolución Mexicana, Introduction by Hilario Medina, 2 vols. (México, D.F.: Talleres Gráficos de la Nación, 1960), 2:1211.

CONTRIBUTORS

Louise Año Nuevo Kerr, Associate Vice Chancellor for Academic Affairs and Associate Professor, Department of History, University of Illinois at Chicago. Ph.D. in history from the University of Illinois at Chicago. Fellowships include: Woodrow Wilson (1964), Ford Foundation (1972-73), National Research Council (1980-81). Former member of the National Council of the National Endownment for the Humanities and the Illinois Humanities Council. Taught at Loyola University of Chicago, Colorado College, and Northeastern Illinois University. Many of her publications have appeared in scholarly journals.

Marisol Arbeláez, Instructor of sociology at the Universidad Nacional Autónoma de México. Investigadora, Dirección de Estudios Históricos of the Instituto Nacional de Antropología e Historia. She teaches Mexican and Latin American history at the Universidad Autónoma Metropolitana at Iztapalapa. Presently, she is conducting research on working women in Mexico City.

Lourdes Arguelles, Associate Professor and MacArthur Chair in Women Studies at Pitzer College, Claremont, California. Ph.D. in behavioral sciences/human relations from New York University. Dissertation on "Cuban Political Refugees in the U.S.: A Study of Social Mobility and Authoritarianism." Former Senior Lecturer in the School of Social Work, University of California, Los Angeles.

Former director of Women's Programs at the AIDS Research and
Educational Project, Long Beach and former director of Research
for the Ministry of Human Resources, British Columbia, Canada.
Taught at several American and Canadian universities and
colleges; consultant to national and international human rights
service organizations. Has published on women and racial and
ethnic relations in popular and academic journals. Dr. Arguelles is
a licensed psychotherapist.

Iris Blanco, Ph.D. Candidate, Department of History, University
of California, San Diego. M.A. in history from the Universidad
Nacional Autónoma de México, Mexico City. Taught at the
University of California, San Diego. Presented "Elitismo y
misoginismo de misioneros y caciques" at the Casa de la Cultura in
Ensenada (1978). Publications include: "Participación de las mujeres
en la sociedad prehispanica" (1977), "La Mujer en los Albores de
la Conquista de México" *Aztlan* (1980), and co-authored "O te
aclimatas o te aclimueres," *Fem.* (1984).

Roberto R. Calderón, Ph.D. Candidate, Department of History,
University of California, Los Angeles. Teaching Assistant,
Department of History, University of California, Los Angeles.
Fellowships include: UCLA Chicano Studies Research Center
Graduate Fellowship (1984), National Hispanic Scholarship Fund,
Scholar of the Year (1984), UCLA Dissertation Year Fellowship
(1988). Has published in popular and scholarly journals.

Antonia Castañeda, Ph.D. Candidate, Department of History,
Stanford University. M.A. in Latin American Studies from the
University of Washington. Taught at the University of
Washington, Stanford University, University of California at Davis
and various community colleges. Dissertation title "Presidarias y
Pobladoras: Spanish-Speaking Women in Frontier Monterey,
California, 1770-1875." Publications include (co-editor) *Literatura
Chicana, Texto y Contexto: Chicano Literature, Text and Content*
(1972); (co-author) "Chicano Historic Sites in California" in *Multi-
Cultural Survey of Historical and Cultural Sites in California*
(forthcoming); "Comparative Frontiers: The Migration of Women
to Alta California and New Zealand," in *Western Women: Their
Land, Their Lives* (forthcoming).

494

Carmen Castañeda García, former director, Archivo Histórico de Jalisco, Guadalajara. Ph.D. in history from El Colegio de México, Mexico City (1974). Investigadora, Centro de Estudios Educativos, Mexico City (1975). Editor, *Boletín del Archivo Histórico de Jalisco* and *Guía de los Archivos Históricos de Jalisco*. Publications include: "La Casa de Recogidas de la ciudad de Guadalajara," in *Boletín del Archivo Histórico de Jalisco* (1978); collaborator, *Historia de la educación en México* (1976); "Los archivos de Guadalajara," in *Historia Mexicana* (1975).

Juan Gómez-Quiñones, Professor, Department of History, University of California, Los Angeles. Served in various posts in higher education including the Accreditation Commission for Senior Colleges and Universities and the Board of Trustees for the California State University System. Founder of *Aztlán: International Journal of Chicano Studies Research*. Has published several seminal articles on historiography, labor, Chicano Studies, culture and politics. Book length studies include *Sembradores*, and *Porfirio Diaz, los intelectuales y la revolución*. Forthcoming are *Aspects of the Formation of the Mexican Nation, Nationalism and its Crisis of 1910* and *Thyme's Season, a Commentary on the Political History of the Mexican People in the United States*.

María R. González, Ph. D. Candidate, Department of Literature, University of California, Irvine. M.A. in Spanish from the University of California, Santa Barbara. Has studied at the Universidad Nacional Autónoma de México, Mexico City. Taught at the University of California at San Diego and Santa Barbara, and San Diego State University. Has published articles and poetry in various journals and anthologies.

Ramón Gutiérrez, Associate Professor, Department of History, University of California, San Diego. Ph.D. in history from the University of Wisconsin at Madison (1980). Dissertation on "Marriage, Sex and the Family: Social Change in Colonial New Mexico, 1690-1846." Has studied in Mexico, Peru and Ecuador. Awards include: Hayes Foundation Fellowship (1981); Mexican Ministry of Foreign Relations Beca Lincoln-Juarez (1977); Danforth Graduate Fellowship (1974-1980); Fulbright-Hays Fellowship (1973); MacArthur Prize (1983). Social Science

Research Council (1981). Author of *When Jesus Came, The Corn Mothers Went Away: Marriage, Conquest and Love in New Mexico, 1500-1840.* Currently working on Hispano folk religion in the Southwest.

J. Jorge Klor de Alva, Professor, Department of Anthropology, Princeton University. Former director, Institute for Mesoamerican Studies, State University of New York, Albany. Ph.D. in history from the University of California, Santa Cruz. Fellowships granted by the John Simon Guggenheim Memorial Foundation (1987-1988), Fullbright, Mexico (1976), National Endowment for the Humanities, Ford Foundation, National Science Foundation, Danforth, and Wenner-Gren Foundation. Author of numerous articles and books on colonial Nahua culture contact and change and among contemporary Latinos in the United States. Publications include: *Sociocultural and Service Issues in Working with Hispanic American Clients* (1985) and *The Work of Bernardino de Sahagún: Pioneer Ethnographer of Sixteenth-Century Aztec Mexico (1988).*

Helen Lara-Cea, doctoral student in Ethnic Studies, University of California, Berkeley. M.A. student, Department of History, University of California, Davis. Has been a Reader in Latin American history and in Chicano Studies.

José E. Limón, Associate Professor, Department of Anthropology, University of California, Santa Cruz. Chair of American Studies, University of California, Santa Cruz.

Elsa Malvido, Investigadora, Instituto Nacional de Antropología e Historia, Mexico City. Has studied at the Universidad Nacional Autónoma de México and El Colegio de México. Publications include: "El siglo XVI, una nueva patología en America," (1985), co-author "La epidemia de cocoliztli de 1576," (1985) and "El abandono de los hijos, una forma de control de la mano de obra indígena y del tamaño de la familia en la época colonial: Tula, 1683-1780" (1981). She has organized international conferences and seminars on death and epidemics on New Spain's colonial period.

Elizabeth Martinez, Graduate of Swarthmore College. United Nations Researcher on colonialism (1947-52). Books and Arts editor of *The Nation* (1963-64), editor of *El Grito del Norte* (1968-73). Coordinator of the Chicano Communications Center in Albuquerque. Co-author of *Viva la Raza!* (1974) and author of *450 Years of Chicano History* (1976). Visiting professor of Chicano History at Antioch College (1975). Currently administrator of Global Exchange and on the editorial board of *Social Justice* in San Francisco.

Ed McCaughan, M.A. from Stanford University (1974) and doctoral student in sociology, University of California, Santa Cruz. Staff member of North American Congress on Latin America (1975-79). Co-author of *Beyond the Border: Mexico and the U.S. Today* (1979) and author of numerous articles and papers on U.S.-Mexico relations, runaway shops and immigration. Currently on the editorial board of *Social Justice*, the journal of Global Options.

Douglas Monroy, Associate Professor, Department of History, The Colorado College, Colorado Springs. Teaches American West and Southwest History. Has written extensively on the labor movement and southern California's garment industry, his articles have been published in anthologies and the journals *Labor History, The Western Historical Quarterly*, and *Aztlán*. Author of *Thrown Among Strangers: Life, Labor and Acculturation in Spanish and Mexican Southern California, 1769-1900* (University of California Press, forthcoming).

Emma M. Pérez, Ph.D. in history from the University of California, Los Angeles. Taught at Pomona College, University of California at Davis, and University of Minnesota. Her dissertation is titled "Through Her Love and Sweetness: Women, Revolution and Reform in Yucatán, 1910-1918" and surveys women's activities during a socialist era. Currently, she is a visiting scholar in Mexican American Studies at the University of Houston where she is researching the topic "Mexican Women in Houston from 1900 to 1920." Received a Ford Foundation Post-doctoral

Fellowship for Minorities for 1989-90. Dr. Pérez will join the History Department at the University of Texas, El Paso.

Carmen Ramos Escandón, Professor, Department of History, Universidad Autónoma Metropolitana-Iztapalapa, Mexico City. Ph.D. in history from the State University of New York at Stony Brook. Her dissertation is titled "Working Class Formation and the Mexican Textile Industry" (1981). M.A. from The University of Texas at Austin (1972). Currently, she is teaching at the Institute of Latin American Studies at The University of Texas at Austin.

Raquel Rubio-Goldsmith, Instructor, Department of History, Pima Community College, Tucson. L.L.M (law degree) from the Universidad Nacional Autónoma de México, Mexico City. M.A. in philosophy from the Universidad Nacional Autónoma de México. Former member of the Board of Arizona Humanities Council (1979-81) and Manzo (community activist group). Taught at the University of Buenos Aires School of Law. Recipient of National Endowment for the Humanities fellowship to develop a bibliography on Mexicanas in the United States (1975). Has published in various law and academic journals.

Vicki L. Ruiz, Associate Professor, Department of History, University of California, Davis. Ph.D. in history from Stanford University (1982). Co-editor of *Women on the United States-Mexico Border: Responses to Change* and *Western Women: Their Land, Their Lives.* Author of *Cannery Women, Cannery Lives: Mexican Women, Unionization and the California Food Processing Industry, 1930-1950.*

Concepción Ruiz Funes, Investigadora, Instituto Nacional de Antropología e Historia, Mexico City. M.A. in Spanish literature from the Universidad Nacional Autónoma de México, Mexico City. Research at the University of Havana, Cuba (1965-68). Publications include: *La Poesía de Leon Felipe* and two books on Spanish refugees in Mexico: *Palabras en Exilio* and *El Principio y el Final.* Currently working on a project on Mexican women with a research group of seven women, under the auspices of the

Instituto Nacional de Antropología e Historia and the Departamento de Investigaciones Históricos.

Rosaura Sánchez, Associate Professor, Department of Literature, University of California, San Diego. Ph.D. in Romance linguistics from the University of Texas at Austin. Publications on socio-linguistic, literary and cultural topics. Author of several short stories. Co-editor of *Essays on La Mujer* and author of *Chicano Discourse. Socio-historic Perspectives* (1983).

Shirlene Soto, Professor, Department of Chicano Studies, California State University, Northridge. Ph.D. in Latin American history from the University of New Mexico (1977). Taught at California Polytechnic State University and the University of New Mexico. Participated in many innovative teaching programs through the U.S. Department of Education, the National Endowment for the Humanities and others. UCLA Postdoctoral Scholar Fellowship (1985-86) and Ford Foundation Fellowship (1972-76). Publications include: *Emergence of the Modern Mexican Woman: Participation in Revolution and Struggle for Equality, 1910-1940* (forthcoming), "Tres modelos culturales: La Virgin de Guadalupe, La Malinche y La Llorona" (1986) and "Women in Mexico" in *Twentieth Century Mexico* (1986). Author of *The Mexican Woman: A Study of Her Participation in the Revolution, 1910-1940* (1979).

Enriqueta Tuñón, Investigadora, Instituto Nacional de Antropología e Historia (INAH), Mexico City. Currently researching the activism of Mexican women in the twentieth century under the auspices of INAH and the Departamento de Investigaciones Históricos.

Josefina Z. Vazquez, Professor, Department of History, El Colegio de México, Mexico City. Former director, Centro de Estudios Históricos, El Colegio de México, Mexico City. Ph.D. in history from the University of Madrid, Spain; Ph.D. in history from the Universidad Nacional Autónoma de México, Mexico City. Taught at Duke University, The University of Texas, University of Puerto Rico, Goethe Universitat, and Universidad Nacional Autónoma de

México. Publications include: *Nacionalismo y Educación en México* (1970); *Historia Moderna y Contemporanea de México* (Volume 1, 1977); *Mexicanos y Norteamericanos ante la Guerra del '47* (1971, 2nd edition, 1977); and co-authored *The U.S. and Mexico* (1985).

Devra A. Weber, Assistant Professor, Department of History, California State University at Long Beach. Publications include: "The Organizing of Mexicano Agricultural Workers in the Imperial Valley and Los Angeles, 1928-1934: An Oral History Approach" and "Oral Sources and the History of Mexican Workers in the United States." She is currently at work on a book on agricultural workers, to be published by Cornell University Press.

Emilio Zamora, Assistant Professor, University of Houston. Ph.D. in history from The University of Texas at Austin. Former director, Ethnic Studies Center, Texas A & I University, Kingsville, Texas. Fellowships granted by the Ford Foundation, University of California (President's Fellowship), and the Rockefeller Foundation. Publications include: "Chicano Socialist Labor Activity in Texas, 1900-1920" and "Sara Estela Ramírez: Una Rosa Roja en el Movimiento."

BIBLIOGRAPHY

I. *Documents*

Burgess, Ernest W., and Newcomb, Charles, ed. *Census Data of the City of Chicago, 1930.* Chicago: University of Chicago Press, 1933.

California Canners' Directory, July 1936.

California CIO Council, Research Department. *Economic Material on the California Cannery Industry.* Prepared under direction of Paul Pinsky, Research Director, February 1946.

California Governor C.C. Young, Mexican Fact-Finding Committee. *Mexicans in California.* San Francisco: California State Printing Office. 1930. Reprint. San Francisco: R and E Research Associates, 1970.

Chicago Historical Society, University of Chicago. Settlement House Papers. Annual Reports, 1934; 1936; 1937; 1939.

Newcomb, Charles, and Lane, Richard O., eds. *Census Data of the City of Chicago.* Chicago: University of Chicago Press, 1934.

Menefee, Selden C., and Cassmore, Orin C. *The Pecan Shellers of San Antonio: The Problem of Underpaid and Unemployed Mexican Labor.* Washington, D.C.: United States Government Printing Office, 1940.

Proceedings of the Fifth National Convention of the Food, Tobacco, Agricultural, and Allied Workers of America. Philadelphia, Pennsylvania, December 4-9, 1944.

Proceedings of the First National Convention of the United Cannery, Agricultural, Packing, and Allied Workers of America. Denver, Colorado, July 9-12, 1937.

Proceedings of the Third National Convention of the United Cannery, Agricultural, Packing, and Allied Workers of America. Chicago, Illinois, December 3-7, 1940.

Report of Donald Henderson, General President of the Second Annual Convention of the United Cannery, Agricultural, Packing, and Allied Workers of America. San Francisco, California, December 12-16, 1938.

Report of the General Executive Officers to the Third Annual Convention of the United Cannery, Agricultural, Packing, and Allied Workers of America. Chicago, Illinois, December 3-7, 1940.

Social Service Directory and Yearbook. Chicago: Chicago Council of Social Agencies, 1933.

United Nations. *The Determinants and Consequences of Population Trends*, vol. 1. New York: United Nations, 1973.

U.S., Bureau of the Census. *Abstract of the Fifteenth Census of the United States.* Washington: U.S. Government Printing Office, 1933.

U.S., Bureau of the Census. *Current Population Reports. Population Characteristics: Persons of Spanish Origin in the United States: March 1979.* Series P-20, No. 354, October 1980.

U.S., Department of Labor, Women's Bureau. *Application of Labor Legislation to the Fruit and Vegetable Preserving Industries.* Bulletin of the Women's Bureau, No. 176.

U.S., National Youth Administration, State of California. *An Occupational Study of the Fruit and Vegetable Canning Industry in California.* Prepared by Edward G. Stoy and Frances W. Strong under direction of Anne de G. Treadwell, Director of U.S. National Youth Administration, State of California, 1938.

II. *Archival Material*

Berkeley. Bancroft Library, University of California. Arcadia Bandini Brennan Scott Papers.

Berkeley. Bancroft Library, University of California. Arcadia Bandini Brennan Scott Papers. "Guajome" [by Arcadia Bandini Brennan Scott].

Berkeley. Bancroft Library, University of California. Bale Family Collection.

Berkeley. Bancroft Library, University of California. "California in 1834: Recollections" [by Carlos N. Hijar].

Berkeley. Bancroft Library, University of California. "Cosas de California" [by María Inocenta Pico Avila].

Berkeley. Bancroft Library, University of California. "Documentos para la historia de California" [by Cloromiro Soberanes].

Berkeley. Bancroft Library, University of California. Domestic Account Book of Francisca Benicia Vallejo. Vallejo Family Collection.

Berkeley. Bancroft Library, University of California. "Familia Soberanes" [by Irene Sewell Soberanes].

Berkeley. Bancroft Library, University of California. "Geneological Tables of Spanish and Mexican Families [by Thomas Workman Temple].

Berkeley. Bancroft Library, University of California. de la Guerra Family Papers.

Berkeley. Bancroft Library, University of California. Henry D. Fitch Collection.

Berkeley. Bancroft Library, University of California. "The History of the Bear Party" [by Rosalia Leese].

Berkeley. Bancroft Library, University of California. "Los tiempos pasados de la Alta California" [by Apolinaria Lorenzana].

503

Berkeley. Bancroft Library, University of California. "Los tiempos pasados en Alta California" [by Don Mauricio González].

Berkeley. Bancroft Library, University of California. Manuel de Jesus Castro Papers.

Berkeley. Bancroft Library, University of California. Marcelino García Papers.

Berkeley. Bancroft Library, University of California. Marcelino García Papers. "Descripción de un baile en Santa Barbara en 1836" [by Francisca Gómez].

Berkeley. Bancroft Library, University of California. "Memorias sobre la historia de California" [by José María Amador].

Berkeley. Bancroft Library, University of California. "Narración" [by Sra. Viuda del Capitán Enrique D. Fitch].

Berkeley. Bancroft Library, University of California. "Narración" [by Isidora Filomena Solano].

Berkeley. Bancroft Library, University of California. "Narración" [by María Teresa de la Guerra Hartnell].

Berkeley. Bancroft Library, University of California. "Padrones y extractos de libros de misiones de California 1776-1846" [by Zoeth Skinner Eldrege].

Berkeley. Bancroft Library, University of California. Paul S. Taylor Collection.

Berkeley. Bancroft Library, University of California. Provincial State Papers. "Benicia Military: Real Presidio de Monterey."

Berkeley. Bancroft Library, University of California. Regional Oral History Office. "Writings and Revolutionists" [Ethel Duffy Turner interviewed by Ruth Teiser].

Berkeley. Bancroft Library, University of California. Thomas Oliver Larkin Collection.

Berkeley. Bancroft Library, University of California. Vallejo Family Collection.

Berkeley. Bancroft Library, University of California. Will of Edward Turner Bale. Bale Family Collection.

Chicago. Special Collections, University of Chicago. Robert Redfield Papers. "Mexicans in Chicago: 1924-25."

Chicago. Special Collections, University of Chicago. Robert Redfield Papers. "Placida and Severna Gonzales."

Los Angeles. Los Angeles Public Library. Mary M. Bowman Scrapbooks.

Monterey. Mission of San Carlos Borromeo, Archdiocese of Monterey. Book of Marriages.

Salinas. Mexican Archives, Office of the Monterey County Clerk. Civil Records: 1821-1848. Vols. 6-16.

Santa Clara. University of Santa Clara Archives. Mission Santa Clara Parish Registers.

Santa Fe. New Mexico State Records Center and Archives. Archiv es of the Archdiocese of Santa Fe. *Diligencias Matrimoniales*. Microfilm Reel 60.

Washington. National Archives. Records of the Works Progress Administration. Record Group 69. "Mexican Migration to Chicago" [by Edward Jackson Baur].

III. *Books*

Abreu Gómez, Ermilo. Prólogo a *Poesías de Sor Juana Inés de la Cruz*. 2a. ed. México, D.F.: Ediciones Botas, 1948.

Acuña, Rodolfo. *Occupied America: A History of Chicanos*. 2d ed. New York: Harper & Row, 1981.

Alegría, Juana Amanda. *Sicología de las Mexicanas*. México, D. F.: Editorial Diana.

Almaguer, Tomas. *Interpreting Chicano History: The "World System" Approach to 19th Century California*. Berkeley: Institute for the Study of Social Change, Working Paper Series, no. 101, University of California, 1977.

Althusser, Louis. *Lenin and Philosophy and Other Essays*. New York: Monthly Review Press, 1971.

Archibald, Robert. *The Economic Aspects of the California Missions*. Washington, D.C.: Academy of American Franciscan History, 1978.

Aries, Philippe. *Centuries of Childhood: A Social History of Family Life*. Translated by Robert Baldick. New York: Alfred A. Knopf, 1962.

Babel, August. *La mujer en el pasado, en el presente, en el porvenir*. España: Editorial Fontamara, 1980.

Baird, Peter, and McCaughan, Ed. *Beyond the Border: Mexico and the U.S. Today*. New York: NACLA, 1979.

Bancroft, Hubert Howe. *California Pastoral, 1769-1848*. San Francisco: The History Book Company, 1888.

Bancroft, Hubert Howe. *The History of California*. 7 vols. San Francisco: The History Book Company. 1884-90. Reprint. Santa Barbara, Calif.: Wallace Hebberd, 1963.

Bancroft, Hubert Howe. *Register of Pioneer Inhabitants of California, 1542 to 1848*. Los Angeles: Dawson's Book Shop, 1964.

Bandini, José. *A Description of California in 1828.* Translated by Doris Marion Wright. Berkeley: Friends of the Bancroft Library, 1951.

Barnes, Thomas C.; Naylor, Thomas C.; and Polzer, Charles. *Northern New Spain Research Guide.* Tucson: University of Arizona Press, 1980.

Barrera, Mario. *Race and Class in the Southwest: A Theory of Racial Inequality.* Notre Dame and London: University of Notre Dame, 1979.

Barrett, Michele. *Women's Oppression Today: Problems in Marxist Feminist Analysis.* London: Verso Editions and NLB, 1980.

Bartra, Armando. *Regeneración, 1900-1918.* México, D. F.: Ediciones Era, 1977.

Bautista Pomar, Juan. *Relación de Texcoco.* México, D.F.: Salvador Chaves Hayhoe, 1941.

Bustillos Carrillo, Antonio. *Yucatán al servicio de la patria y de la revolución.* México, D.F.: Casa Ramirez Editores, 1959.

Beiharz, Edwin A., and DeMers, Donald O., Jr. *San Jose California's First City.* Tulsa, Oklahoma: Continental Heritage Press, 1980.

Berger, Monroe. *La novela y las ciencias sociales.* México, D.F.: Fondo de Cultura Económica, 1979.

Billington, Ray Allen. *Westwood Expansion: A History of the American Frontier.* New York: MacMillan, 1949.

Black, Ester Boulton. *Rancho Cucamonga and Dona Merced.* Redlands, Ca.: San Bernardino County Museum Association, 1975.

Bourdieu, Pierre. *Outline of a Thoery of Practice.* Cambridge: Cambridge University Press, 1977.

Boxer, C.R. *The Church Militant and Iberian Expansion 1440-1770*. Baltimore: John Hopkins University Press, 1978.

Bridenthal, Renate, and Koonz, Claudia, eds. *Becoming Visible: Women in European History*. Boston: Houghton Mifflin, 1977.

Brownmiller, Susan. *Against Our Will: Men, Women and Rape*. New York: Simon and Schuster, 1975.

Cabello-Argandoña, Roberto; Gómez-Quiñones, Juan; and Herrera Duran, Patricia, comps. and eds. *The Chicana: A Comprehensive Bibliographic Study*. Los Angeles: Chicano Studies Center Publications, University of California, 1975.

Cabeza de Baca, Fabiola. *We Fed Them Cactus*. Albuquerque: University of New Mexico Press, 1954.

Calderon de la Barca, Fanny. *Life in Mexico: The Letters of Fanny Calderon de la Barca*. New York: Doubleday, 1966.

Camarillo, Albert. *Chicanos in a Changing Society: From Mexican Pueblos to American Barrios in Santa Barbara and Southern California, 1848-1930*. Cambridge: Harvard University Press, 1979.

Camarillo, Albert. *Chicanos in California*. San Francisco: Boyd & Fraser, 1984.

Cardoso, Ciro F.S. *Los métodos de la historia*. México, D.F.: Editorial Grijalbo, S.A., 1977.

Carroll, Berenice A., ed. *Liberating Women's History: Theoretical and Critical Essays*. Urbana: University of Illinois Press, 1976.

Castles, Steven, and Kosack, Godula. *Immigrant Workers and Class Structure in Western Europe*. Oxford: Oxford University Press, 1973.

Centro de Estudios Históricos del Movimiento Obrero Mexicano. *La mujer y el movimiento obrero mexicano en el siglo*

XIX: Antología de la Prensa Obrera. México, D.F.: CEHSMO, 1975.

Chodorow, Nancy. *The Reproduction of Mothering: Psychoanalysis and the Sociology of Gender*. Berkeley: University of California Press, 1978.

Cleland, Robert Glass. *The Cattle on a Thousand Hills: Southern California, 1850-1880*. San Marino: Huntington Library, 1941.

Cockcroft, James D. *Mexico: Class Formation, Capital Accumulaton and the State*. New York: Monthly Review Press, 1983.

Comisión Nacional para la Celebración del Sesquicentenario de la Proclamación de la Independencia Nacional y del Cincuentenario de la Revolución Mexicana. *Diario de los Debates del Congreso Constituyente, 1916-1917*. 2 vols. México, D.F.: Talleres Gráficos de la Nación, 1960.

Congreso Feminista de Yucatán. *Anales de Esa Memorable Asamblea*. Mérida: Talleres Tipográficos del "Ateneo Peninsular," 1916.

Cook, Sherbourne F. *The Conflict Between the California Indian and White Civilization*. Berkeley and Los Angeles: University of California Press, 1976.

Cook, Sherbourne F. *The Population of the California Indians 1769-1970*. Berkeley: University of California Press, 1976.

Cook, Sherbourne F., and Borah, Woodrow. *Essays in Population History*. 3 vols. Berkeley: University of California Press, 1971-1979.

Cordova, Teresa; Cantú, Norma; Cardenas, Gilberto; García, Juan; and Sierra, Christine M., eds. *Chicana Voices: Intersections of Class, Race and Gender*. Austin: National Association for Chicano Studies, Center for Mexican American Studies, University of Texas at Austin, 1986.

Cotera, Martha P. *Diosa y Hembra: The History and Heritage of Chicanas in the U.S.* Austin, Texas: Information Systems Development, 1976.

Cotera, Marta. *Profile on the Mexican-American Women.* Austin, Texas: National Educational Laboratory Publishers Inc., 1976.

Cott, Nancy. *The Bonds of Womanhood: Women's Sphere in New England, 1780-1835.* New Haven: Yale University Press, 1977.

Cowan, Robert G. *Ranchos of California: A List of Spanish Concessions 1775-1846 and Mexican Grants 1822-1846.* Fresno: Academic Library Guild, 1956.

Cruz, Sor Juana Inés de la. *Obras Completas.* 2a. ed. México, D.F.: Ediciones Botas, 1948.

Cue Cánova, Agustín. *Historia social y económica de México: 1521-1854.* México, D.F.: Editorial Trillas, 1971.

Dakin, Susanna Bryant. *Rose or Rose Thorn? Three Women of Spanish California.* Berkeley: Friends of the Bancroft Library, 1963.

Dana, Richard Henry, Jr. *Two Years Before the Mast.* 1840. Reprint. New York: Airmont Publishing Company, Inc., 1965.

Daniel, Cletus. *Bitter Harvest: A History of California Farmworkers, 1870-1941.* Ithaca: Cornell University Press, 1981.

Davis, Angela Y. *Women, Race, and Class.* New York: Random House, 1981.

Davis, William Health. *Seventy-Five Years in California.* San Francisco: John Howell, 1929.

Degler, Carl N. *At Odds: Women and the Family in America from the Revolution to the Present.* New York and Oxford: Oxford University, 1980.

Delphy, Christine. *Close to Home. A Materialist Analysis of Women's Oppression.* Amherst: The University of Massachusetts Press, 1984.

DeNevi, Donald. *Sketches of Early California.* San Francisco: Chronicle Books, 1971.

Deutsch, Sarah. *No Separate Refuge: Culture, Class and Gender on an Anglo-Hispanic Frontier in the American Southwest, 1880-1940.* New York: Oxford University Press, 1987.

Dorantes, Alma. *Intolerancia religiosa en Jalisco.* México, D.F.: Instituto Nacional de Antropología e Historia, Dirección de Centros Regionales, Centro Regional de Occidente, 1976.

Dublin, Thomas. *Women at Work: The Transformation of Work and Community in Lowell, Massachusetts, 1826-1860.* New York: Columbia University Press, 1979.

Durán, Diego de. *Historia de las Indias de Nuevas España e Islas de la Tierra Firme.* 2 vols. México, D.F.: Editorial Porrúa, 1967.

Eldredge, Zoeth Skinner. *History of California.* 2 vols. New York: The Century History Company, 1915.

Emparan Brown, Madie. *The Vallejos of California.* San Francisco: Gleeson Library Association, University of San Francisco, 1968.

Engelhardt, Fr. Zephyrin. *The Franciscans in California.* Harbor Springs, Michigan: Holy Childhood Indian School, 1897.

Evans, Sara. *Personal Politics.* New York: Vintage Books, 1980.

Faragher, John Mack. *Women and Men on the Overland Trail.* New Haven: Yale University Press, 1979.

Farnham, Thomas Jefferson. *Travelers in California and Scenes in the Pacific Ocean.* 1844. Reprint. Oakland, Calif.: Biobooks, 1947.

Febre, Lucien. *Combates por la historia.* Barcelona: Editorial Ariel, 1970.

Fernández, Raul A. *The United States-Mexican Border: A Politico-Economic Profile.* Notre Dame: University of Notre Dame Press, 1977.

Fernández, Sergio E. *Homenaje a Sor Juana, López Velarde, a José Gorostiza.* México, D.F.: SEP, 1972.

Fernandez-Kelly, Patricia. *For We Are Sold: I and My People.* Albany: SUNY Press, 1983.

FitzGerald, Frances. *Fire in the Lake: The Vietnamese and the Americans in Vietnam.* New York: Random House, 1973.

Flores Magón, Ricardo. *Artículos Políticos,* 1917. México D.F: Ediciones Antorcha, 1981.

Foner, Philip S. *Women and the American Labor Movement.* New York: The Free Press, 1979.

Fonseca, Omar, and Moreno, Lilia. *Jaripo: Pueblo de Migrantes.* Jiquilpan, Michoacan: Centro de Estudios de la Revolución Mexicana "Lázaro Cardenas." A.C., 1984.

Foulcault, Michel. *The History of Sexuality,* vol. 1. New York: Random House, 1980.

Foulcault, Michel. *Power/Knowledge: Selected Interviews and Other Writings, 1972-1977,* edited by Colin Gordon. New York: Pantheon Books.

Fox Keller, Evelyn. *Reflections on Gender and Science.* Hartford: Yale University Press, 1985.

Frank, Andre Gunder. *Crisis: In the Third World.* New York: Holmes and Meier, 1981.

Freud, Sigmund. *A General Introduction to Psychoanalysis.* New York: Washington Square Press, 1964.

Friedlander, Peter. *The Emergence of a UAW Local: A Study in Class and Culture.* Pittsburgh: University of Pittsburgh Press, 1975.

Friedrich, Paul. *Agrarian Revolt in a Mexican Village.* Chicago: University of Chicago Press, 1970.

Galarza, Ernesto. *Merchants of Labor: The Mexican Bracero Story.* Santa Barbara, Calif.: McNally & Loftin, 1964.

Galindo, Hermila. *Estudio de la Srita. Hermila Galindo con motivo de los temas que han de absolverse en el Segundo Congreso Feminista de Yucatán.* Mérida: Imprenta del Gobierno Constitucionalista, 1916.

Gamboa Ricalde, Alvaro. *Yucatán desde 1910.* 3 vols. Veracruz: Imprenta Standard, 1943–1955.

Gamio, Manuel. *Mexican Immigration to the United States: A Study of Human Migration and Adjustment.* 1930. Reprint. New York: Dove, 1971.

García, Mario T. *Desert Immigrants: The Mexicans of El Paso, 1880–1920.* New Haven: Yale University Press, 1981.

Gates, Paul. *California Ranchos and Farms.* Madison: The State Historical Society of Wisconsin, 1967.

Geertz, Clifford. *The Interpretation of Cultures.* New York: Basic Books, 1973.

Geiger, O.F.M., Maynard. *Franciscan Missionaries in Hispanic California 1769–1848.* San Marino: The Huntington Library, 1969.

Genovese, Eugene D. *Roll, Jordan, Roll: The World the Slaves Made.* New York: Pantheon Books, 1974.

Goldman, Marion S. *Gold Diggers and Silver Miners: Prostitution and Social Life in the Comstock Lode.* Ann Arbor: University of Michigan Press, 1981.

Gómez-Quiñones, Juan. *Sembradores: Ricardo Flores Magón y El Partido Liberal Mexicano, A Eulogy and Critique.* Los Angeles: Chicano Studies Research Center Publications, University of California, 1973.

Gómez-Quiñones, Juan, and Maciel, David. *Al norte del río bravo, pasado lejano, 1600-1930.* México, D.F.: Siglo XXI Editores, 1981.

Gordon, Ann D.; Buhle, Mari Jo; and Schrom dye, Nancy. *Women in American History.* Somerville: New England Free Press.

Grebler, Leo; Moore, Joan W.; and Guzman, Ralph C. *The Mexican-American People: The Nation's Second Largest Minority.* New York: The Free Press, 1970.

Grele, Ronald J. *Envelopes of Sound: The Art of Oral History.* 2d. ed. Chicago: Precedent Publishing, 1981.

Griswold del Castillo, Richard. *The Los Angeles Barrio 1850-1890: A Social History.* Berkeley: University of California Press, 1979.

Guest, Florian O.F.M. *Fermin Francisco de Lausen 1736-1803.* Washington, D.C.: Academy of American Franciscan History, 1973.

Gurley Flynn, Elizabeth. *I Speak My Own Piece.* New York, 1955.

Gutiérrez Casillas, José. *Historia de la Iglesia en México.* México, D.F.: Editorial Porrúa, 1974.

Hahner, June E., ed. *Women in Latin American History: Their Lives and Views.* Los Angeles: Latin American Center Publications, University of California, 1976.

Hall, Frederic. *History of San Jose.* San Francisco: A.L. Bancroft and Co., 1871.

Hammond, George P., ed. *The Larkin Papers, 1845-1846,* vol. 4. Berkeley: University of California Press, 1953.

Hansen, Roger D. *The Politics of Mexican Development*. Baltimore: John Hopkins University Press, 1971.

Harding, Sandra, and Hintikhan B., Merrill, eds. *Discovering Reality, Feminist Perspectives on Epistomology*. Hingham: Reidel, 1983.

Hart, James. *American Images of Spanish California*. Berkeley: Friends of the Bancroft Library, 1960.

Hart, John. *Anarchism and the Mexican Working Class, 1860-1913*. Austin: University of Texas Press, 1978.

Hartman, Mary S., and Banner, Lois, eds. *Clio's Consciousness Raised: New Perspectives on the History of Women*. New York: Harper Colophon Books, 1974.

Heizer, Robert F., and Almquist, Alan F. *The Other Californians*. Berkeley: University of California Press, 1971.

Heller Committee for Research in Social Economics of the University of California. *How Mexicans Earn and Live*. University of California Publications in Economics 13, No. 1, Cost of Living Studies 5. Berkeley: University of California Press, 1933.

Herr, Michael. *Dispatches*. New York: Alfred A. Knopf, 1977.

Hirschorn, L. *Beyond Mechanization: Work and Technology in a Post-industrial Age*. Cambridge: MIT Press.

Hobsbawm, E. J. *Labouring Men: Studies in the History of Labour*. New York: Basic Books, Inc., 1964.

Hogden, Margaret T. *Anthropology, History and Cultural Change*. Tucson: Wenner-Gren Foundation for Anthropological Research, 1979.

Hollenbaugh Aviña, Rose. *Spanish Mexican Land Grants in California*. New York: Arno Press, 1970.

Hooks, Bell. *Ain't I a Woman?: Black Women and Feminism*. Boston: South End Press, 1981.

515

Hoopes, James. *Oral History: An Introduction for Students.* Chapel Hill: The University of North Carolina, 1979.

Hughes, Elizabeth Ann. *Living Conditions of Small Wage-Earners in Chicago.* Chicago: City of Chicago, Department of Public Welfare, 1925.

Hughes, Elizabeth Ann. *Illinois Persons on Relief in 1935.* Works Progress Administration, Project No. 165-54-6018. Chicago: Works Progress Administration, 1937.

Hutchinson, Alan C. *Frontier Settlements in Mexican California: The Hijar-Padres Colony and its Origins, 1769-1835.* New Haven: Yale University Press, 1969.

•Israel, J.L. *Race, Class, and Politics in Colonial Mexico.* London: Oxford University Press, 1975.

Ixtlixochitl, Fernando de Alva. *Obras Históricas.* 2 vols. México, D.F.: Secretaría de Fomento, 1892.

Jackson, Helen Hunt. *Ramona.* Boston: Roberts Brothers, 1884.

Jackson, Helen Hunt. *Glimpses of California and the Missions.* Boston: Little, Brown & Co., 1907.

Jackson, Helen Hunt. *A Century of Dishonor: The Early Crusade for Indian Reform.* New York: Harper & Row, 1965.

Jackson, Sheldon G. *A British Ranchero in Old California: The Life and Times of Henry Dalton and the Rancho.* Azuza, California: A.H. Clark Co., 1977.

Jacobs, J. *Cities and the Wealth of Nature.* New York: Vintage Books, 1985.

Jameson, Fredric. *The Political Unconscious: Narrative as a Socially Symbolic Act.* Ithaca: Cornell University Press, 1981.

Jeffrey, Juliet Roy. *Frontier Women: The Trans-Mississippi West, 1840-1880.* New York: Hill & Wang, 1979.

Johannson, Robert W. *To the Halls of the Montezumas: The Mexican War in the American Imagination.* New York: Oxford University Press, 1985.

Jones, Oakah L., Jr. *Los Paisanos: Spanish Settlers on the Northern Frontier of New Spain.* Norman: University of Oklahoma Press, 1979.

Joseph, Gloria I., and Lewis, Jill. *Common Differences: Conflicts in Black and White Feminist Perspectives.* Garden City, New York: Anchor Books, 1981.

Kearney, Michael. *The Winds of Ixtepeji: World View and Society in a Mexican Town.* New York: Holt, Rinehart and Winston, 1972.

Kelves, Bettyann. *Females of the Species.* Cambridge: Howard, 1986.

Kerver, Linda K., and DeHart Mathews, Jane. *Women's America: Refocusing the Past.* Oxford: Oxford University Press, 1982.

Kessler-Harris, Alice. *Women Have Always Worked.* New York: The Feminist Press, 1981.

King, T. Butler. *Report of Hon. T. Butler King, on California.* Washington, D.C.: Gideon and Co., 1850.

Knaster, Meri. *Women in Spanish America: An Annotated Bibliography from Pre-Conquest to Contemporary Times.* Boston: G.K. Wall, 1977.

Kollontai, Alejandra. *Sobre la liberación de la mujer.* España: Editorial Fontamara, 1979.

Kroeber, Alfred L. *Handbook of the Indians of California.* Washington, D.C.: Government Printing Office, 1925.

Kushner, Sam. *Long Road to Delano.* New York: International Publishers, 1975.

Lange, Dorthea, and Taylor, Paul. *An American Exodus*. New Haven: Yale University Press, 1969.

Laslett, Peter; Oosterveen, Karla: and Smith, Richard. *Bastardy and its Comparative History*. London: Edward Arnold, 1980.

Lavrin, Asuncion, ed. *Latin American Women: Historical Perspectives*. Westport, Conn.: Greenwood Press, 1978.

Leiss, William. *The Limits to Satisfaction: An Essay on the Problems of Needs and Commodities*. Toronto: University of Toronto Press, 1976.

Lens, Sidney. *The Labor Wars*. Garden City, New York: Anchor Books, 1974.

Lerner, Gerda. *The Woman in American History*. Menlo Park, Calif.: Addison Wesley, 1971.

Lerner, Gerda, ed. *Black Women in White America: A Documentary History*. New York: Pantheon Books, 1972.

Lerner, Gerda, ed. *The Female Experience: An American Documentary*. Indianapolis: Bobbs-Merrill, 1977.

Lerner, Gerda. *The Majority Finds Its Past: Placing Women in History*. New York and Oxford: Oxford University Press, 1979.

López de Gómora, Francisco. *Historia General de las Indias, Conquista de México*, vol. 2. Barcelona: Editorial Orbis, 1985.

López y Rivas, Gilberto. *Los chicanos: una minoria nacional explotada*. México, D.F.: Editorial Nuestro Tiempo, 1971.

Lummis, Charles F. *The Spanish Pioneers and the California Missions*. Chicago: A.C. McClurg and Co., 1936.

MacFarlane, Alan; Harrison, Sarah; and Jardine, Charles. *Reconstructing Historical Communities*. London: Cambridge University Press, 1977.

Macias, Anna. *Against All Odds: The Feminist Movement in Mexico to 1940.* Westport, Conn.: Greenwood Press, 1982.

Maciel, David, ed. *La otra cara de méxico: el pueblo chicano.* México, D.F.: Ediciones "El Caballito," 1977.

Maciel, David, and Bueno, Patricia, eds. *Aztlán: historia del pueblo chicano, 1846-1910.* México, D.F.: SepSetentas, 1975.

Madsen, William. *The Mexican-American of South Texas.* New York: Holt, Rhinehart, and Winston, 1964.

Marsh, Margaret S. *Anarchist Women, 1870-1920.* Philadelphia: Temple University Press, 1981.

Martinez, Oscar. *Border Boom Town: Ciudad Juarez Since 1948.* Austin: University of Texas Press, 1978.

Martinez-Alier, Verena. *Marriage, Class and Colour in Nineteenth-Century Cuba.* Cambridge: Cambridge University Press, 1974.

Marx, Carlos; Engels, Federico; Lenin y otros. *La emancipación de la mujer.* México, D.F.: Editorial Grijalvo, 1970.

Marx, Karl. *Pre-Capitalist Economic Formations.* New York: International Publishers, 1965.

Marx, Karl. *A Contribution to the Critique of Political Economy.* New York: International Publishers, 1976.

Marx, Karl. *The Marx-Engels Reader,* edited by Robert C. Tucker. New York: Norton.

Marx, Karl, and Engels, Frederick. *The German Ideology.* Moscow: Progress Publishers, 1976.

McKenna, Teresa, and Ortiz, Flora Ida, eds. *The Broken Web: The Educational Experience of Hispanic American Women.* Claremont and Berkeley: The Tomás Rivera Center and Floricanto Press, 1988.

McKittrick, Myrtle M. *Vallejo, Son of California*. Portland, Oregon: Binfords & Mort, 1944.

McWilliams, Carey. *Factories in the Field: The Story of Migratory Farm Labor in California*. 1935. Reprint. Archon Books, 1969.

McWilliams, Carey. *Ill Fares the Land*. New York: Barnes and Noble, 1941.

McWilliams, Carey. *North from Mexico: The Spanish-Speaking People of the United States*. New York: Greenwood Press, 1968.

Melville, Margarita B., ed. *Twice a Minority: Mexican American Women*. St. Louis: The C.V. Mosby Co., 1980.

Méndez Plancarte, Alfonso. *Obras completas* (de Sor Juana). 2 vols. México, D.F.: Fondo de Cultura Económica, 1951-57.

Méndez Plancarte, Alfonso. *Poetas novo-hispanos*. México, D.F.: Universidad Nacional Autónoma de México, 1964.

Mendieta Alatorre, María de los Angeles. *La mujer en la revolución mexicana*. México, D.F.: Talleres Gráficos de la Nación, 1961.

Mendoza, Vicente T. *Lírica infantil de México*. Lecturas Mexianas No. 26. México, D.F.: Cultura SEP, 1980.

Meyer, Michael C., and Sherman, William L. *The Course of Mexican History*. New York: Oxford University Press, 1979.

Miller, Elaine K. *Mexican Folk Narrative from the Los Angeles Area*. Austin: University of Texas Press, 1973.

Mirandé, Alfredo, and Enriquez, Evangelina. *La Chicana: The Mexican-American Woman*. Chicago and London: University of Chicago Press, 1979.

Mitchell, Juliet. *Women's Estate*. New York: Vintage Books, 1971.

Mitchell, Juliet. *Psychoanalysis and Feminism.* New York: Pantheon Books, 1974.

Montejano, David. *Anglos and Mexicans in the Making of Texas, 1836-1986.* Austin: University of Texas Press, 1987.

Mora, Magdalena, and Del Castillo, Adelaida R., eds. *Mexican Women in the United States: Struggles Past and Present.* Los Angeles: Chicano Studies Research Center Publications, 1980.

Moraga, Cherrie, and Anzaldua, Gloria, eds. *This Bridge Called My Back: Writings by Radical Women of Color.* Watertown, Mass.: Persephone Press, 1981.

Morgan, Robin, ed. *Sisterhood Is Powerful.* New York: Random House, 1970.

Morner, Magnus. *Race Mixture in the History of Latin America.* Boston: Little, Brown and Co., 1967.

Mowry, George. *The California Progressives.* Los Angeles: University of California Press, 1951.

Muriel, Josefina. *Conventos de monjas en la Nueva España.* México, D.F.: Editorial Santiago, 1946.

Muriel, Josefina. *Los recogimientos de mujeres.* México, D.F.: Universidad Nacional Autónoma Metropolitana, 1974.

Myerhoff, Barbara. *Number Our Days.* New York: Simon and Schuster, 1978.

Nash, June, and Fernández-Kelly, Maria Patricia, eds. *Women, Men and the International Division of Labor.* Albany: SUNY Press, 1983.

Northrop, Marie E. *Spanish-Mexican Families of Early California: 1769-1850,* vol. 1. New Orleans: Polyanthos, 1976.

Oakley, Ann. *Women's Work: The Housewife, Past and Present.* New York: Vintage Books, 1976.

Ord, Angustias de la Guerra. *Occurences in Hispanic California*, translated and edited by Francis Price and William H. Ellison. Richmond, Virginia: Academy of American Franciscan History, 1956.

Ots Capdequí, J.M. *El estado español en las Indias*. Cuba: Edición de Ciencias Sociales, 1975.

Panuzio, Constantine. *How Mexicans Earn and Live*. University of California Publication in Economics 13, no. 1, Cost of Living Studies V. Berkeley: University of California, 1933.

Paz, Octavio. *The Labyrinth of Solitude: Life and Thought in Mexico*. New York: Grove Press, 1961.

Pecheux, Michel. *Language, Semantics and Ideology*. New York: St. Martin's Press, 1982.

Peña, Devon, G. *Maquiladoras: A Select Annotated Bibliography and Critical Commentary on the U.S.-Mexico Border Industry Program*. Bibliography Series 7-81, Center for the Study of Human Resources, University of Texas at Austin, 1981.

Pesotta, Rose. *Bread Upon the Waters*. New York: Dodd, Mead, & Co., 1945.

Pfandl, Ludwig. *Sor Juana Inés de la Cruz: la décima musa de México. Su vida. Su poesía. Su psique*. México, D.F.: Universidad Nacional Autónoma de México, 1963.

Phillips, D.L. *Letters from California: Its Mountains, Valleys, Plains, Lakes, Rivers, Climate and Production*. Springfield, 1877.

Phillips, George H. *The Enduring Struggle: Indians in California History*. San Francisco: Boyd and Fraser, 1981.

Pitt, Leonard. *The Decline of the Californios: A Social History of the Spanish-Speaking Californians, 1846-1890*. Berkeley: University of California Press, 1971.

Poniatowska, Elena. *Fuerte es el silencio.* México, D.F.: Editorial Era, 1980.

Poole, David. *Land and Liberty: Anarchist Influences in the Mexican Revolution: Ricardo Flores Magón.* Sanday, U.K.: Cienfuegos Press, LTD., 1977.

Price, Glenn W. *Origins of the War with Mexico: The Polk-Stockton Intrigue.* Austin: University of Texas Press, 1967.

Raat, Dirk W. *Revoltosos: Mexico's Rebels in the United States, 1903-1923.* College Station: Texas A & M University Press, 1981.

Rascón, María Antonieta. *La mujer y la lucha social.* En *Imagen y realidad de la mujer,* compilado por Elena Urrutia, pp. 139-174. México, D.F.: SepSetentas/Diana, 1979.

Richman, Irving Berdine. *California Under Spain and Mexico, 1535-1847.* 1911. Reprint. Boston and New York: Cooper Square Publishers, 1965.

Robinson, Alfred. *Life in California.* 1846. Reprint. Santa Barbara, Calif.: Peregrine Press, Inc., 1970.

Robinson, Cecil. *With the Ears of Strangers: The Mexican in American Literature.* Tucson: University of Arizona Press, 1963.

Robinson, W.W. *Ranchos Become Cities.* Pasadena: San Pasqual Press, 1939.

Robinson, W.W. *Land in California.* 1949. Reprint. Berkeley: University of California Press, 1979.

Rocard, Marcienne. *Les Fils du Soleil.* Paris: Maisonneuve et Larose, 1980.

Rodriguez O., Jaime E. *Down from Colonialism: Mexico's Nineteenth Century Crisis.* Los Angeles: Chicano Studies Research Center Publications, University of California, 1983.

Rolle, Andrew. Introduction to *Life in California*, by Alfred Robinson. 1846. Reprint. Santa Barbara, Calif.: Peregrine Press, Inc., 1970.

Rowbotham, Sheila. *Women, Resistance and Revolution*. New York: Pantheon Books, 1972.

Rowbotham, Sheila. *Woman's Consciousness, Man's World*. Baltimore: Penguin, 1973.

Rowbotham, Sheila. *Hidden from History: Rediscovering Women in History from the Seventeenth Century to the Present*. New York: Pantheon Books, 1976.

Rowland, Lenore. *The Romance of La Puente Rancho*. Covina: San Gabriel Valley News, 1948.

Ruiz, Vicki L. *Cannery Women, Cannery Lives: Mexican Women, Unionization, and the California Food Processing Industry, 1930-1950*. Albuquerque: University of New Mexico, 1987.

Ruiz, Vicki L., and Tiano, Susan, eds. *Women on the U.S.-Mexico Border: Responses to Change*. Boston: Allen & Unwin, 1987.

Saenz Royo Xochitl, Artemisa. *Historia Política-Social-Cultural del Movimiento Feminino en México, 1914-1950*. México, D.F.: M. León Sánchez, 1954.

Sahagún, Fray Bernardino de. *Historia General de las Cosas de Nueva España*. 4 vols. México, D.F.: Editorial Porrúa, 1956.

Samuel Raphael, ed. *People's History and Socialist Theory*. London: Routledge and Kegan Paul, 1981.

Sanchez, Nellie Van de Grift. *The Spanish Period*. Chicago and New York: The Lewis Publishing Company, 1930.

Sanchez, Nellie Van de Grift. *Spanish Arcadia*. New York: Arno Press, 1976.

Sanchez, Rosaura, and Martinez Cruz, Rosa, eds. *Essays on La Mujer*. Los Angeles: Chicano Studies Center Publications, University of California, 1977.

Sargent, Lydia, ed. *Women and Revolution: A Discussion of the Unhappy Marriage of Marxism and Feminism*. Boston: South End Press, 1981.

Schneider, David. *American Kinship: A Cultural Account*. Chicago: University of Chicago Press, 1968.

Scott, Ann Firor. *The Southern Lady*. Chicago: University of Chicago Press, 1970.

Secrest, William B. *Juanita: The Only Woman Lynched During Gold Rush Days*. Fresno, Calif.: Saga-West Publishing Company, 1967.

Security-First National Bank of Los Angeles. *El Pueblo: Los Angeles Before the Railroads*. Los Angeles: Equitable Branch of the Security Trust & Savings Bank, 1928.

Shanon, Lyle, and Shanon, Magdaline. *Minority Migrants in the Urban Community*. Beverly Hills: Sage Publications, 1973.

Siguenza y Góngora, Carlos. *Relaciones Históricas*. México, D.F.: Universidad Nacional Autónoma de México, 1940.

Spearman, Arthur Dunning S.J. *The Five Franciscan Churches of Mission Santa Clara, 1777-1825*. Palo Alto, Calif.: National Press, 1963.

Spender, Dale. *Man Made Language*. London: Routledge and Kegan, 1980.

Stimson, Grace. *Rise of the Labor Movement in Los Angeles*. Los Angeles: University of California Press, 1955.

Sweezy, Paul M. *The Theory of Capitalist Development*. New York: Monthly Review Press, 1970.

Takaki, Ronald. *Iron Cages: Race and Culture in 19th-Century America*. New York: Alfred A. Knopf, 1979.

Taylor, Paul. *Mexican Labor in the United States-Imperial Valley*, vol. 6, nos. 1-5, vol. 7, nos. 1-2. Berkeley: University of California Press, 1928-32.

Taylor, William. *Drinking, Homicide and Rebellion in Colonial Mexican Villages*. Stanford: Stanford University Press, 1979.

Terkel, Studs. *Hard Times*. New York: Avon Books, 1970.

Therborn, Goran. *The Ideology of Power and the Power of Ideology*. London: Verso Editions and NLN, 1980.

Thompson, E.P. *The Making of the English Working Class*. New York: Vintage Books, 1963.

Thorne, Barrie, and Henley, Nancy. *Language and Sex Difference and Dominace*. Massachusetts: Newbury House Publishers, 1975.

Tilly, Louise A., and Scott, Joan. *Women, Work and Family*. New York: Holt, Rinehart and Winston, 1978.

Toor, Frances. *A Treasury of Mexican Folkways*. New York: Crown Publishers, 1947.

Trejo, Raul. *El movimiento obrero: su situación y perspectivas en México hoy*. México, D.F.: Siglo XXI, 1981.

Turner, Ethel Duffy. *Revolution in Baja California: Ricardo Flores Magón's High Noon*. Detroit: Blaine Ethridge Books, 1981.

Turner, John. *Barbarous Mexico*. Chicago: Charles H. Kerr and Company, 1910.

Turner, Victor, and Turner, Edith. *Image and Pilgrimage in Christian Culture*. Oxford: Basil Blackwell.

Urrutia, Elena. *Imagen y realidad de la mujer*. México, D.F.: SepSetentas/Diana, 1979.

Vankleffens, E.N. *Hispanic Law*. Edinburgh: Edinburgh University Press, 1968.

Vansina, Jan. *Oral Tradition: A Study of Historical Methodology*. Chicago: Aldine Publishing Co., 1965.

Vásquez, Carlos, and García y Griego, Manuel, eds. *Mexican-U.S. Relations: Conflict and Converge*. Los Angeles: Chicano Studies Research Center Publications and Latin American Center Publications, University of California, 1983.

Velez-Ibañez, Carlos G. *Rituals of Marginality: Politics, Process, and Cultural Change in Urban Central Mexico*. Los Angeles and Berkeley: University of California Press, 1983.

Vera Fortino, Hipólito. *Apuntamientos Historicos de los Concilios Provinciales Mexicanos y Privilegios de América*. 5 vols. Amecameca: Imprenta del Colegio Católico, 1893.

Vidal, Mirta. *Chicanas Speak Out: Women, New Voice of La Raza*. New York: Pathfinder Press, 1971.

Wallace, Elizabeth. *Sor Juana Inés de la Cruz: poetisa de corte y convento*. México, D.F.: Ediciones Xóchitl, 1944.

Ware, Caroline F. *The Early New England Cotton Manufacture*. Boston: Houghton Mifflin Company. 1931. Reprint. New York: Johnson Reprint Corporation, 1966.

Ware, Carolyn. Introduction to *Class, Sex and the Woman Worker*, edited by Milton Cantor and Bruce Laurie. Westport: Greenwood Press, 1979.

Weaver, Thomas, and Downing, Thomas. *Mexican Migration*. Tucson: University of Arizona Bureau of Ethnic Research, 1976.

Webb, Edith Buckland. *Indian Life at the Old Missions*. Los Angeles: W.F. Lewis, 1952.

Weber, David. *Foreigners in Their Native Land*. Albuquerque: University of New Mexico Press, 1973.

Weber, Devra Anne. *The Struggle for Stability and Control in the Cotton Fields of California: Class Relations in Agriculture, 1919-1942.* Ithaca: Cornell University Press, forthcoming.

Welter, Barbara. *Dimity Convictions.* Athens, Ohio: Ohio University Press, 1976.

White, Hayden. *Metahistory: The Historical Imagination in Nineteenth-Century Europe.* Baltimore and London: John Hopkins University Press, 1973.

Winther, Oscar O. *The Story of San Jose: California's First Pueblo, 1777-1869.* San Francisco: California Historical Society, 1935.

Wolf, Eric R. *Sons of the Shaking Earth.* Chicago: The University of Chicago Press, 1959.

Woodcock Tentler, Leslie. *Wage Earning Women: Industrial Work and Family Life in the United States, 1900-1930.* New York: Oxford University Press, 1979.

Wright de Kleinhans, Laureana. *Mujeres Notables Mexicanas.* México, D.F.: Tipografía Económica, 1910.

Zavella, Patricia. *Women's Work and Chicano Families: Cannery Workers of the Santa Clara Valley.* Ithaca: Cornell University Press, 1987.

Zenker, E.V. *Anarchism.* London: Methuen & Co., 1898.

IV. *Articles and Pamplets*

Albertson, Dean Howard. "Dr. Edward Turner Bale, Incorrigible Californian." *California Historical Society Quarterly* 28 (1949): 250-269.

Alexander, Sally. "Women's Work in Nineteenth-Century London: A Study of the Years 1820-50." In *The Rights and Wrongs of Women*, edited by Juliet Mitchell and Ann Oakley. New York: Penguin Books, 1976.

Allen, Ruth. "The Labor of Women in the Production of Cotton." *University of Texas Bulletin* No. 3134, September 8, 1931.

Allen, Ruth. "Mexican Peon Women in Texas." *Sociology and Social Research* 16 (September/October 1931): 131-142.

Alurista. "Must be the Season of the Witch." In *Fiesta in Aztlan: Anthology of Chicano Poetry*. Santa Barbara: Capra Press, 1981.

Alvarez, Alejandro. "El movimiento obrero ante la crisis económica." *Cuadernos Políticos* Núm. 16 (abril-junio 1978): 31-43.

Apodaca, Maria Linda. "The Chicana Women: An Historical Materialist Perspective." In *Women in Latin America: An Anthology from Latin American Perspectives*, edited by William Bollinger et al., pp. 81-100. Riverside, Calif.: Latin American Perspectives, 1979.

Aragon de Valdez, Theresa. "Organizing as a Political Tool for the Chicana." *Frontiers* 5 (Summer 1980): 7-13.

Arguelles, Lourdes, and Angulo, Julio. "Undocumented Mexican Workers in the United States Southwest: A Preliminary Report on Their Migratory Experience." *Women's Studies* 1 (Fall 1985).

Aries, Philippe. "Le mariage indissoluble." En *Sexualites Occidentales*, pp. 148-168. Paris: Seuil, 1982.

Arizpe, Lourdes. "Mujeres migrantes y economía campesina: análisis de una cohorte migratoria a la ciudad de México, 1940-1970." *América Indígena* 38 (abril-junio 1978): 303-326.

Arizpe, Lourdes. "The Rural Exodus in Mexico and Mexican Migration to the United States." *International Migration Review* 15 (1981): 626-649.

Arnaz, José. "Memoirs of a Merchant." Edited and translated by Nellie Van de Grift Sanchez. *Touring Topics* 20 (September 1928): 14-19.

Arrom, Silvia M. "Marriage Patterns in Mexico City, 1811." *Journal of Family History* 4 (Winter 1978): 376-391.

Arroyo, Anita. "La mexicanidad en el estilo de Sor Juana." *Revista Iberoamericana* 17 (febrero-junio 1951): 53-59.

Arroyo, Laura E. "Industrial and Occupational Distribution of Chicana Workers." *Aztlan: Chicano Journal of the Social Sciences and the Arts* 4 (Fall 1973): 343-382.

Arroyo, Laura E. "Industrial and Occupational Distribution of Chicana Workers." Reprinted in *Essays on La Mujer*, edited by Rosaura Sanchez and Rosa Martinez Cruz, pp. 150-187. Los Angeles: Chicano Studies Center Publications, University of California, 1977.

Arroyo, Luis Leobardo. "Chicano Participation in Organized Labor: The CIO in Los Angeles, 1938-1950. An Extended Research Note." *Aztlan: International Journal of Chicano Studies Research* 6 (Summer 1975): 277-303.

Arroyo, Luis Leobardo. "Notes on Past, Present and Future Directions of Chicano Labor Studies." *Aztlan: International Journal of Chicano Studies Research* 6 (Summer 1975): 137-149.

Atondo, Ana María. "Algunos grupos desviantes en el México Colonial." En *Familia y sexualidad en Nueva España*, pp. 275-283. México, D.F.: Cultura SEP, 1982.

Baca Zinn, Maxine. "Chicanas: Power and Control in the Domestic Sphere." *De Colores* 2 (1975): 19-31.

Baca Zinn, Maxine. "Political Feminism: Toward Sex Role Equality in Chicano Families." *Aztlan: International Journal of Chicano Studies Research* 6 (Spring 1975): 13-26.

Baca Zinn, Maxine. "Field Research in Minority Communities: Ethical, Methodological and Political Observations by an Insider." *Social Problems* 1 (1979): 217-218.

Baca Zinn, Maxine. "Gender and Ethnic Identity Among Chicanos." *Frontiers* 5 (Summer 1980): 18-24.

Baker, Charles C. "Mexican Land Grants." *Historical Society of Southern California* 9 (1914): 236-243.

Barakat, Robert A. "Aztec Motifs in La Llorona." *Southern Folklore Quarterly* 29 (1965): 288-296.

Barbieri, Teresita de. "Notas para el estudio del trabajo doméstico." *Demografía y Economía* 34 (1977).

Bauman, Richard. "The Field Study of Folklore in Context." In *Handbook of American Folklore*, edited by Richard M. Dorson, pp. 363-368. Bloomington: Indiana University Press, 1983.

Baxandall Krooth, Ann, and Greenberg, Jaclyn. "Interview with Elizabeth Nicholas." *Harvest Quarterly* 3 & 4 (September-December 1976).

Bell, Colin, and Newby, Howard. "Husbands and Wives: The Dynamics of the Deferential Dialectic." In *Dependence and Exploitation in Work and Marriage*, edited by Barker and Allen, pp. 152-168. New York: Longman, 1976.

Berger, John. "Towards Understanding Peasant Experiences." *Race and Class* 19 (1975): 352.

Borah, Woodrow, and Cook, Sherbourne F. "Marriage and Legitimacy in Mexican Culture: Mexico and California." *California Law Review* 54: 946-1008.

Blanco, Iris. "Participación de las mujeres en la sociedad prehispánica." In *Essays on la Mujer*, edited by Rosaura Sanchez and Rosa Martinez Cruz, pp. 48-81. Los Angeles: Chicano Studies Center Publications, 1977.

Bovenschen, Silvia. "The Contemporary Witch, the Historical Witch, and the Witch Myth: The Witch Subject of the Appropriation of Nature and Object of the Domination of Nature." *New German Critique* 5 (1975): 83-119.

Bowman, J.N. "Prominent Women in Provincial California." *Historical Society of Southern California* 39 (June 1957): 149-166.

Bowman, J.N. "Juana Briones de Miranda." *Historical Society of Southern California* 39 (September 1957): 227-241.

Bowman, J.N. "The Resident Neophytes of the California Missions (1769-1834)." *Historical Society of Southern California Quarterly* 40 (June 1958): 138-148.

Briones, Brigida. "A Carnival Ball at Monterey in 1829." *Century Magazine* 41 (1890): 468-469.

Briones, Brigida. "A Glimpse of Domestic Life in 1827." *Century Magazine* 41 (1890): 470.

Brophy, Brigid. "The Rococo Seducer." *The London Magazine* 2 (May 1962): 54-71.

Burkett, Elinor C. "In Dubious Sisterhood: Class and Sex in Spanish Colonial South America." In *Women in Latin America: An Anthology from Latin American Perspectives*, edited by William Bollinger et al., pp. 17-25. Riverside, California: Latin American Perspectives, 1979.

Bush, Rod. "Racism and the Rise of the Right." *Contemporary Marxism* (1982).

Bustamante, Jorge. "Undocumented Migration from Mexico: A Research Report." *International Migration Review* 11 (1977): 149-178.

Campbell, Leon. "The First Californios: Presidial Society in Spanish California, 1769-1822." *Journal of the West* 2 (October 1972): 582-595.

Candelaria, Cordelia. "Six Reference Works on Mexican-American Women: A Review Essay." *Frontiers* 5 (Summer 1980): 75-80.

Carrasco, Pedro. "The Joint Family in Ancient Mexico: The Case of Molotla." In *Essays of Kinship in Mexico*. Pittsburgh: University of Pittsburgh, 1976.

Carroll, Berenice A. "Mary Beard's Woman As Force in History: A Critique." In *Liberating Women's History: Theoretical and Critical Essays*, edited by Berenice A. Carroll, pp. 26-41. Urbana: University of Illinois Press, 1976.

Casavantes, Edward. "Pride and Prejudice: A Mexican American Dilemma." In *Chicanos: Social and Psychological Perspectives*, edited by Carrol A. Hernandez, Marsha J. Haug, and Nathaniel N. Wagner. St. Louis: The C.V. Mosby Company, 1976.

Cesar, Julio. "Recollections of My Youth at San Luis Rey Mission." Translated by Nellie Van de Grift Sanchez. *Touring Topics* 25 (November 1930): 42-43.

Chodorow, Nancy. "Mothering, Male Dominance and Capitalism." In *Capitalist Patriarchy and the Case for Socialist Feminism*, edited by Zillah R. Eisenstein, pp. 83-106. New York: Monthly Review Press, 1979.

Clark, E. Culpeper; Hyde, Michael J.; and McMahan, Eva M. "Communication in the Oral History Interview: Investigating Problems of Interpreting Oral Data." *International Journal of Oral History* 1 (1980): 31-32.

Clark, Harry. "Their Pride, Their Manners, and Their Voices: Sources of the Traditional Portrait of the Early Californios." *California Historical Quarterly* 53 (Spring 1974): 71-82.

Cobarrubias, Sebastian de. "Definición de mujer." En *Tesoro de la Lengua Castellana Española*. Madrid y México, D.F.: Editorial Turner, 1984.

Códigos Españoles. "Titulos y leyes de la Quarta Partida." En *Código de las Siete Partidas*, vol. 2 & 3. España: Imprenta de la Publicidad, 1848.

Contreras Suarez, Enrique y Silva Ruiz, Gilberto. "Los recientes movimientos obreros mexicanos por independencia sindical y el reformismo obrero." *Revista Mexicana de Sociología* 34 (julio-septiembre, octubre-diciembre 1972): 845-879.

Coronel, Don Antonio. "Things Past." Translated by Nellie Van de Grift Sanchez. *Touring Topics* 22 (May 1930): 22-26.

Cortés, Carlos E. "Mexican Americans in Twentieth-Century California." *Masterkey: Anthropology of the Americas* 60, nos. 2 & 3 (Summer/Fall 1986): 36-48.

Corwin, Arthur. "Mexican American History: An Assessment." *Pacific Historical Review* 42 (August 1973): 269-308.

Cotera, Marta. "Feminism: The Chicana and Anglo Versions, A Historical Analysis." In *Twice a Minority: Mexican American Women*, edited by Margarita B. Melville, pp. 217-234. St. Louis: The C.V. Mosby Co., 1980.

Coyle, Laurie; Hershatter, Gail; and Honig, Emily. "Women at Farah: An Unfinished Story." In *Mexican Women in the United States: Struggles Past and Present*, edited by Magdalena Mora and Adelaida R. Del Castillo, pp. 117-144. Los Angeles: Chicano Studies Research Center Publications, University of California, 1980.

Davin, Anna. "Feminism and Labour History." In *People's History and Socialist Theory*, edited by Raphael Samuel, pp. 176-181. London: Routledge and Kegan Paul, 1981.

De Jong, G., and Ahmad F. "Motivation for Migration of Welfare Clients." In *Internal Migration: The New World and the Third World*, edited by Anthony H. Richmond and Daniel Kubat. Beverly Hills: Sage Publications, 1976.

Del Castillo, Adelaida R. "Malintzin Tenepal: A Preliminary Look into a New Perspective." Reprinted in *Essays on La Mujer*, edited by Rosaura Sanchez and Rosa Martinez Cruz, pp. 124-149. Los Angeles: Chicano Studies Center Publications, University of California, 1977.

Del Castillo, Adelaida R. "Mexican Women in Organization." In *Mexican Women in the United States: Struggles Past and Present*, edited by Magdalena Mora and Adelaida R. Del Castillo, pp. 7-16. Los Angeles: Chicano Studies Research Center Publications, University of California, 1980.

Del Castillo, Adelaida R. "Sterilization: An Overview." In *Mexican Women in the United States: Struggles Past and Present*, edited by Magdalena Mora and Adelaida R. Del Castillo, pp. 65-70. Los Angeles: Chicano Studies Research Center Publications, University of California, 1980.

Del Castillo, Adelaida R., and Mora, Magdalena. "Sex, Nationality, and Class: La Obrera Mexicana." In *Mexican Women in the United States: Struggles Past and Present*, edited by Magdalena Mora and Adelaida R. Del Castillo, pp. 1-4. Los Angeles: Chicano Studies Research Center Publications, University of California, 1980.

Del Castillo, Adelaida R. "Sobre la experiencia educativa chicana." *Fem.: Publicación Feminista Bimestral* 48 (octubre-noviembre 1986): 7-10.

Dinnerman, Ida. "Patterns of Adaptation Among Households of U.S. Bound Migrants from Michoacan, Mexico." *International Migration Review* 12 (1978): 620-644.

Dixon, Marlene. "On the Superexploitation of Women." In *Women in Class Struggle*. San Francisco: Synthesis Publications, 1978.

Dixon, Marlene. "On the Situation in the USA Today." *Our Socialism* 2 (October 1981): 16-31.

Dixon, Marlene; Jonas, Susanne; and McCaughan, Ed. "Reindustrialization and the Development of a

Transnational Labor Force." *Contemporary Marxism* (Summer 1982).

Duhaut-Cilly, Auguste Bernard. "Duhaute-Cilly's Account of California in the Years 1827-28." Translated and edited by Charles Franklin Carter. *California Historical Society Quarterly* 8 (1929): 306-336.

Dunbar Ortiz, Roxanne. "Female Liberation as the Basis for Social Revolution." In *Sisterhood Is Powerful*, edited by Robin Morgan, pp. 477-492. New York: Random House, 1970.

Dunbar Ortiz, Roxanne. "Toward a Democratic Women's Movement in the United States." In *Mexican Women in the United States: Struggles Past and Present*, edited by Magdalena Mora and Adelaida R. Del Castillo, pp. 29-35. Los Angeles: Chicano Studies Research Center Publications, University of California, 1980.

Eisenstein, Zillah. "Developing a Theory of Capitalist Patriarchy and Socialist Feminism." In *Capitalist Patriarchy and the Case for Socialist Feminism*, edited by Zillah R. Eisenstein. New York: Monthly Review Press, 1979.

Elshtain, Jean Betke. "The New Feminist Scholarship." *Salmagundi*, No. 70-71 (Spring-Summer 1986): 3-26.

Ewing, J. Andrew. "Education in California During the Pre-Statehood Period." *Historical Society of Southern California* 11 (1918): 51-59.

Fischer, Christine. "Women in California in the Early 1850s." *Southern California Quarterly* 60 (Fall 1978): 231-254.

Foppa, Alaíde. "El Congreso Feminista de Yucatán, 1916." *Fem.: Publicación Feminista Bimestral* 3 (noviembre-diciembre 1979): 55-59.

Frisch, Michael H. "The Memory of History." *Radical History Review* 25 (October 1981): 9-23.

Frisch, Michael H. "Oral History and Hard Times: Review Essay." *Red Buffalo* 1 & 2.

Garcia, Mario T. "The Californios of San Diego and the Politics of Accommodation, 1846-1860." *Aztlan: International Journal of Chicano Studies Research* 6 (Spring 1975): 69-81.

Garcia, Mario T. "Racial Dualism in the El Paso Labor Market, 1880-1920." *Aztlan: International Journal of Chicano Studies Research* 6 (Summer 1975): 197-218.

Garcia, Mario T. "La Familia: The Mexican Immigrant Family, 1900-1930." In *Work, Family, Sex Roles and Language.* National Association for Chicano Studies, pp. 117-139. Berkeley: Tonatiuh-Quinto Sol, 1979.

Garcia, Mario T. "The Chicana in American History: The Mexican Women of El Paso, 1880-1920--A Case Study." *Pacific Historical Review* 49 (May 1980): 315-337.

Garcia-Bahne, Betty. "La Chicana and the Chicano Family." In *Essays on La Mujer*, edited by Rosaura Sanchez and Rosa Martinez Cruz, pp. 30-47. Los Angeles: Chicano Studies Center Publications, University of California, 1977.

García Morruz, Fina. "Mexicanidad de Sor Juana." *Sin Nombre* 7 (1976): 6-36.

Garr, Daniel J. "A Rare and Desolate Land: Population and Race in Hispanic California." *Western Historical Quarterly* 6 (April 1975): 133-148.

Gómez-Quiñones, Juan. "Toward a Perspective on Chicano History." *Aztlan: Chicano Journal of the Social Sciences and the Arts* 2 (Fall 1971): 1-49.

Gómez-Quiñones, Juan. "The First Steps: Chicano Labor Conflict and Organizing, 1900-1920." *Aztlan: Chicano Journal of the Social Sciences and the Arts* 3 (Spring 1972): 13-49.

Gómez-Quiñones, Juan. *On Culture.* Los Angeles: Chicano Studies Center Publications, University of California, 1977.

Gómez-Quiñones, Juan. "Critique on the National Question, Self-Determination and Nationalism." *Latin American Perspectives* 9 (Spring 1982): 62-83.

Gómez-Quiñones, Juan, and Arroyo, Luis Leobardo. "On the State of Chicano History: Observations on Its Development, Interpretations, and Theory, 1970-1974." *Western Historical Quarterly* 7 (April 1976): 155-185.

Gómez-Quiñones, Juan, and Ríos-Bustamante, Antonio. "La comunidad al norte del Rio Bravo." En *La otra cara de México: el pueblo chicano*, editado por David Maciel. México, D.F.: Ediciones "El Caballito," 1977.

Gonzales, Sylvia Alicia. "The Chicana Perspective: A Design for Self-Awareness." In *The Chicanos: As We See Ourselves*, edited by Arnulfo D. Trejo, pp. 81-99. Tucson: University of Arizona Press, 1979.

Gonzalez, Rosalia. "Chicanas and Mexican Immigrant Families: Women's Subordination and Family Exploitation." In *Decades of Discontent: The Women's Movement, 1920-1940*, edited by Joan Jensen and Lois Sharf, pp. 59-84. Westport, Conn.: Greenwood Press, 1983.

Gordon, Ann D., and Buhle, Mari Jo. "Sex and Class in Colonial and Mid 19th-Century America." In *Liberating Women's History: Theoretical and Critical Essays*, edited by Berenice A. Carroll, pp. 278-300. Urbana: University of Chicago Press, 1976.

Gordon, Ann D.; Buhle, Mari Jo; and Schrom Dye, Nancy. "The Problem of Women's History." In *Liberating Women's History: Theoretical and Critical Essays*, edited by Berenice A. Carroll, pp. 75-92. Urbana: University of Illinois Press, 1976.

Gordon, Linda. "A Socialist View of Women's Studies: A Reply to Editorial." *Signs: Journal of Women in Culture and Society* 1 (Winter 1975): 559-566.

Griswold del Castillo, Richard. "A Preliminary Comparison of Chicano, Immigrant and Native Born Family Structures,

1850-1880." *Aztlan: International Journal of Chicano Studies Research* 6 (Spring 1975): 87-95.

Griswold del Castillo, Richard. "La Familia Chicana: Social Change in the Chicano Family of Los Angeles, 1850-1890." *Journal of Ethnic Studies* 3 (Spring 1975): 41-58.

Griswold del Castillo, Richard. "Myth and Reality: Chicano Economic Mobility in Los Angeles, 1850-1880." *Aztlan: International Journal of Chicano Studies Research* 6 (Summer 1975): 151-171.

Griswold del Castillo, Richard. "The Del Valle Family and the Fantasy Heritage." *California History* 50 (1980): 2-15.

Gruzinsky, Serge. "Matrimonios y sexualidad en México y Texcoco en los albores de la conquista o la pluralidad de los discursos." *Cuadernos de Trabajo* 35 (1980): 19-76.

Gruzinsky, Serge. "La conquista de los cuerpos." En *Familia y sexualidad en Nueva España*, pp. 177-206. México, D.F.: Cultura SEP, 1982.

Guest, O.F.M., Florian F. "The Establishment of the Villa de Branciforte." *California Historical Quarterly* 40 (March 1962): 29-50.

Guest, O.F.M., Florian F. "The Indian Policy Under Fermin Francisco de Lasuen, California's Second Father President." *California Historical Quarterly* 45: 195-224.

Gutierrez Girardot, Rafael. "Teoría social de la literatura, esbozo de sus problemas." *Escritura: Teoría y Crítica Literaria* 1 (enero-junio 1976): 42.

Hall, Stuart. "Culture, the Media and the Ideological Effect." In *Mass Communication and Society*, edited by J. Curran et al. London: Arnold, 1977.

Harding, Susan. "Women and Words in a Spanish Village." In *Toward an Anthropology of Women*, edited by Rayna Reiter, pp. 283-308. New York: Monthly Review Press, 1975.

Hart, John. "Working-Class Women in Nineteenth Century Mexico." In *Mexican Women in the United States: Struggles Past and Present*, edited by Magdalena Mora and Adelaida R. Del Castillo, pp. 151-157. Los Angeles: Chicano Studies Research Center Publications, University of California, 1980.

Horcasitas, Fernando, and Butterworth, Douglas. "La Llorona." *Tlalocan: revista de fuentes para el conocimiento de las culturas indígenas de México* 4 (1963): 204-224.

Hornbeck, David. "Land Tenure and Rancho Expansion in Alta California, 1784-1841." *Journal of Historical Geography* 4 (1978): 371-390.

Hornbeck, David. "The Patenting of California Private Land Claims, 1851-1885." *Geography Review* 69 (1979): 434-448.

Hough, John C. "Charles Henry Brinley: A Case Study in Rancho Supervision." *Historical Society of Southern California* 40 (June 1958): 174-179.

Jameson, Elizabeth. "May and Me": A Working Paper on Relationships with Informants and Communities." Working Paper, Southwest Institute for Research on Women, University of Arizona, 1982.

Jensen, Joan M., and Miller, Darlis A. "The Gentle Tamers Revisited: New Approaches to the History of Women in the American West." *Pacific Historical Review* 44 (May 1980): 173-213.

Jonas, Susanne, and Dixon, Marlene. "Proletarianization and Class Alliances in the Americas." *Contradictions of Socialist Construction*. San Francisco: Synthesis Publications, 1979.

Jordan, Rosan A. "The Vaginal Serpent and Other Themes from Mexican-American Women's Role." In *Women's Folklore, Women's Culture*, edited by Rosan A. Jordan and Susan J. Kalcik, pp. 26-44. Philadelphia: University of Pennsylvania Press, 1985.

Kaplan, Temma. "Female Consciousness and Collective Action: The Case of Barcelona, 1910-1918." *Signs: Journal of Women in Culture and Society* 7 (Spring 1982): 545-566.

Kearney, Michael. "La Llorona as a Social Symbol." *Western Folklore* 27 (1968): 199-206.

Kelly-Godal, Joan. "The Social Relation of the Sexes: Methodological Implications of Women's History." *Signs: Journal of Women in Culture and Society* 1 (Summer 1976): 809-823.

Kessler-Harris, Alice. "Organizing the Unorganizable: Three Jewish Women and Their Union." In *Class, Sex, and the Woman Worker*, edited by Milton Cantor and Bruce Laurie. Westport, Conn: Greenwood Press, 1977.

Kirtley, Bacil F. "La Llorona and Related Themes." *Western Folklore* 19 (1960): 155-168.

Knaster, Meri. "Women in Latin America: The State of Research, 1975." *Latin American Research Review* 11 (1976): 3-74.

Konetzke, Richard. "Documentos para la historia y crítica de los registros parroquiales en las Indias." *Revista de Indias* 25 (1946): 581-586.

Kuhn, Annette, and Wolpe, Ann Marie. "Feminism and Materialism." In *Feminism and Materialism: Women and Modes of Production*, edited by Annette Kuhn and Ann Marie Wolpe, pp. 1-10. London: Routledge and Kegan Paul, 1978.

"La Chicana: The Brown Woman and Today's Struggle." In *The Chicanos: Life and Struggles of the Mexican Minority in the United States*, edited by Gilberto López y Rivas, pp. 168-170. New York: Monthly Review Press, 1973.

Laclau, Ernesto, and Mouffe, Chantal. "Post-Marxism Without Apologies." *New Left Review*, no. 166 (November/December 1987): 79-106.

Lacy, James H. "New Mexico Women in Early American Writings." *New Mexico Historical Review* 34 (1959): 41-51.

Lane, Ann J. "Women in Society: A Critique of Frederick Engels." In *Liberating Women's History: Theoretical and Critical Essays*, edited by Berenice A. Carroll, pp. 4-25. Urbana: University of Illinois Press, 1976.

Langellier, John Phillip, and Meyers Peterson, Katherine. "Lances and Leather Jackets: Presidial Forces in Spanish Alta California, 1769-1821." *Journal of the West* 20 (October 1981): 3-11.

Langum, David J. "Californio Women and the Image of Virtue." *Southern California Quarterly* 59 (1977): 245-250.

Larguia, Isabel, and Dumoulin, John. "Toward a Science of Women's Liberation." In *Mexican Women in the United States: Struggles Past and Present*, edited by Magdalena Mora and Adelaida R. Del Castillo, pp. 45-61. Los Angeles: Chicano Studies Research Center Publications, University of California, 1980.

Lawrence, Eleanor. "Mexican Trade Between Santa Fe and Los Angeles, 1830-1848." *California Historical Society Quarterly* 10 (March 1931): 27-39.

Leal, Luis. "El 'Tocotín Mestizo' de Sor Juana." *Abside* 18 (enero-marzo 1954): 51-64.

Le Compte, Janet. "The Independent Women of Hispanic New Mexico, 1821-1846." *Western Historical Quarterly* 12 (January 1981): 17-35.

Leddy, Betty. "La Llorona in Southern Arizona." *Western Folklore* 7 (1948): 272-277.

Leonard, Irving A. "A Baroque Poetess." *Baroque Times in Old Mexico*. Ann Arbor: The University of Michigan Press, 1966.

Lerner, Gerda. "New Approaches to the Study of Women in American History." In *Liberating Women's History:*

Theoretical and Critical Essays, edited by Berenice A. Carroll, pp. 349-356. Urbana: University of Illinois Press, 1976.

Lerner Gerda. "Placing Women in History: A 1975 Perspective." In *Liberating Women's History: Theoretical and Critical Essays*, edited by Berenice Carroll, pp. 357-367. Urbana: University of Illinois Press, 1976.

"Letter to Our Readers." *Frontiers* 5 (Summer 1980): iv.

Levine, Andrew; Sober, Elliot; and Olin Wright, Erik. "Marxism and Methodological Individualism." *New Left Review*, no. 162 (March/April 1987): 67-84.

Levine, Susan. "Labor's True Woman: Domesticity and Equal Rights in the Knights of Labor." *Journal of American History* 70 (September 1983): 323-339.

Lidoff, Joan. "Her Mother's Voice: Reading Towards a Feminist Poetics, Tillie Olsen and Grace Paley." In *Fluid Boundaries: The Origins of a Distinctive Women's Voice in Literature*. Chicago: University of Chicago Press.

Limon, José E. "El Primer Congreso Mexicanista de 1911: A Precursor to Contemporary Chicanismo." *Aztlan: International Journal of Chicano Studies Research* 5 (Summer 1974): 85-117.

Livingston, M. M. "The Earliest Spanish Land Grants in California." *Historical Society of Southern California* 9 (1914): 195-199.

Lizarraga, Sylvia S. "From a Woman to a Woman." In *Essays on La Mujer*, edited by Rosaura Sanchez and Rosa Martinez Cruz, pp. 91-95. Los Angeles: Chicano Studies Center Publications, University of California, 1977.

Lomax-Hawes, Bess. "La Llorona in Juvenile Hall." *Western Folklore* 27 (1968): 153-170.

Longauex y Vasquez, Enriqueta. "The Mexican-American Woman." In *Sisterhood Is Powerful*, edited by Robin Morgan, pp. 379-384. New York: Random House, 1970.

Lopez, Ronald W. "The El Monte Berry Strike of 1933." *Aztlan: Chicano Journal of the Social Sciences and the Arts* 1 (Spring 1970): 101-114.

López Cámara, Francisco. "La conciencia criolla en Sor Juana y Sigüenza." *Historia Mexicana* 6 (1957): 350-373.

Lugo, José del Carmen. "Life of a Rancher." *Historical Society of Southern California* 32 (September 1950): 185-236.

Luz Aniaga, María de la; Velasco, Edur; y Zepeda, Eduardo. "Inflación y salario en el régimen de LEA." *Investigaciones Económicas* 36 (julio-septiembre 1977).

Macias, Anna. "Mexican Women in the Social Revolution." In *History of Latin American Civilization: Sources and Interpretations*, edited by Lewis Hanke. 2 vols. Boston: Little, Brown and Co., 1973.

Mackinnon, Catherine A. "Feminism, Marxism, Method and the State: An Agenda for Theory." *Signs: Journal of Women in Culture and Society* 7 (Spring 1982): 515-544.

Malvido, Elsa. "El abandono de los hijos, una forma de control de la mano de obra indígena y del tamaño de la familia en la época colonial: Tula 1683-1780." *Historia Mexicana* 81 (1981): 251-561.

Malvido, Elsa. "El siglo XVI, una nueva patología en América." En *La ciencia moderna y el Nuevo Mundo*, pp. 367-378. Madrid: CDICJSLHCT, 1985.

Marcus, Jane. "Storming the Toolshed." In *Feminist Theory: A Critique of Ideology*, edited by Nannerl O. Keohane, Michelle Z. Rosaldo and Barbara C. Gelpi. Chicago: University of Chicago Press, 1982.

Marquez, Evelina, and Ramirez, Margarita. "Women's Task is to Gain Liberation." In *Essays on La Mujer*, edited by

Rosaura Sanchez and Rosa Martinez Cruz, pp. 188-194. Los Angeles: Chicano Studies Center Publications, University of California, 1977.

Marx, Karl. "A Reader in Marxist Aesthetics - Selected Texts." In *Marxism and Art*, edited by Maynard Solomon, pp. 22-75. Detroit: Wayne State University Press, 1979.

Mason, William M. "Alta California During the Mission Period, 1769-1835." *Masterkey: Anthropology of the Americas* 60 (Summer/Fall 1986): 4-14.

Maza, Francisco. "Prólogo a Sor Juana Inés de la Cruz, de Ludwig Pfandl." *Norte* 265 (1975): 21-23.

McDonough, Roisin, and Harrison, Rachel. "Patriarchy and Relations of Productions." In *Feminism and Maternalism: Women and Modes of Production*, edited by Annette Kuhn and Ann Marie Wolp, pp. 15-18. Boston: Routledge and Kegan Paul, 1978.

McGinty, Brian. "The Carrillos of San Diego: An Historic Spanish Family of California." *Historical Society of Southern California* 39 (1957).

Melville, Margarita B. "Selective Acculturation of Female Mexican Migrants." In *Twice of Minority: Mexican American Women*, edited by Margarita B. Melville, pp. 155-163. St. Louis: The C.V. Mosby Co., 1980.

Melville, Margarita B. "Mexican Women Adapt to Migration." In *Mexican Immigrant Workers in the U.S.*, edited by Antonio Ríos-Bustamante, pp. 119-124. Los Angeles: Chicano Studies Research Center Publications, University of California. 1981.

Meyer, Doris L. "Early Mexican American Responses to Negative Stereotyping." *New Mexico Historical Review* 53 (January 1978): 75-91.

Miller, Michael. "Variations in Mexican American Family Life: A Review Synthesis of Empirical Research." *Aztlan:*

International Journal of Chicano Studies Research 9 (1978): 209-231.

Mindiola, Tatcho. "The Cost of Being a Mexican Female Worker in the 1970 Houston Labor Market." *Aztlan: International Journal of Chicano Studies Research* 11 (Fall 1980): 231-247.

Miranda, Gloria. "Gente de Razon Marriage Patterns in Spanish and Mexican California: A Case Study of Santa Barbara and Los Angeles." *Southern California Quarterly* 63 (Spring 1981): 1-21.

Mirandé, Alfredo. "The Chicano Family: A Reanalysis of Conflicting Views." *Journal of Marriage and the Family* 39 (November 1977): 747-756.

Mitchell, Juliet. "Four Structures in a Complex Unity." In *Liberating Women's History: Theoretical and Critical Essays*, edited by Berenice A. Carroll, pp. 385-399. Urbana: University of Illinois Press, 1976.

Mitchell, Juliet. "Femininity, Narrative and Psychoanalysis." In *Feminist Literary Theory*, edited by Mary Eagleton, pp. 100-103. New York: Basil Blackwell, 1986.

Molina, Daniel. "La política laboral y el movimiento obrero, 1970-1976." *Cuadernos Políticos* Núm. 2 (abril-junio 1977).

Molyneux, Marine. "Socialist Societies: Progress Toward Women's Emancipation." *Monthly Review* 34 (July-August 1982): 56-100.

Mongió, Luis. "El negro en algunos poetas españoles y americanos anteriores a 1800." *Revista Iberoamericana* 22 (1957): 245-259.

Monroy, Douglas. "La Costura en Los Angeles, 1933-1939: The ILGWU and the Politics of Domination." In *Mexican Women in the United States: Struggles Past and Present*, edited by Magdalena Mora and Adelaida R. Del Castillo, pp. 171-178. Los Angeles: Chicano Studies Research Center Publications, University of California, 1980.

Monroy, Douglas. "An Essay on Understanding the Work Experience of Mexicans in Southern California, 1900-1939." *Aztlan: International Journal of Chicano Studies Research* 12 (Spring 1981): 59-74.

Mora, Magdalena. "The Tolteca Strike: Mexican Women and the Struggle for Union Representation." In *Mexican Immigrant Workers in the U.S.*, edited by Antonio Ríos-Bustamante, pp. 111-117. Los Angeles: Chicano Studies Research Center Publications, University of California, 1981.

Moraga, Cherrie. "La Guera." In *This Bridge Called My Back: Writings by Radical Women of Color*, edited by Cherrie Moraga and Gloria Anzaldua. Watertown, Mass.: Persephone Press, 1981.

Murillo, Nathan. "The Mexican American Family." In *Chicanos: Social and Psychological Perspectives*, edited by Carrol A. Hernandez, Nathaniel N. Wagner, and Marsha J. Haug, pp. 15-25. St. Louis: The C.V. Mosby Co., 1976.

Navoa, Juan Bruce. "Interview with Jose Antonio Villareal." *Revista Chicano-Riqueña* 4 (Spring 1976).

Nelson, Howard J. "The Two Pueblos of Los Angeles: Agricultural Village and Embryo Town." *Southern California Quarterly* 59 (Spring 1977): 1-12.

Nelson-Cisneros, Victor B. "La clase trabajadora en Tejas, 1920-1940." *Aztlan: International Journal of Chiano Studies Research* 6 (Summer 1975): 239-265.

Nelson-Cisneros, Victor B. "UCAPAWA and Chicanos in California: The Farm Worker Period, 1937-1940." *Aztlan: International Journal of Chicano Studies Research* 7 (Fall 1976): 453-477.

Nieto-Gomez, Anna. "La Feminista." *Encuentro Femenil* 1 (1974): 34-47.

O'Malley, P. "Social Bandits, Modern Capitalism, and the Traditional Peasantry: A Critique of Hobsbawn." *Journal of Peasant Studies* 6 (1979): 489-501.

"On the Brown Women's Struggle!: Statement from the Brown Women's Venceremos Collective." In *The Chicanos: Life and Struggles of the Mexican Minority in the United States*, edited by Gilberto López y Rivas, pp. 171-174. New York: Monthly Review Press, 1973.

Obledo, Mario. "Mexican Americans and the Media." In *La Causa Chicana*, edited by Margaret M. Marigold. New York: Family Service Association of America, 1971.

Ortega, Sergio. "El discurso del Nuevo Testamento sobre el matrimonio, la familia y los comportamientos sexuales." *Cuadernos de Trabajo* 35 (1980): 77-104.

Osorio Urbina, Jaime. "Superexplotación y clase obrera: el caso mexicana." *Cuadernos Políticos* Núm. 6 (octubre-diciembre 1975): 5-23.

Padilla, Raymond V. "A Critique of Pittian History." *El Grito: A Journal of Contemporary Mexican-American Thought* 6 (Fall 1972): 3-44.

Padilla, Raymond V. "A Critique of Pittian History." Reprinted in *Voices*, edited by Octavio I. Romano-V, pp. 65-106. Berkeley: Quinto Sol Publications, 1973.

Paredes, Américo. "Estado Unidos, México y el machismo." *Journal of International Studies* 9 (1967): 65-84.

Paredes, Américo. "Mexican Legendry and the Rise of the Mestizo." In *American Folk Legend: A Symposium*, edited by Wayland D. Hand. Berkeley and Los Angeles: University of California Press.

Paredes, Américo. "On Ethnographic Work Among Minority Groups: A Folklorist's Perspective." In *New Directions in Chicano Scholarship*, edited by Raymond A. Paredes and Ricardo Romo, pp. 1-32. La Jolla: Chicano Studies Center, University of California at San Diego.

Paredes, Raymond A. "The Mexican Image in American Travel Literature, 1831-1869." *New Mexico Historical Review* 52 (January 1977): 5-59.

Paredes, Raymond. "The Origins of Anti-Mexican Sentiment in the United States." *The New Scholar* 6 (1977): 139-165.

Paz, Octavio. "América Latina y la democracia." *Vuelta* 1 (junio 1982): 38.

Peña, Devon. "Las Maquiladoras: Mexican Women and Class Struggle in the Border Industries." *Aztlan: International Journal of Chicano Studies Research* 11 (1980): 159-229.

Peña, Devon. "Tortuosidad: Shop Floor Struggles of Female Maquiladora Workers." In *Women on the U.S.-Mexico Border: Responses to Change*, edited by Vicki L. Ruiz and Susan Tiano, pp. 129-154. Boston: Allen & Unwin, 1987.

Peregrina, Angélica. "Notica de los establecimientos para la educación de niñas en el Departamento de Jalisco en 1866." *Boletín del Archivo Histórico de Jalisco* 2 (1978): 17-22.

Pérez, María Esther. "Elementos folklóricos indígenas en las loas introducidas al teatro religioso de Sor Juana. En *Lo americano en el teatro de Sor Juana Inés de la Cruz*. Nueva York: Eliseo Torres e Hijos, 1975.

Pérez de Guillen, Eulalia. "Keeper of the Keys." Translated by Nellie Van de Grift Sanchez. *Touring Topics* 21 (January 1929): 24-27.

Pescatello, Ann. "The Female in Ibero-America: An Essay on Research Bibliography and Research Directions." *Latin American Research Review* 7: 125-141.

Phillips, George Harwood. "Indians in Los Angeles, 1781-1875: Economic Integration, Social Disintegration." *Pacific Historical Review* 49 (August 1980): 427-451.

Porter Benson, Susan. "'The Customers Ain't God': The Work Culture of Department Store Saleswomen, 1890-1940." In

Working Class America, edited by Michael H. Frish and Daniel J. Walkowitz. Urbana, University of Illinois Press, 1983.

Puccini, Darío. "Los villancicos de Sor Juana Inés de la Cruz." *Cuadernos Americanos* 24 (1965): 223-254.

Quintana, José Miguel. "Sor Juana en América." *Cuadernos Americanos* 28 (julio-agosto 1946): 219-222.

Ramirez, Arthur. "Estella Portillo: The Dialectic of Oppression and Liberation." *Revista Chicano-Riqueña* 8 (Summer 1980): 106-114.

Ramos, Reyes, and Ramos, Martha. "The Mexican American: Am I Who They Say I Am?" In *The Chicanos: As We See Ourselves*, edited by Arnulfo D. Trejo, pp. 49-66. Tucson: University of Arizona Press, 1979.

Reyes, Alfonso. "Virreinato de filigrina." En *Letras de la Nueva España*. México: Fondo de Cultura Económica, 1948.

Ridington, Juana Machado Aliapaz. "Times Gone By in Alta California." *Historical Society of Southern California* 41 (September 1959): 195-240.

Ríos-Bustamante, Antonio. *Mexicans in the United States and the National Question: Current Polemics and Organizational Positions*. Santa Barbara, Calif.: Editorial La Causa, 1978.

Ríos-Bustamante, Antonio. "The Barrioization of Nineteenth-Century Mexican Californians: From Landowners to Laborers." *Masterkey: Anthropology of the Americans* 60 (Summer/Fall 1986): 26-35.

Rischin, Moses. "Continuities and Discontinuities in Spanish-Speaking California." In *Ethnic Conflict in California History*, edited by Charles Wollenburg, pp. 43-60. Los Angeles: Tinnon-Brown Publishers, 1969.

Rivera, Feliciano. "The Teaching of Chicano History." In *The Chicanos: Mexican American Voices*, edited by E. Ludwig and James Santibanez. Baltimore: Penguin Books, 1971.

Rodriguez, James. "La búsqueda de identidad y sus motivos en la literatura chicana." En *Chicanos: antología, historia y literatura*, compilado por Tino Villanueva, pp. 200-208. México, D.F.: Fondo de Cultura Económica, Colección Tierra Firme, 1980.

Romo, Ricardo. "Responses to Mexican Immigration, 1910-1930." *Aztlan: International Journal of Chicano Studies of Research* 6 (Summer 1975): 173-194.

Rosaldo, Renato. "Grief and a Headhunter's Rage: On the Cultural Force of Emotions." In *Text, Play, and Story: The Construction of Self and Society*, edited by Edward M. Bruner. 1983 Proceedings of the American Ethnological Society. Washington, D.C.: American Ethnological Society, 1984.

Rosales, Francisco A., and Simon, Daniel T. "Chicano Steel Workers and Unionism in the Midwest, 1919-1945." *Aztlan: International Journal of Chicano Studies Research* 6 (Summer 1975): 267-275.

Rowbotham, Sheila. "The Trouble with 'Patriarchy.'" In *People's History and Socialist Theory*, edited by Raphael Samuel, pp. 364-369. London: Routledge and Kegan Paul, 1981.

Rubin, Gayle. "The Traffic in Women: Notes on the 'Political Economy' of Sex." In *Toward an Anthropology of Women*, edited by Rayna R. Reiter, pp. 170-184. New York: Monthly Review Press, 1975.

Rubio Goldsmith, Raquel. "Shipwrecked in the Desert: A Short History of the Mexican Sisters of the House of the Providence in Douglas, Arizona, 1927-1949." In *Women on the U.S.-Mexico Border: Responses to Change*, edited by Vicki L. Ruiz and Susan Tiano, pp. 177-195. Boston: Allen & Unwin, 1987.

Ruiz, Vicki L. "Working for Wages: Mexican Women in the American Southwest, 1930-1980." Working Paper No. 19, Southwest Institute for Research on Women, University of Arizona, 1984.

Ruiz, Vicki L. "Obreras y Madres: Labor Activism Among Mexican Women and Its Impact on the Family." In *La Mexicana/Chicana*. Renato Rosaldo Lecture Series, Vol. 1, Series 1983-84, Summer 1985, pp. 19-38. Tucson: Mexican American Studies and Research Center, University of Arizona.

Ruiz, Vicki L. "By the Day or the Week: Mexicana Domestic Workers in El Paso." In *Women on the U.S.-Mexico Border: Responses to Change*, edited by Vicki L. Ruiz and Susan Tiano, pp. 61-76. Boston: Allen & Unwin, 1987.

Ryan Johansson, Sheila. "'Herstory' as History: A New Field or Another Fad?" In *Liberating Women's History: Theoretical and Critical Essays*, edited by Berenice Carroll, pp. 400-430. Urbana: University of Illinois Press, 1976.

Salinas, Judy. "The Image of Women in Chicano Literature." *Revista Chicano-Riqueña* 4 (Fall 1976): 139-148.

Sanchez, Federico A. "Rancho Life in Alta California." *Masterkey: Anthropology of the Americas* 60 (Summer/Fall 1986): 15-25.

Sanchez, Rosaura. "The Chicana Labor Force." In *Essays on La Mujer*, edited by Rosaura Sanchez and Rosa Martinez Cruz, pp. 3-15. Los Angeles: Chicano Studies Center Publications, University of California, 1970.

Schlein, Lisa. "Los Angeles Garment District Sews a Cloak of Shame." In *Mexican Women in the United States: Struggles Past and Present*, edited by Magdalena Mora and Adelaida R. Del Castillo, pp. 113-116. Los Angeles: Chicano Studies Research Center Publications, University of California, 1980.

Schofield, Ann. "Rebel Girls and Union Maids: The Woman Question in Journals of the AFL and IWW, 1905-1920." *Feminist Studies* 9 (Summer 1983): 335-355.

Schrom Dye, Nancy. "Creating a Feminist Alliance: Sisterhood and Class Conflict in the New York Women's Trade Union

League, 1901-1914." In *Our American Sisters: Women in American Life and Thought*, edited by Jean E. Friedman and William G. Shade. 2d ed. Boston: Allyn and Bacon, Inc., 1976.

Schulman, Alix Kates. "Dancing in the Revolution. Emma Goldman's Feminism." *Socialist Revolution* 12: 31-44.

Secombe, Wally. "The Housewife and Her Labour Under Capitalism." *New Left Review* 82 (January-February 1974): 3-24.

Segura, Denise. "Labor Market Stratification: The California Experience." *Berkeley Journal of Sociology* 29 (1984).

Sepúlveda, Ygnacio. "The Spanish Californians: An Historical Memoir (1874)." *Touring Topics* 21 (November 1929): 31, 53-54.

Shay, Anthony. "Fandangos and Bailes: Dancing and Dance Events in Early California." *Southern California Quarterly* 64 (Summer 1982): 99-113.

Sicherman, Barbara. "Review Essay: American History." *Signs: Journal of Women in Culture and Society* 5 (1975): 461-485.

Smith, Hilda. "Feminism and the Methodology of Women's History." In *Liberating Women's History: Theoretical and Critical Essays*, edited by Berenice A. Carroll, pp. 369-384. Urbana: University of Illinois Press, 1976.

Smith, Margo L. "Domestic Service as a Channel of Upward Mobility for the Lower-Class Woman: The Lima Case." In *Female and Male in Latin America*, edited by Ann Pescatello. Pittsburgh: University of Pittsburgh Press, 1973.

Smith-Rosenberg, Carroll. "The Female World of Love and Ritual: Relations Between Women in Nineteenth-Century America." *Signs: Journal of Women in Culture and Society* 1 (Autumn 1975): 1-30.

Soeiro, Susan A. "Recent Work on Latin American Women: A Review Essay." *Journal of Interamerican Studies and World Affairs* 17 (November 1975): 497-516.

Solares, Ignacio. "Entrevista con Mario Vargas Llosa." *Vuelta* 1 (junio 1982): 26-29.

Solórzano-Torres, Rosalía. "Female Mexican Immigrants in San Diego County." In *Women on the U.S.-Mexico Border: Responses to Change*, edited by Vicki L. Ruiz and Susan Tiano, pp. 41-59. Boston: Allen & Unwin, 1987.

Sosa Riddell, Adaljiza. "Chicanas and El Movimiento." *Aztlan: Chicano Journal of the Social Sciences and the Arts* 5 (Spring and Fall 1974): 155-165.

Stanley, Liz. "Whales and Minnows: Some Sexual Theorists and Their Followers, and How They Contribute to Making Feminism Invisible." *Women's Studies International Forum* 7 (1984): 53-67.

Staples, Robert. "The Mexican-American Family: Its Modification Over Time and Space." *Phylon* 37 (1971): 179-192.

Stephenson, Terry E. "Tomas Yorba, His Wife Vicenta, and His Account Book." *Historical Society of Southern California* 23 (September-December 1941): 126-155.

Sutherland, Elizabeth. "Colonized Women: The Chicana - An Introduction." In *Sisterhood Is Powerful*, edited by Robin Morgan, pp. 376-379. New York: Random House, 1970.

Sweeney, Judith. "Chicana History: A Review of the Literature." In *Essays on La Mujer*, edited by Rosaura Sanchez and Rosa Martinez Cruz, pp. 99-123. Los Angeles: Chicano Studies Center Publications, University of California, 1977.

Tancer, Shoshana B. "La Quisqueyana: The Dominican Woman, 1940-1970." In *Female and Male in Latin America*, edited by Ann Pescatello. Pittsburgh: University of Pittsburgh Press, 1973.

Taylor, Paul S. "Mexican Women in Los Angeles Industry in 1928." *Aztlan: International Journal of Chicano Studies Research* 11 (Spring 1980): 99-131.

Taylor, Paul S., and Kerr, Clark. "Documentary History of the Cotton Strike." In U.S., Congress, Senate, Subcommittee of the Committee on Education and Labor, *Hearings on S. Rec. 266, Violations of Free Speech and the Rights of Labor*. Report no. 1150, 77th Congress, 2d sess. Washington, D.C.: Government Printing Office, 1942.

Tjarks, Alicia. "Comparative Demographic Analysis of Texas, 1777-1793." *Southern Historical Quarterly* (April 1977): 297-338.

Torres, Manuel. "Incidents of Life in Young California." Translated by Nellie Van de Grift Sanchez. *Touring Topics* 22 (May 1930): 22-26.

Torres Ríoseco, Arturo. "Sor Juana Inés de la Cruz." *Revista Iberoamericana* 12 (febrero 1947): 13-38.

Torres Ríoseco, Arturo. "Tres dramaturgos mexicanos del período colonial (Eslava, Alarcón, Sor Juana)." En *Ensayos sobre literatura latinoamericana*. México, D.F.: Fondo de Cultura Económica, Colección Tezontle, 1954.

Trejo, Arnulfo D. "As We See Ourselves in Chicano Literature." In *The Chicanos: As We See Ourselves*, edited by Arnulfo D. Trejo, pp. 187-211. Tucson: University of Arizona Press, 1979.

Trulio, Beverly. "Anglo American Attitudes Toward New Mexican Women." *Journal of the West* 12 (1973): 229-239.

Turner, Kay. "Mexican American Home Altars: Towards Their Interpretation." *Aztlan: International Journal of Chicano Studies Research* 13 (1982): 309-326.

Turner, Victor W. "Forms of Symbolic Action." In *Proceedings of the 1969 Annual Spring Meeting of the American Ethnological Society*, edited by Robert F. Spencer, pp. 3-25. Seattle: University of Washington Press, 1969.

Turner, Victor. "Hidalgo: History as Social Drama." In *Dramas, Fields, and Metaphors: Symbolic Action in Human Society*, edited by Victor Turner. Ithaca: Cornell University Press.

Uhlenberg, Peter. "Marital Instability Among Mexican Americans: Following the Patterns of Blacks?" *Social Problems* 20 (Summer 1972): 49-56.

Urdaneta, Maria Luisa. "Chicana Use of Abortion: The Case of Alcala." In *Twice a Minority: Mexican American Women*, edited by Margarita B. Melville, pp. 33-51. St. Louis: The C.V. Mosby Co., 1980.

Vasquez, Carlos. "Women in the Chicano Movement." In *Mexican Women in the United States: Struggles Past and Present*, edited by Magdalena Mora and Adelaida R. Del Castillo, pp. 27-28. Los Angeles: Chicano Studies Research Center Publications, University of California, 1980.

Vasquez, Mario. "The Election Day Immigration Raid at Lilli Diamond Originals and the Response of the ILGWU." In *Mexican Women in the United States: Struggles Past and Present*, edited by Magdalena Mora and Adelaida R. Del Castillo, pp. 145-148. Los Angeles: Chicano Studies Research Center Publications, University of California, 1980.

Velez-I., Carlos. "Se me acabó la canción: An Ethnography of Non-Consenting Sterilization Among Mexican Women in L.A." In *Mexican Women in the United States: Struggles Past and Present*, edited by Magdalena Mora and Adelaida R. Del Castillo, pp. 71-91. Los Angeles: Chicano Studies Research Center Publications, University of California, 1980.

Velez-Ibañez, Carlos G. "Ourselves Through the Eyes of an Anthropologist." In *The Chicanos as We See Ourselves*, edited by Arnulfo D. Trejo. Tucson: University of Arizona Press, 1979.

Vischer, Edward. "Edward Visher's First Visit to California." Edited and translated by Erwin Gustav Gudde. *California Historical Society Quarterly* 19 (September 1940): 193-216.

Wagner, Roland M., and Schaffer, Diane M. "Social Networks and Survival Strategies: An Exploratory Study of Mexican American, Black, and Anglo Female Family Heads in San Jose, California." In *Twice a Minority: Mexican American Women*, edited by Margarita B. Melville, pp. 173-190. St. Louis: The C.V. Mosby Co., 1980.

Waldman, Elizabeth. "Profile of the Chicana: A Statistical Fact Sheet." In *Mexican Women in the United States: Struggles Past and Present*, edited by Magdalena Mora and Adelaida R. Del Castillo, pp. 195-204. Los Angeles: Chicano Studies Research Center Publications, University of California, 1980.

Wallerstein, Immanuel, and Hopkins, Terence. "Patterns of Development of the Modern World System." *Review* 1 (Fall 1977).

Weber, David J. "'Scarce More than Apes': Historical Roots of Anglo-American Stereotypes of Mexicans." In *New Spain's Far Northern Frontier*, edited by David J. Weber, pp. 293-304. Albuquerque: University of New Mexico, 1979.

Weber, Devra Anne. "The Organization of Mexicano Agricultural Workers, The Imperial Valley and Los Angeles, 1928-1934, An Oral History Approach." *Aztlan: Chicano Journal of the Social Sciences and the Arts* 3 (Fall 1972): 307-347.

Weber, Devra Anne. "Oral Sources and the History of Mexican Workers in the United States." *International Labor and Working Class History* 23 (Spring 1983): 47-50.

Weber, Msgr. Francis J. "Sources for Catholic History of California: A Biblio-Archival Survey." *Southern California Quarterly* 57 (Fall 1975): 321-335.

Weiss, Lawrence D. "Industrial Reserve Army of the Southwest: Navajo and Mexican." *Southwest Economy and Society* 3 (Fall 1977).

Weissman, David. "Boyle Heights - A Study in Ghettos." *The Reflex* 6 (July 1935).

Welter, Barbara. "The Cult of True Womanhood." *The American Quarterly* 18 (1966): 151-174.

Whiteford, Linda. "Mexican American Women as Innovators." In *Twice a Minority: Mexican American Women*, edited by Margarita B. Melville, pp. 109-126. St. Louis: The C.V. Mosby Co., 1980.

Wiesen Cook, Blanche. "Female Support Networks and Political Activism: Lillian Wald, Crystal Eastman, Emma Goldman, Jane Adams." In *Women and Support Networks*. Brooklyn: Out and Out Books, 1977.

Wilson, Joan Hoff, and Donovan, Lynn Bonfield. "Women's History: A Listing of West Coastal Archival and Manuscript Sources - Part II." *California Historical Quarterly* 55 (Summer 1976): 170-185.

Wittenberg, S.N.D., Sister Mary Ste. Therese. "A California Girlhood: Reminiscences of Ascensión Sepúlveda y Avila." *Southern California Quarterly* 64 (Summer 1982): 133-139.

Wolf, Eric R. "The Virgen de Guadalupe: A Mexican National Symbol." *Journal of American Folklore* 71 (1958).

Womack, John, Jr. "Who Are the Chicanos?" *The New York Review of Books* 19 (August 1972): 12-18.

Ybarra, Lea. "When Wives Work: The Impact on the Chicano Family." *Journal of Marriage and the Family* 44 (February 1982): 169-178.

Yorba, Tomás Antonio. "Will of Don Tomás Antonio Yorba, Year of 1845." Translated by M. R. Harrington. *Historical Society of Southern California* 33 (March 1951): 67-73.

Young, K. "Economía campesina, unidad doméstica y migración." *América Indígena* 2 (abril-junio 1978): 279-302.

Zamora, Emilio. "Sara Estela Ramirez: Una Rosa Roja en el Movimiento." In *Mexican Women in the United States: Struggles Past and Present*, edited by Magdalena Mora and Adelaida R. Del Castillo, pp. 163-169. Los Angeles: Chicano Studies Research Center Publications, University of California, 1980.

Zavella, Patricia. "Doing Chicana Life Histories: Refining the Insider's Perspective." Working Paper No. 5, Southwest Institute for Research on Women, University of Arizona.

Zavella, Patricia. "'Abnormal Intimacy': The Varying Work Networks of Chicana Cannery Workers." *Feminist Studies* 11 (Fall 1985): 541-557.

V. *Theses and Dissertations*

Almaguer, Tomas. "Class, Race, and Capitalist Development: The Social Transformation of a Southern California County, 1848-1903." Ph.D. dissertation, University of California, Berkeley, 1979.

Boone, Lalla Rookh. "The History of the Santa Clara Valley: The Spanish Period." Master's thesis, University of California, Berkeley, 1922.

Burkett, Elinor C. "Early Colonial Peru: The Urban Experience." Ph.D. dissertation, University of Pittsburg, 1975.

Castaneda, Antonia I. "Presidarias y Pobladoras: Spanish Speaking Women in Frontier Monterey, California, 1770-1850." Ph.D dissertation, Stanford University, in progress.

Castillo, Pedro. "The Making of a Mexican Barrio: Los Angeles, 1890-1920." Ph.D. dissertation, University of California, Santa Barbara, 1979.

Francis, Mrs. Jessie Davis. "An Economic and Social History of Mexican California, 1822-1846." Ph.D. dissertation, University of California, 1936.

Gómez-Quiñones, Juan. "Social Change and Intellectual Discontent: The Growth of Mexican Nationalism, 1890-1911." Ph.D. dissertation, University of California, Los Angeles, 1972.

Gutiérrez, Ramón A. "Marriage, Sex and the Family: Social Change in Colonial New Mexico, 1690-1846." Ph.D dissertation, University of Wisconsin, 1980.

Lederer, Lillian Charlotte. "A Study of Anglo-American Setttlers in Los Angeles County Previous to the Admission of California to the Union." Master's thesis, University of Southern California, 1927.

Lothrop, Marian Lydia. "Mariano Guadalupe Vallejo, Defender of the Northern Frontier of California." Ph.D. dissertation, University of California, Berkeley, 1926.

Lynch, Henry. "Six Families: A Study of the Power and Influence of the Alvarado, Carrillo, Castro, de la Guerra, Pico, and Vallejo Families in in California, 1769-1846." Master's thesis, California State University, Sacramento, 1977.

Miranda, Gloria E. "Family Patterns and the Social Order in Hispanic Santa Barbara, 1784-1848." Ph.D. dissertation, University of Southern California, 1978.

Ríos-Bustamante, Antonio. "Los Angeles, Pueblo and Region, 1781-1850: Continuity and Adaptation on the North Mexican Periphery." Ph.D dissertation, University of California, 1985.

Ruiz, Vicki L. "UCAPAWA, Chicanas, and the California Food Processing Industry, 1937-1950." Ph.D. dissertation, Stanford University, 1982.

Sanchez, Frances Nelda. "Motivational and Demographic Factors Which Influence Mexican American Women to Enroll in Higher Education." Master's thesis, Texas Woman's University, Denton, 1983.

Soto, Shirlene. "The Mexican Woman: A Study of Her Participation in the Revolution, 1910-1940. Ph.D. dissertation, University of New Mexico, Albuquerque, 1977.

Tremayne, Frank Gilbert. "History of the Santa Clara Valley: The Mexican Period." Master's thesis, University of California, Berkeley, 1923.

Ybarra, Lea. "Conjugal Role Relationships in the Chicano Family." Ph.D. dissertation, University of California, Berkeley, 1977.

Zavella, Patricia. "Women, Work and Family in the Chicano Community: Cannery Workers of the Santa Clara Valley." Ph.D. dissertation, University of California, Berkeley, 1982.

VI. *Unpublished Papers*

Abascal, Anita. "Parteras, Llaveras y Maestras: Women in Provincial California." Paper delivered at the Conference of the West Coast Association of Women Historians, Los Angeles, California, May 1976.

Alexander, Cheryl. "The Lower Class Mexican Family of the Southwest during the 1850s." Unpublished manuscript, 1982.

Arguelles, Lourdes. "Once the Block is Carved: Third World Immigrants in Advanced Capitalist Societies." Unpublished manuscript.

Cardenas, Gilbert. "Immigrant Women in the Labor Force." Unpublished manuscript, University of Texas, Austin, 1981.

Gómez-Quiñones, Juan. "Notes on the Political Economy of Mexican Women in the Far North, 1500 to 1900." Unpublished manuscript, 1986.

Gonzalez, Rosalinda Mendez. "A Review of the Literature on Mexican and Mexican-American Women Workers in the United States Southwest, 1970-1975. Unpublished manuscript, University of Irvine, 1976.

Hembold, Lois Rita. "The Work of Chicanas in the United States: Wage Labor and Work in the Home, 1930 to the Present." Seminar paper, Stanford University, 1977.

Martinez, Edward. "Domesticity and Mexican Women in the Northern Frontier." Unpublished manuscript, 1982.

McBane, Margo. "History of Women Farm Workers in California." Unpublished manuscript, 1974.

Moch, L. Page, and Tilly, Louise Alice. "Immigrant Women in the City: Comparative Perspectives." Paper prepared for the Conference on Women, Work, and City Environment. Paris, 23-25 October 1979.

Pesquera, Beatriz. "A Border Society in Transition: The Maquiladoras of Tijuana." Paper delivered at the Conference on the Cultural Roots of Chicana Literature: 1780-1980, Oakland, California, 16 October 1981.

Romero, Gloria, and Arguelles, Lourdes. "Women Without Work: Implications for Praxis." Unpublished manuscript.

Sewell, William. "Dock Workers of 19th Century Marseilles: Rise and Fall of a Labor Aristocracy." Seminar paper, University of Texas at El Paso, 22 March 1984.

Tuñon, Esperanza y Zurita, Gloria Alejandra. *La mujer obrera en México. Una propuesta.* Ponencia presentada en el Segundo Encuentro México-Sudamérica sobre Historia Obrera, México, 18-21 de agosto de 1981.

Ybarra, Lea. "The Status of Research on Chicanas." Unpublished manuscript, 1981.

Zavella, Patricia. "I'm Not Exactly in Love With My Job": Chicana Cannery Workers in San Jose, California." Paper delivered at the Ninth Annual Meeting of the National Association of Chicano Studies, Riverside, California, April 2-4, 1981.